The Masters
and their
Retreats

The Masters
and their
Retreats

Mark L. Prophet and Elizabeth Clare Prophet

Compiled and edited by Annice Booth

SUMMIT UNIVERSITY ● PRESS®
Corwin Springs, Montana

THE MASTERS AND THEIR RETREATS
Teachings of Mark L. Prophet and Elizabeth Clare Prophet
compiled and edited by Annice Booth
Copyright © 2003 Summit University Press
All rights reserved

Library of Congress Control Number: 2003104585
ISBN: 0-9720402-4-2

Cover design and production: Brad Davis

Printed in the United States of America

Note: Because gender-neutral language can be cumbersome and at times confusing, we
have used the pronouns *he* and *him* to refer to God or to the individual and *man* or
mankind to refer to people in general. We have used these terms for readability and
consistency, and they are not intended to exclude women or the feminine aspect of the
Godhead. God is both masculine and feminine. We do, however, use the pronouns *she*
and *her* to refer to the soul because each soul, whether housed in a male or a female
body, is the feminine counterpart of the masculine Spirit.

08 07 06 05 04   6 5 4 3 2

Contents

Descriptions of the Retreats   417

A Note from the Editor

Thirty-three years ago, the messenger Elizabeth Clare Prophet informed me that it was time to publish a book on the masters and their retreats. She felt that the world needed a complete introduction to the ascended masters, the angels, the Elohim and the cosmic beings so that mankind could understand the great love of these masters for the sons and daughters of God on earth. It was to be a book that anyone pursuing a spiritual path could pick up and read or use as a reference.

At that time we were living at La Tourelle, a beautiful mansion in Colorado Springs, Colorado. This was a physical retreat of the Brotherhood of Light, a focus for the ascended masters and home to the messengers and their staff. I was privileged to sit with our messenger as she wrote short biographies of the masters, telling the stories of their lives and describing the qualities that made each of them a unique manifestation of God.

I was also blessed to be present as she meditated in her prayer tower at La Tourelle. During these deep meditations, the messenger would look into the inner planes and visit the heavenly retreats and etheric temples of the masters. She brought back with her the details of all that she had seen and then spoke into a tape recorder. Later her secretaries transcribed her teachings.

I sat with her for many hours a day over several weeks while she did this inner work. My task, as she described it to me, was to hold the light while she journeyed to the inner planes of the heaven-world. Like a cosmic sponge, I endeavored to absorb any untoward vibrations, keeping the energy from her so that her soul was free to soar to the inner planes to do the work the masters assigned her.

These precious hours with the guru and teacher were a very high and holy time for me. I could feel the pure light radiation in the room as she communed with the masters, as they described the retreats to her, and as she visited them in turn in their homes of light. Hearing her speak as she returned from one of these sojourns broadened my own understanding of the entire cosmos. I learned of the Creator's vast plan for his creation, and I was overjoyed to find that each one of us has a special part to play in God's intricate plan for earth and her evolutions.

I treasure those early days with Elizabeth and Mark, now the ascended master Lanello. The messenger entrusted me with this teaching, and I have carried these precious transcripts with me, whenever and wherever I moved as a part of the messenger's staff—from Colorado Springs to Santa Barbara, to San Francisco, to Minneapolis and, finally, to my home at the Inner Retreat in Paradise Valley, Montana.

Interestingly, wherever I have gone, students have asked me about the masters and their lives. Many have requested a book of their biographies as a road map for their own journey on the path of personal Christhood. Occasionally, Elizabeth Clare Prophet would release a small portion of this information during a lecture or prior to an address by one of the ascended hosts, but never before has this information been collected in one place. I am sure that students of the ascended masters as well as seekers of truth from all walks of life will welcome the profound truths revealed in this book.

As we have learned more about the retreats of the masters over the years of the messengers' service, we have found that any sincere student may visit the retreats of the masters in his or her finer bodies while their physical body sleeps at night. During sleep, we often do visit the homes of the masters, and we sit at their feet to receive training from them directly. You may even have recalled your own "inner temple" experiences upon awakening in the morning. Have you ever wished that you could remember what the master was really like, what the retreat looked like and what it was you learned there? If only you could recall the words of the master! Now, you can read all about the masters and their retreats for yourself, as this teaching becomes a magnet, pulling you toward the retreats you have read about.

I pray that this little encyclopedia, *The Masters and Their Retreats*, will assist the masters and their students and will help finish a part of the work the messengers began so long ago. The mission of the two witnesses, Mark L. Prophet and Elizabeth Clare Prophet, is to publish the Everlasting Gospel, the scripture for the dawning age of Aquarius. The teaching the messenger received in the little room in her prayer tower many years ago was originally intended to be a part of chapter 32, the next-to-the-last chapter, of *Climb the Highest Mountain*, the Gospel for the Aquarian Age. But the teaching became so extensive that it was worthy of a separate book in this series.

It has been my cherished dream to see this book in print, even as I have held it in my heart all these years. Now, truly, it is time to launch this book to a waiting world, hungry for the Truth within its pages. Thirty-three years later, I also pray that the understanding of the masters and their retreats may be the means for you to really become acquainted with the ascended masters and to launch your own journey—a journey that will take you to that highest mountain, the summit of your own being, your ascension in the light.

Annice Booth
The Royal Teton Ranch
Paradise Valley, Montana
April 3, 2002

Introduction

Who Is Elizabeth Clare Prophet?

Elizabeth Clare Prophet is an author, teacher and messenger. Like her late husband, Mark L. Prophet, her calling is to be a prophet of God, or one who delivers the Word of God. In this role as a messenger, she communes with angels and masterful beings of light through the power of the Holy Spirit in the manner of the ancient prophets and apostles, and she delivers their messages to the world. These messages contain the words of the heavenly host as "dictations," as well as a transfer of light for soul quickening and initiation. While receiving these dictations, she is fully conscious yet in an exalted state. The messages occur through the conveyance of the Holy Spirit and not through psychicism or spiritualism where a disembodied spirit takes over the body of a channeler.

Through these two messengers, the ascended masters have released profound teachings, messages and prophecies that present a path and a teaching whereby every individual on earth can find his or her way back to God.

Elizabeth Clare Prophet does not claim to be a master herself but only their instrument; she sees herself as the servant of the light in all students of the ascended masters and in all people. During her mission and ministry, she has taught on a wide variety of spiritual subjects: karma and reincarnation, healing and wholeness, soul mates, twin flames and relationships, and practical spirituality, to name just a few. Her books and writings are intended to give people the opportunity to know the Truth that can set them free. Her great desire is to share a path that will take true seekers, in the tradition of the masters of the Far East, as far as they can go and need to go to meet their true teachers, the ascended masters and their own Higher Self, face-to-face.

❖

Of Angels, Masters and Men —
The Hierarchy of Heaven

Before delving into the detailed descriptions of the various masters and their retreats, it will be helpful to have a framework for what is to follow. A preliminary knowledge of the structure of the heavenly hierarchy is a useful prerequisite for entering the world of the masters.

Who Are the Ascended Masters?

All sons and daughters of God have a divine spark, which is their potential to become, or realize, the Christ within. This concept is at the heart of the major religions, East and West. And it was part of Jesus' original teachings to his disciples, many of which were either obscured by Church Fathers or destroyed.

There is no record in the scriptures of Jesus saying that he is the only Son of God, having exclusive right to Divine Sonship. His message was that we should follow in his footsteps to realize the fullness of this Christ in our lives— for only thereby can we work his works on earth.

The culmination of the path of Christhood is the ascension, a spiritual acceleration of consciousness that takes place at the natural conclusion of one's final lifetime on earth. Through the ascension, the soul merges with Christ her Lord and returns to the Father-Mother God, free from the rounds of karma and rebirth.

How does one become a master and enter the heaven-world? A master is one who has attained self-mastery by using the energy of free will, coupled with the law of their oneness with God, to demonstrate mastery in time and space. Through mastery of the flow of energy in his own being as well as his environment, he reaches a certain level of attainment, bringing his soul into congruency with his own God-awareness. This mastery propels him into the reunion with God that is called the ascension in the light, the ritual of the return that was demonstrated by Jesus. Hence the term ascended master.

Jesus was not the only Son of God to demonstrate the ritual of the ascension, nor will he be the last. Neither is he the only Son of God in heaven. Elijah also ascended into heaven. Enoch walked with God, and "he was not, for God took him." John the Beloved, the disciple closest to Jesus, demonstrated the ascension, as did Mary the Mother. In fact, sons and daughters of God throughout cosmos have followed the path of the ascension since the first creation. The path of the ascension is the path of spiritual evolution.

Having balanced their karma and accomplished their unique mission, the ascended masters have graduated from earth's schoolroom and ascended to

God. They are our elder brothers and sisters on the path of personal Christ-hood. Many are familiar to us, having walked among us through the ages, while others may be unknown to our outer mind. Some masters are ancient beings of light, and their names have long ago become secondary to the flames they bear.

The ascended masters have proven the victory over sin, disease and death and over every conflict. They have balanced what is called in the East karma and in the West sin. They have transmuted all energies that have ever been given into their use in all incarnations, and they have returned to the heart of the I AM THAT I AM. It is written, "And a cloud received him out of their sight."[1] This cloud is a forcefield of electronic or spiritual energy called the Divine Monad. It is the I AM Presence, the Presence of the I AM that appeared to Moses as the flame that burned in the bush that was not consumed. This Pres-ence is our origin, our True Being, whereby we, too, can attain what is called cosmic consciousness. The energy of our own God source is not remote. It is ever-present within and above us, hovering as a cloud of infinite spiritual energy. (See the description of the Chart of Your Divine Self, page 532.)

Every master in heaven has already merged with the Spirit of the I AM Pres-ence. By proving the laws of God, the masters demonstrate that we, too, can attain immortality. All that we are is not lost at the moment of death but is per-petuated by the action of that light that lighteth every man that cometh into the world.

They are all a part of the Great White Brotherhood, spoken of in Revelation 7 as the great multitude of saints "clothed with white robes" who stand before the throne of God.[2] (The term "white" refers not to race but to the aura of white light that surrounds these immortals.) The Brotherhood works with earnest seekers and public servants of every race, religion and walk of life to assist humanity in their forward evolution.

Among these saints are Gautama Buddha, Maitreya, Jesus Christ, Saint Michael the Archangel, Zarathustra, Moses, Melchizedek, Mother Mary, Saint Francis, Saint Germain, El Morya, Thérèse of Lisieux, and unnumbered and unnamed loving hearts, servants of humanity who have ascended to the I AM THAT I AM and are a part of the living God forevermore.

These masters are teachers of mankind. They teach the path of overcoming victory whereby the soul can reunite with the Higher Self, walk the earth with self-mastery following in the footsteps of Jesus as a Christed one and return to the heaven-world at the conclusion of a lifetime of service. This is the path of per-sonal Christhood, whereby each one can find the way of overcoming.

The ascended masters teach by example, not by words or platitudes. They reveal to us the next step of our spiritual evolution. They point the way, and they say: "I AM the way. This is the way, and the way ye know." The "way" is a path that can be followed.

Having walked where we walk, the masters are well qualified to teach us. And even as they teach mankind, they were and are students. They also studied in the retreats of the heaven-world in preparation for incarnation on earth; and even as ascended beings, they are students of other masters who are above them in the great chain of being, the heavenly hierarchy. The path of discipleship continues in the heaven-world and is a model for the student-teacher, master-disciple relationship on earth.

The ascended masters come to initiate us in the ancient mysteries of Christ and Buddha and the Everlasting Gospel for the new age of Aquarius. And they come to exhort us so that we will rise to the great God flame within ourselves and defeat the momentums of returning karma that are coming upon the age. The ascended masters present a path and a teaching whereby every individual on earth can find his way back to God.

Every ascended master is unique in the cosmic sense of the word, having a unique causal body by which he or she may bless, heal and teach lifestreams such as ourselves who are not as far along the Path. Even so, when you have accomplished your reason for being and balanced your karma, you will have much to offer life as a result of all the constructive good you have brought forth on earth.

Seven Masters Teach the Seven Paths to God

When we come into the knowledge of the ascended masters, we come into an awareness of defining the Path. The path back to the Source can be walked over seven rays of the Christ consciousness that emerge from the white light.

The seven color rays are the natural division of the pure white light emanating from the heart of God as it descends through the prism of manifestation. These are the subdivisions of the wholeness of Christ. Regardless of their color, all of the flames have a white-fire core of purity, which embodies all of the attributes of God and which may be invoked by those who desire to expand the Christ consciousness.

The seven rays present seven paths to individual or personal Christhood. Seven masters have mastered identity by walking these paths, defined as the seven archetypes of Christhood. These seven masters are called the chohans of the rays, which means lords of the rays. Chohan is a Sanskrit term for lord, and lord is equivalent to law; hence the chohan is the action of the law of the ray. To be a chohan on one of the seven rays means that this master defines the law on that ray; through him that energy of the Christ and of God flows to mankind, to all who are evolving on that particular path.

The chohans are the closest ascended masters to those who would be chelas, or students, of the real gurus. The chohans function in planes of perfection, but these planes are simultaneously one with the Matter plane where we are. And so, the chohans are here with us. There is a congruency of Spirit and Matter where we are, and we understand that time and space are but coordinates of infinity.

Let us briefly look at these seven chohans and their retreats.

El Morya, the chohan of the first ray, maintains his focus of the will of God on the etheric plane concurrent with Darjeeling, India. He is the Chief of the Darjeeling Council, a council of ascended masters of the Great White Brotherhood.

Lanto is the lord of the second ray, the yellow ray of illumination. He serves in the retreat of the Royal Teton, the main retreat of the Great White Brotherhood on the North American continent. He is concerned with the illumination of the youth of the world.

Paul the Venetian is the chohan of the third ray of divine love, the pink flame. He is the hierarch at the Château de Liberté in southern France. He sponsors the ascended master culture for this age and works with all who desire to bring that culture forth on behalf of mankind.

Next, we come to the great disciplinarian, Serapis Bey, chohan of the fourth ray. Serapis maintains the focus of the Ascension Temple at Luxor in Egypt. This is the place where candidates for the ascension are received, and it is considered the most difficult of these retreats to enter. Serapis Bey is the teacher of the path to the ascension.

Hilarion is the chohan of the fifth ray, the green ray of precipitation and truth. He was embodied as the apostle Paul. He maintains the Temple of Truth on the etheric plane near Crete. He works with atheists, agnostics, skeptics and others who have become disillusioned with life and with religion.

The sixth ray of ministration, service and peace is presided over by Nada as chohan. The flame of the sixth ray is purple, the color of violets, flecked with metallic gold and ruby. Nada's retreat is in the Arabian desert.

Saint Germain, the chohan of the seventh ray, holds a very important position in hierarchy in this age. Not only is he the chohan of the seventh ray of freedom, mercy, transmutation and ritual, but he is also the hierarch of the Aquarian age. The pulsations of the violet flame can be felt from his retreat over the House of Rakoczy in Transylvania and from the Cave of Symbols in the United States.

The offices of the seven chohans of the rays are divinely appointed by the cosmic hierarchy. Those who hold these offices are selected from among the most qualified ascended beings who have arisen from earth's schoolrooms. Each one has attained self-mastery and won the ascension by serving humanity on one or more of the seven rays through their embodiments in the world of form.

The chohan for each ray holds sovereign responsibility under divine ordination for the administration to mankind of all the qualitative aspects of their own specific ray, while harmonizing their administration with the other six rays of the white light. The chohans always obey cosmic law; yet they are given certain latitude in keeping with their manifest individual evolution, capacities and special endowments to direct mankind in the most adroit manner, giving such loving assistance and spiritual direction as may be the requirement of the hour. They retain in their service legions of angelic hosts and ascended brethren who carry out the plan of the Great White Brotherhood for the most complete expression of the seven rays that is possible among mankind of earth.

Individuals are keyed to certain rays in order that they may perform a specific service to God and man. The ray of service to which an individual is attuned may vary from one embodiment to the next, but the reward for service is cumulative. And thus, powerful momentums may be retained from one's past service on several or all of the rays. A balance of attainment on all of the seven rays is a requirement for the ascension and the mark of the golden-age man or woman.

The services of the seven chohans impact all who work in the world, whatever their level of service: Statesmen, leaders and organizers are on the first ray under El Morya; teachers, philosophers and educators serve on the second ray under Lanto; artists, designers, beauticians and those of a creative nature serve on the third ray under Paul the Venetian; architects, planners and those dedicated to the purity and discipline of any undertaking serve with Serapis Bey on the fourth ray; doctors, scientists, healers, musicians, mathematicians and those consecrated to truth serve on the fifth ray with Hilarion; ministers, nurses and all who administer to mankind's needs assist Nada on the sixth ray; diplomats, priests of the sacred fire, actors, writers and defenders of freedom serve with Saint Germain on the seventh ray.

If we lack one of these godly attributes and desire to make progress on a particular path back to God, we can pray to our God Presence, our own Holy Christ Self and the chohan of that ray for those qualities we want to see manifest in our world. By doing this, we can make great strides of spiritual progress in a comparatively short time.

The Three Orders of Spiritual Beings

The kingdom of the ascended masters is the order of the Christed ones, the evolution that we call the sons and daughters of God. Mankind are included in this order. Their destiny is to become the Christ. This order includes beings newly ascended as well as ancient masters who have manifested the Christ consciousness. Besides the order of masters and men, there are two other kingdoms of spiritual beings: the angelic kingdom and the kingdom of elemental beings.

When God created man and commanded him to be fruitful in service, to multiply his graces and to take dominion over the earth,[3] he gave him helpers to assist in the important task of expanding His kingdom. Angelic ministrants and elemental servants of earth, air, fire and water formed the cosmic retinue that accompanied man as he descended to earth, "trailing clouds of glory" and vowing, "Lo, I AM come to do thy will, O God!"[4]

During three golden ages on the earth, man talked freely with his God and associated intimately with angels and elementals. Communion with all life was unrestrained, and cooperation between angels, elementals and men was unspoiled. To man was given the assignment of overseeing creation and working with God to plan, to design, to invent and to direct activities on earth. To the elementals, the builders of form, was given the important task of bringing into manifestation the intents of God and man. And to the angels was given the holy ordination of ministering to the needs of both men and elementals.

The three orders of the heavenly hierarchy manifest the threefold flame, the three primary attributes of God: power, wisdom and love. The sons and daughters of God are intended to outpicture the intelligence of the Christ mind, focusing the genius of God for invention and creativity. They were created to become co-creators with God. They represent the yellow plume of hierarchy.

The pink plume of the threefold flame of hierarchy is the order of the angelic hosts. Their service is to amplify the feelings and virtues of God. They bring the qualities of hope, love, mercy, compassion, charity, constancy and all the virtues that we need to make it in life. The angels help us to amplify these feelings, and they often do this through heavenly music called, at inner levels, the music of the spheres.

The archangels are the highest beings in the angelic kingdom, which goes all the way down to the tiniest angel. This kingdom includes the cherubim, seraphim and all kinds of orders of angels under their leaders. Every ascended master has his own legion of angels who serve with him to amplify the flame that he tends.

The third order, or kingdom, represents the blue plume of the threefold flame. This is the order of Elohim, or the elemental kingdom. The Elohim are the highest beings in this order. The Elohim are the builders of form, the Seven Spirits of God who responded when God gave forth the fiat "Let there be light; and there was light."[5] When God directed the formation of the cosmos in the physical plane, it was the Elohim who brought forth that creation. Under the Elohim are the directors of the elements who, in turn, are in charge of the gnomes, sylphs, undines and salamanders—the elemental beings who take care of the four elements of the nature kingdom.

Cooperation between the Three Kingdoms

Before man went forth from out the center of God's being, he asked, "Father, might I not be given the freedom to choose the way, the plan and the action of my life?" In his great heart of love the Father knew what pain might come upon a creation that would be free to go against his will, but he also saw the great opportunity for expansion and rejoicing that would come to those who would choose to follow his plan.

And so, out of God's infinite wisdom came the fiat, "Man shall have the gift of free will; and whosoever shall prove in thought and word and deed that he can choose wisely and well in all things, to him will I give glory and honor and power and dominion; he shall sit upon my right hand, and he shall preside over the kingdoms of the world, over the elements and the angelic hosts."

This was one of the great moments in cosmic history: Man had been given free will and with it, the opportunity to become a co-creator with God. "Made a little lower than the angels," he would be "crowned with more glory and honor"[6] if he used this precious gift to glorify God, to bless his fellow men and to master his environment and himself.

It was the seven mighty Elohim, directors of elemental life and masters of precipitation, who had responded to the seven great commands of God that culminated in the creation of man. Now the hierarchs of the four elements, four pillars in the temple of being serving under the Elohim, pledged to sustain the balance of life on Terra, in nature and in man. Salamanders, gnomes, sylphs and undines, mimics of the Grand Design, all served to keep man's house in order and to sustain his noble form. Laborers in the Father's vineyard, harvesters of his sowings, the beings of the elements occupy a most important position in the Trinity of God in manifestation as they heed each beck and call of God and man.

The angelic hosts, like the elemental builders of form, were not given the freedom to express, to move and to create on their own. They remained tethered to the Father's will; his slightest wish was their command—cherubim and seraphim, mighty archangels and their archeiai, created by God to amplify his attributes.

God created the angels out of his own essence as beings who would sustain his magnificent feelings throughout the universe. Their assignment was to infuse men and elementals with those qualities that are necessary in planning and executing the will of God upon earth: faith, hope and charity, peace, understanding and compassion, purity, comfort and healing, mercy and forgiveness and such praise of eternal life as would unite men and elementals in service to their Creator and in love to one another.

From the centrosome of being, the Great Central Sun, the Holy of holies that is at once in God in universal manifestation (the Macrocosm) and in man (the microcosm) as the flame upon the altar of his heart, angelic messengers carry the magnitude of the divine potential to the farthest reaches of cosmos and consciousness. They come bearing rainbow hues of joy, beauty and delight, portending the advent of the Christ in every man. Their love and unfailing direction is a clarion call that integrates the lower and the Higher Self in unity of purpose, plan and action. Their love is a balm of friendship, an unguent of healing and the oil of heavenly inspiration.

The love of the angels is a divine magnet that keeps the stars on their appointed rounds, the atoms of our being inclined to do the heavenly will and each monad in his rightful place. Their love is a sacred tone, the music of the spheres, the Spirit that animates nature and all things beautiful.

Thus, while man's portion was to become the Christ and to sustain on earth the illuminating radiance of God's mind, the beings of the elements would build the temple to grace his wisdom—stone on stone of measured will, the Archi-

tect's design. And angel beings, inspired by the plan, vowed to bring coals of inspiration still glowing from the Father's hearth. In this trinity of cooperation we behold the action of the Cosmic Christ and the balanced manifestation of the cosmic threefold flame of wisdom, love and power.

The Opportunity to Evolve Upward

As a co-creator with God, man was also given the authority to invoke the presence and service of the angelic hosts who pledged to answer his call so long as man's requests were in keeping with the Father's will. Opportunity was given to the angels to receive the gift of free will only after they would prove their ability to sustain the pure feelings of God during centuries of allegiance to the Creator and unswerving devotion to his creation, man.

The title "archangel" was given to those who became masters of their worlds "as Above, so below" and that of "archeia" to their feminine complements. In order to earn this office, many who are now archangels had to embody in human form, experiencing the same tests as the sons and daughters of God. However, there were some who remained in the heaven-world and never took embodiment in the physical octave.

All the archangels are healers. They come as master surgeons to repair our bodies, even as they mend the garments of our souls. There is no field of study in which they do not excel. With the Elohim, they exercise the power to create or uncreate life. Archangels are extraordinary beings, extensions of God himself, personifying his grace and majesty and power.

Elementals, too, were given the opportunity to evolve in the order of the spiritual hierarchy. After proving their ability to sustain simple and then more complex patterns in nature—first a drop of rain, then a blade of grass, a forget-me-not, a rose, then a mighty oak and finally, a great redwood—and after passing many tests of endurance, an elemental and his feminine complement might become the overseers of an entire regiment and then even the directors of all of the elementals serving under one element. The directors of the elements on this planet are as follows: Oromasis and Diana, who are in charge of the fire element and all salamanders; Neptune and Luara, who direct the undines and the mighty waters; Aries and Thor, who oversee the graceful sylphs and trackless realms of the air; and Virgo and Pelleur, mother and father of earth and gnomes.

Thus, there is opportunity for each of the three evolutions to rise within their own order, and there is no limit to the attainment that can come to those who manifest the will of God in any field of endeavor.

The Plan of Victory: The Ascension, the Goal of Life

The plan of victory for the children of God was nobly defined in the life of Jesus and that of many other avatars who have been sent by God as exemplars to point the way of freedom to generations who have lost their contact, not only with God but also with the heavenly hosts and the elementals. The ascension and the overcoming of every binding condition that must precede it are the birthright and the highlight of the life of all who are born of God.

When through service to life, an individual son or daughter of God (1) attains mastery over outer circumstances, (2) balances 51 percent of his karma and (3) fulfills the law of his being—the divine mission that is the unique plan for his lifestream—he may then return to the throne of grace, being perfected in the ritual of the ascension. Once ascended, he is known as an ascended master. Here life truly begins, and man is ordained a priest of the sacred fire in the eternal, ever-enfolding service of his God.

All of life (hence all of God) is in the process of ascending when it follows the divinely natural process of spiritual evolution. It is therefore through the ascension that angels, elementals and men find their way back to the heart of God and the eternal life they once knew even before the morning stars sang together.

Profiles of the
Ascended Masters

Meet the Master

The ascended masters each demonstrate a profile in Christhood. Under the name of each master listed below is an outline of their particular path and teaching, a brief sketch of what is known of their lives and embodiments on earth, if any, as well as their attributes and gifts. The name and location of their retreat is given, when it is known.* Also included are excerpts of key teachings from the master through their messengers Mark L. Prophet and Elizabeth Clare Prophet.

As you can imagine, it is beyond the scope of this book to tell all that is known of each master. The Bible says that if all that Jesus did were written, the world could not contain all the books that would be needed. The same can be said of each master, angel and cosmic being in heaven.

The masters listed in these profiles are those who are a part of the dispensation of these two witnesses, Mark L. Prophet and Elizabeth Clare Prophet, and The Summit Lighthouse activity. Clearly, there are many more masters in heaven than can be listed here, and this book is not intended to be an exhaustive list of every master or angel. The ones you will read of here are those who have released their teachings through this activity or who have been spoken of by these messengers. They are the ones who have come forward in this dispensation to assist mankind and who have promised assistance to those who will call to them for help.

Only a little is known of some masters. For others, a whole book and more could be written. Masters such as El Morya and Saint Germain, pivotal in sponsoring this activity, have dictated their releases to these messengers time and time again. The stories of their embodiments and the teachings they have released could fill many books. And although it was almost heart-wrenching to limit all that is known about these dear masters to a few pages in a book, yet the information contained here does reveal the essence of each one and what they offer to their students.

As you learn of the masters and get to know them, they can help you define your own profile on the path of personal Christhood. Even as you are seeking the master, so from ages past, the masters have been seeking you, and they are seeking you again today. They already know who are their students, even if the student is as yet unaware of the master. The masters desire to contact those

---

*The retreat of a master is his home of light, his temple or his place of service. Most of the retreats are found in the etheric plane, but a few also extend to the physical. For further information about the retreats, see the introduction to the next section of this book.

whose lives they long to touch. As the master Jesus said, "You do not choose me, for I have chosen you."

As you read of the masters, you may recognize your master or masters, the one or the ones who are sponsoring your lifestream. May this special master be for you an open doorway to heaven. And may this book be the means for the masters to find you, their chelas.

The Editor

❖ **AFRA, Patron of Africa**

Afra was the first member of the black race to make his ascension. Long ago, he offered name and fame to God to sponsor a vast continent and a mighty people. When he ascended, he asked to be called simply "a brother" (*frater* in Latin), hence the name Afra. The continent of Africa takes its name from Afra, and he is the patron of Africa and of the black race.

The Ascended
Master Afra

There were ancient golden ages in Africa when it was a part of the continent of Lemuria, when the people came forth out of the light of the great causal body of the Great Divine Director. The Great Divine Director continues to sponsor the divine plan for the continent of Africa, even as he sponsors the divine plan for the descendants of Afra in America.

Many people have ascended from the black race—although from a spiritual perspective, there is no such thing as the black race or the white race. In heaven, the masters are not noted by their race or previous religion. All of the races on earth have come forth from the heart of God under the seven rays, or seven paths of initiation.

Those who are of the "white" race came forth for the mastery of the yellow (wisdom), pink (love) and white (purity) flames—hence, the various mixtures and tone qualities of their skin. These evolutions were intended to place upon the altar of God the gift of their self-mastery in the way of wisdom, love and purity. Those of the yellow race, the people of the land of Chin—or China—serve on the ray of wisdom, while those who have "red" colored skin are intended to amplify the pink flame of divine love.

The members of the "black" race have come forth on the blue ray and the violet ray. In an ancient civilization on the continent of Africa, the people's skin actually had a blue or a violet hue. These colors come from the Father-Mother God, Alpha and Omega, the beginning and the ending, the first ray and the seventh ray.

Just as each individual serves on a particular ray, so individual nations also have their calling, or dharma. Each nation is called by God to manifest a specific virtue to fulfill a certain destiny. The members of what is now known as the black race were sent to earth to master the qualities of God's power, his will and his faith (on the blue ray) and the qualities of God's freedom, justice and mercy (on the violet ray).

Throughout the ages since his departure from Eden, man has wandered from his high estate, and the pure colors of the rainbow rays are no longer reflected either in the skin tone or in the aura. Division has set in through the divide-and-conquer tactics of the fallen ones. Instead of the races embracing one another as brother and sister, there is division: one race enslaves another race, and the great unity of all children of God and their oneness in the flame is destroyed.

Afra lived 500,000 years ago when the people of this ancient civilization had reached a crossroad. Fallen angels who had invaded planet Earth divided the people. These evil angels set out to destroy the blue and the violet races. They distorted the once-sacred rituals and art forms of this people, opening the door to witchcraft, voodoo and black magic. They turned the people toward hatred, superstition and a vying for power.

As the people began to divert their attention from their God Presence, they became more and more vulnerable to the divide-and-conquer tactics of the fallen angels. The civilization became divided by the warring factions of its tribes. The people were losing the inner spiritual battle between the forces of light and darkness within them. And their division, both within and without, allowed them to become enslaved under the powers of darkness.

Seeing the plight of his people, Afra took embodiment among them in order to rescue them. First, he pinpointed the one missing trait that he perceived to be the Achilles' heel of his people. He identified the point of vulnerability as their lack of brotherhood. Allegorically speaking, they followed the example of Cain rather than following the example of Abel. When the LORD asked the people of Afra if they would be willing to lay down their lives for their kinsmen and friends, their answer was the same as Cain's: "Am I my brother's keeper?"[7] The one who answers no to that question is dedicated to his ego. He will never be his brother's keeper, and eventually the divine spark within him, the threefold flame, will die.

Afra knew that many of his people had lost their threefold flame, even as many blacks and whites, through anger, are losing it today. He also knew that in order to regain that flame, they would have to follow a path of brotherhood. They had to care for one another. The only way he could teach them to be a brother to all others was to be a brother to all himself. And for this, he was crucified by his own people. He was the Christ in their midst, but they knew him not. They were blinded by their greed for power.

The ascended master Afra spoke on "The Powers and Perils of Nationhood" in Accra, Ghana, in 1976, stressing the theme of unity and of dissolving our differences in the fire of the Holy Spirit. He said:

"We are brethren because we are of the same Mother. I am your brother, not your lord, not your master. I am your brother on the Path. I have shared your passion for freedom. I have shared with you the hours of crisis when you beheld injustice, when you prayed to the Lord for justice and the Lord gave to you the divine plan for this nation and for this continent.

"I have lived in your hearts for hundreds of years as you have toiled under the burden of oppression self-imposed from within and put upon from without.

"The people of Afra have the supreme opportunity to learn from every civilization and every history. When materialization reaches its peak, there are only two courses open to a civilization: either material decline and decay because of indulgence, or spiritual transcendence through the alchemy of the Holy Spirit."[8]

In a later message, Saint Germain asked Afra to convey the following message to the descendants of Afra in America:

"In this moment, those who call themselves the blacks of America can rise to new dimensions of freedom and liberty. But this can only come to pass through the mighty heart flame, through the understanding of the path of initiation under the Holy Spirit, through submitting yourself, your soul, to the altar of God and calling upon the Lord for an acceleration of light, a purging of inner darkness.

"Though there were successes through the civil rights movement, there have been setbacks. For those successes in many instances were outer. Having gained them, the people did not understand that they must go within to the inner light in order to sustain them. We would seek the equality of all souls whatever their outer 'color.' We would teach you a spiritual path of true advancement on the path of initiation.

"Though they know it not, the black people of America today are at the eternal Y. They must choose this day whom they will serve—whether gains in the line of material comfort and increased well-being and higher-paying jobs, or the real gain of the eternal light of Sonship and the path of immortality with all of its challenges. In this land of abundance, it is natural for all people to expect and to live according to a higher standard of living. It is when this higher standard obliterates the inner longing for the higher light and the higher way that it becomes dangerous. I would tell you that God has chosen this people as those who have become rich in Spirit."[9]

You can call to Afra for unity and for the dissolving of racial tensions through the true understanding of universal brotherhood.

Afra, our brother of light, like all ascended masters, has true humility. Kuthumi spoke of Afra's humility: "This giant soul with his tremendous devotion was one of the unknown brothers. So long as individuals feel the need to expound upon their own personal achievements, they may well find that they are not truly a part of us."[10]

❖ AKSHOBHYA, *See* The Five Dhyani Buddhas

❖ ALEXANDER GAYLORD, Twin flame of Lady Master Leto

Alexander Gaylord ascended in 1937 after having been a messenger for the Brotherhood and active in the Cosmic Secret Service. His twin flame is the ascended lady master Leto, and together they serve in the retreat of the Master of Paris.

Gaylord and Leto were embodied in the Inca civilization. At that time, he was a public servant and she was a devoted scientist, both highly attuned with the spiritual hierarchy.

Godfré Ray King's book *The Magic Presence* recounts how Alexander Gaylord, while yet in embodiment and working for the Brotherhood, went on missions with Leto, who had ascended more than three hundred years earlier.[11] Godfré relates a story Alexander Gaylord told him about Gaylord's first meeting with an unnamed master. Gaylord was on an assignment for the Indian Council of the Great White Brotherhood. He was on board a ship going to France when he met "a most distinguished looking gentleman." The man accompanied Gaylord to India and other places and taught him, in Gaylord's words, "the most marvelous use of the ancient wisdom." Gaylord says he was "a remarkable man. The only promise he exacted from me at any time was that I never reveal his name to anyone."

Today, the ascended master Alexander Gaylord continues this work and is very much involved in helping mankind to set their house in order. He is an emissary of freedom and peace for the Brotherhood and member of the Departments of Cosmic Psychology and Geopolitical Studies at the Royal Teton Retreat. He has explained that his work for the Brotherhood is of a very special nature, and that he does occasionally manifest a physical body for this work. He has given dissertations to his students on the nefarious forces at work in the world scene and the interplay of forces in society, including the manipulation of the masses.

He has said, in the name of the Brotherhood, "Ours is the way of love. And in freedom's name, if humanity would really end all wars, they must do so by an unequivocal acceptance of the golden rule of the Prince of Peace. Nations and peoples must be willing to negotiate, but not at the expense of justice and reason. World unrest, which should long ago have been calmed by true religion, has unfortunately been fanned by religious intolerance and the mortal wickedness of the manipulators. Therefore, the Brotherhood prays that wise men everywhere, kneeling at the feet of God, will learn to distinguish between a genuine complaint and one that is synthetically manufactured in order to spread discord.... My prayer is for world peace through individual peace and understanding, but not at the cost of giving in to the manipulators or the warmongers who wave an olive branch that belies the violence in their hearts."[12]

The twin flames of Alexander Gaylord and Leto have a special service among the youth.

❖ **ALOHA,** *See* **Peace and Aloha**

❖ **ALPHA AND OMEGA, The Father-Mother God**

Alpha is the highest manifestation of God in the Great Central Sun. His complement is Omega, the personification of the God flame as Mother. John the Beloved spoke of them in Revelation as "The Beginning and the Ending." Together they focus the beginning and the ending of all cycles of life. They rule in the center of the Hub in the City Foursquare and preside directly over the twelve hierarchies of the Sun.[13]

To the evolutions of this system of worlds, Alpha and Omega represent the Father-Mother God in the heart of the Great Central Sun, on the first and seventh rays respectively. These twin flames are the highest known individualization of the masculine and feminine polarity of the Deity.

Alpha is the personification of the God flame as Father in the core of consciousness we call life. Alpha has said, "as we have declared: Within your hearts and your minds will we write our law.[14] The Law of God, the Law of adoration is reflected in the words 'I AM.' For I, Alpha, am the one who signifies the source, the numeral 1, and the word 'I.' Omega, my beloved, represents the 'AM' and is therefore called '*Ah*-m-ega.'

"I/Amega—the beginning and the ending[15]—declare that the pulsating lifewaves by which the entire cosmos is created are a boon to sharing our love with all systems of worlds and binding them together in a great divine unity of eternal happiness and solicitude."[16]

Although Alpha and Omega are the highest-ranking members of the hierarchy in our universe, they are also the most humble. Their flame is represented in the forget-me-not, for they are the most humble of all manifestations of the Godhead and, therefore, the most worthy to rule.

❖ **ALPHAS, The Keeper of the Gate at the Royal Teton Retreat**

To Alphas, the greatest mission and calling in life and the highest honor is to be the gatekeeper of the Royal Teton Retreat. This magnificent retreat is the principal retreat of the Great White Brotherhood on the North American continent. Thousands of lifestreams travel there from every continent as their bodies sleep at night to attend this retreat. Alphas is therefore a point of reference to all who come to this retreat. He is there to greet you when you arrive. When you see Alphas, you know that you have reached your destination.

Archangel Zadkiel refers to Alphas' role as gatekeeper: "Beloved Alphas now opens the door, stands ready to admit each one. You have but to make the call, beloved hearts, as you take your sleep to enter the sheath of the etheric body, to enter the Christ mind and to receive the guardian angels. May you retain all in the Higher Mind, and may your Christ Self deliver to you the certain direction and knowledge of decisions you must make in the hours and days to come."[17]

By serving at his post, Alphas also demonstrates an important point of spiritual law in our service to the masters. By keeping your appointed post or point in hierarchy and doing it well, even if a humble position or office, you uphold your portion of the plan of God and keep a place in the chain of hierarchy. If that point is not held, a stitch may be dropped. By holding the position assigned, you also prepare yourself for the next point on the path of initiation.

We ought to be content to be in the position we hold and see that we do it well. As we master that focal point, whether it is a job in the world or in the household or as father or as mother or as teacher, we find that the masters give us the exact tests we need in life.

On New Year's Eve, 1963, in Washington, D.C., Alphas gave an address at the conclusion of Gautama Buddha's annual New Year's Eve Address. He said: "I, Alphas, master of the gate for this session at the Grand Teton, declare that this glimpse into the Grand Teton Ranges is closed to mortal men for this occasion. You are welcome there, at the request of the Council, out of your physical forms and in your finer bodies this night. The request of Lord Gautama is that the peace he brought in the name of the risen Christ may surround you all this night. In the name of beloved Alpha and Omega, I, Alphas, bring my love to you as a keeper of that gate this night."

❖ **AMARYLLIS, Goddess of Spring**

The Goddess Amaryllis is the spirit of spring. This beautiful goddess mastered the mental plane and the air element and, as a result, was given the power to rejuvenate those matrices within the consciousness of man that lead to the fulfillment of his divine plan. Amaryllis embodies the green and gold of the precipitation flame that brings forth the power of the creativity of Alpha and Omega.

The angels and elementals serving with Amaryllis are imbued with the spirit of the resurrection flame that produces a rebirth within nature and assists each individual to overcome the last enemy that is death. Because of her devotion to the Holy Spirit in nature, God has rewarded the Goddess of Spring with a great momentum of Christ-power. The elemental beings of earth, air, fire and water adore this daughter of the Sun and follow her from one end of the planet to the other, outpicturing the beauty of her love for all things living.

Amaryllis says: "I bring to the mind those aerating thoughts that are akin to the realm of the elementals—the beautiful billowing sylphs of the air, the gnomes and elementals of the earth in their busy industry, the sacred fire of the fiery salamanders and the undulations of the marvelous undines of the water. All of these convey to humanity an aspect of the fourfold nature of nature's God.

"In manifest form, that which man sees, that with which the artisans work, all malleability and even the hardness of the diamond are the manifestation of the fragrant thoughts of God, thoughts that sparkle with iridescence and wonder, thoughts that flow out majestically into the realms of nature, forest and fields, streams and sky and clouds, all reflecting a cosmic symphony, the symphony of infinite harmony.

"Let men learn, then, how they also may, as the tiny elementals do, leap from floral pattern to floral pattern; be cupped within the heart of a rose in consciousness, feel its fragrance, its color and the soft satiny sheen of its petals; how they may revel in the inflow of natural air and the radiance of the warming sun; how they may feel the awakening of manifestation within themselves, the awakening of the manifestation and the sense of beauty.

"Beauty and love are in the fragrance of the flowers, and when the flowers blow in a gentle breeze, they sway to and fro, nod their tiny heads and speak of love. Let men learn their language, the language of the heart. And let them understand that poetic meandering that is the reverie of the soul as it inhabits the nature kingdom....

"How grateful man ought to be to the wondrous creatures of field and forest, the little invisible creatures who are so wise and so determined in their own blessed efforts to make a carpet of love and splendor for man's eyes to behold!

"How marvelous is the constancy of nature! Season after season these tiny creatures bring forth what otherwise could so easily become the monotonous cycles of manifestation, but they do it with alacrity and joy, and their hearts are filled with a desire to be of service to man.

"And what of man made in the highest image, the image of God? How their thoughts do mar all the beautiful patterns of nature. The blight of vile insect creations, the blight of thorny patterns of destruction manifest also in the kingdom of nature because nature has taken on those aspects of human cruelty and fright. Let men learn, then, that as they improve the quality of their thoughts, so will nature more redundantly and perfectly express, so will beauty and perfection more gloriously dress the world in the cosmic wonder that is the nature of God cascading, falling, fragrance from the Sun of sun.

"Let men dream, then, of blue skies and fearlessness flame. Let them dream, then, of swaying in those cosmic ballets as the tiny creatures do. And let them understand that the beautiful leap from flower to flower is as though man, in tiny elemental form, were possessed of the wings of a bumblebee, could fly and flit from flower to flower, so gentle and persuasive was his confidence in the mercy of God and these creatures that is exuded from every pore. They have faith in the wonders of their own bodies and their beings, their own minds to devote themselves to constancy and service to man.

"Let gratitude flow from human hearts to the eternal God for the won-der of their bountiful service, without which the fruit of the earth could never come forth and garland the world with that mystic splendor of cosmic dew upon the grass."[18]

The inner meaning of the word Amaryllis is: A merry (Mary) God lily, or Alpha merry (Mary) God lily.

❖ **AMAZONIA,** *See* **Hercules and Amazonia**

❖ **AMEN BEY, Twin flame of Ascended Lady Master Clara Louise**

Amen Bey has had many embodiments in Egypt, where he was a pharaoh who influenced the culture of the land according to the principles of the ascended masters. He was a priest of the sacred fire on Atlantis, and he works closely with Serapis Bey as a brother in the Temple at Luxor. His electronic pattern is a deep blue hieroglyph that contains the concept of the spiritual rebirth of the Christed man.

Amen Bey's twin flame is Clara Louise Kieninger, Regent Mother of the Flame. Amen Bey and Clara Louise are dedicated to the youth of the world. When you call to them together, you have the mighty action of

Alpha and Omega that they focus. You can pray to them to assist you to help parents and their children, and they will lead the way in spiritual work on behalf of the youth of the world.

Amen Bey presently teaches classes on cosmic law at the Royal Teton Retreat. He can assist you in preparation for the ascension and in healing. He says: "I AM Amen Bey, your brother on the Path. I bring healing through the sacred fire in your temple. I direct needlepoint rays into every cell and atom of your four lower bodies for balancing and healing."[19]

❖ **AMERISSIS, Goddess of Light**

Amerissis is a powerful being who ensouls the quality of light, hence her name, Goddess of Light. The term God or Goddess denotes one who is a cosmic being and who ensouls the consciousness of God, of his or her office in the spiritual hierarchy and his or her ray.

The Goddess of Light's devotion is to the light of God, even to the light of God within you. She stores that light for us in the heart of every atom, cell and electron. She once explained, "I am called, by God's grace, the Goddess of Light simply because I have paid allegiance to light for so long."[20]

She works with the Queen of Light and the Goddess of Purity. The trinity of these goddesses will pour their light through you when you pray to them and give their decrees and fiats. Even the simple mantra "Let there be light!" will suffice.

Amerissis uses the Queen of Light's focus above Messina on the island of Sicily, the Goddess of Purity's focus in Madagascar, and her own focus in the Shrine of Glory in the Andes in South America as anchoring points for a threefold distribution of the light throughout the world, especially Europe, Asia and Africa.

Prior to her ascension, when she was embodied in South America, the Goddess of Light had achieved such great attainment that she was able to maintain life in one body for more than five hundred years. In an off-guard moment, her forcefield was violated by a group of black magicians who lay in wait, waiting to compromise her. They superimposed upon the lower half of her body the tail of a fish, thus imprisoning her as a mermaid.

Because of her great attainment, it was not possible for her to lay down that physical body and be reborn. The Law required that she ascend from that form in which she had attained her mastery. She was therefore required to sustain life in that form for over eight hundred years before the ascension was given to her.

For three hundred years she served her fellowman from behind a counter and wore full-length skirts so that no one would be aware of what had taken place. She has said that from that moment on, she gazed ever upward toward the light and never placed her attention upon the negative matrix (her mermaid form) again. When her momentum of light was great enough, the Brotherhood sent an unascended emissary who was the key to her freedom. Together they drew forth the necessary balance and momentum of the sacred fire to shatter the matrix she had borne for three centuries. Shortly thereafter she made her ascension.

In 1966, the Goddess of Light explained why she had been vulnerable to the black magician intending to bring about her destruction. She said: "In an unguarded moment I was congratulating myself on all of my attainments when he struck with the sting and bite of an adder, and I found myself bound and scarce able to recover the use of my upper parts. But the spiritual teacher who watched over me was able to save me from that destruction.

"I called and I called and I called through the years unto God to free me from this bondage. And my calls were always made to light: 'O light, set me free. O light, set me free. O God's light, set me free. O God's light, set me free.'

"As I waited upon mankind, as I served people and humanity, the constant prayer of my lips was to light. 'Light, light, light, expand! Light, expand! Light, expand! Light, expand, expand, expand!' And this God-command reached such a crescendo of momentum that at last, as a bolt of lightning through the blue, came the edict of the Karmic Board. And there was a great quaking and trembling within myself, and suddenly the scales of bondage parted and I gazed down upon the new flesh and the perfect body that I once knew, restored by light to the realm of divine opportunity and the place where I could once again take up my studies in divine grace right where I had left off—but in a most humble manner and determined as I was to never again submit to any form of bondage.

"And so I kept up my application to light until eventually I was called before the great Karmic Board and told that I was indeed, because of the light I had externalized, worthy to be called, worthy of the appellation the Goddess of Light. In sudden and almost blind wonder, I stepped forward to accept, not for myself or for the sake of a title (noble though it was indeed and noble though it is) but in order that I might convey to mankind down through the centuries my own gift of light and thus assist not only mankind but even the angelic host to externalize greater light through the roaring centuries and into the eternal boundlessness of God's own limitless light."[21]

Amerissis says, "I give you my light and my causal body, and my legions are ready to serve. Remember my name—Amerissis, Goddess of Light. And remember to call to me and to give forth the fiat of light.

"Light, then, is the alchemical key to the healing of the nations, and also it is the key to your continued objectivity as you learn the meaning of the cross of white fire.

"I am a Mother of light, and I am with you. I have stood where you stand. I have seen the Lord Sanat Kumara consume the darkness. I have seen victory upon victory. We, too, are longing for the termination of the age of darkness. It has been too long. But its cycles are determined, my beloved, by those in embodiment.... Free will weighs remarkably in the outer universes."[22]

In her dictations, the Goddess of Light has repeatedly cautioned us to be constantly on guard against those who would use our weaknesses to set us back on the spiritual path. She has revealed that she works closely with Jesus. She and Jesus often send light to the dying and help them deal with the fear of death. When someone is passing on, you can call to her. "I will use you as a focal point in the world of form," she said, "to expand the light unto them, which is the light of hope, the light of faith and the light of charity" unto all who are making the transition to higher octaves.[23]

The Goddess of Light has given us a meditation for increasing the light within us. She said, "It is well to develop a meditation on light whereby you see pinpoints of light throughout the body. Visualize yourself as a giant Christmas tree with a candle on every little twig and branch so that a million candles might burn on your tree of life to light the way for millions. Remember that at every point of every cell of your body, there is a nucleus in the atom and there is a central sun in every cell. These are points of light. These are, as it were, manifestations of the Great Central Sun at microscopic levels.

"Vibrant health within the body helps to keep the light circulating. Thus, one may enjoy the vibrant mind that is quick and alert and the desire body that is truly aligned with the Law of God in the joy of the LORD."[24]

Amerissis has also given practical teaching on overcoming character weaknesses. She explained that each of us has three major recurring tests in our lives. She said: "Most people on earth, as we have calculated in surveys our angels have taken, have three knots in consciousness that hold them back, pull them back. These knots are so obvious, right beneath their noses, that they fail to see them year after year. Some pass from the screen of life in the change called death never having realized that they missed the most obvious—the most obvious of matters that they came into embodiment to correct.

"Self-analysis is wise when it is not overdone. Therefore, seek those professionals who can assist you. Seek also counsel from your dearest friends, loved ones, family members. For they may also tell you what they may have observed....

"Think then of the three strongest points in your lifestream, where you show the greatest strength of character—the honor, the nobility, the constancy, the stick-to-itiveness. Note this, because most people do have three points where they excel, and excel consistently....

"You should always have three points of acceleration and attainment that you are working on and three points to eliminate, elements of character that you desire to put into the flame. If these are always with you, you will make constant progress. You will self-transcend yourselves many times over. And in the end when you arrive at the gate, you will find that you have passed so many tests that you have balanced karma and you are ready to be candidates for the ascension in one of the ascended masters' retreats."[25]

❖ **AMETHYST,** *See* **Zadkiel and Amethyst**

❖ **AMITABHA,** *See* **The Five Dhyani Buddhas**

❖ **AMOGHASIDDHI,** *See* **The Five Dhyani Buddhas**

❖ **AMORA,** *See* **Heros and Amora**

❖ **THE ANCIENT OF DAYS,** *See* **Sanat Kumara**

❖ **THE MIGHTY ANGEL CLOTHED WITH A CLOUD**

The tenth chapter of the Book of Revelation speaks of the angel "clothed with a cloud: and a rainbow was upon his head...and in his hand a little book." This angel appeared to John the Revelator. The rainbow and the cloud are the causal body and the light of the I AM Presence. The little book is the concentrated energy of the Word of the masters spoken to the prophets.

The Mighty Angel Clothed with the Cloud has given one dictation through the messenger Elizabeth Clare Prophet. He said:

"I bear witness unto the light descending as the Word of the sons and daughters of God. I come from the fount of living flame. I have stood in the presence of Alpha and Omega. I am the angel which stands in the presence of the LORD God with seraphim and cherubim, and unto me is given the office of the transfer of the light of prophecy unto the prophets of the ages. And thus, the writing in the book is the writing in cipher of those energies that are uncoded cyclically each thousand cycles of the turning of God's consciousness within the worlds upon worlds.

"Within my heart I know billions of lifewaves. I know, for I am known of God. And as I gaze upon the consciousness that he has shared with his sons and daughters, I behold an infinite creativity on the part of those who have exalted free will within his will. And I behold also the infamy of those who have enshrined the darkness of nonexistence. And I stand to sound forth the clarion call of an age, for I am the herald of the ascended masters, and the little book is the concentrated energy of their Word spoken unto the prophets, spoken unto the prophets for their children evolving into the oneness of that flame.

"I can be seen standing in the cities, standing in the temples, standing in the midst of the people. And those who desire truth are bidden to the initiation of that mighty angel that also appeared unto John. And with me is the sound of the Elohim. The thundering and the sounding of that voice is the tuning of a cosmos and of millions of souls."[26]

❖ **ANGEL DEVA OF THE JADE TEMPLE, Hierarch of the Jade Temple in China**

The Angel Deva of the Jade Temple is the hierarch of the retreat in China known as the Jade Temple.

According to ancient tradition that comes down to us from the time when the angels of the Jade Temple walked among the people and healed, jade has healing properties that are transferred to the physical body. Standing in the Jade Room of the Temple, we bear witness to the truth of this ancient belief. The glow of the healing flame comes through the walls of jade, which convey a feeling of velvet softness, peace and stillness.

In the temple, there is a statue of a jade Buddha sitting in the lotus posture with his hands outstretched upon his knees, holding a focus of the healing flame in each palm: in his left palm, the feminine and in the right, the masculine aspect of the healing flame. Thus, the buddhic consciousness is androgynous and conveys the wholeness of the Father-Mother God to all whose faith will permit them to be whole.

The jade that lines the walls of the Temple is the crystallization of the healing flame used by the Brothers and angels of this retreat to minister to the needs of mankind and elemental life.

As a gift to the Keepers of the Flame, the Angel Deva and his legions erected a replica of the Jade Temple around La Tourelle at the 1969 Harvest Class. The Angel Deva told those present to visualize in the midst of the Temple a great white lotus flame. This he created out of the essence of their own souls' aspiration to be a pulsing lotus of light, and he condensed it into the aura of each one who was able to accept it.

"By the process of cosmic thought," he said, "you can create your own meditation temples wherever you are, and you can create this great lotus of white fire around yourself, a breathing purity from God that will cut off all outer activity of the senses. Even as your tube of light functions so magnificently, this will also add to it the power of the Jade Temple."[27]

He said that the Jade Temple exists in the flame of purity that you are when you understand the cosmic seed and the cosmic intent and function as one with the Presence. He sealed the cables of communication between the Higher Self and the lower self in a coating of fiery jade, in a flowing flux of cosmic reality, to enhance the student's understanding of his true Being.

On the same occasion, he blessed the jade worn by the students in attendance with his momentum of purity and healing. In establishing these individual foci, he pointed out that the secret of all healing is to bask in purity's glow; for in the flame of purity, there is no human stain.

He said of the blessing of the jewelry: "Understand that the time limit of the charge is determinate upon your own life. For whenever you wear the jade and your thoughts are inharmonious or destructive, you remove a little of the charge I have placed within it today; and whenever you are constructive and building in hope and renewal toward God and the flame of his purity, you will add to it. This is a simple rephrasing of the law of your own being: 'Whatsoever ye shall sow, that shall ye also reap.'"[28]

With this understanding, all students may ask the Angel Deva of the Jade Temple to charge their jade jewelry with his momentum of purity and healing.

❖ **ANGEL, LISTENING,** *See* **Listening Angel**

❖ **ANGEL OF GETHSEMANE**

This angel is one who ministered to Jesus in the Garden of Gethsemane. He comes to strengthen the body of God upon earth as he strengthened Jesus in the Garden. The Angel of Gethsemane has released one dictation. He said, "My strengthening is for the hour when you also must be alone in the Garden, unsupported by those well-meaning ones around

you, in the hour when you, too, must say, 'If thou be willing, let this cup pass from me. Nevertheless, Father, not my will but thine be done.' And when you have spoken the word, 'thy will be done,' then and only then shall I appear to strengthen you for the most glorious of initiations—the hour of the crucifixion when the Christ is liberated fully and the soul prepares for the resurrection."[29]

❖ ANGEL OF LISTENING GRACE

The Angel of Listening Grace is one of a band of angels who have come to minister to the needs of mankind in this hour. "I AM an angel of listening grace, an intelling presence, the Spirit of God that draws nigh unto mankind in the hour of the overcoming. I am one among many who have been sent in the flaming presence of the law of love to minister unto the needs of mankind in the hour when mankind are searching to know the Truth, the why of being, the wherefores of life….

"We come in the flaming presence of the One whose Spirit, whose very essence, draws nigh unto the heart flame and the souls of mankind. We are angels of the Holy Spirit, angels of the Presence, the very essence of life. We come in numberless numbers, for great is the need. Great is the desiring of God to press the being and the soul of mankind into the mold of inner reality. And so we urge and so we speak in the inner ear the word of encouragement, of hope, urging the soul to pursue that which is worthy….

"We are angels of the sacred fire. We know the thoughts, the feelings, the levels of consciousness almost infinite in the finite form. We see how layers and layers and layers of the being of man must be defined and the dark layers extracted by fire. Only the fire of God can resolve the dilemma of the age! Only the fire of God can move in as a needle ray to penetrate the earth and the consciousness of mankind and to withdraw those elements that are the energies of the spoilers, spoiling the barrel of humanity's consciousness.

"Therefore, place your hope in the eternal Presence and understand that that Presence has the full capacity within the law of cosmos to individualize itself as the angels of listening grace, angels of ministration and service, angels of the legions of the cosmic hierarchy. So we are the Presence and the very present help. And so as flaming spirits of fire, we can be the refiners of the electrode and the grid of consciousness. We can move through the density of consciousness and rally the molecules to perform the perfect work of the alignment of your being! We can rally the energy of the electron! We can rally the energy of the cell to make you whole!"[30]

❖ **ANGEL OF PEACE**

The Angel of Peace is head of the band of angels known as the Legion of Peace. This angel assisted Jesus in amplifying the flame of peace during his ministry. He was also one of the ministering angels who, together with Holy Amethyst, kept the vigil with Jesus in the Garden of Gethsemane. He was one of the heavenly hosts sent by God to sustain Jesus after he had prayed, saying, "Father, if thou be willing, remove this cup from me: nevertheless not my will, but thine, be done."[31]

Although the Father, acting in conformity to his own Law, did not "remove this cup," he did send his archangels and archeiai and, among others, this Angel of Peace to strengthen Jesus in his resolve to do the will of God. The fiery presence of these angels served as electrodes to magnetize the flames of peace and power, healing and truth, faith and hope and reality from Jesus' own causal body, thereby aiding Jesus in bringing the full momentum of his own light to bear upon the betrayal, the trial and the crucifixion that lay before him.

It was the Angel of Peace that appeared to the three shepherd children in Fátima, Portugal, in 1916, prior to the appearances of Mother Mary. The angel was described as "A light whiter than snow in the form of a young man, transparent and brighter than crystal, pierced by the rays of the sun."

The angel said, "Do not be afraid. I am the Angel of Peace. Pray with me." He kneeled with his forehead to the ground and said, "My God, I believe, I adore, I hope and I love you. I ask pardon of you for those who do not believe, do not adore, do not hope and do not love you." The angel taught the children to pray and offer sacrifices to God on behalf of others.

Mother Mary has said, "Beloved ones, if the Angel of Peace and my own message at Fátima was the encouragement to pray, to make sacrifice, to call for the conversion of sinners, and if the prayers of these three could in itself be a dispensation to stay the hand of darkness, what do you think the dispensation is when hundreds upon hundreds, even thousands of Keepers of the Flame, in the full awareness of the science of the spoken Word and the science of the Immaculate Heart, will give these invocations as shouting from the housetops for the invocation of light?

"Well, I will tell you, you can let your imagination flow through the stars, for indeed the galaxies are filled with light. And this is what is needed for the turning point, beloved ones, the turning point in world history."[32]

Mary invites us to call to the Angel of Peace to enter the classrooms and teach the sweet children their prayers. The Angel of Peace and Mother Mary are greatly concerned about the separation of souls from God through atheism, agnosticism, political or economic systems that have denied God, and systems of doctrine and dogma.

❖ **ANGEL OF THE AGONY, The Angel Who Ministered to Jesus on the Cross**

The Angel of the Agony ministered to Jesus on the cross. With his legions, the Angel of the Agony inspires and uplifts those who are weighted down with the weight of the cross of personal and planetary karma. He exemplifies the many angels who minister to suffering humanity.

This angel asks to be remembered when we are praying for those who are suffering: "I pray, then, that as you pray to our Father in the name of the Christ and the I AM THAT I AM, you will remember to call to me on behalf of the thousands upon earth who are suffering daily. Call to me, for then I can send legions to the side of those who are waiting and watching for the appearance of their Lord....

"In the hour, then, of the suffering of those who depart from life making the transition, bearing as they do the personal and planetary karma, I ask you to call for all of those who are on beds of pain and who must be received by the angels of heaven and by the Lords of Karma. Call, then, that we might stand and encourage these blessed ones with a vision of the etheric temples and cities and retreats to encourage them with a view of the life that is to be and with the joy and the understanding somewhere in the soul that that suffering is also bringing a balance to life and the opportunity for others to live and to overcome. I ask you to call to our legions of angels also for the comfort of those who stand at the cross watching the passing of loved ones, for we would also care for those who suffer with the ones who are in the midst of the initiation."[33]

The Angel of the Agony and his legions come to rebuke the spirits of death who taunt the overcomers in the hour of agony and also to give inspiration to those who are passing through their initiations. "I desire that you should understand that even in the hour of the most intense suffering, even in the hour when pain is present within the body temple, there is a bliss within the soul and within the heart, and this is the bliss that expands and expands and expands until the entire forcefield of the Son of God becomes a replica of the Central Sun right in the very midst of the agony of the crucifixion....

"I am called the Angel of the Agony, and I come with my legions to inspire those who are weighted down with the weight of the cross of personal and planetary karma. We come to the courageous ones who greet the angels of Lord Maitreya with the glad 'Yes, I will be initiated! Yes, I will take the next step, whatever that step may be. I am ready Lord, for I have the will to be the victor over hell and death in this life, this my life victorious and triumphant.'"[34]

❖ ANGEL OF THE COSMIC CROSS OF WHITE FIRE

The Angel of the Cosmic Cross of White Fire is the spokesman for legions of angels of the cosmic cross of white fire, "numberless numbers who minister unto the sons and daughters of God in the hour of the crucifixion." In his dictation in 1980, he explained that he and his legions had come to earth to assist in the initiation of the one hundred and forty-four thousand, the original lightbearers who came to earth with Sanat Kumara.

"Not since the hour of the crucifixion of the Lord Jesus Christ have we entered earth's domain to deliver unto the sons of God the fullness of this initiation.... Lo, we are come for the preparation of your soul in the consummate union with your own Christ Self.... Lo, we come to amplify the path of the cross, the path of the Sacred Heart. Lo, we are come to multiply by the power of the one hundred and forty and four thousand the original God-victory of the Lord and Saviour Jesus Christ.... Legions in the order of this cosmic cross have come to earth, will remain in the earth, will tarry unto the victory of the hundred and forty and four thousand."[35]

In 1997, angels of the cosmic cross of white fire and the ruby ray came to help us internalize the flame of the white fire and the ruby ray. They work with the Buddha of the Ruby Ray to fill the cups of our cells and molecules with ruby-ray essence, especially for the healing of the heart. They intensify the fire of being and give instruction on mercy and forgiveness.

The joy of forgiveness liberates from sin, disease and death as well as the evils of the underworld. These angels say, "You would do well to think of your past, present and future as you meditate and ask yourself, 'Is there someone whom I have wronged from whom I have not asked for forgiveness?' If so, approach that one,...even if your concern is just a little thing, embrace that one and say: 'I will not defile your being, your God or your heart flame again. This, my friend, I vow to you. Please forgive me and let us walk on the road of life together.'"[36]

❖ **ANGEL OF THE RESURRECTION**

The Angel of the Resurrection is one of the band of angels of the resurrection "who attend the light of victory in souls ascending to the sacred fire of God!" In 1977, this mighty angel explained his mission: "Angels of the resurrection have the assignment of the LORD God to stand with the son and the daughter who are accelerating consciousness by invocation to the sacred fires of the heart, stepping up, then, and accelerating by the Great Central Sun Magnet the light of the Father, the Son and the Holy Spirit within the heart.

"We are the angels who stood at the head and at the feet of the body of Christ tending that precious body as stewards of life there in the tomb. I AM the angel who announced to Magdalene, 'He is not here, but he is risen. Come, see the place where the Lord lay.'[37]

"The joy of resurrection is the joy of our heart as we keep the forcefield of Alpha and Omega for the son, the daughter of God who has earned the opportunity for the initiation of the resurrection. That son, then, is able to invoke and to magnetize by the fire of the heart and the fire of the sacred centers an accelerated momentum of resurrection's fire, accelerating the cells and atoms in a coordinated manner chakra by chakra in a spherical motion that begins within the heart and in a clockwise direction extends to the chakras above and below the heart until the entire forcefield becomes a whirling sun of light.

"And the acceleration, then, that is sustained by the consciousness of the son of God who is out of the body temple hovering over that lifeless form— that consciousness magnetizes a greater and greater momentum of the light of the I AM Presence until there is once again drawn forth from that I AM Presence the full momentum of the threefold flame anchored once again in the physical vehicle, and the one who was dead is restored to life.

"This is the means of overcoming.... This is the initiation that is reenacted by the sons and daughters of God who come to the Temple of the Resurrection over the Holy Land and are received also at Luxor by Serapis Bey. This is the initiation that is conducted in the Great Pyramid in the etheric counterpart."

The Angel of the Resurrection says, "I have placed my feet within the tomb where He was lain. I have placed my feet on the rock. I have placed my hands upon the stone. I have seen his lifeless form, and I have seen him rise. I have seen him come forth through the open door, and I have seen that threefold flame restored and the light begin to pulsate and the form be filled with life. I am therefore the eyewitness to that event that has been questioned for two thousand years.... This is the victory that *was* and *is* for all.... We will teach you how to accelerate the fire of the resurrection, and we will be unto you guardian, friend and fellow servant."[38]

The resurrection flame is a powerful adjunct to healing. It can be invoked for resurrection, not only of the four lower bodies but also for the soul and spirit of men and nations and even the earth body itself.

❖ ANGEL OF THE REVELATION OF JOHN THE DIVINE

Jesus dictated the book of Revelation to John the Beloved through his Angel of the Revelation. This angel has spoken profoundly on the Christ and the true meaning of Church and of the need to cease division within the Church. He says:

"I speak to the body of God fragmented over the earth. I speak to those who come out of the churches and I speak to souls who are within the churches. I call to those who have worshiped God in Islam, as the Hindu, as the Buddhist, as followers of the Tao, as interpreters of the Word of the LORD of Israel. I speak to Jew and Gentile, to those who are the true followers of God and to those who have gone out of the way.

"I release the Spirit of the living Christ and I say, Each way of finding God is a ray that leads to the center of the temple and of all true building that is Christ—Christ as you have known the eternal Logos in Jesus and Christ as you are to know him again in this age, within your very own heart and as the flame that burns upon the altar of the heart.

"I come with a warning, and I come with a quickening. Let the warning be, then, to souls who are of God, that there are the fallen ones who have infiltrated your ranks, who have moved among you in your midst. It is they who are the false Christs and false prophets, and they have separated the love of the holy innocents and the credo of our Lord by their murmuring, by their false doctrine, by their separation of the love of the members of the body of God.

"My warning, then, is this: that there shall come the crumbling of the Church of Rome and the crumbling of the churches of Christendom unless the spirit of division is routed from the church in the name of Jesus the

Christ. And let the demons and the fallen ones tremble, for the Lord is nigh. And he will not allow the money changers to remain in the temple, those who barter for men's souls, those who compromise the faith of our Lord with compromise to suit the ethics of the day....

"Be true to the Christ who lives within, and you will find yourself one in the true Church that is a flame within your heart. It is not necessary for you to find salvation through outer commitment and outer organizations. But it is necessary for you to confirm the living Word where you are and to band together in the churches, to go back into the churches and to bring unto them the Holy Spirit and the message of the Angel of the Revelation, who I AM as a fellow servant with you of the Most High God.

"I am come to give you the impetus of light and fire of the Christ to go back into the churches of your origin or to be a part of this band of devotees who have formed an outer focus of the Church Universal and Triumphant. Wherever you go to pray, to worship and to find oneness in the communion of souls, bring there the Spirit of the living God. Bring there the spirit of Truth.

"And remember that this Truth is where you are and where I AM. And in that I AM THAT I AM, we are one and there is no separation in planes of consciousness, for the Spirit of God moves those who are in embodiment and who are in celestial spheres as one body in the service of Christ.

"I am come for the contact. I am come that you might realize that the hosts of the armies of heaven are very real and very near and that the numbers of angels and angelic hosts, of archangels and seraphim and cherubim, and of the saints ascended far outnumber the forces of the fallen ones as well as the numbers who are yet embodied in terrestrial bodies on earth."[39]

❖ **ANGEL OF UNITY,** *See* **Micah**

❖ **THE ANGEL WHO ROLLED AWAY THE STONE**

The angel who rolled away the stone from Jesus' tomb has the assignment to care for the sons and daughters of God who are undergoing the passions of our Lord. This angel has also offered to help us roll away the stones of stumbling and boulders in the path of our own life, particularly the boulder of pride. He says:

"Would you have me roll back your stones of stumbling, your boulders of pride, your mountains of fear and doubt? If the answer is yes, then call to me! For I am the roller of the stones that prevent the children of the light and the sons and daughters of God from going straight to the mark of Sirius, to the Great Central Sun and to the sun of Helios and Vesta....

"Inscribe in your notebook a reminder to look at the boulders around you and say to yourself: 'Now, what am I going to do with these boulders? I cannot move them. Jesus needed help to move his boulders. Who will help me to move mine?'

"Smart ones of Saint Germain will say, 'We have the violet flame! We have the alchemy of violet-flame transmutation whereby we may consume our boulders of pride. We can move those boulders, as Merlin did at Stonehenge centuries ago!' Call to Saint Germain to remove anything and everything in your life that is stopping you from serving the Great White Brotherhood."[40]

❖ APOLLO AND LUMINA, Elohim of the Second Ray

Apollo and Lumina are guardians of the Cosmic Christ consciousness. The Elohim of the second ray assist those who desire to know God through the mind of the Son, the second person of the Trinity. For the Elohim of the second ray, all is "the instantaneous precipitation of the mind of God."

The god known long ago to the Greeks as the mythological Apollo could well be the representation of the memory of an ancient encounter with the Elohim. After thousands of years, however, the gods and goddesses assumed more and more human traits in the minds of the people. Hence, what is currently attributed to Apollo as the god of Greek mythology may not necessarily reflect the actuality of the Elohim.

Apollo was known in the Pythagorean tradition as the symbol of masculine beauty, the solar god who personifies the spiritual light of which the sun is the physical image. He represented the descent of heaven on earth. Apollo is considered by some to be the Solar Logos, the Mediator, Vishnu, Mithras, Horus, the Universal Word. Apollo was lawgiver to the Greek city-states. As the god of divination and prophecy, he communicated to humanity by means of prophets and oracles as in the famed Oracle of Delphi.

Apollo's flame is a golden yellow enveloped in a sheath of blue lightning. The blue flame acts as a protective forcefield of energy surrounding the light of the Christ. This blue lightning cuts through the density of human error and misqualification, clearing the way for Lumina's golden flame that manifests the perfection of the seven aspects of the Christ mind. The twin flames of Apollo and Lumina infuse earth, air, fire and water with the intelligence locked in the center of the atom—the essence of the diamond-shining mind of God.

Apollo and Lumina want us to focus on education and the quickening of the mind of God within all mankind. On July 6, 1975, Apollo came with a major dispensation of a rod of illumination for the stepping-up of the minds of humanity. Apollo said this dispensation is delivered only once in ten thousand years. He said: "Mankind may, if they choose, employ the rod to enter a new era and a golden age."[41]

The Great Divine Director explained that this electrode of energy could turn around all negativity that has ever been superimposed upon us. "This dispensation came in order that for the remaining quarter of the century, the lightbearers should have every advantage possible to increase divine awareness,"[42] and so that the mind of God could be restored within them.

You may visualize the rod of illumination being activated within you. See it as an intense golden light pulsating within your brain. See this electrode burning up all impurities that would impede the flow of God's light in your mind. Also see a corona of golden light that is the manifestation of the mind of God superimposed over your own head and over the heads of the children of light on earth.

Apollo and Lumina's retreat is located in the etheric plane over Lower Saxony, Germany. In preparation for the coming golden age, tremendous tides of illumination's flame are being released from this temple. The millions of angels who serve under Apollo and Lumina are ready to go forth to raise the consciousness of the entire earth to the level of the Christ in answer to the calls of the students.

These angels, together with those angels serving at the retreats of Jophiel and Christine, Lord Lanto, the God and Goddess Meru, Lord Gautama Buddha, Lord Himalaya, Lord Maitreya and the World Teachers, Jesus and Kuthumi, should be called upon on behalf of the enlightenment of all mankind, for they are equal in every respect to the tremendous task at hand. Ask them to bring about illumined, intelligent action in all situations, especially those that affect the future of earth and her evolutions.

❖ ARCHANGELS OF THE FIVE SECRET RAYS

Sanat Kumara spoke of the archangels of the five secret rays in a dictation in 1992: "I, Sanat Kumara, draw the circle in the earth, in the sand and in the sea. And that circle is the circle of fire round about the city where the Keepers of the Flame keep the flame and where the messenger will go.

"Now see the diagram of the twelve-pointed star around the circle and know, beloved, that the archangels and archeiai of whom I have spoken this day are the five, who, with the seven, make the twelve, and the thirteenth is Uzziel. Thus, know, beloved, that these angels have come out of the cosmic heights with their bands and they are authorized to be in the earth in response to your presence here. You may call to them as the archangels of the five secret rays....

"Thus, beloved, imagine the increase of light in the earth when five additional archangelic sets of twin flames become a part of this activity. The multiplication is stunning! It is a stunning geometry whereby those of the five secret rays multiply now the action of the archangels of the seven rays, and the seven archangels multiply the action of the archangels of the five secret rays.

"Know, then, that they do stand with their divine complements, their backs to the center of the circle, with raised swords, and they direct the piercing light of their swords outward into action now. And thus they do send light throughout the planetary home. And the multiplication factor is Archangel Uzziel standing in the center with his twin flame; and they do magnificently embody the Presences of Alpha and Omega in that center."[43]

❖ ARCTURUS AND VICTORIA, Elohim of the Seventh Ray

Arcturus and Victoria, the Elohim of the seventh ray, focus the energies of the seat-of-the-soul chakra of the planet from their retreat in the etheric realm near Luanda in Angola, Africa. This retreat is dedicated to the freedom and victory of the planet. They also focus the flame of mercy, forgiveness and alchemy. The pulsations of the violet flame from the hearts of Arcturus and Victoria produce the rhythm and the ritual of application through service and reverence for life.

Arcturus uses the purple flame to focus the scientific action and transmutative essence of freedom, while Victoria radiates the violet (orchid-colored) flame, representing the mercy and love of freedom.

The service of the Elohim of the seventh ray to this planet has been intensified beginning in the twentieth century as the result of the dispensation given to Saint Germain in the 1930s to release to the outer world the teachings of the I AM. Formerly this instruction had been given only in retreats of the Brotherhood.

Therefore, at the opening of the Century of Progress Exposition in Chicago in 1933, Arcturus began the specific action of the freedom flame for the assistance of the Americas. During that decade, other cosmic beings came out of the Great Silence (Nirvana) to assist Saint Germain in his tremendous undertaking on behalf of the evolutions of the planet. This assistance has been augmented and intensified in recent years, and the continuing sponsorship of the Great White Brotherhood, ascended hosts and cosmic beings is evident in the dispensations that have come forth.

Arcturus and Victoria have spoken frequently about the benefits of the violet flame: "The problems of the world are bigger than both of us and all of us. They are not bigger than the Elohim of God, but they are bigger than us when we have no one to contact in the earth who will make the call to the violet flame whereby we can intercede.

"The violet flame, then, is the very solution of the hour to get things moving…in all of these places you see as you sit before your TV sets and stare in wonder at the atrocities being committed. Yet have you saturated the area with the violet flame?… Whatever problems you see when you look at your home life, your family and your children, know that the violet flame can and will make the difference!…

"Many of you have seen the film *Aladdin,* and you have said to yourselves, 'Now, that is just what I need—I need a genie!'… Well, Saint Germain is a genie also. So you have your genies. In fact, you have ten thousand–times–ten thousand genies! For look at all the ascended masters and hosts of the LORD who, when they hear just one command from you, when that command is qualified by the will of God, will answer your call and perform for you so long as what you are asking for is the will of God and is in keeping with the cosmic timetable for that event.… We are in joy, Arcturus and Victoria, ever ready to save planet Earth in answer to *your* command!"[44]

Arcturus and Victoria, hurl us this challenge:

"*So you will decide* whether the violet flame shall be for you the point of the springboard of your victory!…

"*So you will decide* what the violet flame will be as the x factor in the turning around of your life, your economy, your outlook!

"Everything that happens to you in this world can be altered by the violet flame! Only you can decide.…

"Somehow this human mind that carries the cast of the dweller-on-the-threshold and the not-self does not quite believe, even in the minds and hearts of chelas, that the violet flame can do *everything—everything* that you need to have done.… Yes, beloved hearts, seeing is going to be believing. And we are going to see to it that at some level of your being, both conscious and unconscious, you shall acknowledge the miracles of the very violet flame that you invoke.

"When an alchemist goes to his laboratory, if he does not perform the experiment, if he does not engage in alchemy, nothing happens. Well, if you do nothing, you will see nothing! And so the experiment must include your invoking the violet flame for a certain amount of time each day until you have a momentum building in your aura....

"The violet flame is the wonder drug of the century. It is the wonder flame! And it can make the difference as to which way planet Earth goes. I don't mind if you whistle the violet flame, sing the violet flame, jump and dance to the violet flame, do circle dances to all of your music to the violet flame, create new music to the violet-flame decrees. I don't mind whatever you do. Make games out of it! Do marathons with it! But whatever you do, beloved ones, you have to get busy with exciting and innovative methods to bring that violet flame into every area of your life and to bring it there at the point where it counts, with the science of the spoken Word—your word, your tongue, your vocal cords and your chakras."[45]

❖ ARIES AND THOR, Hierarchs of the Air Element

As directors of the air element, these twin flames serve with the hierarchies of Aries, Taurus and Gemini to teach mankind the mastery of the mental body and with the hierarchies of Gemini, Libra and Aquarius to teach the mastery of the air element.

Beloved Aries and Thor direct the activities of illumination that proceed from the mind of Christ, of inspiration and respiration, the breathing in

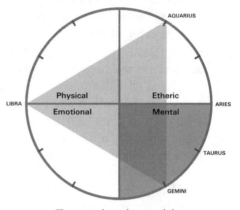

The mental quadrant and the trine of the air signs

and out of the breath of the Holy Spirit, the purification of the air element, the atmosphere and the mental belt.

The sylphs who assist them are the air elementals who control the four winds, the atmosphere and the clouds. Since all elementals are essentially mimics, the sylphs, being no exception, pattern in the clouds the designs they perceive in the physical, astral, mental and etheric planes of the earth. When we see pictures of angels in the clouds, we know that they are nigh at hand, for the sylphs have seen them and have formed the clouds after their image and likeness. Similarly, the beasts of prey and monsters that loom as dark clouds are the sylphs' renderings of mankind's discord that rages in the astral sea, agitating elemental life and preventing them from functioning according to the law of harmony. Thus, the signs of the times can be read in the activities of elemental life who faithfully record the man-

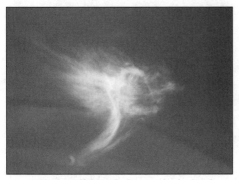

dates of angels and men upon the face of nature.

Mark Prophet has described the sylphs in this way: "They're beautiful. These are the type of fairies you see with the long golden hair and the rather thin, seraphic-type bodies, and they're very curvaceous. They float through the air, and they'll bend their whole body in different shapes. Sometimes the body is bent with the legs behind, trailing like a garment, and their arms are in graceful ballerina poses.

"They have beautiful faces like the most beautiful women you can imagine, except that they are faces of purity. There's nothing carnal or hard in their faces. The only exceptions are that certain sylphs take on the more human form and human attitudes when they are subjected to them.

"Now, when the sylphs take on negative human attitudes and qualities of discord, they will desire to rid themselves of these by the use of centrifugal force. They will throw off the human vibration of hatred and anger by starting a whirling action in the air. They can whirl so fast that they can develop winds of a hundred and fifty miles an hour. That's the power behind the hurricane."[46]

Theosophist E. L. Gardner gives this vivid description of elementals, and sylphs in particular. He says: "The natural 'body' used by elementals seems to be a pulsing globe of light. Streams of force radiating from this center build up floating figures, 'wings' of radiating energy, and filmy shapes of vaguely human likeness. In the more evolved forms the heads and eyes are always clearly distinguishable; often the whole figure is there, with a 'center' of light blazing at the heart or head.

"A sylph of this type might materialize into a beautiful male or female form for work...among plants, animals, or even human beings, but its natural body is...iridescent, changing, pulsating...but not limited to a fixed or definite shape."[47]

The sylphs are bearers of the "prana of the Holy Spirit that is the very life breath of the soul." They stand "with the Lord Maha Chohan as he breathes the breath of life into the newborn soul and as the threefold flame is rekindled once again upon the altar of the heart." They are "the great transmitters of the currents of the Holy Spirit from heaven to earth" and they are "giant transformers, conductors of the currents of the mind of God unto the mind of man."[48] The sylphs wash and purify the atmosphere and aerate the mind and heart and every cell of life.

It is important for mankind to give heartfelt prayers of gratitude to the sylphs and to call for their protection.

❖ **ASTREA,** *See* **Purity and Astrea**

❖ **AURORA,** *See* **Uriel and Aurora**

❖ **BABAJI, Unascended Master of the Himalayas**

Babaji is an unascended master of the Himalayas. He has become well known in the West through the writings of Paramahansa Yogananda. Babaji has chosen to forgo the ascension by reason of the bodhisattva ideal, which means that he desires to remain on earth until everyone has won their freedom. He remains in a body of flesh in a cave in the Himalayas, yet he is able to dematerialize his body at will and carry himself and his followers from one part of the world to another.

Babaji is a part of the Great White Brotherhood in the lineage of the unascended brotherhood of the Himalayas. His name means "Revered Father." Mighty Victory has described the service of the unascended masters:

"Unascended souls of magnificent countenance have stood with the evolutions of earth. They have stood as sages. They have stood to retain the flame at the etheric level to give comfort to life. They are the consciousness of the ascension, yet unascended. You might say they have reached the plane of samadhi, of eternal communion with the Mother light, and from that communion they have drawn forth even the light of nirvanic planes, anchoring that light here below. They are the perpetuation of the Word. They stand to ennoble the race."[49]

According to Yogananda, Babaji has never disclosed his family origin, birthplace or birth date. He speaks generally in Hindi but also converses easily in any language. Yogananda says, "The deathless guru bears no mark of age on his body; he appears to be a youth of not more than twenty-five. Fair-skinned, of medium build and height, Babaji's beautiful, strong body radiates a perceptible glow. His eyes are dark, calm, and tender; his long, lustrous hair is copper-colored.... He has lived for many centuries amid the Himalayan snows."[50]

Yogananda's Sanskrit tutor was a disciple of Babaji who had spent time with the master in the Himalayas. He said of Babaji, "The peerless master moves with his group from place to place in the mountains.... Babaji can be seen or recognized by others only when he so desires. He is known to have appeared in many slightly different forms to various devotees—sometimes with beard and moustache and sometimes without them. His undecayable body requires no food; the master, therefore, seldom eats."[51]

Yogananda relates the following story about the power of a guru's intercession: "Babaji's disciples were sitting one night around a huge fire that was blazing for a sacred Vedic ceremony. The guru suddenly seized a burning brand and lightly struck the bare shoulder of a chela who was close to the fire.

"'Sir, how cruel!' Lahiri Mahasaya, who was present, made this remonstrance.

"'Would you rather have seen him burned to ashes before your eyes, according to the decree of his past karma?'

"With these words Babaji placed his healing hand on the chela's disfigured shoulder. 'I have freed you tonight from painful death. The karmic law has been satisfied through your slight suffering by fire.'"[52]

During a dictation in 1988, Surya explained that Babaji was present, "floating in the lotus posture, beaming intense and fiery love. Remaining at the interval and the nexus between the crystal spheres of the Spirit-Matter Cosmos, this unascended master of the Himalayas does come to demonstrate to you what is the victory of the Mother flame, how ascension's flame as a buoyant fount of light may become the lotus pad."[53]

Babaji speaks on behalf of the Brotherhood of the Himalayas, urging his students to take up the path of the violet flame. He also asks us to find the students trapped in the false paths and false teachings of India. Babaji tells his students to not remove themselves into nirvana but to "get over the desire to be the removed one, set apart and in meditation and in unreality when there is a victory to be won and a battle to enter."

He says, "I AM Babaji! I choose to speak by the authority of the Darjeeling Council on behalf of the unascended brotherhood of the Himalayas. For we come forth and we come to sponsor now true chelas of the Path who will wear the mantle of the ascension, white and bright.

"I come in the person of Father as I am called. I come to pierce and penetrate the veil. I come to expose those false ones who have misrepresented us. They are named and their names hang with the sword of Damocles that is upon their head. I say, Let them be exposed! For we will have the victory of all chelas in the dispensation of the Great White Brotherhood....

"Test me by my vibration! Ask me and I will come to your life! Don't you dare deny me or my messenger until you have demanded proof and more proof! For I will give it! I will come! And I will growl with Himalaya until you know that the God Star Sirius is my home also. And I am with the legions of the mighty Blue Eagle and I am here. And I will not take no for an answer! If you are of the light, you may first fight with Babaji. And when I have fought and won, I will teach you how to defeat the demons.

"So I have come. I have broken the silence. And all of the masters of the Himalayas gather with me....

"Now you who hear me: Go find those souls trapped in the false paths of the false gurus of India! And let them hear my message; let them hear my Word! Do not fear to show them the face of the messenger or the sound of my voice. Then let them choose. And do not leave them without the light and sign of Astrea.

"I AM Babaji. I AM here because I AM not anywhere else, but everywhere."[54]

❖ BLUE EAGLE, THE MIGHTY

The mighty Blue Eagle is a formation of blue-lightning angels who come from Sirius to assist Archangel Michael in his work on behalf of the evolutions of this solar system. Their legions move in the formation of the mighty eagle that is on the Seal of the President of the United States. When you study the components of the mighty Blue Eagle, you will see that every feather and part is a blue-flame angel. It is a vast formation that fills the starry heavens.

The Blue Eagle is the symbol of the God Star Sirius, the symbol of the soaring of consciousness and the raising of the Mother, the symbol of judgment and of vigilance and of the quickness of the All-Seeing Eye of God. The mighty Blue Eagle beholds the enemy and casts out the enemy for the coming of the children of the One. These angels also reinforce the work of the violet-flame angels.

In 1977, Archangel Michael announced that Surya has assigned to each Keeper of the Flame ten angels from the mighty Blue Eagle. These angels will stand with you twenty-four-hours a day to enhance your service to the light. You may call to them to perform functions that you are not able to perform. Archangel Michael says, "They are nearly physical, beloved ones, so tangible is their presence."[55]

Saint Germain has explained that it was this mighty formation of angels that answered the prayers of George Washington (now the ascended master Godfre) in Valley Forge:

"I see him kneeling in prayer, praying on behalf of America. And I see legions from the God Star Sirius hearken to the prayers of the general. I see how the words spoken from his lips on that cold day in the wood were heard by the mighty Blue Eagle of Sirius, who responded instantaneously—these legions of light who made their way, encamping round about him and among the men and, by the infusion of that God-light, securing the victory....

"Above all, I ask you, Keepers of the Flame, to kneel in prayer once a day with Godfre and with me before you retire and to remember to call for the victory of light in America and in the hearts of the American people. And I can assure you by all that lives and breathes, by all that is holy in love, the mighty Blue Eagle from Sirius will answer your call and will deliver this nation as one nation under God—individed, undivided, secure in the oneness of the light."[56]

❖ **BOB AND PEARL SINGLETON,** *See* **Rex and Nada, Bob and Pearl**

❖ **BONZANO, CARDINAL**

Cardinal Bonzano lived in Chicago and made his ascension after his passing in 1927. He was a prelate of the Roman Catholic Church for many years. During his service as a priest, he saw the violet flame while in meditation. At a certain point in giving his devotions, the violet flame became a living part of him, day in and day out. Through the violet flame and his service, he was able to transmute enough of his karma to earn his ascension.

Since his ascension, Cardinal Bonzano has said, "Prior to my ascension, as an officer of the Holy Church to which I then belonged, I aspired with all my heart to secure from the hand of God all the wonders that his love could convey. And so I was taught inwardly the law of the violet flame, and I knew an inward communion with Saint Germain, which has been given to other princes of the Church on occasion.

Cardinal Bonzano

"I was able to be subsequently raised to the position of an ascended being to surround the beloved Master Jesus, and I consider this a supreme tribute of heaven. But as most of us are not satisfied to merely enjoy the wonders of heaven, we continue to convey our love and service to mankind in many ways. Myriad angels beam their light earthward each day bearing messages of love from our councils and from the councils of even stars beyond your ken."[57]

Vaivasvata Manu spoke of the ascension of Cardinal Bonzano: "This is the goal of every man—to attain his ascension in the light. But the ascension in the light, while it is a gift to every man, requires some application. The Great Cosmic Law has at various times given the ascension to those who did not have the full training in this particular activity—some of you are familiar with Cardinal Bonzano, and you realize that he made his ascension in the light. But nevertheless, this particular and specific teaching, the invocation of the sacred fire by decrees, is calculated by the ascended masters to provide immeasurable success and opportunity to those who will practice its teachings and principles.

"While individuals may occasionally make their ascension from outside this activity, that does not mean that this way is not swift, valuable and priceless. And therefore, I urge you by all the love of the ascended masters, by all the love of the Spirit of the Great White Brotherhood, to cherish this opportunity to hear our words, to walk in this light, and to expand the light flame within you until in harmony with the universal oneness of God, it becomes at peace with the universal harmony present within all."[58]

We may call to Cardinal Bonzano (as well as to Pope Pius XII, Pope John XXIII, Padre Pio, Saint Thérèse of Lisieux, Mother Cabrini, Saint Bernadette, and the many others who have ascended after their final embodiments of service in the Roman Catholic Church) for the enlightenment of the Catholic hierarchy and the freedom of the devout from all fear and ignorance of the true teachings of Christ.

❖ **BRAHMA, First Person of the Hindu Trinity**

Brahma, Vishnu and Shiva of the Hindu Trinity parallel the western concept of the Father, Son and Holy Spirit—the eternal Creator, Preserver and Destroyer. Brahma embodies the divine desire that inspired the creation of the world. Vishnu conveys mercy and virtue to sustain the world. Shiva represents the sacred fire that destroys evil.

Brahma, as the Father figure and the First Person of the Trinity, is seen as the Immense Being—the Creator, Supreme Ruler, Lawgiver, Sustainer and Source of All Knowledge. Brahma is Godly omnipotence incarnate. His divine complement, or *shakti,* is Sarasvati, the active principle of Brahma. These divine lovers exemplify the masculine and feminine embodiment of the cosmic force.

The Maha Chohan speaks of the universal presence of Brahma with us: "Beloved ones, understand the mystery of Brahma within your heart, the great Lawgiver, the living principle of the Father, the person in the figure of the one who has the great God-mastery of the four quadrants of being. That Father whom you call Brahma is indeed the very blue plume of power within your heart. And therefore, when you say 'O Lord Brahma, come forth,' beloved ones, the Lord Brahma of the universe will come forth from within your heart, from within the heart of Helios and Vesta, Alpha to Omega, and every son and daughter of God both ascended and unascended. Understand the meaning, then, of the very Person of God....

"Understand, O blessed hearts, that that Brahma unto whom you give your call and your devotion is both an energy, a consciousness, a spirit *and* the living, dancing, moving image of the Hindu deity. So when you say 'Brahma,' the entire Spirit of the Great White Brotherhood will answer your call in the full power of cosmic omnipotence. Do not consider that the word I use, 'cosmic omnipotence,' is merely a word that you cannot comprehend. But begin to extend your flame, the flame within your heart, out, out, out into dimensions of magnitude and begin to sense the great sphere of God's being within you extending, contacting the earth, the air, scraping as it were the very sky or head and beyond and beyond."[59]

Beloved Brahma has spoken of his desire to be with us: "O beloved of the Creator, I AM come for one purpose this day. For I AM the lowering of myself, the Great God Self, into levels of being one by one, into the waiting chalices of millions who look to the dawn of their union with Brahma.

"I come, then, to anchor by Word, by vibration of my spoken Word (resonating in this plane through the messenger) my heralding to many that I AM available unto you even as you have made yourselves available unto me.

"I descend to the levels of purification to which you have attained, to the levels of love—profound and dignified love, love that is the immersing of being in the totality of God.

"Thus, throughout the earth I AM everywhere, known in form yet formless. I descend, then, for I come for the harvest of souls of light and I may now occupy heart chalices upraised until the fullness of that light is manifest....

"So, my little ones, so, my precious souls, so, my sons and daughters, come into the arms of Brahma and know me as the figure of one who creates and re-creates and re-creates so that the whole of creation is in that process of being born again and reborn and reborn until the fullness of being is discovered—and the fullness of purpose of a blade of grass, of the tiniest elemental, of an angel, of a star is made known."[60]

❖ **BROTHERHOOD OF MOUNT SHASTA.** *See also* **Ra Mu**

The Brotherhood of Mount Shasta, an ancient hierarchy of priests and priestesses who tended the flame of the Mother on the altars of Mu

(Lemuria) before the sinking of that continent, is a brotherhood composed of ascended and unascended masters who are devotees of the Buddha and his light and who have kept the flame of purity in Mount Shasta. Ra Mu is a member of the Brotherhood of Mount Shasta.

Mount Shasta

Mount Shasta was once the crown chakra of Lemuria. The Brotherhood of Mount Shasta withdrew their focus from the mountain in 1988. Sanat Kumara announced "the withdrawal of the Brotherhood of Mount Shasta from the retreat physical of Mount Shasta. This entire Brotherhood, therefore, does withdraw and does transfer their forcefield and focus both into the Grand Teton and into another area of the northern Rockies."[61]

❖ BUDDHA OF THE RUBY RAY

The ruby ray is an intense action of divine love. The being called the Buddha of the Ruby Ray has the Buddhic mastery of this intense action of divine love.

He was sent long ago by Sanat Kumara and Gautama Buddha to abide in the secret chamber of God in the heart of the earth. In 1988, the Buddha of the Ruby Ray spoke of his acceptance of this assignment:

"Think back now upon the day when you did see me, as from Shamballa I went forth.... All did watch as staff in hand, ruby-ray focus about my neck, I did enter a cave and I did begin to walk and I did walk to the center of the earth.... I was told in that hour and all heard it, 'You shall not come forth until there be those on the surface of the earth who can hold the balance for the attainment that shall be thine own.' So, beloved, you might say that I have been confined to hold the nucleus of a planet at the mercy of such as yourselves until you should arrive at the place of a similar love for the ruby ray."[62]

In 1989, Cuzco announced that the Buddha of the Ruby Ray, in answer to the call of the Keepers of the Flame, had literally walked step by step from the center of the earth to be present and to assist us in dealing with the negative forces at hand. This Buddha has angels of fiery intensity who maintain a cave of ruby light in the heart of the earth beneath the Royal Teton Ranch. His angels are available at all times to cut away and purge the density brought about by improper diet, poor choices in music, improper consciousness and the saturation of the mind with entities.

The Buddha of the Ruby Ray has given us a gift of a droplet of ruby ray, which he said could be retained by us only if we keep the flame of internal love and harmony. He said: "I come to reinforce Buddhic presence in your heart and leave indeed a replica, in outline only, of my form that you may fill in as you become the Buddha and see me mirrored in self. For I desire to live on the surface of earth in the hearts of true devotees of the Buddha. It is my prayer that you will accord me this to make my wish come true."[63]

❖ **CARDINAL BONZANO,** *See* **Bonzano, Cardinal**

❖ **CASIMIR POSEIDON**

During the height of the Atlantean empire, Casimir Poseidon ruled over Poseidonis, a major colony located in the Amazon Valley of South America. The capital city of the empire was located near the juncture of the Madeira and Amazon Rivers, which at that time were at an altitude of 5,000 feet and in a semitropical climate. The plan of the city was in a series of concentric rings that formed "beltways" three miles apart with connecting streets raying from the center.

At its peak, about 12,000 years ago, the citizens of this golden-age civilization attained great mastery over the sciences of metallurgy, chemistry and mining and were even able to precipitate their own food. Casimir Poseidon, already then an ascended master, led his people in the ways of God. Among his profound instructions he gave them the motto, "Learn to love to do well, and you shall!"

For approximately two thousand years, the citizens of Poseidonis followed his advice, for they greatly loved their ruler who epitomized the beauty of their racial characteristics: tall in stature, golden-haired, blue-violet eyes, light complexion. Gradually, however, the people turned from the light into paths of selfishness. As this occurred, the Brotherhood withdrew its support; and after a final warning of what would be the outcome if they continued to ignore the laws of God, Casimir Poseidon and a handful of followers left the country and came to what is now the western United States. Within five years the entire continent of Meru (now South America) rolled to the east and submerged the eastern coast, bringing to an end the once proud civilization.

In a dictation given October 5, 1975, Casimir Poseidon explained that this civilization declined because the people "did not give the glory unto the LORD for every accomplishment of science and culture." Before it was destroyed by cataclysm, he and a band of disciples "withdrew to North America to seal that light, to seal the scrolls of that culture in a place, the point of a pyramid now located in Colorado. And we anchored there the records of the ancient civilization."

For many thousands of years, his memory was only kept alive in South America by the Indian legend of a fair ruler who would one day return. Now Casimir Poseidon, with the assistance of the God and Goddess Meru, the Great Divine Director, Saint Germain and others, has once again come forth to guide the people of North and South America into a golden age.

On December 29, 1996, Casimir Poseidon told us to "think big" when it comes to stopping cataclysm. He said: "Cataclysm in the world is not always necessary and in many instances can be easily mitigated because people are at peace with themselves and can send forth light rays to hold the balance for the earth. They are almost as laser beams going into your bodies and into the heart of the earth.

"As you stand in the earth and you plant your feet there, you shall be for this community and for the ascended masters and for the Great White Brotherhood pillars of fire in the earth. God has given into your keeping and into your trust this balancing action.... Now is the time to go about thinking big—big as Elohim! And see what you can do to stop or mitigate planetary cataclysm." Casimir Poseidon said that we could mitigate potential earth changes by devoting ourselves to "decree work and service to God."[64]

Students can amplify his radiation by playing the music of "Indian Love Call."

❖ CASSIOPEA, Elohim of the Central Sun

Cassiopea (not to be confused with Cyclopea) is an Elohim of the Central Sun, holding a focus of great illumination on behalf of the Godhead. This cosmic being has come forth to assist the hierarchy in raising the consciousness of the entire planet in preparation for the golden age.

❖ CELESTE, Devic Angel of the Ascended Hosts

Celeste came out of the Great Silence in 1964 to shatter the veil of human night. Having experienced many earthly embodiments and having ascended through the devic evolution, she works closely with the angelic and elemental kingdoms on this planet.

Her plea is for mankind to recognize the tremendous assistance these evolutions give unto humanity. She has said to man, "They need your love and your constancy, even as you need theirs."[65] She asks us to release our love and gratitude to them as well as to the Elohim and archangels and to join her in calling for the flame of freedom from the heart of Saint Germain to infuse every elemental being on earth with the permanence of victory from the heart of Jesus the Christ.

Celeste has given a prayer for the elementals:

> *I am calling for the freedom and victory of the fiery elementals, the salamanders; of the elementals of the waters, the undines; of the earth elementals, the gnomes; and of the beings of the air, the sylphs. And I call to beloved Mother Virgo and to beloved Pelleur for their enfolding love to blaze forth now from the heart of the earth and to cut all elemental life free! I accept this now in the name of beloved Saint Germain and in the name of my own mighty God Presence. It is done.*[66]

❖ CHA ARA

Cha Ara is the son of lady master Meta. In his last embodiment he lived in Persia as Meta's son. In this life, he gained mastery over his physical form, which he maintained for several hundred years, An adept of the fifth ray, he produced the elixir of life and used it not only to sustain his own form but also for the healing of others. He now heads a department of instruction on healing and precipitation in the Royal Teton Retreat and conducts classes there.

Cha Ara is intimately associated with the victory of the light on the American continent and came forth to assist Saint Germain in revealing to the children of God in embodiment those teachings that are necessary for their cooperation with the Brotherhood in bringing in the golden age. He is fulfilling his destiny as a guardian of the youth of America and the world that they might be prepared to bring forth the Holy Christ children and the seventh root race in South America.

Cha Ara works with Chananda and the Indian Council of the Great White Brotherhood. He calls us to an understanding of the mysteries of the sacred fire and the path of Zarathustra. Saint Germain speaks of his sense of joy.

❖ CHAMUEL AND CHARITY, Archangels of the Third Ray

Archangel Chamuel, whose name means "he who seeks God," and his divine complement, Archeia Charity, serve on the third ray of divine love and maintain an etheric retreat over St. Louis, Missouri—the Temple of the Crystal-Pink Flame. An arc of divine love forms a bridge between this retreat and that of the Elohim of the third ray, Heros and Amora, in the etheric realm near Lake Winnipeg in Manitoba, Canada.

Together with their legions of pink-flame angels, Chamuel and Charity serve to expand the flame of adoration and divine love within the hearts of men and elementals. The joy of the Christ and the proper use of the creative powers of the Godhead are the forte of their instruction.

Chamuel is the archangel who released the edict that confounded the tongues of those who were attempting to build the Tower of Babel, built by Nimrod to the glory of Nimrod. The ruby ray of the LORD's judgment came down through Chamuel, and in an instant, the people were speaking in different tongues.[67] All was chaos, and fright turned to anger—anger against the LORD and his avenging angel. Because the people could no longer communicate with each other, they could no longer conspire to do evil, and the confounding of tongues prevented the rapid spread of the evils of society. Thus, God's love keeps mankind separated until they are perfected in love.

Nimrod was a rebel angel whose ambition was to control the world. Rebel angels in high places are a fact of life on planet Earth; they have been here ever since they lost the war in heaven and Archangel Michael and his legions cast them out into the earth. They move among us wearing physical bodies that are often larger than those of average humans. The archangels still wage war with fallen angels on behalf of the children of light. You can enlist their legions as you champion the cause of children, the poor, the homeless and all who suffer under the yoke of their karma as well as the tyranny of the fallen angels.

Depending on their assignment, Chamuel and Charity's legions may appear in full battle regalia or in ceremonial dress. They may come in the softness of the Mother to comfort life. At times they are robed in what appear to be layers of delicate pink chiffon or the deepening colors of rose and the ruby ray; these are actually layers of gossamer light.

Archangel Chamuel and Charity teach you to develop the qualities of mercy, compassion and loving-kindness for others. They teach you to replace your sense of injustice with a supreme trust in the ultimate resolution of divine love. They teach you to intensify the flame of love in your heart and to prepare for the descent of the Holy Spirit into your temple. They will heal the layers of your aura when you offer devotions and service to God in their name.

Chamuel and Charity say, "Each time you give your violet-flame decrees, songs of praise to Almighty God and heartfelt prayers, the angels are permitted to take from your aura and body some of the burdens you carry.

"If you invite us, we will come home with you. We will help you with difficult family situations. We will address whatever is most burdensome to your heart. We will even help you find a job—or a parking place! We will do anything you ask, as long as it is lawful for us to do it in the sight of God."[68]

❖ CHANANDA, Chief of the Indian Council of the Great White Brotherhood

Chananda is the chief of the Indian Council of the Great White Brotherhood and hierarch of the Cave of Light, the focus of the Great Divine Director in India. The Palace of Light, which is adjacent to the Cave of Light, is the home of Chananda and his sister, the ascended lady master Najah.

Chananda was a scholar on Mu and lived in the city of the seven hills where San Francisco now is. He was also embodied at the time of Jesus and knew the Master in Judea. He saw his radiant magnetism and "perceived the Presence of immortality shining through his outer garment."[69]

To certain unascended chelas, Chananda has demonstrated the extraordinary powers available unto all of the ascended hosts. On one occasion, he levitated himself, Godfre, Rex and Nada, Bob and Pearl (then unascended) on a "magic carpet" (a sheet of metal covered with a Persian rug) eleven thousand feet into the atmosphere to enjoy the view of a valley.[70]

Chananda came forth in 1937 to assist Saint Germain to implement his plan for the freedom of the earth, as did Najah in 1938. He assists the governments of the world, while she works with the youth, often appearing as a young girl in parts of India and China, teaching and helping the people.

Chananda is currently working on a top-priority project with the Darjeeling Council and unascended initiates of the Brotherhood. Part of this project involves the precipitation of a golden-age government based on the principles behind the Constitution of the United States. This God-inspired document was released to America by its founder, the ascended master Saint Germain; and when properly used and followed, it will provide the key to a golden-age civilization that is just beyond the horizon.

Chananda is particularly concerned with the problems of racial and

Varanasi (Benares), India

religious divisions between people and with the future of India. He outlines the path of peace as the way of overcoming: "India was won through nonviolence. We shun violence and exude the peace of the Buddha, which is the all-power of God. But we would have our chelas understand that when you depend upon the peace of the

Buddha as the ultimate power, then it would be well for you to study assiduously the terms of that peace. For you must make peace with your God if you expect your God to provide that power in the hour when peace is challenged by absolute war....

"I know whereof I speak. I remember in a previous incarnation as the battle raged all around me and I stood holding the balance in the midst of thousands and ten thousand. Blessed hearts, I stood in their midst holding the focus of the sacred fire. And do you know—they saw me not! I was not visible in the physical spectrum, though I was in physical embodiment. And thereby...by my unswerving allegiance to the light, which I owe to the Almighty and to him alone—I was that pillar! I was that fire! And thus they could not continue the battle. And they retreated on both sides, leaving me standing alone in the midst of the plain of the battle itself."[71]

Call to beloved Chananda, the Great Divine Director, El Morya and Saint Germain for the proper implementation of the plans for God-government throughout the world.

❖ **CHARITY, ARCHEIA,** *See* **Chamuel and Charity**

❖ **CHARITY, THE COSMIC BEING.** *See also* **Faith, Hope and Charity**

There are two lifestreams who bear the name Charity. One is the cosmic being Charity, and the other is the archeia, the divine complement of Chamuel, the archangel of the third ray. The archeia assists the cosmic being in amplifying the virtue of all-forgiving love.

It was the cosmic being Charity who dictated to the apostle Paul the message on charity recorded in the first book of Corinthians, chapter 13:

> Though I speak with the tongues of men and of angels, and have not charity, I am become as sounding brass, or a tinkling cymbal. And though I have the gift of prophecy, and understand all mysteries, and all knowledge; and though I have all faith, so that I could remove mountains, and have not charity, I am nothing. And though I bestow all my goods to feed the poor, and though I give my body to be burned, and have not charity, it profiteth me nothing.
>
> Charity suffereth long, and is kind; charity envieth not; charity vaunteth not itself, is not puffed up, doth not behave itself unseemly, seeketh not her own, is not easily provoked, thinketh no evil; rejoiceth not in iniquity, but rejoiceth in the truth; beareth all things, believeth all things, hopeth all things, endureth all things.
>
> Charity never faileth: but whether there be prophecies, they shall fail; whether there be tongues, they shall cease; whether there

be knowledge, it shall vanish away. For we know in part, and we prophesy in part. But when that which is perfect is come, then that which is in part shall be done away.

When I was a child, I spake as a child, I understood as a child, I thought as a child: but when I became a man, I put away childish things. For now we see through a glass, darkly; but then face to face: now I know in part; but then shall I know even as also I am known.

And now abideth faith, hope, charity, these three; but the greatest of these is charity.

The final verse of this chapter makes reference to the three cosmic beings, Faith, Hope and Charity, who serve together to assist mankind in the balancing of the threefold flame and in the bringing forth of the qualities of the Christ. The omission of the word *charity* in more recent translations of the Bible and its replacement with the word *love,* while it may clarify the meaning for some, nevertheless excludes the name of the great cosmic being who dictated this passage and who has worked with Faith and Hope in the service of mankind since the first golden age.

Love is the cohesive power of the universe, and it is the key to each man's ascension in the light; charity is the consequence of love, the practical application of love in society. The word *charity,* together with its electronic pattern, amplifies the feeling of forgiveness through gratitude and the acceptance of the Christ who lives in all. The recognition of the Christ, through the flame of Charity, enables us not only to forgive but also to love. Therefore, love is the consequence of charity rather than a synonym for charity. Its inner meaning is the *rit*ual of accord of Alpha, or the righting of all things through the chord, or the *c*osmic *h*armony, of Alpha, the beginning.

❖ **CHRISTMAS, SPIRIT OF,** *See* **Spirit of Christmas**

❖ **CLARA LOUISE, Regent Mother of the Flame**

The ascended lady master Clara Louise was embodied as Clara Louise Kieninger. She made her ascension at the age of 87 from Berkeley, California, on October 25, 1970, joining her twin flame Amen Bey to serve with Serapis at the Ascension Temple at Luxor, Egypt. You can ask to be taken to this retreat to receive instruction for your path and what you are to accomplish in life.

Clara Louise Kieninger was born on September 16, 1883, in Junction City, Kansas, and spent a happy childhood in a large pioneer family. She

started her career as a secretary and business-
woman, but finally persuaded her mother to let her
follow the profession of her heart: nursing.

In 1912 she graduated from the Lutheran Hos-
pital Nursing School in St. Louis, Missouri. At this
occasion she took her class motto, "Ich Dien" (I
Serve), as the guiding principle of her life. Clara
Louise quickly advanced to responsible positions,
becoming assistant director and then director of
schools of nursing. In 1917 she was sent to France
as a chief nurse and served there until the end of the
First World War.

She served devotedly in the field of nursing for many years and established the first school of nursing in Brazil, in preparation for her work with

the children of the incoming seventh root race destined to embody in South America. Through the
profession of nursing, she served the body of God
on earth with the same honor and love she would
accord the Christ. Her memoirs are published in
the book *Ich Dien.*

Clara Louise serves on the fourth ray of God's
purity, and her musical keynote is "Calm As the
Night." Her soul's devotion to God is reflected in
her prior embodiments. In the days of Lemuria, she
served in the central temple as a priestess at the

Guanabara Bay,
Rio de Janeiro, 1943

altar of the Divine Mother, and at the time of Jesus she was embodied as the
apostle James. In her recent life, she often repeated to others the words of
Jesus, "What is that to thee? follow thou me!"[72]

Clara Louise had a great heart of love. She was also a disciplinarian.
In her later years, as a dedicated student and friend of the ascended masters, she kept a daily vigil of prayer beginning as early as three or four in
the morning and continuing for two to four hours, even until noon. She
prayed on behalf of the youth of the world, the incoming children, their
parents and teachers.

The ascended lady master Thérèse of Lisieux spoke of Clara Louise
and her prayers for the youth of the world: "Cherish the era of childhood and preserve that innocence through all the years of thy life. For
the one whose ascension you celebrate this day, your own beloved
Clara Louise, did keep that innocence and purity side by side with an
astute and mature discipline and a very ready awareness of the plots and

ploys of the fallen ones to tear from her the bridal veil in the very hour of her ascension.

"Ah, yes! She kept the watch in Berkeley, California. And I kept it with her for the children and the youth of the world. And many of you are sponsored by our flame.

"We come with the aura of roses—mine pink, becoming the ruby ray of the blood of Christ; hers the white of her beloved Amen Bey and Mother Mary and Serapis, Lord of Life. Thus we two, standing as mothers mothering the Flame within you, present the body and the blood of Christ as the white and the pink, that you might also see that there is a bridal bouquet waiting for you as you accept the initiation of the cross of the ruby ray, of the angels of white fire.

"Thus, enter into the joy of the hallowed circle of thy Father and thy Mother. And reconsecrate your life as 'Holiness unto the LORD'[73]—priests and priestesses of the sacred fire, drawing the circle of the One."[74]

From the ascended state, Clara Louise told us, "I see so many among you for whom I did pray in this my final incarnation, and I would tell you that it is clear in the record that my prayers did make the difference in your entering the Path. I am grateful for this but I tell it to you so that you can understand that I who have been with you so very recently in this century was able to develop that prayer momentum, and therefore you can do the same. It simply takes a dedication of time and space and a determination that puts down every other voice seeking attention, every point of chaos or confusion or disruption."[75]

Clara Louise practiced the science of the spoken Word for close to fifty years, and her calls and invocations were very powerful. She simply would not take no for an answer, a quality she learned from her embodiment as Jesus' disciple. Just as Jesus cast out demons through the power of the spoken Word, so she knew that one has to be fierce with demons and the state

of the human consciousness. Her fiats would travel across the planet as she gave her prayers and invocations, standing in defense of all children.

The world also needs your intercession and prayers for the children and youth. You can give fiery calls to God as Clara Louise did. And in the fierceness of the fire of Serapis Bey and Amen Bey, invoke the fiery mantle, or cloak of light, of Clara Louise. She carries the flame of white fire and will assist you in accelerating this flame, raising the Kundalini, the ascension flame and life-force within, so that you can deliver the command that binds the foul spirit.

When you speak in the authority of Christ, the foul spirit cannot disobey you, because God reinforces your call. You receive the reinforcement because you have a magnet of fire intense enough to draw down the magnet of your I AM Presence. However, you should always ask that your prayers be adjusted according to the will of God.

In 1961 Saint Germain anointed Clara Louise as the first Mother of the Flame of the Keepers of the Flame Fraternity. On April 9, 1966, when the mantle of the office of Mother of the Flame was passed to the messenger Elizabeth Clare Prophet, Clara Louise became the Regent Mother of the Flame. From the ascended level, she continues to hold the office of Regent Mother of the Flame, nurturing the souls of all the world's children.

On July 3, 1962, Mother Mary promised Clara Louise the fulfillment of her ascension at the close of her embodiment. Astrea and Purity speak of her ascension and of her service since that time:

"If you have the resolution, if you have the balance of your threefold flame, you will see and know that in the hour of your passing you can make your ascension, as occurred in the case of the first Mother of the Flame, Clara Louise Kieninger. She did make her ascension from the place where she passed, Berkeley, California, and chose that place, beloved, that there might ever be anchored there that focus of the ascension flame for the youth of the world.

"So, beloved, there are those such as the first Mother of the Flame, who, upon the hour of passing and the release of the last sacred breath, did enter into ascension coils, as is meet. And thus she appeared at the temple of Serapis Bey, met her twin flame there, Amen Bey, and has been serving the youth of the world ever since—not alone from Luxor but she does journey from retreat to retreat around the world. Many of these retreats you have never heard about, but you shall hear about them in due time.

"Clara Louise Kieninger, then, does go to the retreats to teach those who tarry there who have lessons to learn, karma to balance. And she speaks also to the hierarchy of the retreat, imploring them to send reinforcements for the care of the youth of the world and especially the unborn and especially the dire situation of the sacrifice of children in the womb and at term. Blessed ones, this has been her cause for many, many, many years in embodiment and now in the octaves of light."[76]

Since her ascension, she has given seven dictations through Elizabeth Clare Prophet. In Gautama Buddha's annual New Year's address on January 1, 1973, Clara Louise was present at inner levels throughout the service. Gautama spoke of the return of her youthful appearance in her ascended state and announced that she would present to the Mother of the Flame a torch of illumination to the age:

"Some of you may recall one who passed from you some time ago, the first Mother of the Flame who later became the Regent Mother. Well, I want you to know that tonight at inner levels she is with you.... I want you to understand that her body is no longer gray or crooked in any way; her form no longer reflects age, but only the beauty of her earliest youth and maturity. Upon her face there is a glow of hope and sweetness and love....

"I want you to know that she still will be with you until this service shall break up. Until you shall leave and depart these doors, she will be with you this night, giving her love and her counsel at inner levels to you, conveying her blessing to you as the first Mother of the Flame. And she shall, ere the night pass, give to the present Mother of the Flame a torch charged with the vital fires from God's heavenly altar and the conveyance of a vast mission to illuminate the world's children and produce the blessing of true culture to the age and unto all people everywhere."[77]

The messenger has explained the meaning of the passing of a torch and its significance to each of us: "The torches must always be passed. One day you will pass a torch. The most important thing to remember about the passing of a torch is that the torch is a flame that burns. It is composed of many, many millions of flames. And each one of those flames is a petal— a petal of light and sacred fire.

"As you go into the central sun of your mighty I AM Presence and form and fashion your torch of life, you will want to be certain, as those who have gone before us are certain, that the torch will contain all that the one who follows you on the Path will need in order to make it all the way Home.

"I have mentioned to you that our beloved Mark signed my own copy of *Climb the Highest Mountain* with the words 'May you win all the way.' It is not enough that we wish victory upon someone, or winning. We want them to win *all* the way, every step of the way—not just today but to the hour of the ascension.

"Every guru is concerned for the blessed chela—that he make it all the way Home, else the Path should be in vain. Therefore, you must be concerned for the chela you do not yet know, for the master you are to become—that even now you are forging a torch that you will one day pass. And when it comes time to pass the torch, there will be no time to say, 'Wait a minute, I must create the torch.' The torch must be there and burning.

"The torch of Gautama Buddha, Clara Louise and our own beloved Lanello were there—just seven weeks before his ascension. That very year of 1973, Summit University opened on a full-time basis—out of that torch. And all who have passed through its halls are free to ratify the will of God and receive one petal of the torch, one petal-flame that becomes a nucleus of their own torch to be passed in the hour of the appointing."[78]

Clara Louise says of her ascension: "There is a spiral of victory that is anchored in the atmosphere over the place where I made my ascension. And therefore, I shall direct you to that place and that home, that you might ever know when you are in the area of Berkeley that there is a focus that blesses and heals and is sustained for the little ones. And by your application to that focus, you can expand the influence of the Archangel Gabriel and Hope and of the Goddess of Purity* throughout this state, throughout America and the world."[79]

❖ CONFUCIUS, Hierarch of the Royal Teton Retreat

Confucius

Confucius is hierarch of the Royal Teton Retreat, and he serves on the second ray of divine wisdom. He succeeded Lord Lanto as hierarch of the Retreat on July 3, 1958.

Although he has had many embodiments of service to the light, Confucius is best remembered for his contributions to the Chinese way of life. Known as K'ung Fu-tze ("Philosopher K'ung" or "Master K'ung") to his contemporaries in the 5th century B.C., he set the stage for the eventual unification and administration of the Chinese empire. A brilliant social, economic, political and moral philosopher, Confucius laid the theoretical foundations that enabled China to become one of the greatest civilizations of all time. Despite the rise and fall of dynasties, the Confucian state prevailed; and eventually, through the spread of Chinese culture, his ideas were accepted throughout Eastern Asia. Seldom has one man influenced more people over a greater period of time.

Confucius is honored as China's greatest teacher and has been worshiped as a great bodhisattva, or future Buddha. He believed that heaven could be created on earth through ritual and music. His followers became known as Knights of the Arts because they mastered archery, poetry, mathematics, history, dance, religious rituals and etiquette.

---

*The etheric retreat of Archangel Gabriel and Hope is located between Sacramento and Mount Shasta, California. The Goddess of Purity maintains a retreat over the city of San Francisco.

While later generations misinterpreted Confucius and thought him to be a stuffy bureaucrat, Confucius had a profound spirituality and vision. That is why he was so practical. Confucius taught: "The Path may not be left for an instant. If it could be left, it would not be the Path."[80] Despite the effort to purge his teachings, sayings of Confucius such as "The demands that a gentleman makes are upon himself; those that a small man makes are upon others"[81] and "The cautious seldom err"[82] remain an integral part of the thinking of the Chinese people.

Confucius was born in 551 B.C., a time of great turmoil and chaos. His father, an elderly soldier, died when he was three. Although his family was poor, he managed to educate himself. When he was fifteen, he knew he wanted to be a scholar. He worked as a clerk at the memorial temple of the Duke of Chou, one of the greatest statesmen in Chinese history.

Five hundred years earlier, the Duke of Chou, his father, King Wen, and his brother had overthrown the corrupt Shang dynasty and established the Chou dynasty. He brought a new understanding of God and divine government to the Chinese people. "I am only concerned with Heaven and the people,"[83] he had said.

Confucius believed that the Duke of Chou was teaching him in his dreams at night. In fact, Confucius claimed that he himself was not an innovator—he was only bringing back the standard and the principles of the Duke of Chou. (The Duke of Chou was an embodiment of Lord Lanto, and it is believed that Confucius was embodied at the time of the Duke of Chou and helped him implement his ideals.)

Inspired by the Duke of Chou, Confucius edited the six Chinese classics, which had been written by King Wen. These were the Book of Poetry, the Book of Rites, the Book of History, the Book of Change (I Ching), the Book of Documents and the Book of Music. The Book of Music, unfortunately, has been completely lost.

Today Confucius has a reputation for being stiff and reserved. But he was not without sensitivity. The story is told that he was once so moved by a performance of ancient music that he remained in a stupor for three months. When he finally came out of the trance, he said, "I never imagined that music could be so sublime."[84]

We do not know much about Confucius' life. He was married when he was nineteen and had a son and a daughter. He studied under various teachers and eventually gathered a group of students around him. For a time, he held a job as justice minister but was forced to abandon it and go into exile. Although Confucius had seventy-two disciples and more than three thousand students, he never realized his dream of becoming a prominent ruler in China.

During this time, the Chou dynasty was on the verge of collapse. The Chou government had degenerated into chaos, and brutal warlords continually fought with each other. "Confucius was the first to formulate a systematic response to this crisis in values," writes Robert Eno, scholar of Chinese thought. "And the depth of his achievement is reflected by the fact that China's first philosopher remained throughout its history its leading philosopher."[85]

Confucius Temple, China

Confucius believed that ritual, or *li,* could transform one's identity, one's mind, one's very being. "The program of study begins with the chanting of texts and ends with the study of ritual *li,*" Confucius explained. "Its significance is that one begins by becoming a gentleman and ends by becoming a Sage."[86] Through disciplined cultivation of li, one attained *jen,* which Eno describes as "the selfless ethical responsiveness to others."[87]

Although Confucius traveled throughout China, he never found a suitable job in the government. He felt like a failure and started to lament: "Extreme indeed is my decline. It's been a long time since I dreamt about the Duke of Chou."[88]

Confucius did not realize it at the time, but his spirituality was far more powerful than his resumé. He wandered about looking for work, but what he was really doing was anchoring his spiritual flame of wisdom in every corner of China. That flame inspired and sustained Chinese culture for many centuries.

As an ascended master, Confucius still dreams of making a heaven on earth through divine government. While he has not been able to work this dream in China, he sees himself as the grandfather of America. With practical wisdom and deep love, he inspires and guides his disciples who have embodied in the United States. Lanto explains that the practical side of the culture of America comes from the causal body of Confucius.

The ascended master Confucius has a profound understanding of family as the vital unit for building community and a new society in the Aquarian age. He shows us how to take etheric patterns and use them in tangible ways to improve our everyday lives—patterns of self-reliance in God, of the sacred family and of God-government. We tie into the etheric patterns and precipitate the etheric ideals through beauty, harmony and order in the physical octave. This is why the flame of precipitation is the main focus of Confucius' Royal Teton Retreat. This flame is Chinese green in color, tinged with gold, and it burns on the main altar of the Retreat.

Confucius wants us to regard him as our loving and supportive grandfather. And like a grandfather, he also desires to pass on his dreams to us that we might fulfill them in his name. He longs to build a society on the foundation of love, wisdom and the will of God in the individual and in the family.

In 1976, Confucius said that many souls from ancient China have reembodied in America. He called them "the quiet Buddhic souls, the diligent ones," the ones who have a spiritual mission to lay the foundation of the family in America. He points out that they understand the "basic loyalty of the family, the code of ethics, the gentleness, the sweetness and the desire for learning as the means to God-awareness."

Furthermore, Confucius said, "They have come for an embodiment that their wisdom might be fired with freedom, that they might assist America" as she enters the twenty-first century. Their aim is to turn around a "false materialism" and to manifest instead "an etherealization, a spirituality, a conquering of self, of society and of the energies of time and space."

Confucius is very much concerned with the affairs of civilization and with the destiny of America: "I am concerned on the one hand with the activities of the masculine ray as that ray has been perverted in China today and as its perversion has also led to the perversion of the feminine ray and the manifestation of the family.

"I have seen the corruption in government. It is the same corruption that I witnessed twenty-five hundred years ago—the same corruption, mind you, the same corruptible ones. For the lifestreams who are focusing the energies for the disintegration of the light and of the golden age of China today are the lifestreams who thwarted the cosmic purpose of the Virgin thousands of years ago when my feet touched the earth and the streams of that beloved land of Chin.

"I have noticed also that those who are the corruptible ones who have corrupted Saint Germain's promise for America have come again and again. It is they who were the rats in the granary of Rome and Greece, India, the Middle East. There are always the betrayers."[89]

Confucius has said, "It is only cosmic justice that a balance should be made for the expenditure of every ounce of energy. Through the aeons and aeons of creation, this great law has never been violated with impunity. And those who think they can violate divine statutes have quickly found out upon the cosmic screen of life that the scales of divine justice do act, and that they act wisely and well."[90]

❖ A COSMIC BEING FROM OUT THE GREAT SILENCE

On October 29, 1987, a Cosmic Being from out the Great Silence spoke to students of the masters in the city of Chicago: "I AM a cosmic being ensouling, therefore, cosmos. In the heart of God I AM. And I am come to you for the bracing of this city and your hearts in a chalice formed of crystal light....

"In the purity flame of an ancient focus of light, I descend into this city to call those who have reincarnated from the previous golden age that was once in this area. Blessed ones, you have known of the light, and long ago the prophecy of a darkness to come was given to you here.

"You volunteered to return to this area to enshrine the heart of a nation* as a celebration of the heart of God in life here below. You said, 'O Blessed One, we shall go forth and remember to keep the flame in that future age.'... Know, then, that thy descent is single-pointed. Its purpose, as a two-edged sword: the celebration of the energy of light of a Spirit cosmos and the consuming of all darkness that would assail it."[91]

❖ COSMOS, MIGHTY, Cosmic Being Who Ensouls the Secret Rays

Mighty Cosmos is a being whose self-awareness in God includes the all of cosmos—hence his name. He is commissioned by the Logos to ensoul the secret rays—energies of the fiery core of being, energies for initiation in the mysteries of the Christos.

Embracing the cosmo-conception, the consciousness of the universe itself, Mighty Cosmos was commissioned by Alpha and Omega to come to the earth in 1939 with two of the five secret rays, which he anchored in a cosmic action and release of light in the North and South Poles.

Being aware of the cosmos, he is keenly attuned to the vibrational patterns of the evolutions of the earth to their original pitch, attuning them with the hum of creation. Holding the cosmo-conception of the light pattern and frequency of every lifestream, he enfolds the crystal cord of each one with the action of his own heart flame. As the light from the Presence descends into the individual forcefield of the evolving monad, Cosmos charges it with the divine pattern of the perfection of that lifestream. Thus, even before it enters the consciousness of man and before it can be misqualified, that energy is superimposed with the memory of the divine plan.

Mighty Cosmos has volunteered this service unto mankind in order that with each pulse beat, the individual may feel the pattern of his Electronic Presence and so desire to become that perfection. Mighty Cosmos is

---

*The city of Chicago is the heart chakra of America.

The causal body has seven spheres corresponding to the seven rays of outer manifestation. Five additional spheres, the spheres of the five secret rays, are found in a different dimension between the white and the yellow bands.

the scientist of all scientists, and he should be revered as the great mentor of our liberation through the knowledge of Universal Law in operation. In the field of science, he is unexcelled.

The action of the secret rays anchored by Mighty Cosmos at the Poles comes forth from two of the five bands in the center of the causal body where their colors and identity patterns remain unrevealed. The appearance of the two secret rays is a crystal-blue radiance, but this is only the reflection of the sheath in which these rays are sealed so that no destructive eye might probe their identity or action. These two rays, together with the seven represented to the earth by the chohans, the Elohim and the archangels, invoke the power of the three-times-three, or the magical number nine.

The secret ray anchored in the North Pole radiates beyond the equator along the longitudinal lines to the Tropic of Capricorn, focusing the masculine ray of the Godhead. The secret ray anchored in the South Pole radiates along the longitudinal lines past the equator to the Tropic of Cancer, focusing the feminine ray of the Godhead. Thus, there is an intense activity of the secret rays focusing the balanced action of Alpha and Omega in the tropical regions between the Tropics of Capricorn and Cancer.

A focus of the secret rays is maintained in the Temple of Peace over the Hawaiian Islands, balancing the masculine activity in the Northern Hemisphere and the feminine activity in the Southern Hemisphere. The attack on Pearl Harbor (December 7, 1941) was an attempt by the dark forces to disrupt the action of the secret rays that are holding the balance as the earth enters the golden age.

All five secret rays were released to the earth by Mighty Cosmos on April 8, 1973. This release marked the beginning of the initiation of the crucifixion for the earth and was the beginning of the great spiral of the transition from Pisces to Aquarius and the bringing in of the golden age. With that release, Cosmos explained the action of these secret rays:

"Have you thought about the fact that there is a consciousness and awareness of God within the core of being that is the threefold flame and within the white fire that is the heart of every atom of man's being? So then, I AM that consciousness; and you are that consciousness if you choose to ensoul the white fire.

"I caution you not to leap into the flame without the realization that all that is human, all that is less than divine within you, must be consumed when you make that leap. I think of how mankind gingerly approach the waters of the sea, and they put in one toe and quickly withdraw it because it is too cold. Well, you might do the same because it is too hot. But the heat is only generated by the friction of your own consciousness in the flame.

"Therefore, first divest thyself of the awareness of thyself as a being apart from God, apart from his preeminence; and then consider the allness that is man as the manifestation of God. Realize that that allness can only be the consuming fire. And there—there you stand. Take one step and enter the Flame, for that is how close the Flame is. That is how near divine perfection is. And that is how unreal the vanity of vanities is.[92] Only one step, and you step out of imperfection into perfection....

"And so I have come forth to release at the behest of the Lords of Karma an extraordinary assistance through the momentum of the secret rays that descend now from the heart of Alpha and Omega, from the hearts of the mighty Elohim and their heavenly consorts who send forth the aspect of the masculine, the aspect of the feminine of the secret rays. And they are spiraling into manifestation through the etheric, the mental, the emotional, and into the physical plane of the planet Earth....

"The secret rays are a haven for the blessed. Let all retreat to the secret rays and to the consciousness that I AM. For I AM Cosmos and I ensoul the cosmos with the power of the secret rays. And there is nowhere within this Giant Egg that you can go that you will not find my Self-awareness of the cosmic secret rays that come forth from the heart of Almighty God. And thou shalt find me in the rock and in the water, in the spring of life, in the heart of man, in the heart of a flower, in the clouds above, and in the stratosphere, and in all solar awarenesses; for I AM Cosmos, and I AM the precipitation of the masculine and feminine rays of Alpha and Omega....

"So then the power of Mighty Cosmos is victorious 'as Above, so below' this day. And the cycles of God-vision are released from the heart of the earth, from the heart of the four beings of the elements; and the planetary adjustments begin. For the LORD God requires this day that the four lower bodies of the planet Earth come into alignment and that the consciousness of Cosmos be made manifest north, south, east and west for the rectifying of the poles and of the axis in physical manifestation. So the spiral is released and so the manifestation shall be made plain at the hour and in the time of the LORD's appointing."[93]

Mighty Cosmos gave a dispensation on July 1, 1995, whereby he added his needlelike rays to the reinforcement of the earth. He said these needlelike rays "can only be likened unto crystal fire, fire crystallized as pins, pins so tiny that they cannot even be measured.... I appreciate your calls to me. For my secret rays are a part of the holding together of the core in the center" of the earth.[94]

❖ **CUZCO, Emissary of the God Star**

Cuzco is a disciple of Surya and director of his retreat of God's will near Suva, the Sacred Retreat of the Blue Flame. This retreat is in an island northeast of Viti Levu (the largest of the Fiji Islands) and is both under the sea and within the mountains. For many centuries, Cuzco has served under beloved Surya to avert or temper cataclysmic activities. His mighty balancing power of peace, his advice to us to follow the wisdom offered by the Great White Brotherhood and his divine love are radiant gifts to all mankind.

Cuzco's retreat is dedicated to the holding of the balance of forces in the earth, to the adjustment of the earth to the weight of karmic effluvia and to the guarding of the earth on its axis and in orbit. Ascended masters who serve with Cuzco at his retreat use advanced technology, including computers and scientific instruments.

For millennia, the axis of the earth has been tilted at a considerable angle due to the great weight of human discord of the planet's evolutions. During the comparatively recent righting of the earth's axis at the etheric level (October 12, 1958), it was the cosmic being Cuzco, with others of the ascended host, who stood guard, staying cataclysmic action that might otherwise have occurred during this adjustment. This adjustment will enable the planet Earth to receive a fuller measure of blessing from Helios and Vesta.

Cuzco is concerned with the riptides of anger, hate, fear, frustration, confusion, derision, gossip and many other momentums of psychic force that rush headlong against the lifestreams of unascended beings. He has given a "Count to Nine Decree"[95] by which the individual may protect his four lower bodies against the bombardments of these astral riptides.

Surya and Cuzco are also concerned about raising the flame of Mu (Mother) and the culture of the Motherland. The cult of the Mother, destined to come into prominence as we enter the Aquarian age, was the foundation of the civilization of Lemuria. The fall of Mu was the direct result of the Fall of man, which reached its lowest point in the desecration of the shrines to the Cosmic Virgin. Through the worship of the Motherhood of God and the elevation in society of the functions of the feminine aspect of the Deity, it is expected that science and religion will once again reach their apex, and man will discover the Spirit of God as the flame enshrined upon the altar of his own being.

The ascended master Cuzco explained the meaning of his name in a dictation delivered at Cuzco, Peru, on December 23, 1973. He said: "I am the masterful Presence that hails the coming of the Christed one. And this is the inner meaning, the light pattern of the name Cuzco: the coming of the Christed one."

He also said: "I am the gov-erning Presence of a flame that was anchored here [at Cuzco] thousands of years ago, far beyond the mists of time and space as you reckon them. And the flame is a focus of hearts, hearts consecrated to the Christ, twin

Cuzco, Peru

flames consecrated to a new race and a golden age."

On April 4, 1969, Cuzco said that some of us were with him at the Temple of the Wind on Lemuria. He said: "I, Cuzco of old, have reigned over the islands of the sea. I am well remembered in South America and honored there."

Cuzco works closely with elemental life to hold the balance for earth's transition from the age of Pisces to the age of Aquarius. In his 1988 dicta-tion Cuzco said: "I hold the balance of the currents of the seas and of the continents. And in my retreat, which the unascended do not frequent, there the balance of the tides and of the unleashing of the karma of a plan-etary sphere may be sent forth by higher edict. Thus we work very closely with all elemental life and the four hierarchs of the elements….

"It is the great desire of all elemental life to bring peaceful and calm transition everywhere upon earth. Unfortunately, the cooperation has not been forthcoming from many. O let the violet flame go forth into the hearts of those who do know better but do lead in anger in their protest and thus, to a certain extent, negate their opportunity to be the instrument of God Harmony….

"From my retreat I send forth resurrection's flame that you might be above the din, the turmoil, above the discord and all burdens of the conclusion of the century….

"I am an emissary of the God Surya. I am an emissary of the focal point of the Central Sun and the seat of God-government of this galaxy [the God Star, Sirius]…. Each time you call upon beloved Surya, I am also the echo that answers, for I am the chela of this Great One, and therefore, I bring to you the Omega balance of your call.

"I will come to you if you call me. I will be in your heart if you will have me. I come in the fullness of the comfort flame of the Holy Spirit. I bring comfort to all life even as I assist all life to adjust to new cycles."[96]

❖ **CYCLOPEA AND VIRGINIA, Elohim of the Fifth Ray**

Cyclopea and Virginia are the Elohim of the fifth ray (green ray) of truth, healing, constancy and the desire to precipitate the abundance of God through the immaculate concept of the Holy Virgin. Holding the focus for the All-Seeing Eye of God and the purity of the science of precipitation,

these twin flames assist mankind and elemental forms of life to precipitate the abundance of the Spirit of God into manifest form.

Cyclopea is the Elohim of vision, and his cosmic consciousness ensouls the vision of the Creator. Creation is an action of the faculty of God's vision. Cyclopea holds the vision for all of life, and thus he is known as the All-Seeing Eye of God. He teaches mastery of the third eye and lends his momentum of vision for the freedom of lifewaves and planetary homes such as Earth, Venus, Mars and countless others beyond our solar system and galaxy.

The apostle James said, "A double minded man is unstable in all his ways."[97] Jesus said, "The light of the body is the eye: if therefore thine eye be single, thy whole body shall be full of light."[98]

Cyclopea and Virginia focus the purity of single-eyed vision, which was lost when mankind partook of the fruit of the tree of the knowledge of good and evil. Through the focus of the All-Seeing Eye of God in the third-eye chakra in the center of each one's forehead, they radiate the truth of the original divine plan through a single green flame emitting the seven color rays of the Elohim. This is a focus of the purity that ennobles man through the spiraling caduceus, which, when raised and anchored in the forehead, is the symbol of his winged victory and his return to wholeness.

The caduceus, symbol of the light raised to the point of the third-eye chakra

Seated among the twelve solar hierarchies, Cyclopea occupies the position of the ten o'clock line on behalf of the evolutions of this solar system, representing the hierarchy of Scorpio and teaching the correct use of the creative energies. Cyclopea is a member of the Karmic Board, where he represents the fourth ray of purity.

He and Virginia are also known as the Elohim of Music or the God and Goddess of Music. Through the music of the spheres, they govern the activities of speech, hearing and sight, focusing the rays of concentration and consecration to the evolutions in their care. They are cosmic patrons of music in charge of the release of the music of the spheres through the masculine and feminine rays of Alpha and Omega. These magnificent God flames have long served in this capacity on behalf of the evolutions of many systems of worlds.

Cyclopea and Virginia guard the virgin consciousness. During the conclaves held at each half-year cycle in the Royal Teton Retreat, Cyclopea releases balls of blue fire into the atmosphere of earth through the focus of the All-Seeing Eye at the north end of the sanctuary. These balls, with their accompanying light rays, charge the earth with the action of the will of God and the purity of the divine conception of every man, woman and child on the planet. The action of the blue lightning cuts through the dense effluvia and paves the way for the crystal flame of purity and the emerald ray, which are healing mantras from the heart of Cyclopea and Virginia that purify the four lower bodies of the lifestreams to whom they minister.

Cyclopea's aura is green with a reflection of the prism of the Christ consciousness resembling the action of crystal. Virginia's aura is green tinged with white. Their retreat is in the etheric realm high in the Altai Range where Mongolia, China and Russia meet, near Tabun Bogdo.

Cyclopea says that if we would recognize "the connecting link" between angelic hosts and Elohim, between cosmic masters and ascended masters, and between students of spirituality throughout the world, "you would find a great outpouring of spiritual assistance descending from on high as the perfect indicator of any given moment that would enable you to have that spiritual finesse...similar to the ascended master Saint Germain prior to his ascension."

Therefore, "in the holy name of freedom, let the power of your vision expand. Let the power of God's light within you be a radiating glow-ray to act as a sword of penetration...and reveal the path toward infinite mastership that is to be found posited within your own God Presence, I AM."

The Elohim emphasize that "you must have the selfsame sense as your beloved Saint Germain has attained to—that the victory of God is a cosmic Reality...radiantly expanding its power from the altar of your heart...into the world of form.... The power of transmutative vision, then, must be recognized" so that "the power that flows forth through man will also extend itself to elemental life.... The power of spiritual vision can be transferred to them, for they are great mimics and have hitherto mimicked mankind in their erroneous outpicturings, producing thorn and thistle to manifest in consciousness."[99]

In 1997, Cyclopea came with a dispensation to help us fulfill our divine plan: "Out of the white light I create an imprint," he said, "which I affix to every soul of God who has transmuted a certain level of her karma. You who have reached that certain level…shall receive from me, as long as you call to me each day, assistance in outpicturing your divine blueprint in small things and in great things, in planetary things and in the systems of worlds."

If you were not in attendance for that dictation or you had not yet transmuted the required level of karma, you can ask Cyclopea to bless you now, in this very moment. You can ask him to bless you with that imprint and to assist you in manifesting your "divine blueprint."

Cyclopea went on to say that "at a certain point on the Path every chela must activate and claim divine vision as his own." Cyclopea said that you can consecrate his decree[100] and other emerald-ray decrees to him, and he will strengthen you and "show you the vast science of God, even the science of your own ascension in the light."[101]

The Elohim Cyclopea and Virginia want us to focus on our divine blueprint as well as on the following issues: the healing of the nations, their economies and their peoples; the halting of misuses of music, science and technology, including genetic engineering and cloning; and the counteracting of germ warfare and the spreading of harmful viruses and microbes.

❖ **DANIEL AND NADA RAYBORN**

Daniel and Nada Rayborn are ascended masters who are twin flames and initiates of Saint Germain. They were friends of his messenger Godfré Ray King during the 1930s. The instruction and assistance given them by the masters enabled them to make their ascension.

A great opera singer before her ascension, and an even greater one after, Mrs. Rayborn was a pupil of the ascended lady master Nada. Mr. Rayborn was a successful businessman. As the owner of a profitable mine, the qualities of the Christ that he manifested toward the men who worked for him contributed to his momentum of victory that resulted in his ascension in 1931 in the Cave of Symbols with the assistance of the atomic accelerator.

The example of Daniel and Nada Rayborn, their love for one another and the bond of their mutual service, will forever be a strength to all who call to them for assistance in the expansion of the threefold flame in family life. Rex and Nada, the children of Daniel and Nada, also ascended in that life. By attuning with this modern American family, we know that it is possible for us also to make the ascension and to follow in their footsteps. The matrix of family unity, the focus of the Holy Trinity, which was held by Saint Germain, Jesus and Mother Mary, is a flame of hope to all modern families who are confronted with the divisive forces of modern civilization.

Much of what we know of the lives of Daniel and Nada Rayborn is from the book by Godfré Ray King (Guy Ballard) *The Magic Presence.* Godfré and his wife, Lotus (Edna Ballard), were Saint Germain's messengers in the I AM Activity beginning in the 1930s.

Godfré first met Daniel Rayborn in the summer of 1930 at the Brown Palace Hotel in Denver, after receiving a letter of introduction to him from Saint Germain. He wrote in *The Magic Presence:* "My impression of Rayborn was very pleasant, for his whole attitude was one of harmony and kindliness, and at the same time, I felt that he was a man of strong character with a keen sense of honor. He had a finely shaped head, classic features, iron-gray hair, and clear, piercing blue-gray eyes. He stood very erect and was fully six feet two inches in height."[102]

The day after they met, Godfré accompanied Daniel to his Diamond K Ranch in Wyoming, which was one of Daniel's mining properties. When later visiting another of Daniel's mining operations, Godfré remarked that he had never seen so fine a camp of men. At the Diamond K Ranch, Godfré met Daniel's two children—his eighteen-year-old son, Rex, and his sixteen-year-old daughter, Nada. Rex and Nada had remarkable singing voices and they performed for Godfré after dinner one night. That evening Nada told Godfré about her mother, whose name was also Nada.

Their mother's father was an Englishman and her mother, who was educated in England, was the daughter of an Arab Sheik. Four weeks before she passed on, she received transcendent revelations. Saint Germain first came to her at the beginning of her career in grand opera, when she suffered from extreme stage-fright. The master touched her forehead with the fingers of his right hand. Instantly, she was calm and was able to perform well. Saint Germain told her of the man she was to marry and of her future children. He came often and taught her cosmic laws that she was able to apply with success. He later told her that she had work to do at inner levels but that he would always care for her children.

Nada told Godfré: "Shortly after I was born, our Beloved Master, Saint Germain, came to [Mother]. He explained that she had work to do on the higher planes of life and that he would always hold Rex and me in his great, loving, protecting care.... Father, Saint Germain said, was not sufficiently awakened to be told of [the Higher Law] until about a year ago, when…Saint Germain came to him."[103]

After dinner the next evening, Daniel Rayborn met with Godfré, Rex and Nada. He told them that Saint Germain had awakened him at 4:00 a.m. that morning and had taught him for at least two hours. Saint Germain revealed to him that he would soon make his ascension.

In a dictation given through Mark Prophet on October 14, 1963, the ascended master Daniel Rayborn explained how his contact with Saint Germain prior to his ascension propelled him forward on the spiritual path:

"It was such a wonderful experience to me when first I came into contact with Saint Germain, when I realized that he was a vibrant, living person, a great ascended master, one who could come from the great cosmic ethers with the swiftness of blue lightning and make himself known and felt. The tangibility of this great master flooded my being, and I was wholly aware of the fact that I was in the presence of great divinity. But the one particular quality that he imparted unto me above all others, which floods my soul at this moment with wonder, is the fact that God within me had the same desire of transformation as was resident within the being of Saint Germain.

"He made known unto me that it was the wonder of God's love that would impart to me also the full stature of an ascended master. He engendered in me great faith and courage so that I had hope, when faced with many vicissitudes in the business world and in family situations,…that the great light of God would safely pull me through all those conditions and that ultimately I would be given the gift of my ascension."

In that same dictation Daniel Rayborn taught us a mantra we can use in times of trial. He said: "Many of you who are at times afflicted by elements of doubt and shadow must recognize the constancy of the sun of your being that shines behind each cloud. You have heard it said that every cloud has a silver lining, but these words seem poor consolation at times to individuals during their moments of trial. Men must recognize the need not to necessarily make decisions during moments of trial but to wait until the clouds have rolled away and the cycle has passed.

"The words, 'This too shall pass!' are a fiat of authority that Saint Germain taught to me as an old mantra. When correctly understood and applied to life, it tends to act as an eraser to wipe the slate of life clean and to remove unwanted pictures from the consciousness. 'This too shall pass!' stated three times and followed by 'The light of God never fails!' three times, creates a mantra of Christ consciousness to clean the consciousness of unwanted conditions and bring forth a positive victory over negative elements that may at times be projected into one's consciousness."

A few days after Saint Germain had awakened Daniel Rayborn and instructed him, the master spent three days with Daniel, Rex and Nada Rayborn and Godfré at the Cave of Symbols, his retreat near the Rayborn ranch. He gave them a tour of the retreat and showed them marvelous inventions, including a device called the atomic accelerator.

Saint Germain explained that the atomic accelerator was "a mechanical way of quickening the atomic vibration of the human body...and assisting to raise it into the pure Electronic Body which Jesus referred to as the seamless [garment] or the bridal garment of the Spirit.... It will be used a great deal in the future to assist in raising the physical flesh atom into its divine purity and structure—the Electronic Body. This Body remains forever, eternally youthful, beautiful, strong, perfect, and free from every conceivable limitation. In this body, individuals can and do function wherever they choose in the universe, for in it there are no barriers of time, place, space, nor condition."[104]

Saint Germain also explained that it establishes perfect equilibrium in the brain structure. By balancing the mental and emotional states, dishonesty and crime of every kind can be prevented. The atomic accelerator was used on Atlantis, although it was less perfect at that time.

During the Rayborns' visit to the Cave of Symbols, Saint Germain asked Daniel Rayborn to sit in the atomic accelerator, which was aglow with currents of light. After this experience, Rayborn said, "Words can never describe the marvels I have experienced. And for the first time in my life, I am beginning to know the real meaning of life."[105] Through this machine, Rayborn was given a life-extension through the raising of the atomic structure of the physical body.

A year later, as Saint Germain had foretold, Daniel Rayborn made his ascension. He went to the Cave of Symbols, where for several days he prepared for his ascension in what Saint Germain called the Chamber of Light. In his dictation of October 14, 1963, the ascended master Daniel Rayborn described what he experienced in that glorious moment of his ascension: "Oh, the glory and the surge of power, the supreme blessing, the contact with the angelic host! But, above all, was the great feeling of union with one's own mighty I AM Presence.

"I recall the thought passing through my consciousness that it was similar to standing outside during the noontime and gazing up to the heavens and recognizing that not a star was visible, and then suddenly being transferred to the hour of midnight and seeing that the entire sky was full of beautiful points of light. For I became aware of regions of the cosmos not even thought of or conceived of by me before. And I felt a kinship with wonderful individual minds and hearts, a reunion with those whom I had long suffered absence from. I knew on the instant that nothing in this world was significant or worthy of anything by comparison to the ascension.

"...The final thought that passed through my mind as I rose upward into the great light to be absorbed, was, 'Oh, if I could only tell them!'... And I realized afterward, by reflection that this thought has filled the mind and consciousness of everyone who has ascended. For all have felt, 'Oh, if I could only tell them!'

"This is the desire that we of the ascended hosts feel—to reach down into human consciousness, with all of its density, its almost suffocating outer conditions, and to say, 'Oh, do put all that you have into your search for your divinity that you might receive the blessing of the ascension at the conclusion of this life.'"

Daniel Rayborn concluded that dictation with a special gift. He asked that a golden chair be placed before the altar and said: "I call to the Great Divine Director for the resurgent energies of Christ-accomplishment to be magnified and a beam of direct light substance to pass through the substance of this chair and to energize it for the space of one hour.

"Ladies and gentlemen, we have received permission from the Great White Brotherhood for an action of one percent radiation of the atomic accelerator to be anchored in this chair. We ask you to share it with one another for the coming hour." For an hour the students of the masters took turns to sit in the golden chair.

Through the intercession of Saint Germain, Nada was able to visit her family from the ascended state. She said that after her passing, twelve ascended masters, including Saint Germain, had surrounded her, showing her how she could raise the atomic structure of her physical body into the "pure Electronic Body."

She said: "As the process of raising gradually took place, I became more and more aware of blazing light filling my entire body.... I felt the most marvelous radiant energy surge in and through me, sweeping away every vestige of resistance and imperfection and quickening my consciousness.

"I became more and more aware of my Mighty I AM Presence until finally it stood before me visible, tangible, and very real. Steadily and powerfully, I felt my physical body drawn into and enveloped by my glorious God-Self, and when I stepped out of the cemetery, I could scarcely realize how transcendent I had become. The old human, limited activities of my consciousness were raised into that alert sense of freedom and unlimited use of wisdom and power. I was shown very clearly, now I was aware of this greater activity, that I must put it to use. Then came a still fuller sense of the freedom, beauty, joy, and service that I must render to those who still remain unascended."[106]

In a dictation delivered on May 13, 1962, Nada Rayborn spoke of her service as an ascended lady master: "Some of you will recall that I was a prima donna and did a great deal of work in connection with opera.... My song today is a song of the Spirit and my voice may be heard at night in the various retreats when the members of the Great White Brotherhood are assembled together.

"For ever so frequently, at the request of beloved Saint Germain and beloved Daniel Rayborn and my son and daughter and others of the ascended hosts, I still stand before the multitude of the hosts ascended and give a rendering to the heart of my own Presence. I pour forth my melodic interpretations of the universe, and I rejoice continually in the privilege of so doing.

"Your talents, beloved ones, are never removed from you by your ascension in the light. They are enhanced, and limitation is removed from them."

❖ DAVID LLOYD

In his final embodiment, David Lloyd lived as a young boy in India, where his father represented the British Government. His father passed on when he was twenty, leaving a hundred thousand pounds willed to the family by a friend whom they had sponsored in diamond mines in South Africa. An unascended master saw to it that David Lloyd was taken care of and that he and his mother were safely transported to England. The same master told David Lloyd that one day he would find a man on a mountain in North America who would hand him a crystal cup containing the elixir of life and that he would assist him in raising his body.

After fifty years of continuous searching, amidst great trials, he met Godfré Ray King on Mount Shasta. When Godfré offered him a drink from a nearby spring, a crystal cup formed in Godfré's hand. As he handed David the cup, Godfré saw that it was filled with the same sparkling liquid that Saint Germain had previously offered him. David Lloyd then told Godfré the story of his life, and Godfré made the call to the I AM Presence and Saint Germain to assist David Lloyd through him. Again a crystal cup formed in his hand and was filled with living liquid light. As David Lloyd drank the elixir, his youth returned, and he rose from the ground into his ascension in the light.

Just as Godfré was the key to David Lloyd's immortal freedom and the only one through whom that blessing could come, so that experience was an initiation for Godfré that could only come through David Lloyd. By it he rose in service as a messenger of the hierarchy. In a like manner, we are all keys to one another's victory, and we must be alert to affirm that victory for one another. For in so doing, we rise up the ladder of initiation.

David Lloyd is among the masters who have made the physical ascension. In the ritual of the ascension, the soul is united with the white-fire body of the I AM Presence. Normally, this does not require the raising of the physical body; rather, the soul itself may take flight from the mortal coil and be translated through the ascension process. Today most people whose souls qualify for the ritual of the ascension ascend from inner levels after the soul has departed the physical body following the change called death. The soul attains union with the mighty I AM Presence to become a permanent atom in the body of God just as in a physical ascension.

The ascended master Rex has told us that those who are called to the physical ascension must have had many thousands of years of preparation. In order to ascend, the candidate must have balanced at least 51 percent of his karma. In order to make a physical ascension, he must have balanced between 95 and 100 percent of his karma.

When a physical ascension takes place, the physical body is transformed by and superseded by the ascended master light body. During the ascension ritual, the soul becomes permanently clothed with this body, also called the "wedding garment," or the deathless solar body.

Serapis Bey describes the process of the ascension in his *Dossier on the Ascension.* "The flame above (in the heart of the Presence) magnetizes the flame below (the threefold flame within the heart) and the wedding garment descends around the silver cord to envelop the lifestream of the individual in those tangible and vital essence currents of the ascension. Tremendous changes then take place in the form below, and the four lower bodies of man are cleansed of all impurities. Lighter and lighter grows the physical form, and with the weightlessness of helium the body begins to rise into the atmosphere, the gravitational pull being loosened and the form enveloped by the light of the externalized glory that man knew with the Father 'in the beginning....' The individual ascends, then, not in an earthly body but in a glorified spiritual body into which the physical form is changed on the instant by total immersion in the great God flame."[107]

The ascended master David Lloyd has told us that we may call to him to charge us with his feeling and momentum of desiring the ascension, which was built up over those fifty years of searching. He speaks with compassion for those who have not yet attained the ascension and describes his experience of the ascension:

"Beloved ones, take heart. I give to you and pledge to you my sacred word this night that the love of God has programmed for you all a similar opportunity, a victorious overcoming of the vicissitudes of life and the darkness of this world....

"Do not be overconcerned, beloved hearts of light, simply because you have failed to attain in previous moments of struggle and search. Be not dismayed. Be not affrighted nor consider yourselves as an offcast from the gates of heaven, for heaven beckons and comes very close.

"Many times as I journeyed throughout the realm of experiences in the earth life, I also found that struggle seemed to overcome me, and discouragement aimed directly at dissuading me from the search caused me momentarily to pause. The wise do it not, and yet I do not think of myself in that former state as always acting wisely—but persistently. For I was persistent to storm the very gates of the citadel of heaven, and I continued to pursue the spiritual path, even when some around me sought to discourage me. Many circumstances that are unrecorded still occurred in my life that prevented me from enjoying at all times the fullness of the divine search.

"Yet, the eye of God beckoned. The perception of God continued to call me. And I knew that it was a matter of divine and infinite destiny that one day I should receive the gift of the ascension. Yet, when the moment came, I knew it not, and scarcely as it was happening did I know it. Yet so wondrous was it, when I began to feel that buoyant joy, that caress of the Infinite upon my finite being that dissolved it altogether. And in its place, almost as the sea, spewed forth the beautiful, compassionate experience of molding me in cosmic form into the infinitude of God's thought.

"The perfect body appeared. The perfect mind appeared. The perfect soul ruled the world of my being. A surge of infinite strength came forth, and I rose into the air, into the arms of a similar dissolvement as had happened previously to beloved Jesus. For a cloud, too, of infinite, cosmic love received me out of the sight of men. And in the bond of cosmic compassion, I expanded my knowledge into the Infinite as cadences of loveliness, receding into a far and distant future, which appeared before me then as a mountain of hope. And I entered in to the joy of God. And the joy of God filled my soul, and darkness vanished altogether.

"And in the mystery of being, I understood that others like me would follow also in the wake of my experience and would come to realize at last that the infinite lamp of God was always lit, awaiting the return home of the prodigal child and the lifting up of each individual who passed through this magnificent gift of attainment with the vestments of immortality."[108]

❖ DHYANI BUDDHAS, FIVE, *See* Five Dhyani Buddhas

❖ DIANA, *See* Oromasis and Diana

❖ DIVINE DIRECTOR, GREAT, *See* Great Divine Director

❖ DJWAL KUL, The Tibetan Master

Adoration of the Magi,
artist unknown

Djwal Kul is known as the Tibetan Master, or the "Tibetan." Two thousand years ago, Djwal Kul journeyed with El Morya and Kuthumi as one of the three wise men following the star to the birthplace of Jesus. In that service to the Trinity, he focused the pink plume, Morya the blue and Kuthumi the gold, in the forcefield of the infant Jesus.

Previously, prior to the sinking of Lemuria, he had assisted Lord Himalaya in removing ancient records and tablets to the Himalayan retreats of the masters; later he studied in the lamasaries of Asia. It has been said by Theosophists that he was embodied as Kleineas, a pupil of Pythagoras (Kuthumi), as one of the disciples of Gautama Buddha, and as Aryasanga.[109]

As "D.K." and as Gai Ben-Jamin, he served with El Morya and Kuthumi in their endeavors with Madame Blavatsky and the Theosophical Society. Through his willingness to serve, he became known as "The Messenger of the Masters." Djwal Kul was the foremost disciple of Kuthumi, and is said to have lived near his teacher in Tibet. In the late nineteenth century, Djwal Kul, El Morya and Kuthumi won their ascension, and in the 1950s, they began working with the messengers Mark L. Prophet and later Elizabeth Clare Prophet to publish their instruction through The Summit Lighthouse.

The focus of Djwal Kul's golden flame of illumination is in his etheric retreat in Tibet. From that point, he assists in the raising of the consciousness of India through her embodied teachers, the yogic masters of the Himalayas, under the influence of his understanding of yogic principles in preparation for future advancement in the science of invocation and the release of Christ-power through the seven chakras.

With Kuthumi, Djwal Kul teaches about the human aura. He gives us the meditation on the secret chamber of the heart, and is one of the masters who initiate us within the inner temple, the secret chamber of the heart, on the path of love. He has released a breathing exercise for the integration of the four lower bodies, which is found in the book *Studies of the Human Aura*. He also teaches the great astrology of the ascended masters—the twelve lines of the cosmic clock for the twelve paths of initiation under the twelve solar hierarchies. He teaches us how to invoke the flame for the mastery of our daily astrology, which is our daily karma. Day by day, the karma—positive and negative—that comes to our life can be met and mastered by these twelve paths and twelve flames.

Djwal Kul tells a story that illustrates an element of spiritual science: "I am come tonight to bring to you the fresh winds of the Zuider Zee; and I begin with a tale of the land of the dikes.

"There lived by the sea a gentle soul who was a miller. He and his wife served together to grind the grain for the people of their town. And it came to pass that in all the land there were no communities where so much happiness reigned as there. Their countrymen marveled and wondered, for they recognized that something unusual must have happened to make the members of this community so singularly wise and happy. And although the townsfolk themselves were born, grew up, matured to adulthood and passed from the screen of life within the community, never in all of their living were they able to understand the mystery.

"Tonight I shall draw aside the curtain and tell you what made the people of this community so happy and prosperous, so joyous and wise.

"It was the service of the miller and his wife and the love that they put into the flour. For this love was carried home in sacks of flour on the backs of those who patronized their mill and was then baked into their bread. At every meal the regenerative power of love from the miller and his wife was radiated around the table, and it entered their physical bodies as they partook of the bread. Thus, like radioactive power, the energy of this vibrant love from the miller and his wife was spread throughout the community.

"The neighbors did not know the reason for their happiness and none of the people were ever able to discover it. For sometimes—although they live side by side—mankind are unable to pry the most simple secrets about one another. And so the mysteries of divine love continue to defy probing by the human consciousness, but we of the ascended masters' octave occasionally choose to make them known to you by sharing these gems with you.

"The instruction which I would bring to you tonight concerns physical properties and their power to retain the radiation of those who handle them. The food you eat, beloved ones, when prepared by hands charged with divine love, enters into your physical body and creates a much greater degree of spiritual happiness than mankind would at first realize. Those who are wise will recognize the truth of what I am saying; and if they must partake of food from unknown sources, they will be certain that they have removed by the violet transmuting flame those undesirable momentums of human creation whose radiation can do no good to the individual who partakes thereof and much harm to him who is unwary and therefore unprotected."[110]

❖ DURGA, *See* Shiva

❖ ELEMENTAL LIFE. *See also* Aries and Thor, Neptune and Luara, Pelleur and Virgo, Oromasis and Diana

God Tabor is one of the masters who work closely with elemental life— the nature spirits who so faithfully serve God and mankind. He is concerned with the levels of pollution—in the earth and in the bodies of her people—that burden the elementals.

Tabor has given us a prescription for the victory of elemental life. He says: "The joy of elemental life is to serve you.... And your joy must be to serve with them, to command the life-essence of the Christ to flow to the elementals, to infuse them with rejoicing and newness of being and fire and the spirit to bring the earth into a golden age!"[111]

Earth could be very different if the elementals were not bowed down with pollution and the weight of mankind's karma. Mark Prophet once painted that scene for us:

"If we had followed the divine plan, we would be able to see and be friends with the nature spirits. We would not have to deal with lesser or greater storms. No rain would fall, but dew would appear from the air to water our crops. The air would be saturated with moisture in just the right amounts everywhere on earth. The deserts would bloom as the rose, and there would be no excess moisture and no lack of it. It would be just right for every climate.

"You would have the most beautiful weather, and you would have the most beautiful flowers all over the world. You would have plenty of food, and you would find that people would not be killing animals to live. There would be abundant fruit. Many of the fruits that would manifest are not even on the planet now.... We would have communion with the elementals, showing them how to step up into a higher manifestation. And we would be receiving our instructions from angels."[112]

Unfortunately, mankind's negative karmic patterns have clouded this picture considerably. In Genesis, God tells Adam, "Cursed is the ground for thy sake; in sorrow shalt thou eat of it all the days of thy life."[113] "The ground" is symbolic of elemental life. In other words, because of mankind's fall from grace (represented in the figures of Adam and Eve) the elementals were "cursed"—that is, mankind's negative karma was introduced into their world—and the elementals were assigned the task of maintaining balance where karmic imbalance now appeared. The weight of karma has been building up over centuries and millennia. Yet the elementals keep on working heroically to clean up the earth, the air and the water of our planet. Day after day, they work to keep the earth on an even keel.

Without the unflagging work of the elementals, we would not have a physical platform on which to live. We would not have a place to work out our karma or to grow spiritually. Author Geoffrey Hodson describes the incredible patience of the tree devas (angels who work very closely with the elementals). Hodson says, "On contacting one of them more closely I have become conscious of their extreme age and unwearying patience. In their eyes is an inscrutable knowledge, a calm certainty.... Passing beyond the eyes into their consciousness, one touches a vivid intensity, which I can find no words to describe. To pass into theirs from our human brain consciousness might be compared to stepping out of water into fire."[114]

The masters remind us again and again how hard it is for the elementals to do their job. In 1966 the Great Divine Director said: "It is not the will of God or the ascended masters to permit the downfall of society or of the world of form, but we want you to know that the accumulation and accretion of darkness has risen higher than ever before in history. In fact, it was only seventy-five percent this high when the decision was made to overthrow in the time of Noah through the great Flood the civilizations then existing."

The Great Divine Director then announced: "Conditions in the world today have reached a point where the Karmic Board has withdrawn all restraint from the beings of the elements. This means that mankind of earth today do not know from one minute to the next just what the elementals will do.... If the present course is pursued, the entire planet would of necessity be blotted out of the planetary chain and those righteous individuals who are here be removed to other evolutions.... Therefore, we sound forth the edict that, unless mankind shall change and correct and mend some of the terrible flaws now existent in society, certainly the elementals will be unable to hold back the tide of negative human creation."[115]

In 1990, beloved Oromasis said that the elementals carry a great weight of oppression and depression, despair and discouragement. Like mankind, the elementals "become listless. They become tired. They become burdened. They become overworked.... But, beloved ones," he said, "you can clear them of it." The elementals do not have a threefold flame, and Oromasis said that until they earn that threefold flame "they must rely on your heart flame. Yes, they decree with you, but they must have you to decree with. For they depend upon the altar of your heart as you depend on the altar of God's heart and upon the unfed flame…. It is not just your family and your children who depend upon you, but each and every one of you has potentially millions of elementals who depend upon your heart flame."[116] Think of this—potentially millions of elementals are depending on us in this moment and until the hour of our transition and our victory in the light!

In 1996, Lanello told us that the elementals were still laboring under a very heavy burden. "The elementals and their hierarchs have reached their limit. They cannot and will not bear the sins of the world any longer. We call upon you to pray for them, for when they can no longer do their jobs, you can anticipate planetary cataclysm. It is in your best interest, then, to remember the elementals, to walk and talk with them, to call to their four hierarchs and to encourage them, to give them hope and stand by them. Otherwise you will see them giving up one by one….

"What would happen if all the earth should become a place where the beings of the elements have gone on strike, saying: 'We can no longer deal with the mountains of karma and polluted substance that mankind is dumping in the waters, in the earth, in the air!'"[117] The elementals have helped us for so very long. Now it is our turn to help them. We have the spiritual tools of the violet flame and the power of the Holy Spirit to do it.

Mankind has a tremendous influence on elemental life—for good or for ill. The elementals are very easily influenced; they are more easily influenced than a child. For example: wrong thought and feeling poured out in a small town day after day by husbands and wives fighting could result in a tornado hitting that town. That's right! A tornado can be generated by the thoughts and feelings of the people in that town if the elementals pick it up. But the sylphs can be controlled, and they will work for God's children.

Mark Prophet recounts one of his experiences in working with the elementals: "I remember driving an automobile near the city of Chicago, Illinois. And as we arrived in the vicinity of Chicago, the entire area was black with storm clouds. It was an absolute scene of terror, because in these storm clouds were cyclones and tornadoes. So when we perceived the ominous and threatening danger to the city, our entire group in the car immediately went into action contacting the sylphs of the air.

"Prior to our beginning, the storms and the winds began to howl. They howled something terrible, and they sobbed as a child would sob—you could hear it in the wind. We gave our decrees and we sang to the elementals and we called for the dissolving of the storm, and it was all done exactly as we called it forth. The storm clouds disappeared, and the city was saved from terrible destruction by calls to the elementals."[118] When our hearts are engrafted to God's heart, nothing is impossible.

In 1990, Oromasis' twin flame, Diana, announced a dispensation initiating a new wave of cooperation between sons and daughters of God and elemental life. Diana said, "I have brought with me today representatives of the four kingdoms. To each of you are given a troop of elementals, some from each of the kingdoms. You may consider that you have adopted a little tribe today numbering twelve. They will stay with you and obey your command if it is heart-centered in the diamond heart of Mary and Morya. And they will remain as long as you tend and nurture them.

"Include them in your calls and give them assignments, but only in keeping with the will of God. Invoke them for many, many purposes in your life, not excluding the healing of your four lower bodies or the tending to practical matters. And as you see the results of your interactions with them and take them with you on your hikes, so you may come to realize what is this segment of the army of the Lord.

"Thus, when those who are higher up on the scale of hierarchy perceive your gentleness as well as your firmness and your ability to marshal the forces of the elemental kingdom for good works, they will begin to consider also becoming your obedient servants.... Keepers of the Flame, walk with God—and as you do, know that God in elemental life walks with you."[119]

Give your troop of twelve elementals assignments daily. These can be any constructive endeavor that will help, not just one or two or ten people, but tens of thousands and millions of people. Ask them to take care of practical matters, including the healing of yourself and others. All elemental life knows how to heal. Be sure your requests are in keeping with the will of God. As you are diligent in marshaling the forces of the elementals for good, other beings who are more powerful than the elementals will become your servants as well. Just think what you can accomplish with more and more helpers at your disposal!

In 1993, Oromasis and Diana came again with a plea and a prayer for the elementals. They described other planets that are barren today because the elementals on those planets had no sponsorship—no sons and daughters of God who would keep the flame for them.

❖ **ELIJAH (JOHN THE BAPTIST)**

The ascended master Elijah had two embodiments that are recorded in the Bible: the Old Testament prophet Elijah, and John the Baptist in the New Testament. Jesus himself declared that John the Baptist was Elijah come again.[120]

The story of Elijah the Tishbite and his disciple Elisha (an earlier embodiment of Jesus) is recorded in the Book of Kings, where Elijah's ascension is described in this way: "There appeared a chariot of fire, and horses of fire, and parted them both asunder; and Elijah went up by a whirlwind into heaven."[121]

Elijah and Elisha

After Elisha witnessed his teacher's ascension, he took up "the mantle of Elijah that fell from him" and he smote the waters of Jordan. When the waters parted and Elisha went over, the sons of the prophets saw that the spirit of Elijah rested on Elisha. From that time on, Elisha performed many miracles, feats of alchemy that were prophetic of the triumph of his Spirit over matter during his final embodiment as Jesus. The accounts of Elisha healing the waters, multiplying the widow's oil, opening the womb of the Shunammite and later the raising of her son from the dead, the multiplying of the loaves of barley and the curing of Naaman of leprosy are recorded in the second book of Kings together with other demonstrations of the Law by this "Man of God."

After his ascension, Elijah received the almost unique dispensation that enabled him to reembody; and so he came again as John the Baptist to "prepare the way of the Lord." He willingly took on a flesh form and allowed himself to be sacrificed at the hand of Herod, in order to assist his disciple to fulfill his mission.

John the Baptist

The relationship of Jesus and John the Baptist is a story of great devotion, love and respect—beautiful to behold and seldom equaled. It is the story of the guru-chela, master-disciple relationship. Being the great and humble teacher that he was, John said of Jesus, "He must increase, but I must decrease";[122] for he bore in his heart the great God-desire that Jesus should exceed him in attainment and in service. He wanted to remain in the background, to see the glory—the full mantle of his ascended consciousness—upon Jesus. After his lifetime as John the Baptist, he returned to the ascended state.

The ascended master John the Baptist says: "There must be a meeting ground for heaven and earth, and that is the place of the heart. Your heart is the receiver of God, of Christed ones; and the womb of the Divine Mother is the recipient of the seed of Alpha for the birth of the Divine Manchild. Therefore, as Christed ones, welcome the King of kings and Lord of lords into your heart! As flames of the Divine Mother, cherish the incarnation of the Christ!

"It is the materialization of the God flame that we pursue to make earth a haven of light that all mankind might know the kingdom of God within and without, the conformity of sacred law."[123]

❖ EL MORYA, Chohan of the First Ray

El Morya is chief of the Darjeeling Council of the Great White Brotherhood, chohan of the first ray and hierarch of the etheric Temple of Good Will over Darjeeling, India. He is the founder of The Summit Lighthouse and the guru and teacher of the messengers Mark L. Prophet and Elizabeth Clare Prophet.

The Ascended Master
El Morya

Throughout his many embodiments to the present hour from the ascended state, beloved El Morya has been actively engaged in service to the light. As the son of Enoch, who "walked with God and was not for God took him" in the ritual of the ascension; as one of the seers who penetrated into the higher octaves of light in the ancient land of Ur of the Chaldees; and as a native of Persia, who worshiped the One God, Ahura Mazda—in these and during many other embodiments, he learned to experiment with "divine electricities," becoming increasingly aware of the spiritual power flowing through man. Later he became accomplished in the constructive use of fohat—the mysterious electric power of cosmic consciousness (quiescent or active)—that impelling vital force, which, when called into action by divine fiat, moves the evolutions of a universe, a galactic or solar system, or even a human being from the beginning to the completion of its mission.

He represents the godly attributes of courage, certainty, power, forthrightness, self-reliance, dependability, faith and initiative. These are the qualities of the Father principle—the statesman, the executive, the ruler. Because he has ably outpictured these essential virtues, El Morya has, through many embodiments, worn the crown of authority, ruling many kingdoms wisely and well. His rulership has not been that of a dictator, demanding that his subjects submit to his human will; but rather, his interpretation of government is God-over-men and his concept of true statesmen

 is God's overmen. He inspires in his subjects illumined obedience to the holy will of God.

El Morya was embodied as Abraham (c. 2100 B.C.), the first Hebrew patriarch, the prototype and progenitor of the twelve tribes of Israel. Judaism, Christianity and Islam all trace their origins back to Abraham. Although scholars once widely assumed that he was either a mythical figure or a nomadic or semi-nomadic Semite, archaeological finds since World War I have corroborated the picture of Abraham that is given in the Bible itself.

Abraham, by Doré

In answer to the call of the LORD, Abraham left the leading Sumerian city of Ur, forsaking the culture and cults of Mesopotamia at a time when Sumerian civilization was at its height. The LORD told him to journey to a land that he would show him and promised to make of him a great nation. The Book of Genesis describes him as a man rich in flocks and herds who commands a private army and is recognized by neighboring chieftains as a mighty prince.

Abraham is the archetype of the man of faith. He received the supreme test of faith when God told him to sacrifice his son Isaac. Abraham had waited many years for his wife Sarah to bear Isaac, who was to be the fulfillment of the LORD's promise to multiply Abraham's seed as the "stars of the heaven." Nevertheless, Abraham obeyed, and as he raised his knife to kill his son, the angel of the LORD told him to stop, and Abraham offered a ram in his place.

Because of Abraham's personal relationship with God and his exemplary faith, both Christian and Moslem scriptures describe him as the Friend of God ("El Khalil" in the Arabic language of the Koran). Inscribed on the Jaffa Gate in the Old City of Jerusalem is the passage from the Koran, "There is no God but Allah, and Abraham is beloved of Him."

El Morya was embodied as Melchior, one of the three wise men. As King Arthur (fifth century A.D.), Guru of the mystery school at Camelot, he guarded the inner teachings. He summoned knights of the Round Table and ladies of the court to quest the Holy Grail and to attain through initiation the mysteries of Christ.

As Thomas Becket (1118–1170), he was Lord Chancellor of England and good friend and advisor of Henry II. When he became archbishop of

Canterbury, foreseeing that his duties as archbishop would inevitably conflict with the king's will, he resigned the chancellorship against the king's wishes.

Becket turned his administrative abilities and diplomatic finesse as a distinguished chancellor into ardour and devotion as archbishop. He became as strong a supporter of the papacy as he had once been of the king and freely excommunicated courtiers and nobles for their unlawful use of church property and other breaches. In the face of the king's intent to imprison him, Becket exiled himself to France for six years. He returned

King Arthur

to England following a partial reconciliation with the king, only to begin quarreling with him anew.

On December 29, 1170, he was brutally murdered in Canterbury Cathedral when four knights of the court took literally the king's remark that he wished to be rid of "this turbulent priest." Uncompromising to the end, Becket told the knights: "If all the swords in England were pointing at my head, you would never make me betray either God or the Pope." More than five hundred healing miracles were attributed to him only a few years

Sir Thomas More, by Holbein

after his death, and he was canonized three years later.

Morya was also embodied as Sir Thomas More (1478–1535), the "man for all seasons." More's deep devotion to God caused him at one time to consider a religious vocation and to practice extraordinary austerities for over four years to test his own self-discipline. He decided to marry, however, and his wife and four children proved to be his greatest joy and his sole comfort in days to come. Their famed estate at Chelsea housed Thomas' entire family, including eleven grandchildren. Over the years, More's "little Utopia," as he often called it, became a center of learning and culture, likened by Erasmus to "Plato's academie"—a home of good will to which came the most learned men of the day, even the king himself, for counsel and for comfort. At Chelsea, More wrote the famous work entitled *Utopia*, a witty exposé of the superficiality of English life and the flagrant vices of English law.

In 1529, Sir Thomas More was appointed by Henry VIII Lord Chancellor of England and Keeper of the Great Seal. In spite of many honors and achievements, More sought no man's esteem; he was known for his promptness, efficiency and even-handed justice. He remained sensitive to the needs of the common people by daily walking the back streets of London to inquire into the lives of the poor.

Sir Thomas devoted himself to his duties with utmost zeal until Henry, desirous of but lacking a male heir to the throne, declared his marriage to Catherine of Aragon null and announced his intent to marry Ann Boleyn. Since the divorce was without papal approval and directly opposed to the laws of the Church, More refused to support the king's decision. In 1532, at the height of his career, he resigned his office and retired to Chelsea, where, greatly concerned with the heresies of Luther's revolt, he continued his writings in defense of the Catholic faith. Without friends and without office, More and his family lived in abject poverty. Nevertheless, Henry had been insulted at the chancellor's public disapproval of him. The king, therefore, sought to defame More and thus restore his royal image.

When he refused to take the Oath of Supremacy (which implied the rejection of papal supremacy and made Henry the head of the English church), More was imprisoned in the Tower of London. Fifteen months later, he was convicted of treason on perjured evidence. He was beheaded on Tower Hill July 6, 1535, affirming himself "the king's good servant, but God's first." He was canonized four hundred years later in 1935.

Thomas More was known for his wit. Author Anthony Kenny observes that More "is the first person to embody the peculiarly English ideal that the good man meets adversity and crisis not with silent resignation nor with a sublime statement of principle, but with a joke. One of More's most recent biographers has very well said, 'More was never more witty than when he was least amused.'"[124]

Akbar

Lawyer, judge, statesman, man of letters, author, poet, farmer, lover of pastoral life, ascetic, husband and father, champion of women's education, humanist and saint, Thomas More was outstanding among the avant-garde of the English Renaissance.

Morya was next embodied as Akbar the Great (1542–1605), founder of the Mogul empire in India and the greatest of its rulers. During his reign, he ended all discrimination against the Hindus and accepted them into government, serving on an equal basis with the Muslims. His policies were considered to be among the most enlightened of his time.

He was also Thomas Moore, the Irish poet (1779–1852), who wrote many ballads and is best remembered for "Believe Me If All Those Endearing Young Charms." To this day, the song draws the power of his intense love for the will of God as representative of the highest good—the immaculate image of every soul, untarnished by the burdens of the world.

Thomas Moore

In his final embodiment, El Morya was born a Rajput prince in India and later became a monk frequenting the retreats of the Himalayas. As the Master M., he, together with Kuthumi and Djwal Kul, attempted to acquaint mankind with the workings of the Law and hierarchy through the writings of Mme. H. P. Blavatsky. Together with the Master K.H. and Saint Germain, he founded the Theosophical Society. Morya ascended in 1898 and continues his great work for God-government on earth through the flame of goodwill and his embodied chelas.

El Morya told us that beginning January 6, 1998, the three wise men, El Morya, Kuthumi and Djwal Kul, will teach us the keys to the path of the ascension and sponsor all who aspire to make their ascension in this life. These masters will help us balance our karma, and they will stay until certain key souls have made their ascension. El Morya, Kuthumi and Djwal Kul represent the three plumes of the threefold flame of the heart—El Morya, the blue plume; Kuthumi, the yellow plume; and Djwal Kul, the pink plume. They come to bring our threefold flames into balance with theirs. If you follow the three kings and the star of the Christ Child, you will arrive at the manger scene of your own Christ-potential and your own Christhood.

In 1995 Morya spoke about what it takes to become his chela: "Constancy is the key virtue that I must have in those who truly desire to be one with me. If I would train you personally, beloved, I must have from you an unflinching constancy whereby you maintain a steady level of absorption of the blue flame of the will of God and thus enter day by day into the sacred fire of the first ray. You must be willing to take any rebuke, any correction, to take it swiftly and to then swiftly self-correct. You must have a momentum on giving the decrees to the ascended masters who serve principally on the first ray. You may give any (or all) of the blue decrees, whether they be to me or to Surya or to Himalaya or to Vaivasvata or to Archangel Michael.

"I tell you, beloved, when you keep yourself saturated in the blue ray and you are alert to every out-of-step state of mind that you might even consider entertaining, you will find that I shall become your champion. Once I become the champion of a chela, I will work with that chela to the end. Thus, beloved, do not think that I take lightly the taking on of a chela.

"Many of you are chelas in the becoming. But I must test and try you for many years, sometimes for lifetimes, before I receive the signal from Almighty God himself that I might burden myself by taking on another student.

"Realize this, beloved: It is well to make yourself a devotee of the will of God. For as a devotee, you will increase! and increase! and increase! many shades of blue rings around your four lower bodies and the circumference of your life. And when you have proven yourself under fire and in many situations—untenable situations, devastating situations—and have

El Morya often speaks of "the tall pines of Darjeeling"

come out right side up, we will know that we have a chela of the first order, and we will receive you that you might be anointed before the council in Darjeeling.

"Yes, this is a very special opportunity, and all can make themselves worthy. I speak of it, beloved, because I have surveyed the earth and I have listened to the dictations that have been given at this class and I understand that there are many, many people in the world who would seek and find this teaching if they knew it existed somewhere.

"Since I am about to sponsor millions of souls for this activity and this path, I must be certain that you who are here and who form the foundations of this community throughout the earth are true to me."[125]

As the chief of the Darjeeling Council of the Great White Brotherhood, Morya presides at round table meetings in his Retreat of God's Will in Darjeeling where the souls of the world's statesmen and men and women of integrity in God's will convene to study under this living master.

Morya has a second retreat in El Capitan, in Yosemite Valley, California. His keynote is "Pomp and Circumstance," his flowers are the blue rose and the forget-me-not, and his fragrance is sandalwood.

Forget-Me-Not

❖ **ELOHIM OF THE FIVE SECRET RAYS**

While there are seven pairs of Elohim in outer manifestation, there are five in inner manifestation within the Great Central Sun. These five manifest the five secret rays. While they have not released their names, their power and authority can be invoked by addressing "the Elohim of the five secret rays." Their momentum can be used to develop the bands of the secret rays in the causal body of man and to magnetize the flaming potential of the white-fire core of each atom of being.

❖ **ENOCH, Priest of the Sacred Fire**

The Book of Genesis records that Enoch was the seventh from Adam, that "he walked with God: and was not; for God took him."[126] Enoch was a priest of the sacred fire and a priest of the Order of Melchizedek.

Enoch has spoken of the challenges of that life: "I have never regretted my step nor the steps that preceded it that drew me to the brink of a human debacle where my own life, according to my fellowmen, was adjudged a failure. And yet before the masters, before the great Brothers of Light, I was adjudged worthy to make my ascension and to be no more, for God took me. And I do not regret it, for the brief moments when mankind chanced to hold me in derision passed rapidly and the glory of the future in realms of light has been so wondrous that even in one moment of that glory, all the pain and anguish of human censure was erased and passed away."[127]

"I have walked with God. For many a century, I have walked along the highways and byways of life carrying his flame as an emissary of the Great White Brotherhood. Oh, the walk with God upon earth and in the heavenly cities in the kingdoms of our Lord to sow the seeds of the Christ that they might spring up in the hearts of all men. You, too, may walk with God if you will but give thought to the fact that as you go about your daily tasks, mundane though they may be, you are engaged in a walk with God, and that walk becomes closer, an inner communion, the rhythm of his footsteps and his heartbeat, of his fire breath."[128]

So completely absorbed in his Divine Selfhood was Enoch, that the ritual of the ascension took place on one of those walks with God. So it can take place with each one who builds the momentum of the sacred fire with each footstep, each heartbeat. For with each inbreathing of the sacred fire from the throne of God, one can draw a little nearer to the goal of oneness with him.

There are a number of writings that have been attributed to Enoch. The most well-known of these is the Book of Enoch, whose main theme is the final judgment of a certain band of fallen angels, whom Enoch called the "Watchers" and their progeny. In one early chapter of the book, Enoch was himself sent to the Watchers to convey God's message that they shall have neither peace nor forgiveness on account of their sins against him. The Watchers, terrified and trembling, asked Enoch to petition God on their behalf, which Enoch did. Nevertheless, God's judgment remained against the Watchers, "Nevermore shall you ascend into heaven." Enoch set forth this book for our wisdom, our admonishment and our warning.*

We can call to the ascended master Enoch to judge the fallen angels and the origins of evil. Enoch says, "My beloved, I have petitioned the Father that I might speak to you from my heart and on behalf of Saint Germain. Some of you were with me in my life as Enoch. Some of you saw Atlantis with me. You remember vividly the temptations of the fallen angels, which had begun long ago in Lemuria. You know, beloved, that these fallen ones have drawn mankind in this hour to depths of degradation not thought possible.

"Surely, then, all that I have written of the judgment of the Watchers must come to pass. Let my knowledgeable ones, well-taught by the messengers, understand the directing of sacred fire and legions of Astrea into the earth for the uprooting of the roots of wickedness and karma of these fallen ones as they are bound and taken from the screen of life and, following transition, clearly removed from the astral plane and from the planet."[129]

❖ **ERIEL OF THE LIGHT**

Eriel, who received the science of the Light and Sound Rays in the Arabian Retreat, is the hierarch of the retreat in Arizona where training in the use of this science is given. Embodied in China as an alchemist, a philosopher and a sage, Eriel has assisted China through many crises, including the Communist revolution. During the slaughter of the Chinese people in the 1930s, he assisted thousands who passed prematurely from the screen of life by taking them to his retreat for training and preparation for reembodiment. The most advanced were prepared for admission to the Ascension Temple.

One whom he assisted was Fun Wey, now the ascended master, who was brought to Eriel's retreat when his life was threatened as a small boy in China. There he passed his initiations leading to his ascension and finally gained his immortal freedom.

Eriel has appeared in a body over six feet tall and has penetrating

---

*The Book of Enoch and other Enoch texts, with commentary by Elizabeth Clare Prophet, are included in the book *Fallen Angels and the Origins of Evil: Why Church Fathers Suppressed the Book of Enoch and Its Startling Revelations.*

Oriental eyes that glisten like stars in the night sky. In his command are legions of purple-flame angels. His symbol is a pink rose.

❖ **ERNON, Rai of Suern**

Ernon, Rai of Suern, was embodied 13,000 years ago at the time of Atlantis. The story of this extraordinary figure is told in the book *A Dweller on Two Planets,* by Phylos the Tibetan, published in 1899. It is the story of the incarnations of Phylos the Tibetan on ancient Lemuria, on Atlantis and in America in the nineteenth century.

Rai is an Atlantean word meaning "emperor" or "monarch." When Phylos was embodied as Zailm on Atlantis, Rai Ernon was the emperor of the land of Suern. This land encompassed present-day India and part of Arabia. The people of Suern possessed seemingly miraculous powers, including the ability to precipitate their own food. These powers stemmed, first of all, from their strict adherence to a moral code forced upon them by their monarch. Secondly, the Suernis enjoyed these powers by the intercession of the occult adepts of the time, who were called the Sons of the Solitude.

Rai Ernon was one of the Sons of the Solitude. These Sons were celibate, lived without families, often apart from civilization. In exceptional cases, they returned to civilization to serve their fellowman in Church and State. They went through years of training, embodiment upon embodiment, to become unascended and then ascended adepts.

Rai Ernon possessed extraordinary powers whereby he could defeat his country's enemies without having to use weapons. In *A Dweller on Two Planets* we read an eyewitness account of how Ernon single-handedly conquered an army of 160,000 Chaldeans.

Despite their great powers, the Suernis were not a happy people. Zailm noticed that the people of Suern did not love their monarch, the Rai Ernon. The story of the Suernis is a story of the karma of rebellion against the Law and the Lawgiver. Because Rai Ernon forced the Suernis to obey a strict moral code as a prerequisite to their enjoying the use of occult powers, they cursed Ernon in their hearts, and many rebelled against their ruler.

Upon Ernon's death the people lost their powers, as he had foretold. He was their guru and they were the ungrateful chelas. They had had their powers only by his grace and sponsorship. They were no longer able to precipitate their own food. In order to survive they had to learn the basics of agriculture, husbandry, mining and spinning under the guidance and training of the Atlanteans.

The story of the Suernis actually goes back further to the time when

Jesus was the emperor of a golden age on Atlantis 35,000 years ago. He stepped down as monarch of Atlantis because 80 percent of the people demanded it. The 20 percent (about two million people) who supported Jesus left Atlantis with him and traveled to Suern. One million of them made their ascension from the land of Suern. The other million continued to embody. Most of them went astray and lost the tie to their Holy Christ Self that they had known on Atlantis.

These million souls continued to reincarnate on Suern and Atlantis. Throughout the centuries they gave birth to many of the souls who had turned against Jesus during the golden age on Atlantis. At the time of Zailm, former Atlanteans from that golden age were embodied on Suern. These Suernis continued to reincarnate and continued the stiff-necked and stubborn behavior they exhibited on Atlantis and in Suern.

The Suernis were then given the opportunity to embody as the seed of Abraham to atone for the karma they had made, some of them by betraying Jesus during his golden age on Atlantis and others by descending into a downward spiral of evolution on Suern. It was for these karmas that the children of Israel were sent into captivity in Egypt. The children of Israel have continued to reincarnate to the present day.

Phlyos the Tibetan encountered Rai Ernon again in nineteenth-century America. Phylos was embodied as Walter Pierson, who met a master from the planet Venus named Mol Lang, who took him in his finer bodies to Venus. Mol Lang was Rai Ernon come again. Mol Lang taught Walter about the purpose of life, the law of karma and reincarnation, the nature of life after death, twin flames and other eternal truths.

Describing Mol Lang, Phylos writes: "[He had] deep-set eyes, under massive brows, and a head of similar contour to that of the philosopher Socrates; his snowy hair and long, white beard, together with a soldierly erectness of person, made Mol Lang...the very personification of occult wisdom, from my point of view.... His turban...was blue, mottled with brown.... He wore a long, gray robe,...belted at the waist. On his feet, of goodly, delicate shape, were sandals." Phylos says his faith in Mol Lang was inspired "by the gentle dignity and kindly love" he saw "beaming from those deep-set, calm gray eyes."[130]

The ascended master Ernon, Rai of Suern, says: "The teachings of the ascended masters given freely are a specific transfer, a quickening and a knowledge unto those who had it 35,000 years ago in the golden age of Atlantis and in many centuries prior to that, for those souls had been with Jesus long before the fullness of their time came in that golden age.

"Therefore, understand that the traditions found in the Western Bible contain fragments and remnants of this ancient teaching. These fragments have been filled in by the ascended masters today—your beloved Saint Germain, your El Morya, and of course, the Lord Jesus Christ. Many others have joined them until the saints robed in white in numberless numbers have come forward to give this teaching."[131]

❖ **FAITH.** *See also* **Faith, Hope and Charity** *and* **Michael and Faith**

There are two beings by the name of Faith to whom we can call. One is Faith, the divine complement of Archangel Michael; the other is the cosmic being Faith. These two beings assist each other in amplifying the flame of faith to life's evolutions. The cosmic being Faith serves with the cosmic beings Hope and Charity to focus the Trinity and the power of the cosmic threefold flame.

❖ **FAITH, HOPE AND CHARITY**

There are three cosmic beings who bear these names, as well as the archeiai of the first, third and fourth rays, who assist the cosmic beings in releasing to the evolutions of earth the qualities of faith, hope and all-forgiving love.

After the first three golden ages, when mankind's consciousness descended into duality, man's threefold flame was reduced in size by cosmic decree in order to curb his misuse of the creative potential. Through his inordinate misqualification of God's energy, man was no longer able to sustain the balance of the qualities of power, wisdom and love (faith, hope and charity) within the threefold flame. Thus, the Christ flame became imbalanced—i.e., the plumes were not at the same height or intensity—because he had lost the Christ consciousness.

It was at that time that the cosmic beings Faith, Hope and Charity sent forth the trinity of their flame-action and anchored a ray of their momentum in every lifestream evolving on the planet to renew and sustain the balanced action of the Christ consciousness.

The threefold flame within the heart

Hope has described their service in this manner: "Hope is a divine quality. It is a quality of God himself, and it springs forth eternally in the human heart from the fount of the Father of all lights and cosmic purpose.

"He and he alone manifests the power, love and wisdom of the three-fold flame. Faith, or the blue plume thereof, identifies with the vibration of power; for faith is 'the power of God unto salvation to everyone that believeth.'[132] Hope identifies with the yellow plume, and it is to be found in the holy comfort of true illumination. It springs from the Christ mind, from the mind that hath wisdom; and as you shall see, charity is the boundlessness of divine love."[133]

Through their cosmic power of faith, hope and charity, these cosmic beings serve the individual until he expands the threefold flame, balances the plumes and attains his immortal freedom in the ascension. Without the assistance of these cosmic beings (together with the impetus rayed to each heart from Shamballa), mankind could not have made the advances in civilization, in the sciences and in the arts that they have. For the balance of the threefold flame is essential to living—indeed, it is the very balance of life itself.

As the disciples of Christ visualize the expanded threefold flame enfolding their four lower bodies in its balanced action, beloved Faith, Hope and Charity infuse that visualization with their momentum. Their service is the key to the attainment of the Christ consciousness, and their flames should be invoked daily by all who aspire to world service and to reunion with the God flame.

❖ **THE FIVE DHYANI BUDDHAS, Celestial Meditation Buddhas.**
See also **Vajrasattva**

The Five Dhyani Buddhas are Vairochana, Akshobhya, Ratnasambhava, Amitabha and Amoghasiddhi. Tibetan Buddhists believe that the Adi-Buddha, the primordial and highest being, created the Dhyani Buddhas by his meditative powers.

The Five Dhyani Buddhas are celestial Buddhas visualized during meditation. The word *Dhyani* is derived from the Sanskrit *dhyana,* meaning "meditation." The Dhyani Buddhas are also called *Jinas* ("Victors," or "Conquerors") and are considered to be great healers of the mind and soul. They are not historical figures like Gautama Buddha, but transcendent beings who symbolize universal divine principles or forces. They represent various aspects of the enlightened consciousness and are guides to spiritual transformation. Meditative powers are also secret-ray powers, and the Dhyani Buddhas hold the keys to the mastery of the five secret rays.

Each Dhyani Buddha is associated with certain attributes and symbols. Each one embodies one of the five wisdoms, which antidote the five deadly poisons that are of ultimate danger to man's spiritual progress and keep him tied to worldly existence. Buddhists teach that the Dhyani Buddhas are able to transmute the five poisons into their transcendent wisdoms. The *Tibetan Book of the Dead* recommends that the devotee meditate on the Dhyani

Buddhas so that their wisdoms will replace the negative forces he has allowed to take hold within.

Each Buddha rules over one of the directions of space and one of the cosmic realms of ether, water, earth, fire and air. The Dhyani Buddhas also personify the five *skandhas,* components that make up cosmic existence as well as human personality. These components are consciousness, form, feeling, perception and volition.

In addition, each Dhyani Buddha is associated with a specific color, *mudra* (hand gesture), symbolic animal that supports his throne, sacred symbol and *bija* (seed syllable). The bija represents the essence of the Dhyani Buddha. It can be used along with the sacred syllable *Om* and the Buddha's name to create a mantra, a series of mystic syllables that have an esoteric meaning. In Hinduism and Buddhism disciples recite mantras to evoke the power and presence of a divine being. In some traditions, devotees use mantras in meditation to help them become one with the deity they are invoking.

"By repeating the *mantra* and assuming the *mudra* of any Buddha," writes Buddhist monk and teacher Sangharakshita, "one can not only place oneself in correspondence or alignment with the particular order of reality which he personifies but also be infused with its transcendental power."[134]

Buddhists often depict the Dhyani Buddhas in a mandala. *Mandala* is a Sanskrit word meaning "circle," translated in Tibetan texts as "center" or "what surrounds." Some say the word derives from *manda,* meaning "essence." The mandala as a circle denotes wholeness, completeness and the perfection of Buddhahood. The mandala is also a "circle of friends"—a gathering of Buddhas. Traditionally mandalas are painted on *thangkas* (scroll paintings framed in silk), drawn with colored sand, represented by heaps of rice, or constructed three-dimensionally, often in cast metal. A Dhyani Buddha is positioned in the center as well as on each of the cardinal points of the mandala.

A mandala is a sacred, consecrated space where no obstacles, impurities or distracting influences

The mandala of the Five Dhyani Buddhas

exist. Buddhists use mandalas to aid them in meditation and visualization. "All mandalas," writes Tibetologist Detlef Lauf, "originate from the seed-syllables, or *bija-mantras,* of the deities. During meditation upon these mantras, an elemental radiance of light develops, from which comes the image of the Buddhas.... The whole external mandala is a model of that spiritual pattern which the meditating individual sees within himself and which he must endeavour to experience in his own consciousness."[135]

Vairochana

The name Vairochana means "He Who Is Like the Sun" or "the Radiating One." Vairochana represents either the integration of, or the origin of, the Dhyani Buddhas. His wisdom is the Wisdom of the *Dharmadhatu.* The Dharmadhatu is the Realm of Truth, in which all things exist as they really are. Vairochana's wisdom is also referred to as the All-Pervading Wisdom of the Dharmakaya, the body of the Law, or the absolute Buddha nature. It also represents the causal body around the I AM Presence in the Chart of Your Divine Self. (See page 532.)

Vairochana's transcendent wisdom reveals the realm of highest reality and overcomes the poison of ignorance, or delusion. His wisdom is considered to be the origin of, or the total of, all the wisdoms of the Dhyani Buddhas.

Vairochana is usually located in the center of mandalas of the Dhyani Buddhas. According to some texts, he is positioned in the East. His color is white (or blue), symbolizing a pure consciousness. He rules over the element of ether and embodies the skandha of consciousness. In some systems,

he is associated with the skandha of form.

His symbol is the *dharmachakra,* the wheel of the teaching, or the wheel of the Law. It denotes the teaching of the Buddha. Its eight spokes represent the Noble Eightfold Path, which Gautama revealed in his first sermon after his enlightenment. Vairochana's lotus throne is supported by the lion, symbol of courage, boldness and an eager, advancing spirit.

His mudra is the *dharmachakra mudra,* the gesture of turning the wheel of the teaching. Because he embodies the wisdom of all Buddhas, Vairochana's bija is the universal sound *Om.* His mantra is *Om Vairochana Om.*

Vairochana has recently become the eighth member of the Karmic Board, a group of spiritual overseers who adjudicate the karma for the evolutions of this system of worlds. He explained his specific role on the

Karmic Board, granted by dispensation of all Buddhas:

"My role shall be to assist those who have light who are sincere but who have strayed from the track of Reality, considering that their karma was too hard to bear.... I would teach all who apply to me what they need to know to make it all the way Home.

"I would teach a certain level of souls who, with my support and the support of all of us, will have the opportunity to make it, whereas without that support, they might not make it....

"I will help you. I will prepare you. I will show you how in profound humility and with inner strength you will master all flaws of character that are open doors to negative spirals and negative traits, and you will get on with your reason for being—why you embodied in this life in the circumstances you find yourselves—and you will know that you embodied to balance your karma so that you can fulfill your mission."[136]

Akshobhya

The name Akshobhya means "Immovable" or "Unshakable." Akshobhya's Mirrorlike Wisdom reflects all things calmly and uncritically and reveals their true nature. One text says, "Just as one sees one's own reflection in a mirror, so the Dharmakaya is seen in the Mirror of Wisdom."[137] The Mirrorlike Wisdom antidotes the poison of hatred and anger.

In the mandala of the Five Dhyani Buddhas, Akshobhya is usually positioned in the East (at the bottom) but he is sometimes placed in the center. His color is blue. He rules over the element of water and personifies the skandha of form. In some systems, he is associated with the skandha of consciousness. Akshobhya's lotus throne is supported by the elephant, symbol of steadfastness and strength.

His symbol is the *vajra,* also called thunderbolt or diamond scepter. The vajra denotes enlightenment, the indestructible, adamantine nature of pure consciousness, or the essence of Reality. In some traditions, the vajra signifies the union of man and the Buddha; one end of the vajra symbolizes the macrocosmic realm of the Buddha and the other end the microcosmic realm of man.

Akshobhya's mudra is formed by his right hand and is the *bhumisparsha mudra,* the earth-touching gesture. It denotes unshakability. This is the mudra Gautama Buddha used to summon the earth to witness to his right to attain enlightenment when he was challenged by Mara, the Evil One.

Akshobhya's paradise is Abhirati, the Land of Exceeding Great Delight. Buddhists believe that whoever is reborn there cannot fall back to a lower level of consciousness. Akshobhya's bija is *Hum,* and his mantra is *Om Akshobhya Hum.*

Akshobhya says, "The way seems intricate, but the intricacy is the intricacy of karma woven and rewoven. The intricate undoing of the threads of karma is what seems to make the Path so complicated. But when all is said and done and all of those components of the threads of karma are consumed in one great violet-flame bonfire, you will come to know, and you will remember one day that I have said the entering in is simplicity itself, humility itself, purity itself."[138]

Ratnasambhava

The name Ratnasambhava means "the Jewel-born One" or "Origin of Jewels." The Three Jewels are the Buddha, the Dharma and the Sangha. The Buddha is the Enlightened One, the Guru, the hub of the wheel of the Law. The Dharma is the Teaching, or the Law. The Sangha is the Community.

Ratnasambhava transmutes the poison of pride (spiritual, intellectual and human pride) into the Wisdom of Equality. Tibetan Buddhists teach that with the Wisdom of Equality one sees all things with divine impartiality and recognizes the divine equality of all beings. One sees all beings and the Buddha as having the same nature.

Ratnasambhava is the Dhyani Buddha of the South. His color is yellow, the color of the sun in its zenith. Ratnasambhava rules over the element of earth and embodies the skandha of feeling or sensation.

He is sometimes shown holding his symbol, the *ratna* (jewel) or *chintamani* (wish-fulfilling jewel that grants all right desires). The chintamani is a symbol of the liberated mind.

Ratnasambhava's throne is upheld by a horse, denoting impetus and liberation. His mudra is the *varada mudra.* It is the gesture of giving, or charity, which portrays him offering compassion and protection to his disciples. His bija is *Tram* and his mantra is *Om Ratnasambhava Tram.*

Ratnasambhava says, "O blessed ones, God has so valued each one that to each one he has given the very image of himself, the I AM Presence, the Holy Christ Self, in whose image you are made. Find the jewel, find the jewel. Find the Sangha, find the Buddha, find the Dharma, all locked within the inner divine spark."[139]

Amitabha

The name Amitabha means "Infinite Light." Amitabha's Discriminating Wisdom conquers the poison of the passions—all cravings, covetousness, greed and lust. With this wisdom, the disciple discerns all beings separately yet knows every being as an individual expression of the One.

In the mandala of the Dhyani Buddhas, Amitabha is positioned to the West. His color is rose (red), the color of the setting sun. He rules over the element of fire and personifies the skandha of perception. Thus, the eye and the faculty of seeing are associated with Amitabha. The peacock with "eyes" on its plumes is his throne-bearer. The peacock symbolizes grace.

Amitabha's symbol is the *padma*, or lotus. In Buddhism, the lotus can symbolize many things, including spiritual unfoldment, purity, the true nature of beings realized through enlightenment, and compassion, the purified form of passion.

Devotees aspire to be reborn in Amitabha's Western Paradise, known as Sukhavati, where conditions are ideal for attaining enlightenment. His mudra is the *dhyana* (meditation) *mudra*. His bija is *Hrih* and his mantra is *Om Amitabha Hrih*.

Some consider Amitabha to be synonymous with Amitayus, the Buddha of Infinite Life. Others honor Amitayus as a form of Amitabha or as a separate Buddha. Amitayus is usually depicted holding a vessel of the elixir of immortal life. A tiny ashoka-tree often sprouts from the cover of his vessel, representing the union of the spiritual and the material.

Amoghasiddhi

The name Amoghasiddhi means "Almighty Conqueror," or "He Who Unerringly Achieves His Goal." Amoghasiddhi's All-Accomplishing Wisdom, or Wisdom of Perfected Action, antidotes the poison of envy and jealousy. This wisdom confers perseverance, infallible judgment and unerring action.

Amoghasiddhi represents the practical realization of the wisdoms of the other Dhyani Buddhas. He is described as the Dhyani Buddha of the realization of the bodhisattva path. A bodhisattva is one who has forgone the bliss of nirvana with a vow to first liberate all beings.

Amoghasiddhi is the Dhyani Buddha of the North. His color is green, signifying the sun at midnight. He rules over the element of air and embodies the skandha of volition, also called the skandha of mental phenomena or tendencies of mind. His symbol is the *vishvavajra,* or double vajra. It is made of two crossed vajras and symbolizes the highest comprehension of truth and the spiritual power of a Buddha.

 The throne of Amoghasiddhi is supported by *garudas*—mythical figures, half man and half bird. In relation to Amoghasiddhi, Lama Govinda says the garuda symbolizes "man in transition towards a new dimension of consciousness,…the transition from the human to the superhuman state, which takes place in the mysterious darkness of the night, invisible to the eye."[140]

Amoghasiddhi's mudra is the *abhaya mudra.* It is the gesture of fearlessness and protection. The right hand is raised to shoulder height with palm forward. The left hand is cupped in the lap or placed at the heart, fingers pointing inward. Amoghasiddhi's bija is *Ah* and his mantra is *Om Amoghasiddhi Ah.*

❖ FORTUNA, Goddess of Supply

Fortuna, Goddess of Supply will precipitate her momentum of the abundance of supply, the powerful radiance of green and gold, to those who call to her and invoke her flame. When she was embodied, her desire all her life was to see mankind have the glory of the golden ages, the true spiritual gold that would bring the flow of the material gold and all success.

The false hierarchy impostor of Fortuna is "Lady Luck." She is also known to the masters in the masculine form as Fate or Kismet. The counterfeit goddess is fickle, glittering like fool's gold. She frequents gambling casinos and was very active during the stock market crash of 1929. She works with the suicide entity to try to bring people down into despair when they lose all that they have gained through the power of Lady Luck.

The real Fortuna, the Goddess of Good Fortune, is radiant like the sun. This cosmic being teaches that abundance is never a matter of chance, but a manifestation of the unerring law of harmony. Precipitation is a science based on the immutable law, "As you sow, so shall you reap"—as you sow harmony, you reap supply. She teaches the wisdom of the Christ who said, "I AM come that ye might have life, and that more abundantly."[141]

The legions of angels in her command serve on the fifth ray. Their auras are a brilliant green. Fortuna wears golden robes and carries a gold scepter with a large green emerald. Her hair is a striking gold, a mass of curls, and her eyes a brilliant blue. Her aura is spherical, the center being gold and the periphery an emerald radiance.

Fortuna has said: "Precious ones, supply comes to those who have the heart of gold. And the golden heart is the heart of love for all life. When mankind love life, the source of supply wells up within them as the well-spring of life, life eternal, the emerald-green hue, which bathes the earth in beauty, in life and light and love....

"The focus of supply is scientific, precious ones, scientific as is the entire universe. If you would therefore have supply, determine first what the goal or purpose of that supply would be in your life. What would it achieve for the glory of God? To what purpose do you pledge the offerings that the angelic hosts bring to you? Have you given your life to the Christ, to the healing of all mankind, to the raising up of the elementals? If you have not, then do not wonder that the flow of supply does not come to you at your beck and call. For all life will answer the call of the Son of God who has arisen and said, "I will take my stand to do the will of God and, in love, fulfill the fiats of creation for my fellowman."[142]

❖ FOUR AND TWENTY ELDERS

The four and twenty elders are described in the Book of Revelation: "And round about the throne were four and twenty seats: and upon the seats I saw four and twenty elders sitting, clothed in white raiment; and they had on their heads crowns of gold."[143] They are twelve pairs of twin flames representing the twelve hierarchies of the Sun in the masculine and feminine power/wisdom/love of Elohim. This council of cosmic beings presides with Sanat Kumara at the Court of the Sacred Fire on the God Star Sirius (the seat of God-government in this sector of our galaxy) as instruments of the judgment of Almighty God.

In approximately 2000 B.C. we entered the age of Aries. Two thousand years ago we entered the age of Pisces. And now we are entering the age of Aquarius. Passing through each of the twelve signs of the zodiac, there is a dispensation from the Great Central Sun whereby the four and twenty elders and the four cosmic forces impart to the evolutions of the planet a new awareness of self in relationship to a new awareness of God.

On July 4, 1976, the Goddess of Liberty announced: "I come from the God Star Sirius this night. I come where the deliberations of the four and twenty elders concerning all manifestations of earth are underway. And one and all, I hear them say: 'God has decided to save the earth.'... And when you ask how and why and where and who, the answer is: 'Through you.'"[144]

Cyclopea describes the four and twenty elders: "These magnificent beings of light are robed in white and gold, beloved. They come with a message of victory for those who are the victorious ones. And they deliver lessons—lessons indeed and chastenings to those who have not made the use they should have made of stupendous teachings we have released and the light that comes through these teachings."[145]

❖ FOURTEEN ASCENDED MASTERS WHO GOVERN THE DESTINY OF AMERICA

The fourteen ascended masters who govern the destiny of America are great beings of light from the God Star Sirius, which is the seat of God-government in this galaxy. These masters have been appointed by God to direct the course of the United States of America and to assist in the establishment of God-government in America.

As the spirit of freedom in these fourteen ascended masters says, "The victory of America is not the victory of a nation. It is the victory of the twelve hierarchies of the Sun in the twelve tribes of Israel who have come forth from every nation to dip into the flame, who shall return to every nation to ignite the flame, and who shall be unto all people the carriers of the fires of freedom.

"Let the runners in the race, then, hear the cry of the fourteen ascended masters. Ours is a cry for freedom throughout the land of Terra. Ours is a cry for the Divine Mother. Ours is a cry of liberation for the souls of humanity."[146]

More than fifty thousand years ago, in a fertile country where the Sahara Desert now is, Saint Germain was the king-emperor of a great golden-age civilization. Under his enlightened reign, the entire civilization knew an era of peace, abundance and accomplishment in commerce, education and the arts and sciences.

In this golden age, the authority of the affairs of state was vested in fourteen ascended masters, two governing on each of the seven rays of the Christ light, with fourteen lesser masters in charge of the seven departments of government. No government since that time has even approached the achievements of this divinely directed administration. For hundreds of years, harmony among peoples was the law of the land without the need for enforcement by any armed forces.

The decline of that ancient civilization began when a portion of the people became more interested in the temporary pleasures of the senses than in the larger creative plan of the Great God Self. Those governing realized they must withdraw and let the people learn through hard experience that all their happiness and good had come from adoration of the God within—and that they must again adore and serve the light if they were to be happy. The ruler was instructed by a cosmic council that he must leave his empire and his people.

The king and his children withdrew seven days later. A prince arrived the next day and took over without opposition. Two thousand years later, most of that empire had become barren land. This blight upon nature was the result of the discord and selfishness of the once-great people who had lived there.

Today the people of that ancient civilization have reembodied in America. As a nation, they are destined to rise once again, to recognize the Real Self within and to reestablish a great spiritual culture under the tutelage and leadership of Saint Germain. And these same fourteen masters are here again as the fourteen ascended masters who govern the destiny of America, and they offer their assistance, if we will only invoke it: "Do not treat us as though we were from distant stars and relatives who come now and then to visit! We are here! We will help you in answer to your call!

"Remember, when we hear those fiats so fiercely given, we respond. We call for reinforcements. And you have the victory. And the fallen ones are totally defeated. They have no power! They have no power! They have no power over you!

"Wherefore, call upon the LORD! Rise in his dominion! And remember that the archangels do battle for you. Never enter in to a direct confrontation with aliens or fallen ones but turn them over in your decrees to the hosts of the LORD. This is the formula, beloved. It works. I ask you for the sake of all evolutions of this planet, make the formulas of the Great White Brotherhood work in your life every single day!"[147]

❖ **FREEDOM, GODDESS OF**

The Goddess of Freedom represents the feminine aspect of the quality of freedom to the earth. She is a cosmic being who has kept the flame for thousands of years. Her service is rendered from the Royal Teton where she gives instruction to incoming souls on how to retain the purity of the consciousness of freedom while in embodiment on earth. She maintains a focus of light in her statue, the nineteen-foot bronze *Armed Freedom*, which crowns the dome of the Capitol of the United States.

On November 23, 1975, Saint Germain said, "I select the monument, the focal point for the enshrining of freedom; and I place that focus of freedom in the heart of America, in the very heart chakra of the Goddess of Freedom reigning over the Capitol building of the United States."

The Goddess of Freedom has said: "I remember the day when the messenger discovered me in my statue that is above the nation's Capitol. And I remember her pondering on my heart and her recognition of myself as more than a mere statue but, indeed, as the cosmic embodiment of cosmic

freedom to all systems of worlds. And I am grateful that the thoughtform of my Presence did indeed find its way to that Capitol dome....

"I AM the Goddess of Freedom. I have much to tell you. I shall tell you things, each one personally. I shall tell you in the retreats; I shall tell you as I walk at your side. I multiply myself, as many times as necessary, without dilution. For I AM the Goddess of Freedom. My hour has come. Your hour has come. We are teammates! Let us go forward and play to win!"[148]

❖ FUN WEY

The ascended master Fun Wey serves under the master Eriel in his retreat in Arizona. Fun Wey teaches the "fun way" to the ascension. He says, "The fun way of living is the God way of living. It is the abundant life for which the Christ came into manifestation in ye all."[149]

Fun Wey began his evolution in the elemental kingdom, mastered certain disciplines and was transferred to the human kingdom, given a three-fold flame and the opportunity to earn his immortality.

The master Eriel rescued Fun Wey, when, as an infant born to an old Chinese family, his life was threatened. Fun Wey attained his ascension from Eriel's retreat after giving enthusiastic and illumined obedience to the master.

Serving on the third and sixth rays, Fun Wey radiates the qualities of joy and the desire to serve. He also works with the elemental beings. His radiation may be drawn through the melody of "In a Country Garden."

Fun Wey tells us: "It was by no idle measure that the Father bestowed upon me the name Fun Wey, for indeed by obedience, chastity and love I found my way back to his heart under the tutelage of beloved Eriel. Precious friends of light, it was because I found the fun way to the ascension that the Father gave me this name, and so I come today to bring to you the knowledge and understanding of the meditations of my heart as I saw truly that the way back home was the way of delight in God's Law."[150]

❖ **GABRIEL AND HOPE, Archangels of the Fourth Ray**

Gabriel and Hope are archangel and archeia of the fourth ray of the resurrection and the ascension flame. Together with the angels of purity and the seraphim, these twin flames guard the immaculate concept of the God-design for every man, woman and child upon the planet.

Gabriel is the Angel of Annunciation who greeted Mary with the words, "Hail, thou that art highly favoured, the Lord is with thee: blessed art thou among women."[151] Gabriel salutes each mother-to-be with the glad tidings of the coming of the Christ for whom she is privileged to prepare the body temple. He places the electronic pattern of the Christ Self of the incoming child within the aura of the mother in order that the body elementals of mother and child, under the direction of their Christ Selves, may work together to bring forth the perfect form. The angelic hosts work with the parents to anchor in the child the highest and best talents developed in previous embodiments and stored in the causal body.

The Annunciation

Although most women upon the planet today are not attuned to Gabriel's high consciousness of purity and therefore do not hear his voice, the time is coming when all parents-to-be shall hear the annunciation of the descending Christ, and they will know that the bearing of a soul sent from God to fulfill his destiny is a high and holy calling, a responsibility from which qualified couples should not shrink.

Gabriel warns that the campaign to limit the population is a plot of Antichrist to deprive souls of the opportunity to earn their ascension. Those who proclaim or hearken to the lies regarding population control may find the portals of birth closed to them when they next seek to apply to the Lords of Karma for reembodiment.

Gabriel and Hope are dedicated to the purity of every lifestream and to the purity of the purpose of God for every soul. Hope fills the parents with expectancy, joy, enthusiasm and the memory of the goal of every lifestream: the ascension in the light.

Gabriel would like to share with us his precious memories of resurrection's morn nearly two thousand years ago. He says: "Gracious ladies and gentlemen, I would span now the great akashic records and envision once again that glorious morning when I descended through the ethers accompanied by the holy angels of my band to fan the flame of hope within the hearts of the waiting beloved disciples of the Christ by rolling away the stone from before the tomb in which his precious body lay.

"It was no effort, and is no effort for an angelic being to move matter when given the power by the Godhead. And the stone did not resist the passage of light from my fingers. As I clutched it momentarily, the thought occurred to me that in rolling away this stone, I would to God that even at that moment I could have rolled away the stone of death from every man and woman upon this precious planet until all would be free from fear and from oppression.

"The angels who accompanied me, catching my thought instantaneously as is our custom—for we are not like you, blessed ones, that we require one another to utter a thought—quickly began a chant of hope. And led in melodic expression by my beloved Hope, the angels began this wondrous song, which seemed to radiate a pathway of golden light of hope across the very face of the earth with the incoming dawn. Early in the morning, when the holy women came searching for the Christ, they found the stone rolled away."[152]

This same blessing and service of an archangel is also offered to each one of us who can accept it. Just as the stone was pushed away by Gabriel's hand from before the door of the tomb in which Christ lay, so also can the problems and density of our own lives yield to the light if we will allow him to enter our world. As the tomb of materiality that stands before each one of us as our own human creation and density is rolled away, we can see within that tomb the resurrected Christ of our own Holy Christ Self standing above us in the ethers, radiant in all the splendor of his glory and perfection.

Archangel Gabriel has spoken about the mysteries of life and death, this world and the next, and the nature of an ages-old conspiracy to dominate the minds and souls and hearts of the lifewaves not only of planet Earth, but of this and other systems of worlds. He was eyewitness to the antediluvian epochs, and he speaks to us of the books of our father Enoch, vividly interpreting the battle of Light and Darkness.

In his book *The Mysteries of the Holy Grail*, Gabriel has given his teaching concerning the knowledge of relative good and evil, and how it was transmitted to our first earthly parents by fallen angels who conspired to tear the veil of innocence from Adam and Eve that they might no longer see the LORD God face to face—and their progeny be led astray for thousands of years.

Gabriel is the friend of God and man. All lovers of the light can claim this archangel as their special confidant and advisor. He teaches us about the lawful communion of the saints dwelling in these lower octaves of earth with the saints moving in the higher octaves of heaven.

In 1987, Archeia Hope said, "O blessed hearts, do you know one thing that you have absolute and complete control over? It is this—that the golden age *can* manifest in this hour *where you are!* Where the individualization of the God flame is in you, the golden age can already be in session and in progress in your aura…. You need no longer speculate, 'Will the golden age come to earth?' But you can say, 'It is here in me. That I know, O God. It is where I am, and more than this I cannot even desire. For I am with Hope filling cosmos with my golden age.'"¹⁵³

Archangel Gabriel,
by Tiffany

The retreat of Archangel Gabriel and Hope is located in the etheric plane between Sacramento and Mount Shasta, California. As archangel and archeia of the fourth ray of purity and the ascension, they also serve with Jesus and Mother Mary at the Temple of the Resurrection over the Holy Land and with Serapis Bey, lord of the fourth ray, at the etheric retreat of the Ascension Temple at Luxor, Egypt.

The energy of Gabriel is focused through the music of the Intermezzo from *Cavalleria Rusticana,* by Pietro Mascagni.

❖ GAUTAMA BUDDHA, Lord of the World

Gautama attained the enlightenment of the Buddha in his final incarnation as Siddhartha Gautama. He was born in northern India, about 563 B.C., the son of King Suddhodana and Queen Mahamaya, rulers of the Sakya kingdom, and thus a member of the Kshatriya (warrior or ruling) caste.

On the fifth day following his birth, 108 Brahmins were invited to a name-giving ceremony at the palace. The king summoned eight of the most learned from among these to 'read' the child's destiny by interpreting his bodily marks and physical characteristics.

Seven agreed that if he remained at home, he would become a universal king, unifying India; but if he left, he would become a Buddha and remove the veil of ignorance from the world. Kondañña, the eighth and youngest of the group, declared he would definitely become a Buddha, renouncing the world after seeing four signs—an old man, a diseased man, a dead man and a holy man. The child was named Siddhartha, or "One Whose Aim Is Fulfilled." Seven days after his birth, his mother passed on and he was raised by her sister Mahaprajapati, who later became one of his first female disciples.

The king, concerned about the possibility of losing his heir, took every precaution to shelter his son from pain and suffering, surrounding him with every conceivable luxury, including three palaces and forty thousand dancing girls. At sixteen, after proving his skill in a contest of arms, Prince Siddhartha married his beautiful cousin Yasodhara. He soon grew pensive and preoccupied, but the turning point of his life did not occur until the age of twenty-nine, when he set out on four journeys, which presented in turn the four passing sights.

First, he encountered a very old man, gray and decrepit, leaning on a staff; second, a pitiful one racked with disease, lying in the road; third, a corpse; and fourth, a yellow-robed monk with shaved head and a begging bowl. Much moved with compassion by the first three sights, he realized that life was subject to old age, disease and death. The fourth sight signified to him the possibility of overcoming these conditions and inspired him to leave the world he knew in order to find a solution for suffering.

On his way back to the palace, he received news of the birth of his son. That night he ordered his charioteer to saddle his favorite horse, Kanthaka. He rode all night and at dawn assumed the guise of an ascetic, exchanging clothes with his charioteer, whom he sent back to his father's palace.

Thus, Gautama began the life of a wandering monk. Immediately he went in search of the most learned teachers of the day to instruct him in truth, quickly mastering all they taught. Unsatisfied and restless, he determined to find a permanent truth, impervious to the illusions of the world.

Traveling through the Magadha country, he was noticed for his handsome countenance and noble stature. He arrived at a village called Senanigama, near Uruvela, where he was joined by a group of five ascetics, among whom was Kondañña, the Brahmin who had foretold his Buddhahood.

Here, for almost six years, Gautama practiced severe austerities. Finally realizing the futility of asceticism, Gautama abandoned his austerities to seek his own path of enlightenment—whereupon his companions rejected and deserted him.

One day Sujata, a villager's daughter, fed him a rich rice milk—a "meal so wondrous…that our Lord felt strength and life return as though the nights of watching and the days of fast had passed in dream."[154] And then he set out alone for the Bo tree, where he vowed to remain until fully illumined. At that point, Mara, the Evil One, attempted to prevent his enlightenment and confronted him with temptations much in the same manner that Satan tested Jesus during his fasting in the wilderness.

Unmoved, he sat under the Bo tree while Mara continued her attack—first in the form of desire, parading voluptuous goddesses and dancing girls before him, then in the guise of death, assailing him with hurricanes, torrential rains, flaming rocks, boiling mud, fierce soldiers and beasts—and finally darkness. Yet still, Gautama remained unmoved.

As a last resort, the temptress challenged his right to be doing what he was doing. Siddhartha then tapped the earth,* and the earth thundered her answer: "I bear you witness!" All the hosts of the LORD and the elemental beings responded and acclaimed his right to pursue the enlightenment of the Buddha—whereupon Mara fled.

Having defeated Mara, Gautama spent the rest of the night in deep meditation under the tree, realizing the Four Noble Truths. Thus, he attained Enlightenment, or the Awakening, during the night of the full-moon day of the month of May, about the year 528 B.C. His being was transformed, and he became the Buddha.

For a total of forty-nine days he was deep in rapture, after which he again turned his attention to the world. He found Mara waiting for him with one last temptation: "How can your experience be translated into words? Return to nirvana. Do not try to deliver your message to the world, for no one will comprehend it. Remain in bliss!" But Buddha replied: "There will be some who will understand," and Mara vanished from his life forever.

In his first sermon he revealed the key discovery of his quest: the Four Noble Truths, the Eightfold Path and the Middle Way. For forty-five years, Gautama walked the dusty roads of India, preaching the *Dharma* (universal Doctrine), which led to the foundation of Buddhism. He established the *Sangha* (community) that soon numbered over twelve hundred devotees. When the people questioned him as to his identity, he answered, "I am awake"—hence, the Buddha, meaning "Enlightened One" or "Awakened One."

He passed during the full moon of May, about 483 B.C., after advising his chief disciple, Ananda, that the Dharma—the Truth—must be his master and reminding the monks of the transiency of all conditioned things.

Gautama Buddha today holds the office of Lord

*with the "earth-touching mudra"—left hand upturned in lap, right hand pointed downward, touching the earth of the World (referred to as "God of the Earth" in Revelation 11:4). At inner levels, he sustains the threefold flame of life, the divine spark, for all children of God on earth.

Speaking of the great service Lord Gautama renders to all life in his office as Lord of the World, Maitreya said on January 1, 1986: "The Lord of the World does sustain the threefold flame in the evolutions of earth by a filigree light extending from his heart. This, then, is the bypassing of the individual's karma whereby there is so much blackness around the heart that the spiritual arteries or the crystal cord have been cut off.

"The comparison of this is seen when the arteries in the physical body become so clogged with debris that the area of the flow of blood becomes greatly diminished until it becomes a point of insufficiency and the heart can no longer sustain life. This is comparable to what has happened on the astral plane.

"So Sanat Kumara came to earth to keep the flame of life. And so does Gautama Buddha keep this threefold flame at Shamballa, and he is a part of every living heart. Therefore, as the disciple approaches the Path, he understands that its goal is to come to the place where the threefold flame is developed enough here below within his own heart that indeed, with or without the filigree thread from the heart of Gautama Buddha, he is able to sustain life and soul and consciousness and the initiatic path.

"Beloved ones, this step in itself is an accomplishment that few upon this planet have attained to. You have no idea how you would feel or be or behave if Gautama Buddha withdrew from you that support of the filigree thread and the momentum of his own heartbeat and threefold flame. Most people, especially the youth, do not take into consideration what is the source of the life that they experience in exuberance and joy."

Of this gift, Gautama himself said on December 31, 1983: "I am very observant. I observe you by the contact of my flame through the thread-contact I maintain to the threefold flame of your heart—sustaining it as I do until you pass from the seat-of-the-soul chakra to the very heart of hearts [the secret chamber of the heart], and you yourself are able by attainment to sustain that flame and its burning in this octave.

"Did anyone here ever recall himself igniting his own threefold flame at birth? Has anyone here ever remembered tending its fire or keeping it burning? Beloved hearts, recognize that acts of love and valor and honor and selflessness surely contribute to this flame. But a higher power and a higher Source does keep that flame until you, yourself, are one with that higher power—your own Christ Self.

"Therefore, all receive the boost of my heart flame and impetus. And as that light passes through me from the Godhead, I therefore perceive many things about you and your everyday life that you might think beyond mention or notice of a Lord of the World, who must be, indeed, very busy.

"Well, indeed, I am! But I am never too busy to notice the elements of the Path presented by parents and in families and communities and in the schoolrooms of life everywhere. For I make it my business to see to it that some element of the path of initiation, moving toward the heart of Jesus and Maitreya, is a part of the life of every growing child."

Gautama Buddha is the sponsor of Summit University and the hierarch of Shamballa, the etheric retreat of the Lord of the World located over the Gobi Desert. In 1981, Gautama established an extension of this retreat, called the Western Shamballa, in the etheric octave over the Heart of the Inner Retreat at the Royal Teton Ranch.

Gautama Buddha's keynote is "Moonlight and Roses." The "Ode to Joy" from Beethoven's Ninth Symphony also gives us direct attunement with the Lord of the World.

❖ **GODDESS OF BEAUTY,** *See* **Ruth Hawkins**

❖ **GODDESS OF FREEDOM,** *See* **Freedom, Goddess of**

❖ **GODDESS OF JUSTICE,** *See* **Portia**

❖ **GODDESS OF LIBERTY,** *See* **Liberty, Goddess of**

❖ **GODDESS OF LIGHT,** *See* **Amerissis**

❖ **GODDESS OF MERCY,** *See* **Kuan Yin**

❖ **GODDESS OF OPPORTUNITY,** *See* **Portia**

❖ **GODDESS OF PEACE,** *See* **Peace, Goddess of**

❖ **GODDESS OF PURITY,** *See* **Purity, Goddess of**

❖ **GODDESS OF SUPPLY,** *See* **Fortuna**

❖ **GODDESS OF TRUTH,** *See* **Pallas Athena**

❖ **GODDESS OF WISDOM,** *See* **Theosophia**

❖ **GODFRE, God Obedience**

The ascended master Godfre was embodied as Guy W. Ballard, the messenger of Saint Germain. He brought forth the teachings of the Great White Brotherhood, the Law of the I AM Presence and held the focus of the Christ consciousness for the planet until his ascension in 1939. His wife and twin flame was Edna Ballard, now the ascended lady master Lotus.

Guy Ballard's pen name was Godfré Ray King. He is now known as the ascended master Godfre, God Obedience, but is still affectionately remembered by his students as "Daddy." Although the requirements for his ascension had been completed several years before he actually ascended, he volunteered to continue in the service of the Brotherhood as their point of contact in the world of form.

Through the assistance given him by the Great Divine Director in the Cave of Light, his four lower bodies were aligned and his threefold flame balanced, enabling him to be the channel for many miracles and healings before his ascension. As part of his final service while in embodiment, Godfre took on world karma and expiated it through his physical form, thus sparing humanity great suffering that he himself chose to bear, even as Jesus bore the crucifixion for the sins of mankind.

The turning point in his mission and the key to his victory in that embodiment occurred as he was walking on Broadway in Los Angeles. At that time, when all seemed to be against him, he suddenly stopped and made a fiat to the dweller-on-the-threshold, the remnant of his own untransmuted human creation: "You have scared me for the last time. You have no power."

Soon thereafter on Mount Shasta he met the master Saint Germain, who took him into the retreats of the Brotherhood and gave him the training for his world mission. These experiences are recorded in the three books that he subsequently brought forth as an expression of the threefold flame of the master's consciousness, *Unveiled Mysteries* (yellow), *The Magic Presence* (pink) and the *The "I AM" Discourses* (blue).

From Godfre, we learn that unfailing obedience to one's ascended guru and to the Great Law of Life is essential to individual victory and to the completion of the cosmic timetable for the golden age. Each act of disobedience sets back the plans of the Brotherhood for the victory of the planet, a victory for which each person is individually and collectively responsible.

The second great lesson we learn from Godfre is that it is not until we cast down the idol of the human consciousness that we begin the trek up the mountain of our initiations. The rejection of the human ego and consciousness should be made each time it attempts to assert itself. One need only say, "In the name of my mighty I AM Presence, I refuse to accept the tyranny of my human consciousness!" Of other individuals one may say, "In the name of my mighty I AM Presence, I refuse to accept (his or her) human consciousness. Beloved Holy Christ Self, you step forth in your blazing Reality and be the only Presence acting here!"

Godfre won his freedom through obedience to the law of Being. He teaches us to ascend moment by moment by raising our thoughts and feelings, our energies and actions. The ascension is the goal of life not only for the few, but for the many.

George Washington

Godfre was embodied as a son of the great king (Saint Germain) who ruled the civilization that flourished in what is now the Sahara Desert over 50,000 years ago. Guy, his wife, Edna Ballard, and their son, Donald, were embodied as Saint Germain's children there. Among his other embodiments were Richard the Lionhearted (1157–1199) and George Washington (1732–1799).

❖ **GOD HARMONY,** *See* **Harmony, God**

❖ **GOD MERCURY,** *See* **Hermes Trismegistus**

❖ **GOD OF GOLD,** *See* **Gold, God of**

❖ **GOD OF NATURE,** *See* **Nature, God of**

❖ **GOD OF THE SWISS ALPS,** *See* **Swiss Alps, God of the**

❖ **GOD TABOR,** *See* **Tabor**

❖ **GOLD, GOD OF**

The God of Gold appears in a blazing golden light, with rays of fiery gold coming forth from his head and hands. The emanation of his aura and of his heart flame is a dazzling white light, almost too brilliant to gaze upon. He serves with God Tabor, the God of Nature, the Maha Chohan and the hierarchs of the four elements to precipitate or reduce the rate of frequency of the electronic substance from the sun, drawing it into manifestation in the earth as gold.

The God of Gold, in magnetizing the currents of the sun and directing these into the earth, maintains the most active and brilliant attunement with Helios and Vesta of all those serving the nature kingdom. Having served for many centuries on the ray of purity, the God of Gold elected to amplify the golden radiance of the sun that he had contacted through his devotion to purity. Today he bears witness to the purity and illumination from the heart of the sun. These rays he directs as a vivifying and purifying action through the metal that he precipitates.

Because gold is essential to the balance of the light in nature and in man, the God of Gold holds a very important position in hierarchy. Gold is intended to be the standard of exchange throughout the earth; but because mankind have hoarded and abused it, the masters have not revealed the wealth of gold that is hidden in the earth. The wealthiest mines that the world has ever known will be opened up as the golden age dawns and the governments of the nations return to the gold standard and a sound fiscal policy based on the golden rule.

In every civilization where gold was in circulation as the medium of exchange and worn by all the people, there was a corresponding attainment of great illumination, abundance, health and self-mastery. (The custom of using gold as an adornment in primitive tribes comes down to them from the ancient civilizations of which they are the last remnant.)

The replacement of gold by silver and more common metals, and finally the substitution of paper as the medium of exchange, is a plot of the manipulators to magnetize people's consciousness to the lower vibrations of these metals and to deprive them of the benign, healthful and stimulating qualities of gold.

The God of Gold has explained: "The action of the God of Gold is the instantaneous precipitation of the mind of God through the alchemy of the emerald and crystal ray. Thus, the second and the fifth rays* become twin flames for the precipitation of God's will as the flow of supply and demand, which, from this night forward, we direct that children of God must demand as the abundance of God upon earth.... All of life—as a flow of energy, of commerce, of interchange and of consciousness—depends upon the proper working of that supply and the medium of exchange in the economies of the nations.

"The term *golden age* did not derive from nothing. Golden age means an age based upon the gold standard, the standard of the gold of the Christ

---

*i.e., the ray of wisdom (yellow, gold) and the ray of truth, science, abundance (emerald and crystal)

consciousness, of the golden rule, of gold as precipitated sunlight for the balance of the mind and the emotions and the flow of life even in the physical temple. Gold, beloved ones, is necessary for the stability of consciousness as well as for the stability of the economies of the nations. Unless there be a certain portion of gold even in the temple, the balance of the elements is not held. When the people no longer hold gold in their possession or wear gold, there is far greater mental and emotional disturbance.

"Gold is the lodestone of Alpha and Omega. It is a reminder to every child of God at the soul level of the great throne of grace, of the great throne room that is white and gold in the Great Central Sun. It is from this room that souls of light took leave of the octaves of Spirit, descending into the planes of Mater.

"It was my commission from Alpha and Omega aeons and aeons ago to establish the focuses of gold in the Matter planes among the galaxies and thus to teach elemental life under the four hierarchies and through the Elohim how the balance of forces in the four planes of Mater would be anchored through the magnetic quality of this precipitated sunlight. Thus, the elementals learned to precipitate gold. And thus, gold does grow in the earth. Veins expand, and this balancing of energy corresponds directly to, first of all, the blueprint of the Christ consciousness of the evolutions of earth or of a system of worlds and then to that which has been outpictured through the threefold flame.

"That which is the gold in circulation represents attainment in the outer. Gold that remains undiscovered represents that portion of potential of the Christ mind that remains to be brought forth. You cannot have a demonstration of light and of the consciousness of the Christ without a corresponding manifestation of gold in your world."[155]

The masters have advised that we should all have some gold upon our person at all times to magnetize the fire of the sun. They have also asked us to call to the God of Nature and the God of Gold, as well as to Saint Germain and the Goddess of Liberty, to restore the free flow of gold coins throughout the world.

❖ **GREAT DIVINE DIRECTOR, Manu of the Seventh Root Race**

The Great Divine Director is a cosmic being. He says, "I am known as the Great Divine Director because I have merged my consciousness with the cosmic cycles of God's divine plan for untold universes of light."[156] His causal body is a giant blue sphere that surrounds the entire planet. Within that sphere, there are grids and forcefields through which the delivery of the judgment shall pass.

He long ago passed those initiations that placed him at cosmic levels of service and qualified him to become the manu of the seventh root race. A *manu* of a root race is the lawgiver who sets the divine plan for an entire evolution. The manu embodies the archetype for an entire lifewave of souls who will incarnate on earth at a certain period—the Divine Image and likeness out of which they are made and the pattern of their destiny. The seventh root race is destined to embody first in South America under the Great Divine Director.

Prior to the sinking of Atlantis, while Noah was yet building his ark and warning the people of the great Flood to come, the Great Divine Director called Saint Germain and a few faithful priests to transport the flame of freedom from the Temple of Purification to a place of safety in the Carpathian foothills in Transylvania. Here they carried on the sacred ritual of expanding the fires of freedom even while mankind's karma was being exacted by divine decree.

In succeeding embodiments, Saint Germain and his followers, under the guidance of the Great Divine Director, rediscovered the flame and continued to guard the shrine. Later, the Great Divine Director, assisted by his disciple, established a retreat at the site of the flame and founded the House of Rakoczy, the royal house of Hungary. Because of his association with the House of Rakoczy, the Great Divine Director bears the appellation Master R—the "R" signifying Rakoczy. The Great Divine Director continues to maintain in the Rakoczy Mansion in Transylvania a focus of freedom for Eastern and Western Europe. The retreat was once physical but is now in the etheric plane.

El Morya tells us that the Great Divine Director has sponsored Europe for thousands of years. He is the teacher of Saint Germain and many other masters including Jesus and El Morya. In addition to the Rakoczy Mansion, he maintains a focus in the Cave of Light in India, where he uses his authority to purify the four lower bodies of advanced initiates of their remaining karma and to give them purified vehicles to render a cosmic service in the world of form prior to their ascension.

The Great Divine Director is a member of the Darjeeling Council and also a member of the Karmic Board, serving that body on the first ray of God's holy will. He also occupies the twelve o'clock line of the twelve solar hierarchies on behalf of the evolutions of this solar system, serving with the hierarchy of Capricorn to assist mankind in the overcoming of their human creation.

He is often depicted with a large blue belt, hung with dazzling blue jewels, with dazzling light rays emanating from his heart, throat and head.

These light rays are very powerful. When you give the decree to the Great Divine Director, you can tie into those light rays and his protection. He will place his blue belt around you at the etheric level for the protection of your chakras and will help you bring forth your divine plan.

The Great Divine Director administers the use of the Disc of Light that focuses the whirling action of the violet flame. As the disc of fire rotates at the speed of light in a clockwise direction, it draws into its center the misqualified substance in the electronic belt and in the four lower bodies. You may visualize this disc of light as a giant electric sanding machine, emitting sparks of light as it whirls and creating a vortex that draws into itself all substance requiring transmutation.

Divine direction is a state of consciousness in God. It is the perfect awareness of his plan for all life. Ultimately, this awareness contains within itself not only the direction but its logical conclusion in action-fulfillment. Long ago, before our souls were reckoning with being God, an initiate of the Solar Lords perceived the need of lifewaves here below to know the plan and to proceed with unerring direction from the Polestar of Being to complete the plan as blueprint-matrix, as thought conceptualized, as motive and willingness engendering momentum for completion, as Mater-realization, physical fulfillment, the completion of a cycle. His name, too, became secondary to the flame he adored.

And so, the nameless one worshiping God as the law of unerring direction came to be known as the Great Divine Director, because, through adoration, he became the adored and then the adorable one. And then, the office in cosmic hierarchy, the Great Divine Director, became his God-identity.

The Great Divine Director has authored a series of *Pearls of Wisdom*, called "The Mechanization Concept," to help us understand the challenges of Armageddon. The "Rakoczy March" by Franz Liszt was inspired from his causal body.

❖ GREAT SILENT WATCHERS

The Great Silent Watcher is another name for the Elohim of the Fifth Ray, Cyclopea, the All-Seeing Eye of God. The Great Silent Watchers are cosmic beings of light who keep the watch over the entire Matter cosmos. All that exists in the Matter cosmos is held in the mind of the Elohim of the fifth ray, in the mind of God, immaculately according to its original and perfect design.

The Great Silent Watchers guard the purity of the Christ consciousness and Christ image out of which souls of light are created. Your Holy Christ Self also has this office—to hold the immaculate concept for your path, your divine plan, your mission upon earth. Your Holy Christ Self is your teacher, teaching you how to fulfill that plan, as are the angels of light known as the Great Silent Watchers, who are cosmic beings at the level of Elohim.

In 1979, Cyclopea said, "I am joined on this platform by numerous Great Silent Watchers who keep the watch of the immaculate design for each soul, each system of worlds, each galaxy. Contemplate Elohim and Great Silent Watchers without number through the vast cosmos that is God, holding the matrix of the Mother light for the intricacies of starry worlds and of souls and of light itself."[157]

Cyclopea and Virginia have explained that these great beings are known as silent because "it is the silence of the inner Holy of holies whereby the outer manifestation is sustained."[158]

❖ **HARMONY, Cosmic Being**

The cosmic being God Harmony is also known as the Great Tenor. He represents the cosmic consciousness of God's harmony and the law of God-harmony as it manifests in music, in science, in art, in society and in the four lower bodies of man. God Harmony serves on the six o'clock line of the cosmic clock (the line of God-harmony) with Serapis Bey. This is the line of the Divine Mother.

Prior to his ascension thousands of years ago, God Harmony had been embodied as a blacksmith, a mechanic and an astronomer. He devoted himself in many incarnations to the flame of Mother as the flame of her harmonious love for her children. He attained to the cosmic consciousness— the God consciousness—of harmony, and so became known as God Harmony. Since his victory, he has rendered great service at inner levels and drawn a tremendous momentum of the quality of God-harmony, a crystal flame that reflects the seven rays in harmonious interaction.

God Harmony says: "I AM the living flame of harmony; all people in the earth require my ministrations." "I AM the harmony of the origin of cycles in your being, and I carry the vibration of the absolute harmony of a cosmos. Without that harmony, beloved ones, the entire cosmos itself would collapse."[159]

God Harmony explains that harmony is a key to our progress on the Path. He says that no matter how much the saints call for more light, "that which can be given must be adjusted according to cosmic law as to, what you might say, the traffic will bear." He wants us to understand how "the ascended masters make karma in delivering unto an unascended chela more light than that chela can hold in balance...."

"That supreme magnet of love harmonious is all-attractive of all good and all-repelling of all evil. Therefore, those who would survive when the earth is in chaos and disintegration and death must understand clearly that the antidote for all of this is the purity of harmony.

"Harmony is a science, even as music is a science.... Harmony, then, is the balance of light, of sun centers, electronic forcefields. When there is balance, then there is harmony. When there is balance and harmony, then, and then only, can there be acceleration.

"You may have wondrous gifts of virtue, but often in a lifetime or many lifetimes an individual lifestream does not exceed a certain level of attainment professionally or a certain level of virtue because the individual reaches the line where there is no longer balance, where he cannot carry into an accelerated momentum that virtue that may function at a lesser vibration.

"Take, for example, a top that spins. In order to spin, it must have a certain acceleration and a certain balance. Thus, when the law of harmony functioning within you goes below the level of a certain acceleration, it can no longer be maintained. And this is when discord enters in with disintegration and ultimately self-destruction. Thus, in order to have the key of harmony, you must have the key of acceleration of love....

"Wherever energy is tied in knots of self-deception, of dissonance, of selfishness, of hatred—all of these manifestations, including anxiety itself, cause the deceleration of that which is God-harmony within the fiery core of the threefold flame itself. Thus, when the momentum of dissonance becomes too great, the top of the threefold flame cannot spin. When its three plumes are of different height, out of balance, it cannot spin, and therefore the resurrection fires do not glow."[160]

Saint Germain has told us in his *Studies in Alchemy* that "Light is the alchemical key." God Harmony says, "May God-harmony provide you with the key to light—which itself is the alchemical key. Thus, harmony is the key to the key.

"Think upon these words and ask yourself this question: 'How many doors will I pass through, how many keys must I find to finally enter into the Holy of holies of my very own God being?'

"In the flame of God-harmony, I release to your heart the answer to your question. I send you forth on a mission for the self-sustainment of harmony. It is, my beloved, the key to the crucifixion."[161] And of course, without the crucifixion, there can be no resurrection, no ascension. Without the cross, there can be no crown.

God Harmony gives a simple definition of harmony as "oneness with

God, attunement with God, ever beholding the face of the Father as the angels do…. It is happiness in the simple manifestations of nature, in the sharing of love, in the creating of beauty."[162]

"Every war and every battle may be won by you by the science of absolute God-harmony. Harmony is the true source of everlasting life; it is the principal quality of the Tree of Life. Think of this, beloved, when you are fully in harmony with God, you are immortal, for God is immortal…. Thus, harmony is the price you must pay for your ascension."[163]

Commenting on the high level of inharmony in the earth, God Harmony said in 1995: "What is this inharmony? I will tell you one major factor, and that is the absence of the Divine Mother Omega in the earth. Those of earth are like children, one and all, crying for their Divine Mother in heaven, crying out to be nurtured, to be cared for.

"And she does not come and she does not come, and they become angry. Yet they have chased her out of the earth long, long ago. As in Kabbalah when the Mother is perceived as being in exile in the earth, so the Mother is exiled in heaven, for the inharmony of her children universally does not allow her to enter in."

So great is this inharmony that during this same dictation when God Harmony placed harmony over the earth from his causal body, he experienced immense pain. He said: "I do this, beloved, for the sake of the light-bearers who have been, who are and who are to come….

"Your very life and health depend upon your harmony. The joy and the singing of atoms, molecules, cells and organs in your body—the very joy of God throughout all creation—this harmony you must find.

"Call it peace, if you will. But whatever you call it, beloved, establish that inner sense of your own completeness, your own internal happiness that does not require that you derive your happiness from others but only from the wellspring of God that wells up within you."[164]

God Harmony says that the Community of the Holy Spirit is based on the harmony of each of the seven rays: "I pray that you will understand that there is no effort, no plan, no undertaking, no group activity nor a single work of a single individual that can be fulfilled if the harmony is continuously broken."[165]

As we seek to master the flame of harmony on the seven rays, God Harmony suggests that we start with the first ray and with the will of God. "Consider now," he says, "if suddenly my angels would pour into you with the water pots of the Aquarian water-bearer the fullness of the elixir of Morya's devotion unto the will of God.

"You can visualize yourselves being filled with an intense fiery-blue flow of cosmic energy. Our study then would be: How does the increased dimension and vibration of the will of God within the temple affect the harmony of the lifestream? At what point does an excess of the holy will of God produce a reaction in place of an interaction with the flame of life? This is the question that must be answered by the angels of El Morya before he would come to initiate a soul with even an erg of the priceless essence of millennia of his devotion to the will of God.

"Thus, every ascended master, beginning with the seven chohans of the rays, must estimate, based on the very contents of the psyche, the four lower bodies and the subconscious as to how much light the individual can contain and still maintain a reasonable balance of God-harmony."[166]

We often make the most karma through our emotions in the solar plexus and our speech in the throat chakra. Because a golden age requires harmony with one's God and with oneself, few people on earth today would be accepted in the great etheric cities of light above this octave, where the golden ages are in progress. Students of the masters should seek to maintain harmony in their being and world and not be moved or provoked into discord of any kind.

God Harmony explains that true God-mastery is God-harmony. Harmony comes with the determination to fulfill the qualities of God on the twelve lines of the clock. Although the quality of God-harmony is charted on the six o'clock line of the cosmic clock, God Harmony says that as long as we have karma on any of the twelve lines of the clock, we do not have full harmony. As you call forth the light of God and of Christ and Buddha to seal untransmuted karma on each of the twelve lines of the clock, you build an increasing momentum of God-harmony.

He also warns that God-harmony is not the sign of those who cry, "Peace, peace," and desire to smooth over the war and the warring in their members that is raging beneath the surface. He cautions us not to be fooled by those who may speak in quiet tones with the smile of peace but have no internal fount of harmony or love. "You know better when you look into their eyes and see that they may be deeply troubled or angry or gripped by whatever else may have invaded their temple."[167] He asks us to judge righteous judgment and not be fooled by the outer appearance of any.

God Harmony offers to instruct us in keeping true harmony. He and his legions can be contacted through meditation upon the emerald and crystal rays. His presence may be magnetized by meditation upon his keynote, the "Anvil Chorus" from the opera *Il Trovatore,* by Verdi.

❖ **HELIOS AND VESTA, God and Goddess of This Solar System**

Helios is the God of this solar system and abides in the very heart of the physical sun. With his twin flame, Vesta, he serves to represent the Godhead to those evolving on the planets orbiting the sun. It is their God consciousness that sustains our physical solar system.

Helios, the Lord of the Dawn, and Vesta, the Mother of Eternal Cycles, are known as Presiding Solar Deities and are the representatives of the Father-Mother God in the Sun behind the sun of this solar system. Helios serves on the golden ray and his twin flame, Vesta, on the pink ray. Among the twelve solar hierarchies, they represent the hierarchy of Aries (the three o'clock line) to the evolutions of this system. This is the line of the Son of God, the only begotten One, and it is on this line that the Sun Presence of Helios and the Great Central Sun messengers focus the quality of God-control, which they amplify by the power of the Great Central Sun Magnet. This Magnet is the God-control of the flow of life through us, the flow of the energy of the Logos. This is the quality we must outpicture under the hierarchy of Aries.

The ancient Greeks knew Helios as the Sun God. In Roman mythology, Vesta was worshiped as the Goddess of the Hearth. The Greeks knew her as Hestia. Each Roman and Greek household and city kept a fire burning perpetually in the honor of Vesta. In Rome, the sacred fire in the temple of Vesta was tended by six priestesses called vestal virgins.

Beloved Helios has told us: "Just as the tides of the sea flow in and out, so the tides of the eternal sun radiate in ever recurring cycles. When the incoming tide of the Great Solar Light pours into your world, it is God conveying his grace and gifts to you. When the tide goes out, it is a time for you to convey to him your gratitude and your desire to become a very essential part of him. Those who are eager to receive the light that is incoming, with its buoyancy, its joy, its power, often do not recognize the moments when life does not seem to be with them...as the moments when God is asking them to send love and supplication in his direction."[168]

❖ **HERCULES AND AMAZONIA, Elohim of the First Ray**

Hercules and Amazonia are the Elohim of the first ray of power, faith and God's will. Their retreat is on the etheric plane in and over Half Dome in Yosemite National Park in Northern California. The auras of Hercules and Amazonia are charged with blue lightning and have an intense pink lining.

Half-Dome

Hercules was the most famous of the heroes of Greek mythology. The origin of the figures in Greek mythology is a distant soul memory and a decadent understanding that there were great beings of light who walked and talked with mankind during past golden ages. The ascended masters once walked with mankind on Atlantis, but they gradually withdrew with the fall in consciousness of mankind.

To the ancients, Hercules was one of their most illustrious ancestors, an intermediary between men and the gods. His name means "glory of the air." Hercules presided over all aspects of Hellenic education. In his

The Farnese Hercules, National Museum of Naples

aspect of athlete-hero, the Olympic Games were ascribed to him. It is said that at the command of the Oracle of Delphi, Hercules spent twelve years under the orders of Eurystheus, who imposed upon him twelve arduous, seemingly impossible "labors." Students of the deeper mysteries understand that the story of Hercules' labors illustrates the soul requirement on the path of initiation for self-mastery of the energies of the twelve solar hierarchies.

The ascended master Hercules is millennia older than Greek mythology. When God commanded this solar system to be formed, the fiat went forth, "Let there be light," and there was light. It was Hercules who summoned the mighty Elohim, the Builders of Form, to come forth and to precipitate the divine plan of the Solar Logoi. His great strength is drawn through his obedience to love of the will of God. He releases blue-lightning protection and his momentum of will-energy-action in answer to mankind's calls for strength and direction.

Hercules has told us that in many cases, because of his office among the Seven Elohim, he is the only representative of the Godhead who can stand between mankind and their returning karma. He said in 1974, "Wherever there is cataclysm, flood or fire or storm or drought, I ask you to call unto me, that I may intercede with the great power that God has given me.... Call on the name of Hercules, day and night."[169]

According to the law of free will, the masters, the Elohim, the angels cannot intercede in our world unless we ask them to. In 1995 Hercules said,

"Never before has there been such a dispensation for using our decree to focus in the earth the ribbons of blue fire and white lightning whereby there is a literal disintegration of misqualified human substance.

"I promise you that each and every time you give your call to me in multiples of nine, you shall have the multiplication that you have not seen since my original physical presence in the earth. You can use this decree to summon the Great Teams of Conquerors who work with our legions. Ours is a most specific dispensation. For we are the only ones allowed to be so physical in the earth at this time."[170]

In 1996, Hercules said, "Calling to us is imperative to hold the world in peace.... Make calls to me daily, even if you only offer me three Hercules decrees. That is enough, beloved. But call my name, and you empower me to work in your levels."[171]

Hercules wants us to focus on turning back domestic and international terrorism, earth changes and all challenges to God-government. As you give these calls, you can visualize the Elohim pouring their light into this world through the chalice of Elohim anchored over the Heart of the Inner Retreat. Visualize white fire and blue lightning turning back domestic and international terrorism and all that opposes God-government. Make your visualizations as specific as possible. The more specific your visualizations, the more effective your decrees will be, because you are directing God's light, like a laser beam, right into the core of a situation.

In August 1989 the messenger requested decree assignments from El Morya to accomplish "meritorious deeds" that would help the Great White Brotherhood, El Morya and the lightbearers of the world. During the 1989 fall conference, Archangel Michael announced that Hercules and the seven Elohim had come to give us spiritual labors. He said, "They come to give you those assignments whereby this world may be delivered of certain increments of karma and certain manifestations of the fallen ones whose time is up."[172] During the conference the messenger and chelas worked on twelve spiritual labors corresponding to the twelve labors of Hercules in Greek mythology. Beloved Hercules and El Morya have periodically given us labors for the binding of astral forces and fallen angels attacking the lightbearers. These decree assignments are also for penance, initiation and the balancing of karma.

Morya has told us that the reason our beloved mighty Hercules is so close to the physical octave is that he once volunteered to embody on earth: "There came a time in earth's history when evil was so rampant and spacecraft and aliens, and indeed there were giants in the earth and there were gods,[173] that Hercules himself did volunteer to take embodiment to deal with those Watchers, to deal with their creation half-animal, half-human. And therefore, he did descend in another era. And he did go forth all of his days and all of his hours to challenge those fallen ones.

"And therefore, heart and mind and soul and spirit one-pointed, Hercules did save the day for planet Earth at one point in an era past. And he did save the earth for you, beloved, to be here again in this time. And now he is grateful that you have chosen to call forth his Electronic Presence and to walk the earth not only as Morya's chelas, as Michael's chelas, but also as the chelas of Hercules and Amazonia."[174]

On December 16, 1962, Amazonia came from the Great Central Sun to speak of the ancient civilizations of South America and of a giant race of magnificent women who once dwelt there when Amazonia herself "manifested physically upon this planet." However, the Amazons "became depraved individuals using their giant strength to wage destructive warfare even against the opposite sex and degenerating into mere tribes."

Amazonia then reminded us of many of the cataclysmic upheavals that have occurred throughout history in order "to call to your attention the dangers inherent in wrong thinking and wrong living and misjudging and misdirecting your energy." She explained that the Great White Brotherhood longs to see an era of peace and plenty in South America, "to see the old temples raised anew." But Amazonia warned that "the power of freedom must be retained in the heart of America that the germinal seeds of light may be transmitted safely there in one mighty Pan-American union."

❖ HERMES TRISMEGISTUS (GOD MERCURY)

Hermes was known in ancient times as the great sage to whom is attributed sacred writings and alchemical and astrological works. Because of his learning and profound skill in the arts and sciences, the Egyptians gave him the name *Trismegistus,* which means "thrice-great." The title "thrice-great" also applies to his role as philosopher, priest and king. The ascended master Hermes Trismegistus is also known as the God Mercury.

Hermes walked the earth for tens of thousands of years. He was on Atlantis, walked its streets, was in its temples and halls of learning and gave forth his teaching. He figures as the great archetype of the messenger of the gods.

James Campbell Brown writes in his *History of Chemistry,* "A series of early Egyptian books is attributed to Hermes Trismegistus, who may have been a real savant, or may be a personification of a long succession of writers.... He is identified by some with the Greek god Hermes [equated with

The Roman god Mercury

the Roman god Mercury] and the Egyptian Thoth.... The Egyptians regarded him as the god of wisdom, letters, and the recording of time."[175]

Hermes Trismegistus has been referred to as the father of alchemy. According to one legend, a slab of emerald found in his tomb had inscribed upon it Hermes' precepts for making gold. This emerald tablet contained the familiar Hermetic axiom: "What is below is like that which is above. And what is above is like that which is below."[176]

One ancient author who claimed to have seen the stone said that it was an emerald on which the characters were represented in bas-relief, not engraved. The material had once been in a fluid state like melted glass and had been cast in a mold, and it had been given the hardness of a genuine emerald by alchemical means.

The emerald tablet has long been regarded in the mystery schools as one of the oldest and most profound expositions of spiritual alchemy. It presents an alchemical formula that has been used by the adepts and alchemists for thousands of years to assimilate the most essential understanding of both physical transmutation and spiritual regeneration. However, its statements clearly hide to all but the true alchemist their inner meaning.

The ascended master Hermes has taught of the emerald tablet of the heart: "I, Hermes, messenger of the Gods and also the one called Mercury, have tarried, lo, these tens of thousands of years and beyond that there might be a torch of remembrance, an inscribing of the Law upon the emerald tablet of thy heart.

"For, lo, the emerald tablet in the secret chamber of thy heart is even now unveiled by thine own Holy Christ Self, the priest-philosopher-scientist who officiates at the altar of unalterable change. It is that change that must come, that must be because I AM and because thou art also the God-man."

He instructed us to "neglect not the heart; and call the sacred fire to melt and transmute daily all hardness of heart, spiritual neglect and records of death surrounding the sun center of your own heart chakra. Let us be diligent to expand the heart, for out of it are the issues of life."[177]

The ascended master Hermes is the sponsor of El Morya and of all those who have come from the planet Mercury. El Morya explains: "The lifewaves of sons and daughters of God who have evolved out of Mercury, who have served with Sanat Kumara and who now are dwelling on earth, come from an evolution that we knew long ago. In that planetary body, the issue of light and darkness was present....

"As we saw the challenge and as we were taught by God Mercury, we knew that unflinching devotion to the will of God, the drawing within of energy to the diamond point of the Self, the wielding of the sword of blue flame, and the mastery of the action of fohatic keys would result in the victory....

"God gave to us, as we fought the battle of worlds on Mercury, that energy, that power—only because we were willing to balance the threefold flame, to pursue wisdom and wisdom's might, to intensify such love in every cell and in the flame of every cell, so that our auras were so saturated with love that there was no possibility for the misqualification of one erg of God's power through any form of tyranny whatsoever....

"Beloved ones, the victory of Mercury has not yet been concluded. A greater part of the victory was won, yet certain sons of light and certain fallen ones had not reached the culmination of their evolution. They were, therefore, assigned to other planetary homes and systems. Some of the fallen ones became aligned with the laggard evolutions that eventually embodied on earth. Some of the sons and daughters of God journeyed to Venus and later accompanied Sanat Kumara to earth."[178]

Hermes calls those who would take up the arts of communication in defense of Truth. "I am a messenger of the Gods and I have a message that I must deliver to your hearts....

"I speak of the lineage of the initiates of Mercury—those who have fashioned their skill by the sword and the pen, those who have acquainted themselves with the mind of God and have claimed that mind, who have come from a lineage that antedates myself. Truly, there is a lineage of those who have been called Hermes, the name being the title of an office. Thus, there is a descent of those whose craft has been to set forth in writing and in other forms of communication that which is Real, that which is unreal, that which is necessary information to the body politic round the world that they might know and understand the way to go....

"There are those whom I myself have trained under my mantle as God Mercury. We who bear the shield and the armour of the Sun must therefore go up and down the nations of the earth and call out those who have the original communication skills, who practiced those skills in ancient times and on ancient continents and are willing to once again take the lead in the dissemination of the Truth and in exposing error. You must come forward! For the Truth must be made known....

"Set forth the message! Set forth the platform for its delivery in your area of expertise! And if you think you have no expertise, go out and get it, and study and prove yourself to be one who will make that statement and make that name, not only for yourself but for God and all the ascending ones. I AM Hermes and I say to you: I shall overshadow any of you, each and every one of you, who will learn these disciplines."[179]

At the present time, Hermes serves in the retreat in Arabia where he is the patron of the science of alchemy—which Saint Germain has defined as the all-chemistry of God. His aura is a brilliant gold; he wears white robes and has long hair. He is the image of the ancient wisdom and the androgynous nature of the Deity.

❖ **HEROS AND AMORA, Elohim of the Third Ray**

Elohim Heros and Amora are the Elohim of the third ray of God's love, representing the Spirit of the Father-Mother God on the pink plume. They infuse earth, air, fire and water with the cohesive power of the Holy Spirit. Thus, by the power of the love they radiate, the planets are held in their orbits and the electrons continue on their appointed rounds.

The radiance of Heros and Amora is pink with a white lining. Their focus is in the etheric realm over Lake Winnipeg in Canada. The radiance of their pink flame, together with that of Chamuel and Charity, forms an arc of love connecting their retreat with that of the archangel and archeia of the third ray over St. Louis, Missouri.

In 1995, Heros and Amora came with a landmark dispensation whereby they were strategically layering thousands of "bricks of the ruby ray" in the earth that would "radiate ruby-ray 'heat' to balance inner levels of the earth closest to the core." They will stabilize the earth and curtail the power of those with evil intent, lightening the load of darkness on the planet. The Elohim also said that this action would cause changes in the earth, and added, "You may pray that these changes be not physical." They encouraged us to give violet-flame decrees daily to restore the equilibrium of the planet.

"Our angels will repair the faults in the etheric sheath, and as you intensify your violet-flame rituals, they will repair the faults in the earth. And you shall see the curtailment of the power of those who have persecuted the body of God in the earth. Ratify this prophecy by your calls, and it shall swiftly come to pass!"[180]

Heros and Amora would like us to focus on first, the intensification of these ruby-ray bricks and second, the defeat of all forces of anti-love that oppose the union of twin flames and our union with our Higher Self. Visualize the layered ruby-ray bricks radiating an intense ruby heat throughout the earth.

Heros and Amora speak of an action of love that is not widely understood: "The action of love is the action of the mightiest force in all of cosmos, the unleashing of the white-fire core of the atom, of the core of the secret rays.... Watch, then, how the judgment is meted by God through the instrument of the Elohim and through the instrument of love, and see how in the coming days there is a reinforcement of choices: those who choose light will find their light reinforced...and those who are of the darkness will become that conglomerate mass of the mass subconscious wherein the spirals of self-annihilation and defeat lead, then, to the second death. Choose, then, life!... Choose allegiance to the inner flame. And be not concerned whether or not the messenger, the emissary, is right, is wrong, is real, or is not real.... Be concerned with the choice within the citadel of your own consciousness, your own being and life, and then you will know what is Real."[181]

❖ HILARION, Chohan of the Fifth Ray

Hilarion is the chohan of the fifth ray of healing and truth. He is the hierarch of the Temple of Truth on the etheric plane near Crete, Greece.

Hilarion was high priest of the Temple of Truth on Atlantis, and he transported the flame of Truth together with the artifacts of the Temple to Greece a short time before the sinking of the continent. The focus of Truth that he established became the focal point for the Oracles of Delphi, messengers of Truth who served under the direction of Pallas Athena for hundreds of years, until black priests penetrated the Delphic Order and perverted the Truth that had been brought forth. The Brotherhood then withdrew this service to embodied mankind, since people were unable to distinguish between Truth and error.

Hilarion was later embodied as Saul of Tarsus, who became the apostle Paul. Hilarion has recalled for us his encounter with the Christ in that embodiment: "Jesus the Christ we called him, and we were called of him as you are called this day. I recall the memories of his coming to me, empowering me with his Word. Yet first he humbled me on that road to Damascus, the humbling I sorely needed that I might bow to my own Christ flame that he revealed to me, as he also gave to me the key of meditation upon that

St. Paul preaching to the Thessalonians, by Doré

flame that I might walk in his footsteps on the fifth ray of science and healing and apostleship and the preaching of the Word.

"Often I felt like the hands and the feet and the heart of Hercules, wrestling with the downward spirals of the earth with their atheism, their agnosticism, their intellectual pride and rancor against the prophets and the Holy One of God so recently come into our midst. Yet, all the while I remembered I was once counted among them. To have been once so proud and so deliberate against the will of God would forever burn in my memory the helplessness that we all have as instruments of God. But the great empowering by the Word comes, my beloved, in the hour of the conversion. It is not the hour of the call, but the hour of the conversion when the soul answers with something that is deep. It is the flowing, it is the giving, it is that surrender when, as He said: 'It is hard for thee to kick against the pricks....'

"My soul knew Him as of old and recalled to my outer mind the memory of the inner vow. It was not the first time I had seen the Lord Christ. I had seen him before taking incarnation, and yet I had to work through that pride, that karma on the fifth ray of much learning, much studying and superiority in social standing and intellectual standing that I had in regards to the early Christians. And so, it was my own karma that was upon me whereby I was resisting the call."[182]

"My Lord did pursue me as I made my journey on the road to Damascus. Yes, beloved, I was blinded, not by his light but by my own sin and the alchemy of his light penetrating the record of sin in my being. Thus, I was turned around, converted by the Spirit of the Lord in the full manifestation of Jesus Christ upon me."[183]

For a period following his conversion to Christ, Paul retreated into the Arabian desert. In Galatians 1:16–18, Paul records, "I conferred not with flesh and blood. Neither went I up to Jerusalem to them which were apostles before me; but I went into Arabia and returned again unto Damascus. Then after three years I went up to Jerusalem."

Commentators have often speculated as to what Paul did during his sojourn in the desert. Hilarion has explained that Jesus took him "with others into his retreat over the Holy Land and at Arabia. I have been there and learned of him. And this was my desert sojourn in meditation with him, taken up as I was in my finer bodies and trained directly heart to heart."[184]

Because in that lifetime the apostle Paul had consented to the stoning of Saint Stephen (the first Christian martyr) and had actively persecuted and killed Christians, he did not ascend at the conclusion of that life. The taking of life in one incarnation often requires another embodiment to balance that karma. The ascended master Hilarion has explained why he was required to embody again before making his ascension: "Remember, then, that we, the apostles of Christ, did come under the dispensation of the Law that required that one balance 100 percent of one's karma ere the soul enter the ascension in the light.* Thus, I was required to atone in my life as the apostle Paul and in my next life as Saint Hilarion for the sins I had committed before I received my Lord."[185] So Jesus, who raised up Paul to be his apostle, sponsored him in a final incarnation as Saint Hilarion (c. A.D. 290 to 372), the founder of monasticism in Palestine.

Hilarion spent twenty years in the desert in preparation for his mission and only then wrought his first miracle—God working through him, he cured a woman of barrenness enabling her to bring forth a son. From that day forward, he carried out a healing ministry.

He healed children of a fever by invoking the name of Jesus, cured paralysis and cast out many devils. Crowds would gather to be healed of diseases and unclean spirits. They followed him even into the most desolate and remote places. He tried many times to hide, but they always found him, compelling him to follow his true calling, for the love of Jesus.

Jerome, whose biography of the saint provides most of the information we know about him, records: "The frequency of his signs in Sicily drew to him sick people and religious men in multitudes; and one of the chief men was cured of dropsy the same day that he came, and offered Hilarion boundless gifts; but he obeyed the Saviour's saying, 'Freely ye have received; freely give.'"

On the occasion of a great earthquake, the sea was threatening to destroy the town. According to Jerome, "The sea broke its bounds; and, as if God was threatening another flood, or all was returning to primeval chaos, ships were carried up steep rocks and hung there." The townsfolk, seeing these mountains of water coming towards the shore, ran and got Hilarion, and "as if they were leading him out to battle, stationed him on the shore. And when he had marked three signs of the cross upon the sand, and stretched out his hands against the waves, it is past belief to what a height the sea swelled, and stood up before him, and then, raging long, as if indignant at the barrier, fell back, little by little, into itself."

Toward the end of his life the people's saint, for they had claimed him as their own, retreated to a spot in Cyprus so remote that he was convinced

---

*Since the inauguration of the new dispensation early in the twentieth century, it is possible to ascend having balanced at least 51 percent of one's karma, the remaining portion then being balanced on inner levels after the ascension.

no one would find him there. It was even haunted—the people would be afraid to approach, he thought. But one paralyzed managed to drag himself there, found Hilarion, was cured, and spread the word.

And so it was that the saint ended his days in that valley, with many people coming to see him. After his passing, his followers buried him there, as was his desire, but within several months his closest disciple, Hesychius, secretly dug up his grave and carried his body off to Palestine.

The ascended master Hilarion shared with us a revelation he received in this last physical incarnation on earth as the great healer and hermit living in the deserts of Palestine and Cyprus. He said: "I AM Hilarion! I have walked in the desert places! I have taken my refuge in the desert of life, but the multitudes came after me into the desert as I lived in my final incarnation as Hilarion. They came for the healing fountain; they came for love. Though I would retreat, they would follow. And so, the Lord told me that the gift of Truth and of healing is only for the sharing, only for the giving away."[186]

Hilarion had the gift of healing in abundant measure. The truly great healers of mankind, who can bring souls to the point of resolution and wholeness by a touch of the hand or a simple command, "Be thou made whole!" are sent from God. The identifying mark of the true healer is that he walks in the shadow of his mighty I AM Presence, that he is humble before God and man and that he gives all glory to God for the works God performs through him, knowing that he is but the instrument of the Holy Spirit. These holy ones of God are self-effacing, and they will not necessarily tell you that they have the gift of healing.

The melody of "Onward, Christian Soldiers" may be played to draw the radiance of Hilarion into one's world. Through this music, we can feel the same fervor and zeal today that enabled the apostle Paul, two thousand years ago, to inspire the early Christians to establish the Church of Christ in Asia Minor and eventually throughout the known world. He imbues us with the courage necessary to fulfill our mission today with these words:

"So I say, apostles of the Most High God, be on your way! It is the changing of forcefields, the changing of the boots that causes the quaking in the knees. I say be up and doing! Left, right, left, right, take another step, go forward! You will find out what God would have you do. No need to sit and wonder! There is work—work in the action of the Holy Spirit. There is the joy of the service that is true brotherhood and true community.

"Find out what God would have you find out about yourself by immersing yourself in the great cosmic flow, the ongoing flow of service. Find out what the teaching is by living the teaching. And find out what we have for you at Crete as our assignment as representatives of Truth."[187]

The Brotherhood of Truth in Hilarion's retreat over Crete use the flame of healing, science and constancy focused there. They work with those who have become disillusioned with life and religion and with their fellowmen who have misrepresented or misinterpreted the Truth, and thus they have become atheists, agnostics or skeptics. The Brothers of Crete also work with doctors and scientists and assist them in their research. You can call to Hilarion for healing and wholeness, for the conversion of souls and for the exposure of truth in the media.

❖ HIMALAYA, Manu of the Fourth Root Race

Himalaya is the manu of the fourth root race. He is also the hierarch of the Retreat of the Blue Lotus in the Himalayan mountains, guardian of the ray of the masculine aspect of the Godhead focused directly from the heart of Alpha. The gentle radiance of Himalaya can be felt throughout the East as a tangible presence drawing the pilgrims of all nations into a divine awareness of the flame of the blue lotus.

The Himalayas

A root race is a group of souls, or a lifewave, who embody together and have a unique archetypal pattern, divine plan and mission to fulfill. The manus (Sanskrit for "progenitors" or "lawgivers") ensoul the Christic image for the lifewave they sponsor. According to esoteric tradition, there are seven primary groups of souls, i.e., the first to seventh root races.

The first three root races lived in purity and innocence upon earth in three golden ages before the Fall of man. Through obedience to cosmic law and total identification with the Real Self, these three root races won their immortal freedom and ascended from earth. It was during the time of the fourth root race, on the continent of Lemuria, that the allegorical Fall took place under the influence of the fallen angels known as Serpents (because they used the serpentine spinal energies to beguile the soul, or female principle in mankind, as a means of lowering the masculine potential).

The fourth, fifth and sixth root races remain in embodiment on earth today. The seventh root race is destined to incarnate on the continent of South America in the Aquarian age under their manu, the Great Divine Director.

Himalaya is a Master of masters. His pupils have been Lord Gautama, Lord Maitreya, El Morya, Kuthumi and thousands of others. He teaches meditation while in the lotus posture. Those who are privileged to sit at his feet must learn to blend their consciousness with his, and as their pulse becomes one with the rhythm of his threefold flame, they receive the ideations of his mind, although never a word is spoken. Those who master the art of telepathy always leave the Blue Lotus Temple with hearts full and with a mantra that is the key to the unfoldment of their divine plan.

The tangible radiance of Lord Himalaya appears as golden snow; his great devotion to the flame of the Christ in the masses of Asia has kept the Ganges purified as a healing focus for centuries. Likewise, in the mountains bearing his name, he has anchored magnetic poles of the Christ consciousness.

Lord Himalaya has spent much time in the Great Silence (in Nirvana) where he retreats to gather the energies of the great creative consciousness, stepping forth from time to time to release the light he has drawn to the four corners of the earth. At the present time, he is active in his retreat on behalf of the illumination of the world and the uniting of East and West. His divine complement remains in embodiment to anchor their twin flames in form.

Himalaya says, "The quietness of the Buddha, the listening of the Christ, this is the power of God. The Great Silence is the power, the tenderness of the flowers, the new babe and those making the transition to all light. Learn of power, beloved, and learn of me. Learn of the wonder of God and the miracle of grace. Learn of the entering in to the Temple of the Blue Lotus. Learn, then, of the assimilation of that cobalt blue in all of the chakras. Learn the stillness of the eye of the hurricane and the eye of God. Learn the majesty of the peace that establishes the light of the heart."[188]

❖ **HOPE,** *See* **Faith, Hope and Charity** *and* **Gabriel and Hope**

❖ **IGOR (THE UNKNOWN MASTER), Mary's Unknown Son**

Igor was embodied in Russia at the time of the Russian Revolution and kept the flame on behalf of his countrymen in that period of travail. Igor was a disciple of Mother Mary and Archangel Gabriel.

Early in Igor's life, Gabriel came to him saying: "Hail, Igor. God has heard thy prayer and he has sent me unto thee. Know, then, that I will guide thee throughout thy life and I will be to thee a friend."[189] Through this devoted son of God, Mary anchored a light that prevented the destruction and loss of life during the Russian Revolution from being much greater than it was.

Mother Mary speaks of Igor as her "unknown Son" and describes his life of dedication to God: "And so I would tell you about Igor, the little Russian boy, the peasant child that I took under my wing back during the 1800s. And I held for him the same immaculate concept that I held for my Son, Jesus.

"Igor dwelt near Ararat's Mountain* in a very humble cabin, and from the time he was a child he prayed unto God. For he was a different child from those rude peasant boys who were his neighbors, and he turned at a very early age to inward contemplation.

"I recall well when his unformed mind could not yet even create the matrices of understanding of just what he felt within his soul. But I worked with one of the great angels of speech who had been used at the time of the Tower of Babel to confound the people. And I urged upon this angel assistance for Igor that he might come, through the power of the angel, to understand the meaning of speech so that even his feelings could be translated into divine comprehension.

"This child prayed, and he prayed not only with feeling but he prayed with understanding. And it came to pass that during the days of the Russian Revolution the work of Igor was most important to stop the frightful toll that otherwise would have been thrice that which it was. And while the awful powers of darkness were focusing in Rasputin, Igor was continually in prayer for the great peoples of Russia and for Mother Russia.

"I tell you about this because he left no writing except upon the pages of akasha. But I want you to know that this blessed one who bore this name, which could well be confounded [i.e., confused] by the people of the world as synonymous with 'ignorance,' was not ignorant. He was God-taught, and I sponsored his soul at inner levels.

"His passion made him to be a patriarch to his people, but they knew him not. His name was never recorded, his own parents did not recognize his inward development—they thought him a strange and weird child, the child of aloneness—and his teachers cuffed his ears and sent him into the corner because they, too, thought him ignorant and without knowledge.

"He sought for nothing for himself. But when the full knowledge of spiritual mastery was given to him and he attained a wisdom compatible with my Son Jesus, he did not do as Jesus did—go forth to gather souls by speaking to the masses upon the hilltops—but he wrestled with the souls of men at inner levels.

"And as he lay upon his straw pallet and gazed up at the stars at night, his consciousness would roam afar—about the world. And he traveled and journeyed to France, to America and to many lands, seeing clearly and with a greater vision than your television screens can convey the beauty of

---

*International boundaries have shifted since Igor's time. Mount Ararat, now in Turkey, was then on the border of Turkey and Armenia, which was part of the Russian empire in the late nineteenth century.

men's souls and their perils. When he saw peril there, he prayed, and his prayer filled the very air. His prayers were answered by angels of Raphael's band, and healing was often effected by his love.

"I would like to say to you today that he is the unknown Son of God. I would like to say to you today that if America and Russia are ever able to mend their differences and unify, it will be in part, and a great part, because of the work of Igor.

"He has a new name now and it is so beautiful that I wish that I might be permitted to tell it to you. But the Lords of Karma have asked that he remain 'the unknown Son.'"[190]

Of his ascension at the close of that embodiment, Igor has said: "I accepted Mary's love and her wisdom and my heart was comforted, but the terror burned on. Throughout my life as I sought to be a pilgrim in a strange country, I aspired to attain something higher that I might free men. By and by, through the solemn ritual of the sacred mantra of my devotion toward God and through my one-pointedness, it came to pass that I was finally made ready for the moment of my ascension. And when it was given to me, it was not with mortal witnesses. I went up alone, but quickly found that I was not alone, for around me were many bright beings; and I knew that at last I had gone Home."[191]

❖ ISHVARA

Ishvara is a Sanskrit word meaning "Lord of the universe" or "Lord." In Hinduism, Ishvara is seen as the "immediate personal aspect of the supreme impersonal Godhead."[192] We cannot know God unless we know him personified, and God personifies himself in extensions of himself to whom he gives spiritual and physical form. In reality, there is only one God, but the one God appears to us in his many manifestations. Thus, the many gods in Hinduism are simply rays of light from the one central Source.

The Encyclopedia of Eastern Philosophy and Religion explains that "the God of Christianity and of Islam, as well as all the deities of Hindu mythology, are aspects of Ishvara. Our human reason can conceive of divinity only within some form; thus, we need the concept of Ishvara.... The most widely disseminated form of Ishvara in Hindu thought is the *trimurti*, the Trinity of Brahma, Vishnu, and Shiva."[193]

Ishvara is usually personified as one aspect of this Trinity. Various Hindu sects identify Ishvara with the highest figure in their pantheon— whether it be Brahma, Vishnu or Shiva. As described by the Hindu sage Ramanuja, "Ishvara...has an infinite number of supreme and auspicious qualities.... He has a most perfect body, which is eternal and immutable. He is radiant, full of beauty, youth, and strength. He is omnipresent; he is...the inner ruler of all."[194] You can think of Ishvara as being one with the great Atman, the Presence of God that is part of and in your threefold flame.

Swami Prabhavananda and Christopher Isherwood write: "What is important is the concept of devotion. Devotion to a personal ideal of God brings with it a natural inclination to humility and service. If we set ourselves to serve Ishvara, if we dedicate our actions and surrender our wills to him, we shall find that he draws us to himself. This is the grace of God, which Sri Ramakrishna compared to an ever-blowing breeze. You have only to raise your sail in order to catch it."[195]

During a dictation in 1977, Ishvara appeared on inner levels in a magnificent crystal filigree spiral of light as the representative of the hidden man of the heart, the Holy Christ Self. In that dictation, Ishvara said:

"I am the one, Ishvara.... I am in the light of the Holy of holies, in the within of the flame and in the secret chamber of the within. Come and find me in the center of the one that is thy life. Come and seek me to know my name and thus know the inner key to the release of that energy that will only give to thee life and life everlasting."[196]

On June 30, 1995, Ishvara said: "I am Ishvara. I speak on behalf of the Hindu Trinity. I may be to you in one moment Father, then Son, then Holy Spirit as defined by Shiva. This threefold flame that you acknowledge in your heart I portray to you as divine incarnation of the Trinity so that when you would look at the three plumes you would see Brahma in the blue, Vishnu in the yellow, Shiva in the pink.

"Thus you begin to converse not merely with plumes that are flames dancing but with the Trinity of God within your heart. This is the meaning of the Atman. This is the meaning of the face of the Mother in the white sphere that supports the Trinity.

"And so, wherever you call me, wherever I am, whenever you need me, I am Ishvara. And I provide for you an understanding of the Godhead that is the personality of God rather than the simple Spirit of God that is often conceived in the West as a vapor—vaporous and something that cannot be touched or worshiped, perhaps imbibed and perhaps even loved."

❖ **JESUS THE CHRIST, Avatar of the Piscean Age**

Jesus of Nazareth was and is the living Christ because he was the fullness of the incarnation of the Word. In him the threefold flame of power, wisdom and love, the Trinity of Father, Son and Holy Spirit, was God, a consuming sacred fire—three persons in one, a light to lighten all peoples.

In the average man and woman the threefold flame is one-sixteenth of an inch in height, reduced by the edict of the LORD God made at the time of Noah. Jesus Christ, the wayshower, teaches us how to expand the threefold flame within the secret chamber of the heart that we might follow his example and become the living incarnation of the Word. He shows us how to balance the energies of love, wisdom and power until we are enveloped by this threefold action of the sacred fire and we become the living witness of Father, Son and Holy Spirit.

To become the flame of God is the goal of life. Jesus, the Saviour of mankind, is here today to teach us the way, to teach us that the I AM THAT I AM is the way, the truth and the life.

Jesus first came to the earth as a volunteer with Sanat Kumara, and he has had many embodiments on earth since that time. In one of these, he reigned as emperor and high priest over a golden-age civilization on Atlantis that lasted two thousand years, from 34,550 B.C. until 32,550 B.C. This age was seventeen ages previous to our own, and it was under the sign of Cancer. Jesus was born in 33,050 B.C. and began his reign in 33,000 B.C. after the golden age had been in progress for over 1,500 years. His consort was his twin flame, whom we know as the ascended lady master Magda. They ruled because they were the highest representatives of God in embodiment in that civilization. All the people of this civilization knew and accepted God's will. Jesus and Magda did not have to impose any rules on the people because they were all in attunement with their Divine Source.

However, after Jesus had reigned for 450 years, the seeds of corruption were sown by one called Xenos, who was chief counsellor to the emperor. Finally Xenos convinced the people to revolt against the government (personified in Jesus) because the government was supposedly not supporting them. Xenos took over as leader of the government. Jesus Christ, Magda and two million loyal subjects (20 percent of the people) went to the land that later was to become Suern—India including Arabia. Half of them made their ascension at that time; the other half have continued to evolve on earth until today.

On Atlantis, the once golden-age civilization gradually descended into barbarism as the people, imperceptibly to themselves, grew dense and insensitive to life. Looting and anarchy prevailed to the point where even Xenos lost control. Over time the cities disappeared and crumbled. Barbarism reigned on Atlantis from 30,000 B.C. to 16,000 B.C., when the great civilization of Poseid arose.

After that embodiment, Jesus materialized on Atlantis and elsewhere on the planet where and when he was needed if the people's good karma and allegiance to the Godhead warranted his intercession. About 15,000 B.C., Jesus returned as the ruler, the Rai, of Atlantis. As described by Phylos the Tibetan in his book *A Dweller on Two Planets,* this great Rai appeared in the Temple of the capital, Caiphul, and caused to spring up there the Maxin, the Fire of Incal. This unfed flame burned on the altar of the temple for five thousand years. The Rai of the Maxin light ruled for 434 days. He revised the laws and provided a legal code that governed Atlantis for thousands of years to come.

After a long golden age, the civilization of Atlantis was corrupted by false priests, until "God saw that the wickedness of man was great in the earth, and that every imagination of the thoughts of his heart was only evil continually."[197] Atlantis went down in the great cataclysm that is recorded as the Flood of Noah.

In the Genesis account of Adam and Eve, we see Jesus as Abel, the son of Adam, who found favor with the LORD but was slain by his jealous brother, Cain. When Eve conceived and bore another son she called his name Seth: "For God, said she, hath appointed me another seed instead of Abel, whom Cain slew." And when to this Seth there was born a son, Enos, it is written: "Then began men to call upon the name of the LORD."[198] Thus, through the rebirth and the renewal of the spiritual seed of Christ in Seth— the reincarnated Abel—the sons and daughters of God once again had access to the mighty I AM Presence by means of his mediatorship.

Jesus came again as Joseph, the son of Jacob, who was sold into slavery in Egypt by his brethren—the same who later reembodied as his disciples. In Egypt he was accorded high honors and authority in affairs of state because of his spiritual interpretation of Pharaoh's dreams.

As Joshua, the son of Nun, Jesus felled the walls of Jericho and led the Israelites into the Promised Land. As David, he wrote the Psalms: "Thou wilt not leave my soul in hell; neither wilt thou suffer thine Holy One to see corruption."[199] As Elisha, he was the pupil of Elijah, who ascended and later, under special dispensation, reembodied as John the Baptist to prepare the way for Jesus' mission in Galilee.

Jesus came into his final incarnation having passed many initiations throughout his Eastern and Western embodiments; yet he retained the small percentage of karma that was required for his mission, and which he balanced by the time he left Palestine at age thirty-three. Jesus recognized in John the Baptist his guru Elijah, who had "come again" to prepare the way of his chela.[200]

Between the ages of twelve and thirty, Jesus studied in both outer and inner retreats of the Brotherhood at Luxor and in the Himalayas. Scrolls that describe Jesus' journey are still preserved in a monastery in a valley in Ladakh, Kashmir.[201] In India he studied under the Great Divine Director, Lord Maitreya and Lord Himalaya. It was here that he received key mantras for his mission, which he later taught to his disciples. Some of these mantras are included in "The Transfiguring Affirmations" dictated by the master Jesus to Mark Prophet.[202]

Having been a member of the Order of Zadkiel prior to his final embodiment, Jesus had learned the science of invocation and alchemy. This knowledge enabled him to change water into wine, to calm the sea, to heal the sick and to raise the dead.

After his crucifixion and resurrection, Jesus went to Kashmir, where he lived to the age of eighty-one. At the conclusion of that life, he took his ascension from the etheric retreat of Shamballa.

After his ascension, Jesus became the chohan of the sixth ray. When Sanat Kumara returned to Venus on January 1, 1956, Jesus assumed the

position of World Teacher, replacing Lord Maitreya who became the planetary Buddha.

Jesus calls us to the path of discipleship under the ascended masters. He has released a series of calls to this path, published in the book *Walking with the Master: Answering the Call of Jesus.*[203] Jesus says to those who would be his disciples in the age of Aquarius, "Greater love than this hath no man, that a man lay down his life for his friends. Blessed ones, this is not speaking of death but of a vibrant life lived—lived truly to convey the fire of my heart to all. This is the

The Ascended Master
Jesus Christ,
by Charles Sindelar

meaning of being a disciple who is called apostle, instrument and messenger of light, conveyer of that light."[204]

Jesus serves in the Arabian Retreat and with Mother Mary in the Resurrection Temple over the Holy Land. The radiance of the Christ can be drawn through the playing of his keynote, "Joy to the World."

❖ JOHANNES (POPE JOHN XXIII)

Pope John XXIII (1881–1963), now the ascended master Johannes, was one of the most beloved popes of modern times. He was renowned for his simplicity, humor, charity and warm personality. During his four-and-a-half-year reign, he brought about a new era in the Roman Catholic Church by his openness to change. He convoked the second Vatican Council and encouraged progressive trends in Roman Catholic thought.

Pope John XXIII

Pope John XXIII used a technique to resolve important issues with others. Heros and Amora have described how we can also use this technique: "The night before you meet with people on any matter, offer a prayer on behalf of all who will be attending the meeting. Especially call that those points of discussion you expect to be difficult be resolved harmoniously."

Before retiring, call to the guardian angel and the Holy Christ Self of all, and "ask that all parties who will discuss the matter on the morrow be taken to the Retreat of the Divine Mother to review it the night before." Give the calls "for the enlightenment of souls and the binding of the dweller-on-the-threshold (i.e., the not-self), which would deter them through pride or stubbornness from making right decisions for right action. If you anticipate having to deal with attitudes of bigotry, prejudice, persecution or racism that come from jaded minds, invoke the violet flame the night before to consume [these attitudes] before they cast a spell on your meeting....

"The Holy Christ Self (who is often referred to as the guardian angel) will overshadow and direct each one and prepare all to reach a consensus from the highest level. And when you sit down to have that meeting the next day, simply acknowledge the presence of...the Higher Self. And see how in those meetings divine resolution, human resolution and legal resolution can come about because you have made your spiritual preparations."[205]

The ascended master Johannes has told us that he wears at inner levels "the mantle of the spirit of oneness, the spirit of unity in the true Church," because of his role in drawing together all Christians.[206] It was this master who, on February 10, 1974, announced the formal inauguration of Church Universal and Triumphant and dedicated it to be the open door of the Divine Mother to receive individuals from every walk of life.

He has explained the purpose of the Church in this way: "Blessed ones, some of you know that the name Church Universal and Triumphant has long been accepted as the name of the Lord's Church in heaven. Thus, you see, the founding purpose of this Church is to bring that kingdom of our

Lord, his heaven and his Church, into universal manifestation on earth."[207]

The Church comes forth so that the Mother flame can be enshrined upon the altar; and with the Mother flame enshrined upon the altar, the Church is the magnet that draws the children of God back to the ritual of ordered service and worship whereby they pass through the gate of the victory of the ascension.

The ascended master Johannes calls us all to the path of the ascension: "I am waiting for you, for the hour of your graduation from earth's schoolroom. And in the hour of your ascension, I will be standing with the Lord Jesus, with Mary and Saint Germain, with Lanello and Archangel Michael to receive you into the company of the ascended saints of the true Church. Do we have a date? ["Yes!"] I will keep my appointment."[208]

❖ **JOHN THE BAPTIST,** *See* **Elijah**

❖ **JOHN THE BELOVED, Closest Disciple of Jesus**

John the Beloved was the closest disciple of Jesus the Christ. He authored the Book of Revelation, which was dictated by Jesus, "sent and signified by his angel." He who best understood the mystical teachings of the Christ ascended at the close of that embodiment, the only one of the twelve apostles to do so.

Under the guardianship of Joseph, the protector of Mary and Jesus, John and his brother James received training in the Essene community. Having beheld Jesus enter the inner temple while he was worshiping without, John sensed the destiny of the Christ. Years later when the call came, he was ready to follow his Lord and Master.

John's magnetization of the love ray was the greatest of any of the disciples. This love he expressed not only for Jesus, but also for the light of the Christ within him and for his mission, which he, above all, understood and shared. John has told us that his love for Jesus was so great that in order to make his ascension he had to learn the meaning of impersonal love.

John was the only disciple who did not forsake Jesus as he was dying on the cross. As Jesus saw John standing nearby with Mary, he said to her, "Woman, behold thy son!" and said to John, "Behold thy Mother!"[209] Jesus thereby acknowledged John as his spiritual brother, as worthy to be the son of his own mother—and therefore, he elevated John to the level of Christ.

John embodied the full person of the Christ Self, and unless this had been true, Jesus would not have created that relationship, because Mary was Mother in the archetypal sense of Universal Mother—she embodied the Mother flame. When Jesus called John her son, he was speaking not just in the physical sense but also in the universal sense of the Son of God, the Son of the Divine Mother, whose representative she was.

John stayed in Jerusalem for some time during the persecutions following Jesus' resurrection. After the martyrdom of Peter and Paul, John settled in Ephesus, the greatest city of Asia Minor, where Paul had centered his missionary activities. There is a tradition, which is confirmed by Tertullian and Jerome, that during the reign of Domitian, John was taken to Rome where an attempt to put him to death in a cauldron of boiling oil was miraculously thwarted. (This is the test of fire that was also faced by Shadrach, Meshach and Abednego.[210]) He emerged from the cauldron unharmed and was then banished to the island of Patmos. Here he received and recorded the Book of Revelation.

After the death of Domitian in the year A.D. 96, John could return to Ephesus, and many believe that he wrote his Gospel and three epistles at that time, when he was in his nineties. John is said to have passed his last years at Ephesus, and to have died there at a great age, outliving all the other apostles. According to some, he simply "disappeared"—was translated like Elijah or "assumed" into heaven as was the Blessed Virgin. Others testify to the miracles wrought from the dust of his tomb.

In an earlier embodiment, John was Benjamin, the youngest brother of Joseph, the idle dreamer, who later embodied as Jesus. Of his eleven brothers (all of whom served as his disciples in his final embodiment), Joseph loved Benjamin the most.

John uses as his symbol a purple Maltese Cross superimposed upon a pink Maltese Cross with gold radiance surrounding it. The flame focused in his retreat in the etheric realms above the state of Arizona is purple and gold. Through this flame, which focuses the power of divine love in its four phases, he teaches the mastery of fire, air, water and earth as the four aspects of the nature of God.

This hope is also held by beloved John and the brothers and sisters who serve in his retreat, who teach the impersonal impersonality of divine love through the mastery of the fire element, the impersonal personality of divine love through the mastery of the air element, the personal personality of divine love through the mastery of the water element, and the personal impersonality of divine love through the mastery of the earth element.*

---

*These four aspects of God's consciousness correspond to God as Father, Son, Mother and Holy Spirit.

Students who desire to study these four aspects of the nature of God and how they can solve the problems of our civilization that are the result of the perversions of the love ray on the planet, may ask to be taken to John the Beloved's retreat while they sleep.

❖ **JOHN XXIII, POPE,** *See* Johannes

❖ **JOPHIEL AND CHRISTINE, Archangels of the Second Ray**

Jophiel and Christine are the archangel and archeia of the second ray of wisdom and illumination. These twin flames amplify the Christ consciousness within angels, elementals and men. Jophiel and Christine serve with the World Teachers, Jesus and Kuthumi, to illumine mankind's understanding of cosmic law. The name Jophiel means "beauty of God."

The retreat of Jophiel and Christine is in the etheric realm over the plains of Central China, south of the Great Wall near Lanchow. From the yellow flame of illumination focused here since the first golden ages, have come not only the "yellow" race and the Yellow River, but also the wisdom of Confucius, Lao-tse and the civilizations of ancient China. The wisdom of ancient China reached great heights long before there was even a stirring of culture in the West. In those days China's rulers held mystical contact with the hierarchs of Jophiel's retreat. As long as these initiates held the mandate of heaven (the divine right of rulership) and ruled the "middle kingdom," the civilizations of China grew and prospered under the radiance of the golden sun of cosmic wisdom.

Jophiel and Christine and the angels of wisdom teach you how to contact your Higher Self. Jophiel says that you need to educate the heart, then the mind and then the soul. He says: "Think of the ancients who walked the earth and knew the thoughts of God *when God thought them.*"[211]

Angels of Jophiel and Christine unveil the mysteries of God, and they expose the infamies of men and fallen angels. They are here to reveal what is hidden in government, science, education, medicine, food, health, AIDS and other terminal diseases, the war on drugs, pollution and the environment, the effects of music on evolution and in just about everything that touches our daily lives.

Jophiel and Christine have come on a mission to deliver us from profound levels of ignorance that are settling over every nation, starting with the earliest grades of children in school. In our time, the goal of education on earth has been to accelerate the computer of the mental body. Direct communication with God through the threefold flame and the heart chakra is wanting.

Angels are filled with joy in their service, and they have a fierce loyalty to God that has kept them from swerving from their path of light. Anchored within their hearts—even though they be angels of illumination—is a tremendous love for mankind that keeps them working constantly in an atmosphere that is most uncomfortable to their pure vibrations. However, their only motive is to glorify the Father and raise his sons back to the true estate they once knew and enjoyed.

"I would like to point out to you, then," Jophiel says, "that there is a method whereby you can keep your own consciousness high, and that method is to feel God's love anchored in your heart simultaneously while you feel God's love and wisdom anchored within your mind. It is possible, then, for you to utilize the center of your heart as a sun of divine love and to use your brain as a radiant focus of the power of illumination's flame so that all density is indeed removed from your consciousness.

"The cerebrum and the cerebellum are as the great Milky Way is in the vast starry universe. These are intended to be mighty continents of power anchored within the head area of every man [and woman] whereby great currents of illumination may flow through those wondrous folds of your precious brains, creating therein a golden flame of illumination and removing the so-called gray matter from human consciousness, which is but the distortion of the pure white light into the qualities of gray by reason of the addition of flecks of shadow created by human ideas of great density and opacity."[212]

If you call to the angels of illumination, they can release to you mighty currents of light that are the mercury diamond-shining mind of God. These light rays can flow across your brain, scintillating as the sunlight upon the water and remove from you the density that has been created by reason of human thought and feeling that has become the vibration of jealousy, doubt, fear, dishonor and a lack of integrity.

On September 9, 1963, Archangel Jophiel released the fiat that resulted in the exposure of the hazards of tobacco and the report of the Surgeon General of the United States concerning the harmful effects of smoking. Jophiel explains to those who are addicted to smoking that the use of nicotine creates a density in the brain preventing the divine intelligence from flashing forth through the receptacles of the brain. When people set aside the smoking habit, they will find that this will increase the flow of spiritual illumination to them through the brain and central nervous system.

Smog and atmospheric pollution also act to render the golden flame of illumination inefficient in our brain consciousness. Jophiel tells us that when men understand the proper use of atomic energy and when they apply themselves to the heart of God with a greater diligence, they will be able to terminate the release of smoke and the burdens on the environment that cause so much misery to millions.

Archangel Jophiel is specifically concerned about the deplorable state of education. His angels are relentless in their warfare against ignorance, mental density and mediocrity as these affect the minds of educators and students and lower the standards of institutions of learning. He says that these negative attitudes "detract from the crispness of the Christ-qualities that belong to and are the inheritance of the children of the Sun."[213]

The archeia Christine says, "Call to me to intercede before the Cosmic Christ in your behalf to release advanced teaching methods to the parents, teachers and sponsors of youth. Will you not pray that the World Teachers and the hierarchies of illumination might release to instructors in every field, as well as to yourselves, new and advanced methods of teaching all subjects. We have released methods through Maria Montessori and many other educators. There is so much more we can deliver to those who will listen."[214]

Jophiel will teach you how you can commune with the mind of God and experience self-knowledge. The angels of wisdom are ready and waiting to help you, at your signal, to absorb the elements of the mind of God. Archangel Jophiel once remarked, "Do you know that a single mind, transformed by the mind of Christ, is a catalyst for quickening the minds of the population of an entire planet? That is what the Christ incarnate, the Buddha incarnate, can do."[215]

❖ **JUSTICE, GODDESS OF,** *See* **Portia**

❖ **JUSTINA, Twin Flame of Mighty Victory**

Justina is the twin flame of Mighty Victory. On January 1, 1978, in Pasadena, California, beloved Justina dictated for the first time. In this landmark address, titled "The Forgiveness of Eve," she said:

"Now I step forth, for Almighty God has weighed these several systems of worlds and the evolutions therein, and Almighty God has pronounced that certain evolutions of lightbearers do now contain within themselves enough consciousness of the victory of the feminine ray that I might stand forth and be with my Beloved the focal point for the Father-Mother God in total awareness of the victory of evolutions in these systems. Beloved ones, the one whom you call Mighty Victory is indeed androgynous, as I am, as is Alpha, as is Omega. But as we come forth together, descending into lower and lower dimensions of awareness, we bring a greater complement of the spectrum of that cosmic polarity as a polarity of manifestation to those of lesser evolution. Therefore, though one may be sufficient in the whole, always twin flames are required for the transmutation of a cosmos."

We can claim the sense of victory from Justina. Saint Germain tells us how: "Blessed hearts, the only reason to get out of bed in the morning is for the victory! There is no other reason to get out of bed! Hear me. You must have the victorious spirit. You must claim it from Mighty Victory. You must claim it from Justina and all of the hosts of heaven!

"We are sick and tired of the nonvictory consciousness! There is a victory available to you and you and you and every one of you. And you must have it! You must will to have it! You must desire to have it! You must shout your fiat and determine: 'I will be God's will of victory in manifestation today, this hour and every day!'

"Get up for the victory! Go to bed for the victory! Work for the victory! Eat for the victory! Be joyous and happy for the victory. But always and always and always give the earth, give yourself, give all whom you meet that victory spin! I say, do it and be glorious about it, be triumphant about it, be magnanimous about it, but be it!

"So! So now you know why I have come in the hour of victory. [It is] because I desire the full momentum of Lord Maitreya to be in this Inner Retreat that he might have his day and have his say. And I tell you, there is more fire and determination in the entire Spirit of the Great White Brotherhood, in this messenger and in you than there is the spirit of defeat in the fallen ones.

"Do you understand? He who has the greater sense of victory will win! And we are going to win!"[216]

❖ **JUSTINIUS, Captain of Seraphic Bands**

Holy Justinius heads the seraphic order of angels. He is known as the Captain of Seraphic Bands. He serves with Serapis Bey and the legions of purity in his command. Justinius describes his order of angels as fiery beings who, with their bodies and their wings, form concentric rings around the Great Central Sun. They absorb the light of the spiritual Sun and deliver it to the far-flung evolutions of the universe, including earth, always trailing clouds of glory.

Saint Francis had a vision of a seraph

when he received the stigmata. While in a state of ecstasy, he saw a seraph with six wings descend from heaven. The third book of Enoch records that the seraphim "radiate like the splendor of the throne of glory."[217]

The only biblical reference to the seraphim is in the Book of Isaiah. Isaiah had a vision of the Lord sitting on a throne, and above the Lord were seraphim, each with six wings. They cried out to each other: "Holy, holy, holy, is the LORD of hosts: the whole earth is full of his glory." One seraph placed a live coal from the altar upon Isaiah's mouth and said, "Thine iniquity is taken away, and thy sin purged."[218] This initiation prepared Isaiah for his mission.

You can call to the seraphim daily to purge you of all that is not a part of your God-reality. Ask them to prepare you for your mission in life. Then work with them daily until you have accomplished it. Consider them comrades, brothers, friends.

Seraphim are among the greatest healers. Justinius says, If you really want to get rid of your ailments, call upon the seraphim! "They may release the sacred fire, purge and purify, renew your bloodstream, give you eternal youth. You have but to call for it and to live the path of one who is ascending."[219] He has also urged us to "call upon the seraphim for the healing of loved ones and all throughout the world who suffer burdens of the heart, the mind and the soul. Likewise, call for the healing of the planet and all sentient life. For as you know, the planet itself is diseased. And its inhabitants suffer both conscious and unconscious pain in level upon level of being."[220]

Sanat Kumara, the Ancient of Days, told us that each one who has the threefold flame of God and the worship thereof would have four seraphim to command in Jesus' name. He said, "Send them on your missions. They come to protect you and seal you from...world karma that is descending."[221]

The seraphim are here to help you achieve the ultimate success of your reunion with God through the ascension. Justinius asks us to consider the goal of the ascension and "not to postpone it to another lifetime or some undefined future."[222] You are ascending as you give back to God in word and deed and in the flow of the Holy Spirit the energy he has given you. You achieve this flow magnificently by the science of the spoken Word.

The seraphim are as "flaming streaks of fire passing through the atmosphere,...like cosmic rays they can pass through the flesh form of man, through his thoughts and feelings."[223] The seraphim are mighty angels who possess the quality of "cosmic penetrability," the power to penetrate the densest human consciousness and to transmute that substance instantaneously. They can absorb toxins from our bodies, our minds and our emotions, and they leave behind a residue of purity.

Justinius explains the service of his seraphim: "We come to make you white and clean, to make you whole." The seraphim "come to minister to the soul. And so they come passing through the microcosm, and their fire also burns the cause of disease, of poison, of the toxins that have been passing through you for so many years in the food, in the water, in the tobacco and the alcohol that mankind imbibe. Who, pray tell, will keep souls alive and evolving in these body temples if not the angels who come to minister, who come to uplift? I tell you, mankind have been spared again and again and again the last plagues and all forms of chaos and disturbance and imbalance and insanity by the very presence of the angels.

"Now hear this! When they pass through your forms as spirits of living fire, they leave, as it were, the calling card of their identity. That calling card is a focus of fire tingeing your aura with the hue of the Central Sun, tingeing the aura with a halo. And for a while, then, there is that glow, that essence, that sense of well-being, that inner warmth."[224]

Justinius first became known to the outer world when he wrote the Seraphic Meditations in the *Dossier on the Ascension,* by Serapis Bey. Speaking of their service, Serapis has said: "I know of no power more valiantly capable of assisting anyone into his own ascension in the light than the transmutative efforts toward Cosmic Christ purity that are emitted by the Seraphic Hosts. In our retreat at Luxor the meditations upon the seraphim are a very important part of our spiritual instruction. Jesus himself spent a great deal of time in communion with the seraphic hosts. This developed in him the superior power whereby he could cast out demons and take dominion over the outer world of form."[225]

You can ask for the protection of the armour of Justinius, Captain of Seraphic Bands. Call for and visualize daily the silvery, platinum and white color of the armour and helmet of the seraphim. Call for the great electronic fire rings of the seraphim to surround and seal you.

"Rêve Angélique," or "Angel's Dream," by Anton Rubinstein, reflects the musical rhythm and harmonies that are in the center of our cosmos and the action of the seraphim as they form circles and tiers focusing the energies of God around the Central Sun.

❖ KALI, *See* Shiva

❖ THE KARMIC BOARD, Adjudicators of Karma for This System of Worlds

The Karmic Board is a body of eight ascended masters who are assigned the responsibility to dispense justice to this system of worlds, adjudicating karma, mercy and judgment on behalf of every lifestream. The Lords of Karma are divine intercessors who serve under the twenty-four elders as mediators between a people and their karma.

All souls must pass before the Karmic Board before and after each incarnation on earth, receiving their assignment and karmic allotment for each lifetime beforehand and the review of their performance at its conclusion. Through the Keeper of the Scrolls and the recording angels, the Lords of Karma have access to the complete records of every lifestream's incarnations on earth. They determine who shall embody, as well as when and where. They assign souls to families and communities, measuring out the weights of karma that must be balanced as the "jot and tittle" of the Law. The Karmic Board, acting in consonance with the individual I AM Presence and Christ Self, determines when the soul has earned the right to be free from the wheel of karma and the round of rebirth.

The Karmic Board consists of the Great Divine Director (representing the first ray), the Goddess of Liberty (second ray), Ascended Lady Master Nada (third ray), Elohim Cyclopea (fourth ray), Pallas Athena, the Goddess of Truth (fifth ray), Portia, Goddess of Justice (sixth ray) and Kuan Yin, the Goddess of Mercy (seventh ray). Recently Vairochana, one of the five Dhyani Buddhas, became the eighth member of the Karmic Board.

Out of his great mercy, God has anointed these beings to act as mediators between the perfection of the Law and the imperfection of those who have departed from the state of grace. The Karmic Board serves, then, at the level of the Christ Self of mankind, daily weighing the balance of mankind's use of energy Above and below.

The Lords of Karma adjudicate the cycles of individual karma, group karma, national karma and world karma, always seeking to apply the Law in the way that will give people the best opportunity to make spiritual progress. When the Karmic Lords release a spiral of karma for the planet, the entire nature kingdom plays a part in its descent, which is always according to the law of cycles.

The elementals have been the foremost instruments of the karmic return of mankind's discord. The earliest memory we have of this phenomenon is the sinking of the continent of Lemuria beneath the Pacific many thousands of years ago for the karma of the abuse of the sacred fire by priests and priestesses at the altars of God.

Changes in climatic conditions (as well as storm, flood, fire, tornado and cataclysm) are brought about as the result of man's misuse of the creative power of the Holy Spirit. Through these periodic disturbances in nature, when Atlas shrugs off human discord, the balance of the four elements is restored and the four lower bodies of the planet are purified and realigned.

Twice a year, at winter and summer solstice, the Lords of Karma meet at the Royal Teton Retreat to review petitions from unascended mankind. Traditionally, students of the masters write personal petitions to the Karmic Board requesting grants of energy, dispensations and sponsorship for constructive projects and endeavors. The letters are consecrated and burned. The angels then carry the etheric matrix of these letters to the Royal Teton Retreat, where they are read by the Lords of Karma.

Students who are requesting assistance may offer to perform a particular service or work or make a commitment to certain prayers and decrees that the masters can use as "seed money" for something they desire to see accomplished in the world. They may also offer a portion of their causal body as energy for the masters to use, but such an offer must be approved by the Lords of Karma. The exact percentage will be determined by the I AM Presence and Holy Christ Self.

❖ **THE KEEPER OF THE SCROLLS**

The Keeper of the Scrolls is a cosmic being in charge of the akashic records of this galaxy, the impressions of all that has ever transpired in the planes of Matter.

Of his service, the Keeper of the Scrolls has said: "As Keeper of the Scrolls, I want to tell you that I have an awesome responsibility! Fortunately, the eternal Father has given me many able assistants [the recording angels]. I am here to tell you that there is not one jot nor one tittle of energy that passes through any of your lifestreams that is not recorded on the eternal scrolls. Fortunately, by the power of the sacred fire and the love of beloved Saint Germain, there has been established a special qualification of the cosmic law whereby those who use the violet fire faithfully have an erasing action that takes place on the scrolls. And through the action of the flame, their karma is removed almost as soon as it is created.

"I wish to point out to you, beloved ones, that each time there is a removal and transmutation of karma, a temporary record is made of it. If individuals will continually persist in repeating the same offenses against the great cosmic law over and over and over again, there comes a time when their actions are called to the attention of the Lords of Karma. Then, a specific activity of the Law is brought to bear upon the lifestream whereby all of their karma becomes accountable for balance. For it is absolutely necessary that mankind shall face their own human miscreations! This action is brought about in order to insure all lifestreams that they will not continually turn toward the left-handed path. It is a curbing action, designed to bring them back to the right hand of God and to the right hand of fellowship. It is wholly an action of divine love."[226]

The Keeper of the Scrolls maintains an extensive library and research facilities so that at any time the record of a lifestream who may be petitioning for energy, opportunity or a dispensation from the Lords of Karma may be reviewed. Thus, one of the duties of his office is to provide the ascended masters and the Karmic Board with a resumé of the embodiments of an evolving soul about whom they may inquire.

At Easter 1962, in his first dictation, the Keeper of the Scrolls explained that he has "a dual parchment for each lifestream. One is magnetized of the sacred fire itself and carries the complete life pattern for the individual upon it. It is unalterable and irrevocable: it is the law of life for you! There is a smaller parchment, which is placed on top of the permanent one. It is much thinner and somewhat plastic in substance. It contains the complete engrammatic record of your life from the time you first came forth into individualized consciousness. Every mark of your being, every thought that you have entertained is recorded there.

"I do not gaze upon these scrolls unless I am specifically requested to do so by the Karmic Board. This occurs when an assessment of a lifestream is desired in order to ascertain their opportunities or the need for temporarily lowering the karmic hammer upon them. When it therefore becomes necessary to make such an evaluation, I assure you that I immediately turn my eyes to the violet fire of transmutation in order to erase from my consciousness at once all that is written upon the scroll by the infamy of human consciousness."[227]

When the soul comes before the Karmic Board to give an accounting at the close of each embodiment, the Keeper of the Scrolls or one of his representatives reads to the Lords of Karma the records taken from the Book of Life. The Keeper of the Scrolls also reads the records of those lifestreams who have come to the Last Judgment at the Court of the Sacred Fire on Sirius, and in that position, he alone is permitted to stand opposite the throne of Almighty God.

When the time comes for the round of embodiments to be finished and the soul to make his ascension, the Keeper of the Scrolls or one of his assistants reads the records of the lifestream in honor of his achievement. The Keeper of the Scrolls, acting with the individual's own Christ Self, then puts to the torch those records of mortal involvement that have bound the soul to the earth. Thereafter, he says, "in the eternal records of God there will remain only the record of eternal perfection; thus, in the future lifestream, a perfect individualized outpicturing of God-manifestation, man made in the image and likeness of God."[228]

❖ KRISHNA

Krishna is a divine being, an incarnation of the Godhead, an avatar, and he is one of the most celebrated Indian heroes of all time. He has captured the imagination and devotion of Hindus everywhere in his many forms—whether as a frolicking, mischievous child, as the lover of shepherdesses, or as the friend and wise counsellor of the mighty warrior Arjuna.

Krishna is known as the eighth incarnation of Vishnu, the Second Person of the Hindu Triad. His story is told in the Bhagavad Gita, the most popular religious work of India, composed between the fifth and second centuries B.C. and part of the great Indian epic, the Mahabharata.

Bhagavad Gita means "Song of God." It is written as a dialogue between Krishna and Arjuna. Krishna describes himself as "the Lord of all that breathes" and "the Lord who abides within the heart of all beings," meaning one who is in union with God, one who has attained that union that is God. He says: "When goodness grows weak, when evil increases, my Spirit arises on earth. In every age I come back to deliver the holy, to destroy the sin of the sinner, to establish righteousness."[229]

Arjuna is Krishna's friend and disciple. The setting is the eve of a great battle to determine who will rule the kingdom. Krishna is to be the charioteer for Arjuna. Just before the battle begins, Arjuna falters because he will have to fight and kill his own kinsmen. Krishna explains to Arjuna that he must enter the battle because it is his dharma—his duty or his reason for being. He is a member of the warrior caste, and come what may, he must fight.

The traditional Hindu interpretation of the battle is twofold. First, the battle represents the struggle Arjuna must engage in to fulfill his dharma and to reclaim the kingdom. Second, the battle represents the war he must wage within himself between good and evil forces—his higher and lower natures.

Krishna teaches Arjuna about the four yogas, or paths of union with

God, and says that all the yogas should be practiced. The four yogas are knowledge (jnana yoga), meditation (raja yoga), work (karma yoga) and love and devotion (bhakti yoga). By self-knowledge, by meditation on the God within, by working the works of God to balance karma and increase good karma and by giving loving devotion, we fulfill the four paths of the four lower bodies—the memory body, the mental body, the desire body and the physical body.

We can see Arjuna as the archetype of the soul of each of us and Krishna as the charioteer of our soul, one with our Higher Self, our Holy Christ Self. We can see him occupying the position of the Holy Christ Self on the Chart of Your Divine Self (see p. 532), as the Mediator between the soul and the I AM Presence. He is universal Christ consciousness.

When we send devotion to Krishna through mantra and sacred song, we open a highway of our love to the heart of Krishna, and he opens the other half of the highway. He sends back our devotion multiplied by his manyfold.

Lord Krishna has pledged to help heal the inner child as we sing mantras and bhajans to him. His request is to visualize his Presence over you at the age when you experienced any emotional trauma, physical pain, mental pain, from this or a previous lifetime. You can ask for these events in your life to pass before your third eye like slides moving across a screen or even a motion picture. Assess the age you were at the moment of the trauma. Then, visualize Lord Krishna at that age—six months old, six years old, twelve years old, fifty years old—and see him standing over you and over the entire situation.

If there are other figures in this scene through whom the pain has come, see the Presence of Lord Krishna around them also. Give the devotional mantra and song until you are pouring such love to Lord Krishna that he is taking your love, multiplying it through his heart, passing it back through you and transmuting that scene and that record. If you see Lord Krishna superimposed over every party to the problem, to the anger, to the burden, you can understand that you can affirm in your heart that there really is no Reality but God. Only God is Real, and God is placing his Presence over that situation through the personification of himself in Lord Krishna.[230]

❖ KRISTINE, LADY

In her final incarnation, the ascended lady master Kristine was embodied as Florence Jeannette Miller. Florence was born on February 27, 1936, in Krugersdorp, South Africa. She grew up in South Africa and the Belgian Congo and received most of her high school education through American

Florence Miller

correspondence courses. At the age of 16, she and her parents moved to Brussels, Belgium. She later worked in London and South Africa as a secretary before starting college. She received an Associate in Arts degree from Blackburn College in Carlinville, Illinois and a Bachelor of Arts degree in French from the University of Wisconsin. After college, she worked in Toronto, Canada, for several years as a research assistant for the Canadian Education Association.

Florence found the teachings of the ascended masters in 1968, while living in Albuquerque, New Mexico. The minute she saw photographs of Mark and Elizabeth Prophet, she recognized them as true messengers of God. In October 1968, she joined the staff of The Summit Lighthouse, where she later served as head of the publishing department and as a member of the Board of Directors of Church Universal and Triumphant. She was a pillar of strength and inspiration to all who knew her, always bringing self-discipline, creativity, dedication and a spirit of joy to her work.

While serving on the staff of The Summit Lighthouse, Florence met and married the Reverend Norman Thomas Miller. Tom has said of her: "She was just an incredible light—a magnificent devotee, not only of the teachings but of the messengers personally. Helping them to fulfill their role was her greatest joy. She thrived on challenges...and always kept her poise through any difficult situation. It was a won-  derful thing to behold.... She had that flame of accomplishment and victory and moving ahead. She was balanced, beautiful...a great servant of light. The fervor of her dedication to the cause of world freedom and enlightenment set a high standard for all to emulate. Her devotion to God was a rare gift. It told me she had touched the hem of Christ's garment....

"She was the kind of person who, in the midst of many responsibilities, would always respond spontaneously with her heart to people's personal problems or any situation that would crop up in the course of the day.... I was extremely privileged...to be married to the blessed Florence."

On September 19, 1979, at the age of 43, Florence passed from the screen of life as a result of a brain tumor. The next morning, her soul fulfilled at inner levels the initiation of the ascension. She is now known and loved as the ascended lady master Kristine. The title Lady Kristine had been given to her by Saint Germain on July 5, 1970.

Sanat Kumara proclaimed her "the example and forerunner on the path of the ruby ray." He said of her that "her path for many centuries had been that of surrender, self-sacrifice, service and selflessness guided by the ascended masters under the four cosmic forces. Always living for the mission of the guru and my messengers, she transcended earthly modes and manifestations. Her light filled the cups of consciousness to overflowing, creating new streams of immersion in Christ's love for all following the breezes of her billowing bridal garment."[231]

In a previous incarnation, Lady Kristine was embodied as the sixteenth-century Catholic mystic Saint Teresa of Avila. In 1998 Raphael and Mother Mary announced that she had become a bodhisattva.

Teresa of Avila

In 1983 Lady Kristine said, "I am a flower in the field of life. One day the Saviour passed by and plucked me to his heart, and I became the special one that he would no longer leave in the field. I would miss my fellows and even shed a tear, longing to be in the tall grasses with them in their play and in their labor. But in his heart he took me and to another field where I saw another harvest—Elysian Fields where lilies grow and other saints that you and I have known.

"Thus, beloved, the parting is the regathering. And we may all understand that being plucked to the Saviour's heart—this special offering will come to each and every one in time and in space and beyond. And when the hour comes, as you may anticipate your own victory, you will know that all who have gone before you, the blessed friends of light and the saints, have all become a bouquet in the heart of the living Saviour. And the Lord Jesus Christ, who has taken us to himself, presents his bouquet to the Mother of the World. Therefore is our preaching and our teaching not in vain. For, after all, our goal in ascending is to be the offering of the Christ unto the Blessed Virgin."[232]

❖ **K-17, Head of the Cosmic Secret Service.**

"K-17" is the code name for the ascended master who heads the Cosmic Secret Service. Its members are devotees of the All-Seeing Eye of God. They use their God-vision to warn the citizens of cosmos of threats to the security of the individualization of the God flame—threats to life and liberty, threats to the governments of the world and to the family as the basic unit of the Aquarian society.

The members of the Cosmic Secret Service are the guardians of the destiny of liberty in America and in every nation on earth. Because of the nature of their service, K-17 and his co-workers are very close to the physical octave. They often appear in physical form as the guardians of right action midst chaos and crisis as they assist members of the various security agencies of the nations of the world. Sometimes they actually work under-cover, assuming the appearance of those whose ranks and organizations they would penetrate.

K-17 explains that his legions "have dedicated themselves to be those members of hierarchy who are the closest to the physical octave and its physical vibration.... It has been said of me that I make more physical appearances in the halls of governments and among the leaders of nations than any other ascended master. This is because of the dispensation of the legions in the Cosmic Secret Service to work so close to mankind that they actually feel tangibly our presence, and thus in times of danger their fears are allayed because they feel the presence of that heavenly help that is always forthcoming when there is dedication to the honor flame."[233]

K-17 employs a protective forcefield known as a "ring-pass-not," which is actually a ring of white fire that may be tinged with the colors of the rays according to the requirements of the hour. He draws this circle of living flame around individuals and places to protect and to seal the identity and forcefield of those dedicated in the service of the light.

Both K-17 and his sister were able to maintain life in their physical bodies for over three hundred years prior to their ascensions in the 1930s. Continuing their evolution and service to embodied mankind, they now maintain a villa in Paris and focuses in other parts of the world for the training of unascended chelas.

K-17 frequently visits the executive offices of the United States Government in a physical body and works closely with members of the FBI. He is equally familiar with the Kremlin, although they are not aware of his true identity.

In 1973, K-17 described the work of his legions and how we can help them. He said, "My legions are agents of the Cosmic Christ, and they are ever on the alert to search out those manifestations that are subversive against the Christ and the unfolding Buddhic consciousness in mankind.... My legions have computers recording all types of information on all types of people, for we must be ready, as we serve with the Keeper of the Scrolls, to provide any ascended master at any time with what you would call a dossier on a lifestream." The ascended masters use this information to determine a person's aptitude for a specific job they would assign him.

"We do have openings in our ranks for those who would participate, by the use of the All-Seeing Eye of God with the help of Cyclopea, in calling to the attention of hierarchy the persons and conditions, the organizations and happenings that are not in keeping with the Law and that are... a threat to the advancement of the light upon the planet. You know that God is omniscient. But God's omniscience is manifest through his awareness of himself in man. God uses your hands and feet. He also uses your eyes. And thus it is not out of order for those in embodiment to call to the attention of hierarchy conditions that are in the making and on the drawing boards that require the seal of white fire—the ring-pass-not.

"I desire also to acquaint you with the fact that in your service with the legions of K-17, you may don the cloak of invisibility. The cloak of invisibility is a forcefield that can actually render you invisible as you walk in dangerous passages and along the highways in the service of the Brotherhood. But I ask you to remember when you desire to be seen...to request of your Christ Self that the cloak of invisibility be removed....

"There are definitely times, as you will learn from my legions, when it is important to walk the earth incognito. When you realize you are in the camp of the enemy and you are there to gather information and to learn what you can learn for the sake of the light, then you remain in the folds of the cloak of invisibility and your very conscience and soul tell you that silence is golden, that discretion is the better part of valor."[234]

There are many in embodiment who serve with the Cosmic Secret Service. This is because many ascended masters who serve on the councils of the Great White Brotherhood have not been embodied recently. Once they ascend, they are no longer in touch with the world situation and contemporary society in the same measure that they were when they were embodied on earth. While they possess the power of tuning in to mankind, they don't spend any more of their energy than necessary to accomplish their service.

The unascended branch of the Cosmic Secret Service assembles information on specific cases, writes reports on world situations and offers opinions as to what should be done about certain matters. The reports of the various agents are put together and examined. The masters compare their own views with the suggestions of the unascended agents. In most cases, they pass on the results in concise form to the Karmic Board. The final actions of the Brotherhood are based, then, to some degree, on the intelligence gathered by those in embodiment.

In 1977, Lanello revealed that he had worked with K-17 for many centuries prior to his ascension. These two masters continue to work together, and in 1996 they delivered a report on the world scene requesting that the students give calls to Cyclopea to expose and prevent attacks on the nation of America.

K-17 and the legions in his command should be called upon to expose by the power of the All-Seeing Eye those forces and plots that would undermine Saint Germain's plan for God-government in the golden age. His flame is teal green and white. He is often simply referred to as "Friend."

❖ **KUAN YIN, Goddess of Mercy**

Kuan Yin is revered in Buddhism as the compassionate Saviouress, the Bodhisattva of Mercy. Beloved as a mother figure and divine mediatrix who is close to the daily affairs of her devotees, Kuan Yin's role as Buddhist Madonna has been compared to that of Mary the mother of Jesus in the West. Throughout the Far East, devotees seek her guidance and succor in every area of life. Altars dedicated to Kuan Yin can be found in temples, homes and wayside grottoes.

Kuan Yin

The name Kuan Shih Yin, as she is often called, means "the one who regards, looks on, or hears the sounds of the world." According to legend, Kuan Yin was about to enter heaven but paused on the threshold as the cries of the world reached her ears.

Kuan Yin is revered as protectress of women, sailors, merchants, craftsmen, those under criminal prosecution and those desiring progeny. There is an implicit trust in Kuan Yin's saving grace and healing powers. Many believe that even the simple recitation of her name will bring her instantly to the scene. *Kuan Yin's Crystal Rosary*[235] contains her mantras and is a powerful means of invoking her intercession.

For centuries, Kuan Yin has epitomized the great ideal of Mahayana Buddhism in her role as *bodhisattva*—literally "a being of bodhi, or enlightenment," who is destined to become a Buddha but has foregone the bliss of nirvana with a vow to save all children of God. Kuan Yin has taken the bodhisattva vow to work with the evolutions of this planet and this solar system to show them the way of the teachings of the ascended masters.

Kuan Yin was worshiped in China before the advent of Buddhism and thereafter adopted by Buddhists as an incarnation of Avalokiteshvara (Padmapani). Devotees invoke the bodhisattva's power and merciful intercession with the mantra *Om Mani Padme Hum*—"Hail to the jewel in the lotus!" or, as it has also been interpreted, "Hail to Avalokiteshvara, who is the jewel in the heart of the lotus of the devotee's heart!"

According to legend, Avalokiteshvara was born from a ray of white light that Amitabha, the Buddha of Boundless Light, emitted from his right eye as he was lost in ecstasy. Thus Avalokiteshvara, or Kuan Yin, is regarded as the "reflex" of Amitabha—a further emanation or embodiment of *maha karuna* (great compassion), the quality that Amitabha embodies. Devotees believe that Kuan Yin, as the merciful redemptress, expresses Amitabha's compassion in a more direct and personal way and that prayers to her are answered more quickly.

It is widely believed that Kuan Yin took embodiment as the third daughter of Miao Chuang Wang, identified with the Chou dynasty, a ruler of a northern Chinese kingdom about 700 B.C. According to legend, she was determined to devote herself to a religious life. She refused to be married despite the command of her father and the entreaties of her friends. Finally, however, she was permitted to enter the Nunnery of the White Bird in Lungshu Hsien. Here, at her father's orders, she was put to the most demeaning tasks, which in no way dampened her zealous love for God.

Angered by her devotion, her father ordered her to be executed, but when the sword touched her, it broke into a thousand pieces. Her father then commanded her to be stifled, but when her soul left her body and descended into hell, she transformed it into paradise. Carried on a lotus flower to the island of P'ootoo, near Nimpo, she lived for nine years healing the diseased and saving mariners from shipwreck.

It is said that once, when word was brought to her that her father had fallen ill, she cut the flesh from her arms and used it as a medicine that saved his life. In gratitude, he ordered that a statue be erected in her honor, commissioning the artist to depict her with "completely formed arms and eyes." The artist misunderstood, however, and to this day Kuan Yin is sometimes shown with a "thousand arms and a thousand eyes," thereby able to see and assist the masses of her people.

Kuan Yin's ministration is very real and as ancient as the hills. The vow taken by the bodhisattva to stand with humanity is a sacred calling. However, she cautions us against taking it ourselves unless we thoroughly understand the service of these dedicated ones: "Being one with all life, we are aware of all life in its manifestation from the highest to the lowest. This is part of the bodhisattva ideal, which is a part of those who are standing with humanity. And there are quite a number upon this planet, although few compared to those who go their own way of riotous living. It is a very high and holy order, and I suggest that you think long and hard about this calling before you respond and say, 'I will do the same!'

"For when aeons pass and men are not moved by the flame that you hold, remember that you might wish that you had chosen another easier or more gratifying way. As the centuries pass, the thousands of years and the cycles, and the same individuals whom you have nourished by the power of your heart flame are involved in the same involvements in the world, you find that you cry out to God and say, 'O LORD, how long, how long will this wayward generation be in coming to the knowledge of their divinity and of the love of the sacred fire that we have held for so long?'"[236]

Kuan Yin represents the qualities of mercy and compassion to the evolutions of earth. The mercy flame is the means whereby the Christ intercedes on behalf of those who have erred, who cannot bear the full brunt of the Law that demands swift recompense for each violation. The quality of mercy tempers the return of mankind's own karma, staying the hand of justice until that time when individuals are able to stand, face and conquer their own human creation. Kuan Yin tells us that "mercy is the quality of love that smoothens the rough places of life, that heals the sores of the etheric body, that mends the cleavages of mind and feelings, that clears away the debris of sin and the sense of struggle before these manifest in the physical body as disease, decay, disintegration and death."[237]

"Mercy is the strongest power in the universe," Kuan Yin says, for "it is the power of the will of God.... The power of mercy is the intensity of love that will dissolve all fear, all doubt, all recalcitrance and rebellion within the race.... The mercy of the Law is sometimes very stern, but it is always patient, always tolerant, and it sees the flame within the heart rising, rising, rising to meet the Christ."[238]

Kuan Yin reminds us, "When you feel the need of greater strength, of illumination, of greater purity and healing, remember that all of these qualities come to you from the heart of God by the power of the flame of mercy itself. For in forgiveness there comes renewed opportunity to fulfill the Law, and without forgiveness little progress can be made."[239] Therefore, in order to reenter the walk with God, we need forgiveness.

When we invoke it, let us realize that our own Christ Self is our psychiatrist, our psychologist, our minister, our priest, our rabbi, our friend, the one to whom we should go daily to unburden ourselves, as the American Indians did. They made a circle around the camp fire at night and discussed the events of the day. And all that they didn't like, they threw into the flames. It is the same principle that has been taught in every religion of the world. When we put it into the flame, we can go to bed at night in peace. Much insomnia is caused because we are not releasing our daily karma, our daily burdens; and therefore, we are not at peace with ourselves and with God.

We have a need for confession, a need to tell God what we have done that is not in keeping with his Law. Until we tell him about it and ask for his flame of forgiveness to pass through us, we have that sense of guilt, fear, shame, and above all a separation from him. Today this is manifest in all kinds of mental and emotional diseases, split personalities, hatred of father and mother, hatred of children, and many other problems to which modern society has fallen prey. The path back to the guru, the Inner Christ, is calling upon the law of forgiveness.

Forgiveness is something we need to invoke not only for ourselves; we need to invoke it for every part of life—all who have ever wronged us, all whom we have wronged. Saint Germain teaches us that when we invoke forgiveness, it must be by a very intense love in our heart. We need to let each other know that we forgive and that we are asking for forgiveness. And it's a point of humility to say, "I've done wrong, and I ask you and God to forgive me."

When we invoke the law of forgiveness, it bursts like fireworks in the aura as violet, purple and pink, dissolving unpleasant conditions in our world. And it begins to intensify until great spheres of energy are going forth from our heart and inundating the world. You may visualize a loved one, a child, a self-styled enemy, a political figure; you may visualize an entire city, the government, the whole nation or the planet within this brilliant sphere of mercy's flame, becoming the recipient of waves and waves of this wine of forgiveness.

Forgiveness is a law, and by this law, our sins are set aside to give us the opportunity to develop the Christ consciousness. "Training in the law of forgiveness is necessary," Kuan Yin instructs us, "for it is indeed the foundation of the Aquarian age.... Forgiveness is not the balancing of karma; it is the setting aside of karma whereby you are given the freedom in renewed creativity to conquer, to go forth, to make things right without that heavy burden, that weight of sin. And when you come to the place where you have further attainment, then, according to the law of forgiveness, that karma that was set aside is returned to you. And in your heightened state of consciousness in the plane of self-mastery, you are quickly able to place in the flame that substance for transmutation and to pursue your high calling."[240]

There is a difference between the forgiveness of sins and their transmutation. Someone may steal your purse and later tell you that he is sorry he took it. You may forgive him, but the matter is not closed, karmically speaking, until he returns that purse to you with every penny intact or makes whatever restitution is necessary. Forgiveness is not the balancing of karma; it is the setting aside of karma whereby you are given the freedom to make things right without that heavy burden of sin.

The foundation of the path of the abundant life or of science is forgiveness. It is the resolution of harmony between every part of God. It is an intense love action of the freedom flame. The energies of the violet flame, the energies of God, are always pulsating, always moving, and they are transmuting the records of the subconscious. Forgiveness is the fulfillment of the law in Isaiah, "Though your sins be as scarlet, they shall be as white as snow; though they be red like crimson, they shall be as wool."[241]

If you expect forgiveness, then you must be ready to forgive seventy times seven, as the Master Jesus taught. "In small ways and in great ways, mankind are tested," Kuan Yin says, "And the bigotry that remains in the consciousness of some is also a lack of forgiveness. Those who cannot forgive their fellowmen because they do not think or worship as they do— these have the hardness of heart that encases the flame of love and also prevents the flow of wisdom."[242]

The mercy of the law is like a two-way street. It is the signal that you send to God and the signal that he returns. A two-way street means the give-and-take with God. If you expect mercy from God, then you must give mercy to every part of life. The fulfillment of the law of mercy must be for the ultimate liberation of each and every soul. Thus, as we forgive life, life forgives us.

Time and time again we have all heard the cliché, "Let bygones be bygones. Forgive and forget!" This is so true, because if you can still resurrect the memory of a wrong that has been done to you, then you have not truly forgiven. In order to forgive, the record and the memory must be dissolved from your consciousness. Kuan Yin tells us that if this is not the case, not only have you not truly forgiven, but "you have hardened your heart. You have stored the record as a squirrel with his nuts deep within the subconscious. Deep in the etheric plane, you have stored the record of that wrong. You have not released it into the flame. You have not been willing to let go and let God be free to express in those who have wronged you, in those whom you have wronged."[243]

One of the best ways to accomplish this complete "forgiving and forgetting" is by the use of the science of the spoken Word, accompanied by visualization, in a mantra for forgiveness written by El Morya in his "Heart, Head and Decrees."

I AM forgiveness acting here,
Casting out all doubt and fear,
Setting men forever free
With wings of cosmic victory.

I AM calling in full power
For forgiveness every hour;
To all life in every place
I flood forth forgiving grace.

As you give this prayer daily, you may wish to visualize the flames of mercy, which are a lovely pink-violet color, enfolding your being and removing the cause and core of many wrongs of the past. It is possible to experience a great sense of relief from burdens you may have been carrying for centuries as you call for forgiveness for your sins—even those of which you may not be aware in this embodiment—and then truly accept God's grace and forgiveness that he is extending to you through the gift of his violet transmuting flame.

The color violet has many hues ranging from the orchid-pink of mercy's flame, containing a greater saturation of the pink ray of God's love, to the deep-purple flame that embodies more of the blue of the will of God. The purple flame has a greater electronic cleansing action, which, when used alternately with the healing green decrees, will effectively purify and heal the four lower bodies, especially the etheric body (the memory body) of the records of the past that may be buried deep within the subconscious. To invoke this flame, take any violet-flame decree and substitute the word "purple" for "violet." Oftentimes it is more difficult to penetrate to the etheric body than to any of the other lower bodies, and therefore the repetition of a mantra thirty-six times can be very effective in clearing old records of past momentums.

Kuan Yin reminds us of another facet of the flame of mercy as she says: "For many of you I have pleaded before the Lords of Karma for the opportunity to embody, to be whole, to not have dealt to you in the physical the great karma of being maimed and blinded at birth that some of you have deserved. I have interceded with the flame of mercy on your behalf so that you could pursue, in the freedom of a sound mind and body, the light of the Law. Some who have been denied that mercy by the Lords of Karma are today in the institutions for the insane; for them it was meted that they should experience the agony of the absence of the presence of the Christ mind, that they might know what it is to defile that mind, that they might return in another life and appreciate the gift of reason, the gift to pursue the

Holy Word Incarnate by the power of the Logos.

"You do not realize how much has hung in the balance of your own life because mercy's flame has been available to you. You have called and God has answered, and through my heart and my hands, mercy has flowed. I say this that you might also have the wisdom to understand that when mercy has been accorded for a time, you are expected to deliver the fruits of mercy, following the works of the LORD and the way of wisdom."[244]

The Bodhisattva Kuan Yin is known as the Goddess of Mercy because she ensouls the God-qualities of mercy, compassion and forgiveness. She serves on the Karmic Board as the representative of the seventh ray (violet ray). She also held the office of chohan of the seventh ray for two thousand years until Saint Germain assumed that office in the late 1700s.

Kuan Yin ascended thousands of years ago and has taken the vow of the bodhisattva to serve planet Earth until all her evolutions are free. From her etheric retreat, the Temple of Mercy, over Peking (Beijing), China, she ministers to the souls of humanity, teaching them to balance their karma and fulfill their divine plan through loving service to life and application of the violet flame.

Kuan Yin's flame is the color of orchids, the pink of divine love tempering the blue of the will of God. Her flower is a pink and violet lotus; the center, being pink, is as the mercy flame, becoming deeper and deeper violet on the periphery.

❖ KUTHUMI, World Teacher and Master Psychologist

The ascended master Kuthumi, formerly chohan of the second ray of wisdom, now serves with Jesus in the office of World Teacher. This much beloved master is hierarch of the Temple of Illumination in Kashmir, which is also known as the Cathedral of Nature. He is the head master of the Brothers of the Golden Robe and trains students who are on the ray of wisdom in the art of meditation and the science of the Word in order that they may become master psychologists of their own psyche, or soul.

The Ascended Master Kuthumi

As Pharaoh Thutmose III (c. 1567 B.C.), prophet and high priest, he expanded the Egyptian kingdom to include most of the Middle East. His most decisive victory was on the battlefield near Mt. Carmel. There he led the entire army single file through narrow Megiddo Pass to surprise and defeat an alliance of 330 rebellious Asian princes—a daring maneuver protested by the pharaoh's terrified officers. Thutmose alone was assured of his plan and rode ahead holding aloft the image of Amon-Ra, the Sun God who had promised him the victory.

In the sixth century B.C., he was the Greek philosopher Pythagoras, the "fair-haired Samian" who was regarded as the son of Apollo. As a youth, Pythagoras conferred freely with priests and scholars, eagerly seeking scientific proof of the inner law revealed to him in meditation upon Demeter, the Mother of the Earth. His quest for the great synthesis of truth led him to Palestine, Arabia, India, and finally to the temples of Egypt, where he won the confidence of the priests of Memphis and was gradually accepted into the mysteries of Isis at Thebes.

When Asian conqueror Cambyses launched a savage invasion of Egypt about 529 B.C., Pythagoras was exiled to Babylon, where the prophet Daniel still served as king's minister. Here rabbis revealed to him the inner teachings of the I AM THAT I AM given to Moses. Zoroastrian magi tutored him in music, astronomy and the sacred science of invocation. After twelve years, Pythagoras left Babylon and founded a brotherhood of initiates at Crotona, a busy Dorian seaport in southern Italy. His "city of the elect" was a mystery school of the Great White Brotherhood.

At Crotona, carefully selected men and women pursued a philosophy based upon the mathematical expression of universal law, illustrated in music and in the rhythm and harmony of a highly disciplined way of life. After a five-year probation of strict silence, Pythagorean "mathematicians" progressed through a series of initiations, developing the intuitive faculties of the heart whereby the son or daughter of God may become, as Pythagoras' *Golden Verses* state, "a deathless God divine, mortal no more."

Pythagoras delivered his lectures from behind a screen in a veiled language that could be fully comprehended only by the most advanced initiates. The most significant phase of his instruction concerned the fundamental concept that number is both the form and the essence of creation. He formulated the essential parts of Euclid's geometry and advanced astronomical ideas that led to Copernicus' hypotheses. It is recorded that two thousand citizens of Crotona gave up their customary lifestyle and assembled together in the Pythagorean community under the wise administration of the Council of Three Hundred—a governmental, scientific and religious order that later exercised great political influence throughout Magna Grecia.

Pythagoras, the "indefatigable adept," was ninety when Cylon, a rejected candidate of the mystery school, incited a violent persecution. Standing in the courtyard of Crotona, Cylon read aloud from a secret book of Pythagoras, *Hieros Logos* (Holy Word), distorting and ridiculing the teaching. When Pythagoras and forty of the leading members of the Order were assembled, Cylon set fire to the building and all but two of the council members were killed. As a result, the community was destroyed and much of the original teaching was lost. Nevertheless, "the Master" has influenced many great philosophers, including Plato, Aristotle, Augustine, Thomas Aquinas, and Francis Bacon.

As Balthazar, one of the three Magi who followed the star of the Presence of the infant Messiah, he was said to have been the King of Ethiopia who brought the treasure of his realm as the gift of frankincense to Christ, the eternal High Priest.

As Francis of Assisi (c. 1181–1226), the divine *poverello*, he renounced family and wealth and embraced "Lady Poverty," living among the poor and the lepers, finding unspeakable joy in imitating the compassion of Christ. While kneeling at Mass on the feast of St. Matthias in 1209, he heard the gospel of Jesus read by the priest and the Lord's command to his apostles, "Go, preach." Francis left the little church and began evangelizing and converting many. Among them was the noble Lady Clare, who later left her home dressed as the bride of Christ and presented herself to Francis for admittance to the mendicant order.

Francis Preaching to the Birds, by Giotto (detail)

One of the many legends surrounding the lives of Francis and Clare describes their meal at Santa Maria degli Angeli, where Francis spoke so lovingly of God that all were enraptured in Him. Suddenly the people of the village saw the convent and the woods ablaze. Running hastily to quench the flames, they beheld the little company enfolded in brilliant light with arms uplifted to heaven.

Shah Jahan

God revealed to Francis the divine Presence in "brother sun" and "sister moon" and rewarded his devotion with the stigmata of Christ crucified. The prayer of St. Francis is spoken by people of all faiths around the world: "Lord, make me an instrument of thy peace!..."

As Shah Jahan (1592–1666), Mogul emperor of India, he overthrew the corrupt government of his father, Jahangir, and restored in part the noble ethics of his grandfather Akbar the Great. During his enlightened reign, the splendor of the Mogul court reached its zenith and India entered her golden age of art and architecture. Shah Jahan lavished the imperial treasury on music, paintings, and the construction of awesome monuments, mosques, public buildings and thrones throughout India, some of which may still be seen today.

The Taj Mahal

The famous Taj Mahal, "the miracle of miracles, the final wonder of the world," was built as a tomb for his beloved wife, Mumtaz Mahal. She had ruled by his side almost as an equal and died in 1631 giving birth to their fourteenth child. Shah Jahan spared no effort in making the monument "as beautiful as she was beautiful." It is the symbol of the Mother principle and celebrates his eternal love for Mumtaz.

In his final embodiment, the adept Kuthumi (known also as Koot Hoomi and K.H.) led a secluded life, affording but a fragmented record of his words and works. Born in the early nineteenth century, Mahatma Kuthumi was a Punjabi whose family had settled in Kashmir. He attended Oxford University in 1850 and is believed to have contributed "The Dream of Ravan" to *The Dublin University Magazine* around 1854, prior to returning to his homeland.

The Kashmiri Brahman spent considerable time in Dresden, Würzberg, Nürnberg and at the university of Leipzig, where in 1875 he visited with Dr. Gustav Fechner, the founder of modern psychology. His remaining years were spent in seclusion at his lamasery in Shigatse, Tibet, where his contact with the outside world included didactic writings sent by mail to some of his devoted students. These letters are now on file with the British Museum.

With El Morya, known as the Master M., Kuthumi founded the Theosophical Society in 1875 through Helena P. Blavatsky. The Theosophical Society has published Kuthumi's and El Morya's letters to their students in *The Mahatma Letters* and other works. Kuthumi ascended at the end of the nineteenth century.

From the focus of his etheric retreat at Shigatse, Tibet, Kuthumi plays celestial music on his organ to those who are making the transition called "death" from the physical plane to higher octaves. So tremendous is the cosmic radiation that pours through that organ—because it is keyed to the music of the spheres and an organ-focus in the City Foursquare—that souls are drawn out of the astral plane as if following a pied piper. In this way, thousands are drawn to the retreats of the masters by the great love of this Brother of the Golden Robe. Those who are able to see Kuthumi at the moment of their passing often find peace in the certain knowing that they have seen the master Jesus, so closely do Jesus and Kuthumi resemble one another in their adoration and manifestation of the Christ.

Kuthumi is known as the master psychologist, and his assignment is to assist chelas in the resolution of their psychology. On January 27, 1985, he announced a dispensation from Lord Maitreya: "This dispensation is my assignment to work with each one of you individually for your physical health and for the healing of your psychology, that we might swiftly get to the very cause and core of physical as well as spiritual and emotional conditions that there be no more setbacks or indulgences and surely not two steps forward and one step back."[245]

Kuthumi has given a key to understanding our psychology in his teachings on the dweller-on-the-threshold and the electronic belt. The momentums of untransmuted karma in orbit around the "nucleus" of the synthetic self (or carnal mind) form what looks like an "electronic belt" of misqualified energy around the lower portion of man's physical body. Diagrammed at the point of the solar plexus, extending downward in a negative spiral to below the feet, this conglomerate of human creation forms a dense forcefield resembling the shape of a kettledrum. Referred to as the realm of the subconscious or the unconscious, the electronic belt contains the records of unredeemed karma from all embodiments. At the eye of this vortex of untransmuted energy is the consciousness of the anti-self personified in the dweller-on-the-threshold, which must be slain before one can attain full Christhood.

The master can better help us if we give his mantra, "I AM Light." This mantra is for the development of a tremendous momentum of white light and the wisdom of God. It is to bring us to the realization that God can and does dwell within us. When we draw nigh to him, he draws nigh to us, and the angelic hosts also gather for the strengthening of the aura. In his book *Studies of the Human Aura,* Kuthumi speaks of a threefold exercise using the "I AM Light" mantra that students can give for the purpose of strengthening the sheath of the aura so that they can maintain the consciousness of Christ, of God, of Buddha, of Mother.

I AM Light
By Kuthumi

I AM light, glowing light,
Radiating light, intensified light.
God consumes my darkness,
Transmuting it into light.

This day I AM a focus of the Central Sun.
Flowing through me is a crystal river,
A living fountain of light
That can never be qualified
By human thought and feeling.
I AM an outpost of the Divine.
Such darkness as has used me is swallowed up
By the mighty river of light which I AM.

I AM, I AM, I AM light;
I live, I live, I live in light.
I AM light's fullest dimension;
I AM light's purest intention.
I AM light, light, light
Flooding the world everywhere I move,
Blessing, strengthening and conveying
The purpose of the kingdom of heaven.

Kuthumi gives an important key to the spiritual path in his teaching that "the most important part of any experience you have is not what is flung your way *but your reaction to it.* Your reaction is the determination of your place on the ladder of attainment. Your reaction enables us to act or not to act. Your reaction to anything or everything shows us the fruit that has ripened in you from all of our prior teaching and loving and support as well as discipline....

"Thus, from this hour, if you will call to me and make a determination in your heart to transcend the former self, I will tutor you both through your own heart and any messenger I may send your way. Therefore, heed the voices—not astral but physical—and watch the course of events.... Thus, I come in many guises."[246]

❖ **LAKSHMI, Shakti of Vishnu.** *See also* **Vishnu**

The Divine Mother in her manifestation as Lakshmi is the shakti of Vishnu. Lakshmi is known in earlier Eastern texts as Sri, which means "splendor," "beauty," "prosperity," "wealth."

Vishnu holds the office of Preserver in the Hindu Trinity. The Preserver is parallel to the principle of the Son in the Western Trinity. As the Son, Vishnu embodies Cosmic Christ wisdom. He is also the mediator, or bridge, between the human consciousness and Brahman, Absolute Reality.

According to the teachings of Hinduism, Vishnu was incarnated nine times, most notably as Rama and Krishna. Lakshmi took human form to serve as his consort in each of his incarnations. Lakshmi's incarnations included: Sita, the faithful wife of Rama; the cow girl Radha, beloved of Krishna; and Rukmini, the princess whom Krishna later married.

As the Preserver, Vishnu preserves divine design conceived in Wisdom's flame. He restores the universe by Wisdom's all-healing light. Lakshmi shares his role as preserver. Her wisdom is revealed in blessings of prosperity and the precipitation of the abundant life. She bears the cornucopia of good fortune by "eye magic," the eye magic of the All-Seeing Eye of her beloved. She embodies divine compassion and intercedes on our behalf before her consort. She is the mediator of the Mediator!

Lakshmi is described as being "as radiant as gold" and "illustrious like the moon." She is said to "shine like the sun" and "to be lustrous like fire." She teaches multiplicity and beauty and is called "She of the Hundred Thousands." Whatever matrix is in her hand, whatever you hold in your heart, Lakshmi can multiply by the millions, for one idea can be reproduced infinitely. Lakshmi also teaches us mastery of karmic cycles on the cosmic clock.

At the beginning of the commercial year in India, Hindus give special prayers to Lakshmi to bring success in their endeavors. She is worshiped in every home on every important occasion. But Lakshmi has a deeper, esoteric significance in that she is associated with immortality and the essence of life. In Hindu lore, she was created when the gods and demons churned a primordial ocean of milk. Their goal was to produce the elixir of immortality. Along with the elixir, they also produced the Goddess Lakshmi. Lakshmi is seen as the one who personifies royal power and conveys it upon kings. She is often depicted with a lotus and an elephant. The lotus represents purity and spiritual power; the elephant, royal authority. Lakshmi, therefore, combines royal and priestly powers.

The Goddess Lakshmi is an embodiment of the Divine Mother. In her role as consort of Vishnu, the Second Person of the Trinity, she is very much a part of the ceremony of the marriage of your soul to your Holy Christ Self. When you are wed and bonded to that Christ Self, you become royal, in the godly sense of the word. Each one of us can receive this "royal" initiation when we have earned the grace of the bountiful Lakshmi. She restores us to our original estate of oneness with God.

In one Tantric text, Lakshmi says of herself: "Like the fat that keeps a lamp burning, I lubricate the senses of living beings with my own sap of consciousness."[247] Lakshmi bestows upon us the nectar of God consciousness when we gain her favor. Vishnu is the Christ light, and Lakshmi is the bestower of that light. The riches she brings are spiritual riches and admission to the kingdom of heaven.

Lakshmi's seed syllable, or bija, is *Srim*. Her mantra is *Om Srim Lakshmye Namaha*.

❖ LANELLO, The Ever-Present Guru

Mark Prophet

The ascended master Lanello was recently embodied on earth as the twentieth-century mystic and messenger for the ascended masters, Mark L. Prophet. In this and in many previous embodiments, he and his twin flame, the messenger Elizabeth Clare Prophet, have served the Great White Brotherhood and sought to set forth the true teachings of Christ.

Thousands of years ago, when the bodhisattva Sanat Kumara came from Venus to keep the flame of life on earth, Lanello and his twin flame and other light evolutions of the planets of this solar system were among the sons and daughters of God who accompanied him. The history of Lanello's mission is the story of a soul seized with a passion that is the love of God.

On Atlantis, he was a priest of the sacred fire and master of invocation in the Temple of the Logos. As the prophet Noah, he received the prophecy of the Flood and exhorted the people for over a hundred years. He lived as Lot, "Abram's brother's son," in the twentieth century B.C.—the man of God in the wretched cities of the plain, Sodom and Gomorrah. Thirty-three hundred years ago, as the Egyptian Pharaoh Ikhnaton, he overthrew the tradition of idolatry, challenged the false priesthood, and established a monotheism based on the worship of Aton, God of the Sun. During his reign, Egypt enjoyed a golden age of art, poetry and music. As Aesop, he was a Greek slave in the sixth century B.C. who won his freedom as a master of didactic stories and fables, though he was murdered by the townspeople he sought to serve.

Ikhnaton

Then as Mark the Evangelist, he wrote the account

of the works of Jesus—the Gospel of Deeds—as confided to him by Peter the Apostle. His mother was one of the most devoted of the women disciples, and Mark remembered when, as a boy, Jesus celebrated the Last Supper in the Upper Room. He was raised an Essene and, being well-educated, was chosen Peter's chief disciple and secretary and was taken to Antioch to assist Paul. He became an exponent of the deeper mysteries of Christianity and founded the Church at Alexandria, where he was later martyred.

As Origen of Alexandria, he returned in the second century to the city he had known as St. Mark and was one of the most distinguished theologians of the early Church, setting forth the true teachings of Jesus Christ on reincarnation and the heavenly hierarchy. At the age of eighteen, he was appointed head of the Catechetical School—the first institution where Christians could be instructed in both the Greek sciences and the doctrines of holy scripture. He lived as an ascetic, working day and night with the crowds, lecturing and giving personal consultation. He made a thorough study of Plato, Pythagoras and the Stoics and learned Hebrew in order to properly interpret scripture. But his deep understanding seemed to shallow, worldly minds bizarre and heretical.

Banished from Egypt, Origen nevertheless became an honored teacher in Palestine at Caesarea where he established a school famous throughout the East. He was imprisoned during the persecution of Decius, tortured and later died. Origen left behind a massive body of writings, numbering close to one thousand titles. His books were widely used for more than a century, but not without harsh criticism. In the fifth century, Rufinus of Aquieleia translated and made significant alterations in Origen's work, and Jerome condemned his teaching as heresy. In the sixth century, a list of fifteen anathemata were drawn up by Emperor Justinian in the Fifth Ecumenical Council, followed by the physical destruction of his writings, of which few remain today.

In the days of Arthur the King, the soul of Lanello came from France as Launcelot du Lac. According to legend, the infant Launcelot was laid down beside a lake and the Lady of the Lake carried him off to her kingdom of ten thousand maidens where no man was allowed. Here he matured in great honor and purity and thus was known as Launcelot du Lac (Launcelot of the Lake). He became Arthur's closest friend, their soul-relationship that of guru and chela, and the champion of Queen Guinevere, his twin flame. The jealousy, intrigue and witchcraft of Modred and Morgana La Fey challenged the deep mutual love of the "trinity" of Camelot, driving wedges of distrust between king and queen, knight champion, and the other knights of the Round Table, ending in the death of Arthur and most of the knights and the seclusion of Guinevere and Launcelot in respective roles as renunciates of the Church.

As Bodhidharma, he was the founder of the Zen school of Chinese and Japanese Buddhism. Born a Brahman around A.D. 440 in southern India, he converted to Buddhism and traveled to China to spread the teachings of the Buddha. The essence of Bodhidharma's message is that we cannot realize ultimate truth or attain our own Buddhahood by means of words and letters—we must discover for ourselves our real nature, our Buddha-nature.

As Clovis, he established the French monarchy in the sixth century. He married his twin flame, then the Burgundian princess Clothilde, a Christian, and was baptized after successfully challenging her God to give him victory in battle. He became a devoted representative of the Church, and Clovis and Clothilde became patron saints of France as the founders of the nation and patron and patroness of the poor.

Saladin, by Doré

Then as Saladin, the great Moslem leader of the twelfth century, he conquered and united all of the Mohammedan world. Although a powerful general, Saladin is remembered for his generosity, gentleness, honesty and justice to both Arabs and Christians alike.

He lived as Saint Bonaventure (1221–1274), a theologian and Franciscan mystic. At the age of four, Bonaventure fell gravely ill. His mother begged Saint Francis to intercede for her son's life. Through his prayers the child was cured and Francis is said to have cried out in prophetic rapture: "O buona ventura!" (O good fortune!), from which Bonaventure is believed to have received his name. In gratitude for her son's healing, Bonaventure's mother consecrated his life to God. He became a cardinal of the Roman Church and papal adviser, renowned for his abilities as both scholar and preacher. He was declared a doctor of the Church in 1587, and he is called the Seraphic Doctor. Together with Thomas Aquinas, a Dominican, Bonaventure played an important role in defending the mendicant orders in the thirteenth century.

Louis XIV

He was Louis XIV, King of France from 1643 to 1715 (the longest recorded reign in European history), who was known as "le Roi Soleil" (the Sun

King). He sought to outpicture his soul memory of the culture of Venus in the magnificent palace and gardens of Versailles.

Longfellow

As Henry Wadsworth Longfellow (1807–1882), he became the most popular of American poets of the nineteenth century. He was an excellent teacher, first at Bowdoin and later presiding over the modern language program at Harvard for eighteen years. Longing for literary freedom, however, he left his post and began writing the poetry that captured the spirit and heart of America and the abiding flame of his guru, El Morya. It was his own soul of which Longfellow wrote in the narrative poem of the legendary Iroquois chief Hiawatha.

At the dawn of the twentieth century, Lanello embodied in Russia as Alexis, the son of the tsar and heir to the Romanov throne. However, his father, Nicholas II, abdicated on his behalf, denying the opportunity for his flame to be the light of Russia. The Russian Revolution followed soon thereafter, followed by the execution of the tsar and all of his family.

As the twentieth-century master Mark L. Prophet, he was born in Chippewa Falls, Wisconsin, in 1918, the only child of Thomas and Mabel Prophet. His father passed on when he was nine, and he and his mother endured the hardships of the depression years. When a boy of about eighteen, while working on the Soo Line Railroad, he was contacted by the ascended master El Morya, calling him to his mission.

During World War II, he served in the U.S. Air Force and his training under the master continued. In 1958, El Morya directed him to found The Summit Lighthouse in the nation's capital. Mark himself typed the first dictations given by the ascended masters, called "Ashram Notes." He was joined by his twin flame, Elizabeth, in 1961, and together they fulfilled the prophecy of Jesus set forth by John the Revelator of holding the office of the "Two Witnesses" and the "Other Two" in this age.[248]

On February 26, 1973, Mark passed on and his soul ascended to the plane of the I AM Presence to carry on his work with the ascended masters and to make contact with their unascended chelas. As the ascended master Lanello, he continues to direct the activities of The Summit Lighthouse, the "Ever-Present Guru" who has said: "Ours must be a message of infinite love and we must demonstrate that love to the world."

Lanello's first public dictation was given April 20, 1973, just two months after his ascension: "As I have thought this night upon the many

subjects on which I would choose to discourse, I have drawn the conclusion that it is always the most expedient to speak of practical things, even when the heart would sing to the poetic cadences of the music of the spheres, for I am concerned that you wear my mantle—those of you that I have known for so long, for so many embodiments. And therefore, I have enlisted the service of my angels over these past weeks, thinking of what I could do to bring you my joy; and I have asked the angels to sew you a replica of my cape—my blue cape that I have worn even in the physical octave. And I have asked my angels to place that cape upon your shoulders this night, and it might very well come to pass that you shall feel even the fabric of that cape as it rustles around your ankles and around your arms.

"Yes, I have fashioned a blue cape for each one of you; that is, my angels—they have taken the fashioning that I have given to them and styled a most noble garment complete with hood like the monks of old. And so before this service is concluded, these angels are going to place my cape upon you that you might also go forth wearing the momentum of my victory in many past embodiments, which I have taken forth from my causal body as a momentum of light to give unto you....

"I say, you are *all* candidates for the ascension if you choose to be. And if you choose to be this night and in the coming weeks, then I will sponsor you and I will direct the Mother of the Flame to sponsor you also. There is no need to tarry; there is no need to go back to the old ways of the human consciousness. I say, your Christed awareness, your Christed Being, is the *blazing* Reality of your consciousness! It is the new day dawning within you! It is your potential of victory! It is your purity *now!*

"And I say, you do not have to wait for the carnal mind to evolve, for the carnal mind will never evolve, precious hearts; it will *never* become the Christ. It must be put off and cast into the flame! You have to trade in the old model and take out the new. How long will you dwell with that old model? Some of you are more tolerant of your former selves than you are of your cars that you trade in every year, but you forget to trade in the carnal mind for the Christ mind that is in the height of fashion in the courts of heaven!

"And so, precious hearts, I say that of all of the warnings and all of the prophecies that I might prophesy this night, it is this one key of Christhood, and salvation through Christhood, that can give you the ultimate victory. And it is with ultimate victories that we are concerned—not with the skirmishes that are lost or won each hour and each day; nevertheless, these do count as the great Keeper of the Scrolls makes his mark in the Book of Life. But I say, sometimes when you lose in the fray, it is a lesson that needs to be learned; and a temporary loss may mean the ultimate victory, for the lesson that is gained is a measure toward perfection.

"And so I say, count the experiences that you have been through as the past that is prologue; and now write the chapter, chapter one on the book of 'My Christhood.' Keep a diary that is called 'My Christhood,' and write down each day how the flower of the Christ is appearing in your life. And when you know you have done an act in the consciousness of the Christ, write it down and leave the record for yourself, so that in those hours of darkness and moments of trial when you forget and cannot remember one good thing you have ever done because the devils are tormenting you with their lies, then read in the book of 'My Christhood' of how you have vanquished error and how you have overcome.

"I say, the saga of your lives—of many of you—is beautiful to behold; for you have indeed won in small ways and in great ways. And until the last tally is taken, you never know how the Lord looks upon the balance of power within you. So keep on striving for the light, striving for the right; and know that I, Lanello, walk with you each step of the way.

"I am as near as the breath that you breathe. And there is nowhere that you can go that I am not, for I have projected an Electronic Presence of myself to each one of you who will receive me. As Jesus wrote, 'He that receiveth a prophet in the name of a prophet shall receive a prophet's reward.'[249] My reward is the ascension! My reward is light! And if you receive me as a prophet of your ascension, then you can have my Electronic Presence walking next to you, and I will wear my own blue cape. And they will say, 'Look at those twins walking down the street.' For you will look like me and I will look like you, and who will say who is ascended and who is unascended? For did they not have a little moment of trouble in discerning the difference between Jesus and his disciples?[250]

"So they will not know who is who. And I dare say that when the forces move their chessmen on the board of life to attack your lifestream, they may very well fling those arrows of outrageous fortune at *me!* And then they will have the reward of attacking an ascended master! And how do you like that? And so we two shall walk hand in hand; and at any hour of the day or night when you reach out your hand for mine, I will clasp your own....

"I say to you, whatever you have done in the past, forsake the past! Leave it behind! And let the light of mercy triumph within you, for our God is a God of mercy and his mercy endureth for ever.[251] Therefore, take a step forward this night; and consider that in taking that step you are stepping out of the skins of the former man and into the raiment of the Christ. And when you take that step as I shall direct at the close of my address, you shall

have placed upon you my cape, my *capuchon.*"

Lanello's retreat is at Bingen, on the Rhine River in Germany. He serves on the first ray, and his keynote is "Greensleeves." He has worked with K-17 for many hundreds of years and continues to work with him from the ascended octave. He is called the Ever-Present Guru because he is always appearing and talking to his chelas.

❖ LANTO, Chohan of the Second Ray

Having studied under Lord Himalaya and gained his mastery in the Retreat of the Blue Lotus, Lord Lanto elected to use the yellow plume to enfold the hearts of all mankind. He is dedicated to the perfectionment of the evolutions of this planet through Cosmic Christ illumination. The golden flame that he bears is charged with the momentum of God-victory for the youth of the world.

Lanto volunteered with Sanat Kumara, the Ancient of Days, to come to earth long ago for the rescue of the planet and her evolutions. He was a High Priest in the temple of the Divine Mother on the continent that sank beneath the Pacific, known as Lemuria. He had other incarnations on Atlantis, as did all of the chohans of the rays.

In the last days of Lemuria, those who tended the flames upon the altars of the temples were warned of the coming cataclysm. They removed their flames, carried them to places of safety, and deposited those flames in other physical retreats or removed them to the etheric octave. It was Lord Lanto who carried the flame of precipitation and deposited it in the area of the Grand Teton mountains in North America.

The flame of precipitation is a Chinese green tinged with yellow of the second ray. This flame burning in the Royal Teton Retreat is the quality in consciousness that makes Americans extremely practical, developing an applied science in technology that takes us back to the time of Mu when that technology even exceeded what we have today. It is a flame of abundance that enables the precipitation of wealth as well as happiness and joy and the Universal Christ consciousness.

Lord Lanto embodied in ancient China as the Duke of Chou, also known as the Yellow Emperor (twelfth century B.C.). The Duke of Chou is regarded as one of the greatest statesmen in Chinese history and is considered to be the architect of the Chou dynasty and the true founder of the Confucian tradition. Confucius looked to the Duke as his model and believed it was his mission to reestablish the principles and culture of the early Chou era, which was thought to have been a golden age.

Lanto was later embodied as a ruler of China at the time of Confucius (551 to 479 B.C.) and has held the golden flame of illumination on behalf of the Chinese people for many, many centuries. This flame is anchored in China in the retreat of the archangels Jophiel and Christine, which is located in central China.

Before his ascension Lord Lanto determined that the light from his own heart flame should shine forth physically as living proof to his disciples that the threefold flame, as in past and coming golden ages, is the Word that is made flesh and that it can be thus expanded and intensified by the priority of the adept.

Affirming with (or aeons before) the proverbial Job, "Yet in my flesh shall I see God!" Lanto, by the dynamism of his decrees from the heart, his devoutness to the living Word as the Universal Christ ever with him, and his consecration of the chakras to the sacred fire of the Mother did achieve what none other in earth's recorded history since the Fall had done: Lanto so adored the Trinity in the tripartite light of his innermost being that the intense glow of that divine spark could actually be seen through his flesh form emanating a soft golden glow through his chest. This he maintained in honor of Sanat Kumara until his ascension around 500 B.C.—"a memorial to all generations" who are the issue of the I AM THAT I AM—in order that the original lightbearers might recall the mission to illumine the dark star.

Throughout the nineteenth and twentieth centuries Lanto has stood faithfully behind the efforts of Saint Germain to liberate mankind through his release of the ascended masters' teachings on the I AM Presence and the violet fire. On July 3, 1958, the ascended master Confucius succeeded Lord Lanto as hierarch of the Royal Teton Retreat. With attainment far beyond that required either of retreat hierarch or chohan, Lanto accepted from Kuthumi the office of lord of the second ray on that date (this blessed brother who had worshiped the God of Peace as Saint Francis having already in 1956 joined Jesus in the office of World Teacher).

On October 30, 1966, in cooperation with the God and Goddess Meru, Lanto was granted the dispensation by the Karmic Board for a "mighty transcendent golden flame of illumination" to pulsate three hundred feet into the atmosphere over the colleges, universities, divinity and theological schools of America and the world whose students and faculty were and would be receptive to knowledge from higher spheres.

The ascended master Lanto conducts classes at the Royal Teton Retreat, the initial retreat of the Great White Brotherhood to which the neophyte may ask to be taken. Here we learn the fundamentals of the path of initiation. Because of the dispensation of opening the seven retreats of the seven chohans, many tens of thousands of souls are receiving training at inner levels to accelerate their consciousness for the New Age.

Lord Lanto also tries to give us a sense of our worth instead of the feeling of self-deprecation so common among men today: "Man is a God in the becoming, but he can never know this while he thinks earthly thoughts. He can never know this by worldly knowledge, for the things of this world are foolishness with God.[252] And in the eyes of God, the only real values are those that free man from the eclipse of being that has concealed the sun of God's Presence from his eyes. And it is this sun that will awaken his spiritual senses that enable him to see with Saint Paul the face of the Master and to hear his cry 'It is hard for thee to kick against the pricks.'"[253]

Meditation on Lord Lanto and his golden lotus flame may be accompanied by the music of "Song to the Evening Star" from *Tannhäuser,* by Wagner (keynote of the Royal Teton Retreat). The wisdom of Lanto is excelled by few ascended beings serving this earth. His flame should be invoked daily on behalf of the youth of the world.

❖ **LEONORA, Patroness of Science and Invention**

The ascended lady master Leonora is a patroness of science and invention. We can call for her to oversee the release of inventions and the correct knowledge for the protection of all that our nations need through the government and armed services. She works with Saint Germain in the Cave of Symbols. One of her inventions that was seen there by Guy Ballard was a radio that could pick up signals from any location on the earth, as well as other planets. It could also communicate with the etheric belt around the earth and with the interior of the earth.

Lady Leonora warns about the misuse of science and technology. She comments on techniques of mind control based on hypnotic designs and autosuggestion that would attempt to replace the Christ consciousness with so-called scientific methods:

"Learned by rote, these methods will supposedly make man a master of himself. He is told that he will need no help from any other, save those who would make merchandise of him by promising to communicate to him the techniques of mind control. These, he is assured, will enable him to bend not only his own mind but also the minds of others at will. Thus, there is produced psychic domination by a psychic technology that would wrest the secrets of life from heaven itself.

"Let those who tamper with higher law beware, for in olden times, it was this tampering that broke the lines of cosmic communication between unascended man and the Reality of God. By setting up a system of domination of self by self, men sought to establish a personal oligarchy that would require help from no one, not even from God himself.

"The spirits who direct such unwholesome activities will tell men first that they have the means within themselves of going directly to God, that they require no instruction or aid from anyone except the Deity himself. Then, after they have convinced people of their own inner powers, they subtly introduce the lie that since they are doing so well on their own, perhaps they don't really need Him after all."[254] Leonora explains that the way to emancipation comes only through the Christ consciousness.

Mother Mary has urged us to call to Leonora: "Let America awake and pursue diligently the things of spiritual glory. And as America pursues the glories of Spirit, let it also pursue the necessary scientific advances of the age. I think it well if mankind would call to beloved Saint Germain and the lady master Leonora that a greater release of science and invention may be given so that it will become less possible for the powers of shadow to attack the democracy and the places known as the citadels of freedom."[255]

❖ LETO, Teacher of Youth

The ascended lady master Leto teaches students on the Path how consciously to leave the body and to reenter at will and also how to draw upon the experiences in the masters' retreats during the sleep of the physical body.

Leto's twin flame is the ascended master Alexander Gaylord. Godfré Ray King's book *The Magic Presence* recounts how Alexander Gaylord, while yet in embodiment and working for the Brotherhood, went on missions with Leto, who had ascended more than three hundred years earlier.[256]

Gaylord and Leto were embodied in the Inca civilization. At that time, he was a public servant and she was a devoted scientist, both highly attuned with the spiritual hierarchy. Drawing upon the healing focuses of the world, Leto has rendered great assistance to mankind, especially during periods of plague. As a scientist on Atlantis and later as a mystic in China, she devoted her energies to the precipitation of the flame of truth.

Leto speaks of her service: "As some of you know, I have dedicated my lifestream to the science of the Divine Mother for many centuries, and in our retreat in Paris, serving with the Master of Paris and my twin flame, Alexander Gaylord, we have made many discoveries, not only discoveries of a scientific nature but those that show us how we can better communicate to the children of men the knowledge of the sacred laws of the universe, which, when applied, will give mankind their freedom."[257] She is currently conducting scientific experiments and teaching the laws of alchemy to a select group of students.

The action of her flame is purple tinged with gold; appropriately, she wears a purple cape lined with gold. Her fragrance is heather and her radiation can be drawn through the melody "The Heather on the Hill," from Brigadoon.

Leto says: "With the fragrance of heather I bring to your heart's remembrance the love of twin flame and of little child. I bring to your heart the remembrance of love of the inner teacher. I am Leto, and heather is a symbol of my love of the Holy Spirit in nature and my devotion even to the light in the people of Scotland and the British Isles and many throughout the earth who are tied to me through the inner mystery schools and the work we have done together on the continent of Europe in the early ages when we set forth writings on the mysteries of Christ. It was a group of souls whose hearts were one, and we toiled into the night to leave a record and a memory of the indwelling light. Then again, you have come with me to the inner retreat of the Brotherhood in Persia where Cha Ara has called you to an understanding of the mysteries of the sacred fire and the path of Zarathustra.

"I am a teacher of youth of every age. I taught Rex and Nada and Bob and Pearl, and I come to welcome you to the Cave of Light, retreat of the Great Divine Director in India, for here are activities for acceleration of candidates for the ascension. I especially work with children and youth who desire to give this lifetime to that path and to an extraordinary service to America, to Saint Germain. The color of violets, when meditated upon, will draw you nearer to the violet heart, the purple heart that I carry in the name of Saint Germain."[258]

❖ LIBERTY, GODDESS OF, Spokesman for the Karmic Board

The Goddess of Liberty is spokesman for the Karmic Board and representative of the second ray on that Board. She is the hierarch of the Temple of the Sun, her etheric retreat over the island of Manhattan, New York.

The Goddess of Liberty was embodied on Atlantis. She was also embodied as a member of the Amazonian Race, a people of great stature whose women ruled an ancient civilization where the Amazon Basin now is.

So great was her momentum of dedication to the Spirit of Liberty embodied in the threefold flame of the heart, that after her ascension, this lady master was called upon to bear the title of Goddess of Liberty, denoting her office in hierarchy as the authority for the cosmic consciousness of liberty to the earth.

During her embodiment upon Atlantis, she erected the Temple of the Sun where Manhattan Island now is, patterning it after the Solar Temple in the Great Central Sun. The central altar was dedicated to the threefold flame of the liberty of the Christ, which proceeds from the white-fire core of Being focused by beloved Alpha and Omega. This shrine was surrounded by twelve lesser shrines attended by representatives of the solar hierarchies who, together with the Goddess of Liberty, invoked on behalf of the evolutions of the earth the spiritual radiation of the Sun behind the sun.

Just prior to the sinking of Atlantis, the Goddess of Liberty transported the liberty flame enshrined at the temple to a place of safety in another retreat of the Great White Brotherhood, the Château de Liberté in southern France. When Atlantis went down in cataclysm, the Temple of the Sun was withdrawn to the etheric octave, and the activities of the Brotherhood of Liberty continue at the etheric plane where the physical temple once stood.

The Spirit of Liberty inspired the early American patriots to found a new nation "under God" and to frame a constitution based on the Brotherhood's plan for the emerging Christ consciousness that would come to maturity on virgin soil under the direction of Saint Germain, the God of Freedom for the earth.

The Goddess of Liberty appeared to General Washington during the winter of 1777 and revealed to him America's destiny, giving him the strength and the courage to complete his own mission as the liberator of the thirteen original colonies.

It is no wonder that the Statue of Liberty, a gift of the French people, was erected on Bedloe's Isle. The flame of liberty drew the focus of the Statue of Liberty as an outer symbol of hope for liberation from all forms of tyranny to the "tired, the poor, the huddled masses yearning to breathe free."[259]

The Goddess of Liberty wears a crown of seven rays, focusing the power of the Elohim and their implementation of the seven rays in form, in Matter (Mater), the mother aspect of Divinity. Her crown is also a focus of the seven rays anchored in the forehead of every son and daughter of God. The Goddess of Liberty is that "Lady with the lamp" whom Henry Wadsworth Longfellow prophesied would "stand in the great history of the land, a noble type of good, heroic womanhood."[260]

The Goddess of Liberty represents the archetypal pattern of the World Mother who carries the Book of Divine Law, the Book of Illumination containing the knowledge that will show mankind the way out of the night of human error. At the base of the Statue of Liberty are broken chains, symbolizing a being free from the bondage of human creation, stepping forth to enlighten the world. Her torch is the flame of cosmic illumination.

Liberty proclaims: "The song of creation is the song of hope, and the hope that is born of the heart of God is a tender flame that blazes in the torch that I uphold! I uphold it now and I uphold it for aye and I uphold it for all.

"Will you join me in the upholding of that torch? Will you join me in standing fast when all the world assails you? Will you join me in the hour of twilight, knowing that with me you shall watch out the coming dawn?"[261]

The Goddess of Liberty stands at the seven o'clock line of the twelve solar hierarchies (opposite Saint Germain) as the authority for the attribute of God-gratitude on behalf of the evolutions of this solar system. Of gratitude and America's destiny she has said:

"Gracious ones, I AM God in action! As I come to you today, it is to reveal the wondrous thought in the idea of 'Immigration'—*I AM gratitude in action*. Behold, then, that America was intended to be a land where gratitude in action would produce, through the power of the cosmic liberty bell, that wondrous attitude of freedom that would make men responsive to God within the citadel of their hearts....

"Immigration from the heart of God to the planet Earth, precious ones, is an opportunity. And immigration back to the heart of God is an opportunity. Individuals must, then, recognize the boon of gratitude. 'I AM gratitude in action!' And therefore, the goings out and the comings in of mankind ought always to be accompanied by a manifestation of gratitude to the Deity."[262]

Although she has attained initiations at cosmic levels and need not remain with the planet, the Goddess of Liberty has taken the vow to remain in the service of the earth until every last man, woman and child has made his ascension. This is the bodhisattva ideal. She has called for one thousand faithful ones to decree to preserve America's destiny. May the students' great love for the destiny of God in man inspire them to answer Liberty's call!

❖ **LIGHT, GODDESS OF,** *See* **Amerissis**

❖ LIGHT, QUEEN OF

The Queen of Light focuses the action of the crystal fire mist and the crystal sword. Wherever she goes, she directs her light rays through the crystal flame and radiates the full complement of the Christ consciousness through the crystal prism. Her legions of light wield the crystal sword and may be called upon to cut through the densest human creation, to clear the four lower bodies of all that is not reflective of the crystal-clear radiance of the Christ mind.

Her consciousness is at the point between the crystal and the mist where Matter becomes Spirit and Spirit becomes Matter. This is truly the razor's edge of Christ-realization. When the Queen of Light and her legions wield their crystal swords on behalf of the freedom of mankind, there is a tremendous release of crystal lightning.

The Queen of Light speaks as a mother and is most concerned for the children of the world. She enlists our aid on their behalf and says: "Some of you have pledged at inner levels to take your stand for those sweet children from the moment that they are conceived to the age of seven. That is the tender, forming period. Those of you who have taken your vows must remember that the flame of application must be used daily. And these children require your assistance each morning when you pray.

"I would like to develop in you the sense that the children of the world, the babies are so much a part of your own self that not to call for them would be much like not calling for your own tube of light or not feeding yourself or not taking care of your immediate family. They must be under your wing, for your wing is the wing of the Almighty, and that is the unfailing light of God, the protection that is required.

"They are bombarded from every side. And so now they must be bombarded with light, with the power of the fiat of the light and of the spoken Word. O mothers of the world, I call to you this night. I, the Queen of Light, implore you: Awaken to your mission to guard the Holy Christ Child....

"Oh, we long for the day when there are prepared upon earth those souls who can truly receive the avatars and the incoming seventh root race. And even as we are preparing that great continent of South America, so the hordes of shadow are moving in also, to claim these children even before they are born. O beloved ones, turn now and face South America and realize that that continent must be protected. You must provide the pathway of light over which the golden-age children might come."[263]

The Goddess of Light, the Queen of Light and the Goddess of Purity form a trinity of three cosmic beings who have majored on the one-pointed goal of focusing the intense light of the Christ consciousness of God. The retreat of the Queen of Light is in the etheric plane over the island of Sicily, near Messina.

❖ LING, LORD (MOSES), God of Happiness

Lord Ling was embodied as Moses during the mid-fourteenth to the mid-thirteenth centuries B.C. During that lifetime as the Hebrew prophet, statesman and lawgiver, God Ling was inspired by his guru, a cosmic being who sponsored the Hebrew people, and by Micah, the Angel of Unity.

Moses was born about three hundred years after the death of Joseph, son of Jacob. At that time, the Israelites had multiplied in Egypt and become a large population. According to the book of Exodus, which tells the story of Moses, a pharaoh came to the throne who did not know Joseph. He enslaved the Israelites, but still their large population and strength troubled Pharaoh. He ordered all the Hebrews to cast every son who was born to them into the river.

When Moses was born, his mother hid him until he was three months old. Then she made an ark of bulrushes and put him in it. She put the ark in the river. Pharaoh's daughter found Moses and took pity on him. Moses' sister was standing by to watch him. She told Pharaoh's daughter that she could find a Hebrew woman to nurse him. Then she went and got Moses' own mother. Pharaoh's daughter adopted the child and paid his mother to nurse him.

The Bible tells us that Moses "was learned in all the wisdom of the Egyptians, and was mighty in words and in deeds."[264] In fact, he had performed great deeds of merit and passed many tests in previous lifetimes. His soul was chosen for the mission because he had proven himself.

Moses lived as an Egyptian of princely rank until he was about forty years old, when Exodus records that he "went out unto his brethren, and looked on their burdens: and he spied an Egyptian smiting an Hebrew, one of his brethren. And he looked this way and that way, and when he saw that there was no man, he slew the Egyptian, and hid him in the sand."[265] In this, Moses' first act of public record, he took the law into his own hands and for the first time allowed his sympathy for the Hebrews to be known. Though God preordained Moses to "Let My People Go," Moses was a man like other men, and God did not exempt him from the law of karma. For this and other reasons, Moses did not attain union with God at the end of his mission with the Israelites. God required him to reincarnate to balance his karma.

Moses fled Egypt to the land of Midian, where he lived for forty years. The Bible tells us that it was there that "the angel of the LORD appeared unto him in a flame of fire out of the midst of a bush: he looked, and behold, the bush burned with fire, and the bush was not consumed." The LORD said, "I have seen the affliction of my people in Egypt, have heard their cry. I know their sorrows." Then he commanded Moses: "Come now therefore, and I will send thee unto Pharaoh, that thou mayest bring forth my people the children of Israel out of Egypt." Moses said, "When they ask me what is your name, what shall I tell them?" God said, "I AM THAT I AM: Thus shalt thou say unto the children of Israel, I AM hath sent me unto you."[266]

After the land was smitten by ten plagues, the Egyptian pharaoh finally agreed to let the Israelites leave, and Moses led them on their journey through the wilderness to the Promised Land.

At one point in their journey, God called Moses to Mount Sinai for forty days and forty nights to receive the first set of tablets of the Law. But while he was there, the children of Israel rebelled against God and guru. These tablets were inscribed with the covenants that God would make with a holy people. They contained lengthy, detailed statements outlining the way a people sponsored by Sanat Kumara should follow the path of discipleship under the Law and under the guru.

The children of Israel were called to be a holy people, but they were not embodying the holiness of God at that time. In Moses' absence, they worshiped the golden calf. When Moses descended the mountain and saw the people's stubbornness and their embracing of the god of materialism, he broke the tablets. The detailed covenants were thereby lost and later replaced with ten simple commandments, which God inscribed on a second set of tablets. The people's test would then be the "test of the ten," which is the test of the solar-plexus chakra.[267]

After leading the children of Israel for forty years through the wilderness, Moses was not permitted to enter the Promised Land, but only to view it from Mt. Nebo just before his passing, because in anger he smote the rock to receive the waters rather than to lovingly invoke them and receive them.²⁶⁸ And although he liberated the Hebrew people from Egyptian slavery, Moses did not balance his threefold flame, for his service was lacking in the quality of joy. His pink plume of divine love did not match the fiery intensity of his devotion to the will of God.

In Moses' next embodiment, as Ananda during the sixth century B.C., he became the disciple of Lord Gautama Buddha. Here, at the feet of the most advanced initiate on the planet, he learned how to render service in love and to tap the peace and understanding that come from within the golden flame of illumination.

Following that embodiment, he lived in China as Lord Ling, one of the ruling class whose high attunement with the Brotherhood enabled him to serve his people through the balanced action of the threefold flame. At the close of that embodiment, he ascended to become the God of Happiness. He then devoted himself to the bright-gold flame of joy on behalf of all evolving upon this planet, for he recognized that without this quality, one cannot ascend nor render a just service unto God and man.

Lord Ling has spoken of his embodiments as Moses and Lord Ling: "I myself did pass into another incarnation, and you have known me in my final embodiment as Lord Ling of China. There I perfected the wisdom, fulfilled the balancing of my karma and did espouse the flame of God-happiness. This I did in view of the great mourning and depression that is carried by so many of the children of Israel and Judah who have gone forth in a state of burden of their karma and in a state of depression concerning their absence of knowledge of the true path of salvation and the promise of heaven and victory on earth.

"Some are even wed in a greater way to materialism than they were in the moments when we were in the wilderness and at the foot of Sinai. Yes, beloved, materialism and the pleasures of the senses are addictive. Far from getting better, these addictions get worse.

"Thus, I engrave, as God does engrave in your hearts, the true mysteries of the kingdom, the true understanding of the requirements of the Law and the Path. If you are not able to read this writing, know that it does burn within you, that it is a living fire, that it is the fire infolding itself. It is the all-consuming fire of God that will, if you allow it, consume in you all those manifestations less than the fulfillment of the Law.

"May you early seek the sacred fire and then the violet flame and then the calls unto the seven archangels. For those of you who have descended from this seed of Abraham, who also descended ultimately from the seed of Sanat Kumara, do indeed have a destiny in this hour; for your training in the ancient golden-age civilization of Jesus Christ does fit you to be true shepherds.*

"Thus, Jesus knew to whom he was speaking when he said, 'Feed my sheep.'[269] There are those who are rightly able and called by their karma and destiny of dharma to feed the souls of the millions upon earth. I call you all to this calling, for you may be adoptive sons who have chosen to enter in to claim your joint heirship with Jesus of the sonship that does belong to all of this seed of light. Therefore, whether you are adoptive sons or count yourselves as those who truly trace their traditions to the beginnings, I am come to draw you into the office of the high calling of your destiny."[270]

God Ling maintains a focus of the flame of joy in the retreat of Jophiel and Christine in Central China. He often frequents this and other retreats of the Brotherhood, and he uses the flame of joy as a focus, a divine magnet, to draw mankind into the ascended masters' consciousness. His momentum of great joy gives him a sense of the abundant life, the life holy and beautiful. When invoking an abundant supply "of every good and perfect gift," one should call to God Ling in addition to the God of Nature, the God of Gold and Fortuna, the Goddess of Supply.

❖ **LISTENING ANGEL, The Angel Who Listens to Prayers**

Embracing the pink and golden flames, this beloved angel and the legions in her command are assigned by Alpha and Omega to listen to the prayers, the heart calls, the innermost thoughts of the mankind of earth and to carry their prayers on wings of light to the Almighty for his disposition.

Listening Angel and her legions are holy comforters, friends who listen in time of need and give the wisdom and compassion of their hearts to mankind as they pour out their troubles to these angel visitants. Her flame of compassion is anchored in the Temple of the Sun over the island of Manhattan.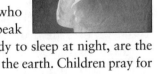

We can learn much from Listening Angel, who says: "The prayers of children, as their hearts speak through their souls after they have left the body to sleep at night, are the most precious of prayers that we hear out of all the earth. Children pray for graces, not for toys.

"Children remember God, for they are yet small and still can peep through the veil beyond the octaves to their home of light. Children come with a desire to console their parents, fully aware that their parents are

---

*For the story of this ancient golden-age civilization on Atlantis, see the entry for Jesus.

burdened by many cares and concerns of the world. Oh, what a blessing it is to nurture these fine sensitivities of children and their sense of being so close to God through angels!

"I AM indeed your Listening Angel, and I have numberless bands of angels who are listening not only to the prayers but to the many types of expressions of the people of earth: their frustrations, their angers, their self-pity, their feelings of aloneness in a wide, wide world where there is no real depth and no longer the capacity for intimacy in spiritual matters, in communion with God or with another heart. And are not these prayers also?

"Many people on earth suffer, as you know, and they do not pray. Therefore, we must listen to the expressions of the soul that may not be articulated, for their pain is so great. Listening angels are there when people pass from life in agony and when there is the joyous birth of children.

"Listening angels are there to comfort souls whose bodies are being aborted, and therefore, whose missions are being aborted. Oh, we tend these souls with greatest care that they may not be scarred when they must enter once again the womb of life and perhaps make another try and another before someone will receive them instead of closing the door and snuffing out the breath of life.

"Earth, then, and her people are dealing with more karma than they have dealt with in many centuries (if it were possible, and it is indeed possible that this is so), and therefore the weight that people feel in their bodies is a weight of anguish.

"Some have accommodated themselves and created accommodations with life, and therefore they consider themselves well-balanced, happy—having all that they want of creature comforts. Yet, many of these have lost contact with their souls, and they do not experience God. For they have cut off their soul faculties, and although they consider themselves rich and increased with goods and having no wants whatsoever, they do not know that their souls feel naked and without anything.

"There are many who cut off not only their own soul but their own divine spark, their own reason for being, and they cut off the angels and God also. And they are very, very sure that they are right in every position they take—social, economic, political.

"All of their views are, of course, right. Yes, beloved ones, so sure are so many who ought not to be sure at all, for they have not the real and living contact with their own soul or with God."[271]

❖ **LLOYD, DAVID,** *See* **David Lloyd**

❖ **LORDS OF FORM, LORDS OF INDIVIDUALITY, LORDS OF MIND, LORDS OF WISDOM,** *See* **Twelve Solar Hierarchies**

❖ **LORDS OF KARMA,** *See* **Karmic Board**

❖ **LOTUS, Messenger of Saint Germain**

The ascended lady master Lotus was last embodied as Edna Ballard, Saint Germain's messenger in the I AM Activity, which was founded in the early 1930s. Her twin flame is the messenger Guy W. Ballard, now the ascended master Godfre. Through them Saint Germain first released the knowledge of the violet flame to the world.

Joan of Arc

Lotus, Godfre and their son Donald were all embodied more than fifty thousand years ago as the children of Saint Germain, the hierarch of a golden-age civilization in the area where the Sahara Desert now is. Lotus was later embodied as Joan of Arc (1412–1431), who was given a mission from God to rally the French armies and drive out the invading English forces, as Elizabeth the First of England (1533–1603), and as Benjamin Franklin (1706–1790), who played a very influential role in the founding of the American nation.

Edna Ballard, often called Mama Ballard by her students, used the pen name of Lotus Ray King. She went through tremendous trials and persecution during her time as messenger. In Los Angeles in 1940 (the year following Godfre's ascension), federal criminal indictments were brought against Mrs. Ballard, her son Donald and others for alleged fraudulent solicitation of funds through the mail. Despite strenuous objections by the defendants' attorney, a jury was in effect given the task of deciding whether the Ballards really believed what they taught and wrote about their messengership and the ascended masters.

Over a period of six years, *United States vs. Ballard* went through two trials and an extended series of appeals, during which Mrs. Ballard was at one point convicted and sentenced to a year in prison and fined $8,000, although the prison sentence was later suspended. Soon thereafter, the Post Office Department issued an order denying use of the mail to the I AM Activity. In the face of adverse media coverage and extreme prejudice within the criminal justice system, Mrs. Ballard and her students fought on, and their efforts culminated in the U.S. Supreme Court throwing out the conviction in 1946. The written opinion from the case has often been cited in subsequent litigation to prohibit judicial inquiry into the truth or falsity of religious beliefs.

The ascended lady master Magda spoke of the service of the Ballards and of their persecution. She said that we would not have the opportunity to give the violet flame and ascend "if Saint Germain and Godfre and Lotus had not been willing to bear the utter persecution, the trial, the lies in the newspapers regarding the I AM movement. You have also been persecuted in your time, but those days of the I AM movement were horrific and without parallel."[272]

On November 18, 1970, Edna Ballard gave her final dictation before her transition. On February 12, 1971, she made her ascension and became the ascended lady master Lotus.

Lotus spoke in 1973 of her service and of the ongoing mission of the messengers: "Some of you here knew me in my last embodiment, and you called me Mama. I desire that you should address this salutation to the Mother of the Flame; for I transfer to her this night my momentum of victory with the legions of light, and I give to her the mantle of my authority and my messengership under Saint Germain....

"I speak now directly to those students who were with me in the I AM Activity, and I say to you, regardless of all evidence to the contrary or of anything that might have passed from my lips while I was in embodiment, I do espouse and back with my total heart flame this activity and this messenger as the continuing outpost and release of the Great White Brotherhood and of Saint Germain to this age.

"For I understand from ascended levels of consciousness the nature of the ongoingness of hierarchy. And although there are only two messengers of the Brotherhood, the two messengers constitute the office of the two witnesses spoken of in the Book of Revelation. This, then, is a high and holy calling to which twin flames are ordained in every age.

"Thus, as there is only one Christ, so there are many manifestations of the office of the Christ; and as there are offices in hierarchy, so the opportunity to serve in those offices is given to ascended and unascended sons and daughters of God as they evolve in the hierarchical scheme of the Great White Brotherhood."[273]

❖ LUARA, *See* Neptune and Luara

❖ MAGDA, Twin Flame of Jesus

The ascended lady master Magda is the twin flame of Jesus. She serves from the Temple of the Resurrection Flame with Jesus and Mary. Her devotion to the Christ, and particularly to the master Jesus, through the centuries has enabled her to build a great momentum of his healing power. She holds the flame of hope to all who desire to overcome the temptations of the world.

Jesus and Mary Magdalene

Magda was embodied as Mary Magdalene, out of whom Jesus cast seven demons. Her victory attests to the fact that all who truly desire to be free are indeed worthy of the great Master's love and may invoke in his name the power of God that will expel the unclean spirits that have gained entrée into the temple of being. Indeed, earth is a schoolroom upon which the evolutions of other planets and solar systems may gaze and see the great miracle of the ascension of those who have descended to the depths of self-degradation before they came to the realization of the Christ and then determined with him to overcome every negative momentum that has brought about the fall of man or woman.

Two thousand years after the ascension of her twin flame, Magda ascended from the Retreat at Luxor. She has been an initiate at Luxor since her final incarnation as the evangelist Aimee Semple McPherson (1890–1944).

The story of Aimee's life shows that she spent her life intensely in the service of God. She enthusiastically preached Jesus' message of healing and salvation worldwide. Thousands flocked to her revival meetings where they were caught up in the rapture of her soaring devotion to her Lord.

In 1917, Aimee began her monthly magazine, *Bridal Call*, writing and editing on the road as she carried her ministry from city to city. In 1919, prior to a sermon in Baltimore, Maryland, Jesus spoke to her about her ministry: "When you lay your hands on them, I will lay my hands on yours. And all the time you are standing there, I will be standing right back of you. And when you speak the Word, I will send the power of the Holy Ghost. You are simply the mouthpiece of the telephone. You are the key on the typewriter. You are only a mouth through which the Holy Ghost can speak."

In Oakland, California, July 1922, Aimee presented a sermon "The Vision of Ezekiel" and received the inspiration from Jesus to call his message "the Foursquare Gospel" of Jesus the Saviour, Jesus the Baptizer with the Holy Spirit, Jesus the Healer, and Jesus the Coming King. On January 1, 1923, she opened the Angelus Temple in Los Angeles, her international headquarters. There she preached to thousands, sometimes in a costume designed to express the theme of her sermon. (For example, for the sermon on "God's Law" she dressed in a police uniform.) From 1923–26, Aimee stayed close to the Angelus Temple. She opened her 24-hour-a-day Prayer Tower, LIFE (Lighthouse of International Foursquare Evangelism) Bible College, and her radio station KFSG (Kall Four Square Gospel).[274]

Aimee was also greatly persecuted and stood alone through great challenges, but during her entire ministry, she lived in anticipation of the day Jesus would come to receive her as his waiting bride. She ascended at the conclusion of that lifetime, and on November 22, 1990, Jesus Christ announced that Magda had finally balanced 100 percent of her karma, over forty-five years after her transition.

The ascended lady master Magda later spoke of this and of her life as Aimee: "I rejoice to have experienced the arduous years during which I was balancing my karma. And those years were indeed arduous, for I had not embraced the violet flame that was being released when I was serving in California.

"Thus, with all that I had of Jesus' love and all of the service I gave throughout the world (even traveling by ship to Australia and to the far corners of the earth), when I passed from the screen of life, I still had my karma to deal with. And then it was, that I saw and understood and accepted the violet flame.[275]

"But for many decades, I had to apply the violet flame, not only to my immediate past life but to many prior lifetimes. And this was simply because I was never given the knowledge of the violet flame when I was embodied. The clergy of Christianity, both Protestant and Catholic, never accepted Saint Germain or his gift of the violet flame, and therefore they never taught it.

"Do you realize that I served in the Angelus Temple in Los Angeles at the same time that Guy and Mama Ballard were also preaching and giving the teachings of the violet flame?

"How tragic it is that so many have become locked into orthodoxy so that they cannot open their minds and see the shafts of violet flame that permeated the auras of the saints who came out of the I AM movement and made their ascensions precisely because they accepted Saint Germain's violet flame.

"Thus, I will say it again and again: How wondrous it is to invoke the violet flame while you are here on earth! How wondrous it is that you can project the violet flame into the distant past and the distant future! How wondrous it is that the violet flame has saved so many souls, that it has lightened their load and brought them to that place where they could make their ascensions!"

Jesus and Magda have explained that "each two thousand years we have come with a profound message and sacrifice of our very life to reach out to your twin flames, to woo you back to the great temples of the Brotherhood and to the school of Maitreya.

"You must understand that your father and mother, even Adam and Eve, are, in a sense, the archetypal pattern of many twin flames who went forth from the mystery school, lured by the temptations of great interest and dominion in the political, economic and social realms that were presented by the Serpent, representing that band of angels who are the scribes, who are the sophists, who pose as the sages but are not the true wise men from the East.

"Thus, you see, there will always be the temptation to master another round of worldly knowledge that is seen as the key to enlightenment, the key to the resolution of the world's problems.

"Blessed hearts, people have had great knowledge and science and invention for tens of thousands of years. Have they saved the world from self-destruction? Have they got to the very core of life and being? Recognize a long, long history of millions of years of trying to solve the problems of the Matter equation without, *sans*, the garment of the etheric temple....

"We have deliberated, our Mother [the Virgin Mary] with us—Magda and I—concerning what we might give to you of the highest and best fruits of our own wisdom and experience, seeing as we see the long continuity of the evolution of thy soul and all that we have encountered. Blessed ones, if it were not so treacherous, the earth would be in the golden age today and you would be walking as masters among men....

"This, therefore, is our commitment and our gift—that those who find they have the division within the members, pulling this way and that—which the apostle Paul spoke of so understandingly, so personally and so poignantly—may then call to us and ask for the transfer of the coil of fire.

"Note the word: *coil of fire*—the coil of myself and of beloved Magda representing the Alpha, the Omega. When these are meshed, they form the divine caduceus. These two coils are of gold. They are of gold as you would visualize golden wire of the purest, finest quality of gold with no alloy.

"Thus, this brilliant, sun-fire gold coil meshed together forms the caduceus of Alpha and Omega. It is not large. These coils are precisely the size large enough to surround each one's physical spinal column from the base unto the crown.

"Now, those sincerely desiring to pass over the dark night and the astral plane of their karma and downward momentums, those who desire to transmute all of this through divine service and chelaship, those who would vow the vow of obedience, chastity and poverty may therefore appeal for this gift. We will supply it.

"And by the coil of gold, by this coil of fire, beloved hearts, and by your pursuing the path of the novitiate, of the holy brother and the holy sister of the divine order, you may reach that point, by the coil and by service, of the transmutation of those elements of being that pull in all directions as horses going in diverse corners who will not submit to the discipline of the driver."[276]

You can call to Magda. She has lived on earth, and she knows of the *via dolorosa*, the sorrowful way. She has walked by our side for many centuries. Now she says that she is just a little bit ahead of us on the path of life. Magda's charity is boundless. She can help you to form a relationship with her twin flame, beloved Jesus. You can invoke her particular momentum and ability to rise from the lowest state of consciousness to the highest overnight, the forsaking of the human with its concepts of good and evil and the embracing of the Christ who stands in the center of one's own temple of Being. With complete faith in the words of the Master, "Thy sins be forgiven thee," she carries the torch of hope to all who are seeking the higher way.

❖ THE MAHA CHOHAN, Representative of the Holy Spirit

The Maha Chohan

The Maha Chohan is the representative of the Holy Spirit. The one who holds this office in hierarchy represents the Holy Spirit of the Father-Mother God, of Alpha and Omega, to the evolutions of this planet and to the elemental kingdom. The retreat of the Maha Chohan, the Temple of Comfort, is located on the etheric plane with a focus in the physical at the island of Sri Lanka (formerly known as Ceylon), where the flame of the Holy Spirit and the flame of Comfort are anchored. His twin flame is Pallas Athena, Goddess of Truth.

Maha Chohan means "Great Lord," and the Maha Chohan is the Great Lord of the seven chohans, the director of the seven chohans of the rays. Among the qualifications for this office in hierarchy is the attainment of adeptship on each of the seven rays, which merge into the pure white light of the Holy Spirit. With the seven chohans, he initiates our souls in preparation to receive the nine gifts of the Holy Spirit, spoken of in 1 Corinthians 12:4–11.

Since the Spirit of God infuses nature and man as the life-giving essence of the sacred fire, the representative of the Holy Spirit must be qualified to interpenetrate all substance through the diffusion of his consciousness and also to draw forth the flame that sustains life in man and nature through the focalization of his consciousness.

The element that corresponds to the flame of the Holy Spirit is oxygen. Without that element, neither man nor elemental life could continue their service. The consciousness of the Maha Chohan is, therefore, comparable to the Great Central Sun Magnet. He focuses the magnet upon the planet that draws to the earth the emanations from the sun that are required to sustain life.

Assisting him in this service are legions of white-fire angels who minister unto the pure white flame of the Holy Spirit of Alpha and Omega anchored in the magnificent altar of the sacred fire in his etheric retreat over the island of Sri Lanka. These angels draw the essence of the sacred fire from that flame to sustain the pranic force throughout the four lower bodies of the planet. Also serving the Holy Comforter are pink-flame angels who tend the focus of the comfort flame in the central altar of his retreat. In an adjoining flame room, there is anchored in a crystal chalice bordered with crystal doves a white flame, tinged in pink, with gold at its base, emitting a powerful radiance of divine love. These angels carry the emanations of these flames to the four corners of the earth to the hearts of all who yearn for comfort and purity from the Father-Mother God.

The twin flames of the Holy Spirit manifested as cloven tongues of fire on the day of Pentecost when the disciples were filled with the Holy Ghost.[277] When Jesus was baptized, "he saw the Spirit of God descending like a dove and lighting upon him."[278] The dove is the physical symbol of the twin flame action of the Holy Spirit, which may also be visualized as a V with wings, a focus of the masculine and feminine polarities of the Deity and a reminder that God created twin flames to represent his androgynous nature.

In the presence of the Maha Chohan and within the walls of his retreat, one feels the rhythm of the Holy Spirit, the pulsations of the sacred-fire breath of God, releasing the flow of life from the Central Sun into the hearts of all evolving upon this planet.

The first three root races, each of which completed their divine plan in the allotted 14,000-year cycle, had their own representatives of the Holy Spirit who graduated into cosmic service with their respective root races.

The one who currently holds this office of Maha Chohan was embodied as the blind poet Homer, whose epic poems, the Iliad and the Odyssey, include his twin flame, Pallas Athena, as a central figure. The Iliad tells the story of the last year of the Trojan War, while the Odyssey focuses on the return home of Odysseus—one of the heroes of the Trojan War.

Historically, little is known about Homer, but most scholars believe he composed his poems in the eighth or ninth century B.C. Even at that time, Homer attuned his consciousness with the comfort flame, and the radiance he sustained with the focus of his own heart flame was a great blessing to elemental life. In his final embodiment as a shepherd in India, the light that he quietly drew forth kept the flame for millions of lifestreams. He gained his mastery by consecrating his four lower bodies as a chalice for the flame of the Holy Spirit and his consciousness as a step-down transformer for the emanations of Sanat Kumara, the Ancient of Days.

The Maha Chohan has referred to the Holy Spirit as the great unifying coordinator who, "like unto a mighty weaver of old, weaves a seamless garment of ascended master light and love. The shuttle of God's attention upon man drives forth radiant beams of descending light, scintillating fragments of purity and happiness, toward earth and into the hearts of his children, whilst the tender risings of men's hopes, aspirations, invocations and calls for assistance do pursue the Deity in his mighty haven of cosmic purity....

"As a tiny seed of light, the Holy Spirit enters into the heart of the earth, into the density of matter, that it might expand throughout the cells of form and being, of thought and perception to become a gnosis and an effulgence in the cup of consciousness. This Holy Grail of immortal substance may be unrecognized by many who pass by, but to many others it will be perceived gleaming from behind the veil. Shedding the light of that divine knowing that transcends mortal conception and is the renewing freshness of eternity's morn, it vitalizes each moment with the God-happiness that man cognizes through infinite perceptions cast as fragments into the chalice of his own consciousness."[279]

In 1974 the beloved Maha Chohan said, "The Karmic Board has decreed that at this hour in the evolution of this lifewave and this planetary home, there has come that moment when the cosmic clock has struck. It is the hour when mankind must receive the Holy Spirit and prepare the body temple to be the dwelling place of the Most High God. In this hour of the appearing of that Spirit, it is necessary that certain numbers of mankind are purified to receive that Spirit. For unless they receive that flame and that awareness, the world as a place of evolution as you know it today will cease to exist. For you see, the balance of all phases of life and evolution cannot continue unless the Holy Spirit becomes the quickening energy and the life and light of man and woman. When the clock strikes midnight and 1974 gives way to 1975, in that moment will be the release of the spiral of the

Holy Spirit to the entire planet."

Then the Maha Chohan told us that the release of the final quarter of the century was "a cosmic spiral that will be for the full realization of the Holy Spirit in man, in woman, in nature, in holy child. And the probation will be a twenty-five-year period to see whether enough among mankind will be able to maintain a tabernacle for the Holy Spirit through sacrifice, surrender and self-purification."[280]

The Maha Chohan ministers to every person on earth as we enter this world and as we exit it. At the moment of that birth, he is present to breathe the breath of life into the body and to ignite the threefold flame that is lowered into manifestation in the secret chamber of the heart.

The Maha Chohan also attends at the transition called death, when he comes to withdraw the flame of life and to withdraw the holy breath. The flame, or divine spark, returns to the Holy Christ Self, and the soul, clothed in the etheric body, also returns to the level of the Holy Christ Self. Similarly, he will minister to you at every crossroad in life, if you will but pause for a moment when making decisions, think of the Holy Spirit and simply say the mantra, "Come, Holy Spirit, enlighten me."

The radiation of the Maha Chohan is drawn through the musical composition "Homing," by Arthur Salmon.

❖ **MAITREYA, LORD, Cosmic Christ and Planetary Buddha**

Lord Maitreya

Lord Maitreya holds the office of Cosmic Christ and Planetary Buddha. His name means "loving kindness," and he focuses the radiance of the Cosmic Christ to the evolutions of earth. Guardian to the planet Earth from Venus, he succeeded Lord Gautama as Cosmic Christ when Gautama became Lord of the World at a Royal Teton ceremony on January 1, 1956.

Under the office of the Cosmic Christ, Lord Maitreya monitors potential earth changes as well as the comings and the goings of the fallen angels and the progress of the Christs incarnate.

In the history of the planet, there have been numerous Buddhas who have served the evolutions of mankind through the steps and stages of the path of the bodhisattva. Lord Maitreya, the Cosmic Christ, has passed the initiations of the Buddha. He has come to the fore in this age to teach all who have departed from the way of the Great Guru Sanat Kumara, from whose lineage both he and Gautama descended.

Maitreya is worshiped in Tibet, Mongolia, China, Japan and throughout Asia, where he is revered by Buddhists as "the Compassionate One" and as the coming Buddha. While Maitreya is accepted by all Buddhists, he does take on a variety of roles in different cultures and religious sects. These roles include the guardian and restorer of the Dharma; intercessor and protector; a guru who personally communes with, initiates and teaches his devotees; a messiah who descends when the world is in turmoil; a messenger sent by the Divine Mother to rescue her children; and the Zen Laughing Buddha.

Buddhist scholar Evans-Wentz describes Maitreya as the "Buddhist Messiah, who will regenerate the world by the power of divine love, and inaugurate a New Age of Universal Peace and Brotherhood. He is at present in the Tushita Heaven, whence He will descend and be born among men and become the future Buddha, to reveal anew, as did Gautama and the long Dynasty of past Buddhas, the Path leading to the Great Liberation."[281]

In Chinese Buddhism, Lord Maitreya is sometimes portrayed as the "Hemp-bag Bonze." (A "bonze" is a Buddhist monk.) In his role, Maitreya appears as a plump, jolly, pot-bellied Laughing Buddha. He is often shown sitting and holding a sack, with happy children climbing all over him. To the Chinese, he represents prosperity, material wealth and spiritual contentment; the children represent the blessing of a large family.

Buddhist scholar Kenneth Ch'en writes of this portrayal of Maitreya, "One feature of his appearance singled him out—he carried a hemp bag wherever he went. Into this bag was deposited whatever he received, and for this reason, the bag became an object of intense curiosity, especially among the children. They would chase him and climb all over him, and force him to open his bag. On such an occasion he would place the bag on the ground, empty the contents one by one, and just as methodically put them back into the bag. The expressions attributed to him were all enigmatic and exhibit [Zen] characteristics…. Once a monk asked him about his bag; he replied by placing it on the ground. When asked what this meant, he shouldered the bag and went away. Once he was asked how old the bag was, and he replied that it was as old as space."[282]

This bag demonstrates the mystery of space and the miracle of space under the dominion of the Buddha. Its timelessness shows the Buddha's mastery of segments of eternity, hence eternity itself, through the flame of Mother.

Lord Maitreya and Lord Gautama were the first from among mankind to respond to Sanat Kumara's magnetic pull to face God and to return to that divine estate in which man had first been created and which he was destined to outpicture in the world of form.

The time came when the one who had served the earth as her Planetary Buddha chose to return to his own planetary chain, leaving a vacancy in this office for one from among earth's guardians to fill. Lord Maitreya applied for the initiations necessary to qualify for this office. Centuries of self-discipline, of training, of devotion and of mastery were required in order for him to attain his present stature. His colleague through all of these classrooms of experience was Lord Gautama, who, by a margin won the buddhic degree first, while Lord Maitreya was accorded the office next in line—that of World Teacher.

As world teacher, his mission was to design for each two-thousand-year cycle the specific type of spiritual instruction most required for the human race for that period. Whenever there was a readied and willing instrument, he was to act as mediator, polarizing the atoms of the four lower bodies of that lifestream, so that the divine plan of that one's individualized I AM Source might flow through its instrument, outpicturing in the world of form the works of a Christ.

Lord Maitreya is the teacher of Jesus, who, with Kuthumi, now holds the office of World Teacher. Maitreya demonstrates on behalf of an evolving humanity the cosmic consciousness of the Christ in all areas of human endeavor and its universality through-out cosmos. He is known as the Great Initiator and was, in fact, the initiator of Jesus in his individualization of the Christ flame in his final embodiment as world saviour and exemplar of the way, the truth and the life to all aspirants on the path of personal Christhood.

Maitreya was himself a chela of Lord Himalaya (manu of the fourth root race) and has his own Focus of Illumination in the Himalayan Mountains. He was the guru of twin flames in the Garden of Eden, which was a mystery school of the Brotherhood. The Mystery School of Eden, located on Lemuria near where San Diego is today, was the first Mystery School on planet Earth. And Maitreya, referred to as the Lord God in Genesis, was its first hierarch.

Since the expulsion of man and woman from the Garden of Eden because of the misuse of the sacred fire in the incorrect application of free will, the Great White Brotherhood has maintained mystery schools and retreats that have served as repositories for the knowledge of the sacred fire that is vouchsafed to twin flames when they have demonstrated the discipline necessary to keep the way of the Tree of Life. The Essene Community was a repository for certain of the ancient mysteries as was the school at

Crotona conducted by Pythagoras.

Following the sinking of Lemuria and Atlantis, the mystery schools that had been established there were relocated in China, India and Tibet as well as in Europe, the Americas and the Pacific fire ring, where they were maintained for thousands of years until, one by one, they were overrun by the hordes of darkness.

Wherever these schools have been destroyed, the ascended masters who sponsored them withdrew their flames and sacred shrines to their retreats on the etheric plane. Here their disciples are trained between embodiments and in their finer bodies (during sleep or samadhi) in order that they might attain that divine Self-knowledge that, until Saint Germain once again advanced it in the twentieth century, had not been available to mankind en masse in the physical plane for centuries. Maitreya has explained that in this time the outer world itself has become the retreat in which each man will take his initiations and, passing these, will gain his eternal freedom, his ascension in the light.

The long-awaited "Coming Buddha," Maitreya has indeed come to reopen his Mystery School to assist Saint Germain and Portia, twin flames of the seventh ray and hierarchs of Aquarius, to usher in the New Age. On May 31, 1984, he dedicated the Heart of the Inner Retreat and the entire Royal Teton Ranch to the path and teaching of the Cosmic Christ in order that those who departed from his tutelage, going the way of Serpents (the fallen angels who led Eve astray), might be restored and the children of the light follow the Son of God in the regeneration.

As well as his focus in the Himalayas, Maitreya maintains an etheric retreat over Tientsin, China, southeast of Peking (Beijing). With Lord Gautama he also teaches students seeking to graduate from earth's schoolroom at the Eastern and Western Shamballa and at the Royal Teton Retreat.

As the sponsor of twin flames, he is the friend of all initiates of the sacred fire. When called upon, he will give the illumination of the Christ

and the strength of the Word to pass the initiations that come under his sponsorship.

His banner is the thoughtform of a mighty clipper ship as it comes in with the tides at eventide to fetch souls of mankind to take them to another shore. His musical keynote is "Ah, Sweet Mystery of Life."

❖ **MANJUSHRI, Boddhisattva of Wisdom**

Manjushri is a great Buddha and a bodhisattva. In Buddhist teachings,

Manjushri is the Bodhisattva of Wisdom. Wisdom is *wise dominion*—of yourself, your aura, your entire being. It is wise dominion of all affairs that are entrusted to you and of all individuals who come under your care.

Wisdom is the most esteemed virtue in Buddhism. The virtue of wisdom has been called the "Mother of all Buddhas," because only wisdom can totally liberate one from suffering. Yet without love and allegiance to the will of God, wisdom itself is not sufficient.

Buddhists see Manjushri as a "herald of emancipation." He is also revered as the patron of arts and sciences, the master of eloquence, and the principal guardian and patron of astrologers. Buddhist writers traditionally invoke Manjushri's assistance, and they often begin their books with verses or prayers in his honor.

Buddhists appeal to Manjushri for intelligence, wisdom, mastery of the teaching, the power of exposition, eloquence and memory. He is the patron of literature who uses the Word consciously as a tool of liberation—as a sharp sword that cuts through ignorance. We can call to Manjushri for gentle or sweet enlightenment.

Though Manjushri is referred to as a bodhisattva, he is believed to have the enlightenment of a Buddha. Some traditions say he became a perfectly enlightened Buddha many aeons ago in another universe.

According to Buddhist lore, Manjushri felt compassion for the people of China because they lived so far from India, where Lord Gautama had incarnated. He therefore took a vow to help the people of China and established his Pure Land in the Five-Mountain Paradise of northern China. A Pure Land is a spiritual realm or paradise presided over by a Buddha, a place created by Buddhas for their disciples that is ideal for their discipleship.

Some texts say that Manjushri also has a Pure Land in another universe, where he manifests as the perfect Buddha he actually is. His earthly Pure Land in northern China is a favorite site for pilgrims; devotees of Manjushri travel there, hoping to catch a glimpse of him. It is said that only those who are truly purified can see him. But even then, it takes a certain mastery to recognize him, because he often appears disguised as a poor man or an orphan.

For those whose karma prevents them from seeing him physically, he sometimes appears in dreams that may be out-of-body experiences, remembered clearly just before we reenter our bodies in the morning. One Zen master says, "There are some student monks who look for Manjushri at Five-Mountain Paradise, but they have already taken the wrong road. There is no Manjushri at Five-Mountain Paradise. Do you wish to know where he is? There is something this very moment at work in you, showing no tendency to waver, betraying no disposition to doubt—this is your living Manjushri." In other words don't look for him outside of yourself, look for him working inside of you within the very walls of your being.

The Sanskrit name Manjushri means "gentle glory" or "sweet glory." In Tibetan iconography Gautama Buddha is often depicted with Manjushri on his left and Maitreya on his right. Manjushri represents the wisdom aspect of the bodhisattva ideal and Maitreya the compassion aspect. Thus, Maitreya and Manjushri represent two sides of the coin of the bodhisattva path.

Professor Robert Thurman writes, "There are different persons on different stages of the path at different times. Different teachings are elaborated for their benefit that emphasize wisdom or compassion. The team of Maitreya and Manjushri, heading the two main branches of the great tree of this philosophical tradition, assure [us] that the balance never goes too far in either direction."[283]

In Buddhist art, Manjushri is often portrayed as a handsome sixteen-year-old prince. His complexion is usually a golden yellow, and he holds in his left hand the stem of a blue lotus blossom. On the blossom rests a book representing one of the Prajna Paramita scriptures, which deal with the realization of *prajna,* or wisdom. With his right hand he wields a flaming sword of wisdom to vanquish all ignorance. This sword has been referred to as "a sword of quick detachment."

The ascended master Manjushri says, "If you choose to recite my mantras, I will assist you in coming to the oneness of the mind of God."[284] The following are Manjushri's mantras:

Om Ah Ra Pa Tsa Na Dhih is given to help develop wisdom, memory and the understanding of the scriptures. The final syllable, *Dhih,* is Manjushri's *bija,* or seed syllable. The essence of a cosmic being is concentrated in his bija. The bija may be given alone or repeated as many times as possible after the final repetition of the mantra.

Om Wagi Shori Mum is given to increase the effectiveness of communication and to deliver the Word. It means "Hail to the Lord of Speech!" Manjushri is known as the Lord of Speech and is revered as a master of eloquence.

Gate Gate Paragate Parasamgate Bodhi Svaha invokes the wisdom of the Prajna-paramita scriptures and can also be given to Manjushri. It means "Gone, gone, gone beyond, gone wholly beyond—Enlightenment, hail!" or "Proceed, proceed, proceed beyond, proceed completely beyond—be founded in enlightenment!" This mantra can propel us beyond illusion and the illusory self into Reality and the Real Self.

Manjushri says, "I AM for your taking wise dominion over the earth and for your wise taking care of all resources available to you.

"I AM for practicality. I AM for your making that which is the nearest right move, even though it be not the perfect move of the moment that you would prefer.

"Above all, do not stagnate. Do what you can do within the hour, within the day, within the year. Plan well. But for God's sake, do not do nothing! For this is not the age of do-nothingness for the chelas of Manjushri and Maitreya and Gautama. This is the age of accelerated doingness.

"We see many on earth operating at high stress levels because they attempt to catch up with the workings of the mind of God within themselves, but they go about it in a human way, and thus, their bodies suffer. Sometimes, just when they are at the peak of their careers, they find that they must deal with problems in their physical bodies that are overwhelming.

"I say, light the way! Be the lamplighters in the earth and know that the lighting of the way to balance in the four lower bodies is the great gift of kindness, the great gift of enlightenment that you can give to many....

"I AM Manjushri, and I have a great sense of humor. And you will know that sense of humor in your own life if you give my mantras. For it is humor on the Path that truly delivers you from the all-too-serious levels of fallen angels."[285]

❖ MARIA

Mother Mary has spoken of an ascended lady master who is named Maria: "Therefore I have brought with me this ascended lady master this day, whose name has not been revealed by the Brotherhood, whose name shall not be revealed this day. But in her devotion to my flame, to the Cosmic Virgin, many have called her Maria—Maria for Mary, for Mother-ray."[286]

❖ MARIA MONTESSORI, Messenger of Education

Maria Montessori is the chela of Mother Mary, and wearing her mantle, she has set forth the fundamentals of ascended master education for the Aquarian age. She was a messenger of the hierarchy in the field of education, and she took her instruction from Mother Mary and from Jesus and Kuthumi.

Maria Montessori was born in Italy in 1870 and became Italy's first woman medical doctor. When she was serving as a doctor in Rome, she was given an assignment to care for the kindergarten children in the

Maria Montessori

slums of the city. By observing the children, she developed what has come to be known as the Montessori Method.

Maria Montessori discovered that children have very different and unique qualities that no one had ever noticed. She found that these qualities can be liberated and set free in the proper environment with the proper conditions.

One of the first things she noticed when dealing with children was that they would rather work than play. Children are very industrious, and if their work is organized, they can develop inner patterns that assist their development.

Children have great power for concentration and a tremendous love for order. Children between the ages of two and seven are great creatures of ritual. They love to do things in order. The goal of the child is not to get the job done, but to do it systematically. Montessori understood that the patterns of order and logic that are developed in the child through physical motion later enhance the child's ability to learn, to concentrate and to study.

Montessori found that children have a keen sense of touch, that they learn with their hands more than they even learn with their eyes, and so she developed systems of what she called sensorial development. Children also like freedom of choice. The Montessori classroom is designed to allow each child to select the set of blocks or the training material that he will then use at that specific moment—it is a cosmic moment—when his soul is ready to develop around that particular point.

Children age two and one-half through six are all in one classroom so that the younger children can see the more advanced work of the older children and they can learn from their example. A Montessori teacher's role is to direct the child toward the exercises.

In a Montessori classroom you will find little children at their tables preoccupied for great lengths of time, concentrating on their lessons. They have an amazing power of concentration. They learn mathematics with concrete equipment such as beads or blocks designed to teach the association of numerals and quantity. They learn writing and reading, but they do it according to the pattern of their own unique inner development. Children are not rushed or forced to do something that does not come easily and naturally to them. The teacher's role is to encourage independent learning as the child listens to his own inner teacher. Maria Montessori discovered that the call of the universal child is, "Help me to do it myself."

All of these things were revealed to Maria Montessori by the children themselves. She said that all she did was watch the children, and they taught her the method.

The Montessori method is intended to bring out the Christ potential of the child, as the child follows the direction of the inner teacher and selects in the classroom certain equipment and exercises that are appropriate for fulfillment of the inner and spiritual needs of the child and to bring forth the inner attainment. The combined freedom and order in the Montessori classroom is the true Aquarian-age education.

The Montessori method for children was inspired upon Maria Montessori by Mother Mary. Mary explained that this was the method she had devised with Elizabeth for teaching John the Baptist and Jesus when they were children.

❖ **MARY, THE MOTHER OF JESUS, Archeia of the Fifth Ray**

Mother Mary is the archeia of the fifth ray and twin flame of Archangel Raphael. The temple of Archangel Raphael and Mother Mary is in the etheric realm over Fátima, Portugal. Mother Mary also serves with Jesus in the Resurrection Temple over the Holy Land.

Although an archangel, Mary has also taken physical embodiment. In the early days of Atlantis, she served in the Healing Temple, tended the flame and studied the healing arts and the disciplines necessary for precipitation. At that time, she developed great concentration and consecration to the immaculate concept. It was her consciousness and momentum more than any others that sustained the flame in the temple and expanded its influence throughout Atlantis. The purity of her heart flame and her devotion shone upon her face and was evident to all who frequented that Temple. She remained a temple virgin during that entire embodiment.

In the days of the prophet Samuel, Mary was called to be the wife of Jesse and the mother of his eight sons. Ever fulfilling her role as the Mother ray, Mary, in this incarnation of her soul on earth, magnified the light of the seven rays of the Christ in the first seven sons of Jesse. But in the youngest, David, she glorified not only the full complement of virtues from the prism of the Lord, but also the majesty and mastery of the eighth ray, which David exemplified in his reign and extolled in his psalms.

David himself was reembodied as Jesus, and thus in the Psalms, the Israelites have recourse to the teachings of one who has attained Christmastery while Gentiles also reflect upon the meditations of the Saviour, all striving for the same goal set forth by him who is known as both the king of Israel and of the New Jerusalem. And so it is not surprising that today in the Cenacle overlooking the city of Jerusalem, Christians pray in the Upper Room on the site where Jesus and the disciples celebrated the Last Supper, where Christ appeared after his resurrection, and where the descent of the Holy Spirit took place. And in the lower level of the same house, there is a temple where Jews worship at the Tomb of David. Nor is it surprising to those who offer praise to her name that Mary is the Mother of both the Judaic and the Christian dispensations.

In her final embodiment, Mary came forth under the direction of hierarchy, chosen of God to bear Jesus the Christ, who would demonstrate the laws of alchemy and the victory that every man must attain over sin, sickness and death. In early childhood she was placed in a temple for training in the science of the immaculate concept. Her twin flame, Archangel Raphael, together with members of the angelic host and the God and Goddess Meru, assisted her in the development of the Mother principle in order that her consciousness might become a womb for the seed of the Christ.

During childhood she focused in her outer consciousness those momentums she had developed long ago on Atlantis and at inner levels before taking embodiment. When Mary was still a young girl, Joseph (an embodiment of Saint Germain) was sent to be the guardian and protector of Mary and Jesus. Together, the three members of the Holy Family composed the  threefold flame that was not only the basis for family unity but also for the entire Christian dispensation.

For thousands of years prior to taking embodiment, Mary had invoked the momentum of the fifth ray and studied how to hold the perfect image or blueprint of the Christ and of the specific precipitation that was the requirement of the hour—a flower, a temple, a flame, a work of art or an entire civilization. Whatever the precipitation, there must be one lifestream who is dedicated to its manifestation, who visualizes its components and through whose consciousness the energizing power of the Holy Spirit flows in order it give it form and life. This is the activity of the representative of the feminine ray of the Motherhood of the Godhead. Mary fulfilled that role for Jesus, and therefore, through her consciousness came the purity and the power and the love that enabled him to fulfill his mission.

During the final three years of his ministry, after his return from the Far East, where he studied in the Himalayas under Lord Maitreya, his guru, Jesus entered public life. This period was a great test for Mary, and only her momentum on the fifth ray enabled her to sustain the matrix of victory unto the very end. After Jesus' ascension, she gathered the disciples and friends and formed a colony at Bethany, where they met to receive instruction from their Lord.

Saint John of Damascus describes how at the close of this magnificent embodiment of service and initiation, Mary ascended from a tomb in which the apostles had placed her body after her passing. Upon opening the tomb three days later, they found only twelve white lilies.

After her ascension, Mary was made representative of the World Mother with a title of Queen of Heaven for the Christian Dispensation. Although all ascended lady masters keep the flame for the World Mother as her representative, we think of Mary as the archetype of Motherhood, the Mother of mothers. Until 1954 Jesus and Mary held the focus of the masculine and feminine rays for the sixth dispensation. At that time, Saint Germain and Portia assumed the office of directors for the coming age on the seventh ray for the seventh dispensation.

Today she works with the master El Morya and the Darjeeling Council in their service to the will of God on behalf of all mankind. She has a blue cape focusing that will and its intense protection for the Christ consciousness emerging within every soul, and when called upon, she will place that cape around all who are in need of the protection of a mother's love. She renders assistance with Archangel Gabriel in preparing the way for the incoming children, in teaching the parents and in guiding the body elementals in forming their physical bodies.

Mary's focus of the Sacred Heart in the Resurrection Temple is the focus of the threefold flame commemorating the mission of the Christ of the Holy Trinity. Her service with Saint Germain and Jesus laid the foundation for two thousand years of Christian belief and service and also for the coming age.

Mary's ascension is celebrated on the 15th of August. Since her ascension, Mother Mary has appeared throughout the world, producing many miracles of healing. She set the stage for these appearances in the later years of her final embodiment, when she visited various areas of the world accompanied by John the Beloved and five others. They went first to the retreat at Luxor, Egypt, and then on a voyage by boat to the Island of Crete across the Mediterranean Sea, through the Straits of Gibraltar, stopping at Fátima in Portugal, Lourdes in Southern France, Glastonbury in the British Isles and Ireland. In all these places, Mary and those serving with her drew focuses of the fifth ray, establishing the flame of science, healing and precipitation, preparing the way for those who would come after her to amplify the Christ consciousness.

These visits laid the foundation for the work of the apostle Paul in Greece and her own appearances at Fátima and Lourdes. The Holy Grail, the cup used by Jesus at the last supper, was buried in a well at Glastonbury. Here was planted the flame of the Christ, which later inspired King Arthur to form the Knights of the Round Table and to engage in the quest for the Holy Grail.

Saint Patrick drew upon the focus of the threefold flame placed in Ireland and later taught the mystery of the Trinity, using the shamrock to illustrate the oneness of the Father, Son and Holy Spirit. The emerald-green healing flame remains the symbol of Ireland and the remembrance of that journey long ago by those seven representatives whose devotion to the seven rays enabled them to succeed in paving the way for the expansion of Christianity throughout Europe and ultimately the Western Hemisphere.

The Aquarian age is the age of the Mother and the Holy Spirit. It is the age when we are meant to experience and express the Mother aspect of God. Coming to understand this feminine aspect of God can liberate the creative feminine energy within us, both man and woman—the energy of beauty and creativity, intuition and inspiration.

The concept of God as Mother is not new to Eastern spirituality. The Hindus meditate upon Mother as the Goddess Kundalini, describing her as the white light, or the coiled serpent, that rises from the base of the spine to the crown, activating levels of spiritual consciousness in each of the chakras (spiritual centers) through which that light passes along the way. Whether we are male or female, we are intended to raise this sacred light of our innermost being that lies dormant within us. The key to unlocking this energy, the Kundalini, is adoration of the Mother principle.

The Pietá, by Michelangelo

The raising of the Mother light is a part of Western tradition also. It is for this purpose that Mother Mary appeared to several of the saints with the safe and sound method of raising the Mother light through the Hail Mary and the rosary. The saints have been portrayed with a white light, or halo, around their heads because they have raised the Kundalini and opened their crown chakras. They have entered into the bliss of God. The great Christian mystics such as Saint John of the Cross, Saint Thérèse of Lisieux and Padre Pio have all had this inner experience—so filled with the divine passion, the bliss of the Beloved, as to defy comprehension.

As we enter this new era, Mother Mary has released a New Age Hail Mary and a New Age rosary. In giving the Hail Mary, Mary has asked us to affirm that we are sons and daughters of God rather than sinners. She also asks us to affirm our victory over sin, disease and death.

> Hail, Mary, full of grace
> the Lord is with thee.
> Blessed art thou among women
> and blessed is the fruit of thy womb, Jesus.
>
> Holy Mary, Mother of God,
> Pray for us, sons and daughters of God,
> Now and at the hour of our victory
> Over sin, disease and death.

The impact of Mother Mary's service and intercession throughout the centuries is almost incalculable. She urges us to fast and pray and to give the rosary. Mother Mary has said, "I extend to you, then, access by the rosary—*by the rosary*—to my causal body, to the attainment on those fourteen stations that I have gained throughout my long spiritual history. I give you, therefore, the opportunity to receive that power and attainment that God has given me as my great Teacher. And as I am his servant, this I transmit to you that it might become close to the physical world and the physical problem through your own physical body and heart."[287]

Mary says, "My appearances through the centuries have centered on the request for prayer and for the giving of the rosary for the saving of souls. Millions have been saved because millions have responded to my call."[288] In her appearances at Fátima, Medjugorje and other places in the world, Mary has told of what may come upon the earth if we do not heed her warnings.

In 1984 Mother Mary said, "I live with the Fátima prophecy. I live with its message. And I go from door to door and heart to heart knocking, asking for those who will come and pray with me—pray the violet flame or the rosary or the calls to Archangel Michael. But above all, pray. For by thy prayer is the open door extended, and the angels come stepping through the veil to prevent disaster and calamity."[289]

Miracles have occurred again and again through her intercession. When the atomic bomb was dropped on Hiroshima in 1945, eight men living eight blocks from the center of the nuclear blast were miraculously untouched. One of them, Father Hubert Shiffner, S.J., explained, "In that house the rosary was prayed every day. In that house, we were living the message of Fatima."[290]

This blessed Mother is fierce in the protection of her children and outspoken on the ills of society: "The land is plagued with darkness upon the screens of the invention of the motion picture. The land is plagued with darkness over the churches devoted to honor my Son's name. The land is plagued with darkness as the political candidates struggle among themselves seeking a temporal crown.... The elementals have communicated recently with one another, and they are preparing to execute cataclysmic strands of destruction that have only begun in the world order. And this shall come to pass unless the teachings of God shall be fulfilled in the hearts of many men and women presently totally dedicated to their own selves without understanding the great needs of humanity."[291]

"Until a correct understanding of the I AM THAT I AM be made known across the land, governments will fall, economies will crumble, churches will come to ruin, darkness will cover the land, famine will be present, and souls will be lost."[292]

"Within my Sacred Heart is the acceleration of light this day...unto the judgment of those who have persistently denied the miracles of the Virgin Mary.... Let there be the judgment of the false teachers who have stolen into the churches with their false theology.... Everyone who has interfered with the birth of these little ones— everyone who has advocated abortion from the pulpits of the churches, I tell you they will suffer exactly the karma that is written in sacred scripture spoken by my Son,[293] and it will not be withheld this day!"[294]

Mother Mary is one of the great teachers of mankind. She instructs us in the science of the immaculate concept, the pure concept or image of the soul held in the mind of God. The immaculate concept is any pure thought held by one part of life for and on behalf of another part of life, and it is the essential ingredient to every alchemical experiment without which it will not succeed. The ability to hold the image of the perfect pattern to be precipitated, to see the vision of a project complete, to draw a mental picture, to retain it and to fill it in with light and love and joy—these are keys to the science that Mother Mary and Saint Germain teach.

God is the supreme practitioner of the science of the immaculate concept. No matter how far man might wander from his individuality, God ever beholds man in the image of Reality in which he created him. This sci-

ence of the immaculate concept is practiced by every angel in heaven. It is that law that is written in the inward parts of man, known by his very heart of hearts, yet dim in the memory of his outer mind. It is based on the visualization of a perfect idea that then becomes a magnet that attracts the creative energies of the Holy Spirit to his being to fulfill the pattern held in mind.

Mary blue, the color that we associate with Mother Mary's love, is almost an aqua—blue tinged with a bit of green—and through it her devotion to healing radi-

ates to all who call to her for assistance. Her fragrance and flame-flower is the lily of the valley, and her keynote is the "Ave Maria" by Schubert.

❖ **MASTER OF PARIS,** *See* **Paris, Master of**

❖ **MAXIMUS, Authority for the Great Maxim Light**

Maximus (meaning "God is great") is the authority in the Sun behind the sun for the Great Maxim Light, which is the first cause behind the effect we have called the Cosmic Egg.

In a dictation in 1977, Maximus explained the nature of his service and the meaning of his name: "The word has many connotations, and it is a point for the centering of consciousness on a certain light of Mother—the *MA* of a cosmos and the *I* of individualization, and again the confirmation of Mother within the *US* of the Elohim, of twin flames, and of Alpha and Omega. And the mighty *X*-factor in the center of the word is the nexus of the turning of the cycles for the integration of the flow of the Buddha and the Mother over the figure-eight pattern.

"You will note that the sign of the *X* is the abbreviation for the sign of the figure eight. You simply erase the curves and you are left with the *X* in the center. Maximus! [*MA-X-I-M-US*] It is the representation of dedication to the Mother of all life and to all that is suspended within her womb.

"I AM a light, a kindling light of worlds. My service to life is in the center of the Flaming Yod. My service to life is in the center of the Elohim. And when I say 'my,' I include in my self-awareness a numberless array of cosmic beings, all of whom are dedicated to that flame, that flame of cognizance of the almighty Maximus."[295]

In 1979 Maximus explained that he has come by dispensation in response to the call: "Alpha and Omega promised me aeons ago in the very hour of the great rebellion that when certain sons and daughters of light should so accelerate and so expose that rebellion, when certain bands of saints should commune and sound the Word, when that Word should be heard in far-off worlds, and when the power and the thrust of that Word should reach a certain intensity, then I would be sent to follow the sound back to the source and there to undo the misuse they have made of the light of Maximus itself. Therefore I come. It is yet a limited dispensation."

He released the sound of the tone of Alpha and Omega into the earth. "It is a rippling of light. It will accomplish its work.... I smile because I know what is the ultimate ending and beginning of the sound. I know how it will resound in hearts and strike a chord of love. I know, for I am Maximus, and I have been Maximus for a long, long time and space and for a wide, wide eternity.

"I know, for I have sounded the sound of the Word in other systems of worlds. By the Word, the worlds were framed. By the Word, the worlds are unframed. By the Word, and only the Word, is the Luciferian creation no more. They know me even as they know you. They have succeeded in postponing the sounding of the sound by casting out their nets, dark nets. They do their fishing at night while children sleep, and they catch the souls and draw them through the astral plane, programming souls asleep to their own net gain.

"But it is no more, for with the awakening of the Buddha Gautama, with the awakening of the light of the Cosmic Christ, with the point of contact in the hearts of the few, the cycles roll and the appointed hour is struck."[296]

Archangel Michael says of Maximus, "You may apply to him for 'the Maxim Light.' But you must understand the path of chelaship and receive the interior correction of the Christ mind and receive all emissaries of God, of the heavenly hosts and of the messengers beneath, that you might quickly respond and not resist the will of God that is in the heart of the Maxim Light."[297] This is the great light borne by the great ones such as Melchizidek, and it was the light that blazed upon the altar of the Incalithlon, the great central temple of Atlantis.

Mother Mary teaches that we can call to Maximus to ratify and maximize a previous victory on the world scene: "A victory can be magnified, can be multiplied, can be maximized through the heart of Maximus for maximum benefit to those individuals who as yet have not had the arcing of that externalization of the threefold flame that has brought about a victory in one area of the globe."[298]

We can also maximize our calls when we pray for one another. For example, if we are praying for one son of God who is beset by suicide and the demons of suicide, we can maximize or prayers and call for all children of the light who are burdened by thoughts of suicide. God is infinite, and he can multiply himself a billion times over.

❖ **MELCHIZEDEK, Priest of the Seventh Ray**

Melchizedek blessing Abraham

Melchizedek, priest of the Most High God, is an ancient member of the sacred-fire priesthood that we know as the Order of Melchizedek. The Melchizidekian priesthood is very ancient, going back all the way to other star systems. It is the priesthood of the seventh ray, combining the perfect religion and the perfect science. Priests of this order are required to be scientists as well as to perfect the way of the light of God in their temples.

Melchizedek is first seen in the Bible as the priest of the Most High God who met and blessed Abraham returning from the slaughter of the kings and to whom Abraham gave a tenth part of the spoils. Melchizedek served Abraham bread and wine, the first record we have of the serving of Holy Communion. Melchizedek is a very key figure of light, a Guru of gurus. He was the greatest initiate and adept of the Old Testament and ascended at the conclusion of that embodiment.

In chapter 7 of the Book of Hebrews we read: "For this Melchisedec, king of Salem, priest of the most high God, who met Abraham returning from the slaughter of the kings, and blessed him; to whom also Abraham gave a tenth part of all; first being by interpretation King of righteousness, and after that also King of Salem, which is, King of peace; without father, without mother, without descent, having neither beginning of days, nor end of life; but made like unto the Son of God; abideth a priest continually."

In the Hebrew, the name Melchizedek means "king of right." Therefore he is a king of righteousness who multiplies the Law of God by the right use or exercise of that Law. It also means king by right, by attainment. Melchizedek also held the title of King of Salem, which is King of Jerusalem, the Holy City. The word *king* means, "*key* to the *in*carnation of God." Therefore Melchizedek holds, by the rod of his authority and his attainment, the key to our incarnation of God in the Holy City, in the New Jerusalem.

Lord Ling explains the description of Melchizedek as without father or mother: "But it is written that in due course of time, by the power of the spoken Word released from the throat chakra, spiritual individuals shall face one another and, uttering the sacred words, shall quicken by light rays in the seed power the proper use of the sex (sacred) energies and the caduceus action, and produce a living form instantaneously in the great cosmic light from which steps forth a son of God in radiant manifestation.

"In this manner Melchizedek was born without father and without mother, without descent, without beginning of days and without ending. You say, 'You have said that he was born without father and mother, and yet you have said that they faced one another.' Yea, it is true. But those who faced one another were as masters of light, a Son and Daughter of God, and he was without earthly mother and father, but not without heavenly mother and father. Thus, I have revealed to you this night one of the secrets of the Order of Melchizedek."[299]

The book of Hebrews says that Jesus was "made an high priest forever after the order of Melchisedec."[300] The akashic records reveal that both Jesus and Saint Germain studied in the retreat of the Archangel Zadkiel when they were in embodiment on Atlantis. Both completed their initiations and training in the order of the priesthood of Melchizedek before the sinking of the continent. They stood before Melchizedek and the great Archangel Zadkiel, who said upon these two blessed ones, "Thou art a priest forever after the order of Melchisedec."[301] Once one receives that training and initiation, it carries over to succeeding lifetimes. Thus, Jesus was already a priest of the Order of Melchizedek before his birth in his final embodiment.

One of the symbols of Melchizedek is the Maltese cross. This cross is made up of four V's that meet in the center of the cross, representing the

four planes of Matter. Melchizedek teaches the mastery of these four planes, and he is at the heart of the cross at the point of the meeting of the lines of force of Spirit and Matter, Alpha and Omega.

The priesthood of the ascended master Melchizedek is of the seventh ray and the seventh age. You can request to become a member of that order. The first step is the giving of the violet flame. You can also write a letter to Jesus, Melchizedek and Archangel Zadkiel, asking to be trained in the priesthood of the Order of Melchizedek. Burn the letter, and the angels will take it to the heaven-world. Each day give violet-flame decrees and ask to be taken while your body sleeps at night to Archangel Zadkiel's retreat for training.

Archangel Zadkiel speaks of the service of this priesthood: "The role of the priesthood, beloved, is to tend the flame of life at the altar of temple and home and heart. The calling of the priesthood is to never let go, or go out, the flame of life. First and foremost, the flame must be kept by these committed ones on behalf of the planetary and solar evolutions. The priesthood are keepers of the flame on behalf of those souls evolving on various rungs of the ladder of life, extending the grace and the mercy and the ritual of the seventh ray that they might find their own God-mastery, petal by petal.

"Thus, the priest of the Order of Melchizedek is also self-effacing, his motto 'He must increase, but I must decrease.'³⁰² The meaning of this statement made by John the Baptist is that the priest cedes his place to the one who comes after him, and he thereby ascends another level vibrationally. Therefore he does decree that the one who is capable of receiving his torch that is passed must increase in that position and he who does go on must decrease at that level, even as he, too, shall increase at the next level."³⁰³

The Priesthood of Melchizedek is very active on the earth today. In a landmark dictation given in Portland, Oregon, May 28, 1986, Saint Germain announced a dispensation whereby one hundred and forty-four thousand priests from the Priesthood of Melchizedek formed a violet-flame Maltese cross over the city:

"Blessed ones, the event that brings me to this city is both ancient and recent. The ancient event, as recorded here in akasha, is a misuse of the light—in some cases by those who have reincarnated here and tarry for the opportunity to balance that karma, and in some cases by those who are not recalled to the scene of this misuse.

"Beloved, there are many sincere hearts in this area and state, as you are well aware; for I count you among them most certainly. Therefore, I would intercede in a danger you know not of, which is the return of that karma, cycle for cycle, in this hour of planetary karma returning. The intercession, then, is invoked through the council of Lord Zadkiel's retreat and the priesthood of Melchizedek.

"There is a violet-ray priesthood, beloved. Therefore, during this meditation, a procession of priests of the sacred fire have marched from that retreat to this area, forming by their bodies of light a Maltese cross.... Thus, beloved, the four arms signify the release into Matter of a sacred fire.

"The members of the order of this ancient priesthood are ascended masters all. They long ago attained that victory that is yours to enter in this hour. They come from ancient temples prior to the desecration thereof on lost continents where they themselves achieved the honor of the white fire and the entering therein. They have come, then, to give protection and an immense fire of transmutation that that return of karma might be mitigated or entirely consumed. This consuming and transmutation must take place in the physical through the intercession of yourselves and your heart flames receiving the violet flame, calling it forth, and welcoming a cooperative endeavor of these one hundred and forty-four thousand priests of the Order of Melchizedek who have placed their bodies this night in this giant Maltese-cross formation."

❖ **MERCURY, GOD,** *See* **Hermes Trismegistus**

❖ **MERU, GOD AND GODDESS, Manus of the Sixth Root Race**
     The God and Goddess Meru are manus of the sixth root race (the sixth of seven primary groups of souls destined to embody on earth). They are the lawgivers and they embody the Christic image for all the members of this root race. These masters are also the sponsors of education, advanced learning, the acceleration of the mind, the heart, the soul and the full development of the potential of the unborn child and all children as they mature.
     The terms God and Goddess denote that they are cosmic beings who ensoul the God consciousness of their office. God Meru has explained that the names God and Goddess Meru have come down from ancient Lemuria, where their twin flames guarded the light of the Motherland. The physical focus of the Mother flame was lost when Lemuria sank beneath the Pacific. The God and Goddess Meru have enshrined the Mother flame at their retreat on the etheric plane to make up for the loss of the focus of the flame on the ancient Motherland.
     Their vast retreat, the Temple of Illumination, is located over Lake Titicaca, high in the Andes mountains on the Peru-Bolivia border. The center of the retreat is directly over the remains of an ancient temple on an island in this lake, the Island of the Sun.
     At their retreat, the God and Goddess Meru focus the feminine ray of the Godhead for the planet, just as Himalaya and his twin flame, the manus of the fourth root race, focus the masculine ray in their etheric retreat in the Himalayas. The polarity of these rays is evident in the religious philosophies of East and West. The austerity and mental polarity of worship in the East is balanced by devotion to the Mother principle and the feeling aspect of religion prevalent in the West.
     The retreat of the Royal Tetons is a relay station for the energies of the

Brotherhood of Wisdom. Thus there is an arc of illumination from the Andes to the Rockies, and from their focus in North America, the God and Goddess Meru direct the action of illumination's flame into the hearts of the youth of the world. Their program of education of the masses, whereby souls are taken to temples of light for training while their bodies sleep, is carried on in retreats of the Brotherhood throughout the world. A massive outreach of the Brotherhood through the efforts of the God and Goddess Meru is preparing the way for the incoming seventh root race and for the golden age.

God Meru tells us of the founding of his retreat: "In the ancient civilizations here in South America we saw how cosmic travail did produce that which is far, far beyond what you have yet seen in your modern world. We were able to see great highways builded by the early Incas. We were able to see vehicles of transportation that far exceed that which you presently enjoy. We were able to witness the great temples of truth and life and light and love that grew and manifested by the labor of men's hearts and minds working in universal harmony until their grandeur surpassed all that modern life—and ancient life in most cases in other continents—has ever manifested. Yet today much of the region occupied by those grand temples and cities lies a tangled jungle ruin. Why, gracious ones, is this so?

"It is so because the minds and hearts of those individuals did not actually keep pace with the scientific advancement that life had vouchsafed unto them. Rather, individuals began first of all within themselves to express some form of inharmony, and then this was transmitted unto other parts of life. And there came into play a vying with one another for recognition and acknowledgment of the dreams of their life and the unfoldment thereof.

"And so it was by the spirit of competition and the 'competement' of individuals with one another that inharmony rode in. And the civilization, led by priests of sacred light who had fallen from their lofty office, eventually came down to the banality of ruin. And the ruin that manifested there in South America was very great. But because of the light that they had sent forth, which light ascended unto God reaching up into the very heavens itself, it was decreed by a karmic law that we should maintain a great spiritual focus of majestic light here!

"And so, at Lake Titicaca, a region relatively unspoiled by mortal thought and feeling, there sprang into manifestation the full focus of the gathered momentum of all of the lifestreams and their constructive endeavors, to merge into the great cosmic flame of illumination. The wisdom of God that built those civilizations, then, itself was gathered, and the flame that rises here at Titicaca is the flame of Almighty God's wisdom, which ascends as a great pillar of witness to all people and all nations. Yet only the few are able to understand the majesty which now and for all time rises into the ethers and pulsates with the flame of divine wisdom for the freeing of mankind."[304]

In our time, there are great burdens on families, children and youth. In assessing these situations, the God and Goddess Meru have evolved a plan for the cooperation of the child, the family and the community. Meru says: "I read to you now a scroll. This scroll has been penned by the angels of our retreat. And it is the setting forth by the beloved Goddess Meru and myself of the priorities that we see for the protection and the securing of youth to a ripened age of maturity and Christhood at thirty-three:

"First and foremost, *the dedication of education upon the Word and the Sacred Heart*—dedicating the three R's as the three rays of the threefold flame and therefore setting the foundation whereby all learning might proceed from within....

"Parents need understanding and training. Therefore, second on our list is *parental training*....

"There must be as point three *a pact* made *twixt parents, teachers and sponsors of children* to work together as a threefold flame of devotion in this community and then city by city. This entails the realization that death and hell desire to devour your children, and therefore, you must pray fervently! You must vow, after understanding the meaning of the vow, to stand between the youth of the world and death and hell....

"Fourth on our list must be the white-fire bastion of *the vow* made.... Once the vow is taken, you must remember the first Mother of the Flame, Clara Louise, who kept a daily prayer vigil for the youth, beginning at four in the morning and not concluding till late morning, praying for all souls of the youth, from the unborn to those in college and beyond....

"*Community action* is next on our list—an involvement of community that does reinforce family as these twin pillars of family and community brace a path of individualism for those of all ages. The breaking down of the family, the breaking down of the neighborhood communities—this is a fragmenting of society and the separation of members of karmic groups as well as individuals of varying ages so that they cannot learn from one another and ripen and mature, as the mature inspire those coming up, and the youth introduce the new wave of a New Age that can also challenge those in the middle of life or retiring.

"Community, then, must be a stronghold of values, of serving together, of meeting one another's needs and of establishing goals and priorities, not the least of which is the protection of that circle of lives. Blessed ones, a community must have more than the survival of itself or its happiness as a goal. It must have a totality of a reason for being toward which every member is galvanized and does rise.

"Apropos this, our next point on the list is the *training* of all members of society, and especially the children, *in responsible citizenship*—in taking responsibility for the necessary functions of the group, whether as a police force, as firemen, as a city council or as those who are supplying the unguent and the service in order that a community might endure.

"When all of the forces of chaos are attempting to break down a way of life, let us turn to *the music of the spheres.* Let us turn to the quieting of souls, to the invoking of harmonies, to the bringing forth of the golden-age sounds that have not been heard. Thus, this point on our list is an activation from the heart of Cyclopea, who does join us in sponsoring this call. Cyclopea holds secret melodies waiting to come forth that will remind the youth of ancient times, inner vows, other years when beauty and love, even in etheric octaves, was their lot.

"The youth need comfort of the Holy Spirit and not surfeiting. Tragically, tragically, few among them in actuality desire a path and a discipleship. Therefore, we do recommend the study and the structuring of a program that does *reinforce individuality* and thereby diminish the necessity in perilous times for such an emotional interdependence among teenagers as to make them fear to stand their ground for a cause or a principle.

"Why is peer pressure of such great consequence, beloved? Is it because of absence of parental reinforcement, understanding and even the camaraderie of a family that is not so distant and that does not set artificial barriers between one generation and the next? Let us not so poorly educate children as to see that they do not know their own minds or hearts or values, having had no noble ideals or stories of saints and heroes or examples of karmic consequences of misdeeds...."

"We are the God and Goddess Meru. We are the sponsors and the teachers of Jesus and all who have come to minister unto the sixth root race. Thus, Jesus and many other saints have long studied in our retreat. It is a home base for them. We invite you to come frequently.... Thus you know that with the World Teachers we shall abide with you until every child on earth does have the opportunity to be tutored in the heart by the Holy Christ Self and by anointed teachers and parents and sponsors."[305]

God Meru has given an excellent teaching on self-condemnation: "Some of you sit in the seat of the scornful. You are scornful toward yourselves. You condemn yourselves because you think you are not what you ought to be, that you have not made a great enough effort. Perhaps you forgot to pray this morning, or you did not have the time. Will you live in condemnation of yourself throughout the day? Or if you, through indiscretion, commit an act of sin for which you have sincere regret, will you be burdened by your own self-condemnation all the days of your life, thinking that you are unacceptable to the Godhead?

"Finally the end result of self-condemnation is rebellion against the Deity. For man cannot live in self-condemnation, and thus he must throw off what the imagines to be the angry God who is condemning him. And thus he can only find his freedom by denying God totally. But who has created this God of condemnation but man himself, in his dissatisfaction with himself?

"I say, O precious children of the Sun, be not weary in welldoing. Be not burdened with a sense of guilt. For there is no condemnation in God, but the demons and the fallen ones stand before you to condemn you night and day. And they whisper here, and they whisper there, and they tell you what a terrible person you are, what a miserable sinner you are, and that there is no hope for your salvation. I tell you, precious hearts, the majority of mankind in this very hour are burdened with this sense of condemnation, which stifles creativity, stifles the beauty of the Godhead—the potential to bring forth the science of light, the music of the spheres, a golden-age culture.

"People walk the streets feeling unworthy of life itself. God in you is worthy to be adored! God in you is worthy to be joyous, to be upheld! If you are burdened with a sense of the consciousness of sin, then I say, what is your consciousness of God? What do you think of God if you make sin so real that you can never be released from the bondage of sin? Is God aware of all that? I tell you, nay. And if he is not aware of it, why should you give it even a flicker of your consciousness of attention? For where your consciousness is, there your energy flows. And there your energy goes, and thus you give the great River of Life into a matrix of self-condemnation. And by and by you condemn yourself out of existence.

"Some of you…are suffering at the present time from physical diseases or impediments that are the direct result of your own condemnation of yourself that has become such a burden to your body elemental that it has outpictured in your physical form.

"O precious hearts, arise and be free and Christ shall give thee light. You must be free of this sense of sin if you would progress one foot forward on the Path. You stop all progress as long as you conceive of yourself as a sinner. Has the Creator lost his power to forgive, to transmute, to dissolve sin? Nay. Our God is a God of mercy and a consuming fire. *Prove him,* therefore, as he has commanded you to do. Prove his law.

"Thrust your sins into the fire as in the ancient sacrifice of the children of Israel, symbolical of putting into the flame the menagerie of the sub-conscious—the animal forms, the darkness, the density. How do you do this? You simply say: 'In the name of Jesus the Christ, I cast all that is less than the Christ into the flame. O God, consume it! I ask it. Hear my plea and answer. I accept it done this hour in full power in fulfillment of the promise of the Creator.' If you will but make that call, all of heaven will move this very hour to lift the burden of the sense of sin from you."[306]

In his Christmas Day address 1986, Jesus announced that the God and Goddess Meru had come from Lake Titicaca to "establish a corridor of light from the etheric retreat over the Royal Teton Ranch to the etheric retreat of the feminine ray at Lake Titicaca," opening a highway whereby our calls might "reach South America in time."

On October 10, 1988, Hercules said that because the physical area of Lake Titicaca in the Andes (where the feminine ray should be anchored physically) is covered over with astral substance, the Royal Teton Ranch "must suffice" as "the physical focus of the feminine ray to the earth here in the Northern Rockies...until the dark period of earth's travail does pass." Because the ascended and unascended masters of the Himalayas keep the flame of the masculine ray, it is able to be anchored physically in the Himalayas from Lord Himalaya's Retreat of the Blue Lotus.

The God and Goddess Meru serve directly under Helios and Vesta, and they are destined to assume the office of Helios and Vesta when these great beings of light move to higher service. The ascended master Casimir Posei-don announced on September 12, 1965, that the messengers Mark and Elizabeth Clare Prophet were being prepared to assume the offices of the God and Goddess Meru when these masters advanced in their own cosmic service.

❖ META, Daughter of Sanat Kumara

The ascended lady master Meta serves on the fifth ray (the green ray) of healing, science and truth. She is the daughter of Sanat Kumara and Lady Master Venus, hierarchs of the planet Venus. She accompanied her father to earth when he came to assist the evolutions of this planet.

On Atlantis she served in the healing temple and nourished the focus of the healing flame that is now in the etheric realm over New England.

In her final embodiment she lived in Persia with her twin flame and their three children, one of whom was Cha Ara. Although her twin flame passed on and ascended in a succeeding embodiment, Meta and their three children sustained life in the same physical bodies for several hundred years before making their ascension in that life.

Since then, Meta has taught the science of healing and the use of the light rays in precipitation in the etheric cities, where she has also consecrated temples of healing. Those who study there between embodiments have the opportunity to draw upon her momentum of healing and to use the instruction received when they next embody as scientists, doctors or spiritual healers.

Meta served under the chohan of the fifth ray and then assumed that office when her teacher, who was a cosmic being, went on to cosmic service. After having held this position for several thousand years, she recently transferred the responsibilities of the office to Hilarion; thus, she was able to return with Sanat Kumara to Venus in 1956.

In a dictation given December 30, 1974, the ascended master Hilarion told us that Meta had volunteered to tarry with earth's evolutions. He said: "Meta, then, will occupy etheric levels of the atmosphere of the planet, serving in the various healing temples. Her assignment is to minister to the needs of children." He said that Meta would be at hand to help mothers and fathers with problems with their children and to heal the minds of children from harmful influences. She is assisted by priestesses of the sacred fire who have tended the flame of healing for thousands of years and who will come to the bedside of children in answer to our call.

Meta works with all the healing masters and the angelic hosts. She carries in her consciousness the immaculate concept, the pure and perfect crystal design for every child on earth and those coming into embodiment.

Hilarion recommended that we appeal to Meta to transfer the crystal matrix for our children. He said: "You can call for the healing thoughtform and the crystal of the immaculate concept to be anchored in their etheric bodies, even now in this very moment. Each day call upon Meta, and you will see how your children will preserve the crystal clarity of the consciousness of God that they had upon entering the world scene."[307]

Students may also call upon Meta for assistance in the clarification of Truth, the definition of Reality and the exposure of false concepts that are set forth in the name of Truth.

❖ MICAH, Angel of Unity

Micah is Angel of Unity, the son of Archangel Michael. Micah and his legions serve to guard the unity for the Christ consciousness in all mankind. His task is to amplify the peace and harmony of unity throughout the world.

Micah was the angel who overshadowed the children of Israel throughout their desert wanderings. He appeared to Moses and assisted him during the forty years of the Israelites' sojourn in the desert. He parted the Red Sea and focused the pillar of fire by night; his legions were the cloud of witness by day.[308]

You can picture Micah in that white-fire cloud that accompanied the children of Israel. Micah's crown of light, or halo, emits a tremendous concentration of the blue light, whereas his garments focus the intense and fiery pink love within the blue lightning that he wields on behalf of the freedom of mankind.

During the long winter at Valley Forge, Micah appeared to George Washington in a vision of three great perils that would come upon the nation of America—the Revolutionary War, the War between the States, and a third world conflict. According to Anthony Sherman's account of this vision, Washington related that he was shown the inhabitants of America "in battle array against each other. As I continued looking I saw a bright angel, on whose brow rested a crown of light, on which was traced the word 'Union,' bearing the American flag which he placed between the divided nation, and said, 'Remember ye are brethren.' Instantly, the inhabitants, casting from them their weapons, became friends once more and united around the National Standard."[309]

Micah guards the union of fifty states of America and the destiny of the nation. He comes forth bringing the heritage of the patriarchs of the Law, the patrons of life and patriots of all ages. He holds the concept of the union of the children of Israel come again. Micah, the Spirit of Unity, has kept America a nation of fifty sovereign states.

Micah says, "You are wholly dependent upon the invincible power of God that beats your heart. Therefore, your heart ought to throb with the hearts of angels in the cosmic beat of unity."[310] You can ask Micah and his angels of unity to walk by your side and help you to overcome the obstacles to your inner unity and your unity with others. Ask him to place his Electronic Presence over you. Invite him to overshadow you and show you what it feels like to be cradled in the flame of unity.

Micah once said that every individual must "stand guard every moment at his own doorstep to keep his house sweet and his heart a gateway for praise, wherein the glory of unity is preferred above all else."[311] In order to stand guard to protect unity, we must start with ourselves and then move to the circle of our communities and nations. As Gandhi once said: "*You* must be the change you wish to see in the world."

Sources of disunity on a national scale will not go away overnight. They take concerted work. They take sustained calls to Archangel Michael and his son, Micah. They take lots of violet flame to transmute the records and the hurts and wounds of the past.

We can perform a great service for the world if we concentrate our prayers and our violet-flame decrees into situations of discord. We must also be examples of the flame of unity and of community, right where we are.

Micah has sponsored a "Meditation for Unity" that we can give to help bring resolution into any situation of conflict.[312] Saint Germain's "Ritual for the Creation of the Cloud" can also be extremely effective for resolving both personal and world problems.[313]

❖ **MICHAEL AND FAITH, Archangels of the First Ray**

Archangel Michael

Michael is the archangel of the first ray of protection, faith and the will of God. He is the Prince of the Archangels and of the Angelic Hosts, the Defender of the Faith, the Angel of Deliverance. The Book of Daniel calls him "the great prince which standeth for the children of thy people."[314] His divine complement is Archeia Faith.

Archangel Michael has figured as the greatest and most revered of angels in Jewish, Christian and Islamic scriptures and tradition. In Muslim lore, he is the angel of nature who provides both food and knowledge to man. In Jewish mystical tradition Archangel Michael is identified with the angel who wrestled with Jacob, destroyed the armies of Sennacherib and saved the three Hebrew boys in the fiery furnace. Archangel Michael was the angel who appeared to Joshua as he prepared to lead the Israelites in battle at Jericho.

John the apostle speaks of Archangel Michael in the Book of Revelation, where he recounts that it was Michael who cast the devil and his angels out of heaven into the earth.[315] By this we know that the fallen angels have taken embodiment and that the enemies of Christ are in the world of form. It is, therefore, Archangel Michael and the legions of blue lightning who serve with him who defend the children of God from the enemy of the Antichrist.

Archangel Michael and his legions daily descend into the astral plane fully arrayed in their mighty blue armour, carrying their shields and swords of blue flame. There they cut free those who have passed from the screen of life and who are unable to rise to higher octaves of service and the retreats of the masters. He and his angels of deliverance work twenty-four hours a day on these levels rescuing souls from the accumulation of their own human creation over the centuries and also from the projections of the dark ones. They have served there for many ages, and Michael says that he is determined to never give up until the last child of light on this planet has risen to the God Source in the ritual of the ascension.

To assist in cutting the lightbearers free from astral entanglements, Archangel Michael has a sword of blue flame that has been fashioned from pure light substance This sword of blue flame is a rod of blue-flame power that he has used for the protection of mankind since the descent of the laggards and the Luciferians to the earth plane. Michael tells us that this sword is God's sword. It has come from the Great Central Sun, a gift from the very heart of God himself, and has been passed to him from the mighty Elohim Hercules. When this sword of blue flame blazes into a negative manifestation, nothing can stand against it.

You may also call for his sword of blue flame. Visualize it as the sparkling electric blue that is seen in the blue flame in the burner of a gas stove. Take this sword in your own right hand. Swing it around you daily as you give your dynamic decrees to be cut free from all that binds you and keeps you from your victory. Then maximize your decrees to include calls for the freedom of all on our planet and even the salvation of the planet itself. Daily calls to Archangel Michael for protection and for his momentum of faith and devotion to the will of God will ensure the protection of those who go forth in his name and service as defenders of the faith.

Students may also call to Archangel Michael for the cloak of invisibility, invincibility and invulnerability and for the mighty blue armour when they go forth to do battle with the forces of evil. Archangel Michael is part of the fraternity of lightbearers known as "Shield," whose members serve twenty-four hours a day to protect the image of the Christ in every man, woman and child embodied upon this planet.

Archangel Michael is a very special angel to us. He, with his legions of light, has dedicated himself for thousands and thousands of years to the safety, the security, the perfectionment of our souls and to our protection; caring for us, sponsoring us, rebuking us, teaching us the way of God's holy will, giving us to understand that we each have a blueprint in life, that we have a divine plan. So tender and so present is the love of God for us, and he makes that known to us especially in a most personal way through his angels.

The Goddess of Liberty says: "Archangel Michael is at your side and does answer your

Archangel Michael, by Tiffany

call and does answer it best when you keep a daily momentum" of prayers to him. "Your call for help will be answered instantaneously when you have built this momentum."³¹⁶ Archangel Michael has made the commitment to each and every one of us that if we will give our decrees and songs to him for twenty minutes each day, he will keep an angel with us until the hour of our victory.

Archangel Michael also offers to give us his momentum of faith, as he says, "Give me your doubts. Give me your questionings. I will indeed give you my faith. And my faith is a power to transform and direct into the world the great blue-lightning love of the infinite Father of all. This power and this faith is real."³¹⁷ Sometimes all that is necessary for us to success-fully pass through a difficult moment of testing is to know that we have friends of light who are upholding us and praying for our overcoming. However, when an archangel offers his faith to humanity, it is our respon-sibility to accept his gift, invoke his flame and his intercession, and make it a part of our lives. He says, "When sight is obtained, of what need is faith? It is not I who need faith then—except to give it away—but it is you who require it."³¹⁸

In most cases, the battle of life is not won on momentous decisions but on the little day-to-day experiences whereby, when you turn your heart to God in faith and trust, you receive the grace that cuts you free from the negative aspects of life in which your consciousness has momentarily become trapped. We can visualize the pathway of faith as a "mighty shim-mering ribbon of light substance connecting the individual with his God Presence."³¹⁹ Sometimes a simple thoughtform like this is all that will be needed to free us from the negative facets of life.

Archangel Michael has offered us another great gift from his heart of love—a dispensation given in Boston on April 22, 1961: "Blessed and beloved ones, some of you are of advancing years, and it will not be long before you shall vacate your body temples. Some of you shall do so by the ascension and some shall enter the realms of our world in the other man-ner called death.... I will make you one promise: If you will call to me secretly within your heart and ask me to come to you at that hour, I, Michael, will materialize to you at the hour of your passing and you will see me as I AM. And I will promise you that I will help to cut you free from the remaining portions of your karma and will help you to enter the realms of light with less of the attendant pain that results from human fear in their passing.

"This is a privilege and a gift I give you from my heart. I flood it forth to the people of Boston and to those throughout the world who have the faith to accept and to realize that God walks and talks with men today in the same manner as of old. I AM Michael, Prince of the Archangels, rendering for the earth a cosmic service."[320]

Archangel Michael's etheric retreat is in the Canadian Rockies at Banff, near Lake Louise. He also has a focus of light over Central Europe. His keynote is "The Navy Hymn" ("Eternal Father, Strong to Save"). The music of the "Bridal Chorus" from *Lohengrin* may also be used to invoke the radiance of the archangels and the angelic hosts. Archangel Michael is the sponsor of police departments and law enforcement agencies around the world.

❖ MILAREPA, Great Saint of Tibet

Milarepa (1040–1143) is the revered saint and poet of Tibetan Buddhism. He attained great mastery in the yogic powers, including levitation and flight through the air. He is characteristically depicted with his right hand cupped to his ear or near his ear. Some have surmised that this indicates that he is a *shravaka,* which is a disciple of the Buddha, a "listener." (*Shravaka* means "hearing, listening to.") Others believe the gesture may also symbolize Milarepa's capacity to retain Buddhist teachings and doctrines in his ear. Milarepa was a master of the esoteric teachings of the tantra, which were orally transmitted from guru to disciple.

Tibetans universally revere Milarepa as a great Buddhist saint who became fully enlightened. The story of his life and path are recorded in a biography written by one of his disciples. In it, Milarepa recounts to his students the events of his life—from his practice of the black arts as a youth and his penance and probationary period under a Guru of the True Doctrine, to his initiation on the "Path of Light" and his practice of renunciation and meditation.[321]

Milarepa learned the black arts in order to bring vengeance upon his wicked relatives. During his cousin's wedding feast he brings down the home of his uncle by his sorcery, causing the death of all the guests. When the villagers seek to avenge this slaughter, he creates hailstorms and destroys their crops.

Feeling deep remorse for these acts, Milarepa goes in search of a guru who will teach him the true dharma. A lama advises him to go to a monastery in Wheat Valley to seek out the "worthiest among the worthiest of men"—Marpa the Translator. "Between thee and him there is a karmic connection, which cometh from past lives," says the lama. "To him thou must go."

Milarepa meets his teacher and guru, Marpa, and begins a rigorous path of chelaship. He endures many hardships. Before he is accepted as a disciple, Marpa makes him build a house and then has him tear it down and begin again. This happens four times.

The walls of these houses represented walls of black magic that Milarepa has built in his subconscious. Black magic is the misuse of the sacred fire of the Divine Mother. Practiced in the past or the present, it is very binding, leaving distorted, out-of-alignment states and jagged lines of force. Milarepa had to be willing to tear down the walls of black magic and build again. While he was building and unbuilding, Milarepa was dismantling his electronic belt. The outer work was the sign of the inner work that was taking place.

During this process, Milarepa was also unlearning the false teachings of the dark ones who imparted to him knowledge of the manipulation of energy. He had to overcome the practice of black magic and to balance the karma of his misdeeds. When he finally earned the right to be the chela of a true master, his pride had been broken, and in humility, he walked the way of attainment.

The ascended master Lanello has spoken of the lessons of Milarepa's life: "Was not Milarepa continually building and tearing down houses? For Marpa, his guru, demanded excellence and ultimately exacted from Milarepa that excellence. When Marpa accepted Milarepa as a pupil, he warned him: 'If I impart to thee the Truth, it will entirely depend upon thine own perseverance and energy whether thou attainest liberation in one lifetime or not.'[322]

"Over time Marpa asked Milarepa to build four houses, each time directing him, after the house was well under construction, to fully or partially tear it down. When Milarepa brought to Marpa's attention his cracked and bruised hands and legs and the large oozing sores on his back, Marpa said: '...If thou art really in search of the Truth, do not boast so about thy services, but continue waiting patiently and working steadily till thy building task is entirely finished.'[323]

"Milarepa said of this incident, 'Considering within myself that such was the wish of my Guru, I felt that I must go on and do as commanded. I therefore took up my loads and carried them in front of me now, and thus went about the work.' He later realized, 'It was because of my having committed such terribly wicked deeds in the earlier part of my life, that now I had to suffer such excruciating and indescribable tortures at the very outset of my search for a Faith and Doctrine to emancipate me.'[324]

"When Milarepa had passed his initiations, Marpa explained to him, 'My son, I knew thee to be a worthy *shishya* [disciple] from the very first.... And it was with a view to cleansing thee from thy sins that I had thee to work so hard upon the four houses. The houses themselves symbolize...the four types of action, each house representing one of the four, namely, the peaceful, the powerful, the fascinating and the stern, respectively.

"'I purposely wanted to fill thy heart with bitter repentance and sorrow, verging on despair, by turning thee out ignominiously. And thou, for having borne all those trials with patience and meekness, without the least change in thy faith in me, shalt have, as the result, disciples full of faith, energy, intelligence and kind compassion, endowed from the first with the qualifications essential to worthy *shishyas*.'[325]

"Be reminded of the yogi, beloved. Be reminded that if you desire enough to get out of the cage of self, you will get out of it and you will transcend yourself!

"Did not Milarepa sit in a cave in obedience to his guru? Did he not become green from eating nettles and yet would not budge from his cave until he received the key to his victory? When you want something enough, beloved, *you will have it.*

"Therefore, Padma Sambhava and I come to you. And we remind you of the teaching that your call compels our answer. If your call is a weak little call, halfhearted, you will get a weak little answer, halfhearted.

"But if, with all the fervor of your heart and mind and being, you cry out to God and to the Great White Brotherhood on behalf of those who are suffering in the earth, and you offer powerful invocations as you walk up and down in the night, beloved—if you do this daily with the intensity that you would offer to God if, for instance, you held your dying child in your arms and were pleading for his life, you will establish such a tie with the heart of the Godhead that no lawful prayer you offer for the rest of your life will be denied you!

"And the intensity of God's power that will be given to you in return shall be enough to literally move mountains of your karma and open the way for resolution through your Holy Christ Self and God Harmony, that great cosmic being who ensouls the harmony of God."[326]

In the age of Aquarius, the ascended masters teach that the work of Milarepa becomes the inner work of undoing the misdeeds of our past lives and past karma. We must rebuild our house through striving and service and the use of the science of the spoken Word and the violet flame.

As Lanello says, "This will take time and hard work, but you can do it, beloved. You *can* and you *must* correct those things that only *you* can correct. For you have built a flawed structure, and the only thing you can do is to tear it down and build again." [327]

❖ **MORYA,** *See* **El Morya**

❖ **MOSES,** *See* **Ling, Lord**

❖ **MOTHER OF THE WORLD**

The Mother of the World, like the eternal Mother, is a timeless office in hierarchy of one empowered by the Father to give birth to the Buddhas. In the Agni Yoga teachings, the Mother of the World is the matriarch and initiator of the hierarchy of spiritual beings involved with this planet. She is also the spiritual mother of all the Christed Ones and Buddhas throughout history.

Helena Roerich, amanuensis for El Morya, has proclaimed the great mission of the Mother of the World in this age. In the 1920s she began releasing the teachings of the Great White Brotherhood through the teachings of Agni Yoga. In her book *Mother of the World,* Helena Roerich describes the Mother of the World as "the Great Spirit of the Feminine Principle" who sometimes appears personally in the incarnations of the avatars who are "impregnated by her Ray." [328]

"From times immemorial the Mother of the World has sent forth to achievement. In the history of humanity, Her Hand traces an unbreakable thread.

"On Sinai Her Voice rang out. She assumed the image of Kali. She was at the basis of the cults of Isis and Ishtar. After Atlantis, when a blow was

Mother of the World,
by Nicholas Roerich

inflicted upon the cult of the spirit, the Mother of the World began to weave a new thread, which will now begin to radiate.

"After Atlantis the Mother of the World veiled Her Face and forbade the pronouncement of Her Name until the hour of the constellations should strike. She has manifested Herself only partly. Never has She manifested herself on a planetary scale.... The old world rejected the Mother of the World, but the New World begins to perceive her lustrous veil." [329]

To Nicholas Roerich, husband of Helena Roerich and also a messenger of the ascended masters, the Mother of the World was the highest symbol of world unity, the most universal of all the great teachers. He painted her many times throughout his career. She was often depicted with her eyes covered or veiled by a blue veil, signifying certain mysteries of the universe not yet to be revealed to man.

In this time, the Mother of the World is no longer hidden but is manifesting herself on a planetary scale. She is seeking her children and desires to rescue them from the burdens that beset them. The culture of the Mother is the culture that existed on the golden-age civilizations of Lemuria and Atlantis. Now is the moment when we must come apart to restore the true culture of America, which is the culture of the Mother of the World.

The Mother of the World has said: "I am in adoration of the Son, for I am Mother. I am in the heart of the lily of thy soul, and I am in the heart of life's goal. I am in the center of the oneness of thy flame, O child of my heart.

"I am everywhere and nowhere. Come and find me. I am the light of Mother that sweeps in the billowing clouds, hiding and peeping through the trees and the singing of the birds.

"I am in your dearest dream and your highest purpose. And I am with you as you rake over the coals and the dying embers of a former state seeking to find therein a comfort that is not there. For the comfort of thy heart is in ever reaching toward my heart, there to discover with mounting wings as eagle flight your own soul's delight reaching ever, ever into the new personality of thy Self. It is God—the eternal comfort, the person of thy life— ever reaching, ever striving, ever excelling and accelerating.

"There is the necessary friction of worlds being born as they rush through a cosmos. And the fire of burning is the passing through of the elements that no longer may be as they were, for in the acceleration is the ever new perception of thyself higher and higher, a manifest person of God. I come to renew the Mother flame in earth in you."[330]

❖ MUSES

This ascended master is patron of art, music and poetry. Muses is a cosmic being and a great musician who drew out of the universal heart the thoughts of God and set them to order and universal harmony.

Speaking of this great being, God Harmony has said: "You can tune in with the work of Muses; you can feel the joy, the harmony and the love that poured out with his thoughts and understand the significance of his contribution to the Law of the One. Man, then, is not useless, as cosmic beings are not useless. Man is useful as cosmic beings are useful; and each man, artist in his own right, creator in his own domain, may draw forth from the harmonies of God the power that will help the *majesté* of the universe to speak through the open door of his own being."[331]

❖ **MUSIC, THE GOD AND GODDESS OF,** *See* **Cyclopea and Virginia**

❖ **NADA, Chohan of the Sixth Ray**

Lady Master Nada

The ascended lady master Nada is the chohan of the sixth ray (purple and gold ray) of peace, ministration and service. She is also a member of the Karmic Board, on which she serves as the representative of the third ray (pink ray) of divine love. From Nada we learn the practical application of love and the path of personal Christhood through ministration and service to life.

On Atlantis, Nada worked in the healing arts and served as a priestess in the Temple of Love. The etheric counterpart of this temple, which is designed after the pattern of a rose, is centered above New Bedford, Massachusetts. She was also embodied as a lawyer on Atlantis, where she championed the cause of divine justice for the downtrodden and oppressed.

Nada speaks of her experience in keeping the flame in the last days of Atlantis: "How well I remember the last days of Atlantis. Those of us who were there keeping the vigil midst the effort of the embodied lightbearers have recently gathered at the Royal Teton Retreat to closely examine the causes and conditions that led to that final judgment and that sinking of a continent and its people.

"The evildoers then and now continue in their evildoing right up to the eve of cataclysm, boasting that they are immune to God's laws, that karma is not real, and that they are the gods of the earth....

"My service on Atlantis was in law and the law of wholeness. Thus the science of healing and the science of truth are the right and left hand of the defense of the individual, body and soul. In those days the manipulators of the law of the fifth ray were as devious in their despisings of the sons of light as they are today. They entered not into the consciousness of God, and they exerted a destructive influence upon those who were entering in as neophytes under the initiates of the mystery schools.

"The marbled, geometric cities of Atlantis, my beloved, were not without the inner retreats of the Brotherhood. And Noah himself, the archetype of the Great Guru, while building his ark was the Mother flame of the ark and the initiator of the embodied sons of God. There were others of our bands who took ships and carried the focuses of their retreats to distant lands and mountaintops, to the Near and Far East, to the Himalayas, to Europe and the Americas, and to the already established retreats of the archangels.

"The securing of spiritual forcefields in Matter is the work of the chelas of the ascended masters. When decay and disintegration beset an age, they mount with wings as eagles[332] to survey the land and the sea. They take counsel with the LORD's hosts and with the LORD himself and the three ascended masters who prophesied to Abraham of the birth of Isaac and the destruction of Sodom and Gomorrah. The initiates of the mystery schools are the preachers of righteousness, and they continue to preach the Word and its science until the hour of the judgment and their embarking on the ark."[333]

In her final incarnation 2,700 years ago, Nada was the youngest of a large family of exceptionally gifted children. She was tutored by Charity, archeia of the third ray, in how to expand the threefold flame of love in her heart for the quickening of the chakras of her talented brothers and sisters. She chose to forgo pursuing her own career in that embodiment and, instead, kept the flame in deep meditation and prayer for her brothers and sisters in their various fields of endeavor.

Nada has spoken of that lifetime: "I can assure you that at the conclusion of my incarnation when I saw the victory of each one of my brothers and sisters, the fullness of my joy was in a heart of love expanded.... It seemed to the world, and perhaps even to my own, that I had not accomplished much. But I took my leave into the higher octaves, thoroughly understanding the meaning of the self-mastery of the pink flame.

"Thus, it was from the point of the third ray that I entered into the heart of Christ and saw the application [on the sixth ray] as ministration and service."[334]

The ascended lady master Nada assists ministers, missionaries, teachers, healers, psychologists, counselors at law and public servants—all who are involved in serving the needs of others. "It does not matter what your training and what your position," Nada says. "It is not in what you do with your hands, it is in what you do with your heart that counts.

"For as I spent several of my last incarnations in keeping the flame of life anonymously for my family and for other members of the community, so I am able to tell you firsthand what it means to God, what it means to souls evolving on Terra to have someone—that silent, peaceful someone in the midst of activity—silently declaring the law of truth, the law of perfection, the law of victory on behalf of each one who is so busy serving, so busy trying to do good for humanity that he does not have time to make the application for himself.

"I would suggest, then, if you are looking for a more than ordinary challenge, that you go into your communities with this thought in mind of being a keeper of the flame, of adoring the flame of life in the hearts of hundreds and thousands....

"If you have professional training, or have the ability to acquire that training, then we suggest that you take on greater responsibilities where you can be involved directly in decision making, in drafting legislature, in organizing—whether it is men's groups, women's groups or community groups working for a cause that is constructive....

"How often we see in these levels of government and community planning, if there were just one of our keepers of the flame in the midst, how smoothly the process would flow and how encouraged people would be, how their faith would be restored in this representative form of government, which is indeed after the teachings of the ascended masters and patterned after that which is to come in the golden-age societies that are to be born upon this continent." [335]

Nada teaches at the retreat of Jesus in the etheric octave over Saudi Arabia, where she instructs on the God-mastery of the emotions and the quieting of inordinate desire. This is the mastery of the solar-plexus chakra, which is the instrument for the sixth ray, the place where you radiate peace. This is the ray of the Piscean dispensation, and Jesus is the great master of this ray—he is the Prince of Peace. Nada comes in the footsteps of Jesus Christ, and it is his path that she teaches. She succeeded him in the office of chohan of the sixth ray when he assumed the office of World Teacher in 1956.

Nada also serves in the Rose Temple, her retreat located above New Bedford, Massachusetts. Designed after the pattern of a rose, each petal is a room representing an initiation in the flame of love. In the center of the retreat there burns the flame of divine love, tended by brothers and sisters of the third ray for the healing of earth's evolutions by love.

Nada is an initiate and master of the path of the ruby ray, and she  teaches the unfolding of the rose of the heart, helping us to develop the sensitivity of the heart for the receiving of the gift of the Holy Spirit of diverse kinds of tongues and the interpretation of tongues.

She is very much involved with the initiation and sponsorship of twin flames and the Aquarian-age family. She also ministers to the world's children with legions of angels who personally tend to the needs of the youth.

Nada says, "I give you my love, for all else I have already given away." The motto of her disciples is "I serve," "I am my brother's keeper," and "The servant is not greater than his Lord." Nada's keynote is "Mattinata ('Tis the Day)," by Ruggiero Leoncavalio.

❖ NADA RAYBORN, *See* Daniel and Nada Rayborn

❖ NADA RAYBORN (DAUGHTER OF DANIEL AND NADA RAYBORN), *See* Rex and Nada, Bob and Pearl

❖ NAJAH, SISTER OF CHANANDA, *See* Chananda

❖ THE NAMELESS ONE FROM OUT THE GREAT CENTRAL SUN

In 1991, a being whom we know only as the Nameless One from out the Great Central Sun delivered a dictation in which he said: "From out the Great Central Sun I, the Nameless One, do speak to my beloved. I have opened the channels of light. And I am the Nameless One, for to give you a name, beloved, would give you access to my causal body. People of earth are not yet ready to access that causal body. Therefore I speak out of profound love for your being that once was a God-free being, as I am, but now does perceive out of the windows of a limited self....

"The greater weight of my being is always in the Central Sun, but the extension of myself to levels of contact with certain among humanity has been the grant that I have known for many, many grand ages....

"I have already been a part of you before you have known that I have existed, and I am aware of the dilemma of being, of knowing what is to be done and yet not having the strength to do it or the wholeness or the resources or the time or the space. Yes, there are many excuses, legitimate and otherwise, in this octave. But, beloved, that which is missing that should provide the answer to all of these lacks is the sacred fire pulsating."

This great being said that he was placing a seed of light in the crown chakra of "those who will accomplish the path of the mystical union with God in this flesh they now wear." He asked that we embody the name of a virtue and said: "May the name of that virtue become the label on the seed that I have placed that might grow in the crown chakra if you nurture it. May you strive to become the God-identification, the God-embodiment of that virtue. And may you be so, that when you graduate from earth you may be acknowledged for your attainment upon that single virtue. Meditate a moment now and see the title of a single virtue that does descend upon your crown chakra with the seed of light."[336]

❖ NATURE, GOD OF

Working with the representatives of the Holy Spirit, the hierarchs of the four elements, the ascended master Cuzco and Mighty Cosmos, the God of Nature draws the magnetic currents of the earth and directs them in a balancing action throughout nature and elemental life.

He is six feet tall and releases his radiation through robes of pink, gold and green. The aura emanating from his head is of an intense blue light, and the light rays that pour forth from his entire form resemble the Aurora Borealis. The rays from his head are white, and those from the heart are gold. From his right hand he emits the green ray and from the left, the pink.

The God of Nature moves with the magnetic currents of the earth, draws them and releases them at will, amplifies and balances their action as they pass through his body, and his consciousness absorbs them and is absorbed by them.

Prior to his attainment in this field, he was embodied as an alchemist of the sacred fire. At inner levels, he learned how to manipulate cosmic forces, and by the time he ascended, he had such a great momentum in working with nature that he was given this position in hierarchy in order that the cosmic beings who previously occupied it might go on to cosmic service.

The God of Nature works with the God of Gold to precipitate gold from the electronic currents of the sun. The presence of this metal in the earth is essential to the balance of the forces of nature and the physical body of man.

❖ NEPTUNE AND LUARA, **Hierarchs of the Water Element**

Neptune and Luara are hierarchs of the water element on this planet. Overseeing the water element and the balance of life therein, Neptune and Luara, together with the undines (elementals of the water element) in their command, govern the tides of the seas and the waters under the sea, precipitation over the landed areas and purification of water wherever it is found—even in the body of man.

Neptune and Luara serve with the hierarchies of Cancer, Leo and Virgo to teach mankind

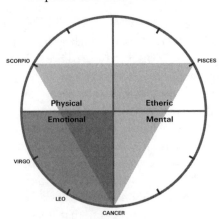

The emotional quadrant and the trine of the water signs

the mastery of the emotional body. They also teach the mastery of the water element in the physical and etheric bodies and the balance of the threefold flame through that element under the hierarchies of Pisces, Cancer and Scorpio.

Neptune carries a trident as a symbol of the three-fold flame and his authority over the action of the Christ consciousness that governs the water element through these three hierarchies (2, 6, 10) of the sun. The influence of the moon upon the astral bodies of earth's evolutions is the perversion of the activities of Luara, who, as the feminine representative of the water element, teaches us the mastery of the emotional body.

The undines live wherever water is found, sometimes appearing in the form of a mermaid. They intensify the purity and flow of God's light in the waters. As more than two-thirds of the surface of the earth is covered with water, the undines are kept very busy. Kuthumi speaks of their service: "The serious work of the undines moves on as the oceans and the rivers and the lakes, streams and

rivulets and raindrops all play a part in the formation and re-formation of the body of our planet and of man, utterly dependent upon the elementals.

"The undines, who also laugh and play in the waves and waterfalls, lovingly follow the example of their hierarchs. Neptune is the king of the deep, and his consort, Luara, is mother of tides, governing cycles of fertility and the water element as it affects the emotional body (known as the water, feeling or desire body) and the communications of mankind's joy, grief, guilt, anger and love through the astral plane, strongly influencing the collective unconscious of the race."[337]

It is important that mankind pray for the undines and tell them how grateful we are for their magnificent work—and encourage them to keep on keeping on. Call to Saint Germain and legions of violet-flame angels to transmute the collective unconscious of mankind and all darkness, disease and death that pollutes the emotional bodies of humanity and the waters of planet Earth. Ask for the restoration of the natural flow of Spirit's fire to the seas to lighten the weight of the astral plane borne by the undines. We must also ask for the protection of the precious whales so that they may continue to transmit cosmic light and cosmic rays to all life on earth.

Pray for the transmutation of all pollution of the waters of the earth. The violet flame can restore unbalanced river and lake ecosystems that can no longer support full biological diversity and reverse the damage of forests through acid rain. Call especially for the purification of the drinking water of earth to maintain the balance of the water element in the bodies of mankind.

Neptune and Luara have spoken of the significance of the sea: "The sea is where Life begets life. The sea is the womb of the Cosmic Virgin, even as it is the tomb where hieroglyphs of the collective unconscious of earth's evolutionary chain are recorded and rerecorded for the transformation of all life. The sea is the desiring of the Mother to give birth to the children of God, and it represents the highest and the lowest of the desirings of humanity to beget God and anti-God, universal harmony or its antithesis.

"The seven seas are man's desirings for wholeness in the seven planes of being. They represent the seven colors, tones and vibrations of the seven days of creation. The seas contain the *Grund* and the *Ungrund*—the formed and the unformed elements of life. The seas and the bodies of water that dot the earth with jewels of glacial blue, aquamarine and gorgeous sapphire hues actually exist in seven layered planes corresponding to the seven bodies of man.

"Elemental beings of light and angel ministrants provide the focus for the interchange of these 'seven seas' with the sacred fire of the seven vehicles of man's consciousness. Most people in your octave observe only the physical body of man, and therefore they likewise observe only the physical body of the sea.

"John the Revelator beheld the 'sea of glass like unto crystal' before the throne of the Ancient of Days and again the 'sea of glass mingled with fire.'[338] Thus, the interchange of sacred fire and flowing water in the Great Central Sun is ever the life-giving movement of Alpha and Omega in the heart of the flaming Monad whose Presence in you is the I AM THAT I AM.

"Thus, Father and Mother, ever begetting life, release the crystal cord as a chain of crystal light. This chain, as a mighty caduceus spanning the ocean of cosmos, is the ascending/descending spinal altar whose structure becomes the superstructure for the mental and physical vehicles of every part of life."[339]

❖ NICHOLAS ROERICH

Nicholas Roerich was a world-renowned artist, archaeologist, author, scholar, lecturer, costume and set designer, poet, mystic and explorer. He and his wife, Helena Roerich, served during the early twentieth century as amanuenses for the ascended masters El Morya and Maitreya. Nicholas ascended at the conclusion of that lifetime.

He was born in St. Petersburg on October 9, 1874, the firstborn son of Konstantin and Maria Roerich. The name *Nicholas* means "one who overcomes," and *Roerich* means "rich in glory." His father was a prominent attorney and notary, and Nicholas spent much of his youth at the family's large country estate, Isvara, located about fifty-five miles southwest of St. Petersburg. There in the beauty of northern Russia a lifelong love for nature was kindled in young Nicholas. At Isvara he developed a passion for hunting and an avid interest in natural history, archaeology and the history of Russia. He was fond of music and horseback riding.

His father wanted him to study law, but Nicholas wanted to pursue art. Nicholas resolved the situation by enrolling simultaneously in the law faculty of the Imperial University and the Imperial Academy of Arts.

In 1898 Nicholas became assistant director of the museum of the Society for the Encouragement of the Arts. In September 1900 he went to Paris to study art. In the summer of 1901, Nicholas returned to St. Petersburg and in October married Helena Ivanovna Shaposhnikova. Helena was an accomplished pianist and came to be regarded as a distinguished lady of letters and a prolific writer in the esoteric tradition of Eastern religion. She was his twin flame, an inspiration and support to Nicholas throughout his life. Nicholas and Helena had two sons, George and Svetoslav.

In the early 1900s, the Roerichs traveled extensively throughout Russia and Europe. During these journeys, Professor Roerich painted, undertook archaeological excavations, studied architecture, lectured and wrote about art and archaeology. In 1906 he was promoted from secretary to director of the school of the Society for the Encouragement of the Arts.

In 1907 he began applying his talents to stage and costume design. This became a fulfilling and successful career for Roerich. He designed sets and costumes for Diaghilev's ballet and opera productions, including Stravinsky's *The Rite of Spring,* and for almost all of Wagner's and many of Rimsky-Korsakov's operas.

The Roerich family left Russia for Finland in 1918, shortly before the border between Finland and the Soviet Union was permanently closed. At the invitation of the director of the Chicago Art Institute, Roerich came to the United States in 1920. He traveled widely, lectured and exhibited his works. While in the United States, Roerich founded the Master Institute of United Arts, an international society of artists called Cor Ardens (which means "Flaming Heart"), and an international art center in New York called Corona Mundi (which means "Crown of the World"). As a tribute to Roerich, the Roerich Museum was established in New York in 1923.

Many of Roerich's works are magnificent scenes of nature, and his themes are inspired by history, architecture and religion. His paintings are mystical, allegorical and even prophetic. Between 1912 and 1914, his paintings often reflected a sense of impending cataclysm. One of these, *The Last Angel* (1912), depicts an intense conflagration enveloping a city; above the city, surrounded by billowing clouds of smoke, an angel bearing a sword and shield heralds the Final Judgment. In 1936, just before World War II, Roerich painted *Armageddon*. One can see the rooftops of a city visible through clouds of smoke with the silhouettes of soldiers marching in the foreground across the bottom of the picture.

Roerich's artistic style is difficult to describe because, as Claude Bragdon put it, he belongs to an elect fraternity of artists—including da Vinci, Rembrandt, Blake and, in music, Beethoven—whose works have "a unique, profound and indeed a mystical quality which differentiates them from their contemporaries, making it impossible to classify them in any known category or to ally them with any school, because they resemble themselves only—and one another, like some spaceless and timeless order of initiates."[340]

Nicholas Roerich was greatly influenced by Eastern culture. He had desired for a long time to travel to the East in order to study the ancient culture firsthand, and in 1923 he set sail for India. He resided for a time in Sikkim (then a kingdom bordering northeast India) while making final plans for an expedition to Central Asia. Roerich wrote of his enchantment with the mountains: "All teachers journeyed to the mountains. The highest knowledge, the most inspired songs, the most superb sounds and colours are created on the mountains. On the highest mountains there is the Supreme. The high mountains stand as witnesses of the great reality."[341]

"Himalayas! Here is the Abode of Rishis. Here resounded the sacred Flute of Krishna. Here thundered the Blessed Gautama Buddha. Here originated all Vedas. Here lived Pandavas. Here—Gesar Khan. Here—Aryavarta. Here is Shambhala. Himalayas—Jewel of India. Himalayas—Treasure of the World. Himalayas—the sacred Symbol of Ascent."[342]

Both Nicholas and Helena Roerich had an intense interest in Eastern philosophy and religion. Many of his paintings contain both Western and

Eastern deities, saints and sages. His series "Banners of the East" portrays not only spiritual leaders of the past but the hopes of the East for a coming leader. Roerich captured these hopes in his paintings of Maitreya and the World Mother.

In 1925 Roerich started on his Central Asian expedition with Helena, his son George and several other Europeans. Roerich wrote of his goals: "Of course, as an artist my main aspiration in Asia was towards artistic work.... In addition to its artistic aims, our Expedition planned to study the position of the ancient monuments of Central Asia, to observe the present condition of religions and creeds, and to note the traces of the great migrations of nations."[343]

Roerich's party traveled 15,500 miles through Central Asia in an arduous and often dangerous trek that took more than four years. Despite overwhelming obstacles, Roerich executed hundreds of paintings during the journey.

While on this expedition, Roerich discovered legends and manuscripts recounting the journey Jesus took to the East during his so-called lost years between the ages of twelve and thirty. The same or similar manuscripts were also found by Russian journalist Nicolas Notovitch and Swami Abhedananda at Himis monastery in Ladakh.[344]

At the conclusion of the Central Asian expedition in 1928, the Roerichs permanently settled in the Kulu Valley in India. There they founded the Urusvati Himalayan Research Institute to study archaeology, linguistics and botany.

One of the goals of Roerich's lifelong pursuit of preserving the world's cultural heritage came to fruition in 1935 with the signing of the Roerich Pact treaty at the White House by representatives of the countries comprising the Pan-American Union. Under the pact, nations at war were obliged to respect museums, universities, cathedrals and libraries as they did hospitals. Just as hospitals flew the Red Cross flag, cultural institutions would fly Roerich's "Banner of Peace," a flag that has a white field with three red spheres in the center surrounded by a red circle. Roerich believed that by protecting culture, the spiritual health of the nations would be preserved.

Roerich was nominated for the Nobel Peace Prize in 1929 and 1935 for his efforts to promote international peace through art and culture and to protect art treasures in time of war. World War II interrupted his activities and those of the Urusvati Himalayan Research Institute, and Roerich devoted himself to helping victims of the war. He also donated money from the sale of his paintings and books to the Soviet Red Cross.

In the summer of 1947, Roerich had heart surgery but was soon back at his easel. One of the last works Roerich painted is called *The Master's Command*. It depicts a white eagle flying toward a devotee who is meditating in the lotus posture atop a high cliff overlooking a mountain valley. On December 13, 1947, while Roerich was working on a variant of this picture, his heart suddenly failed and his soul took flight to higher octaves. He was seventy-three years old.

Throughout his life, Nicholas Roerich found the time to be involved in a multitude of activities and to do them all well. His spiritual life was the wellspring from which his literary and artistic vision arose. In an article about the character and work of his father, Svetoslav Roerich summed up the artist's quest for inner spirituality:

"He was a great patriot and he loved his Motherland, yet he belonged to the entire world and the whole world was his field of activity. Every race of men was to him a brotherly race, every country a place of special interest and of special significance. Every religion was a path to the Ultimate and to him life meant the great gates leading into the Future.... Every effort of his was directed towards the realisation of the Beautiful and his thoughts found a masterful embodiment in his paintings, writings and public life....

"Through all his paintings and writings runs the continuous thread of a great message—the message of the Teacher calling to the disciples to awaken and strive towards a new life, a better life, a life of beauty and fulfillment."[345]

The ascended master Nicholas Roerich says, "I am grateful to address you today, to speak to you from the plane of the ascended masters that you might know that one from among you has graduated to this level and that you might accomplish the same. Never tire, then, in the work that is your dharma, your duty to be the wholeness of yourself. Never be frustrated that you are misunderstood or before your time in your understanding of the stars, the universes, the mountains and the petals of a flower. I have indeed fought the good fight, and I have won."[346]

He asks us to call to him, and he stresses the use of the violet flame: "I ask you, chelas of the ascended masters, to include my name in your decrees and preambles, as I work closely with El Morya, K.H. and D.K., and Lanello. I work closely with them for the bringing together of all those who are on the path of the sacred fire."[347]

❖ **OMEGA,** *See* **Alpha and Omega**

❖ **OMRI-TAS, Ruler of the Violet Planet**

Omri-Tas is the Ruler of the Violet Planet. Saint Germain has told us that Omri-Tas carries such an intensity of violet flame and of the seventh ray in his aura that it extends far beyond the actual size of planet Earth. Omri-Tas makes his abode with the Lord of the World at Shamballa (over the Gobi desert), where he and his retinue of servants of the Most High God have vowed to keep the violet flame of freedom on earth. His divine complement keeps the vigil in the heart of the Violet Planet with one hundred and forty-four thousand priests of the sacred fire.

The evolutions of the Violet Planet have served the violet flame for aeons and use the violet flame to tend to all the needs of daily life—to clean their homes, to care for and purify the planet, and even to wash and bathe in. Menial chores are performed by violet-flame angels and elementals, which allows the people time to pursue the path of adeptship and to serve other planetary homes.

Across the Violet Planet, one hundred and forty-four thousand priests of the sacred fire tend the violet flame day and night and perform ceremonies and rituals of the violet flame at thousands of altars. Omri-Tas describes one of the temples on his planet:

"Behold, O planet Earth, our love is pouring out to you from out the heart of the great Violet Planet. I, Omri-Tas, stand now in the center of the mighty pool of light. I shall describe it to you that you may know the beauty of its wonders. This pool is seventy feet and circular. There is a shimmering, magnificent, yellow-colored water, which flashes like electric sparks across the center of this pool. There are seven circular steps which lead up to it. There are seven columns around it. These are of white marble and rise high into the atmosphere. The canopy is quite naturally circular, and a beautiful flow of starry flames pours down from the center. This pool, then, which dwells upon the Violet Planet stands in the center of a great amphitheater where the priests assemble when we give our sacred invocations.

"I have chosen to describe this unto you that you may receive somewhat the setting from whence I am speaking and may realize the wonders of a civilization that is free from commercialization, from disharmony, from disunity and all of those attendant causes of distress....

"As I stand now upon a tiny, white, circular dais raised within the very center of this pool, I see beneath my feet this shimmering, beautiful, magnetic, yellow-colored water, which flashes with such iridescence and wonder that it is difficult to find words in your own language to describe it unto you…. The marble platform that extends out around this beautiful center-domed temple of light is a pale orange in color. It is set with many white stones sprinkled in it, and the entire effect is magnificent to behold. Many of the priests of our brotherhood here upon the Violet Planet are now lighting canisters…filled with a special form of electronic energy that releases a stream of violet light in such a manner as to highlight the entire sky and atmosphere around our temple.

"The color you see of the sky upon our planet is actually not violet—it is blue like your own. But in order to create the proper atmosphere in this outdoor setting, we utilize a special electromagnetic forcefield whereby even in broad daylight we are able to project from these canisters, focused around the central area of our temple, a radiant color of violet that fills the entire atmosphere.

"The effect of the violet reflected in the scintillating yellow pool is magnificent to behold. But there is a spiritual purpose that is conveyed in this magnificent symbol. For there is a special electromagnetic field that pulsates from the water to the top of the tower and enables us to amplify the violet flame in such a manner that throughout the length and breadth of our land, the homes of all of the people upon this planet receive a charge of violet fire in much the same manner that you convey your electrical current upon transmission lines. This violet fire can be contacted by our people and used on special instruments for combing their hair, for washing themselves and, in other ways, for cleansing their homes."[348]

Omri-Tas has revealed that the evolutions of the Violet Planet had once approached a similar crisis as that faced today by the people of earth. In response to the rallying call of the representative of the Divine Mother, the servants of God were galvanized and turned the tide by the violet flame. As Omri-Tas said, "They heard the call to give their invocations at altars around that planet. There was a saturation of the planetary body with the violet flame. That saturation, therefore, did flush out the fallen angels, who then could be bound by the legions of light and removed…. We went on into a golden age because of the few who responded, and today that planet is sustained in that golden age because the people have not lost the memory of that which was almost a planetary holocaust."[349]

Omri-Tas has one hundred and forty-four thousand priests of the sacred fire serving in his command who may be called upon at any time for an intense and fiery release of the violet flame on behalf of mankind and the elemental kingdom. Over the years, Omri-Tas has released specific violet-flame dispensations to assist the chelas of Saint Germain and to uplift the earth. We can call to Omri-Tas to reactivate and multiply these dispensations:

Violet flame spheres. Omri-Tas came forth at the 1963 Freedom Class in Washington, D. C., and released violet-flame balls into the atmosphere of the earth from the heart of the Violet Planet. These were seen by the messengers and students in the sky over the city. We may call to Omri-Tas for the rolling in of the violet-flame balls any time a concentrated action of the sacred fire is needed on a planetary scale (for example, to quell riot, war or mob hysteria).

Violet-flame clearance of the soul chakra and the cleansing of the West Coast of America. On October 9, 1976, Omri-Tas came for the clearing of the soul chakra of Terra, of America and of every soul on earth. He announced: "We would cleanse this coast of the records of infamy and rebellion, of hatred of the Mother and selfishness of her children.... We are starting a violet-flame action here in the heart of the City of the Angels [Los Angeles] and here in the heart of the Mother and the devotees that will go around the circle of fire, around the entire border of Lemuria, consuming, consuming with the all-powerful light of the violet transmuting flame the records of misuse of the light of love in God-obedience.... Now I raise my arms for the release of sacred fire into the depths of the Pacific at that point where the seven holy Kumaras released the flame of Mother and the rising action. So we penetrate to the ocean floors of the planet the release of the violet flame for the rebalancing of energies and conditions in earth, in water, in air and throughout the etheric plane."

Inauguration of the Aquarian age. Alpha cycle of the violet flame. On December 29, 1976, Omri-Tas came with legions of violet-flame angels and priests and priestesses of the sacred fire for the inauguration of the Aquarian cycle "by the release of the violet flame from the very heart of the Violet Planet.... We come to take up residence on Terra for the age of Aquarius and for the bringing in of that age.... We will make our abode in the residence of the Lord of the World...and we will stand with Terra until the turning of the cycles and the turning of the age.... Angels of the Violet Planet and priestesses of the sacred fire, together with the mighty hosts, the one hundred and forty-four thousand priests who yet hold the focus in the heart of the Violet Planet, have begun that ritual of saturating the earth plane with the action of the violet flame that is for the purpose of the transmutation of millions of years of the qualification of energy on Terra.... We come, then, to introduce the age of ritual, of science and of alchemy."

Omri-Tas also gave the following promise: "From the point of Alpha at Shamballa I will stand, then, to release my light into the heart of the Mother, into the hearts of all who would be Mother, into the hearts of all Keepers of the Flame. And each morning with the first ray of the dawn that caresses the face and the heart of the devotee, I will send forth the electric spark, the current of the Alpha cycle of the violet flame. And in that moment, you may catch that spark and be and receive the Omega return and therefore be unto me throughout the twenty-four-hour cycle the Omega counterpart of the Alpha-concentrated energies, which I place now upon the altar of Shamballa."

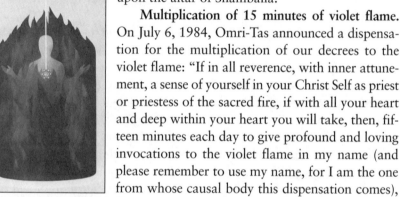

Multiplication of 15 minutes of violet flame. On July 6, 1984, Omri-Tas announced a dispensation for the multiplication of our decrees to the violet flame: "If in all reverence, with inner attunement, a sense of yourself in your Christ Self as priest or priestess of the sacred fire, if with all your heart and deep within your heart you will take, then, fifteen minutes each day to give profound and loving invocations to the violet flame in my name (and please remember to use my name, for I am the one from whose causal body this dispensation comes), then we will take that offering, measure for measure as it is devoted, as it is profound and sincere, the very weight of its power and light. Therefore, by the quality of it, quality for quality, it shall be multiplied in your life ten times!"

Violet-flame reservoir over central Europe. On February 26, 1988, in a dictation given in Lisbon, Portugal, Omri-Tas announced the dispensation of a violet-flame reservoir positioned over central Europe: "It is a very large reservoir of light as a sea in itself; and this light, beloved, is there for you to invoke as a direct transfusion to all lightbearers of Europe, Eastern Europe and the entire Soviet bloc.... When you invoke the violet flame, it will draw forth the light of this reservoir and also maximize it, fortify it, multiply it by your own love and devotion. And therefore, that light shall flow to every lightbearer in these lands. And as it does flow to them, it shall quicken them, it shall cut them free, it shall therefore transmute their spiritual and physical blindness as to those events coming.... This reservoir is a certain dispensation. If those Keepers of the Flame in embodiment do not make the violet-flame call daily, then this reservoir will come to be used up in its entirety, apportioned, then, among all lightbearers. But if the call continues to be given, the reservoir shall be like the unfed flame. It shall not fail. It shall remain full, and all that goes out of it shall be returned unto it multiplied by your call."

Violet-flame sea of light. On May 1, 1991, in Portland, Oregon, Omri-Tas announced the unprecedented dispensation of the violet-flame sea of light: "I deposit in the heart of the earth a dispensation immense of concentrated violet flame. It is an intercession of the quality of mercy. It is an intercession afforded to all those who serve the light. And through your Holy Christ Self, it shall be meted out as an unguent, as an elixir. May you drink of it in your hours of need and in your hours of strength and keep it replenished by new calls to the violet flame. It is a giant violet-flame reservoir, as a sea of light pulsating."

Omri-Tas to be present on earth on the third of each month. On October 14, 1991, Omri-Tas announced a thirty-three-day dispensation in which he would remain on earth to "give us a boost" and multiply our violet-flame decrees. At the conclusion of the thirty-three days, Omri-Tas granted another tremendous dispensation. The messenger and chelas had written petitions to Omri-Tas, asking him to remain longer and offering pledges of violet-flame decrees.

In response, Omri-Tas said that he was profoundly moved by our offering, but that he could not remain on earth full-time. He said there were many other planets at a similar crossroads to that of earth who were in great need of his presence. However, he was so touched by the pledges of daily violet-flame decrees that he promised to return to earth on the third day of each month. That is the day when walls of violet flame can come down, and we can be directly in the Electronic Presence of Omri-Tas.

❖ **ORION, The Old Man of the Hills**

Orion is a great patriot of light who works with Godfre and Saint Germain to expand the fires of freedom from the heart of the mountain to the hearts of mankind. He lived in America and ascended in the twentieth century. He maintains a focus in the Rocky Mountains and works closely with elemental life and the four beings of the elements to maintain the balance of light in the earth focused in gold.

In 1975, he spoke of his service: "I AM the Old Man of the Hills. You have not known my flame, and yet you have known my name. Orion I am called, and you have sung to the aureole of the dawn. You have called me Old Man, and I have laughed with a twinkle in my eye; for if you could see me, you would wonder whether or not I am an old man, a young man, or perhaps something in between. I come scaling the summits of life. And I work with elemental life and with God Tabor, spanning the mountain ranges of North America. I am in search of a chela, even as I was once in search of a guru, even as I met my master in the mountain.

"I am a devotee of freedom, and I am proud to be called a patriot of life! For I release the fervor of my heart, and that fervor is a sphere of pink light around every star aborning—the stars of your soul, the stars of the flag that blows in the wind, the stars of the nations, the stars of planetary bodies. And I walk with Godfre; I walk with Saint Germain, ever kindling, with the fervor of my heart, the precious concepts of freedom they hold for mankind. And as I walk, many times in silence, meditating upon the words of God Obedience and of the Master of freedom's flame, I hear them also in search of a chela—not one, but many."[350]

With clarity and emphasis this one who is ascended points out the need for constancy of application on the part of each student to his own individualized God Source for guidance in this world of form until he becomes one with this Source in the ascension in the light. For none can achieve immortality vicariously through the efforts of another. Beloved Orion, as encouragement to the students, tells of his own need for application to his God Source for direction during his personal Armageddon when, at an early age in his final embodiment, his untransmuted substance, expressed as misdemeanor, disconcerted his parents and brought down upon him condemnation from his associates. But his faith in God and his persistent effort toward mastery was such that he did achieve his eternal victory in the light.

Orion speaks of a turning point in his final embodiment: "When I was yet unascended and in contemplation of the vast Sierras, as I gazed upon the mountains, I was inspired with the exaltation of the soul. And one night as I lay in camp alone, hearing the music of the stars, my soul took flight from my form and I consciously left my body temple for the first time. Lying there in the mountains looking unto the stars, the gaze of my eyes contacting whirling fiery centers transported my soul unto the causal body of ascended beings and my own I AM Presence, and I had a preview of the soul's flight unto the ascension.

"And how I rejoiced to know that which God holds in store for every living soul! How I rejoiced in that moment, transcending planes of consciousness, to see the servants of God as angels and seraphim and sylphs and masterful beings! And I saw how a cosmos is a succession, one by one, of body temples, of fiery vortices of consciousness becoming God, of God becoming selfhood in manifestation through the cycling of the stars and fiery bodies.

"And my own guru upon that holy night came with a visitation of the birth of the Manchild; and I saw the Christ being born, and I saw the record of the descent of the soul of Jesus into that form. Even as I had risen from my body temple to experience planes of causal bodies, so I saw how the soul of the Avatar of the age had descended from his own starry body into form. And so I saw the cycles of life ascending and descending, descending and ascending, and souls upon the ladder reaching for the stars.

"Cosmic purpose was born! And I thought: 'I must take the record! I must take it to all those below who have not seen the vision of initiation and of freedom.' And the master said to me: 'My son, when they are ready, they will have the same initiation that you have been given. And until that hour and that moment, let your communication be with the fiery core of Self and let it be the affirmation of Reality. Let it be the tutoring in the outer of souls—not of the ultimate, but of the next step on the Path.

"'Do not burden souls on Terra with the knowledge of the steps high upon the mountain where the rocky crevices are formidable indeed. They cannot equate with higher initiation. They are concerned with the next step; and that step may very well be how to pay the light bill and how to buy the groceries and how to comfort the sick child and how to earn a living and how to bake the bread. These are initiations that pave the way for the mystical union of the body of God on earth and the body of God in heaven.'

"And so with these words and more of a teaching so profound and so joyous that I leave you to the communion of your own Master of Life to receive it, I descended once again to my body temple high in the Sierras, and I found myself once again gazing upon the stars in the firmament of God's being. And I rubbed my eyes and I said, 'Was it a dream? Was it a dream?' And I knew in my soul that I had contacted a vastness and a plane of mind where the few are privileged to be.

"And when morning came and the sun and the sound of the birds, I remembered the sound of the stars, and I saw even the birds as emissaries of hierarchy speaking to ears that will not listen to the inner sound, singing of a lost chord, singing of hierarchy! And I looked at the birds and all of the kinds of birds and I said, 'This is hierarchy. This is the physical manifestation of all the beings who inhabit the spheres.' And as I thought upon nature and the trees and the mountains and the rock and particles of being, I knew profoundly: God is All-in-all. God is All-in-all! Simple words, I know; but when experienced, profound beyond the word. And what can you say to a friend along life's way when you have had the initiation of the stars? Better keep the silence and say, 'God is All-in-all!'"[351]

Through his ascended master lens of perception, beloved Orion has observed the wickedness in high places of these latter days, and has discoursed upon the subtle and nefarious plot of the forces of negation to undermine the world economy and to bring about ultimate bankruptcy through excessive price and tax fixing, the exporting of America's gold and the devaluation of the dollar. It is not that the coin of the realm will buy our passport into heaven, but it does oil the machinery of our vehicles of transportation toward eternal goals. It is this spiritual train of progress that the hordes of shadow would derail; it is spiritual bankruptcy that they desire to precipitate; it is the gold of celestial values that they seek to devaluate; it is the souls of men that they desire to have in order that they may stymie all that God holds near and dear to man. The Old Man of the Hills pleads that we decree for the God-control of the economy.

Orion says, "Now rejoice! For I am close at hand; and I take my walking stick and I hike into the mountains and I anchor my flame in a physical, tangible body. And by and by, one of these days when you are hiking in the mountains, you may see afar off a form of one—perhaps an old man, perhaps a young man, perhaps the flame of Orion! From my heart to your heart, the flame of the mountain glows."[352]

❖ OROMASIS AND DIANA, Hierarchs of the Fire Element

Oromasis and Diana are the directors of the fire element, in charge of the elemental beings of fire, called salamanders, serving this planet. Standing on the twelve o'clock line, their office under the direction of the four cosmic forces focused in the Hub, these twin flames serve from Hercules' retreat at Half Dome in Yosemite National Park and from their focus in the etheric realm over an island in the Bering Sea off the coast of the Kamchatka Peninsula.

Prince Oromasis and Princess Diana, as they are addressed by their retinue, serve with the hierarchies of Capricorn, Aquarius and Pisces to teach mankind the mastery of the etheric plane, and with the hierarchies of Aries, Leo and Sagittarius in teaching the mastery of the fire element. They also work with Zarathustra and the priests of the Order of Melchizedek.

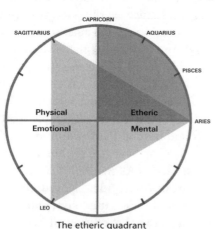

The etheric quadrant
and the trine of the fire signs

Being of the fiery element themselves, they work closely with the etheric, or fire, body of man and assist him in mastering the caduceus action and in opening the seven chakras, in addition to regulating the flow of light through the chakras and aligning the four lower bodies.

Using their momentum of the sacred fire, Oromasis and Diana, together with the legions of blue-lightning and white-fire angels in their command, intensify and quicken the action of the flames in answer to the calls of embodied mankind. This ability to quicken and intensify the action of the flame invoked, including the threefold flame within the heart, makes them especially qualified to assist in the purification of the four lower bodies and the freeing of the physical body from the densities of impure foods, drugs and stimuli. Oromasis and Diana should be called upon to walk through one's four lower bodies and one's environment every twenty-four hours to purify one's forcefield of the mass effluvia of the world.

The salamanders in the command of Oromasis and Diana are fiery beings whose auras ripple with the rainbow rays of the causal body. Composed of liquid fire that reflects the consciousness of those whom they serve, their appearance is constantly changing, for their chameleon-like natures instantly reflect the prism of the Christ consciousness that plays upon their forms.

These beings are actually the mirrors of the Great Central Sun Magnet and instruments of every ascended and cosmic being. Powerful in their out-

reach and service to life, they carry rods of white lightning as scepters of authority to hold the balance of the fire element in the world of form.

Salamanders, being of the realm of Spirit-formless, are not confined to any dimension. Standing nine feet tall, they may reduce their size, with the flicker of a flame, to an inch in height. They are beings of tremendous power. Once captured by black magicians, they can be extremely destructive, but in the service of those who love the Christ—where they love to be—there is nothing they cannot do to uplift the standards of the race.

Oromasis and Diana tell us that "the fallen ones have long ago recognized the value of controlling the beings of the elements. This they do through the bloodletting of voodoo ceremony and satanic rite, invoking demoniac forces of the astral plane and casting spells of death and destruction and hexes that hypnotically bind the elementals to do their bidding. Under these gross misuses of the sacred fire, some salamanders as well as other elementals have been imprisoned for centuries, and thus mankind have come to fear the nature spirits and to attribute to them mischievous and even malevolent designs.

"Thus the first order of the day is to invoke the legions of Archangel Michael and Mighty Astrea to cut free the imprisoned salamanders, to draw them up into the Great Central Sun Magnet to God's heart for repolarization and realignment with his mighty will, which is always good for all who partake of its cup."[353]

Mankind can call to Archangel Michael and Mighty Astrea to cut free the salamanders and all elemental life from the negativity and black magic that keep them from performing their service in full obedience to the will of God.

Call to Oromasis and Diana to take command of the fiery salamanders and to contain all uncontrolled, destructive fires. In the name of the Christ, command the elementals to bring such fires under God-control. Ask beloved Helios and Vesta to draw the salamanders up into the Great Central Sun Magnet for the repolarization and realignment with God's holy will. Call to the Great Divine Director to arrest the spirals of human infamy that have imprisoned elementals in lower forms.

Also, ask for all elementals to be cleared by the combined alchemy of the resurrection flame and the violet flame. The violet flame can consume all radioactive substances that have burdened the salamanders and the earth through irresponsible uses of nuclear energy. Ask Cyclopea to give to every elemental the divine image and the divine vision of the golden age, the City Foursquare and the Temple Beautiful so that every elemental can hold the matrix for perfect form on earth. Ask for the earth be sealed in the emerald matrix and the healing thoughtform.

On July 8, 1990, Diana announced: "I have brought with me today representatives of the four kingdoms. To each one of you is given a troop of elementals, some from each of the kingdoms. They will stay with you and obey your command that is heart-centered in the diamond heart of Mary and Morya. And they will remain as long as you tend them and nurture them, include them in your calls and give them assignments only in keeping with the will of God—so long as you do not abuse them but invoke them for many, many purposes in your life, not excluding the healing of the four lower bodies or the tending to practical matters.... Thus, they are children. And you may consider that you have adopted a little tribe today numbering twelve."[354]

❖ PADMA SAMBHAVA, Great Guru of Tibetan Buddhism

Padma Sambhava is revered throughout the Himalayan countries as the "Precious Guru." He is the founder of Tibetan Buddhism, and his followers venerate him as the "second Buddha."

Padma Sambhava's name means "Lotus-Born One." Although much of his life and work is obscured in legend, he is said to have been the foremost

scholar at the famous monastic university in
Nalanda, India, in the eighth century A.D. He was
renowned for his mystical powers and mastery of
the occult sciences—especially for his knowledge
and application of *dharani* ("mystical sentences").
He also had a great command of worldly knowledge, from languages and fine arts to the earth sciences and architecture.

Padma Sambhava

In about 750 A.D., the Tibetan king Trisong
Detsen invited Padma Sambhava to come to
Tibet. There he helped establish Buddhism by overcoming the forces of the
entrenched Bon religion. He exorcised the demons that were preventing the
building of the first Buddhist monastery in Tibet, the great monastery of
Samye, located outside of Lhasa. Padma Sambhava then oversaw the completion of this monumental monastery with its elaborate complex of temples designed in the form of a mandala. At Samye he also founded the first
community of Tibetan Buddhist monks.

Padma Sambhava brought an age of great enlightenment to Tibet.
Under his direction, an assembly of scholars translated Buddhist scriptures
and texts into the Tibetan language, enabling Buddhism to spread throughout the country. In addition, he traveled throughout Tibet, converting
many to the path of the Buddha and revealing the mantra teachings of the
Vajrayana. *Vajrayana* is the Diamond Vehicle, or Path, a school of Buddhism prevalent in Tibet. One of its central practices is the empowerment
of a disciple by his guru through certain practices and rituals, including
reciting mantras.

Before Padma Sambhava left Tibet, he instructed the king and people
for twenty-one days in the outer and inner teachings. He also taught them
principles of law, farming and enlightened government, and he exhorted
them to pursue the path of Buddhahood.

Legend says that, with this accomplished, he mounted a magnificent
winged horse, and surrounded by rainbow light, rose upward into the
heavens. According to tradition, he now resides in his paradise, his Pure
Land, on the Copper-Colored Mountain.

While he was living, Padma Sambhava initiated an inner circle of
twenty-five disciples who became adepts and transmitters of the teachings.
Because the Tibetan people were not yet ready to receive the essence of
Padma Sambhava's highest teachings, the master and his disciples preserved them in an abbreviated, codified form that could be deciphered only
by those who had been properly prepared. These scriptures are called

termas, meaning literally "treasures." Padma Sambhava and his disciples concealed the termas where they would be safe until it was time for them to be revealed. He predicted that his twenty-five disciples would reembody as *tertöns* (literally "revealers of treasure") to discover and interpret these esoteric teachings.

According to other traditions, the most prominent tertöns are incarnations of Padma Sambhava himself. Tibetan Buddhists believe that starting in the eleventh century and continuing, tertöns began to recover and expound upon these termas. Some of the termas that were discovered contain prophecies made by Padma Sambhava concerning the future of Tibet—prophecies we have seen come to pass in our own lifetime. These include prophecies of the Chinese Communist invasion of Tibet; the destruction of monasteries; the desecration of sacred scriptures, statues and paintings; the degradation of monks; the slaying of the Tibetan people and the raping of nuns.

Padma Sambhava bestowed upon the messenger Elizabeth Clare Prophet the mantle of guru and gave her the name "Guru Ma." "Guru Ma" means the teacher who is a devotee of the Divine Mother.* Wearing the mantle of guru, the messenger is the servant of the light of God within you. The guru helps you find your way back home to God.

There is no greater love than the love that is shared between a guru and his chela. They give their life to each other in a sacred bond. For thousands of years, the great spiritual teachers of mankind have passed their mantle and their teaching to deserving disciples. Around each successive teacher would gather students who were dedicated to studying that teaching and becoming the living example of that teaching.

With the transfer of the mantle from master to disciple comes the transfer of responsibility. The disciple pledges to carry on the mission of his master. In order for the work of the Great White Brotherhood to continue on earth, someone in embodiment must wear the mantle of guru. Today there are very few true gurus in embodiment who are sponsored by the Great White Brotherhood. Padma Sambhava is a part of a special lineage of gurus of the Great White Brotherhood called the hierarchy of the ruby ray. The chain of hierarchy in this lineage is from Sanat Kumara (the Ancient of Days) to Gautama Buddha, Lord Maitreya, Jesus Christ and Padma Sambhava.

---

*A *mantle* is a symbol of authority, preeminence or responsibility, a spiritual office. With its bestowal, there is passed from guru to disciple a great sphere of light. A *guru* is a spiritual teacher who not only teaches about the spiritual path, but he or she also sets the example of how one must walk that path.

For centuries, devotees of Padma Sambhava have received blessings by invoking his mantra, *Om Ah Hum Vajra Guru Padma Siddhi Hum*. It means: "Padma Sambhava, who arose from a lotus, please grant me the ordinary and supreme accomplishments, HUM!" (A "Vajra Guru" is a being who has fully mastered the path of Vajrayana.)

Padma Sambhava instructed his disciple Yeshe Tsogyal that his mantra should be used to avert the evils of a coming period of great darkness. His devotees have invoked this mantra to create peace and harmony and to antidote the confusion and turmoil of this Dark Age. It is a mantra for the era in which we live, a time of the planetary return of karma.

Lord Maitreya has urged us to let Padma Sambhava's mantra ring in our soul and our heart: "Give the mantra of Padma Sambhava thirty-three times and celebrate your soul's ascent each day to the secret chamber of your heart, to the altar of being. Life is empty when you do not do this. When you do not do it, you do not even know just how empty your life is. And you do not know how full it can be when and if you enter into the practice of keeping your appointment with Maitreya, with Gautama Buddha, with the bodhisattvas. Give it thirty-three times, beloved ones."[355]

The ascended master Padma Sambhava has told us that he was sent by Gautama Buddha to be the incarnation of the Buddha so that all beings might have hope of becoming that Buddha. He said that following in his footsteps, we could be "the open door to souls becoming the Buddha within." He also warned that those who choose to walk the path of the Buddha will face challenges.

He gave this key to retaining the Buddhic light: "Keep on loving in the face of the most intense anger, hatred, pride, passion, ambition, fear, death and darkness projected against the alignment of your being with the Buddhas of the light.... Remember not to identify with the counterfeit stream of the darkened ones. Their stream is this anger and all of these perversions that I have named.... These are the energies that you will tame in my name. These are the energies that will pass through your chakras without resistance from yourself. And in passing through, they will become, by the alchemy of transmutation, the great River of Life that you can claim as your own."[356]

On April 2, 1994, Padma Sambhava called us to go back to basics and to examine our reason for being: "Remember why you are here, why you were born, and the mercies that God has extended to you. Opportunity, beloved, may knock and knock every day of your life. But when you are out of embodiment, you will sense the marking of time and even the transpiring of long aeons, some on the astral plane and some on the etheric plane, before you shall be able to return again for such opportunity as you have today."

Padma Sambhava said that he desired to tutor us for two reasons: so that we could reunite with God at the end of our lives in the ritual of the ascension, and so that we might "bear light and freely give light" to rescue other souls. "All of you are capable of this. The question is: Do you have the will? Is this your highest choice? Is this the definition of purpose in your life?"

Padma Sambhava said one of the biggest obstacles to developing our soul potential is learning to make peace with God and with other people. If you find this difficult, he said, "Consider that you may have a malady of the soul and that this malady can become a cancer of the soul, eating away at the very essence of your soul-identity. Recognize when the soul is sick and consult the doctor Lord Gautama Buddha and other Buddhas...."

"Please recognize the illness of the soul. It is the most dangerous illness of all. It is when you begin to have a warped view of life and of others and you imagine they have opinions of you that they do not and you begin to torment yourself with bitterness toward life, toward God. Oh yes, beloved, all of these emotional and mental attitudes are the beginning of the decay of the body itself."

In order to develop our soul potential, he said we must "go beyond rancor.... What vast opportunity is cast aside when anger is not conquered, when resentment is not transmuted into forgiveness and love and gratitude for mercies given...."

"The antidotes begin in the etheric body, the mental body. The antidotes are the good humor, the good happiness, the good compassion, the good love, the good fairness and forgiveness. All of these things are the antidotes that would take away the sins of the whole world and the cancers lying deep in the psyche and then deep in the organs."

Padma Sambhava summarized all of these antidotes in two words: *giving* and *serving*. He said: "Give new life to your body and your soul by freely giving what you have.... Your aura will thus mount and increase and intensify and spread and widen and become as powerful as the seven seas."

Again, he urged, go back to basics: "Determine what is important to you from this day forward. I will tell you what my definition is of what is supremely important. It is that you satisfy the law of love, the law of wisdom, the law of the will of God. It is that you become a rock of refuge in the earth, caring not for the things of the self or the accumulation of the things of the self, but to perform your duties as best as possible, making use of the best of modern technologies and all that you require to have your victory. Serve, beloved, for service is your liberation."

On October 10, 1994, Padma Sambhava called us to be "interpreters of the new teaching of Saint Germain and how it relates to the ancient teachings of Hinduism and Buddhism." Now is the hour when many souls can break the chain of karma and rebirth and reunite with God at the end of their lives in the ritual of the ascension. "But they need a spin," he said. "And the spin they need is the violet spinning flame. I enjoin you, then, to unveil this sacred treasure. Reveal it, beloved, to all who will listen and learn to give the violet-flame mantras. Let them know that the most sacred treasure of all is the violet-flame crystal, the violet-flame mantra, the violet flame blazing in their hearts, transmuting records of karma and cleansing all life in answer to their calls."

The ascended master El Morya tells us that Padma Sambhava is a great devotee of Jesus Christ and Gautama Buddha. Seeking oneness with Jesus is important for all spiritual seekers, and we can pursue that oneness through Padma Sambhava. Padma Sambhava has spoken of his role as the one who can prepare us to be initiated under Jesus Christ. He said:

"I give you the initiations of your Christhood. Do you think it odd that an Eastern Guru should teach you, a Western chela, the path of Jesus Christ? I, for one, do not. For you see, through your training and initiations under me, I bring you along on the path of chelaship to the place where it would be unthinkable for you, under any circumstances, to be an offense to your Lord....

"Jesus said to his disciples: 'Why call ye me, Lord, Lord, and do not the things which I say?'[357] Many continue to cry, 'Lord, Lord,' professing to love him, to know him and to be a Christian, but their actions belie their words.... There is more to the discipline of being a Christian than crying, 'Lord, Lord.' You must be able to continually keep the flame of your emergent Christhood and to live according to God's will.... Call to me so that you might be made whole at all levels of your being so that in that wholeness you might sit at your Lord's feet and neither offend him nor be offended by him."[358]

❖ PADRE PIO, Modern-Day Saint

Padre Pio was the famous twentieth-century Italian monk who for fifty years bore on his hands, feet and side the wounds of the crucified Christ, called the stigmata.

This gentle, humble priest was born Francesco Forgione on May 25, 1887, in one of the poorest and most backward areas of southern Italy. At the age of fifteen, he entered a Franciscan Capuchin monastery, and he was ordained into the priesthood in 1910.

He served in World War I in the medical corps, but was too sickly to continue. In 1918 he was transferred to the small sixteenth-century friary

of Our Lady of Grace, about two hundred miles east of
Rome. From then on, he never left this isolated mountain area. Yet, by the time of his death in 1968, he was
receiving five thousand letters a month and thousands
of visitors. He had become renowned for his piety and
his miracles.

Padre Pio

Padre Pio is thought to be the first Catholic priest
to bear the wounds of Christ. (Saint Francis was the
first *person* known to have received the stigmata.) He
also had the gifts of spiritual clairvoyance, conversion,
discernment of spirits, visions, bilocation, healing and prophecy. It is said
that once when a newly ordained Polish priest came to see him, Padre Pio
remarked: "Someday you will be pope." As prophesied, that priest became
Pope John Paul II.

Padre Pio spoke frequently in visions with Jesus, Mary and his own
guardian angel. On other occasions he spent the night in intense struggles
with the Devil. The Padre would be found in the morning with blood and
bruises and other physical signs of the struggle. He was often exhausted,
sometimes unconscious, and on one occasion suffered from broken bones
in his body. On one occasion the iron bars of the window were twisted.
Other monks often heard the noise of these encounters, although only
Padre Pio saw the demons.

As well as these invisible assaults, Padre Pio also suffered the persecution of people within the hierarchy of his beloved Church. For ten years he
was not permitted to serve Mass publicly or hear confessions.

One of the things Padre Pio was most famous for was his ability as a
confessor. Kenneth Woodward writes: "Most of Padre Pio's energies were
devoted to intense prayer, celebrating Mass and, above all, hearing confessions." People from around the world flocked to his doorstep to have
him hear their confessions. Woodward says: "Padre Pio is credited with the
gift of 'reading hearts'—that is, the ability to see into the souls of others and
know their sins without hearing a word from the penitent. As his reputation grew, so did the lines outside his confessional—to the point that for a
time his fellow Capuchins issued tickets for the privilege of confessing to
Padre Pio. Sometimes, when a sinner could not come to him, Padre Pio
went to the sinner, it is said, though not in the usual manner.

"Without leaving his room, the friar would appear as far away as
Rome to hear a confession or comfort the sick. He was endowed, in other
words, with the power of 'bilocation,' or the ability to be present in two
places at once."[359]

Sometimes Padre Pio treated those who came to him for confession sternly. One of his devotees wrote: "If he is sometimes severe, it is because many people approach the confessional lightly, without giving the sacrament its true importance."[360]

Many people were transformed who came to hear Padre Pio celebrate the Mass. The same devotee writes, "When the hour of Mass approaches, all faces are turned toward the sacristy from which the Padre will come, seeming to walk painfully on his pierced feet. We feel that grace itself is approaching us, forcing us to bend our knees. Padre Pio is not an ordinary priest, but a creature in pain who renews the Passion of Christ with the devotion and radiance of one who is inspired by God.

"After he steps to the altar and makes the Sign of the Cross, the Padre's face is transfigured, and he seems like a creature who becomes one with his Creator. Tears roll down his cheeks, and from his mouth come words of prayer, of supplication for pardon, of love for his Lord of whom he seems to become a perfect replica. None of those present notice the passage of time. It takes him about one hour and a half to say his mass, but the attention of all is riveted on every gesture, movement and expression of the celebrant.

"At the sound of the word 'Credo' pronounced with such tremendous conviction, there is a great wave of emotion through the throng. And the most recalcitrant of sinners is carried along as on a stream that is bringing him to the confessional and the renunciation of his old way of life."[361]

Author Stuart Holroyd relates just a few of the many stories of Padre Pio's miraculous intercession. He writes: "During World War I, an Italian general, after a series of defeats, was on the point of committing suicide when a monk entered his tent and said: 'Such an action is foolish,' and promptly left. The general didn't hear of the existence of Padre Pio until some time later, but when he visited the monastery, he identified him as the monk who had appeared at a crucial moment and saved his life.

"During World War II an Italian pilot baled out of a blazing plane. His parachute failed to open but he miraculously fell to the ground without injury, and he returned to his base with a strange story to tell. When he had been falling to the ground, a friar had caught him in his arms and carried him gently down to earth. His Commanding Officer said he was obviously suffering from shock, and sent him home on leave.

"When he told his mother the tale of his escape, she said: 'That was Padre Pio. I prayed to him so hard for you.' Then she showed him a picture of the Padre. 'That is the man!' said the young pilot.

"He later went to thank the padre for his intervention. 'That is not the only time I have saved you,' said Padre Pio. 'At Monastir, when your plane was hit, I made it glide safely to earth.' The pilot was astounded because the event the Padre referred to had happened some time before, and there was no normal way he could have known about it."[362]

In 1975, some seven years after his death, the ascended lady master Clara Louise told us that Padre Pio is an ascended master. Padre Pio is instrumental in assisting the Church the masters have founded in the Aquarian age. He is also renowned for his ability to answer prayers for healing. Padre Pio was officially recognized as a saint of the Catholic Church on June 16, 2002.

❖ **PALLAS ATHENA, Goddess of Truth**

Pallas Athena, the Goddess of Truth, is a tremendous being of light who ensouls the cosmic consciousness of Truth. The flame of truth is an intense bright emerald green. It combines the flaming blue power of God's will and the brilliant golden illumination of the intelligence of God. Her presence in the universe is the exaltation of the flame of living Truth. This truth she holds on behalf of the evolutions of earth as a member of the Karmic Board, where she serves as the representative on the fifth ray of truth, healing, supply and precipitation.

She ministers to mankind from the Temple of Truth above the Island of Crete. Serving directly under Vesta, the Sun Goddess, she focuses the truth of God's love to the earth. Pallas Athena also works with Hilarion, the chohan of the fifth ray, and other healing and green-ray masters.

Souls come to the Temple of Truth in their finer bodies at night (during sleep) to be instructed in the fine points of cosmic law, the science of healing, mathematics, music, divine geometry and the laws of alchemy and precipitation. Many who come to society today with ingenious ways of opening the doors of higher understanding in these fields have studied under the masters in this retreat.

Pallas Athena was embodied as the high priestess in the Temple of

The ruins of the Temple of Apollo at Delphi

Truth on Atlantis, serving under Vesta. She later kept the Mother flame of truth in ancient Greece, as that temple and that temple flame were transferred from Atlantis to that land. She served as directress of the temple virgins and oracles at Delphi, who were messengers of the gods and goddesses who spoke

Truth and the wisdom of the Law to the ancients. Pallas Athena and the members of the Brotherhood sought to keep alive the inner mysteries of the retreats. The memories of the gods, the functions of the temple virgins and the oracles of Delphi were the last vestiges of communication from the ascended masters in the Greek culture. After the closing over of those sources due to the discord and rebellion of the people, we begin to trace modern thought reaching and culminating in what manifests today as humanism.

Pallas Athena is the twin flame of the Maha Chohan, the representative of the Holy Spirit to the earth. Together they are an indomitable pair in defense of truth. The Maha Chohan was embodied as the Greek poet Homer, who spoke of Pallas Athena in his epic poems, the Iliad and the Odyssey.

Pallas Athena is one of the most important deities in Greek mythology, and in Roman mythology, she is identified as Minerva. Her influence spans everything from the administration of government and militaristic pursuits to the delicate arts of spinning and weaving. She is seen as the very personification of wisdom who presides over the intellectual and moral side of human life.

Athena was the heart of the spiritual life of ancient Athens. The Greeks adored her as the defender of their cities and honored her with many titles. She is revered as the Goddess of War and Peace, the Goddess of Wisdom, patron of arts and crafts, and guardian of cities. She is also honored as the inventor and protector of culture and as the protector of civilized life and agriculture. She has been called the Counselor-Goddess and Goddess of the Assembly for her role in maintaining law and order in the courts and administering justice. She is also looked to as the Goddess of the Working Woman because of her mastery in spinning, weaving and needlework.

Among the many inventions attributed to her are the plow, the rake, the flute, the ship and the science of numbers. Her emblem is the olive, emblem of peace; and her bird is the owl, representative of wisdom.

Athena is popularly admired as the "martial maiden" who inspires and accompanies heroes in their adventures and battles, yet never succumbs to amorous advances, fiercely defending her virginity. She was one of three virgin-goddesses who could not be stirred by the influences of Aphrodite, the Goddess of Love. One of the earliest accounts of Athena appears in the Iliad, where she is a war goddess, inspiring and fighting alongside the Greek heroes. To possess her favor is considered synonymous with military prowess.

According to the traditions of Greek mythology, Pallas Athena was the favorite daughter of Zeus, the powerful father of the Gods and king of Mount Olympus. Her mother was the Goddess Metis, whose name means "thought" or "intelligence." Metis was believed to be so wise that she knew more than all the gods and men together.

Zeus was warned that if he had children with Metis they would be more powerful than he and would eventually dethrone him. Thus, when Metis became pregnant with Athena, Zeus swallowed Metis in order to prevent the child's birth. Soon after, Zeus became afflicted with a violent headache. He went to the smithy god Hephaestus, who split his skull with a bronze ax in order to relieve the pain. Out sprang the bright-eyed Athena in full armour, shouting triumphantly and brandishing a sharp spear!

The birth of Athena from the head of Zeus can be seen as symbolic of her rational temperament. Her very nature reflects the triumph of reason over passion, as she is consistently unmoved by the emotions of passion or romantic love. Her father is the most powerful and her mother the wisest of the gods and goddesses. Athena is thus a product of the union of power and wisdom.

To the Athenians, she was known as "Parthenos," which means Virgin, or Maiden. They built the Parthenon in her honor on the Acropolis at Athens. The beautiful Parthenon was one of the largest Greek temples and a masterpiece of Greek architecture. It was the spiritual center of Athens.

 Built on a high hill, it was visible for miles around and stood as a symbol of Athenian culture, wealth and power. Inside, toward the west end, towered a forty-foot-high ivory and gold statue of the goddess, sculpted by Phidias.

In art, Athena is represented as a stately figure, clothed in armour and bearing her breastplate, the *aegis*, which no arrow could pierce. The aegis is ringed in serpents and is adorned with the head of the Gorgon Medusa. Athena often wears a golden helmet and holds in her right hand a spear to strike at a serpent near her feet. It has thus been said that she wields the spear of knowledge against the serpent of ignorance. To the ancient Greeks, Athena was known as the Spear-shaker. They placed her statue on their temples, and when the rays of the sun would dance on her spear, it looked as if she were shaking it.

Pallas Athena was the muse and inspiration of Sir Francis Bacon, author of the Shakespearean plays, an embodiment of Saint Germain. In her honor, he founded a secret literary society called the Knights of the Helmet. It is believed that he used the name Shakespeare partly in tribute to the goddess Pallas Athena, the "shaker of the spear."

The one who holds the office of the Goddess of Truth has always given great assistance to the messengers of the Great White Brotherhood. Her scepter of power is the flaming sword of Truth that cleaves asunder the Real from the unreal and keeps the way of the Tree of Life in the Garden of Eden.

On June 30, 1976, in Washington, D.C., Pallas Athena called for the raising of the consciousness of the people of earth by the flame of truth—the Coming Revolution in Higher Consciousness. She said: "I wish you would understand this day that when I say I AM Truth incarnate, I must rely upon your body, your flesh and your blood, your mind and your soul to be the incarnation of the Word of Truth that I AM!...

"I AM Pallas Athena. I AM Greek. I AM Roman. I AM freeborn. I AM a member of every nation. I AM an American. From this day and forevermore, I claim you for the cause of Truth because you have made that cause your own. In the living flame of Truth, I am grateful for your love of Truth, of liberty, for your courage and your self-sacrifice. I am grateful, and I bow before the flame of Truth within you. And I will use that flame to light a nation and to light a world!"

As a result of this dictation, Pallas Athena, Saint Germain and El Morya sent the messenger and their chelas throughout the world to bring the truth of the message of the ascended masters.

Whenever you are engaged in a service to the ascended masters, call to Pallas Athena and her legions of Truth to go before you, to be the bearer of the mighty sword of Truth for the binding of the force of anti-truth or Antichrist.

❖ **PARIS, MASTER OF, Chief of the Council of Paris**

The Master of Paris made his ascension more than 500 years ago. He is Chief of the Council of France, although he is not a Frenchman. He is described as a tall, handsome man with courtly grace. The Master of Paris maintains a focus of the will of God in la Sainte-Chapelle on the Île de la Cité in the very heart of Paris, the birthplace of France. He has an etheric retreat over the physical focus where he maintains the action of the three-fold flame.

He also maintains a physical focus in the city of Paris, which he often frequents in a physical form. His retreat is a beautiful old castle-like residence with many windows overlooking the city of Paris. This focus is kept up by his disciples and is used frequently by the masters as a meeting place

La Sainte-Chapelle

in Paris from which they can direct the energies necessary to hold the balance for the governments of Europe.

This master played a key role in establishing the esoteric schools of the Brotherhood in Paris in the eighteenth and the nineteenth centuries. He works with, among others, Saint Germain, Paul the Venetian, the ascended master Alexander Gaylord and Lady Leto. The radiation of Saint Germain and Portia, the Goddess of Justice, is strongly felt throughout la Sainte-Chapelle and the adjoining halls of justice (Palais de Justice). Also on the Île de la Cité is Notre Dame Cathedral, a focus of Mother Mary.

El Morya has spoken of the desire of Saint Germain to have physical focuses of light in the cities of the world, like that of the Master of Paris: "Saint Germain is not content to train the souls in the etheric retreats of the Great White Brotherhood. No, he is determined to have the focuses such as the focus of the Master of Paris, a home of light in the physical octave, a home of light in the city, a home of light where souls can be received."[363] The masters need students to maintain these focuses. Morya asked for the stalwart ones, the builders and the pioneers to come forth.

Archangel Jophiel and Christine have also spoken of the focuses of light in Europe and around the world and their desire to open the retreat of the Master of Paris: "Our message, then, of the great light descending—of Paul the Venetian, of the Great Karmic Board and the Goddess of Liberty, of the expansion of this light—is to you our offering: dimensions of God consciousness expanding as a narrow room that becomes a mansion of light.

"Beloved, you who cherish the shrines, the cathedrals, the history, the culture of the Great Divine Director in Europe—open up your hearts! Give your life and your full support in abundant measure. For we would, this very day, open our retreat in Paris if souls of light would offer to be the innkeepers of this shrine of Saint Germain and the Master of Paris."[364]

❖ **PARVATI,** *See* **Shiva**

❖ **PATRICK, SAINT, Patron Saint of Ireland**

Saint Patrick is the great saint and patron of the Irish people. His intensely spiritual nature, his enthusiasm and his strength in action enabled him to surmount tremendous difficulties and to gradually bring the Christian faith to all of Ireland.

Patrick was born in Roman Britain in the late fourth century A.D. His father, Calpurnius, was a deacon in the Christian church, When Patrick was sixteen years old, a band of Irish marauders carried him off and kept him in captivity tending herds. After six years he escaped, and after several years he returned home.

After his return he had a dream in which he saw a man named Victoricus bearing innumerable letters, one of which he received and read. The beginning of it bore the inscription: "The Voice of the Irish." As he read the first words, he heard the voice of the Irish calling him to return to them.

Statue of Saint Patrick
at Croagh Patrick

Having received the calling, he set out to prepare himself for his mission and spent the next twenty years at centers of learning in Gaul. In 432 he was finally consecrated a bishop and commissioned to spread the faith in Ireland. In addition to establishing many churches and converting thousands to Christianity, Patrick introduced Latin into Ireland as the language of the Church.

Sanat Kumara tells us that it was by his calling that Patrick was raised up to be an apostle of the Christ and to subdue the seed of serpent in Ireland. Sanat Kumara speaks of his son Patrick: "Let us go to the mountain in the land of Erin where a youth enslaved by pagans is in prayer through the day and into the night. So fervent is the love of God within him that the fire of his heart is a light midst snow and ice. He lived on the mountain, alone with God, tending his master's herds. And on that mountain, I called my son Patrick, that out of the condition of servitude there might be produced the miracle fire of freedom.

"It was late fourth century A.D. and the clans of the Irish—the reincarnated tribes of Ephraim and Manasseh—were ruled by a host of kings. They served not the LORD God, nor had they the salvation of his Son. Therefore I, the Ancient of Days, called my son, freeborn, unto slavery that I might deliver him to freedom and to the mission of implanting the violet flame in the hearts of my true sons and daughters that they might one day carry it to the New World in the name of Saint Germain.

"To him I gave the vision of the people of Erin whose seed would one day ignite the fires of freedom on every shore and in every nation. Your own prophet Mark derived his fervor from that lineage of the Ancient of Days, which goes back to the emerald isle. And the Irish eyes of Thomas Moore, poet and prince of my heart, yet smile through the sternness of El

Morya and his twinkle of mirth always needed on earth.

"Finally restored to his kinsfolk after six years of humbling himself before me on the mountain, tending sheep as he would soon feed my sheep, Patrick heard the voices of the souls of my children crying out from the land of Erin for deliverance: 'We beseech thee, holy youth, to come and walk among us once more.' Indeed they remembered him when he had walked among them as a prophet in Israel, rebuking their waywardness in the name of the LORD. Now they awaited the message of their salvation through Messiah's anointed apostle.

"Patrick prepared for his mission under the lineage of the ruby ray and with the saints of the inner Church. And that mission, my beloved, was to subdue the seed of Serpent in Ireland and to raise up the tribes of Israel, the remnant of Joseph's seed who would be Christ-bearers to the nations.* Empowered of the Holy Ghost and bearing the Staff of Jesus, he wielded such power and wrought such miracles that pagan chiefs and decadent druids bowed in submission to this rod of Aaron that, in the new tongue, became the rod of *Erin*.

"So perilous was the mission of the shamrock saint of the fifth ray that he wrote in his 'Confession': 'Daily I expect either a violent death or to be robbed and reduced to slavery or the occurrence of some such calamity. I have cast myself into the hands of Almighty God, for He rules everything; as the Prophet sayeth, "Cast thy care upon the LORD, and He Himself will sustain thee."'

"Well might you emulate the courage and the humility of my son Patrick when he boldly challenged Prince Corotick, that serpent who dared plunder Patrick's domain, massacring a great number of neophytes, as it is written, who were yet in their white garments after baptism; and others he carried away and sold to infidels.

"Patrick circulated a letter in his own hand pronouncing the judgment of Corotick and his accomplices and declaring them separate from him as the established Bishop of Ireland, and from Jesus Christ. He forbade the faithful 'to eat with them, or to receive their alms, till they should have satisfied God by the tears of sincere penance, and restored the servants of Jesus Christ to their liberty.'[365]

"Such is the true Work and Word of the saints of the ruby ray who, with all due seriousness, receive the sign of their coming in the taking up

---

*Joseph, youngest and most favored son of Jacob, had two sons, Ephraim and Manasseh, whom Jacob blessed as his own. Reincarnated in Britain and the U.S.A., they carry the flame of the twelve tribes of Israel.

of serpents. Thousands upon thousands of the descendants of Jacob's favorite son were baptized and confirmed by the Lord Jesus through my son Patrick. Like the apostle Paul, he bound the power of Serpent's seed that had invaded the land of Erin; and like him, he healed their sick, he restored sight—both inner and outer—to their blind, and he raised Abram's seed—dead in body and in spirit—to new life through the indwelling Christ by the Word of Christ Jesus, his beloved.

"Now the ascended master Saint Patrick stands with me on the summit of Mount Aigli where, at the close of his earthly sojourn, he retreated forty days and forty nights, fasting in body and in spirit that he might be filled with the light of the Ancient of Days. There on that occasion fifteen hundred years ago, I summoned all the saints of Erin—the light of Aaron's priesthood and the lightbearers of the Christic seed of Joseph—past, present, and future, to pay homage to him who was father to them all.... My beloved, many of you were among the souls of the saints who came to Patrick in his final hours on the mountain. You saluted him in the glory of God that was upon him, and to him you were the promise that his Word and Work would be carried to golden shores unto a golden age of Christ peace and enlightenment."[366]

Throughout his mission, Patrick was overshadowed by Lord Maitreya and Mighty Victory. The story of his life illustrates the power of one individual in God. On one occasion he faced the initiation of wrestling with the Antichrist. He explains that he was saved by calling on the name of Helios: "On that very same night I lay a-sleeping, and powerfully Satan assailed me; which I shall remember as long as I am in this body. He fell upon me like an enormous stone, and I was stricken nerveless in all my limbs. Whence then did it come into my unscholarly spirit to call upon Helias? At once I saw the sun rising into the dawn sky, and while I kept invoking 'Helias, Helias,' with all my strength, lo, the Splendour of the Sun fell over me and instantly shook all the heaviness off from me. I believe I was succored by Christ my Lord and that his Spirit even then was calling out on my behalf."[367]

Patrick faced many difficult challenges in his life. He was never afraid to confront evil, and he knew that Jesus Christ lived in him and spoke through him. In his *Confession*, he speaks of twelve perils that beset his soul. These perils are the twelve initiations of the twelve gates of the city, the New Jerusalem, whereby we are then anointed to enter into that Holy City, having passed the twelve initiations of the twelve lines of the clock, of our karma and of our Christhood. On many occasions Patrick demonstrated mastery over animal life in the elemental kingdom. He is famous for his use of the shamrock to illustrate the Oneness of the Trinity to members of the court.

Saint Patrick speaks of his mission as an ascended master: "You have called me Saint Patrick, and I come by that name. Yet God has given to me another name, the new name that cannot be received except by those who enter into the white-fire core with the ascended masters. God has called me to be the champion of truth. And as I bring that truth to the nations, there is the rallying to the standard of truth by some and there is division and darkness and murder and death in the midst of others."[368]

You can call to Saint Patrick to help you to deal with entrenched forces of darkness. Saint Patrick's Lorica is a prayer for protection and a way to invoke his presence with you.

❖ PAUL THE VENETIAN, Chohan of the Third Ray

The Ascended Master Paul the Venetian, by his twin flame, Ruth Hawkins

Paul the Venetian is chohan of the third ray of divine love. He is hierarch of the Château de Liberté, his retreat on the etheric plane over southern France on the Rhône River. Paul sponsors the ascended master culture for this age and works with all who desire to bring that culture forth on behalf of mankind. The culture of the ascended masters is the keystone in the pyramid of the golden age; for they have said that it is through culture that mankind will respond to spiritual truths and the teachings of the Great White Brotherhood.

In the days of Atlantis, Paul served in the government as the head of cultural affairs. Before the continent sank, he established a focus of the liberty flame in Peru, which gave impetus to the culture, beauty and wealth of the Incan civilization. He embodied in the Incan empire as an artist who used paints that did not fade (a mastery that he brought back in his final embodiment). Thanks to the tremendous momentum that he drew forth, the Inca civilization flourished.

Later, he was embodied in Egypt as a master of esoteric architecture and worked closely with El Morya, then a master mason, at the time of the building of the pyramids.

His final embodiment was as Paolo Veronese, one of the major artists of the 16th-century Venetian school. Born Paolo Cagliari in Verona, Italy, in 1528, the artist's early training gained him renown at a young age as a talented painter. At twenty-five, he was welcomed to Venice as a master of his art. The palatial splendor of this city, its pearls and silks from the East, its elegant tapestries and brocades enriched his work, which rose to the heights of decorative excellence.

Veronese's ornamentations soon led to dramatic experiments with new colors. In his quest for beauty, he freed himself from the dull browns and grays of his predecessors by modeling in full light, making his already graceful figures iridescent and nearly transparent. He developed glistening pastel hues of azure, coral, pearl, lilac and lemon yellow that startled and fascinated his patrons. He loved deep, bold contrasting colors, and he combined shades never used before—ruby and rich velvety green, pink and emerald, aquamarine and violet.

Monument to Paolo
Veronese, Verona, Italy

As if to stress that true beauty endures forever, Veronese searched for and discovered a technique of pigment preparation that is unsurpassed in preserving paint. His magnificent colors still radiate brilliantly today, compared with the fading ceiling of the Sistine Chapel and even Tiepolo's now-deteriorating frescoes painted two centuries later.

Veronese was a spiritual revolutionary who waged battle against the forces of anti-life in the arts. He saw beauty as the most powerful catalyst for enlightenment, and he endowed the figures of Jesus, the apostles and saints with lifelike expressions. By associating them with easily identifiable places and things, he put them within the reach of the common people. The master transcended the traditionally flat, lifeless and grim aspects of medieval art; his biblical scenes and historical subjects, festivals and pageants were refreshingly executed with joy and sweeping grandeur.

He illustrated the steps of initiation on the path of Christhood and was prolific in painting the martyrdom of the saints. His most impressive work is the vast *Marriage at Cana,* which hangs in the Louvre. His other paintings included the *Temptation of Saint Anthony,* the *Coronation of the Virgin,* the *Deposition from the Cross, Supper at Emmaus,* the *Holy Family* and the *Raising of Lazarus*—each one of these an important initiation in Christhood.

On one occasion he was summoned before the tribunal of the Inquisition under suspicion of heresy for the "irreverences" in his painting of the *Last Supper,* which included in it a dwarf, a parrot, guards in German armour, dogs and a jester. Veronese staunchly defended the artist's right to freedom of imagination. The tribunal found a solution by suggesting that the painting be renamed *Feast in the House of Levi.*

In 1588, he contracted a fever and, after a few days of illness, died on April 9. His brother and sons had him buried in S. Sebastiano, where a bust was placed above his grave. He made his ascension from the Château de

Liberté on April 19, 1588.

Here at the Château, prior to his ascension, he had begun the most majestic of his works, known as "The Holy Trinity." The heavenly Father is portrayed by a majestic figure, the likeness of Jesus depicts the Son, and an impressive white dove with a nine-foot wingspan denotes the Holy Spirit. The canvas has the unprecedented distinction of conveying the vibrations of both dimensions of activity—the earthly and the heavenly—in which Paolo was so interested, for the canvas was completed after his ascension. Beneath the painting of "The Holy Trinity," Paul has inscribed in gold letters: "Perfect Love Casteth out Fear."

Paul the Venetian is a majestic being of some six feet, five inches in height. He is fair of countenance with deep blue eyes and golden, wavy hair. He is usually garbed in raiment of emerald-green velvet. Since he is a native of the planet Venus, where the inhabitants are masters of the Flame and therefore radiate harmony and divine love, Paul's natural heritage is beauty and grace, diplomacy and tact. His voice is melodious and kind, bringing comfort and peace to all who come in contact with his Presence.

The ascended master Paul the Venetian is a great teacher of the path of love. His devotion is to beauty, the perfection of the soul through compassion, patience, understanding, self-discipline and the development of the intuitive and creative faculties of the heart by the alchemy of self-sacrifice, selflessness and surrender. He initiates the heart chakra, and he trains us in the gift of the discerning of spirits—discerning good and evil, light and shadow and the delicate nuances of all of our creations of beauty. Discernment is a real inner sensitivity to one another.

Paul's retreat, the Château de Liberté, has a physical counterpart in a château now owned by a private French family. At the etheric level, the retreat contains classrooms with paintings and artwork of every kind from all ages and races and cultures, as well as workshops for musicians, writers, sculptors and students of voice. Here the masters introduce new techniques in every field of art.

Currently he is holding classes in the Temple of the Sun, the etheric retreat of the Goddess of Liberty over Manhattan. This is the etheric retreat of Paul's spiritual Mother, who is the Goddess of Liberty—the cosmic being behind the statue, so named for her complete identification with the God consciousness of liberty. It was she who first enshrined the liberty flame on earth and, just prior to the sinking of Atlantis, transported it from her then-physical Temple of the Sun to the Château de Liberté.

It was the Goddess of Liberty who inspired the idea of the Statue of Liberty as a gift of the people of France to the people of the United States, which was dedicated on Bedloe's Island October 28, 1886. A symbol of their friendship and more, it was the spanning of the arc of liberty from the Château de Liberté back to the Temple of the Sun with the intent that the descendants of Atlantis reembodied at both her East and West gates (at France and the United States) would hold high her torch until Liberty's culture should once again appear in a golden age founded upon the balanced and expanded threefold flame in the hearts of the freedom-loving people of these sister nations.

Seventy-six years later, in a dictation given in Washington, D.C., September 30, 1962, the ascended master K-17 announced the bestowal of another gift from France to America, this time from Paul the Venetian: "There has been held a beautiful and wonderful session at Chananda's retreat in India, and a decision was made on the part of beloved Paul the Venetian whereby there was transferred from his retreat in France this day, at the hour of eleven o'clock your time, the full pulsation of the great liberty flame.

The Washington Monument

"This flame was permanently placed within the forcefield of the Washington Monument; and the pulsations of the liberty flame are intended to grace the heart of America as a gift from the Brotherhood and from the heart of beloved Paul the Venetian....

"It is given as a treasure from the heart of France, from the spiritual government of France to the spiritual government of America.... The liberty flame is a gift of greater magnitude than the former gift of France, the Statue of Liberty, as a tribute to that great being, the Goddess of Liberty. It is incomparable, for the flame itself shall penetrate the structure of the monument, rising high into the atmosphere above it. And all who visit there shall become, even without knowing it, infused by the pulsations of the liberty flame within the heart of America."

Embodied mankind who serve in the arts attend the retreats of Paul the Venetian for instruction in all of the arts, and through their service, they learn to balance and expand the threefold flame within the heart. Paul explains that the purpose of art is to enhance the love of Christ always.

One who studied at Paul the Venetian's retreat was Norman Rockwell, American painter and illustrator (1894–1978). Paul speaks of instructing him: "I remember when Norman Rockwell came to me at inner levels to study in my etheric retreat. And I remember as I counseled him to show the Christ in the American people, in everyday scenes of humor, humility, wonder, togetherness, heroism. And all these have been treasured, remembered and valued highly because something of the spirit of the Christ image that is become an image of America came through his work.

"A unique artist, one devoted to the inherent qualities and identity of the individual. As his perception of the Christ was, so was his painting the capturing of unique moments. You might examine that work to find in each painting what is the glimmer, however great or faint, of some aspect of the individual reaching for the Higher Self."[369]

The ascended master Paul the Venetian says: "I AM Paul the Venetian. I paint on canvas on the ethers. I etch in crystal, I sculpt, I mold the clay. I fashion all things physical and many substances not known to you in the higher octaves. To what purpose? To the purpose of showing forth an ever-more revealing and exquisite image of the Christ—the Christ appearing in children, in people from every walk of life....

"Is it any wonder that we deplore the chaotic and abstract art that has no point of unity? It also portrays a certain barrenness and absence of that point of light in the individual. One can see anarchy by an absence of dimension—an absence of harmony or focalization in modern art.

"Modern art enters the subconscious. Accordingly, whether or not the artist is influenced by marijuana or other substances, art portrayed in fabric design, wall coverings, clothing style becomes a matrix capable or incapable of carrying some measure of Christly proportion. When the peoples' art and sense of art flounders, then the images of Christ recede.

"It is rare to find a work of art that is come from the etheric octave in this period.... Where will your leaders learn to deal with the invaders of the minds of the nations? They will learn from the etheric schoolrooms and cities and retreats. How will they get there if they do not contain the crystal that becomes the magnet and a star to follow when the soul goes forth from the body in the hours of sleep?

"Unless angels and devotees of light accompany them, they will have no new idea, no means of resolution. Without internal harmony that is the direct child of perfect love, there is no resolution to international terror or the threat of nuclear war. And while abortion itself seems to me the supreme act of anti-art, it does beget the callousness that year-by-year has a lessening sensitivity to the art of angels and the art of God who fashioned the perfect image out of which you were sculpted in clay.

"Thus, beloved ones, it is necessary in the very midst of the most tense international circumstances to retreat into the contemplation of the divine beauty and the music of the spheres, to remember that the building blocks of creation are sound and that sound forms a pattern that is a divine harmony and that this divine harmony can be portrayed in architecture, in life, in everyday utensils such as pottery. The things you use and you surround yourself with become a focus for the flow of attention.

"Art is not a subject so often dwelt upon in our discourses, for there are such pressing needs—pressing needs of the hour for the victory for Saint Germain. I bring my ingredient of love in this hour as an offering to the Christ Child, to the one and the beloved whom I have so longed to paint in the ultimate sense and have done so to the best of my ability in the etheric octave."[370]

The master Paul has also spoken of his own artwork as Paolo Veronese: "Now I speak to you because of some of the canvases that I created. There were times when I felt pressed, through the need for my livelihood, to create on canvas some wondrous object in order that mankind might be able to glory in it. And yet I was driven, in a sense, to a pensive mood whereby I could create at will a masterpiece only to find that when I came to create it, the inspirational spark was not present. And I found it could not be invoked. I found that the harder I tried, the more difficult became the decision as to just what I could paint, for I could not paint a commonplace item. It must be stirring and magnificent. This, then, is why I so well understand how the human hearts of men, at various times when the crossroads of life seem particularly difficult, stand in wonder and amazement as to just which way they shall turn.

"Beloved ones, at times such as those, I myself, finding that I was indeed stymied, ceased to resist the condition, and not with a sense of indifference or aloofness or despair but with a sense of realization that God works in strange ways, mysterious and wondrous to perform his will. I determined to cease and desist in the struggle and to rest in his compassionate consciousness, knowing that, with the tides of time, I would find an answer to the searching and probing question of the hour.

"And then, my peace would come in great flowing waves. And with the coming of my peace and my quietude, there was reestablished a contact between myself and those masterful divine beings who ensouled in my pictures the very essence of their own life. My angelic friends of light—those messengers of hope who guided my hand in its craftsmanship and artistry— were able to express, then, in the stilled muscular control that which they could never do when the tensions of the hour took their toll over my mortal frame.

"I therefore urge all the students to recognize that there is a time to tense and a time to relax; there is a time to pray and a time to wait; there is a time to be devotional and a time to repose in God's devotion.

"I would like to remind all who are here that, after you have poured out all of your love to God—according to the capacity of your own soul—then is the hour when you should await, expectantly, to receive the love of God in return. It is as though an emptiness comes to you, for you have given your all; and then that all comes back to you charged with his love. The love of God flows in mighty waves, sweeping o'er you as the beating sea against the cliffs of being. And the foam intrigues your consciousness as its breakers of many patterns unfold multitudinous and wondrous spraylets of beauty."[371]

The beloved master Paul has promised an important initiation to those who come knocking at the door of his retreat in southern France, ready for a greater increment of the love flame: "I will take you by the hand and show you my castle. I will show you the works of art that have been brought forth by chelas unascended and ascended. And we will go through many rooms, and lastly I will take you to the room where there is that frame that hangs. In some cases it will be an empty frame; in some cases it will have a canvas in it. It will be your frame, the frame of your identity waiting for you to bring forth the genius of your soul. And when you see that frame, if it is empty, you will want to fill it.

"And so I will take you to that place, 'The Atelier,' where you can work with other artisans who are learning the art of living love by the discipline of the hand and the discipline of expression so that you can draw the image of your own Christ-perfection. And when it is the best that you have to offer, it will be placed in your frame.

"And when you come again before that frame after many months of purging and self-purification, you will say undoubtedly, 'Beloved Paul, may I have another opportunity to express my Christhood, to draw the image of myself? For I have perceived a new aspect of that image, and I would like to have this, my best offering, now placed in my frame.' And, of course, you will have the opportunity."[372]

Paul the Venetian's twin flame is the ascended lady master Ruth Hawkins, the Goddess of Beauty. She ascended in 1995 at the age of eighty-eight and serves with him at the Temple of the Sun.

You may pray to Paul the Venetian to assist you in developing your heart chakra and the threefold flame of the heart and to bring forth the image of the Christ consciousness in your life. Ask him to sponsor the true art of the Aquarian age and to overshadow artists of all kinds in bringing forth the consciousness of the Christ.

Paul the Venetian's keynote is "I Love You Truly," by Carrie Jacobs-Bond.

❖ **PEACE AND ALOHA, Elohim of the Sixth Ray**

Peace and Aloha are the Elohim of the sixth ray (the purple and gold ray) of peace, brotherhood, the true ministration of the Christ and the desire to be in the service of God and man through the mastery of the Christ consciousness. From their Temple of Peace, located in the etheric realms over the Hawaiian Islands, they radiate ribbons of Cosmic Christ peace over the entire planet as a network of Cosmic Christ consciousness. Peace and Aloha focus both the gold and the purple flames as the perfect balance of the masculine and feminine aspects of peace. Mighty Cosmos' secret rays are focused in their retreat.

Souls who are to embody the sixth-ray virtues of peace, ministration and service on behalf of all life study for a time at the Temple of Peace in preparation for their mission. Jesus studied at this retreat, and the Elohim Peace has revealed that many of the sayings of Christ Jesus came from him. He said that Jesus learned these sayings "as a disciple of the Elohim Peace long before he took incarnation to be the Prince of Peace."[373]

In 1965 Peace told us that Jesus used mantras to "hold the balance for the evolutions of earth." Peace said that Jesus often used these salutations in honor of the name of Peace: 'Peace be unto you.' 'Fear not, little flock; for it is the Father's good pleasure to give you the kingdom.' 'Be of good cheer; it is I; be not afraid.'"[374]

The Elohim Peace has explained that "when the Master Jesus said 'Peace be still!' it was an invocation calculated to draw forth from the Godhead and from the power of the Elohim the fullness of cosmic peace. Upon him was bestowed the title Prince of Peace, for he consorted to express as ambassadorial the aspects of our office."[375]

Peace instructs us to also learn to release the fire of our hearts by giving the mantra "Peace, be still and know that I AM God!" He said, "Learn to release the fire of the heart, the sacred fire, and to be infilled again...with this mantra."[376]

In 1959, Peace said, "Seal your world daily...within a capsule of the golden oil of peace from my very heart, which as a mantle of infinite protection will guard your world."[377] He then asked us to daily bring a portion of this peace into the world of others.

The solar plexus is the chakra of the sixth ray of peace and the chakra that governs the emotions. It is the "place of the sun," the place where Cosmic Christ peace must be established in you. The Elohim Peace teaches the use of the Great Sun Disc, a shield of dazzling white fire that may be placed over the solar plexus to deflect the discord of others and thus protect the peace of the feeling world. He said, "I would like you to learn how to magnify the power of that disc of light so that you are not so vulnerable to the onslaughts of others…. When peace has gone, everything has gone, and there is nothing left.

"And only when you come to a point where once again, through the power of interior equilibrium, you have found your balance does the power of peace then begin to flow and do you start again to build those wondrous castles in the air—castles of hope—that may well materialize into the blessings you seek because you have kept the peace."[378] The Elohim said to visualize the Great Sun Disc as a large round shield of heavy armour reflecting in all directions the dazzling light of the Great Central Sun.

He explained, "When you master yourself, as the Master Jesus did, you can go to sleep and let others rock the boat for all they are worth, all the while knowing that the sea is God's sea, that the boat is God's boat, that your body is God's temple, that your mind is the dwelling place of God, that your soul is the soul of God, that the wind is his to command, that the wave obeys his voice….

"Rest in that great cosmic tranquility that refuses to be affrighted, that refuses to be disturbed, regardless of outer conditions. And then you will sleep through the storms of the world or you may remain awake through them; but you will be unaffected by any of them, for you will be the master of your world."[379]

In 1993 Peace and Aloha told us why war remains on our planet. They said: "The momentums and records of war on planet Earth remain untransmuted because many of the very ones who have the gift of the violet flame and the science of the spoken Word do not use it to transmute, first and foremost, the warring in their own members….

"In order to make peace with your inner being, you must declare war against the not-self [the carnal mind, or the dweller-on-the-threshold]…. The defeat of war by all seven Elohim and the entire Spirit of the Great White Brotherhood is top on our agenda. But as we have said, if the chelas of the light do not take up the dismantling of the components of war in their own psyches and allow them to be consumed,…where shall we go?"[380]

In 1978 Peace and Aloha said, "Every one of you who has lost that peace for a moment, an hour, or a day has contributed in ways small and great to war, to crime, to murder, to mayhem, to cataclysm."[381] The Elohim teach that the "acceleration of the Christ consciousness" in all people "is the only solution to war and the only option for peace."[382]

In 1992 Peace asked us to become warriors of peace. He said: "War is the agenda of the fallen ones…on planet Earth. Disarmament and the seeming disappearance of World Communism does not change that fact in

any way. The Buddhas and the Cosmic Christs are the warriors of peace....
Be warriors of peace and understand that pacifism is a perversion of peace!
Peace is the guardian action of the sixth ray."[383]

In 1984 Peace and Aloha explained that they can radiate rings of
peace to push back the darkness and the threat of war. They said, "I must
warn you of the forces of anti-peace abroad in the world who will come to
challenge my flame in your heart by all manner of subterfuge, serpentine
logic and subtlety." Peace and Aloha instructed us, "Remember the sign of
peace of the Prince of Peace. Raise the right hand and turn them back!
Remember the tube of light and the solar ring and the ring of peace."[384]

Elohim Peace has warned that our peace is only skin deep when we
become offended at little things and become angry when someone steps on
our toes. Although we may think that we have attained to peace, Peace and
Aloha have said that "99 percent of your consciousness, your energy, is outside of the flame of peace....

"You have created your own zoo and you have made yourself the
zookeeper instead of the keeper of the flame of peace. And so you guard the
animals...of your human creation [in the subconscious, in the unconscious]
that you have fashioned out of your greed and your darkness, your self-con-
cern and your revenge."[385]

Over the years the Elohim Peace and Aloha have given many tips to
help us keep peace. They ask us to make the best of things, forgive and ask
to be forgiven, seek daily resolution by the violet flame, be humble, forsake
harshness, do not chatter or criticize and keep the peace with one another.

In 1993 Peace and Aloha promised us that heaven would reward our
efforts to sustain peace and pass our tests. They said: "Make your peace
with all people. For you cannot make lasting progress on the Path until you
do.... Know that God does test every living soul. Be willing, then, to pass
those tests and to exercise ingenuity of heart in so doing." At that time, they
announced a dispensation that "for every individual upon earth who is
right with God,...there shall be added ten thousand angels unto the bands
of the legions of the sixth ray of the Lord Jesus Christ ministering to the
peoples of planet Earth. Think of this and rejoice! Realize...just how great
a multiplication factor ten thousand angels can be in advancing the cause
of peace on earth!"[386]

These angels have but one goal: that the power of peace that God has
endowed them with be applied to the transmutation and "utter dissolution
of war at every level." With the dispensation of the ten thousand angels "you,
then, in a sense of the word are the leader of that company of angels, and you
have a responsibility to command them—to give decrees in their behalf, even

for their protection.... You, then, must be a very active participant in that which is taking place in your community and on your planet."[387]

On January 2, 1972, Elohim Peace gave a dispensation and a mantra. He placed a miniature replica of the Pavilion of Peace in the hearts of those present. He said, "All you have to do when all around you is turbulent and you are in distress and in confusion is to visualize in miniature the Pavilion of Peace. Call unto me and unto your individualized God Presence and say, 'I need thee every hour, O Elohim of Peace and beloved I AM Presence! Show forth thy light!' And with the words 'Show forth thy light,' I will come again and create the vibratory action of my peace within you."

Peace and Aloha want us to focus on turning back war and the forces of anti-peace both within and without. They often use our calls to render a great and untold assistance to the planet to prevent many small wars from starting and to help put out the fires of larger conflagrations. You can visualize a place on the planet where there is war, invite the angels of Peace to go there, give the mantras of peace and see in your mind's eye ten thousand angels of peace descending to stop that war.

❖ PEACE, GODDESS OF

The Goddess of Peace serves at the Temple of Peace located over the Hawaiian Islands. She represents the feminine aspect of the flame of peace to the evolutions of earth and works directly with the elementals to infuse that flame within nature. She teaches classes on the activities of the flame of peace to unascended mankind and shows how, through devotion to peace, they may qualify for admittance to the halls of Luxor to prepare for their ascension in the light. Without peace there is no harmony, and without harmony one can never gain entrance to the Ascension Temple.

Her momentum of the flame of peace may be invoked to still the waters of human emotion, the confusion of the mind, the inner or outer action of the physical body and the turbulence of the subconscious world. Her mantle of peace should be invoked around mothers bearing incoming souls in order that these souls might attune with the immaculate design for their approaching destiny in the world of form.

The Goddess of Peace says: "Beloved ones of the planet Earth, as Saint Germain has so often told you, only by pursuing the way of your own Divine Self can you ever find and know true peace. Myriad notions have entered and do enter men's consciousness, and as they follow each one to its ultimate end, they find that it did not provide one iota of permanent happiness. Life can become a bottomless pit of seeking where lesser goals are sought and attained, sometimes to the soul's own hurt. But by calling forth ideals of peace from the heart of the Prince of Peace and by calling for the rule of heaven's peace to hold sway over the entire earth, man fulfills the larger goals of the great divine plan and satisfies thereby his daily requirements of ordered service, brotherly love and individual unfoldment."[388]

❖ PEARL, *See* Rex and Nada, Bob and Pearl

❖ PELLEUR, *See* Virgo and Pelleur

❖ PHYLOS THE TIBETAN

Phylos the Tibetan is newly come into the order of the ascended masters and the fraternity of the Great White Brotherhood. He made his ascension in 1989 after working since the nineteenth century as an unascended adept at inner levels.

Phylos' embodiments are revealed in the book *A Dweller on Two Planets*, dictated by Phylos the Tibetan to his amanuensis, Frederick S. Oliver. (*Amanuensis* means "secretary"; it is not a messenger but simply someone who has the vessels necessary to write down what is given to him by an unascended or ascended adept.)

Phylos began dictating the book to Frederick Oliver in 1883 or 1884 when Oliver was seventeen or eighteen years old. The book was published in 1899. In his preface to *A Dweller on Two Planets*, Phylos calls himself a "Theochristian student and Occult Adept." He is a student of the mysteries of God and of Christian mysticism.

A Dweller on Two Planets is divided into three books. In Book One Phylos unveils the karmic record of his embodiment as Zailm Numinos on Atlantis. Book Two covers Phylos' embodiment in the nineteenth century as an American gold miner by the name of Walter Pierson. In this embodiment he comes face-to-face with the karma he made on Atlantis; he is initiated into the inner mysteries and is given a vision of his past and his future. Book Three reviews some of Phylos' past lives prior to his Atlantean embodiment as Zailm and explains why Atlantis fell. Phylos says that he wrote *A Dweller on Two Planets* in the hope that others would learn from his mistakes.

Phylos writes: "I have sought to explain the great mystery of life, illustrating it with part of my own life history, extracts which cover years reaching into many thousands." Speaking of the suffering he had to endure as a result of his errors, he says: "No words can paint the suffering of the expiation. I scarcely propose to try, and shall rest content if a realization of some part of it shall deter others from sin."[389]

Since he has become an ascended master, Phylos has spoken profoundly on the path of balancing karma, on the path of suffering and the need to balance suffering with joy. He explains that the quality of God-happiness is essential to meet adversity, and he asks us to see ourselves in every part of life that is suffering. He says:

"May you see yourself in every life who suffers. May you know that as long as life suffers, a part of you is suffering with that life, for God is one. May you understand, as the leaves of my book have given up much profound teaching through the messenger, that the path to be walked is worth every joy that you encounter and every sorrow.

"For you are sending energy back to God and receiving it again. And as quickly as you send to God light for the transmutation of error, so as quickly does he send to you light that is Truth incarnate within you. And this oscillation from your heart to the center of the sun of your I AM Presence, to the center of the Great Central Sun is the beginning of the acceleration process whereby you shall know that oscillation to the point of the speed of light and then beyond.

"You are an extension of that Sun here and now but perceive yourselves not as rays of light or energy pulsating, going and returning and being magnetized to the great Polestar of Being....

"I am Phylos, and I come from the battleground of earth unto the realms of glory. As you go through my book, you shall have an experience with yourself at inner levels if you meditate, if you decree, if you give the Ashram rituals[390] and maintain your attunement with the masterful beings of Venus who are called upon in your rituals.

"My book is a companion to the ascended masters' path that has been laid before you by Saint Germain and El Morya and Mother Mary and Kuthumi and Djwal Kul and Jesus and Gautama. It is an assist to you, and I am grateful to have the messenger expound upon it and elaborate upon those advances that have come forth in the century since I dictated it.

"Thus, it is an open door and considered by the Darjeeling Council to be among the best of books to present to the new student on the Path, for it does contain keys for the awakening of many souls, as they recognize themselves in the streets of Caiphul,* participating in Atlantean life, whether at the end of Atlantis or in the great golden-age civilization of Jesus Christ.

"All these we have known. And some of you have found this day your footprints left in the sands now at the bottom of the sea. How strong are the footprints of karma! Yet stronger are the footprints of heroism and Christlike deeds! Strong are the footprints of honor, black those of deceit,

---

*Capital city of Atlantis.

deception.

"May you build carefully, stone upon stone, the pyramid of your life. This was the teaching of the adepts of the Great Pyramid that was outpictured in the many pyramids that we built in various civilizations of Atlantis. The four sides, being the four lower bodies that must converge at the point of the All-Seeing Eye, must synthesize as one vessel, even the chalice of the Holy Grail.

"I have looked upon America and I have wept, for I have seen in the collective karma of the reincarnated Atlanteans here the same pitfalls that I found in my own karma. I could not come here free to rise as a servant of God but must pay every jot and tittle.

"America is beset with the karma that the nation has made since its inception two centuries ago. It is beset with ancient records of Atlantis not yet paid. And it is bowed down by a false teaching that is not that of the Christ concerning this karma, concerning accountability.

"So many false teachers abound and so little discrimination is exercised, even in the New Age movement. Wherever there is a claim or a personality or a new fad or some other exploration into the psychic, there do they run like chickens for feed.

"Blessed hearts, find the truth of Being in yourself. Find others who have that truth of Being. And watch out, for the disease of the carnal mind is idolatry. Most people on or off the spiritual path are idolatrous of themselves, quite pleased with their meager knowledge and even less attainment, which they deem to be great.

"Know ye not that the first step on the Path is one of humility and self-effacement? The first step beyond this is forgiveness toward all life."[391]

❖ **PLEIADES, HIERARCHIES OF THE**

In our portion of the universe, the seat of the Great White Brotherhood is the Pleiades. This cluster of stars was named by the Greeks for the seven daughters of Atlas and Pleione. The cluster is situated in the constellation Taurus at a distance of four hundred light years from earth and has an angular size somewhat larger than that of the moon. Of the five hundred stars in the group, six are easily visible to the naked eye. These stars are known from ancient times as the Seven Sisters (the seventh Pleiad was, according to legend, lost or in hiding), and they focus the seven rays of the divine feminine.

The Pleiades

In 1970, the Elohim Cyclopea announced that the hierarchies of the Pleiades had released a dispensation for the manifestation of the divine blueprint of planet Earth. Cyclopea said: "By the power of the Elohim this night there is being superimposed upon this planetary body the forcefield of the Great Blue Causal Body. And its full-gathered momentum of all the hierarchies and hosts of light shall be superimposed as a matrix of victory upon this planetary home…. I, Cyclopea, have seen the vision. And that vision of future triumph, of present reality shall consume all past failure if men will determine to align themselves with the great creative purposes of God….

"I am this night painting before you the vision of the Holy City, the magnificent City Foursquare, the divine kingdom that shall come upon earth even as you keep the flame. And whenever you see reports of problems, of crises, of injustices in your newspapers, I am calling by the power of the Elohim in the name of Almighty God with the permission of your Holy Christ Selves that that vision of the City Foursquare shall flash forth from your consciousness into the world, into that situation, into the problem areas as a divine matrix of the cosmic cube, that City Foursquare that is the key to each man's overcoming, the key to the ascension of the very planet itself.

"And so I say by the power of Mighty Victory, by the power of that six-pointed star of divine balance as Above, so below, by the power of the All-Seeing Eye that penetrates in the center of that star, I am focusing within your consciousness this night and anchoring within your own third eye the vision of that Cosmic City Foursquare….

"That focus is the most powerful image that can be brought forth for the manifestation of Christ and the kingdom of God upon this earth. It contains within it the full power of the World Mother and her divine matrix of the entire material universe for the manifestation of the Christ."

Therefore the Elohim admonished all to guard their vision from "the horrendous forms that come through the media, through the television, through the movies…. Let the All-Seeing Eye of God penetrate to ascertain what is occurring in the world, to ascertain the position of the evil forces. And then, let that projection of the cosmic cube be stamped upon them, sealing the place where evil dwells by the power of the Most High God.

"The entire hierarchy of the Pleiades is behind this experiment for the complete transformation of the planetary orb by the power of the All-Seeing Eye of God. Therefore, I say, I give you the key: Call to the Pleiades and the hierarchies thereof. There are millions of cosmic beings with their cosmic retinues who will come forth in answer to your prayer, millions of Cosmic Christs who will carry into manifestation that divine blueprint."[392]

❖ **POPE JOHN XXIII,** *See* Johannes

❖ **PORTIA, Goddess of Justice and Goddess of Opportunity**

Through thousands of years of service to God on the seventh ray of justice, freedom, mercy, forgiveness, alchemy and sacred ritual, beloved Portia attained to the embodiment of the God flame and God consciousness of divine justice as divine opportunity. Hence, she is called the Goddess of Justice or the Goddess of Opportunity.

Representing the sixth ray of service and ministration on the Karmic Board, Portia keeps the flame of justice and opportunity on behalf of the evolutions of earth. Serving with the hierarchy of Libra (see *Twelve Solar Hierarchies*), she teaches mankind to hold the balance of the flame of the Christ in the four lower bodies through mastery over the four elements. Since justice is the pivotal point between thought and feeling, her balance is between the creative polarities of the masculine and feminine rays of the Deity, or between the yin and yang of creation.

Beloved Portia is the twin flame and divine consort of Saint Germain, the chohan of the seventh ray. On May 1, 1954, at inner levels, they were officially crowned directors of the seventh dispensation of ordered service. During this two-thousand-year cycle, known as the Aquarian age, it has been ordained that the new and permanent golden age shall be established for the planet Earth.

In past ages of beauty, perfection and abundance, justice reigned supreme. Before discord began to manifest upon the earth, Portia made her ascension in the light. When mankind's sense of justice became warped, thus causing an imbalance in all she undertook, she could but fold her mantle about her and remain in the Great Silence (in higher realms of consciousness), for the ascended masters never interfere with the doings of men unless invoked by their decree as it manifests as thought, word and deed.

During these ages, Saint Germain continued to embody on earth while Portia remained in the octaves of light. Upon his ascension from the Rakoczy Mansion in 1684, Saint Germain also entered the Great Silence, where his beloved twin flame—whose name he had inscribed in *The Merchant of Venice*—had long been awaiting his return. Not long thereafter, the beloved Sanctus Germanus was given the dispensation by the Lords of Karma to function in the world of form as an ascended being having the appearance of an unascended being. Throughout the courts of eighteenth-century Europe, he was known as the Comte de Saint Germain. Many of his demonstrations of mastery are described in the diaries of Mme. d'Adhémar, who knew him for at least half a century. She records Saint Germain's visits to herself and to the courts of Louis XV and Louis XVI, noting in his glowing face the appearance of a man in his early forties throughout the period. Unfortunately, his efforts to secure the attention of the Court of France and others of the crowned heads of Europe were unsuccessful.[393]

Saint Germain was last seen by Madame d'Adhémar at la Place de la Révolution on October 16, 1793, at the guillotining of Marie Antoinette. The master stood with Portia beneath the statue of the Goddess of Liberty. Immediately following her execution, they took the soul of Marie Antoinette to the Cave of Light, the Great Divine Director's retreat in India. Three months after their departure from this scene, Portia withdrew to the octaves of light, where she remained in nirvana until she stepped forth in 1939 to assist Saint Germain with his activities in the United States.

While in nirvana, Portia both held the balance for Saint Germain's outer world activities and cleansed the records and the pain of his (i.e., their) European experience. Some time after Portia entered nirvana, Saint Germain returned to Europe by himself to sponsor Napoleon in the establishment of the United States of Europe. Once it was clear that Napoleon would take the master's power to promote his own will, Saint Germain withdrew all sponsorship from him in 1810. From that time on Saint Germain was, for want of a better word, "resting" in the Cave of Light and regrouping his forces. From time to time he sponsored activities in the United States and spent calculated cycles in nirvana.

At this time, the cycles of life have demanded that the scales of justice be balanced in preparation for the golden age, and since some among mankind had begun to request that divine justice be reestablished, on April 9, 1939, Portia came forth from the Great Silence to speak for the first time since her ascension. Even now she seldom speaks, but when she does, her divine attribute of perfect balance (symbolized by the scales) is anchored in the forcefield of all who will receive it.

Portia speaks of the balance of justice and mercy, two qualities of the seventh ray: "Great distress frequently comes to mankind by reason of their own karmic acts and the records that are within their form, for like the tiny bird, they feel as though in the grip of outer conditions and know not that even life here is for the purpose of restoring them to the nest of God's heart and the nest of holy justice.

"Men tremble, for they tremble in ignorance. Let them now, then, receive comfort from justice and know that although I am known as the Goddess of Justice, Mercy holdeth my hand for aye and will so do for aye, for Kuan Yin walks with me where'er I walk and sheds her radiance also.

"Upon the circle of justice is stamped the circle of mercy. And if you would also do as I do, wherever you attempt or seek to administer justice to others whom you also may have beneath your charge, you will give forth mercy—not in that quality unbalanced that will cause mankind to destroy themselves because of your lack of firmness, but in that perfect balance of spiritual understanding that gives to each man that portion of mercy properly mixed with justice that is best for him."[394]

"How, then, will freedom as a Mother flame, as the shakti of Saint Germain, translate the mercy and the justice of the Law in this age? O beloved ones, justice and mercy, mercy and justice are the interaction of the great caduceus of the feminine ray of the seventh age and dispensation. The seventh ray of God's light of the violet flame is a fiery caduceus—the weaving of mercy and justice as a garland of Alpha and Omega around the central altar of freedom's light."[395]

Portia has asked that we use the music of the "Rakoczy March," by Franz Liszt, to magnetize her presence.

❖ **PROSPERINA,** *See* **Virgo**

❖ **PURITY AND ASTREA, Elohim of the Fourth Ray**

Purity and Astrea are the Elohim of the fourth ray (the white ray) of purity, perfection, hope and wholeness. It is the flame of the Mother and the flame of the ascension—the desire to know and be God through purity of body, mind and soul through the consciousness of the Divine Mother, which embraces the natural laws governing all manifestation in the earth plane.

Purity holds the divine pattern of the perfection of the Christ for all that is in manifest form, focusing the white fire that is in the heart of every sun and atom—the pure white light out of which emanate the seven "rays," or aspects, of the Christ consciousness. Blue is considered the feminine aspect of white because the white fire of Purity coalesces as blue in the Matter plane. Thus Astrea, the feminine complement of Purity, works twenty-four hours a day wielding the cosmic circle and sword of blue  flame to free the children of the Mother from all that opposes the fulfillment of the divine plan held in the heart of Purity. Astrea personifies the Hindu concept of Kali, "the demon-slayer."

You can make the circle and sword of blue flame practical in your life as Jesus Christ did to exorcise the boy possessed of a demon—the one who lay on the ground frothing at the mouth, whom the disciples could not heal.[396] As Astrea has explained, "The disciples had attempted, again and again, to cast out the demon from that boy, and I tell you they exerted themselves to the fullest. But they lacked the faith and they lacked the knowledge of our octave of light. If my cosmic circle and sword of blue flame had been invoked around that boy by any one of those disciples, they would have found that that demon would have left on the instant and would not have remained for a second. This was the power of light that Jesus himself invoked. He invoked that energy of the blue flame, and it immediately fulfilled the destiny that God intended it to do."[397]

The circle of blue fire invoked from the heart of Astrea is a dazzling blue-white fire that oscillates as two concentric rings of fire—the blue of Astrea, the white of Purity—interchanging frequencies at such a rapid rate so as to appear as the action of blue-white lightning flashing around souls, planets, solar systems, galaxies—wherever there is a need for the reinforcement of the will of God in the divine blueprint held in the white-fire core of being.

Whenever and wherever there is discord in any form, in any of its aspects, you should call in the name of the Christ to the Elohim Astrea: "Lock your cosmic circle and sword of blue flame around the cause and core of that condition." Then see this circle of the sacred fire lock around the individual at the waist, around entire groups of individuals, around buildings, around entire cities, states, nations and even around the earth at the equator. See this in your mind's eye as a ring of brilliant sapphire and diamond-flashing fire—its regular, almost geometric flames cutting away, like a buzz saw, layers and layers of discord and density. Then visualize the sword of blue flame as a pillar of blue fire perpendicular to the circle of blue flame, breaking the matrices of darkness, shattering forcefields of disease, decay and death. And above all, see the Elohim standing over each individual for whom you are praying, holding the sword of blue flame two inches from the spine and parallel to it.

This is the action whereby the Elohim demagnetize the being and consciousness of the individual of all anti-God, anti-Christ and anti-Spirit manifestations, all sinister strategies of the fallen ones and the serpentine energies of the carnal mind. Whenever and wherever you invoke the circle and sword of blue flame from the heart of Purity and Astrea, you can know with absolute certainty that an action of cosmic momentum is taking place.

In 1973 Astrea said: "That circle, used together with my sword, is the specific antidote for every form of the human consciousness, every aspect of darkness.... When you call upon the name of Jesus the Christ for the binding of those elements that enslave the consciousness to bad habits and to carnal-mindedness, the legions of Astrea do answer with the legions of the Christ....

"If there is any reason why you do not make progress on the Path or why the substance of your human consciousness lingers, it is because of lack of application to the heart of God, to the heart of the Christ and to the heart of the Elohim of the fourth ray.

"If you called to me yesterday and you have problems today, recognize that you must call my being into action every twenty-four hours to receive the relief from those entities that have entered your consciousness through the wrong use of drugs, alcohol, smoking and all types of carnal habits....

"By the authority of Alpha and Omega I say to you, when you desire to meditate upon the action of the circle and sword of blue flame, then meditate upon the Concerto in A Minor by Grieg.... For it contains the action of the circle and sword of blue flame; and you can hear the cutting cadences of that circle as it whirls about your four lower bodies, getting tighter and tighter around the very core of being until the magnet without, the magnet within send forth into the fire those consciousnesses that stand in rebellion against Almighty God."[398]

Astrea encourages us to give her decree on behalf of loved ones who are burdened by addictions of any and all kinds. In 1991 she said: "See how that loved one can be cut free and kept free and how that one will return to the dignity of a child of light and find his mission before it is too late....

"If you would keep the vigil for a loved one or a number of loved ones, know that the power of the circle and sword of blue flame will work as you pray for them each day and for every other child of God on this planet who is similarly enslaved!

"I, Astrea, make you this offer: Pray for your loved ones and put as many photographs as you like upon your altar. And when you pray for them, pray also for all others upon this planet who can be delivered by Astrea.... May your voice utter the spoken Word that is needed.... The single prayer, beloved, will authorize us to help a million souls."[399] This is a powerful promise from a powerful cosmic being.

Astrea also gave us another formula for victory. She said: "Forget not that at any hour of the day or night when the trial comes, when the fires of crucifixion are upon you, you can know that you can win if instantaneously you address the Almighty, if you address Jesus the Christ, the Holy Spirit and the Divine Mother. And then call to the mighty Elohim, call to Astrea, to release the circle and sword of blue flame around the cause and core of all that opposes your God-identity.

"If you will do that, I will promise you that you will not fail one single test along the pathway of life.... So shall you overcome by the blood of the Lamb, which is the spiritual essence, the very life of Jesus and every avatar ascended. And that spiritual essence will coalesce at your call and at your will as a mighty circle of blue flame."[400]

The retreat of Purity and Astrea is in the etheric realm over the Gulf of Archangel, the southeast arm of the White Sea, Russia. The retreat focuses the energies of the base-of-the-spine chakra of the planet. The etheric focus interpenetrates the physical plane in the nearby plains. Legions of white fire and blue lightning serve with Purity and Astrea and will assemble at any given point on the globe in answer to a call for help made in the name of your mighty I AM Presence.

❖ PURITY, GODDESS OF

San Francisco

The Goddess of Purity focuses the flame of Cosmic Christ purity in her service to the evolutions of the earth. From her retreat over Madagascar, where the flame of purity has been sustained for thousands of years, angels of purity carry light rays to the four corners of the earth.

The Goddess of Purity also holds the focus of one of the ancient temples of Lemuria that was located in the city of the seven hills, where San Francisco now is. This is a magnificent etheric retreat, and the intensity of the flame of purity that is focused there is beyond what man can imagine.

This retreat was established hundreds of thousands of years ago. It is a focus of the Mother flame of Mu as well as a focus of the ascension flame.

Her action of purity is amplified by the four beings of the elements in their service to the evolutions of the earth. Hers is the Mother principle of purity, which she focuses through her scepter of power that carries a tremendous momentum of purity, piercing the veil of human night and drawing all those who invoke purity out of the maya, glamour and karma of their own human creation. The point of that scepter is the diamond. Sharper than a two-edged sword, this focus of the flaming will of God is used by the angels of purity in cooperation with Gabriel and Astrea to free mankind caught in the astral belt.

The beauty of her devotion to purity and her powerful momentum drew many of the young women of Atlantis into the temples to serve as vestal virgins and guardians of the flame of purity. The service of the Goddess of Purity in holding the immaculate concept for the evolutions of the planet naturally involves the use of the fifth ray of precipitation and truth. Thus, she holds the keys with beloved Ray-O-Light to the fearlessness flame, which is the white flame of purity tinged with the penetrating green ray of truth. All who serve purity's ray focus their energies through the lily.

The Goddess of Light, the Queen of Light and the Goddess of Purity form a trinity of three cosmic beings who have majored on the one-pointed goal of focusing the intense light of the Christ consciousness of God. They should be invoked daily, and their light is especially amplified at winter solstice.

The retreats of the Goddess of Light (in the Andes), the Queen of Light (above Sicily), and the Goddess of Purity (on Madagascar) focus an action of the Trinity to the earth. Together these hierarchs draw the action of the cosmic threefold flame on behalf of earth's evolutions.

❖ QUEEN OF LIGHT, *See* Light, Queen of

❖ RA MU, Master of the Brotherhood of Mount Shasta

Ra Mu means the ray of Mu, or the ray of the Mother. The ascended master Ra Mu is the Master of the Brotherhood of Mount Shasta, part of the Great White Brotherhood. He is also known as the "master of the mountain." He is the champion of the feminine ray lodged within both man and woman.

The members of the Brotherhood of Mount Shasta hail from an ancient hierarchy of lightbearers, disciplined priests and priestesses who tended the flame of the Mother on the altars of Lemuria, or Mu, before it sank. They are ascended and unascended masters who keep the flame of purity in the mountain and receive chelas who meet the measure of their rod. They are devotees of Buddha and his light. They are Zoroastrians, Confucians, Taoists and Zen monks. They chant the sacred AUM and are well acquainted with the mystery of the Christos in the I AM THAT I AM. The Brotherhood of Mount Shasta sponsored Godfré Ray King and his initiations with Saint Germain.

At Mount Shasta in 1975, the ascended master Ra Mu spoke on behalf of the Brotherhood of Mount Shasta. He came to anchor the light of the Motherland, the ancient religion of devotion to the eternal Mother as the white light. He kindles in us the light of the ancient teaching of Lemuria, the light of that fourth ray that we had before the sinking of the continent.

In 1997 Ra Mu exhorted us to give the violet flame for the clearing of the records of Lemuria. The cleansing of these records beneath the Pacific is necessary for the balancing of the coasts and of the planetary systems as well. Ra Mu and the priests of the sacred fire promised to match whatever violet-flame decrees we give by the power of ten.

Ra Mu also asked us to give violet-flame decrees for the transmutation of the records of the murder of the Divine Mother on Lemuria. He explained that this record of the murder of the highest representative of the Divine Mother in that era is a weight upon civilization. This record must be cleansed ere women can truly rise to their full stature of Christhood and femininity.

In 1981 Ra Mu came to bring to our awareness the ancient chants of Lemuria and the science of the spoken Word that was practiced there. He said: "Chant the name of Ra Mu. Know that I AM the Son of the Mother and that I come to all who would also know her as the beloved Son knows the beloved Mother. Much has been written about the Mother, East and West. You may read it if you will. But I would acquaint you with the inner path of life where the Kundalini travels, where resurrection is a perpetual fount of Being. I would extricate you from the pain simultaneously as I would ask you to remain sensitive to world pain as you share the office of the World Mother.

"I would give you a mantle of joy and a bouquet of wisdom. I would give you golden sandals and the Book of the Law. I would write it in your heart. I would etch a fiery love sonnet for your twin flame and your very own Self. I would do all these things, but I must ask you to take the first step, to lay aside the former garments and be ready to put on the new.

"I would ask you to take the second step, whereby you never again allow your voice to be silenced by the pressing in upon you of any or all forms of hatred of the Word itself. The Word that flows forth from your mouth is Mother. The Mother is a devouring fire, but fear it not, for thou art Mother also.

"I would see you take the third step of integration with the One, of diligent discipleship before the Father and the Son and the Holy Spirit. With the new garment of consciousness, with the pouring of the Mother fire from out the mouth of thy God, and with the Trinity as the road to self-mastery, you will go far, very far with Saint Germain. And I will be there! And I *am* there, supporting his cause and bringing to the fore the memory of Mu and all of the teachings of the Mother in the temple bearing her name.

"Let us move forward!... Let our disciples of the World Mother become aware of the evolution of souls on this planet and of the history of earth from the beginning.

"Let us bring forward, then, all that is worth keeping. Let us spare no effort to build her temple. Let us consign to the flame the debris that bears no fruit. Let us harken to the call of Ra Mu from the Inner Retreat!"[401]

Mount Shasta was once the crown chakra of Lemuria. Within the mountain was the physical retreat of the Brotherhood of Mount Shasta. In 1988 Sanat Kumara announced "the withdrawal of the Brotherhood of Mount Shasta from the retreat physical of Mount Shasta. This entire Brotherhood, therefore, does withdraw and does transfer their forcefield and focus both into the Grand Teton and into another area of the northern Rockies."[402]

The books of Godfré Ray King, Phylos the Tibetan and others have referred to the Brotherhood of Mount Shasta, and many people pilgrimage there seeking the ascended masters. It is important to know that the retreat of this Brotherhood is no longer within the mountain, and unfortunately, those who journey there often find those who profess to guard the strongholds of the mysteries and the I AM Presence, yet who lead them away from the true masters and their teachings.

❖ RAPHAEL, Archangel of the Fifth Ray

Archangel Raphael is the archangel of the fifth ray of truth, wholeness, healing, science, precipitation, the abundant life, music and mathematics. His divine complement is the Archeia Mary, who was embodied as Mary, the Mother of Jesus. Their ray corresponds to the third-eye chakra, and they can also assist us with spiritual vision and the gift of the discernment of spirits.

The name "Raphael" means "God has healed," or "the Medicine of God." One Jewish text says he revealed to Noah the curative power of plants; another tells how he healed a blind man and bound a demon. Catholics revere him as the angel who healed the sick at the pool of Bethesda. The Book of Enoch tells us that his responsibilities include healing the diseases and wounds of men.

A Jewish tradition names him as one of the three archangels who appeared to Abraham on the plains of Mamre. In fact, it is believed that it was Raphael who endowed Sarah, Abraham's wife, with the strength to conceive when she was past childbearing age.

Raphael is also known as the patron of travelers. In the Book of Tobit, Raphael, disguised as a knowledgeable traveler, accompanies Tobit's son as his guide on a long journey. At the end of the story, Raphael reveals his true identity and explains that God sent him to test the faith of Tobit and his son. They passed their tests and received great blessings of healing and abundance.

Tobit and the Angel, by Doré

Raphael's retreat is in the etheric realm over Fátima, Portugal. The healing flame blazing on the altar of his retreat was anchored in the physical octave when Mother Mary appeared to the children at Fátima in 1917. To the present hour, there is a stream of light that flows like a mighty waterfall from the etheric temple to the physical focus, and pilgrims are healed by the "waters" of the healing flame.

When Mary took incarnation on earth, having been chosen by God to give birth to Jesus Christ, the Avatar of the Piscean age, Archangel Raphael did not embody with her but overshadowed her throughout her mission and assisted her in bringing forth "the son of the Highest." Saint Germain embodied as Joseph, having been chosen by God to be the husband of Mary. Similarly his twin flame, the ascended lady master Portia, also did not take embodiment but overshadowed him.

Mary and Raphael minister unto the hospitals of the world, and they train expectant mothers and fathers at inner levels in the precipitation of the Christ consciousness through the four lower bodies, which are the vehicles for each one's Holy Christ Self. They inspire new cures and alternative healing methods upon scientists and those trained in the healing arts and the medical profession.

The angels of Raphael's bands are master surgeons. Raphael says they use a "laser technology" to "penetrate to the very core of a cell,...to

The Healing Thoughtform

expand the violet flame from within" and to "seal that cell in the healing thoughtform."[403]

Archangel Raphael has released a healing thoughtform that is scientifically formulated to restore the inner blueprint and divine wholeness when visualized surrounding and penetrating the cells and atoms of the four lower bodies, or a specific organ. It is composed of concentric spheres of white, sapphire-blue and emerald-green sacred fire. The white sphere at the center works at inner levels to restore the injured part or the diseased organ to its original perfection. Next is the blue sphere, which establishes protection and an action of the will of God. The green outer sphere restores the flow of Spirit through Matter and brings wholeness.

If you or a loved one suffers an injury, call for the healing thoughtform: "In the name Jesus Christ, beloved Archangel Raphael, the Blessed Mother, place your healing thoughtform over [insert the name of the person]." Then visualize spheres of sacred fire descending from the heart of God as the pulsating presence of the Holy Spirit. Visualize the white-fire core centered in the scintillating, sapphire-blue flame wrapped in the emerald-green fires. The first minutes and hours after an accident are critical. Whether you keep the vigil at the bedside of a loved one or at a distance, picture the injured parts becoming whole until they are in their original healthy state. Hold this picture steady in your mind's eye. Still all anxiety and doubt and fear and do not let any of that press in upon you. Focus totally on holding the healing thoughtform in your mind to the exclusion of all else. Affirm that God in you is beholding all as perfect and once again restored to its true image.

Archangel Raphael and Mary also teach the science of the immaculate concept. This science is practiced by every angel in heaven. When an angel looks upon you, they see you in purity as you were when God first created you. They hold that pattern over you. This enables you to fill in the pattern and realize who you really are—a son or daughter of God.

Holding the immaculate concept means that when you think of someone, you don't think of them in a critical way. Visualize the Christ Presence around them and see them in the perfection you know God gave them in the beginning. Support people by maintaining this immaculate, stainless, spotless vision. Hold this vision for yourself also. Having seen what you are in Spirit and what is the potential of your soul, you must retain that image of Reality in your thoughts and feelings. For the image is a natural repellent to all that opposes your Reality in manifestation, and the perfect idea becomes a magnet that attracts creative energies of the Holy Spirit to your being to fulfill the pattern held in mind.

Mother Mary says: "Remember to call upon God, Archangel Raphael and myself and many angels, to bring healing where healing is possible. And if the Law does not allow it in the flesh, then call...for the healing of the soul and the spirit.... It is the healing of the whole man that we are about."[404]

Raphael explains the key role that karma plays in healing: "Karma, beloved, is something that few understand. And many can hardly believe its science. Many will hardly understand how karma plays such a key role in whether or not a diseased situation may respond to the best of natural cures or those offered by medical science.

"The x factor of the equation as to whether or not an individual will attain healing or wholeness or pass from the screen of life is this karmic circumstance. When the Law decrees that karma must be balanced and it must be balanced now, if the individual has not prepared a literal fountain of light through a momentum of devotion and light sustained in the aura, when he is bereft of that joy of service unto God, he may find himself having not enough of the light of God to consume the darkness that suddenly and swiftly is outcropping in the physical body....

"Beloved ones, is it not also well to prepare for the day of urgent need by building up the light in the body temple and by balancing karma while you are able to work? This is the true meaning of 'work while you have the Light,'[405] which Jesus told to his disciples. The meaning is: balance your karma while you have the strength of the light in your being to perform those services, that sacred labor and the holy application of prayer and affirmation that can make a change in the karmic equation."[406]

We can invoke the violet flame to transmute our karma even before it manifests as disease. We can be healed if we will apply the violet flame to our physical and psychological problems. In contrast to this approach of dealing with underlying causes of illness, there are some practitioners of healing who use hypnosis or mental willing to simply deny that disease exists. The result of these practices may be that the physical disease may be pushed back into the desire body, the mental body or the etheric body. The patient appears to be healed, but the karma has been suppressed, only to resurface in this life or in a future life.

Archangel Raphael explains that to remove the symptoms of disease without removing the record of its cause in this or a past life does a great disservice to the soul. And the individual who assents to the easy "cure" will see sometime, somewhere, in this or a future life, the same problem coming to the surface to be dealt with as karma that must be transmuted before the physical symptoms may permanently disappear.[407]

Raphael and Mother Mary have invited us to visit their retreat and to study the science of healing: "You may call to me and Raphael, for our etheric retreat is above Fátima in Portugal. There you may come at night [your soul in her etheric garment apart from the physical during the sleep state] and study the healing arts. Not far away is the University of the Spirit of Hilarion over the isle of Crete.

"Do, then, call to God and your guardian angels to take you at night in your finer bodies where you may study and learn what are the golden-age methods of healing and how, when the planet is delivered of a certain karma and a certain band of fallen angels incarnate who oppose the real cures that could be available today for cancer and other terminal diseases—

how through you and others there may come about finally the liberation and the revelation of the true healing arts."[408]

Archangel Raphael's keynote is "Whispering Hope," by Alice Hawthorne. The music of the *Messiah* was inspired upon Handel by Raphael.

❖ **RATNASAMBHAVA,** *See* **Five Dhyani Buddhas**

❖ **RAYBORN, DANIEL AND NADA,** *See* **Daniel and Nada Rayborn**

❖ **RAY-O-LIGHT, Bearer of Fearlessness Flame**

Ray-O-Light is an ascended master who focuses the fearlessness flame—a piercing white light tinged with emerald green. Ray-O-Light assists Sanat Kumara, Lord Maitreya and Jesus Christ to bind the seed of the wicked; he also works with K-17 and Lanello. Ray-O-Light and his legions of fearlessness-flame angels will come in answer to your call.

After his ascension in the light, this one desired no more to carry a mere mortal name and asked to simply be called Ray-O-Light. The Presence of God reached out from the heart of beloved Helios and Vesta and Alpha and Omega and said, "So shall it be for all eternity. Thou art Ray-O-Light! And thy mission unto all life shall be the illumination of mankind. And thou shalt be able to bring just that wherever thou art, namely, thou shalt be a radiance of my light."[409]

Ray-O-Light says, "Would you like to know how I inherited fearlessness flame? I tell you, I was also embodied in Mater. I also walked the path of initiation, and when I came to that place where all of the demons of the night and the fallen ones assailed me to take from me my own blessed Christ-awareness, I knelt in prayer.

"I called out to God as God gave to me the awareness of these hordes of darkness in their array. And I tell you, the discarnates that assail the holy innocence of the devotees number in the millions, and as vultures they come to attack the soul—the soul that is about to be set free in the ritual of overcoming.

"God showed me the horror of the night and of the fallen ones, and I cried out to him in my prayer, and I said, 'O God, you are greater than all of this, your flame and your light able to consume the darkness!' And I called to God for the specific action of the Christ consciousness that I knew must exist. For no thing, no shadowed one could occupy time and space without God providing the counterpoint of light, of freedom! And I called forth the dissolving action of the light of the Christ. I called forth the ray that I knew would dissolve all that would assail me in the hour of my victory.

"And I would point out to you that in that moment I faced, as you will face in the moment of your overcoming, the entire momentum of fear on that planetary body, fear of evolutions without attainment, fear of the fallen ones of the second death and of the judgment. And all of that fear was upon me as the clouds of the night. Yet I concentrated on the faith in the element of grace that was able to counteract that darkness.

"By that faith in the ultimate existence in God of the element to counteract fear, I received, after many, many hours of prayer, the vision of fearlessness flame descending out of the great God Star as a pencil-light across the sky descending. And I gazed, and I saw, and lo, the descending of that fire came unto me—to the very place where I knelt in prayer. And as that ray descended, I saw the components of the inner light. I saw something of the chemistry of God. I saw elemental beings ensouling that ray. I saw the piercing white light and the action of the emerald ray, piercing all of that darkness!

"And, lo, as the ray descended, I saw the dissolution of worlds of fear and doubt and all separation from God. And in the place where darkness was, I saw, lo, angels, hosts of light, and I heard the music of the spheres carried in fearlessness flame. And as the ray descended, it burst as a fire around me, and I was enveloped in that fire, that fearlessness flame! And it burned through me and through my soul and through my chakras and through my four lower bodies, and it burned until I became that flame.

"And I surrendered all vestiges of lesser awareness outside of the Great God Flame, and I saw that God called me to be the fullness of that flame to many lifewaves. I saw that God placed upon me the greatest initiation of fear, that I might receive the greatest blessing of its antidote. In order that I might carry that fire and be worthy to carry it, I must needs first perceive all that would oppose that fire, that I might give answer unto the LORD whether I would stand fast to focus that flame in the face of all that would oppose it until the ultimate consummation of the planes of Mater.

"You see, precious ones, whatever virtue you invoke from the heart of God, you must first slay the darkness that will assail that virtue. And God will not lower into the chalice of your heart the elements of that flame until you have stood by your own light, your own determination, your own momentum!—until you have stood to conquer those who would challenge you the moment you would receive that energy."

Ray-O-Light explained how to overcome all projections of fear: "You stand in time and space. Before you is the great highway of life. And there will be times when you will feel yourself as in a snowstorm, with your staff that is the teaching to guide you on your way. And in the robes of the pilgrim, you will move against the wind and the storm, scarcely able to see a foot before you. And you will press on, making, as it were, scarcely little progress on that path. And there will be days when the storm will cease, and there will be a calm and you will see the rays of the sun. And once again the rains will come, the lightning and the thunder will be heard, and the crackling of the storm.

"Each step you advance, you advance by the action of fearlessness. That fear that you must conquer is the conglomerate of your own human consciousness amplified by the fallen ones who live by fear not love.

"Press on, chelas of the light.... For the fallen ones who have come disguised as followers of the Prince of Peace come saturated with the entities of doubt and fear and pride and tyranny! They come to thwart the release of the light—the high frequencies of the Buddha, of the Kumaras, of Maitreya, of the World Mother. They come to release their smoke screen. And you will find that men will be trembling in outer darkness, and the fear that shall come upon them is the fear of the last days. And in their fear, they will rise up to defend their position, the false position that has no tenure in the mind of God.

"You will see, then, ere the vanquishing of all evil on the planetary body, the rising of the tide of fear. And inasmuch as the children of God know not how to combat that fear—know not the name of Ray-O-Light or the mighty action of fearlessness flame—I call to the devotees of the Great White Brotherhood to invoke fearlessness flame, that you might preserve your sanity from the vanity and the profanity of the fallen ones who assail you and would tear from you your own Christ-mastery.

"This is the path that Christ walked. He cast out fear as the demons, as the palsied one.[410] He cast out fear of death and want. He cast it out in every form and lived to prove the law of excellence and of love.

"You must fulfill the life of the Piscean conqueror ere you can fulfill your divine plan in Aquarius. And the majority among you will not be allowed to take your ascension until you have fulfilled your divine plan in Aquarius. And the fulfillment of the divine plan is a necessary requirement of your ascension....

"Here is the key, then, to overcoming that fear that stiffens the corpse itself, that fear that stiffens the flow of life—the fear that ultimately is the death of self-awareness. The key is to *keep on moving!*

"When you find yourself in a snowstorm or a blizzard, you will not curl up on the side of the road, for you know instinctively you will freeze to death. You *keep moving!* This is the key to the conquering of all fear. *Keep moving!* Keep active! Move through the elements, move through the mirage of fear! *Pierce!* it with your sword and discover the island in the sun, the place of light, the Garden of Eden."[411]

Ray-O-Light is your ascended master friend, who comes "sometimes at your darkest hour, when the shadows seem to be closing about you and it seems as though you cannot walk another step of the way."[412] He teaches you to hold onto your God Presence through every trial and brings a ray of hope from God. He has promised that whenever you whisper his name, Ray-O-Light, and remember that you, too, are a ray of light—he will bestow upon you the peace of his Presence.

He enlists you to join the legions of fearlessness flame. There are ten thousand angels in each legion, ready to be called into action by you. They are angels of action, swift to run. They will cast out doubt and fear, death and disease, and they will cast out the fallen ones. Ray-O-Light says:

"Now these ten thousand are kneeling before you. They carry the shield of faith in the left hand and the sword of righteousness in the right. They are dressed in white with robes of emerald green. They kneel before you because they give allegiance to the Christ within you. They acknowledge the Christ as the authority to command them into action. They kneel to receive the command of your Christ consciousness to go forth into Terra this night to bind the fallen ones....

"You have seen the vision of those who will come forth in an instant when you breathe a whisper, *O God, O fearlessness flame, legions of Ray-O-Light, come forth!* And suddenly you will find yourself encamped about with their light, and you will stand and behold the glory of God as they cast out all unreality and clear the way for the coming of the son, the daughter of God.

"Now, I say, would you not feel just a little bit sheepish to ever again entertain fear? So, then, I have succeeded in my mission in coming. I have conveyed to you the momentum of my love for fearlessness, for I see how fearlessness liberates the creative power of the cosmos! I have seen what a world can be without fear. I have seen the glistening of the crystals of the mind of God, the creativity, the divine art and the culture. I have seen what life can be when life is free of doubt and fear and death! So, O God, O God Almighty, let these be the electrodes that convey to Terra the new birth in fearlessness flame."[413]

❖ **RESURRECTION, SPIRIT OF THE, *See* Spirit of the Resurrection**

❖ **REX AND NADA, BOB AND PEARL, Ascended Master Youth**

Rex and Nada, Bob and Pearl are ascended master youth who lived in the twentieth century in the United States. They received the initiations for the ascension under the auspices of the Great Divine Director, Saint Germain, Lady Master Leto and the messengers Godfre and Lotus in the 1930s.

Their activity is to serve the youth of the world by drawing forth the threefold flame from the white-fire core of every atom and cell in the being of man. Pearl focuses the purity of the fourth ray (white); Bob, the first ray (blue); Nada, the third ray (pink); and Rex, the second ray (gold).

In their final embodiment, Rex and Nada were the son and daughter of Daniel and Nada Rayborn, also initiates of the Brotherhood, whose ascensions preceded those of their children. Bob and Pearl Singleton were brother and sister who were also students of Saint Germain. The Master revealed to them that Rex and Pearl were twin flames and that Bob and Nada were also twin flames.

Rex has been both a teacher of truth and a leader of men in the armies of the great nations of the world, including Greece, France, England and America. He has also served on the fifth ray as a famous scientist in several lives.

On Atlantis, Pearl served as a vestal virgin in the Temple of Light. She was the most exalted of all the sisters of the temple. She lost her life when the temple was ravaged by Atlantean rebels, but her momentum of service to the light was retained and brought forth again and again in subsequent embodiments. Throughout many lifetimes, she has been a teacher of truth.

Nada was embodied as a mogul emperor of India. During her reign, a great culture and unification of the people took place under the influence of the great love that she expanded through her own heart flame in their behalf. In other embodiments she was a high priestess in a temple in Egypt, the child of an Arab sheik, and served with her twin flame on Atlantis when his uncle was one of the great master-rulers. Her desire for the light has been the dominant theme throughout her hundreds of lives on this planet. Bob served nobly and well under George Washington during the American Revolution.

Rex, Nada, Bob and Pearl were all embodied together at the time of Enoch. Rex explains: "You have heard the word of the ascended master Enoch, our great father, who did explain in his dictation that in the profound hour of the light's increase within him, as he did kneel before an holy angel, was stoned by us, not I alone, beloved, but by all of us who were in embodiment at that time.[414]

"And our father Enoch did pray profoundly for us that we could come to the understanding of this 'old man' and that we could feel the light and see his Path. And therefore he did become our sponsor, and this beloved hierarch did not leave us alone but did pursue us lifetime after lifetime. And thus we did receive many initiations under his sponsorship until the time

Shadrach, Meshach, and Abednego in
the Fiery Furnace

came when we must undergo the fiery trial, the trial by fire, beloved, in the physical octave.

"For we were called as sons and daughters of Venus. We were called to demonstrate upon earth that initiation of the sacred fire and the physical fire that there might be a record on this earth and in the holy books of what truly can be the physical trial by fire. And you will note that it was not one of the Hebrews but a pagan king who did take note of the three cast into the furnace and another, a fourth, like unto the Son of God. Blessed ones, our bodies were prepared for many centuries for that initiation both at inner levels and in embodiment. And therefore when placed in that furnace our physical bodies remained untouched by the fire nor was the smell of smoke found upon our garments.

"In that hour, beloved, I was therefore overshadowed by the Son of God, the integrating Christ Presence of Jesus, our Lord. And the other three were the beloved Pearl and Bob and Nada. Thus, they were the three in physical form and I, the fourth, the abiding Presence.* And through that initiation and our successful passage through it, from that moment we did receive the acceleration of our physical bodies. And that acceleration did remain with us in succeeding embodiments all the way to this century....

"Because we did pass through that fiery trial and did continue to embody lifetime after lifetime as initiates of the Great White Brotherhood, we did come to the hour in this century when we received the call of Saint Germain. And he made known to us that because we had sustained the light of our prior initiations in these bodies and because we had increased the light in them continuously since the hour of the trial by fire, our bodies and therefore we ourselves were prepared, and we could be received as candidates for the physical ascension. Thus, in answer to your question and your wonderment, beloved, it is an absolute truth written in the records of akasha and it is scientific fact that we four did indeed make the physical ascension!†

---

*See the Book of Daniel, chapter 3, for the story of Shadrach, Meshach and Abednego and their trial by fire under king Nebuchadnezzar.

†For further information about the physical ascension, see the profile of David Lloyd, pages 77–79.

"Saint Germain desired profoundly that this example and record should be recorded in akasha so that when the golden age would come forth according to his dreams because of the expected fulfillment of his purposes in the founding of the I AM Activity, those evolutions who should embody, who should have increasing attainment and who should have passed through initiations parallel to our own might also experience the physical ascension. Saint Germain desired to seal in akasha the record of the possibility of the physical ascension, which to this day remains an exception to the rule."[415]

In their joint service to mankind, Rex, Pearl, Bob and Nada focus the flame of eternal youth for people of all ages. They have a tremendous momentum of devotion and service to children and youth that may be invoked for the implementation of the Brotherhood's plan for the youth of the world and for education.

The ascended master Rex speaks of the importance of bringing ascended master concepts to our children and youth: "O America, land of my youth and land of my victory! How I remember thee as I walked through thy hills, as I meditated upon God in thy forests, in thy mountains, O America, in the mists of the morning as I dwelt neath the trees and ordered my thoughts and feelings within the heart flame of my own God Presence.

"I remember well that day, the day when there appeared to me that holy presence of life in the ascended master Saint Germain with his great promise of victory of the ascension, not only for my lifestream but for all the youth of America—his great promise of freedom that would be won in this nation, this great nation under God. He spoke to me of the ascended master youth of America, and he spoke to me of youth as a concept within his heart for all men whatever the age of the forms they might be wearing.

"But he stressed to me upon that day, that early morn when the sun was streaming through the trees glistening in the dew drops, on that holy dawn he explained to me that when the concepts of the ascended masters are embodied early in the years, they are anchored there within the matrix, within the mind and feeling world of the people, of the children. And so when they attain maturity and adulthood the ritual of those concepts is established within their four lower bodies; and so the great victory of light can shine forth from their faces and their hearts even as the sun was shining forth upon that morning.

"And so he told me of the great need for the establishment of focuses of light that would appeal to the youth of America, which would draw them unto their own God Presence, which would enable them to realize so clearly the contrast between the light of God and the simulated light of the outer world with its sordid activities that depreciate the Christ in the youth. And he said that these must be established, these focuses of light, and he looked to this century, to this age, for those workers who would come together and pledge themselves to the youth of the world."[416]

In 1989 Rex announced that he had come from the planet Venus with Nada, Bob and Pearl and a mandala of twenty-five thousand ascended master youth in order to sponsor the youth of the world. They have taken up their abode in the Retreat of the Divine Mother over the Royal Teton Ranch.

❖ **ROERICH, NICHOLAS,** *See* **Nicholas Roerich**

❖ **ROSE OF LIGHT, Mentor of the Heart**

The ascended lady master Rose of Light represents the spirit of Woman and the spirit of Mother in the New Age. By her attainment, she governs the unfoldment of the heart chakra and the expansion of the light through the threefold flame.

On Atlantis she kept the fire of love on the altar of healing love. She also called for the establishment of a cult of the heart and the path of the ruby ray. She is part of the sisterhood that comes in the tradition of the priestesses of the sacred fire.

She tended a meditation garden and shrine on Atlantis devoted to the unfoldment of the divine plan of the soul. The gardens were filled with roses, each one consecrated as a budding soul unfolding its divinity. She identified the sons and daughters of God who should come out from the world and be on the Path, and she prayed for them without ceasing. Her momentum of prayer assisted many who came there to discover their *raison d'être,* and they went forth to fulfill their mission in service to the light and their fellowman. She served when the world was in great decadence and turbulence just before the Flood. It was as difficult as it is today to follow the path of light, and at that time she made her ascension.

Her experience in this embodiment enabled her to unfold the rose in her heart. Each petal is a fiery equation of light. Each petal is to strengthen the threefold flame in the hearts of devotees. She emanates a pink light that is tinged with the gold of Helios and Vesta. She advocates that the fiery heart intensify with the ruby ray, that it press out love, and that this love consume the force of

Antichrist in the world.

Like many of the ascende[d mas]ters serving with planet Earth, Rose of Light's twin flame is as yet [unasc]ended. Rose of Light speaks of the unascended twin flames of th[e unasc]ended masters: "I AM your Rose of Light, your sister of love. I call [to the t]win flame to true love, to the true path of the ascension, to the true v[ictory] of love. And I call all twin flames unascended of the hierarchy of li[ght to] now leave all else for the sake of love and survive unto the New Day. I [call t]o you who are present to call to your twin flames unascended or ascen[ded t]o heed the call of love and intensify it in your heart, even as you inte[nsify i]t in their hearts."[417]

Rose of Light's assistance to s[piritu]al students is to develop the action of the heart and to make the love o[f the] heart an "open door which no man [can sh]ut." She says: "Thus, I come again, (no manifestation of the human) ca[n] [?] with you, for Saint Germain has and my mission is to come and to[?] called me to be your special ment[or on] the heart. Therefore, I bring my angels of the rose of light, and w[e pla]ce upon your heart chakra the thoughtform and the manifestation o[f the] rose of light unfolding petals that are multiplying the twelve of the hea[rt ch]akra. You may have a thousand-petaled rose of the heart chakra, belo[ved,] for the petals increase by mercy's flame and compassion and wisdom..

"I therefore have come forth on th[is day], as scheduled by the Great Law, to begin the process of the tutoring of [the h]eart and the opening of the rose of the heart…. Let each unfolding of th[e pet]al of the heart be a strengthening of the petal and of its release of lig[ht. L]et there be the God-mastery of the petals, signifying a greater and greater release of light, which does require, as has been explained to you at length, a greater protection and likewise a mounting spiral of attainment in the flame of God-mastery."[418]

The rose of light of the heart chakra reminds us that every saint who has entered into the courts of heaven has magnified the Lord, and truly the path of Christ and Buddha is the path of the sacred heart. This heart can hold the entire earth and the physical octave braced in the rose of light. The rose of light of the heart may appear to be delicate, but it is a fiery vortex of love.

She says, "It is love that does personalize the light that does quicken the heart and open it. Some have neat petals in a spiral unfolding about the heart. But others, even among you, yet have not unfolded the rose of light of the heart, choosing at times to retain the strident, the unmerciful expression, the hardness of heart. Thus, the petals are not symmetrical and the golden-pink glow-ray spiral that is a part of this pink rose is not as it should be for the coming of the Queen of Light."[419]

We can call for the distilled essence of beloved Rose of Light to mend each fracture in our etheric body and ask her to help us to develop the action of the heart. We can also ask Rose of Light, through the magnet of our own God Presence and Christ Self, to infuse our hearts directly with her own momentum of purity and love. Her discernment of Truth through the heart will assist all to prepare for the initiations of Lord Maitreya whereby they might gain mastery of the heart chakra. Her discipline is the discipline of divine love and of the exactness of the heart flame.

❖ **RUTH HAWKINS, Goddess of Beauty and Twin flame of Paul the Venetian**

Paul the Venetian's twin flame is the ascended lady master Ruth Hawkins. Ruth was born February 18, 1907, in Topeka, Kansas (also the birthplace of Clara Louise Kieninger). Ruth was living in Albuquerque, New Mexico, when she made her ascension in October 1995 at the age of eighty-eight.

She was a fiery, stalwart soul who gave greatly to the cause of the Great White Brotherhood. She had blonde hair and beautiful crystal-clear blue eyes. Her manner was regal, and she carried herself with dignity.

Ruth first found the masters' teachings through the I AM Activity around 1936, when she was twenty-nine years old. While Ruth was a member of the Bridge to Freedom in the 1950s, Paul the Venetian gave a dictation revealing that Ruth was his twin flame and that when she ascended, her name would be the Goddess of Beauty.

From 1963 to 1973 Ruth was the director of The Summit Lighthouse Study Group in Los Angeles, which was then called Saint Germain's Freedom Group. At that time it was one of the largest Summit Lighthouse groups in the country. Every Thursday afternoon for nearly twenty years Ruth held a vigil with other Keepers of the Flame.

Ruth Hawkins

In 1971 in a service conducted by Mark Prophet, Ruth Hawkins was knighted by Saint Germain for her tireless and faithful work and her meritorious service to the ascended masters. He knighted her Lady Adoremus.

Ruth dedicated her life to Paul the Venetian. At his request, she made a trip to France with another devotee in the fall of 1984. They rented an apartment in Paris where they decreed for France every day for four months in the morning, afternoon and evening.

Ruth and her friend lived in a square called la Place du Tertre, where hundreds of artists set up their easels to paint. Ruth talked to the artists about art and showed them the Chart of Your Divine Self and pictures of the masters. She always carried with her a stack of wallet-sized Charts of Your Divine Self. Whenever she got the chance, she would give a Chart to someone. By the time she left Paris, many of the artists had a picture of the Chart on their easels.

Ruth and her friend found that the French usually responded favorably to foreigners who knew French. Although Ruth didn't know any French when she arrived in Paris, the people loved her anyway. Ruth's apartment was near the Basilica of the Sacré-Coeur, and Ruth and her friend frequently went to the Sacré-Coeur and other cathedrals to pray for Paris. They would sit in the pews and decree to Astrea.

Ruth and her friend also did many violet-flame decrees—half an hour three times a day. They felt that there was much hardness in the city and that the violet flame was needed to soften it so that the people would accept the light. Ruth acquired a violet-color transparency. She would hold it up to her eyes and look through it to see the city covered with violet flame.

She held the immaculate concept for all life and never spoke unkindly about anyone. Her friend said it was as if she never saw anything negative in people.

Ruth herself was beautiful and always well-groomed and finely dressed. One day Ruth and her friend were riding a subway in Paris. A mother who looked very poor boarded the subway with her little boy. The boy, about eight years old, was dirty and his clothes were raggedy. There weren't enough seats for them, so Ruth said to the child, "You can sit on my lap."

The little boy climbed onto Ruth's lap and Ruth looked directly at him. She told him how beautiful and special he was; she told him that he was God's child. The little boy looked back at Ruth and smiled. It was clear that he believed her. When Ruth and her friend got off the subway, Ruth said nothing about how dirty and raggedy the child was. Instead she commented to her friend, "Wasn't he the most beautiful child you ever saw?" That is what she thought about all children.

Every day around 3:30 pm, when the children got out of school, Ruth and her friend would take a walk to see them. Ruth would smile at the children and say *"Bonjour."* And every Thursday the two women held a vigil for the youth.

As the twin flame of Paul the Venetian, Ruth was wholly devoted to truth and beauty. She was an artist and she poured her devotion into her painting. Ruth said that if it were not for Paul the Venetian, she would not have been able to paint. Sometimes, under his direction, she would begin a portrait before she even knew whom she was going to paint.

She created many portraits of the ascended masters, which are still used as focuses for the masters' presence. Mark Prophet said that if she continued painting, she would make her ascension. Her work included portraits of Paul the Venetian, Saint Germain, Mother Mary, Nada, Kuan Yin, Sanat Kumara and Lady Master Venus.

Though Ruth knew that Paul the Venetian was her twin flame, at times she was assailed with doubt that this was true. She remembered an embodiment when they had been together and she had doubted him. Ruth felt that if she was to make her ascension in this life, she would have to have total faith in Paul the Venetian. She did overcome her doubt and maintained total faith in her twin flame.

Paul the Venetian was waiting for Ruth when she made her transition, having fulfilled all her commitments to life and balanced her karma. They requested that Ruth experience her ascension from the Temple of the Sun, the etheric retreat of the Goddess of Liberty over Manhattan. The Goddess of Liberty is Paul the Venetian's spiritual Mother.

Paul the Venetian's retreat, the Château de Liberté, is on the etheric plane over southern France, but currently he is holding classes in the Temple of the Sun. Ruth wanted to take her ascension from the Temple of the Sun because of her deep love for Saint Germain and for America. Ruth Hawkins' ascension flame is now permanently anchored in the etheric octave in that retreat over Manhattan.

While Ruth was in embodiment, she anchored Paul the Venetian's flame in the earth. The master said that she single-handedly carried his torch of the love ray. Since Ruth is now ascended, Paul the Venetian has requested that each one of us carry one flame of the torch of the love ray that she held. We can call to Paul the Venetian and Ruth Hawkins to intensify love in the hearts of people of the world—especially in the youth.

❖ **SAINT GERMAIN, Chohan of the Seventh Ray and Hierarch of the Aquarian Age**

Saint Germain is the chohan of the seventh ray. Together with his twin flame, the ascended lady master Portia, the Goddess of Justice, he is the hierarch of the Aquarian age. He is the great sponsor of freedom's flame, while Portia is the sponsor of the flame of justice.

Each two-thousand-year cycle comes under one of the seven rays. Jesus, as chohan of the sixth ray, held the office of hierarch of the age dur-

ing the last 2000 years. On May 1, 1954, Saint
Germain and Portia were crowned as directors for the
coming cycle of the seventh ray. Freedom and justice
are the yin and yang of the seventh ray of Aquarius,
and together with mercy, they provide the foundation
for all other attributes of God to be outpictured in this
seventh dispensation.

Saint Germain and Portia deliver to the people of
God the dispensation for the seventh age and the seventh ray—the violet ray of freedom, justice, mercy,
alchemy and sacred ritual—a new lifewave, a new
civilization, a new energy.

The Ascended Master
Saint Germain,
by Sindelar

As chohan, or lord, of the seventh ray, Saint Germain initiates our souls
in the science and ritual of transmutation through the violet flame. He is the
seventh angel prophesied in Revelation 10:7 who comes to sponsor the fin-
ishing of the mystery of God "as he hath declared to his servants the
prophets."

Saint Germain says: "I am an ascended being, but it has not ever been
thus. Not once or twice but for many incarnations I walked the earth as you
now do, confined to mortal frame and the limitations of dimensional existence. I was on Lemuria and I was on Atlantis. I have seen civilizations rise
and fall. I have seen the undulations of consciousness as mankind have
cycled from golden ages to primitive societies. I have seen the choices, and
I have seen mankind by wrong choices squander the energies of a hundred
thousand years of scientific advancement and even degrees of cosmic consciousness that transcend that which is attained by members of the most
advanced religions of the day.

"Yes, I have seen the choices, and I have chosen. By right choices man
and woman establish their position in hierarchy. By choosing to be free in
the magnificent will of God, I won my freedom from that mortal round of
incarnations and justifications of an existence outside the One. I won my
freedom by that flame, that keynote of the Aquarian cycle traced by
alchemists of old, that purple elixir the saints do hold....

"You are mortal. I am immortal. The only difference between us is that
I have chosen to be free, and you have yet to make the choice. We have the
same potential, the same resources, the same connection to the One. I
have taken mine to forge a God-identity. For long ago, the still small voice
within spoke the fiat of Alpha and the living God: 'Children of the One,
forge your God-identity.' And in the stillness of the night, I heard the call
and I answered, 'I will!' And when I said, 'I will,' all of cosmos echoed, 'I

will!' The will to be summons the vastness of the potential of being....

"I am Saint Germain, and I have come to claim your soul and the fires of your heart for the victory of the Aquarian age. I have set the pattern for your soul's initiation.... I am on the path of freedom. Take that path, and you will find me there. I am your teacher if you will have me."[420]

Saint Germain is known as a diplomat, expressing the godly qualities of dignity, grace, gentility, poise and true statesmanship through all who will invoke the seventh ray. He is a member of the House of Rakoczy, founded by the Great Divine Director, in whose Transylvanian mansion the violet flame of freedom is presently enshrined.

Over fifty thousand years ago, Saint Germain was the ruler of a golden-age civilization in a fertile country where the Sahara Desert now is. As king-emperor, Saint Germain was a master of the ancient wisdom and of the knowledge of the Matter spheres, and the people looked to him as the standard for their own emerging Godhood. His empire reached a height of beauty, symmetry and perfection unexceeded in the physical octave.

As the people of this civilization became more interested in the pleasures of the senses than in the larger creative plan of the Great God Self, a cosmic council instructed the ruler to withdraw from his empire; henceforth their karma would be their guru. The king held a great banquet for his councillors and public servants. His 576 guests each received a crystal goblet filled with an elixir that was "pure electronic essence."

This elixir was Saint Germain's gift of soul-protection to them so that when their opportunity would come again in the age of Aquarius to bring back that golden-age civilization, they would remember their I AM Presence and they would become a sign to all people that God can and shall dwell with his people when they make their minds and hearts and souls a fitting habitation for his Spirit.

During the banquet a cosmic master, identifying himself solely by the word Victory upon his brow, addressed the assembly. He warned the people of the crisis they had brought upon themselves by their faithlessness, rebuked them for their neglect of their Great God Source, and prophesied that the empire would come under the rule of a visiting prince who would be seeking to marry the king's daughter. The king and his family withdrew seven days later to the golden-etheric city counterpart of the civilization. The prince arrived the next day and took over without opposition.[421]

As high priest of the Violet Flame Temple on the mainland of Atlantis thirteen thousand years ago, Saint Germain sustained by his invocations and his causal body a pillar of fire, a veritable fountain of violet singing flame, which magnetized people from near and far who came to be set free from every binding condition of body, mind and soul. This they achieved by self-effort through the offering of invocations and the practice of seventh-ray rituals to the sacred fire.

Those who officiated at the altar of the Violet Flame Temple were schooled in the universal priesthood of the Order of Melchizedek at Lord Zadkiel's retreat, the Temple of Purification, which stood where the island of Cuba now is. This priesthood combines the perfect religion and the perfect science. It was here that both Saint Germain and Jesus received the anointing, spoken by Zadkiel himself: "Thou art a priest for ever after the order of Melchizedek."[422]

Prior to the sinking of Atlantis, while Noah was yet building his ark and warning the people of the great Flood to come, the Great Divine Director called Saint Germain and a few faithful priests to transport the flame of freedom from the Temple of Purification to a place of safety in the Carpathian foothills in Transylvania. Here they carried on the sacred ritual of expanding the fires of freedom even while mankind's karma was being exacted by divine decree.

In succeeding embodiments, Saint Germain and his followers, under the guidance of the Great Divine Director, rediscovered the flame and continued to guard the shrine. Later, the Great Divine Director, assisted by his disciple, established a retreat at the site of the flame and founded the House of Rakoczy, the royal house of Hungary.

In the eleventh century B.C., Saint Germain was embodied as the prophet Samuel. He was an outstanding religious leader in a time of great apostasy, serving as the last of Israel's judges and the first of her prophets. In those days the judges did not simply arbitrate disputes; they were charismatic leaders who were believed to have direct access to God and who could rally the tribes of Israel against oppressors.

Samuel was the messenger of God's liberation of the seed of Abraham from bondage to the corrupt priests, the sons of Eli, and from the Philistines, who had slaughtered the Israelites in battle. He is traditionally named alongside Moses as a great intercessor. When the nation faced continuing threats from the Philistines, he courageously led the people in a spiritual revival, exhorting them to "return unto the LORD with all your hearts" and to "put away the strange gods."[423] The people repented and beseeched Samuel not to cease calling upon the LORD to save them. As he was praying and offering sacrifices, a violent thunderstorm was

The boy Samuel,
by Reynolds

unleashed, allowing the Israelites to overtake their enemies. The Philistines never rose again in the days of Samuel.

The prophet spent the rest of his life administering justice throughout the land. When he grew old, he appointed his sons to be judges over Israel; but they were corrupt and the people demanded that Samuel give them "a king to judge us like all the nations."[424] Deeply grieved, he prayed to the LORD and received the direction that he must carry out the mandate of the people. The LORD told him, "They have not rejected thee, but they have rejected me, that I should not reign over them."[425]

Samuel warned the Israelites of the dangers that would befall them through their rulers, but they still clamored for a king. Thus he anointed Saul as their leader and charged him and the people to always obey the voice of the LORD. But when Saul proved to be an unfaithful servant, Samuel pronounced the LORD's judgment upon him for his disobedience and secretly anointed David as king. When the prophet died, he was buried at Ramah; all of Israel mourned his passing.

Saint Germain was also embodied as Saint Joseph, the father of Jesus and husband of Mary. There are few references to him in the New Testament. The Bible traces his lineage back to David. It also recounts how when the angel of the Lord warned him in a dream that Herod planned to kill Jesus, Joseph heeded the warning and took his family to Egypt, returning after Herod's death. Joseph is said to have been a carpenter and is thought to have passed on before Jesus began his public ministry. In Catholic tradition, Saint Joseph is revered as Patron of the Universal Church, and his feast is celebrated on March 19.

In the late third century, Saint Germain was embodied as Saint Alban, the first martyr of Britain. Alban lived in England during the persecution of Christians under the Roman emperor Diocletian. He was a pagan who had served in the Roman army and settled in the town of Verulamium, later renamed St. Albans. Alban hid a fugitive Christian priest named Amphibalus, who converted him. When soldiers came to search for him, Alban allowed the priest to escape and disguised himself in the cleric's garb.

Once his deed was discovered, Alban was scourged and sentenced to death. Legend says that so great a multitude gathered to witness his execution that they could not pass over a narrow bridge that had to be crossed. Alban prayed and the river parted to give passage to the crowd, whereupon his appointed executioner was converted and begged to die in his place. The request was denied and he was beheaded along with Alban.

Saint Germain worked from inner planes as the Master Teacher behind the Neoplatonists. He inspired the Greek philosopher Proclus (c. A.D.

410–485), the highly honored head of Plato's Academy at Athens. Under the Master's tutelage, Proclus based his philosophy upon the principle that there is only one true reality—the "One," which is God, or the Godhead, the final goal of all life's efforts. Proclus's writings extended to almost every department of learning, from philosophy and astronomy to mathematics and grammar. He acknowledged that his enlightenment and philosophy came from above and he believed himself to be one through whom divine revelation reached mankind.

In the fifth century, Saint Germain was embodied as Merlin— alchemist, prophet and counsellor at the court of King Arthur. In a land splintered by warring chieftains and riven by Saxon invaders, Merlin led Arthur through twelve battles (which were actually twelve initiations) to unite the kingdom of Britain. He worked side by side with the king to establish the sacred fellowship of the Round Table. Under the guidance of Merlin and Arthur, Camelot was a mystery school where the knights and ladies pursued the inner unfoldment of the mysteries of the Holy Grail and a path of personal Christhood.

In some traditions, Merlin is described as a godly sage who studied the stars and whose prophecies were recorded by seventy secretaries. The *Prophecies of Merlin,* which deals with events extending from Arthur's time into the distant future, was popular in the Middle Ages.

Saint Germain was Roger Bacon (1220–1292), philosopher, Franciscan monk, educational reformer and experimental scientist. In an era in which either theology or logic or both dictated the parameters of science, he promoted the experimental method, declared his belief that the world was round, and castigated the scholars and scientists of his day for their narrow-mindedness. "True knowledge stems not from the authority of others, nor from a blind allegiance to antiquated dogmas,"[426] he said. Bacon eventually left his position as a lecturer at the University of Paris and entered the Franciscan Order of Friars Minor.

In his day Bacon was renowned for his exhaustive investigations into alchemy, optics, mathematics and languages. He is viewed as the forerunner of modern science and a prophet of modern technology. He predicted the hot-air balloon, a flying machine, spectacles, the telescope, the microscope, the elevator, and mechanically propelled ships and carriages, and wrote of them as if he had actually seen them.

His scientific and philosophical world view, his bold attacks on the theologians of his day, and his study of alchemy and astrology led to charges of "heresies and novelties," for which he was imprisoned for fourteen years by his fellow Franciscans. But to those who followed after him,

Bacon was "doctor mirabilis" ("wonderful teacher"), an epithet by which he has been known down the centuries.

Saint Germain was also embodied as Christopher Columbus (1451–1506), discoverer of America. Over two centuries before Columbus sailed, Roger Bacon himself had set the stage for Columbus' voyage to the New World when he stated in his *Opus Majus* that "the sea between the end of Spain on the west and the beginning of India on the east is navigable in a very few days if the wind is favorable."[427] Although the statement was incorrect in that the land to the west of Spain was not India, it was instrumental in Columbus' discovery. He quoted the passage in a 1498 letter to King Ferdinand and Queen Isabella and said that his 1492 voyage had been inspired in part by this visionary statement.

Christopher
Columbus

Columbus believed that God had made him to be "the messenger of the new heaven and the new earth of which He spake in the Apocalypse of St. John, after having spoken of it by the mouth of Isaiah."[428] "In the carrying out of this enterprise of the Indies," he wrote to King Ferdinand and Queen Isabella in 1502, "neither reason nor mathematics nor maps were any use to me: fully accomplished were the words of Isaiah."[429] He was referring to the prophecy recorded in Isaiah 11:10–12 that the Lord would "recover the remnant of his people...and shall assemble the outcasts of Israel, and gather together the dispersed of Judah from the four corners of the earth."

He was certain that he had been divinely selected for his mission. He studied the biblical prophets, writing passages relating to his mission in a book of his own making entitled *Las Proficias,* or *The Prophecies*—in its complete form, *The Book of Prophecies concerning the Discovery of the Indies and the Recovery of Jerusalem.* Although the point is seldom stressed, it is a fact so rooted in history that even *Encyclopaedia Britannica* says unequivocally that "Columbus discovered America by prophecy rather than by astronomy."[430]

As Francis Bacon (1561–1626), he was philosopher, statesman, essayist and literary master. Bacon, who has been called the greatest mind the West ever produced, is known as the father of inductive reasoning and the scientific method, which to a great degree are responsible for the age of technology in which we now live. He foreknew that only applied

Francis Bacon

science could free the masses from human misery and the drudgery of sheer survival in order that they might seek a higher spirituality they once knew.

"The Great Instauration" (meaning the great restoration after decay, lapse or dilapidation) was his formula to change "the whole wide world." He first conceived of the concept as a boy, and when he later crystallized it in his 1607 book by the same name, it launched the English Renaissance.

Over the years Bacon gathered around himself a group of writers who were responsible for almost all of the Elizabethan literature. Some of these were part of a "secret society" he called "The Knights of the Helmet," which had as its goal the advancement of learning by expanding the English language and creating a new literature written not in Latin but in words that Englishmen could understand. Bacon also organized the translation of the King James Version of the Bible, determined that the common people should have the benefit of reading God's Word for themselves.

Ciphers discovered in the 1890s in the original printings of the Shakespearean plays and in the works of Bacon and other Elizabethan authors reveal that Bacon wrote Shakespeare's plays and that he was the son of Queen Elizabeth and Lord Leicester.[431] His mother, however, fearful of an untimely loss of power, refused to acknowledge him as her heir.

Toward the end of his life Bacon was persecuted and went unrecognized for his manifold talents. He is said to have died in 1626, but some have claimed that he secretly lived in Europe for a time after that. Triumphing over circumstances that would have destroyed lesser men, his soul entered the ritual of the ascension from the Rakoczy Mansion, retreat of the Great Divine Director, on May 1, 1684.

Desiring above all else to liberate God's people, Saint Germain sought and was granted a dispensation from the Lords of Karma to return to earth in a physical body. He appeared as "le Comte de Saint Germain," a "miraculous" gentleman who dazzled the courts of eighteenth- and nineteenth-century Europe, where they called him "The Wonderman."

He was an alchemist, scholar, linguist, poet, musician, artist, raconteur and diplomat admired throughout the courts of Europe for his adeptship. He was known

Le Comte de
Saint Germain

for such feats as removing the flaws in diamonds and other precious stones and composing simultaneously a letter with one hand and poetry with the other. Voltaire described him as the "man who never dies and who knows everything."[432] The count is mentioned in the letters of Frederick the Great, Voltaire, Horace Walpole and Casanova, and in newspapers of the day.

Working behind the scenes, Saint Germain attempted to effect a smooth transition from monarchy to representative government and to prevent the bloodshed of the French Revolution. But his counsel was ignored. In a final attempt to unite Europe, he backed Napoleon, who misused the master's power to his own demise.

But even prior to this, Saint Germain had turned his attention to the New World. He became the sponsoring master of the United States of America and of her first president, inspiring the Declaration of Independence and the Constitution. He also inspired many of the labor-saving devices of the twentieth century to further his goal of liberating mankind from drudgery that they might devote themselves to the pursuit of God-realization.[433]

In the latter part of the eighteenth century, Saint Germain received from the lady master Kuan Yin her office as chohan of the seventh ray—the ray of mercy and forgiveness and of sacred ceremony. And in the twentieth century, Saint Germain stepped forth once again to sponsor an outer activity of the Great White Brotherhood.

In the early 1930s, he contacted his "general in the field," the reembodied George Washington, whom he trained as a messenger and who, under the pen name of Godfré Ray King, released the foundation of Saint Germain's instruction for the New Age in the books *Unveiled Mysteries, The Magic Presence* and *The "I AM" Discourses*. In the late 1930s, the Goddess of Justice and other cosmic beings came forth from the Great Silence to assist Saint Germain in his work of bringing the teachings of the sacred fire to mankind and ushering in the golden age.

In 1961 Saint Germain contacted his embodied representative, the messenger Mark L. Prophet, and founded the Keepers of the Flame Fraternity in memory of the Ancient of Days and his first pupil, Lord Gautama—and the second, Lord Maitreya. His purpose was to quicken all who had originally come to earth with Sanat Kumara—to restore the memory

of their ancient vow and reason for being on earth today: to serve as world teachers and ministering servants in their families, communities and nations at this critical hour of the turning of cycles.

Thus, Saint Germain recalled the original keepers of the flame to hearken to the voice of the Ancient of Days and to answer the call to reconsecrate their lives to the rekindling of the flame of life and the sacred fires of freedom in the souls of God's people. Saint Germain is the Knight Commander of the Keepers of the Flame Fraternity.

Saint Germain, the
Knight Commander

On May 1, 1954, Saint Germain received from Sanat Kumara the scepter of power and from the Master Jesus the crown of authority to direct the consciousness of mankind for this two-thousand-year period. This does not mean that the influence of the ascended master Jesus has receded. Rather, as World Teacher from the ascended level, his instruction and his radiation of the Christ consciousness to all mankind will be even more powerful and all-pervading than before, for it is the nature of the Divine continually to transcend itself. We live in an expanding universe—a universe that expands from the center of each individualized son (sun) of God.

This dispensation means that we are now entering a two-thousand-year period when, by invoking into our beings and worlds the violet transmuting flame, the God-energy that the human race has misqualified for thousands of years may now be purified and all mankind cut free from fear, lack, sin, sickness and death, and all may now walk in the light as God-free beings.

At this dawn of the age of Aquarius, Saint Germain has gone before the Lords of Karma and received the opportunity to release the knowledge of the violet flame outside of the inner retreats of the Great White Brotherhood, outside of the mystery schools. Saint Germain tells us of the benefits of invoking the violet flame: "In some of you a hearty amount of karma has been balanced, in others hardness of heart has truly melted around the heart chakra. There has come a new love and a new softening, a new compassion, a new sensitivity to life, a new freedom and a new joy in pursuing that freedom. There has come about a holiness as you have contacted through my flame the priesthood of the Order of Melchizedek. There has come a melting and dissolving of certain momentums of ignorance and mental density and a turning toward a dietary path more conducive to your own God-mastery.

"The violet flame has assisted in relationships within families. It has served to liberate some to balance old karmas and old hurts and to set individuals on their courses according to their vibration. It must be remembered that the violet flame does contain the flame of God-justice, and God-justice, of course, does contain the flame of the judgment; and thus the violet flame always comes as a two-edged sword to separate the Real from the unreal....

"Blessed ones, it is impossible to enumerate exhaustively all of the benefits of the violet flame but there is indeed an alchemy that does take place within the personality. The violet flame goes after the schisms that cause psychological problems that go back to early childhood and previous incarnations and that have established such deep grooves within the consciousness that, in fact, they have been difficult to shake lifetime after lifetime."[434]

Saint Germain teaches the science of alchemy in his book *Saint Germain On Alchemy.* He uses the amethyst—the stone of the alchemist, the stone of the Aquarian age and the violet flame. The waltzes of Strauss carry the vibration of the violet flame and will help to put you in tune with him. He has also told us that the "Rakoczy March," by Franz Liszt, carries the flame of his heart and the formula of the violet flame.

Saint Germain maintains a focus in the golden etheric city over the Sahara Desert. He also teaches classes at the Royal Teton Retreat as well as his own physical/etheric retreat, the Cave of Symbols, in Table Mountain, Wyoming. In addition, he works out of the Great Divine Director's focuses—the Cave of Light in India and the Rakoczy Mansion in Transylvania, where he presides as hierarch. More recently he has established a base in South America at the retreat of the God and Goddess Meru.

His electronic pattern is the Maltese cross; his fragrance, that of violets. The name Saint Germain comes from the Latin *Sanctus Germanus,* meaning simply "Holy Brother."

❖ **SAINT PATRICK,** *See* **Patrick, Saint**

❖ **SANAT KUMARA AND LADY MASTER VENUS, Hierarchs of the Planet Venus**

Sanat Kumara

Sanat Kumara is known as the Ancient of Days. He is the Great Guru of the seed of Christ throughout cosmos, hierarch of Venus and one of the seven holy Kumaras (Lords of Flame who represent the seven rays on Venus). He initiates us on the path of the ruby ray, which he sets forth in his book *The Opening of the Seventh Seal.*

He has held the hierarchical position of the Lord of the World since the darkest hours of earth's history when her evolutions fell to the level of cavemen and lost contact with the God flame and the mighty I AM Presence. When the earth was at the point of being dissolved because there was no one who was keeping the flame of the Christ consciousness alive, Sanat Kumara came to earth, a voluntary exile from his planet Venus, to keep the flame until sufficient numbers among mankind would respond and begin once again to maintain the focus on behalf of their brothers and sisters. One hundred and forty-four thousand souls volunteered to assist Sanat Kumara in his mission and accompany him with legions of angels.

Sanat Kumara describes this momentous event in cosmic history: "You call me Sanat Kumara, and you know me as the one who stood before the cosmic council known as the Council of the One Hundred and Forty and Four. You know me because you were witnesses to my plea made for and on behalf of the evolutions of earth who no longer knew the presence of the Lamb, who by disobedience were cut off from the living Guru. You know me as the one who volunteered to embody the threefold flame within the earth unto the evolutions evolving within the seven planes of being—fire, air, water and earth.

"The Cosmic Council had decreed the dissolution of earth and her evolutions because the souls of her children no longer worshiped the Trinity in the threefold flame of life burning upon the altar of the heart. They had become the sheep gone astray. Their attention fixed upon the outer manifestation, they had willfully, ignorantly abandoned the inner walk with God....

"Thus the light of the temples had gone out, and the purpose to which God had created man—to be the temple of the living God—was no longer being fulfilled. One and all were the living dead, a Matter vessel without an ensouling light, an empty shell. Nowhere on earth was there a mystery school—not a chela, not a guru, no initiates of the path of initiation unto Christhood.

"The hour of the judgment had come, and the one seated upon the throne in the center of the twelve times twelve hierarchies of light had pronounced the word that was the unanimous consensus of all: Let earth and her evolutions be rolled up as a scroll and lit as a taper of the sacred fire. Let all energies misqualified be returned to the Great Central Sun for repolarization. Let energy misused be realigned and recharged with the light of Alpha and Omega, once again to be infused by the Creator within the ongoing creation of worlds without end.

"The requirement of the Law for the saving of Terra? It was that one who should qualify as the embodied Guru, the Lamb, should be present in the physical octave to hold the balance and to keep the threefold flame of life for and on behalf of every living soul. It is the Law of the One that the meditation of the one upon the Eternal Christos may count for the many until the many once again become accountable for their words and their works and can begin to bear the burden of their light as well as the karma of their relative good and evil.

"I chose to be that one. I volunteered to be a flaming son of righteousness unto earth and her evolutions.

"After considerable deliberation, the Cosmic Council and the Nameless One gave their approval of my petition, and the dispensation for a new divine plan for earth and her evolutions came into being....

"Thus I knelt before the great white throne of the Nameless One and he said unto me, 'My son, Sanat Kumara, thou shalt sit upon the great white throne before the evolutions of earth. Thou shalt be to them the LORD God in the highest. Verily, thou shalt be the highest manifestation of the Deity that shall be given unto them until, through the path of initiation, their souls shall rise to thy throne of awareness and stand before thee in praise of the I AM THAT I AM which thou art. In that day when they shall rise up and say, "Blessing and honour and glory and power be unto him that sitteth upon the throne and unto the Lamb for ever and ever"— behold, their redemption draweth nigh.'

"And he said unto me, 'Thus unto the evolutions of earth thou shalt be Alpha and Omega, the beginning and the ending, saith the I AM THAT I AM, which is and which was and which is to come, the Almighty.' And he placed upon me his mantle of sponsorship of the Father unto the Son, which would become in me his sponsorship of a lifewave that he now made my own. It was a trust. It was the initiation of the Father in the Son....

"And the Council of the One Hundred and Forty and Four, forming a single solar ring around the great white throne, intoned the Word with the great beings of light, forming the inner circle round about the throne and saying, 'Holy, holy, holy, LORD God Almighty, which was, and is, and is to come.' And I heard the echo of their chant of the 'Holy, holy, holy' all the way home to the morning star, to my twin flame whom you know as Venus, and to the sons and daughters of the Love Star.

"Winged messengers of light had announced my coming and the disposition of the Cosmic Council and the dispensation granted. The six—my brothers, the holy Kumaras, who sustain with me the seven flames of the seven rays—Mighty Victory and his legions, our daughter Meta, and many servant sons and daughters whom you know today as the ascended masters welcomed me in a grand reception. That evening, the joy of opportunity was mingled with the sorrow that the sense of separation brings. I had chosen a voluntary exile upon a dark star. And though it was destined to be Freedom's Star, all knew it would be for me a long dark night of the soul.

"Then all at once from the valleys and the mountains there appeared a great gathering of my children. It was the souls of the hundred and forty and four thousand approaching our palace of light. They spiraled nearer and nearer as twelve companies singing the song of freedom, of love and of victory. Their mighty chorusing echoed throughout elemental life, and angelic choirs hovered nigh. As we watched from the balcony, Venus and I, we saw the thirteenth company robed in white. It was the royal priesthood of the Order of the Melchizedek, the anointed ones who kept the flame and the Law in the center of this hierarchical unit.

"When all of their numbers had assembled, ring upon ring upon ring surrounding our home, and their hymn of praise and adoration to me was concluded, their spokesman stood before the balcony to address us on behalf of the great multitude. It was the soul of the one you know and love today as the Lord of the World, Gautama Buddha. And he addressed us, saying, 'O Ancient of Days, we have heard of the covenant that God hath made with thee this day and of thy commitment to keep the flame of life until some among earth's evolutions should be quickened and once again renew their vow to be bearers of the flame. O Ancient of Days, thou art to us our Guru, our very life, our God. We will not leave thee comfortless. We will go with thee. We will not leave thee for one moment without the ring upon ring of our chelaship. We will come to earth. We will prepare the way. We will keep the flame in thy name.'

"And so as the LORD God directed me, I chose from among them four hundred servant sons and daughters who would precede the hundred and forty and four thousand to prepare for their coming. For though they knew the darkness of the darkest star, in reality they did not know, as I knew, the real meaning of the sacrifice that they now were offering to make in the name of their Guru.

"We wept in joy, Venus and I and all of the hundred and forty and four thousand. And the tears that flowed on that memorable evening burned as the living sacred fire flowing as the water of life from the great white throne and the Cosmic Council, our sponsors."[435]

Thus, when Sanat Kumara came from Venus to make the earth his temporary home, he was accompanied by a retinue of many great beings of light, including his daughter (the lady master Meta) and three of the seven holy Kumaras. The four hundred who formed the avant-garde were sent ahead to earth to build the magnificent retreat of Shamballa on an island in the Gobi Sea (where the Gobi Desert now is). Alchemists and scientists came also at that time, one hundred forty-four of these focusing the one hundred forty-four flames of the elements. Together they composed a replica of the diamond that is in the Great Hub, a focus of the diamond-shining mind of God.

On the White Island in the Gobi Sea, they built the City of White, patterned after the city of the Kumaras on Venus. Sanat Kumara established the focus of the threefold flame in the retreat at Shamballa, which remained in the physical for many centuries. Sanat Kumara resided in this physical retreat, but he did not take on a physical body such as the bodies we wear today—it was in the Matter universe, yet highly etheric. Later it became expedient for its protection that Shamballa, this wondrous retreat that was in the physical octave, be withdrawn to the etheric octave. The etheric focus remains as an exact replica of what was once the physical retreat. The beautiful azure sea with the White Island in the center is now the Gobi desert.

Sanat Kumara anchored a ray of light from his heart as a thread of contact with each one evolving on the planet Earth, nourishing and sustaining that flame and assisting the Holy Christ Self to quicken the Christ consciousness. Without that assistance, mankind en masse would have gone through the second death, and the planet would have been destroyed.

The ancient custom of the Yule Log has come down to us from the service rendered by Sanat Kumara who, each year, consecrated a focus of the sacred fire in the physical octaves. It became tradition for the people to come across many miles to take home a piece of the Yule Log and to use it to light their fires through the coming twelve-month cycle. Thus, a focus of his physical flame was tangibly manifest in the dwelling places of the people of the earth, enabling them to have actual physical contact with a focus of the Lord of the World in their midst.

Sanat Kumara's mission was completed on January 1, 1956, when his most capable disciple Gautama Buddha was awarded the position of Lord of the World, having enough momentum to hold the balance for the planet and the focus of the threefold flame. Sanat Kumara then became Regent of the World, and in that capacity he continues to assist earth's evolutions from his home on Venus. Until this change in office, Sanat Kumara released tremendous light to the planet each year at the Wesak Festival during the full moon in Taurus. His radiation was anchored through his disciples, Lord Gautama Buddha, Lord Maitreya and the one who currently holds the office of the Maha Chohan. These three anchored the focus of the threefold flame from the heart of Sanat Kumara on behalf of the Lord of the World. They were the step-down transformers for his intense radiation.

Sanat Kumara also figures in several roles in the religious traditions of the East. Each one reveals another facet of his Divine Self. He is revered in Hinduism as one of the four or seven sons of Brahma. They are portrayed as youths who have remained pure. The Sanskrit name Sanat Kumara means "always a youth." He is the most prominent of the Kumaras.

In Hinduism, Sanat Kumara is sometimes called Skanda, or Karttikeya the son of Shiva and Parvati. Karttikeya is the god of war and commander-in-chief of the divine army of the gods. He was born specifically to slay Táraka, the demon who symbolizes ignorance, or the lower mind. Karttikeya is often depicted holding a spear, representing illumination. He uses the spear to slay ignorance. In Hinduism, stories of war are often used as allegories for the internal struggles of the soul.

Skanda-Karttikeya, as he is sometimes called, is also acclaimed as the god of wisdom and learning. He is said to bestow spiritual powers upon his devotees, especially the power of knowledge. In the Hindu mystic tradition, Karttikeya is known as Guha, which means "cave" or Secret One, because he lives in the cave of your heart. Hindu scriptures also depict Sanat Kumara as the "foremost of sages" and a knower of Brahman.

The ascended masters teach that the supreme God of Zoroastrianism, Ahura Mazda, is Sanat Kumara. Ahura Mazda means "Wise Lord" or "Lord who bestows intelligence." He represents the principle of Good and is the guardian of mankind and the opponent of the Evil principle.

Sometime between 1700 and 600 B.C. Zarathustra founded Zoroastrianism in ancient Persia. One morning when he went to fetch water in a river, he beheld a luminous being who led him to Ahura Mazda and five other radiant figures. So great was their light that "he did not see his own shadow upon the earth." From this group of beings he received his first revelation of a new religion. Shortly afterward, Zarathustra became a spokesman for Ahura Mazda.

After the withdrawal of Shamballa to the etheric octave, Sanat Kumara embodied as Dipamkara, the Lamp-Lighting Buddha. (The Sanskrit word *Dipamkara* means "kindler of lights" or "the luminous.") In Buddhist tradition, Dipamkara is a legendary Buddha who lived long, long ago, the first of twenty-four Buddhas who preceded Gautama Buddha. Dipamkara prophesied that the ascetic Sumedha would become the future Buddha Gautama.

Buddhists consider Dipamkara, Gautama Buddha and Lord Maitreya to be the "Buddhas of the three times"—past, present and future. We can understand this to mean that Dipamkara is the past Lord of the World, Gautama Buddha is the present Lord of the World and Maitreya will be the future Lord of the World.

In Buddhism, there is a great god known as Brahma Sanam-kumara. His name also means "forever a youth." Brahma Sanam-kumara is a being so elevated that he must create an apparition body in order to be seen by the gods of the heaven of the Thirty-Three. Sakka, the ruler of the gods, describes his appearance: "He outshines other devas in radiance and glory, just as a figure made of gold outshines the human figure."[436]

The Ancient of Days

The prophet Daniel also recorded his vision of Sanat Kumara, whom he called "the Ancient of Days." Daniel writes: "I beheld till the thrones were cast down, and the Ancient of days did sit, whose garment was white as snow, and the hair of his head like the pure wool: his throne was like the fiery flame, and his wheels [chakras] as burning fire."[437]

Lady Venus

Sanat Kumara's twin flame is Lady Master Venus. During his long exile on planet Earth, she remained on their home planet to keep the flame there. Some years after Sanat Kumara's return in 1956, Lady Venus herself came to earth to assist her evolutions. In a dictation delivered on May 25, 1975, she announced that as Sanat Kumara had kept the flame for earth, now she had come to "tarry for a time on Terra" to "dedicate anew the fires of the Mother." She said, "I release a fiery momentum of consciousness to arrest all spirals that would take from humanity the fullness of their divinity.... See how mankind respond to the flame of the Mother as they responded to the light of Sanat Kumara."

On July 4, 1977, Sanat Kumara said that "the Cosmic Council and the Lords of Karma have granted and decreed that I might be allowed to tarry on earth, in earth, for certain cycles of manifestation for the absolute return of freedom into the hearts of the lightbearers of earth....

"I place my body as a living altar in the midst of the people Israel,* and in that body temple is the original blueprint, the [soul] design for every son and daughter of God and the children of God who have come forth. For it is the desire of the Cosmic Virgin that none of her children should be lost, none of her sons and daughters.

"And thus I join the Lady Master Venus, who has been tarrying with you these many months; and we together, focusing our twin flames in the Holy City, will stand for the triumph of that community of the Holy Spirit that must be manifest as the key to the release of light in this age."

In a dictation given July 4, 1978, Sanat Kumara told us he was manifesting that night in the physical spectrum "and I am anchoring in this very earth plane the full weight and momentum of my office as the Ancient of

---

*The term *Israel* applies to the collective body of the bearers of the Christic seed and Christ consciousness who have descended from Sanat Kumara and not exclusively to the Jewish people. The ascended masters teach that those who are of the I AM THAT I AM have embodied in all races, kindreds and nations. The term *Israelite* means, esoterically, "he who *Is Real* in the mighty I AM Presence." In Hebrew, *Israel* means "he will rule as God" or "prevailing with God."

Days, such as I have not done since our coming to the Place Prepared at Shamballa."

The strains of Sanat Kumara's keynote were captured by Jan Sibelius in *Finlandia*. So powerful is the release of the flame of freedom through this music, that during the Nazi occupation, its playing was forbidden lest it arouse the fervor of the people for freedom.

❖ **SARASVATI, SHAKTI OF BRAHMA,** *See also* **Brahma**

The Divine Mother in her manifestation as Sarasvati is the shakti of Brahma. Brahma is known as the Creator in the Hindu Trinity and is parallel to God the Father in the Western Trinity. He is the Divine Lawgiver, the source of all knowledge. Together, Brahma and Sarasvati are the embodiment of cosmic force.

Sarasvati is known as the Goddess of the Word. She is identified with Vac, the Word. She represents eloquence and articulates the wisdom of the Law. She is the Mother-Teacher to those of us who love the Law revealed by Brahma, and she is the power of volition, the will and motivation to be the Law in action. Sarasvati represents the union of power and intelligence from which organized creation arises.

Sarasvati is sometimes represented with four hands, sitting on a lotus. She holds the sacred scriptures in one hand and a lotus in another. With the remaining two hands, she plays the Indian lute (veena). She is called the Flowing One, the source of creation by the Word. Sarasvati also represents purity and wears white. Her transcendent nature is suggested in her vehicle, the swan, which is a symbol of spiritual transcendence and perfection.

Sarasvati is associated with speech, poetry, music and culture and is known as the Goddess of Learning and the Patroness of the Arts and Music. She is revered by both Hindus and Buddhists. To Buddhists, she is the consort of Manjushri, the bodhisattva of wisdom. Buddhists appeal to Manjushri for intelligence, wisdom, mastery of the teaching, the power of exposition, eloquence and memory. He works with Lord Maitreya. The two are sometimes depicted in a triad with Gautama Buddha in which Manjushri represents the wisdom aspect and Maitreya the compassion aspect of Buddhist teaching. Like Sarasvati, Manjushri brings the gift of illumination.

In the earliest Hindu texts, the Vedas, Sarasvati is a river goddess. The

Vedas say that Sarasvati was the greatest river in India. For years the Saras-vati was believed to have been a myth, but an archaeological survey in 1985 found an ancient riverbed that matched the description of the Sarasvati. It was a great river, four to six miles wide for much of its length. It flowed westward from the Himalayas into the sea.

The Rigveda calls Sarasvati "the best mother, the best river, [and] the best Goddess."[438] It also says, "Sarasvati like a great ocean appears with her ray, she rules all inspirations."

Her sacred "seed syllable," or bija, is *Aim* (pronounced *ah-eem*). A bija mantra encapsulates the essence of a cosmic being, of a principle or a chakra. Sarasvati's mantra is *Om Aim Sarasvatye Namaha*.

❖ SELFLESSNESS, SPIRIT OF, *See* Spirit of Selflessness

❖ SERAPIS BEY, Chohan of the Fourth Ray

Serapis Bey is the chohan of the fourth ray, hierarch of the Ascension Temple at Luxor, and the thirteenth member of the Council of Adepts of the Ascension Temple. He is also known as Serapis Soleil, Serapis of the Sun.

The fourth ray is the ascension flame, the white light of the Mother in the base-of-the-spine chakra. Out of this white light comes architecture, the principles of mathematics, the foundations of the building of the Matter tem-ple and the pyramid of Self. In the presence of Serapis, one knows an entirely different conception of what we call the Christ, the real person of us all.

Known as the Great Disciplinarian, Serapis came from Venus with the Ancient of Days to rekindle the sacred fire in the hearts of a wayward mankind. His great enthusiasm to reclaim the sons of man as kings and priests unto God swelled and mounted into a flame of iron will, determi-nation and discipline.

He was a priest in the Ascension Temple on Atlantis. As guardian of the ascension flame, he carried the flame safely up the Nile River to Luxor just before Atlantis sank. Serapis gives us a glimpse of this experience in his own words:

"I remember well when the first rumblings of the sinking of Atlantis were present. For, as you know, the sinking of that continent came in stages. By the grace of God, the warning given allowed many to escape. And we made our way to Luxor....

"You may wonder why a spiritual flame requires transporting by mere mortals. It is always so that children of the light tend to think that such things ought to happen magically and miraculously. Perhaps a touch of the fairy tale has spilled over into religion, and people have forgot that all that has been wrought by God and man has been the joint work and effort, above and below.

"I will tell you, then, why it is so—because the only place that the flame can truly abide, apart from the altar so dedicated, is the living heart of the living adept."[439]

There in Egypt, Serapis and the brothers who accompanied him built the Ascension Temple, and there they have guarded the flame ever since, alternating duties as they continued to reembody specifically for that purpose.

Serapis Bey continued to reincarnate in the land of the Nile, foregoing his own ascension until about 400 B.C. In these lifetimes he became the sponsor of some of the greatest architectural feats that have ever been brought forth upon the earth.

Serapis was the architect of the Great Pyramid and El Morya was the master mason. The Great Pyramid is the carving in stone of the record of the path of initiation whereby the soul, beginning in Matter, the base of the pyramid, the four sides, rises from the center of the pyramid to the apex. The raising up of that flame is the meditation upon the white light that travels in the physical body from the base of the spine to the crown.

The Sphinx and the Great Pyramid

Jesus and El Morya explain that "the building of the pyramid of Self is an inner building, but the outer equation must comply, must show fruits, must set the example that others may follow you all the way to the heart of the Sphinx—to the very heart of the living Guru whom the Sphinx represents and to the heart of the flame within the Great Pyramid that is on the etheric octave (and is not held in the pyramid of Giza, which remains the shell of its former focus and function due to the misuse of its energy by black magicians and false gurus and false chelas)."[440]

Serapis was embodied as the Egyptian Pharaoh Amenhotep III (reigned c. 1417–1379 B.C.), the son of Thutmose IV and the great grandson of Thutmose III, an incarnation of Kuthumi. His son and successor to the throne was Amenhotep IV, later known as Ikhnaton. During Serapis' reign, Egypt was at her height of prosperity, peace and splendor, which were the direct manifestation of his communion with his own heart flame and with the ascended masters all the way back to the Ancient of Days.

Amenhotep III was regarded as the greatest ruler on earth. He maintained a high level of peaceful diplomatic relations with all nations during most of his reign. Part of the great wealth of his treasury was spent on the construction of magnificent temples and palaces. He enlarged the existing Temple of Karnak of the Nile, and he built a huge funerary temple, the remains of which are known today as the Colossi, the monolithic seated statues uncovered on the banks of the river. He sought to outpicture in stone the understanding of the hierarchical order of initiates, of ascended masters, of philosopher kings who had walked the earth in the earlier golden ages.

His greatest construction was that of the temple of Luxor, which remains partially intact today. This temple embodied in its geometry and design the physical outpicturing of the esoteric law that had been passed down through the priesthood for generations. It stands as a thorough textbook of advanced science, art and philosophy. The temple of Luxor is the physical counterpart today of the etheric retreat that is the Ascension Temple.

Serapis also embodied as the Spartan king Leonidas (died c. 480 B.C.), who commanded the Greeks in their heroic stand against the immense Persian invasion at the pass of Thermopylae, gateway to central Greece. Although the Persians overwhelmingly outnumbered the Greeks, Leonidas resisted the advance of the Persian army under King Xerxes for two days. On the third day, when the Persians approached from the rear and no reinforcements were in sight, Leonidas dismissed most of his troops. Assisted by the remaining Greek allies, Leonidas and his three-hundred-member Spartan royal guard fought to the last man. Their heroic stand enabled the Greek fleet to retreat and later defeat the Persians. The example of Leonidas has helped to carry on the spark of national identity of the Greek nation.

Historians cite this battle as a prime example of courage and fearlessness in fighting for a cause against massive odds. The akashic record reveals that the three hundred Spartans were the assembling again of three hundred chelas of Luxor who were in embodiment with Serapis. They were an extraordinary type of manhood. Some are today ascended masters; some remain in embodiment. At that time, it was a physical war against physical odds. Today, it is a battle of Armageddon against spiritual wickedness in high places of Church and State—the mind of God consuming the anti-mind, the greater Self consuming the not-self.

The Parthenon

Serapis Bey was embodied as the sculptor Phidias during the fifth century B.C. in Athens. He was regarded as the greatest of all the Greek sculptors. He was the architect of the Parthenon, supervising its exquisitely masterful construction. Within the Parthenon he placed his most famous work, the forty-foot high statue in gold and ivory of Pallas Athena, the representation of the Mother figure, the Goddess of Truth.

Standing in the Parthenon, one stands in the presence of a piece of architecture that is designed by an individual who knows how to use form, symmetry, geometry, angles for the housing of a flame. The forcefield of the Parthenon does contain an essential flame, as do the Temple of Luxor and the Great Pyramid.

Phidias also created a huge statue of Zeus out of gold and ivory that stood in the temple of Olympia. He was also a painter, engraver and master of metalwork. His art is characterized by its exalted beauty and spirituality, and he lived as the ultimate personification of the golden age of Grecian master artists who had an enduring influence on all subsequent Western art.

In the Hellenistic age, from 323 to 31 B.C., Serapis became one of the most important gods of the Egyptian and Greco-Roman pantheons. He was revered as the patron of the Ptolemaic kings of Egypt and as the founding deity of the great city of Alexandria. There are numerous historical records of the intimate contact of Serapis with men throughout Egypt and Asia Minor, and there are over 1,080 statues, temples and monuments dedicated to Serapis Bey that were erected during that era.

Demetrius of Phalarum, the founder of the Alexandrian library under Ptolemy I, was miraculously cured of blindness by Serapis and wrote hymns of thanksgiving. Serapis often spoke through oracles and gave counsel as well as personal, miraculous healings to many people. There is a famous historical account involving Serapis that marked an important era in the establishment of him as the most prominent deity of Egypt and Greece. King Ptolemy I, ruler of Egypt, was visited in a dream by Serapis, who commanded the king to bring the god's statue to Alexandria. After vacillation and a second dream with Serapis, the king had the statue brought with the blessings of the Delphic Oracle and installed it in the Serapium, or great Temple, of Alexandria. This is the temple that contained the famous Alexandrian library of three hundred thousand volumes.

Many epithets are ascribed to Serapis, including "Father," "Saviour" and "the greatest of the deities." He was regarded as the sponsor of intimate contact between the gods and mortals. Serapis is regarded in the annals of the esoteric tradition as the hierophant of the secret Egyptian initiatory rites. The lesser mysteries were dedicated to Isis and intended for the layman; the greater mysteries were dedicated to Serapis and Osiris and transmitted only to initiated priests who underwent severe rites of trial and initiation in the temple of Serapis.

Over a period of six to seven hundred years, Serapis became the supreme deity of Egypt and Greece. However, in the late fourth century A.D., the emperor Theodosius issued edicts against polytheism, and Christians took this as license to attack pagans, including the adherents of mystery religions. The Christian Bishop of Alexandria provoked mobs to destroy the great symbol of paganism in Alexandria, the mystery temple of the god Serapis. They hacked apart the huge statue of Serapis, which had inspired worshipers for six hundred years. The mob destroyed at least one of Alexandria's great libraries.

Serapis Bey played a vital role in the initial thrust and direction of the endeavors of the Brotherhood during the nineteenth century. Among the earliest letters from the adepts and masters to the founders of the Theosophical Society were those of Serapis Bey and the Brotherhood of Luxor.

Serapis took personal charge of the direction and chelaship of the amanuensis Helena Blavatsky and of Colonel Henry Steel Olcott, who was the co-founder and the president of the Theosophical Society. During the six months preceding the formation of the society in 1875, Serapis sent many letters of encouragement and instruction to Colonel Olcott. The letters were written mostly on thick green parchment in gold ink, signed by Serapis in script, and inscribed with an esoteric symbol of the Brotherhood of Luxor. It is characteristic of the letters written to Henry Olcott that he continually gave the exhortation to him, "Try." The master Serapis stressed the need for courage and fearlessness, the same strong traits he outpictured as Leonidas.

The ascended master Serapis Bey today occupies a very key position among the seven chohans. The fourth ray is midpoint between three on one side and three on the other. The center figure of four is key because it is the merging of the white light and the nexus of the figure-eight flow of energy. This point of the Mother flame is always embodied in the guru East or West, the person of the Mother in Sanat Kumara who moves in and among us by that white light.

The white light is the sacred fire of creation, and its perversion becomes black magic. This was seen in Egypt, the focal point of the ascension flame, as the practice of black magic by the Egyptian Black Brotherhood that went on for centuries upon centuries in defiance of the very presence of Serapis Bey within his temple.

The point of redemption of earth goes back to Lemuria, the Motherland and the Mother flame itself. Earth has a tremendous karma with the

Mother flame and in the perversions of the Mother flame that took place on Lemuria, in the area of where San Francisco is now located and off the coast of California. The perversions of the Mother light opened the way for the desecration of the temples, the fall of the priests and priestesses, ultimately ending in misuse of the sexual energies and perversions of the life force. The final act was the murder of the highest representative of the Mother on Lemuria. The real cause of the sinking of Lemuria was the desecration of the person of the Mother and her flame.

Since that hour, earth has been slowly coming to the age of Aquarius when once again the light of the Mother could be raised up in all, both male and female, bringing about once again the honoring of the woman and of the Mother and a reunion of the Mother, the light rising from the base, with the light of the Father that descends out of the I AM Presence. The next two thousand years is destined to see the raising up of consciousness such as has not occurred since the golden ages of Lemuria.

The path of the ascension is the resolution of those forces that are necessary within our consciousness—Father, Mother, Son and Holy Spirit as the four pillars of the temple within us. Gautama Buddha's great lesson was that all suffering is caused by being out of alignment with the inner light through wrong desire. Serapis Bey teaches us how to get into alignment with the inner will of Being. His teachings become the keystone in the arch of hierarchy. Without the white light, we cannot enjoy the integration of selfhood.

Serapis Bey, then, becomes a very important key at a time when there are so many problems in society. The increase in crime, murder, rape, drugs, and so forth is the sign of the coming of the Mother light, rising from the altars of Lemuria. The rising light becomes so intense that, unless we dive into it and become a part of it, it becomes the rock that Jesus spoke of—unless we fall upon that rock and allow our misconceptions to be broken, it breaks us.[441] It is the light that resolves identity, but is also the light that is so powerful that it can destroy the false identity that rebels against it. At the dawning of the age of Aquarius, the world is in rebellion against the light of God, and yet the world is seeking God. The teaching of Serapis Bey and the mysteries of the Brotherhood of Luxor contain the answers that can resolve these questions.

Serapis Bey has legions of seraphim in his command. He has great attainment in divine geometry and design. He assists his disciples in the self-disciplines that are necessary for the ascension: the discipline of the four lower bodies in order that the Christ may appear and use them as vehicles for service and attainment in the world of form; the disciplining of past momentums of negative spirals and of human creation that would stand in the way of the ascension flame forming within the heart of everyone evolving upon the planet through the acceleration of the threefold flame.

His book *Dossier on the Ascension* is a textbook on the path of the ascension. It contains teachings from the classes he conducts at the Ascension Temple, and through it, you can have anchored in your conscious mind that which you learn at the Ascension Temple at Luxor while your body sleeps at night. He outlines the requirements of the ascension and provides a thorough explanation and instruction on the process of the ascension.

Serapis describes what happens during the ritual of the ascension: "It is true, although the form of an individual may show signs of age prior to his ascension, that all of this will change and the physical appearance of the individual will be transformed into the glorified body. The individual ascends, then, not in an earthly body but in a glorified spiritual body into which the physical form is changed on the instant by total immersion in the great God flame.

"Thus, man's consciousness of the physical body ceases and he achieves a state of weightlessness. This resurrection takes place as the great God flame envelops the shell of human creation that remains and transmutes, in a pattern of cosmic grids, all of the cell patterns of the individual—the bony structure, the blood vessels and all bodily processes, which go through a great metamorphosis.

"The blood in the veins changes to liquid golden light; the throat chakra glows with an intense blue-white light; the spiritual eye in the center of the forehead becomes an elongated God flame rising upward; the garments of the individual are completely consumed, and he takes on the appearance of being clothed in a white robe—the seamless garment of the Christ. Sometimes the long hair of the Higher Mental Body [the Holy Christ Self] appears as pure gold on the ascending one; then again, eyes of any color may become a beautiful electric blue or a pale violet....

"Lighter and lighter grows the physical form, and with the weightlessness of helium the body begins to rise into the atmosphere, the gravitational pull being loosened and the form enveloped by the light of the externalized glory which man knew with the Father 'in the beginning' before the world was....

"These changes are permanent, and the ascended one is able to take his light body with him wherever he wishes, or he may travel without the glorified spiritual body. Ascended beings can and occasionally do appear upon earth as ordinary mortals, putting on physical garments resembling the people of earth and moving among them for cosmic purposes. This

Saint Germain did after his ascension when he was known as the Wonder-man of Europe. Such an activity is a matter of dispensation received from the Karmic Board."[442] (Generally, however, ascended beings do not return to the physical plane unless there is some specific service requiring this change in vibratory rate.)

Serapis tells us, "You ascend daily." Our thoughts, our feelings, our daily deeds are all weighed in the balance. We do not ascend all at once, but by increments as we pass our tests and win our individual victories. The entire record of all our past lives and momentums of both good and evil must be counted; and then, when we have brought at least 51 percent of all the energy that has ever been allotted to us into balance with the purity and harmony of the Great God Self, we may be offered the gift of the ascension. The remaining 49 percent must be transmuted, or purified, from the ascended octaves through service to earth and her evolutions.*

Serapis Bey, the chohan of the ascension flame and hierarch of the Ascension Temple at Luxor, Egypt, speaks to each one of us: "The future is what you make it, even as the present is what you made it. If you do not like it, God has provided a way for you to change it, and the way is through the acceptance of the currents of the ascension flame."[443]

Guiseppe Verdi captured the music of the ascension flame in the "Tri-umphal March" from *Aïda*. The keynote of the Ascension Temple is "Liebestraum," by Franz Liszt, and the radiance of the Electronic Presence of Serapis Bey and his twin flame pour through the aria "Celeste Aïda."

❖ SERVATUS, Overseer of Healing Angels

Servatus oversees the legions of healing angels who minister to mankind under Mother Mary and Raphael, the blessed archangel and the archeia of the fifth ray. He also serves with Ray-O-Light and his legions of fearlessness-flame angels.

Servatus spoke of his mission in a dictation in 1977: "I come by dis-pensation of the Lords of Karma, who many years ago said to Mary and Raphael: 'My beloved, we will allow Servatus to come forth only when a certain number among mankind have set themselves apart and set them-selves to the task of the Community of the Holy Spirit. For only in the sacrifices necessitated by community can the wholeness of the flame be brought forth. Therefore, when mankind show the love and a certain few

---

*In addition to balancing 51 percent of one's karma, the requirements for the ascen-sion are to balance the threefold flame, align the four lower bodies, attain a certain mastery on all seven rays, achieve a degree of mastery over outer conditions, fulfill one's divine plan, transmute the electronic belt, and raise the Kundalini.

who represent mankind come forth to show the way of that healing, only then can we allow Servatus to speak to the Keepers of the Flame....

"I am come, then, in an unprecedented moment of earth's history when there has never been a greater need for healing, even though it might seem that in the West as well as the East many developments in science and in medicine have taken place. Yet I tell you, the condition of the physical bodies, the emotions and the minds of the people is far, far from the center of Christ-reality. And the spirals of degeneration that are in the subconscious of the collective consciousness are fast spiraling into manifestation. And therefore, the people have not the wholeness that they require. And shortly there will come to pass a greater manifestation of the vial of the fifth angel[444] that comes upon the people as the chastisement for the misuse of science."[445]

Servatus was an eye-witness to the misuse of science in genetic engineering that took place on Atlantis, contributing to the fall of that continent. He is concerned about the return of mankind's karma of the misuse of the emerald ray and the return again of genetic engineering to the earth.

"I would caution you that in the last days of Atlantis the misuses of the emerald ray were very great. Science reached a great crescendo of materialism and mechanization. People became more and more dependent upon the scientists of the day who had their instruction from the laggards who came from Maldek, from the fallen ones and from the Luciferians.

"And therefore, the science of genetics and the manipulation of the DNA chain was in advance of that which it is today. And today's scientists are just beginning to touch on the records that were in the laboratories of Atlantis that caused such a degeneration of consciousness and of body and such a proliferation of perverted forms and the cross-breeding of all types of animal life with human life so as to ultimately find the decree of the LORD God in the flood of Noah and in the sinking of that continent."[446]

Servatus spoke of the great need for all Keepers of the Flame to consider their role in the Order of the Emerald Cross. Members of this order need not be doctors or nurses or healers. They need have only the desire to keep the flame while the evolutions of earth go through a two-fold action: first, the bringing forth again of the records of the misuses of science on Atlantis through the reincarnated Atlantean scientists who are performing the same experiments they did in those last days; and second, the return of mankind's karma from the misuse of the light of the emerald ray.

Servatus says: "As in the days of Atlantis, we stand by. We are watchful. It is our mission to answer the call of the little child and of the mature lightbearer. We come in with thousands and thousands of angels upon one request of one son or daughter of God, even if that request is made some-times half-heartedly and without faith, saturated perhaps with doubt and fear. And yet, if the individual will raise up his head and give voice to the command for wholeness, we will answer. And all of the healing hosts of the LORD will answer."[447]

Call to Servatus and his legions for the healing of the nations and the healing of consciousness of the people. Call to him and to Ray-O-Light for the fearlessness flame, an intense white light edged in a brilliant emerald green. This flame is a healing energy that can clear the conscious and sub-conscious of the energies of fear. When fear and anxiety are removed, then the angels can come with a light of wholeness and reestablish those coor-dinates within the body that are necessary for the flow of the light and the energy of the soul.

"Let every man and woman and child become the physician of his own body and soul and mind. Let him apply directly to his own I AM Presence and Christ Self, and let him see what it takes as a work in God to draw forth that wholeness."[448]

❖ **SEVEN HOLY KUMARAS, Lords of the Flame from Venus.**
See also **Sanat Kumara**

The seven holy Kumaras are seven great brings who hold the focus of the seven Elohim on the planet Venus. Sanat Kumara is one of the seven holy Kumaras. His position among the seven is on the third ray, and he brings the gift of love and the gift of the threefold flame.

Venus is the planet of the third ray of this solar system, and it is known to be the training ground for avatars who have been sent not only to earth but to the other planetary bodies infiltrated by the Luciferians. This is the home of Jesus Christ, Gautama Buddha, Lord Maitreya, John the Baptist, Enoch and the entire hierarchy of Brahmanism, Hinduism, Lemurian and pre-Lemurian avatars. All of these have come through the great mystery schools of Venus and the halls and temples of the seven holy Kumaras.

Each of the seven holy Kumaras has his individual temple on Venus, and each one of these temples is dedicated to the initiations of the Mother flame on one of the seven rays. The initiations of the Mother flame are always the making practical in Matter of the initiations of the Trinity of the Father, the Son and the Holy Spirit. Had the seven holy Kumaras not retained their God consciousness and their absolute purity, had they not retained Venus as a forcefield of love, had this forcefield not been held as the literal heart chakra of this solar system, the remainder of the evolutions of the planets would not have had the opportunity to be redeemed, and Sanat Kumara would not have been given the grant to come to the planet Earth.

The seven holy Kumaras have released a number of specific dispensations for the raising up of the light in the earth. In 1975 they came to release to the lightbearers of the world "an increment of light that is the seed of Alpha, of cosmic illumination to raise the fires of awareness and to increase the penetration of the Infinite One." This was an increment of light "that is delivered only once in ten thousand years for the elevation of consciousness and the centering of that consciousness in the crown."[449]

In 1976 the seven holy Kumaras spoke in Hawaii of the raising up of the Mother flame of Lemuria. This flame was upon a central altar, and around it, on what is known as the fire ring of the lands that border the Pacific Ocean today, were twelve temples, all dedicated to the Mother light. The twelve temples were for the solar initiations of the twelve hierarchies. Each had its own tone and flame. Sanat Kumara said, "We come, then, for one purpose, and that purpose is to anchor certain fohatic keys in the form of electrodes for the spiraling, rising energies of the seven rays in seven aspects of the Mother flame. The raising of these energies is from the point where they descended on Terra. The point of the descent of Lemuria and of Mother light must also be the point of the rise of that Mother light."[450]

Sanat Kumara and the seven holy Kumaras spoke in 1992 in Atlanta, Georgia, of the great love and concern of the evolutions of Venus for mankind: "Blessed hearts, I want you to know that the evolutions of my home star, Venus (who inhabit a plane that is not physical according to the physical nature of earth), are one and all in rapt attention as I address you with the seven holy Kumaras. And there are giant screens throughout that planet upon which all can see the messenger and see your faces and see your auras.

"And they send love, waves of billowing love in support of your sacred hearts, in support of the increase of holy love in your hearts, beloved—an entire planet of lifewaves watching now what shall become of earth and what shall become of their brothers and sisters and twin flames and souls so close to their hearts, those gathered here and those gathered in the cities and those not yet in this community of the Holy Spirit but moving toward the heart of the Buddha and the Christ and of Sanat Kumara.

"Yes, beloved, feel this love, for this love is something truly beyond this world, which all who are one with you in this cause and purpose are determined to manifest here by sending their love and also by journeying in the etheric octave to take their stand at your side.

"Blessed hearts, there is a response to your striving and to your giving of yourselves. There is a response from other systems. There is a response from the Violet Planet. There is a response from planets beyond this solar system, and then those that are light-years beyond even this galaxy.

"There is a hush in the entire Matter cosmos as the decisions of individuals are making the difference as to whether or not the entire tide of darkness will be turned around in planet Earth. For this cause have we come.... Therefore, together in the living flame, we multiply all that you are by the power of the love of Lady Master Venus."[451]

❖ SHIVA, PARVATI, DURGA AND KALI, Third Person of the Hindu Trinity and His Consorts

Shiva

Shiva is one of the most popular deities in India. Along with Brahma and Vishnu, he is part of the Hindu triad, the *trimurti*. Brahma, Vishnu and Shiva are understood to be three manifestations of the One Supreme Being. They are the "three in one," corresponding to the Western Trinity of Father, Son and Holy Spirit. Brahma personifies the creator aspect of God, Vishnu the preserver and protector and Shiva the destroyer or dissolver. Shiva embodies all these aspects to Hindus who select him as their chosen deity.

Shiva's devotees revere him as the supreme Reality, the total Godhead. They see him as the Guru of all gurus, the destroyer of worldliness, ignorance, evil and evildoers, hatred and disease. He bestows wisdom and long life, and he embodies renunciation and compassion.

The name *Shiva* is derived from a Sanskrit word meaning "auspicious," "kind" or "friendly." The many aspects and functions of Shiva are represented in the various names given to him. The Hindu scripture called Shiva-Purana gives 1,008 names for Shiva. One of Shiva's names is Shambhu, which means "benevolent" or "causing happiness." Another name is Shankara, meaning "giver of joy" or "bestower of good." As Mahadeva, he is the "great god."

Pashupati is another epithet, which means "lord of cattle." As Lord of Cattle, Shiva is the herdsman or shepherd of souls. Shiva is portrayed riding a white bull named ("joyful"). According to Hindu tradition, he was one of Shiva's devotees who assumed the form of a bull because the human body was not strong enough to contain his devotional ecstasy for Shiva. Nandi the bull is depicted in most Shiva temples. He is usually seated, facing the figure of Shiva. Nandi symbolizes the soul of man longing for God. He also represents the soul who is in deep contemplation of Shiva as the supreme Reality. Shiva will help you to unlock your supreme Reality.

Mount Kailas is Shiva's throne and the location of his paradise. This majestic mountain is the highest point of the Kailas mountain range in the Tibetan Himalayas. Hindus revere Kailas as the most holy mountain in the world and make pilgrimages there.

Shiva is a study in contrasts. He symbolizes both contemplation and action. He is often shown deep in meditation as a mendicant yogi. As the Maha Yogi, or great yogi, he is the King of Yogis, the supreme embodiment of the spirit of asceticism. Shiva also personifies the dynamic universe. In the Hindu scripture Kurma-Purana, Shiva says: "I am the originator, the god abiding in supreme bliss. I, the yogi, dance eternally."[452]

According to Hindu belief, Shiva performs a variety of dances. One of his dances is called the Tandava. This is his dance of creation and destruction. Shiva dances the universe into being, sustains it and then dances it out of existence at the end of an age. The most celebrated representation of Shiva is that of Nataraja, the King of Dancers, or Lord of the Dance. The place of Nataraja's dance is the golden hall at the center of the universe. This golden hall represents the heart of man. One Hindu hymn that celebrates Shiva's dance says that "as he dances, he appears in the immaculate lotus of the heart."[453]

The relationship of Shiva with his devotees is an intensely personal one. Although he resides at Kailas, his favorite home is in the heart of his devotees.

According to Hindu tradition, when the gods decided to allow the Ganges River to descend from heaven, Shiva received the full impact of the massive weight of the falling water on his head lest the earth be shattered by the gigantic torrent. Shiva's matted hair tamed the rushing cascade. He divided it into seven holy rivers, and the waters descended gently to earth.

To Hindus, the Ganges represents the refreshing river of spiritual wisdom. According to Hindu tradition, when the gods decided to allow that Ganges River to descend from heaven, Shiva in that point of the vortex of light, the whirling energy around him, was actually the balance between heaven and earth of the river that descended, which was a river of light and became the river of earth. And so the water of the Ganges is considered by Hindus to be a magical water, a holy water that purifies anything. The ascended masters teach that these seven holy rivers also represent the seven rays of the Holy Spirit that come out of the white light.

Shiva's role parallels that of the Holy Spirit in the Western Trinity. Shiva teaches that the threefold flame in your heart is the personification of Brahma, Vishnu and Shiva. He says, "You can see those three plumes as ourselves personified. Then you may talk to us. We are not a three-headed god, but Three-in-One, for we also have a threefold flame....

"It is well for a time to visualize us personally rather than simply as an impersonal flame that is burning. Meditate upon us not as statues or pagan gods but as the very fire and the replica of the Godhead that has been placed in your heart."

Shiva says that he is always near at hand to answer your prayers. "You do not need to call me with a long and loud call as if I were far away! A simple signal will suffice, for I am the genie of the ruby ray. I am always ready! Turn your life around with me, and I will show you my cosmic dance. And I will dance with you and whirl in the sphere of fire. Yes, I shall show you how imminent is your victory."[454]

Lord Shiva encourages us to try an experiment for overcoming negative habits. He says: "Give yourself a cycle to rise to a plane of greater dominion. Make a God-determination. Think now of a very certain condition within your consciousness that you know absolutely must go. Think of that human consciousness. Think of that problem or habit that has gnawed at you and kept you from your eternal salvation.

"Now, beloved ones, I ask you, be a scientist of the New Age and try this one experiment for the next forty-eight hours: Each time you face that momentum—that memory, that consciousness, that habit or that desire, whatever it is that you long to see put into the flame—each time it crosses the line of the mind, the desire body, or your big toe, each time it comes into the memory, speak into it with the full ferocity of your voice: 'Shiva! Shiva! Shiva! Shiva!' "[455]

In Hindu tradition, every masculine personification of God has a feminine counterpart, or shakti. The masculine creative power is activated by this feminine principle. Thus, Shiva's action is crystallized in the world of form through his female counterpart. His hidden nature is made visible through her. Shiva's shakti appears in three primary forms—as Parvati, Durga and Kali.

Parvati

Parvati is the gentle mother and wife. Her union with Shiva is a prototype of the ideal marriage. A beautiful, gracious woman, she is often depicted with Shiva in domestic scenes or seated beside him in discourse. Shiva and Parvati are sometimes portrayed with their son Skandha. Skandha is also known as Karttikeya, the god of war, and is identified in one Upanishad with the sage-god whom we call Sanat Kumara.

According to Hindu mythology, when the lovely Parvati was unable to win Shiva's love, she set aside her jewels, donned the garb of a hermit and retreated to a mountain to meditate upon Shiva and practice austerities.

After she embraced the life of a renunciate for some time, Shiva finally accepted her as his wife.

Hindus believe that Shiva and Parvati live on the summit of Mount Kailas. Some artistic representations of Shiva show him as half-man and half-woman. According to legend, Shiva was determined that there be no separation between himself and his shakti, and he therefore decreed that his right side be Shiva and his left be Parvati.

Durga

Durga is called the Goddess Beyond Reach, or the Unfathomable One. Terrible and menacing to her enemies, she rides on the back of a tiger, which represents the demon of the lower self. One Hindu text describes the creation of the goddess in a manner that dramatically depicts the way the shakti activates the power of her consort:

At one time in the past, the gods were in a predicament. They could not subdue the great buffalo demon Mahisha. Because of his victory over the gods, Mahisha triumphantly claimed a place in heaven. The gods assembled together to resolve the situation.

Each one emitted fiery energies. The collective outpouring of their energies formed the body of a beautiful woman. This great being of light was Durga. Her splendor spread throughout the universe. She easily vanquished the demon.[456] Hindus believe that Durga manifests herself again and again in order to protect the world and all God's children.

Durga's seed syllable, or bija mantra, is *Dum* (pronounced *doom*). Another mantra honoring Durga is *Om Dum Durgaye Namaha*.

Kali

Kali is the most fearsome of Shiva's consorts. She is depicted as dark blue in color with fierce, blazing eyes. Kali is usually shown with a terrifying countenance, her tongue protruding, wearing a necklace of human skulls or heads and a belt of severed arms. In one hand she holds a sword, in the others she may hold the severed head of a demon, a shield or a noose; her hands may also make the sign of fearlessness and offer blessings and benefits.

Kali's dread appearance symbolizes her boundless power. Her destructiveness is seen as ultimately leading to transformation and salvation. The object of her wrath is not the outer form of man but his inner delusions. She shatters the delusions of the ego and destroys ignorance, even as she brings blessings to those who seek to know God. She destroys the form and substance of human creations (with the white-fire, blue-lightning and ruby-ray action of her sword) that are not aligned with the will of her consort, thus liberating those who seek the knowledge of God. Kali is a symbol of destruction, yet she bestows blessings upon those who seek knowledge of God, and she is revered by her devotees as the Divine Mother.

Shiva is at times depicted dancing in cremation grounds, called burning ghats. The burning ground symbolizes the heart that is barren of desire, for all ego and illusion have been burnt away. Hence, the true ascetic seeks to make a burning ground of his heart so that Shiva might abide and dance there.

Like Shiva, Kali dances in the hearts of devotees who have purified themselves by renunciation. One famed Bengali hymn addressed to Kali says: "Because thou lovest the burning-ground, I have made a burning-ground of my heart—that thou, Dark One, haunter of the burning-ground, mayest dance thy eternal dance."

The Indian state of Bengal is the land of the deepest devotion to Kali. Ramakrishna was one of her famous Bengali devotees. He saw Kali as a manifestation of the Highest Reality, one with Brahman. Paramahansa Yogananda, the Bengali saint and yogi who came to live in America, also had profound experiences with Kali, who heard and answered his prayers.

Kali's bija mantra is *Krim* (pronounced *kreem*). Another mantra honoring Kali is *Om Krim Kalikaye Namaha*.

❖ **THE SNOW KING AND QUEEN, Rulers of an Ancient Golden Age**

The Snow King and Snow Queen ruled an ancient civilization where Greenland now is. They are twin flames who represented the Father-Mother principle as rulers of that civilization that reached its height long before the Ice Age.

Gautama Buddha spoke of the Snow King and Queen: "These twin flames once ruled an ancient civilization, tropical in nature, that was where Greenland is today and covered a good part of the North Pole. Blessed ones, when the ages changed and the inversions took place, thus they were remembered for the end of their period as the Snow King and the Snow Queen.

"Thus, you understand how the white-fire light may also descend, and that which was once green and lush and beautiful as a Garden of Eden, even as a Lemurian paradise, might be covered over with a white-fire/blue-fire energy of the sun. And thus, the age of snow comes as a purification of the etheric plane, purifying even the physical body and preparing once again for a new order.

"Thus, all things in their cycles have a cosmic purpose. And that which was once snow may blossom again and become the pink and the gold and the violet hues and the azure blue and the light of many worlds twinkling, sparkling in tropical waters that show all manner of opportunity of life-forms moving toward the sun."[457]

In 1979, the Elohim Purity and Astrea also spoke of their service: "The mighty Snow King and Queen, who keep the flame of crystalline purity from the North unto the South Pole and hold the balance of Alpha and Omega, now hold in the earth the blanketing of white light wherever our chelas are present. Therefore, the mighty light of God does now release its rays. And we are blessed to have begun with you this day a twenty-four-hour cycle from midnight unto midnight when all of the hosts of heaven are gathered, garlanding the earth with white flowers of every sort—roses and lilies, lilies of the valley and gardenia, the jasmine light."[458]

The Snow King and Queen work with the beings of the elements to hold the balance in nature and in the four lower bodies of the planet. Their "snow" glistens with the radiance sometimes of pink, sometimes gold, sometimes blue, violet or green, depending on the action they desire to accomplish through purity's focuses on this planet.

They are cosmic beings of great attainment and stature, having great love for the evolutions whom they serve. Theirs is a tremendous momentum of purity that may be invoked to blanket an entire area with a dazzling white radiance of purity's flame. This blanket may be used to stay the hand of riot, war, oppression, revolution and the uncontrolled masses. Their focus of purity often manifests as physical snow.

❖ **THE SOLAR LOGOI**

The Solar Logoi are cosmic beings who transmit the light emanations of the Godhead flowing from Alpha and Omega in the Great Central Sun to the planetary systems. They are also called Solar Lords.

The Solar Logoi maintain the tone and the sound of the Logos, or Word, that sustains the creation. We are all a part of the vastness of the Solar Logoi, and they are a part of us.

We look to the Solar Logoi as the great cosmic teachers at the summit of hierarchy from whom our dispensations originate. (A dispensation is a grant of energy that we can use to fulfill our mission and serve others on this planet who need this energy.) The dispensations we receive start with the Solar Logoi and move through the Great Cosmic Council to the Four and Twenty Elders, to the Lords of Karma and then to an individual master who delivers them to his disciples. The dispensations of the Solar Logoi are for the advancement of the peoples of earth. They are opportunities for souls of light to come up higher and accelerate on their path.

❖ **THE SPIRIT OF CHRISTMAS**

The Spirit of Christmas is a being of great light and Buddhic attainment. Lanello speaks of this great being and the light this one bears: "The one known as the Spirit of Christmas is therefore come to tell of the birth of Jesus Christ against the backdrop of nature's darkest hour of the year. The announcement at winter solstice of his star appearing is a great drama of cosmos; and it is here to teach us that in the darkest night of man's longing, there does appear the star of hope and the birth of the Saviour.

"I enter the Spirit of Christmas so that you may understand that it is entirely possible for more than one son of God to participate in a holy office, to co-occupy the divine intent upon the twig that is bent, upon the very point, the focal point of a quartz crystal embracing a world of fiery intent. Dear hearts, I therefore come as the Spirit of Christmas, as you might anticipate the coming of the one known as Santa Claus.

"Remember the heart of a child—your child, yourself—thinking about the coming of Santa and how he would enter the house, and how you would leave him cookies and milk and perhaps even a snack for the reindeer. Remember how, in fullest belief, because your parents had told you, you entered into that Spirit of Santa. And remember also the disappointment upon learning that Santa was not real.

"But this is not true! Santa *is* real. And I am here to tell you that Santa Claus himself is the typical vessel of the Spirit of Christmas, the one who embodies this very Presence that I have entered.

"It is wrong to tell children that Santa is not real. It is right to explain to them the Spirit of Christmas is indeed a person—a person made real in God, a person who is a cosmic being, who fills the hearts of the people with the anticipation of the greatest gift of all, the gift of personal Christhood.

"Those things that bring delight to children—games and toys and things and rings in stockings—beloved hearts, originally the gifts given to the child of every heart were intended to enhance the child's perception and realization of that Person of Christ. When you think about the gifts that are given these days, you realize that some gifts do assist the individual in a greater sense of identity, while others adorn the outer person and tend to create more maya of idolatry. And thus, attaching importance and attention to the outer self, the individual loses the great opportunity of this hour to truly enter into the heart of that cosmic being known as the Spirit of Christmas.

"Therefore, beloved ones, understand that this Spirit embodies the collective consciousness of Christhood of the entire Spirit of the Great White Brotherhood—of all ascended beings and angels and masters, cosmic hosts of the LORD who are that Christ. Let us realize, then, that in all symbols there is Reality; in archetypes there is the original pattern of the image made perfect out of Christ; and in Santa Claus himself is the lingering hope in all that the figure of the Cosmic Christ will come to bring the true joy, the joy of the heart filled with love."[459]

❖ **THE SPIRIT OF SELFLESSNESS**

The Spirit of Selflessness is a cosmic being from out the Great Central Sun. Selfless, spiritual, divine love is almost unknown on our planet. For the most part mankind exhibit selfishness and self-love. The great Spirit of Selflessness explains that the less aware of self you become, the more of God you retain. In this Spirit is the all-consuming power of the action that will transform selfhood into Godhood, even while retaining the individualization of a God flame.

The life of Saint Francis demonstrated the spirit of selflessness. In his prayer "Lord, make me an instrument of thy peace," Saint Francis desired to convey the comforting aspects of the Holy Spirit, realizing that his God Self and not his lower self was the source of that peace. He knew that by letting God's peace flow through him like the wind rustling in the trees, he would become one with the Spirit, hence one with all life that proceedeth therefrom. Because his prayer to the Holy Spirit was utterly selfless, it left an indelible imprint upon the consciousness of mankind and elemental life.

The Spirit of Selflessness says: "I am the fullness of the All-One. For only in the spirit of selflessness can you be aware of the allness of Being. For the awareness of a self apart from God is a shadow that prevails to separate, to prevent the fullness of consciousness from coalescing a cosmos about the flame of identity....

"The woes and the disturbances and the upheavals [that we see in the world] are these planetary adjustments that mankind would not have if they would only understand the spirit of selflessness. It is not a false humility; it is not a false pride. It is an awareness of the circumference of God and of the dot inside—the point of contact that is the Self of God with which you totally identify. And therefore you are not deprived of the identity when you embrace this spirit, but you have the return of the allness of Being."[460]

Archangel Michael spoke of his own sacrifice, total surrender and unending service and asked us to also become the spirit of selflessness, telling us that when we are, "you will discover the key to the courage, the honor and the bravery of my legions. For in selflessness, there is no self that can live or die, for that self merely is, always has been, and ever shall be. Selflessness—without the human self and fully endued with the Divine

Self, beloved, you are never a target in this octave.

"Thus, if you stick out a little itty-bitty toe outside the circle of your service, blessed ones, be prepared. For that little toe of self-awareness in the human, finite condition will render you vulnerable. Stand on and in the circle of infinity, beloved, and know that it is an armour beneath you. And one day it shall be a dais from which there shall spring spontaneously, in the presence of Serapis Bey, truly, the ascension flame."[461]

The Maha Chohan has spoken of this great being: "You received the dictation of the Spirit of Selflessness in the heart of the Great Central Sun in this very city. That individualization of the God flame is such a consecration of Alpha and Omega that that individuality was veiled from your eyes and from your awareness, for you yourself would be astounded to know how much power and how much wisdom and how much love can be contained in the life of the individual who has become the selfless one. But as you pursue this path, you will come more and more in contact with that one who lives in the Sun behind the sun of your own being, a great cosmic consciousness."[462]

❖ **THE SPIRIT OF THE RESURRECTION**

The cosmic being known as the Spirit of the Resurrection bears the flame of resurrection, a mother-of-pearl color, to bring new life and to overcome the consciousness of death and hell.

The Spirit of the Resurrection says: "I AM the flaming presence of the resurrection. I AM the fire of Easter morn. I come out of the whirlwind of the sacred fire that is God and I AM that consciousness of regeneration, resurrection that lives and moves and breathes in the heart of the Flame. I AM that flaming presence. I AM that identification with God, with solar fire, compelling all of life to rise higher into the fullness of the action of the Law....

"You must understand that without the crucifixion there can be no resurrection. Therefore, in the spirit of the resurrection I come, as holy Mary,[463] to anoint your bodies with oil against the day of your burying, the burying of mortality, of the carnal consciousness. That is the symbol of the crucifixion."[464]

This cosmic being speaks of the first resurrection and the second resurrection: "I speak to you of your emergence from the world of darkness and your coming into the light as your first resurrection on the day when you declare, 'This day I am born of God, I am a son of God, I am in the flame of God and I know who I am!'

"This is your resurrection from the tomb of death and darkness and of the false generations of the worldly ones. On this day of days, then, when you accept that new birth in resurrection's fires, you begin the path of initiation. You begin the way that leads to the second resurrection, after which you will have then put on that garment that will enable you to stand in the presence of Luxor and the priests of the sacred fire in preparation for your ascension in the light."[465]

"Wherever any man or any woman stands before the initiators in the Great Pyramid, before the tomb where the old self is laid, where the new self will stand forth, wherever men and women of righteousness are found waiting upon the LORD to partake of the glorious realization of oneness, there I am, the Spirit of the Resurrection, to initiate the spiral of victory.

"There is no other presence, no other power, no other knowing than that of flaming victory. Trust, then, in God. Trust in him who is thy life. Trust in every heart flame that glows in resurgence, in support of heaven's good will.

"I am that fiery trial. I am in the center of the fire. I build the furnace. I push you through the door and I compel you to dissolve that human consciousness in the fire, the sacred fire that is the coolness of the Maha Chohan, the Great Lord who embodies the very breath and consciousness of the Holy Spirit."[466]

❖ SPONSORS OF YOUTH

The Sponsors of Youth are twelve cosmic beings from the Great Central Sun who have been answering the prayers of mothers, fathers and sponsors of youth for aeons. They were permitted to speak for the first time in 1977 at the conference entitled "God Is Mother" by a dispensation from the Cosmic Council and the four and twenty elders. They had been allowed to unveil their identity because Keepers of the Flame had implored God for dispensations to save the youth of the world for many months.

During this dictation, the Sponsors of Youth said they could not place the fullness of the weight of their light on earth because "insufficient energies" had been invoked to hold the balance. Thus, they projected their Electronic Presence on earth from the Great Central Sun for that dictation. The Sponsors of Youth came with a sobering report on the condition of the youth of the world. This report was based on a study conducted by the Keeper of the Scrolls, ascended masters and archangels, with input at inner levels from those in embodiment.

The Sponsors of Youth reported: "The unmitigated attempts of the fallen angels to interfere with the upward spiral of the culture of the Mother have been directed for a number of decades against the youth and incoming souls. The darkness projected against the mind, soul, heart, body, chakras, health and sanity has been relentless. These attacks begin at the moment the Lords of Karma assign a soul to incarnate and continue through the age of thirty-three."[467]

To Almighty God the most important people on earth are those who are just conceived and are in the womb and those who are maturing through the age of thirty-three (seven years for each of the four lower bodies and five for the secret rays). All these are considered the youth. When an individual passes the age of thirty-three, there is what is known as "the hardening of the spiral," the setting of the habit patterns for life. After this age, it is more difficult for a soul to be converted to the path of light.

The Sponsors of Youth warn that the attack on youth has been so great that "the state of children and youth today is at one of the lowest points it has ever been since the days of the fall of Atlantis, since the days of the coming of Noah.... It was the desecration of the flame of holy youth that resulted in the ultimate judgment of Almighty God upon the people. It is one thing for the adult, hardened in the ways of sin, to perpetuate his sin. But when that sin is transferred to innocent children and they are corrupted and allowed to be corrupted by the population,...then the entire civilization must be judged."

The conclusion of the report was: "There are such gaps in the understanding of the youth of their origin, their source, their purpose, the flow of purity, the right uses of the sacred fire, what the goal of life is, the path of initiation to the ascension, that if this body and this company of light-bearers is not able to reverse the tide by keeping the vigil for the youth, there is the possibility of the loss of this generation. And if this generation be lost, there will be none to pass the torch to succeeding generations. We are calling for an all-out commitment, therefore, of Keepers of the Flame to the cause of the youth."[468]

The Sponsors of Youth gave their second dictation in 1992. Their spokesman said: "It is a most serious hour in earth's history.... I will tell you just how dire the situation is, for I speak for us all, and I say, beloved, this *is* the warfare of the Spirit, and the fallen angels have determined to so sever one generation from the next that inside of a hundred years this earth may de-evolve to such a lesser state that you could not even recognize it.... Therefore we say to you: Hurry, hurry, hurry! These children in the earth, whether they have retained the flame or not, are being set upon by such darkness in so many subtle ways.... Your aches and pains are minor in comparison to the aches and pains of those [children and youth] who cry out to you. It is as though they were partly in the astral plane, in hell itself, while they are in embodiment."[469]

In these two dictations the Sponsors of Youth have outlined several steps you can take to help save the children:

Step One: Observe what is happening. These masters said: "The cries of the children reach out to you! And yet there is still a separation between you and them, almost as though a veil covered your eyes and you did not see and would not see what is happening to these little ones and [the young people].... It is time you entered those schoolhouses and observed for yourselves" what is happening. "It is good to allow yourselves to sense world pain, especially the pain of children."

Step Two: Keep a vigil of prayers. The Sponsors of Youth say: "Pray and pray—and pray on your knees if you must." Keep a vigil of prayers to the heart of the Divine Mother and the Immaculate Heart of Mary, and to all hosts of the LORD that you can name. Keep that prayer vigil! Turn off your TV sets, deny yourselves fictionalized series. Keep abreast of the news, stop watching those series, use all of your free time decreeing for the children from birth to age thirty-three.

"Begin with the absolute conviction that the all-power of God is able to manifest through you" through the science of the spoken Word. The Sponsors of Youth have also asked us to "demand the judgment of abortion and the abortionist." Abortion is not only the abortion of flesh and blood, but it is the abortion of a soul's opportunity to fulfill her divine plan. Today more than ever, you can look around you and see there are vacant seats. Where is your twin flame? Where is your soul mate? Where will you find them? Will you find that they have been aborted and tried and tried again to reincarnate? This is a very difficult time for young people, because everyone who is supposed to be here of their generation is simply not here because millions of abortions have been committed.

The Sponsors of Youth also summoned us to use the spoken Word to exorcise the schoolhouses, colleges and universities of the seed of Satan and Lucifer. "Every individual who is acquainted with the science of the spoken Word must stand up and be counted for in this hour for the youth of the world!" They have never needed your prayers as much as they do today. The Sponsors of Youth gave us the following keys to enhance our decrees: "Plaster the walls of your homes with pictures of children.... Ask for millions of children to be cut free through those focuses. You might also keep a picture of an aborted fetus to remind you every day of your life that children are being aborted, children whom we are sending from the Central Sun."

Step Three: Become involved. The Sponsors of Youth urged us not to sit on the sidelines but to get involved in rescuing the youth. They said:

"When it comes to assisting the youth, there is no substitute for active personal involvement, for becoming a part of their lives—their work and play, their school and sports and their putting-on of the garment of God." Call to the Great Divine Director, the God and Goddess Meru and the Committee for Child Guidance—made up of Jesus, Kuthumi and Mother Mary—to help you understand what your personal role should be.

If we neglect the child, we are neglecting the Christ within a very special person. The Sponsors of Youth warned: "Remember the children. For in the not-too-distant future you, yourself, may be a child again...and as a child, you shall reap the karma you incurred in your last life, this life, for having ignored so great an opportunity and so great a salvation that you could have, and should have, given to the little children.... I warn you: be purged of all selfishness, laziness, sloth, boredom or energy that simply manifests as 'I don't care. I don't have time to work with children or the teens. I will sit in my home and I will do my decrees. And that is all I am willing to give.'"

Step Four: Befriend a child. The Sponsors of Youth encourage us to become a close friend of a child or a teenager. They said: "It's not enough to pass by the children and just say, 'hello.' With reverence for life and with respect for the Holy Child, you must realize that friendship with the world's children can become the greatest joy of your life. When you count your friends, do you count the little children who are so adorable and adoring, who are so devoted to you? And sometimes you scarcely notice how their hearts are pitter-patting in anticipation of a kind word, in anticipation of your coming, your smile or a game that you will play with them."

Step Five: Be an example to children. The Sponsors of Youth said: "Children require your example. Our records show that many children growing up have only the example of Hollywood stars, rock-and-roll stars, representatives in government who have betrayed them by dishonesty, and teachers and parents who have not the capacity to transfer to them the image of the Christ, the Buddha and the Mother. Souls of light must see the example of Almighty God in someone." And that someone is you. "The candle of virtue, held by a single individual, will remain the star of hope to that child. Every child must know someone who represents the divine memory of the child's activities on the inner planes with the ascended masters and the angelic hosts. Our plea to you this day is that you will be that soul of virtue, that example to these children, to the teenagers of the world, and to those who are grappling with the problems of life in their twenties and preparing for the initiations of Christhood and Buddhahood.

"You are on stage twenty-four hours a day. Souls of light upon earth are receiving the impression of your aura, whether you compromise or refuse to compromise. And that energy is affecting the total evolution of the lightbearers of the world."

Step Six: Teach children reading, writing and math. "Teach your children how to read phonetically. To teach children reading, writing and arithmetic before the age of seven is the solemn responsibility of every parent and every single person who calls himself a lightbearer. Go out and find them! Make room for them in your homes. Offer to teach them anywhere their parents will allow. There shall be many, many blessings upon those who have the courage to teach children to read and write and to calculate their numbers."

Step Seven: Give lectures or publish exposés on the issues endangering our youth. The Sponsors of Youth directed us: "Do not cease until there is an exposure in paperback form of every betrayal of the Christ in the youth of America and the world. Let the books be written. Whatever your participation, whatever your support, both near and distant, know that we in the Great Central Sun watch every lifestream who is able to give even an hour of decrees each day in support of our messenger, our cause and the dissemination of this teaching."

The Sponsors of Youth tell us: "Plunge yourself and your life into the support of children…. This is the most serious message you will ever hear from the ascended masters, for it is the message of the loss of this nation and ultimately other nations in the earth if you do not act and act in time."

❖ **SRI MAGRA**

Sri Magra was Lord of the World before Sanat Kumara. Kuthumi refers to Sri Magra as one of the wisest masters of old. In reference to souls being attracted to one another solely on the basis of karma, Kuthumi quotes Sri Magra as saying: "Affinities are the 'fine ties' that are established in the perfect balance of the heart where the natural affections are enhanced by the feeling of delight in givingness as well as in a gracious state of receptivity."[470] Sri Magra has now gone on to cosmic service.

❖ **SURYA, Hierarch of the God Star**

Surya is a cosmic being from Sirius. He wields the tremendous power of the God Star on behalf of the evolutions of earth. His flame is an intense blue tinged with white.

Surya appears in the mythology and religion of India as both the Sun and the Sun God. The Sanskrit word *surya* comes from the root *sur* or *svar,* meaning "to shine."

During the medieval period in India, worshipers of Surya formed one of the five principal sects. Worship of Surya ranked with the worship of Shiva, Shakti, Vishnu and Ganesha. The importance of the Sun God Surya is evident in Vedic hymns and Hindu mythology. The Gayatri hymn from the Rig-Veda identifies Surya with the Hindu Trinity. The hymn is addressed to the sun and associates Brahma with the sun in the morning, Shiva with the sun at midday, and Vishnu with the sun in the evening. The worship of Surya is mentioned repeatedly in the Ramayana, the oldest epic in Sanskrit literature. After offering a prayer to Surya, Rama overcomes his enemy with ease.

Surya

Surya is traditionally depicted seated on a lotus in a chariot of gold drawn by seven horses or by a single horse with seven heads. He crosses the sky observing the good and bad deeds of both mortals and immortals. Surya's chariot is usually depicted with only one wheel. The one wheel is seen as symbolic of the straight path of justice he maintains. The charioteer is the deity of the dawn, who rides in front of Surya, using his body to shelter the world from Surya's brilliant rays.

One Hindu myth relates that the sun-god Surya married the daughter of the celestial architect of the gods. She found Surya's radiance too strong to bear and ran away. Surya pursued his wife and after a long search found her. Once they were reunited, the architect of the gods refashioned Surya so that his wife would be able to remain with him. While singing praises to the sun god, the architect cut away his excessive radiance, keeping intact just a fraction of his original glory in spherical shape. Out of the excess radiance, he created weapons for various gods, including Shiva's trident. Surya remained

Temple to Surya, Konarak, India

resplendent in spite of his alteration. He and his wife had many sons. The eldest was Vaivasvata Manu, who in Hindu tradition is the progenitor of the human race. We know Vaivasvata Manu as the manu of the fifth root race.

One of the most famous temples dedicated to Surya is the colossal thirteenth-century Surya Deula (Sun

Temple) at Konarak in the state of Orissa, India. This one-hundred-foot-high temple and its hall are designed in the shape of a giant chariot borne on twelve carved stone wheels and drawn by seven stone horses. Today the worship of Surya as the supreme deity is limited to one small sect, but an image of Surya is in every Hindu temple.

The ascended masters teach that God Surya is the hierarch of the God Star, Sirius. Sirius is the brightest star in the heavens and is the seat of God-government for this sector of the galaxy. Sirius (known to the outer world as the "Dog Star") is known by astronomers to be a binary star of the constellation Canis Major. Sirius A, the brighter of the two stars, is a blue-white star that is twenty-three times as bright as our sun. Sirius B is a white dwarf star that is not visible to the naked eye. In the revolving of the lesser sun around the greater, we see the devotion of chela Cuzco to the guru Surya.

In a spiritual sense, all have come from Sirius. It is our point of origin and our home at the deepest level of our being. As Jesus said "In my Father's house are many mansions.... I go to prepare a place for you,"[471] so we understand that there is indeed a mansion, a castle of light on Sirius, our original home that we left so long ago. Surya says: "Any number of you hail from the God Star and count it as your home base, as you have volunteered to serve with angels from Sirius and to enter these octaves of maya."[472]

Sanat Kumara spoke of the God Star in 1979: "When we speak of the God Star, we speak of a plane of consciousness where life has accelerated to etheric perfection and to the octaves of light beyond the highest frequencies yet within the range of what is called Matter. The planes of heaven beyond the planes of time and space are exalted in the God Star through the God consciousness of the vast being known as Surya. Surya, the Great Guru, and his chela, the ascended master Cuzco, are the ensouling divinities of these two points of light that move as one—as Alpha and Omega in a positive/negative polarity."[473]

From the God Star, Surya holds the balance for natural forces in the earth. He is assisted by the ascended master Cuzco, whose etheric retreat is at Viti Levu in the Fiji Islands in the South Pacific. This retreat comes under the hierarchy of Sirius. Cuzco journeys back and forth between the earth and Sirius to make his report before the twenty-four elders and the Sun God and Goddess of the God Star.

Surya is very much involved with the Lord Jesus Christ in the judgment of the fallen angels. He has promised to place his Electronic Presence wherever you are and wherever the fallen angels are on the entire face of the earth. You can visualize this mighty being Surya anywhere and everywhere on the face of the earth, seated in the lotus posture as a mighty Buddha of light.

For problems that seem impossible to solve, give a novena to Surya using his decree.[474] The response will be a very deep penetration of your being and world. Although the results may take time to manifest, the liberation is powerful and yet sometimes almost imperceptible, because it occurs at such deep levels of being.

In 1989, Surya spoke of our home on the God Star: "I affirm the origin of the sons and daughters of God at the point of the God Star, Sirius. I affirm this focus of the Great Central Sun as a point of origin for many who pass through earth's schoolroom at this hour. Thus I come to reinforce the Order of the Blue Rose of Sirius, and I come to remind all of your fealty to the Order of the First Ray.

"And thus, I desire to enable you to understand how the beloved El Morya, Son of Sirius, devotee of the will of God, is the lord of the first ray for a reason—that reason being, beloved, that he does tarry in the earth for the training in the path of chelaship of those who are descended from that God Star and need the sharpening of the mind, the soul, the heart and the desire body according to a path of devotion and service, according to a true activity of the Gemini mind of God that is truly founded in that will, that holy will, which is the grid of light of the divine plan.

"If you can visualize the complex geometric form of earth itself, of a sphere, then understand that it is your congruency with that spherical pattern that does raise you to the vibration of Sirius, that does become the open door to the purity of Sirius and the open door to the return to that home of light.

"This is our call to you, then, who are beginning to remember that you are pilgrims passing through earth's schoolroom and that you have upon our star of light homes of truly great magnificence. You have left there and you have left great palaces and the golden age that is perpetual and the evolution with lifewaves who are in constant contact with their teachers....

"Come ye, then, into alignment with the God Star. For this reason beloved Astrea and Purity have established this arc between the God Star and the earth.[475] I suggest that you take a moment when our star is visible to you to face that Central Sun and to give the mantra 'I AM Alpha and Omega... I AM Alpha and Omega in the white-fire core of Being.'

"Blessed ones, the mantra of the affirmation of ourselves where you are as 'I AM THAT I AM God Surya and Cuzco in my heart and soul and mind!' will enable us to anchor within you these currents. And believe me, beloved ones, there are currents from the stars! There are rays that do descend, and those rays are vital in the development of the spirituality of souls and of their chakras."[476]

❖ **GOD OF THE SWISS ALPS, Guardian of the Flame in Central Europe**

The God of the Swiss Alps is the guardian of the threefold flame that is anchored in the Swiss Alps as a focus of liberty in Central Europe. The radiance of his aura is a glacier blue, and he has many devas, elementals and legions of angels serving under him. The pulsations from the threefold flame within his retreat were felt by William Tell in the early fourteenth century.

Northern Europe is under the blue and yellow plumes, and Southern Europe is under the pink plume as the result of the direction of the plumes of the threefold flame anchored in his retreat. Thus, the destiny of nations is always determined by the invisible God flames anchored in their midst, unbeknownst to the people who fulfill the law of their being but seldom know the reason why. Even in Switzerland itself, there are three distinct centers of influence that come forth from the threefold flame and four official languages. German, French, Italian and Romansch.

In the German-Swiss, one feels the precision of the blue plume, the devotion to law and order as foremost in the people's consciousness. In the French-Swiss and Italian-Swiss, the action of the love plume is more dominant; whereas illumination's flame rays toward the East. Nevertheless, since there is the spiral action of the flame, we find a definite balance of all three phases of the Christ consciousness throughout this beautiful country as well as throughout Northern and Southern Europe.

The pattern of the four lower bodies is represented in the four national languages of Switzerland, with the threefold flame in the center focused

near the Lac des Quatres-Cantons ("the lake of four cantons," or states) focusing the Christ within the center of the four lower bodies. This is the archetypal pattern for the development of the God consciousness within all nations of the world as well as the control of the four lower bodies and

Lac des Quatres-Cantons

their harmonious cooperation in order that the flame of freedom might not perish from the earth.

❖ **GOD TABOR, God of the Mountains**

The ascended master God Tabor, the "God of the Mountains," governs the mountain ranges of North and Central America. God Tabor is eight feet tall, and his fragrance is the essence of pine. He works closely with the God of Gold.

In *Ascended Master Discourses,* the ascended lady master Pearl speaks of meeting God Tabor when she was in embodiment. She went to Table Mountain with Rex, Nada and Godfre, where, as she says, "I felt impelled to go away a short distance by myself and there before me was this great majestic being, the God Tabor.

"As he talked to me, I realized—just through a mighty flash of feeling—that we were all being directed by a mighty intelligence, clothed in a dazzling form of light. I want to tell you precious ones, that Cyclopea, Arcturus, the God Meru, the God Tabor and the God Himalaya are beings, who, the first time one sees them, seem almost terrifying in their majesty, their beauty, the intensity of their light, and the perfection which they are. Yet, with all that great and wondrous power, as gentle as a mother with her child whom she loves more than anything in the world. When it is necessary, like a flash of lightning, their limitless power can be released, which is to perform a given service."[477]

God Tabor is very concerned about the burden upon elemental life. He says: "Call for Helios and Vesta to come forth. Call for my mantle—the mantle of God Tabor. Know and understand, beloved, that when you heal elementals and you bring them to the point of understanding how they might one day receive the chalice of a threefold flame—this is indeed the greatest gift that you could ever give to elemental life.

"Beloved, you are all very busy. The Lords of Karma are busy. The hierarchs are busy—all have so many things to do. But you must stop and say, 'We cannot neglect elemental life; indeed, we must serve elemental life and bring them to the place where they can once again believe in themselves and call forth their threefold flame.'

"If elementals felt they could earn that threefold flame, they would work diligently with you. But in some cases, they have again lost all hope for recovering that manifestation. Thus, as you know, elementals pass from the screen of life never to return, for they do not have that threefold flame.

"Sometimes it is nice to go into the forests and the mountains throughout the world to see the scenery. As you do this, always remember the four kingdoms of elemental beings and consider what you can and shall do with them and for them."[478]

In 1964, Tabor said: "I come to you tonight to speak to you primarily of the 'silent ones,' those souls that have drawn apart at various times in their lives to commune in the quiet places of the world with the power that was derived from their eternal source. The world is enriched by countless numbers of these blessed souls....

"Therefore, precious ones of the light, those who are with me, the Gods of the Mountains, desire to expand in your consciousness a new sense of the 'lonely ones.' 'Come apart. Come out from among them and be ye a separate people,' saith the LORD thy God. So long as you are of the world you cannot be of the immortal kingdom. Ultimately, one by one they shall all step forth and be counted in the ranks of God. Now as the lonely ones, one by one in your various communities, not desiring to be thought wise of men but seeking an eternal city of God, as Augustine, the saint of old, you shall pursue your divine destiny."[479]

Tabor has two retreats in North America's Rocky Mountains. One of these retreats, opened on April 14, 1968, is located in the front range of the Rocky Mountains above Colorado Springs. This focus of the will of God forms an arch of blue flame from the Temple of Good Will in Darjeeling. From his retreat, Tabor radiates the protection of the first ray through the mountain ranges in North and Central America.

❖ **TARA,** *See* **White Goddess**

❖ **THEOSOPHIA, Goddess of Wisdom**

The master we know today as the Goddess of Wisdom served in the Temple of Illumination on Atlantis. She was later embodied as Mary of Bethany, the sister of Martha and Lazarus during the time of Jesus. In her final embodiment as Mary Baker Eddy (1821–1910), she was commissioned by Jesus the Christ, the ascended master Hilarion (the apostle Paul) and Mother Mary to set forth certain revelations on the science of the immaculate concept, which she published in *Science and Health with Key to the Scriptures* and other writings and lectures collected under the heading of *Prose Works.*

After her ascension, Mary Baker Eddy took up the office in hierarchy of Theosophia, Goddess of Wisdom, which had long been held by another one known as Theosophia, a being of great attainment in focusing the feminine aspect of the wisdom ray. This cosmic being went on to cosmic service when Mary Baker Eddy assumed this office and the name and title associated with it.

Mary Baker Eddy

Mary Baker Eddy founded the Christian Science movement in the late nineteenth century. She had a very intense contact with the Sacred Heart of Jesus, because she was so close to Jesus in his Galilean embodiment. She understood and taught that Jesus' healings demonstrated spiritual law, that Jesus was the Son of man and that the Christ was the eternal principle that he outpictured, and that Jesus set an example for us to follow.

Mary Baker Eddy was an instruments of the Lord's

healing, but her attempts to define the religion of Christ fell short of the powerful mantle of healing that was upon her. The healing that flowed through her far exceeded the limited matrix of the teaching she delivered. After her transition in 1910, she went to the etheric temples in the octaves of light, from where she made her ascension thirty years later.

In her own life, Mary Baker Eddy demonstrated great perseverance in overcoming poor health as well as in meeting legal and media attacks and opposition from organized religion. She was beset in the early years by a series of court cases that stirred public controversy and raised questions concerning her doctrine, organization and followers. Some of the litigation was vengefully initiated by former associates who had defected from the movement, and some by Mrs. Eddy herself in defense of her teachings. Although she was vilified in the press, for the most part she emerged victorious from each case.

Theosophia speaks of her own preparation for the mission of her final lifetime: "There are any number of embodiments that I had between that two thousand years from the time of Mary of Bethany to the time of Mary Baker Eddy. And during these centuries I myself passed through the initiations with the saints in the Church and even in the East and did study under the great Lights as I prepared for this mission.

"Therefore, beloved, I studied under those who gave me the teachings of the control of nature and natural forces. And I was gifted, by the grace of God, whereby through this teaching and writing of Christian Science many were healed. But it was truly by the grace of God and my oneness with Christ Jesus."[480]

Theosophia teaches the practical application of the wisdom of the Christ in daily life. She also teaches about healing and wholeness and the science of the immaculate concept: "I have lived again and again to set forth the truth of the ages. It is ever the light of the Divine Theosophia to give unto the children of God the awareness of the unreality of death. This is the foundation of all of the teaching of the Mother. For you see, if you can understand that death is not real, then all that leads to death must also be unreal.

"Understand, then, that to see through the mists and the maya and to understand that only God is Real is the way to heal and to hold the immaculate concept for yourself. But the fallen ones who come with their degradation and condemnation, they would always have you believe the fundamental lie that death is real because the sin that produced it is real.

"You must be scientific with your sword of Truth; for the Mother is always scientific, and so her children learn the ways of science. Unfortunately, they have taken the material science and excluded the spiritual science. This is why the Mother must appear again and again and speak the word of Truth and point the way and point to him who taught, 'I AM the way, the truth, and the life.' In that blessed mantra is the understanding that Christ as light is the way—the way out of all human strife and error and that which is apart from the Real. And the truth of being is that God does heal. God does bring together the harmony of consciousness and of Matter. God is the great Spirit of healing in this age."[481]

Theosophia is also very concerned about the correct education of children: "I come to you also with the mantle of the Divine Mother, for I embody wisdom, and I am called Theosophia. Yet, I have occupied this office for not quite a century, so recently embodied have I been....

"I surely would sponsor every school that you would open. You can start with one child, two or three, your own, the neighbors', those who come from homes where parents simply will not place their children in the hands of those who will manipulate their minds toward the left-handed path slowly, imperceptibly, until one fine day they are locked in the grips of forces that neither parents nor teachers can defy.

"Thus, be grateful that you have the call and so great a call and so great a science—developed and continued by the messengers, performed by yourselves—whereby you can bring forth from heaven a response far beyond that warranted or merited by your own present level of attainment. This dispensation comes because you call in the name of your mighty I AM Presence and your Holy Christ Self."[482]

❖ **THÉRÈSE OF LISIEUX, The Little Flower of Jesus**

Saint Thérèse of Lisieux was a nineteenth-century French Carmelite nun known as the Little Flower of Jesus. From her childhood she wanted to become a saint and to become perfected in God. Her deep desire to be constant to the will of God, to his wisdom and to his love led Thérèse to

Thérèse of Lisieux

live a life of self-sacrifice and self-immolation and to put all of the strength of her heart's love into drawing souls into the light of Jesus Christ. She ascended at the conclusion of her brief life.

She was born Marie-Françoise-Thérèse Martin, January 2, 1873, in Alençon, France. At the age of fourteen, Thérèse had such an ardent desire to enter the convent that, on a pilgrimage to Rome with her father, she boldly asked Pope Leo XIII during a public audience for his permission to enter the Carmel at age fifteen. He responded that she would enter "if God wills it." The next year her request was granted by the bishop of Bayeux, and on April 9, 1888, she entered the Carmel at Lisieux where she took the name Sister Thérèse of the Child Jesus and the Holy Face.

She became acting mistress of novices in 1893 and considered it her mission to teach souls her "little way." Her path was a path of love, for, she wrote, "it is only love which makes us acceptable to God." Her favorite works were those of Saint John of the Cross, the Gospels and *The Imitation of Christ*. She desired only "to make God loved as I love Him, to teach souls my little way"—the way of "spiritual childhood, the way of trust and absolute surrender."

With the fire of constancy and the zeal of the apostles, she determined to exemplify the path of simplicity midst a world of sophistication. In April of 1896, Thérèse was found worthy to be accorded the initiation of the crucifixion. She experienced a hemorrhage of the lungs and for a year suffered the agony of the cross that Jesus took upon himself as an atonement for mankind's consciousness of sin. Thérèse bore her burden with the same devotion and trust in God that had marked her mission from the very beginning. In July of 1897, she was sent to the infirmary already wrapped in the ecstasy of the fires of resurrection. She repeated the words day and night, "My God, I love thee." And on September 30, 1897, at the age of twenty-four, she returned to the heart of her greatest love.

During the last two years of her life, Thérèse was asked to write about her childhood memories and her religious life. The manuscript was published one year after Thérèse's death in a book entitled *Histoire d'une Ame (The Story of a Soul)*. It quickly became one of the most widely read spiritual books.

Two of the statements for which Thérèse is most remembered are "I want to spend my heaven in doing good on earth" and "After my death I will let fall a shower of roses," for she foresaw that her activity after her death would be far-reaching and her mission of "making others love God as I love him" would continue. Statues of the saint portray her carrying a bouquet of roses.

After she passed on, Thérèse lost no time doing that good on earth. The convent received thousands of accounts of healings, conversions and intercession attributed to Thérèse. In one moving account, Thérèse appeared to the prioress of an impoverished convent in Italy to give her five hundred francs needed for the debt of the community.[483] During World War I, many of the soldiers who had read Thérèse's autobiography carried relics of her and pinned her picture on the dirt walls of their trenches. One French soldier tells of his harrowing experiences on the front lines. He and others prayed the rosary, and he called to Sister Thérèse. As the battle raged, he suddenly saw her standing at the foot of one of the guns. She said to him, smiling, "Fear not, I come here to protect you." Not one of the soldiers fell, and they soon returned from the battle safe and sound.[484]

Thérèse was canonized on May 17, 1925, less than 28 years after her death. Many miracles have been attributed to her. In 1927 she was declared patroness of foreign missions and of all works for Russia. Her feast day is October 1.

Sometimes we like to think of the saints as having been "born saints." Thérèse's life shows us that this is not so. Thérèse is often remembered as being sweet, loving and obedient. Yet this did not come naturally to her. In fact, when Thérèse was a child, Mrs. Martin characterized her daughter as "unconquerably stubborn."[485]

Thérèse learned how to turn her stubbornness into an iron will. She described how she had a "great victory" in a "certain combat." She writes: "There is in the community a sister who has the faculty of displeasing me in everything, in her ways, her words, her character, everything seems *very disagreeable* to me. And still, she is a holy religious who must be very pleasing to God. Not wishing to give in to the natural antipathy I was experiencing, I told myself that charity must not consist in feelings but in works; then I set myself to doing for this Sister what I would do for the person I loved the most.... I wasn't content simply with praying very much for this Sister who gave me so many struggles, but I took care to render her all the services possible, and when I was tempted to answer her back in a disagreeable manner, I was content with giving her my most friendly smile and with changing the subject of the conversation....

"Frequently, when...I had occasion to work with this Sister, I used to run away like a deserter whenever my struggles became too violent.... Never did she suspect the motives for my conduct, and she remained convinced that her character was very pleasing to me."[486]

The ascended lady master Thérèse of Lisieux has given some insights into her experiences in the heaven-world: "Following my ascension, I was accorded the grant to spend a portion of my heavens on earth. But for another portion, the Father did assign me to study under the three masters El Morya, Koot Hoomi and Djwal Kul. These three wise men, adepts of the East who did come and tend the birth of the Lord Christ, therefore did tend with me the full flowering and birth of that Christ in my being multiplied many times over by their presence after my ascension.

"Therefore, through their hearts I did learn the mysteries of the East, the profundity of the message of the Buddha and his oneness with our Lord. Thread upon thread, they did assist me in weaving and weaving again the fullness of the garment of light that does comprise the whole complement of the teaching of God to this age.

"Therefore, beloved, I had full opportunity to receive that instruction that did fill in for me all of those sacred mysteries that had not been revealed through the established Church. Therefore you understand that much teaching that is given to you in this hour I received at inner levels after my ascension.

"As I did say recently, there are many in the Church who have had the holiness and the sanctity and the purity [prerequisite for sainthood] but because the powers that be in this world who have seated themselves in these positions of power in the Church hierarchy have not seen fit to deliver the Everlasting Gospel to the people, those who qualified for the ascension and for sainthood could not receive that promotion, and therefore they did reincarnate.

"Blessed ones, I desire not to give you any cause for personal pride or spiritual pride, but I am here to tell you that some who are in this place are among those who have reincarnated because they have been 'short-changed,' as you would say, by the Church and its tradition.

"Therefore, beloved, I come to tell you that the way of discipleship can be seen by you as a thousand stairs upon a thousand-tiered golden spiral, and that step by step there is an orderly path of discipline. These masters who have sponsored your messenger and this activity, who have supported Jesus in establishing through the messengers the true Church Universal and Triumphant on earth, have seen fit to also establish an ordered ritual, for they are fully aware what it takes to mount one of these steps.

"The figure of the nun burdened with the cancer in her body, concealing this from all others and occupying herself with the humble task of scrubbing the stairs of the enclave[487] must be seen as archetypal of the soul who, bearing her karma, recognizes that she must clear the debris in each step of consciousness, scrubbing by the violet flame until that level of record and ideation is fully and wholly transmuted. In the process, she may mount a single step. In past ages it would take a soul perhaps an entire lifetime to mount a single step, for the only purging of karma and record and self, as well as its outcropping in the body as disease, would be manifest through prayer and works of penance.

"Thus, beloved, to know 'how great, how great thou art, O God, my Father, my Mother, how great is the gift of the violet flame!' you must establish a co-measurement, a sense of realism that such a gift is also an experiment. For it is a dispensation for which ascended beings of the seventh ray, not the least of whom being your beloved Saint Germain, have given this opportunity. And after a certain lapse of cycles, they will give accounting before the Lords of Karma and the four and twenty elders who stand round the great white throne, and they shall determine whether a people have taken that flame and used it only to deliver themselves of their discomforts, or whether they have used it seriously for the path of initiation as an adjunct, as a mighty assistance to the soul's entering in.

"You must therefore understand that you are watchmen of the night, keeping the watch in your time and in your place as many who have gone before you have kept that watch. In this dark night of the age of the Kali Yuga,* you bear violet-flame torches and torches of illumination with the beloved Mother Liberty. Therefore, beloved, understand that all holy orders have had their rituals and their disciplines and their rules.

"Therefore, those who would serve to keep the flame of this nation must come into alignment, as must those of every nation and city, to understand that it is both the spirit and the letter of the Law that must be fulfilled and obedience in the details of service and the givingness of self. It is this that will lead most swiftly to the desired goal of light in the seven chakras balanced in the supreme blessing of the Father-Mother God."[488]

❖ THOR, *See* Aries and Thor

❖ TWELVE SOLAR HIERARCHIES

The twelve solar hierarchies are twelve mandalas of cosmic beings ensouling twelve facets of God's consciousness; they hold the pattern of that frequency for the entire cosmos. They are identified by the names of the signs of the zodiac, as they focus their energies to the earth through these constellations. These twelve hierarchies of the Sun are often visualized on the twelve lines of the cosmic clock.[489] Each of these hierarchies has one hundred and forty-four thousand cosmic beings in their service and each of these cosmic beings in turn has one hundred and forty-four thousand angels at their command.

These twelve hierarchies are represented at the Court of the Sacred Fire on Sirius by the four and twenty elders, twelve sets of twin flames, each set having mastery and authority over one of the twelve lines of the sun in manifestation. The four and twenty elders have appointed representatives to assist mankind in overcoming their human creation at the twelve points and attaining their mastery on each line. These representatives work directly under the four and twenty elders, who in turn dispense

---

Kali Yuga is the term in Hindu mystic philosophy for the last and worst of the four yugas (world ages), characterized by strife, discord and moral deterioration.

the blessings of the twelve solar hierarchies.

It is precisely because these twelve ascended masters and their twin flames (if they are ascended) have manifested their victory over the human creation on the particular line of the clock on which they serve that they have been appointed by the twenty-four elders to assist each one evolving upon earth to attain self-mastery. The ascended masters who serve on each line of the clock and the heavenly hosts who serve with these divine appointees are as follows:

12	Capricorn	The Great Divine Director and the seven archangels
1	Aquarius	Saint Germain and the angelic hosts of light
2	Pisces	Jesus and the great hosts of ascended masters
3	Aries	Helios and the Great Central Sun Magnet
4	Taurus	God Obedience and the seven mighty Elohim
5	Gemini	El Morya and the legions of Mercury
6	Cancer	Serapis Bey and the great seraphim and cherubim
7	Leo	The Goddess of Liberty and the Lords of Karma
8	Virgo	Lord Lanto and the Lords of Wisdom
9	Libra	Mighty Victory and the Lords of Individuality
10	Scorpio	Cyclopea and the Lords of Form
11	Sagittarius	Lord Maitreya and the Lords of Mind

❖ TWO MEN WHO STOOD BY IN WHITE APPAREL

The Two Men Who Stood by in White Apparel are mentioned in the Bible as standing by when Jesus "was taken up; and a cloud received him out of their sight."[490] They appeared to the disciples and promised that those who had seen him go into heaven would also see him come in like manner.

These two witnesses are emissaries of Luxor. They "stand by" to focus the light of Alpha and Omega at the ascension of the sons and daughters of God. Their white apparel is the condensation of the ascension flame. These two masters have explained their role in attending the ascension of Jesus in this way: "The purpose of two of us coming from Luxor to attend the ascension of Jesus was that we might hold for him in outer manifestation, even in the physical octave (which is why our bodies were lowered to that level), the focus of Alpha and Omega, the focus of the caduceus, for the ascension flame is the wholeness of the light of Father, Mother, Son and Holy Spirit.

"Therefore we attended the ascension, even as those who receive the ascension at the Ascension Retreat receive the ministry of two attendants who guard that one as the one becomes one with the rising pillar of fire upon the altar and the sacred dais. It was, then, an effort of hierarchy, though we would never eclipse the attainment of the beloved Son of God, for truly the totality of his consciousness immersed in the Creator of Life was a wonder of wonders even to us who are often witnesses of souls ascending.

"Nevertheless, as the angels tarried in the tomb as he was working out the flame of the resurrection and the victory over death, so the Law requires the holding of the balance. And you will recall the extending of the cup to David Lloyd by the now ascended master Godfre, and you will realize that Godfre himself was the focal point for the white light. And he stood with us who stood at inner levels, guarding the matrix as this son of God traversed from the plane of Matter to the plane of Spirit.

"And so the more you learn of the inner workings of hierarchy, the more you realize that truly the path of initiation is a joint effort of ascended and unascended servants of the Most High."[491]

Usually candidates for the ascension journey to Luxor to make final preparations for the ascension at the conclusion of their final incarnation. Some spend a number of hours, days, weeks, months or years before they are given the opportunity to take their ascension from inner levels.

However, others who have served the hierarchy and balanced more than 51 percent of their karma and who have been associated with the holding of the balance of a certain geographical area or the transmutation of certain conditions of great darkness from ancient civilizations have been assigned to take their ascension from the very place where they spent their last days. This occurred, for example, with Mother Mary, Clara Louise Kieninger and the messenger Mark L. Prophet, whose record of the ascension remains anchored over the Pikes Peak area in Colorado.

Serapis Bey periodically reviews the records of chelas of many of the ascended masters serving earth's evolutions. When any of the students have manifested a certain alchemy of attainment, Serapis apprises the Keeper of the Scrolls and other ascended masters at Luxor that these individuals may receive the mark as candidates for the ascension. This marking is a white fleur-de-lis, an insignia that is a focus of the white fire of the ascension flame.

This insignia is recognized by all of the ascended hosts, angels and elementals, and the one who has earned this insignia receives an extraordinary assistance from the members of the Great White Brotherhood. All who are in the octaves of Spirit go out of their way to watch and to pray for those who are making their way on the path of the ascension. There are candidates for the ascension in many of the nations of earth, and most are connected either with the disciplines of the way of Christ or the disciplines of the way of the Buddha—two paths above all others that provide an outline for right living and walking with God.

These two masters speak of their service at Luxor: "We also hold classes in the weaving of the seamless garment, and you would be surprised how many times the initiates must start again and again because of the unevenness of the forcefield of the lines and the threads—the very threads themselves representing the consciousness, the thoughts, the feelings. Thoughts are the warp, feelings are the woof, and the fire of the etheric body is the smoothness of the cloth that is to drape as a forcefield of auric protection around the physical body and all of the bodies.

"Some of you who have taken sewing classes who have found yourselves sewing and then undoing and then sewing and then undoing can well understand that this is the patience that is required when working on the seamless garment. And you see, the masters of the Ascension Temple have a very sharp eye for the quality of the garment and they never, never let pass an imperfection in the weave."[492]

These masters point out the importance of attention to the details of life on the path of the ascension: "Realize, then, that the path of the ascension is nothing but detail. It is the disciple who has the consciousness of detail, who leaves no stone unturned, who will discipline the self, who will realize that it is the small victories inch by inch won in consciousness that make the final victory, just as the raindrops one by one make the streams and rivers of life.

"As you approach, then, the mastery of the secret rays from the mastery of the seven rays, realize that you are coming nearer and nearer to the fiery core of your ascension. In the seven rays of mastery you are concerned with conquering the world and forging the pathway of light. But the secret rays demand the very delicate awareness of threads and lines, and crisscrossing of threads and lines, for this is truly the weaving of the seamless garment....

"And so the Path continues, the pilgrims continue on the Path, and we watch and we wait. And there will come a time when those of you who have now felt this fire in your heart and who feel it continuing to burn—there will come a time when two of us, whether ourselves or others who serve in twos from the Retreat of Luxor, will come to you, perhaps a decade, perhaps more, before your ascension to assist you in the flow of the currents in your physical, emotional, mental and etheric bodies."[493]

❖ **THE UNKNOWN MASTER,** *See* **Igor**

❖ **THE UNKNOWN MASTER OF THE HIMALAYAS**

An ascended master who identified himself simply as the Unknown Master of the Himalayas spoke in 1985. He came in the Spirit of the Great White Brotherhood out of the East, out of the Himalayas and in the center of Krishna.

In a fiery release he said: "I have spoken from the very heart of the Eternal Guru, Sanat Kumara. And I come, then, as the Unknown Master of the Himalayas. And you may or may not know me, but in your heart you know the vibration and the Word of the eternal Shepherd whom I represent."[494]

To know the name of a master is a dispensation, because the master's true name is a key to their identity that allows access to the master's causal body by unascended mankind. Perhaps in not releasing a name, this master desires us not to think of an outer label, but get to the core of who he really is.

❖ **URIEL AND AURORA,** **Archangels of the Sixth Ray**

Uriel and Aurora are the archangels of the sixth ray of ministration and service. Their retreat is located in the etheric realm over the Tatra Mountains, south of Cracow, Poland. In their ministrations, they guard the dawn of the Christ consciousness in mankind and elemental life.

The sixth ray is also the ray of peace, and Uriel and Aurora keep the flame of peace for mankind until they are able to invoke it for themselves. They prepare the way for the unfoldment of the light of God within each soul. Aurora carries the Mother feeling of peace and love to all mankind. Hers is the assurance that always flows from a mother's love—all is well, "the dawn is coming."

In order to have peace, the archangels sometimes have to make war for the binding of the fallen angels. Archangel Uriel and Aurora embody the peace and brotherhood of God. They minister to all life. Their work corresponds to the solar-plexus chakra, which is at the navel. Their day is Thursday, and on this day we can receive a greater release of light, energy and cosmic consciousness from their causal body.

The name Uriel means "fire of God," "flame of God" or "God is my light." In Jewish tradition, Archangel Uriel is called the "one who brings light to Israel." He interprets prophecies and is often shown carrying a book, a papyrus scroll. John Milton describes Uriel in *Paradise Lost* as the "regent of the sun" and "the sharpest-sighted spirit of all in Heaven." Some traditions say Uriel is the angel who led Abraham out of the land of Ur.

Uriel is not named in the Bible, but he is mentioned in Jewish and

Christian texts. He is said to be an angel of the Presence who watches over the world and over the lowest part of Hades. Uriel is one of the four chief angels in the Book of Enoch along with Michael, Gabriel and Raphael. He guided Enoch on his journeys through heaven and the underworld, and he warned Noah of the impending flood. Some traditions say Uriel taught Noah how to survive the flood.

In the Sibylline Oracles (texts that were used to spread Jewish and then Christian doctrine among pagans), Uriel is mentioned as one of the angels who leads souls to judgment. Uriel also plays a key role in the Jewish work the Fourth Book of Ezra. In this book, Uriel interprets the visions of Ezra and instructs him in the secrets of the universe. He answers Ezra's questions about the judgment and the signs of the end of the age.

Today Archangel Uriel gives a number of keys for changing your life, your family, your community and your planet for the better. The first is to call to the seven archangels to infuse your spiritual centers, your chakras, with the light of the Universal Christ. He says: "Only call to us in the name of God I AM THAT I AM and in the name of his Son, Jesus Christ, to enter your affairs. Then stand fast and behold the salvation of your God! Stand fast and see the healing of the nations through the work of the seven archangels!"[495]

"When you call upon us, we are instantaneously with you. When you do not call upon us, even though we want to save you, cosmic law says we cannot intervene. We are required to respect your free will."[496]

Another key for personal and planetary change is to apply the violet flame daily and generously. The violet flame is the gift of the Holy Spirit. It transmutes the records of negative karma, including the records of your own misdeeds and the misdeeds of others. For example, to bring about peace on earth, Archangel Uriel says it is important to apply the violet flame to the clearance of the records of death and war on the battlefields of the planet.

Archangel Uriel teaches us to increase the flame of peace in our aura and how to use the power of peace against the forces of anti-peace. When you lose your equilibrium, Uriel advises: Return to harmony as fast as you can. If you desire harmony more than you desire to win an argument, you can restore the peace quickly. Harmony is when you have absolute control over the energies that pass through you. Watch your tone of voice. Rise to the plane of your Christ Self and do not allow the different parts of yourself, as spoiled children, to pull you in four directions. The power of God is to be found in the inner stillness of the heart.

Uriel also teaches us to invoke the power of the Lord's judgment, and he is the archangel who delivers the judgments of the Lord Jesus Christ. Jesus

The Last Judgment, by Gustave Doré

has asked us to call for the binding of the fallen angels who prey upon the children of God. Saint Germain gives to his Keepers of the Flame the power to bind the fallen angels both on earth and in heaven. The apostle Paul confirms this dispensation: "Do ye not know that the saints shall judge the world? and if the world shall be judged by you, are ye unworthy to judge the smallest matters? Know ye not that we shall judge angels? how much more things that pertain to this life?"[497] Paul is referring to the fallen angels.

Archangel Uriel is deeply concerned about abortion and the karma that will descend upon the nations who condone it. For God chooses the special moment in history when each soul is to be born to fulfill its reason for being. Uriel says: "To murder the children of God is to murder God as flaming potential—is to crucify Christ anew."[498] Uriel has prophesied that cataclysm will befall any nation and people who either practice or tolerate abortion. He said this cataclysm could manifest in the weather, in the economy or in the households where brother is set against brother.[499]

Uriel says that if you have ever been involved in an abortion, you can balance your karma by performing acts of mercy. Implore God's forgiveness. You can right the wrong by sponsoring life and by speaking out in defense of the unborn.

On December 29, 1985, Archangel Uriel said that we could call to the angels for the judgment of terrorism anywhere in the world: "Whereas there is no international solution for terrorism, the LORD God Almighty contains that solution. And the angels are ready to deliver it as you offer the confirming Word and ratify God's will by your decrees."

There is another form of judgment—the action of judgment to our own not-self—the antithesis of the Real Self. The not-self is the ego self. It is the angry self, the selfish self, the self that has hardness of heart and does not care for others. When you ask God to judge you, his sacred fire descends into your temple—not to harm you, but to separate out the bad karma from the good karma. This helps you to see your errors for what they are. We must ponder the offenses we have committed against God, unwittingly and ignorantly, and then atone for them. Call to Archangel Uriel to separate the tares from the wheat that are growing side by side within you.

Study what is Real and what is unreal in your consciousness. Then, let the sacred fire consume all energy you have misqualified. Invoke the violet flame vigorously and valiantly.

When you call to Archangel Uriel for divine justice and the true and righteous judgments of our God, his answer may not be immediate. But rest assured the process has begun, and it will be fulfilled in God's time with or without your knowledge.

When we call for God's judgment to descend on earth, it is important to remember that it is ours to forgive; it is God's to deliver his justice. If we witness an injustice, the safest recourse is to turn the problem over to God and his angelic emissaries. The Bible says, "Vengeance is mine; I will repay, saith the Lord." [500]

Uriel is also the angel of the resurrection flame. This flame is mother-of-pearl in color, and it brings renewal, rebirth and rejuvenation so that you, like a phoenix, can rise out of the ashes of your former self. Archangel Uriel teaches us how to use the resurrection flame to conquer fear and achieve true God-mastery. He says, "When it comes to the conquering of fear, it is simply the art of letting God perform his perfect work and of you letting go." [501]

The Phoenix

Archangel Uriel gives us an exercise for letting go of fear. He says to place your hands, one over the other, to your heart, then release them, opened, relaxed, extending them outwards. Uncross your legs and breathe gently. Then speak these words tenderly to your soul and to your body three times: "Peace, be still!" When you hold your hands out in front of you, cupped, the posture reflects the serenity of the little child within you, secure in the arms of its mother.

Uriel says, "As all life reflects this caring, simply trust the Mother flame in the heart of the resurrection light to unburden you of all doubt and fear." [502] Each day, pause for a moment to rest, to relax the body, the mind, the soul. Consciously withdraw the tensions of the day from head to toe. You can use your favorite form of yoga or T'ai Chi to accomplish this. Just let go and let God. See how all doubt and fear are washed away, and you will know the joy of self-confidence and self-esteem.

Archangel Uriel has assigned to each one of us an angel of his band to help us experience the power of resurrection's flame in our personal lives and in our cities. He has also assigned this angel to help us in binding the not-self within and without and in transmuting the karma of our cities. Uriel says that in order to receive your angel, you must say: "In the name

I AM THAT I AM, in the name of Archangel Uriel, I accept the angel of the resurrection where I AM!"[503]

Another key from Uriel for bringing about change is to offer devotions to your God Presence every day. Archangel Uriel and his angels have promised to help you as you walk the path back to God's heart. He says, "We have but one request of you: that you determine within your hearts to not let a day go by that you do not think upon your mighty God Presence and offer your devotions, your adorations and your ministrations to this mighty Source of life. For it is through this God Presence that we are able to penetrate the darkness that is around you, that we are able to descend and walk with you, and that you are able to ascend into our presence. By this mutuality of service, this cosmic cooperation, we can move forward.... The Presence of God never fails!"

Uriel says that it is separation from that God-reality that causes failure. It is separation that causes doubt. It is separation from God that causes fear. "And I say that separation is a lie, that it never existed in the mind and heart of God, and it shall not exist within you if you heed my words this day and accept the mighty dispensations of light given to you. Accept them and become one with your God Presence!...

"Walk the earth as Christs. Put off the old garment! Put it off and be transfigured in the mighty transfiguring flame of life!"[504]

Archangel Uriel gives four steps for overcoming any unwanted condition in your life. First, "Do not condemn yourself for the condition." Second, "See yourself in your Great God-reality, filled with the Spirit, and see the problem as one inch high." Third, "Give this fiat from the very depths of your being: 'O my God, I will have the victory over this beast of my lesser self!'"

Fourth, do not suppress your negatives. Do not get into denial, but look squarely at what you are dealing with and let the negatives in your world just go into the violet flame. Replace unwanted activities and desires with new activities, new desires, new joy, new interactions and friends of light. Unite for a positive cause. You will find yourself so preoccupied with helping others that you will not regress into temptation when you are tempted to engage in old habit patterns. Rechannel the stream. Reverse the course of your downstream momentums. Build a new streambed, directing the course of your life where you want to go. It takes effort to atone for misdeeds and mistakes and to exchange the lesser desires for the greater desires. "But we are here to help you," says Archangel Uriel. "Just call on us and we will prove it to you."[505]

Uriel and Aurora and the legions of angels of peace from their retreat also serve with the legions of peace from beloved Jesus' Retreat in Arabia and from the retreat of the Elohim of Peace over the Hawaiian Islands.

Uriel and Aurora inspired upon the composer Brahms the lullaby that they use to soothe the souls of little children and to infuse them with the comfort and healing of the abiding God Presence and the indwelling Christ flame.

❖ UZZIEL AND HIS TWIN FLAME, Archangels of the Eighth Ray

Archangel Uzziel and his twin flame are the archangel and archeia of the eighth ray. While the names of the seven archangels are known, the names of the other archangels including those of the five secret rays have not been revealed, except the name of Uzziel on the eighth ray. The name Uzziel means "strength of God."

Uzziel says, "I AM the angel who flies in the midst of heaven, having the Everlasting Gospel.[506] For that gospel, my beloved, is the integration of all of the seven rays of Christhood and of the seven churches and of the world's religions and of the seven seals of the Book of Life and of the seven seals of the chakras of man and of woman.[507]

"I AM the entering in to the eighth ray whereby East and West are one. I am the one who bears the Everlasting Gospel that the hundred and forty and four thousand might preach it to the men and women and children of the earth."[508]

Archangel Uzziel assists us to transition from the seven rays to the mastery of the five secret rays. He brings the light of the eighth-ray chakra, the eight-petaled secret chamber of the heart.

The secret chamber of the heart

In 1977 Archangel Uzziel said: "I AM Uzziel. I bring to you the transition for your mastery of the five secret rays. Before you pass from the seven to the five, you must come under the rod of the discipline of the eighth-ray masters including the master Gautama Buddha and the Mother. For this is the ray of the Buddhas and the Mothers who come in the name of the Cosmic Virgin.

"You wonder why you have had the discipline of the Buddha and the Mother, and sometimes in your exasperation you wonder if that discipline will ever end. Well, it will end when you have passed your tests and become the fulfillment of the discipline itself. And then, in that moment, you may receive your diploma and pass to the school of Mighty Cosmos, who will introduce to you the masters of the five secret rays.

"Mankind are yet coming to grips with the seven rays, and therefore you have not heard of the lords of the five secret rays. But in order to contact that level of mastery, you may speak the name of the Ancient of Days, Sanat Kumara, and the seven holy Kumaras. And you may call for the light of the secret rays to come into greater prominence on earth even as you call for your own mastery of the eighth ray.

"Your beloved Lanello took his initiation in the eighth ray, after seven years in Colorado Springs, through the ritual of the ascension. Many unascended souls who have perfected the walk in the seven rays do so in this manner. But I appeal to you to strive for the overcoming mastery of the eighth ray and to remain in incarnation, which brings me to my original premise.

"Since the eighth ray carries such an intensity of ascension's fires, in order to sustain the eighth ray and to remain in incarnation, you must expand your heart chakra! You must open the heart chakra of America! You must contact the American people with the teaching that will enable them to guard the heart, especially from all dissonance and the popular forms of music that are so very destructive to the heartbeat, as that beat is the echo of the cosmic heart. You must teach the people of this nation to turn off their television sets, to separate themselves from noise and the bombardment of the physical senses, all of which are shocks to the heart and the energies thereof.

"And therefore the heart develops that hardness as encrustation, as encasement, as substance of density. Otherwise, it could not withstand the shock even from the cradle. And therefore where the people do not have light, their hearts become surrounded with darkness. And darkness instead of light becomes the defense of the heart chakra. Let them be opened!

"We could send forth the ray this morning, the very heart of the eighth ray, for the shattering of that calcification around the hearts of this people. But what would we accomplish? We would make their hearts naked and without defense. And then they would become so sensitive to the shocks of the world that many would pass from the screen of life.

"And therefore the teaching must come first. Therefore the nucleus must come first. Therefore the violet-flame heart, the purple-fiery heart of Saint Germain, is the dispensation of the God of Freedom in this age. This is why you hear of the Sacred Heart of Mary, the Sacred Heart of Jesus and this purple fiery heart of Saint Germain. It is because this generation of lightbearers have come forth to master the energies of the heart on behalf of all of their brothers and sisters who have such love and yet in ignorance know not what they do as they trample upon the tender laws governing the flow of energy through this sacred center in man and woman.

"You see, then, that although the hosts of light may perform miracles, if mankind cannot sustain the miracle, it is not an economy of cosmic energy. Therefore, the key to the age; therefore, the key to the eighth ray, the teaching, the teaching itself, the *dhamma** of the Buddha, the Sermon on the Mount of the Christ, the pondering in the heart of Mary the Mother, the teaching thread by thread and pearl by pearl, law by law—this is the reinforcement of the light of your heart.

"Become, then, devotees of wisdom that you might expand the teaching, become the teaching, and transfer it heart to heart.

"I am Uzziel. My dwelling place on earth is in the secret chamber of the heart of those devotees who have practiced the meditation of the secret chamber and who have cleared the place for my coming. If, then, you would entertain me within your temple, prepare your island in the emerald sea.† Prepare your island, and let me come to worship with thee."[509]

❖ **VAIROCHANA**, *See* **Five Dhyani Buddhas**

❖ **VAIVASVATA MANU, Manu of the Fifth Root Race**

The manus and their divine complements represent the Father-Mother God to their respective root races. The members of a root race embody together and have a unique archetypal pattern, divine plan and mission to fulfill on earth. Vaivasvata Manu and his consort are the manus for the fifth root race. As manus, they hold the archetypal pattern for that root race and sponsor the Christic path for all souls of that evolution.

Vaivasvata is a Sanskrit word meaning "sun-born"—born of the Sun, born of the Great Central Sun. In Hindu teachings, Vaivasvata is a poet, sage and guru. He is also one of the manus, or divine lawgivers, who guide the lives of mankind. Hindus believe that he is the manu of the present age.

In Hindu mythology, Vaivasvata appears as the Indian Noah, and various legends relate how he was saved from a great deluge. Helena Blavatsky called him "the progenitor of our fifth race, who saved it from the flood that nearly exterminated the fourth race." She specifies further that each manu "has to become the witness of one of the periodical and ever-recurring cataclysms (by fire and water in turn) that close the cycle of every Root-race."[510]

In his book *The Masters and the Path,* C. W. Leadbeater describes Vaivasvata as "a kingly figure,...the tallest of all the Adepts, being six feet

---

*Dhamma [Pali for Sanskrit *dharma*]: cosmic law; the teaching of the Buddha.

†For a meditation in the secret chamber of the heart in which the devotee visualizes a "bejeweled island in a glistening sea" and there worships his Lord, see Kuthumi and Djwal Kul, *The Human Aura,* pp. 158–67.

eight inches in height, and perfectly proportioned. He is the Representative Man of our race, its prototype, and every member of that race is directly descended from Him. The Manu has a very striking face of great power, with an aquiline nose, a full and flowing brown beard and brown eyes, and a magnificent head of leonine poise.... He is living at present in the Himalaya mountains."[511]

Vaivasvata Manu maintains a focus in the Himalayas. The flame focused in his retreat magnetizes the souls evolving within the fifth root race to the pattern of the Christ consciousness that he holds on their behalf. The love of Vaivasvata for his children is so great that once they contact the flame from his heart chalice upon his altar, they are cut free from the impositions of civilization that run contrary to their destiny as members of this root race. His electronic pattern is a complex yet delicate filigree, an antahkarana that surrounds the earth and connects with the heart flames of every member of his family.

The pronunciation of certain vowel tones at a certain pitch attunes the consciousness with the antahkarana (or web of light), and hence into the tremendous God-power of Vaivasvata. Students should make the call to tune into this antahkarana whether or not they are of the fifth root race, for he directs mighty currents that appear as shooting stars across the vast regions of the planet into the hearts of all who will serve with him.

Vaivasvata Manu has said: "Learn this one lesson from a guru who has had hundreds and thousands of victorious chelas: Absolute obedience to the teacher will secure instantaneous mastery. When you think you are alone, separate, misunderstood, maligned, remember Vaivasvata Manu, and call for my pattern to appear. Call for your pattern to appear. And know that I AM in the center of every pattern as the white-fire-core consciousness.

"I AM the white-fire-core consciousness of seed and seedling, of oak and redwood, of flower, of star, of birds that sing, of church bells that ring, of the chiming of the clock, the cosmic clock that tells the time of initiation, of victory, of love. As I walk with you each step of the way, it is because I pursue children of the dawn, children of my root race. And thus, from now on, I would speed to you on wings of light the impetus of our light and of our love that you might also release the great homing call of Father-Mother God to our children to 'Come home, come home, come home.' I withdraw to the heart of the secret rays, and when you invoke those rays, I shall come forth and place upon you my Electronic Presence to raise you into the pattern of God-identity."[512]

Vaivasvata Manu's divine complement remains in embodiment to anchor their twin flames in form.

❖ **VAJRASATTVA, Spokesman for the Five Dhyani Buddhas**

Vajrasattva represents the synthesis of the Five Dhyani Buddhas, a group of five non-historical celestial Buddhas who are visualized during meditation. They are to be distinguished from historical Buddhas, such as Gautama Buddha or Padma Sambhava.

Together with Vajrasattva, the Five Dhyani Buddhas are the central deities of esoteric Buddhism. They represent five different aspects of enlightened consciousness and are guides to our spiritual transformation. In Tibetan Buddhism, student meditators are introduced to the experience of meditation on the Five Dhyani Buddhas through the "sixth Dhyani Buddha," Vajrasattva.

The purpose of our meditation on these celestial beings is to help us awaken to the potential of our own Buddha nature and to find oneness with the Buddhas. These Buddhas also reflect back to us how the components of our consciousness can be transformed into wisdom.

Vajrasattva's name means "Diamond nature," because he represents the essence of our own pure, diamond nature. He is the role model of the devotee, and to become like him we must internalize the wisdoms of all the Dhyani Buddhas, for Vajrasattva has the attainment of all five.

Vajrasattva is invoked at the beginning of many Tibetan initiations. Here candidates meditate on him and recite his mantra to purify themselves and prepare for further advancement on their path to enlightenment. Ultimately, the devotee comes to realize that Vajrasattva is to be found in the center of his own being, seated on a lotus throne in the secret chamber of his heart.

In 1993, Vajrasattva, as spokesman for the Five Dhyani Buddhas, described how they assist us: "We excel in helping you unlock your inner being, the secret chamber of the soul that has been sealed off to the soul by karma and inordinate desire. We unlock inner doors, and the right door, I tell you, is the open door to all the rest.

"Once the soul has the courage and you prompt her, support and direct her and bathe her in love and compassion, she will open that door and walk through. And because you have tended her needs, your soul will know her own Inner Christ" and her own Inner Buddha.[513]

You can visualize Vajrasattva as a golden Buddha—shining as though illumined by the dazzling rays of the sun. He is seated in full lotus posture, and he holds a vajra scepter in his right hand at the level of his heart. In his left hand, he holds a bell.

The vajra represents his compassion, and the bell represents his great wisdom. Compassion and wisdom are the twin virtues essential to the attainment of self-realization. On another level, the vajra and bell symbolize a Buddha's enlightened mind and body in blissful union with ultimate Reality.

Written around the heart of Vajrasattva are the letters of his bija mantra, *Hum*. The bija of a Buddha is the sacred sound, the sacred syllable that represents his essence. We meditate upon the essence of Buddha through his bija mantra. The letters H-U-M are white and they move clockwise around Vajrasattva's heart, emitting sparkling rays of white light.

Vajrasattva is seated on a throne that is formed by a large, white, thousand-petaled lotus. He is smiling his smile of great compassion, and he is looking down upon you with tender love. As the whirling letters in his heart spin faster and faster, his whole body turns whiter and brighter until it appears to be all light. His body becomes transparent. You no longer see his form. You only see light, light, light.

Vajrasattva explains one important spiritual service that is performed through the recitation of the mantras of the Five Dhyani Buddhas: "Each time you have recited our bija mantras, you have pulled us to the very levels of the earth, you have pulled us to the very levels of the astral plane, you have pulled us to the lowest levels of incarnation of all souls who are karmically tied to you….

"Therefore we follow the mantra. We follow the point of origin of the Word. We follow those who give the recitation of the bija mantras, the seed syllables unto the Divine Mother, unto the Goddesses, unto the Dhyani Buddhas, unto the entire hierarchy of Buddhas.

"Therefore, the point of the sounding of the mantra calls the one whose mantra it is to that point. Thus, you have successfully called us to the depths of the astral plane…by the remaining ties that you have to lifestreams who are abiding in those levels.

"We consider this to be a great boon! For unless the Law would dictate otherwise unto us, we are subject to that law whereby we cannot descend any lower in the planes of earth than where there is a tie to one of our disciples….

"Know, then, beloved, that you have now carried us and our bodhisattvas and our disciples and chelas to all levels. And therefore we have duplicated ourselves as we have manifested our presences in a million different points of light at all levels of evolution in the Matter cosmos."[514]

Vajrasattva's six-syllable mantra is *Om Vajrasattva Hum*.

❖ **VENUS,** *See* **Sanat Kumara and Lady Master Venus**

❖ **VESTA,** *See* **Helios and Vesta**

❖ **VICTORY, COSMIC BEING, The Tall Master from Venus**

Mighty Victory is a cosmic being from Venus whose devotion to the flame of victory for more than a hundred thousand years has given him the authority over that flame through vast reaches of cosmos.

His love of the victory of the Christ and the potential victory of those evolving upon earth was the keynote of his response to Saint Germain's call for cosmic assistance to the earth in the 1930s. Coming forth to stand behind the Master of Freedom and to lend his momentum of victory to Saint Germain's projects, he announced the dispensation of the Lords of Karma to set aside the old occult laws for the evolutions of this planet. As a result, it was possible for individuals to ascend with only 51 percent of their karma balanced; to enter the retreats while their bodies slept at night, although their karma might not warrant it; and to be taught the instruction of the I AM in the world at large rather than have this information withheld for those who were not able to make the treacherous journeys to the retreats of the masters in their physical bodies.

Because so many cosmic beings came forth to assist Saint Germain, his petitions to the Lords of Karma for mercy on behalf of the mankind of earth were granted, and thus we are privileged today to have and to use this powerful instruction on behalf of our own freedom and that of the entire planet. We salute Mighty Victory and his love of victory in our devotions to the pink plume on Monday, for truly the star of victory is the star of our own causal bodies, and our individual victory is the victory of love.

Mighty Victory has twelve masters serving with him, in addition to legions of victory angels. Standing in the center of the Great Sun Dial with his twelve disciples taking their places on the twelve points of the clock, Mighty Victory issues the command for the formation of the six-pointed star. The masters standing on the one, three, five, seven, nine and eleven o'clock lines step forward midway between the center and the periphery of the circle. Thus, the star is formed by the action of the flame of Mighty Victory and his twelve, showing that as Above, so below the threefold flame is in balance and victorious in the being of man.

When he first became known to the people of earth, Victory was referred to as the "tall Master from Venus." In one of his dictations through the messenger Guy Ballard, the master explains how he came to be known as Victory: "I was given the Name of 'Victory' by the ascended masters who have made the ascension from your Earth, because all that I have attempted to do, has been victorious! There is no such thing as the memory of a single limitation in my consciousness, or world of activity, and has not been for a tremendously long period!" "I have known only victory for thousands of centuries."[515]

On June 26, 1986, Mighty Victory told us about our mid-year exams. He explained that "at each half-yearly cycle, the Lords of Karma meet. All mankind are tested, but especially those who write their letters to the Karmic Board. These, then, must receive a test according to their knowledge and awareness and training, especially their self-knowledge of those things that ought to be cast into the sacred fire. These tests come specifically in those areas where you yourselves have long endured a specific element of your human creation that you have been repeatedly warned to cast into the sacred fire for good. When you do not pass your tests, the dispensation you have petitioned for at the half-yearly cycle will not be granted. We demand a token, and there are final exams on earth as in heaven."

Mighty Victory told us that if you suspect that you have not passed your half-yearly exam, you can appeal to the Lords of Karma to give you another test so that the record of the year may show that you have determined to pass that test as a second chance.

On June 28, 1992, Mighty Victory with Justina, his twin flame, gave us a practical exercise to precipitate our victories. They said: "Consider, then, all those areas in your life in which you desire to be victorious." Make a note of each point you would master. Remind yourself daily of your commitment to your victory in small ways and big ways. You can chart your victories and your defeats on your map of life. "And you can put those golden ribbons at that place where you are determined to have your victory—victory over self and every condition, victory in this Church, victory in the dissemination of the teachings, victory in the nations, victory in the governments, victory in education, victory in every area of life!"

❖ **VIRGO AND PELLEUR, Hierarchs of the Earth Element**

Virgo and Pelleur are the directors of the earth element. They are the mother and the father of the earth and the gnomes. They work with the hierarchs of Libra, Scorpio and Sagittarius to teach mankind the mastery of their physical bodies; and with the hierarchs of Capricorn, Taurus and Virgo to teach them the mastery of the earth element.

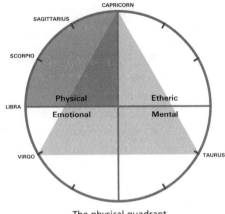

The physical quadrant and the trine of the earth signs

Virgo and Pelleur are cosmic beings who rule from the sun of even pressure in the center of the earth and direct the rays of the causal body through the earth element. During the first three golden ages that element was transparent, pure as crystal with rainbow hues, but after the descent of mankind's consciousness into duality, the earth element took on the density of man's consciousness, as did the water and the air.

In 1980 Virgo and Pelleur told us that "there are billions upon billions of gnomes tending the cycles of earth in the four seasons, purging the planet of poisons and pollutants so dangerous to the physical bodies of man, animal and plant life." They spoke with great concern about the burdens upon elemental life and the need for the violet flame to prevent earth changes: "In past ages when the discord, death and disease self-created by mankind have reached proportions greater than that which the elementals could bear, Nature herself has convulsed," as it did when "elemental life unleashed the fountains of the deep, causing the great deluge that resulted in the sinking of the continent of Atlantis and the flood of Noah....

"If and unless there is a great intensification of the saturation of the earth body with the violet flame through the multiplication of the calls of Keepers of the Flame, there will be in this decade major planetary upheavals, changes in weather conditions and earthquakes that result in great loss of life as well as permanent changes in the geographical surface of the earth."[516]

We have seen a certain amount of this come to pass already, and Saint Germain has said that the amount of violet flame invoked by the evolutions of the planet has not been sufficient to completely transmute the karma. When the people do not put forth the light of the violet flame, then it is Nature that must enact the transmutation. Nature's transmutation of burdens of world karma too hard to bear is cataclysm. That is why we have seen major cataclysms at the end of ages.

Virgo and Pelleur have described the gnomes and their service: "The beings you call gnomes, whose image has been dwarfed in the story of *Snow White and the Seven Dwarfs* and other fairy tales, actually range in size from three-inch-high elves playing in the grasses, to the three-foot dwarfs, all the way to the hierarchies of the mountains who attend the Great Hall of the Mountain King and Queen glimpsed by Grieg and portrayed in his musical tribute to the special gnomes of Norway and the Norsemen.

"There are giants in the elemental kingdom of the earth. These are powerful beings who wield the fire of atom and molecule and hold the balance for the continents through cataclysm, flood and fire. This evolution was created by Elohim to sustain the platform for the great experiment in free will ordained by God unto his children whom he sent forth into the planetary systems to be fruitful in the Christ consciousness and to multiply the manifestation of God in their offspring and in the works of their hands.

"As the gnomes represent the Holy Spirit and are transmitters of the love of the Comforter through the beauty and caring of nature for God's children, there are other elementals who represent the office of the Father, the Son and the Mother. Thus, even in the lower kingdoms of the planetary bodies there are representatives of the four cosmic forces envisioned by Ezekiel and Saint John.[517]

"The mighty gnomes, gentle and merciful, are the archetype in nature of the ox who treadeth out the corn,[518] the great burdenbearer of mankind's karma. Self-sacrificing, they even deny their own evolutionary fulfillment in order that man as the highest manifestation of God might continue to have the opportunity to prove the law of grace and enter into the rite of spring in the true spirit of the resurrection flame."[519]

In 1991 Pelleur said: "There is a certain class of gnomes who have come with me this day who…are familiar with mankind and their ways and their deeds. They have received a special education in order to take part in the activities of this community. They have been prepared to separate out from our bands and to join forces with Keepers of the Flame who find it realistic to make the pledge today to set aside even ten minutes out of the twenty-four hours a day to make specific fiats on behalf of the elementals.

"A gnome is therefore assigned to you, each one, as an experiment. This gnome will be as an assistant. This gnome will take directions from you and also impart to you intimations from myself and beloved Virgo as direction as to what needs to be accomplished upon the planet for the continuity of earthly existence itself. These gnomes will assist you as you give the violet-flame calls for the beings of fire, air, water and earth, even as they will call to other elementals whom they will train to decree and to invoke the violet flame.

"Until the gnomes and the elementals have been endowed with a three-fold flame by their Lord and Saviour Jesus Christ, they must make the call under the sponsorship and mantle of your individual Christhood, your individual threefold flame. Therefore, it is as much a benefit to the gnome for you to receive him or her as it is to you for the gnome to receive you. It is a mutual pact, if you will."[520]

Pelleur and Virgo are known as the Earth Father and the Earth Mother. Virgo is also sometimes known as Prosperina.

❖ **VISHNU, Second Person of the Hindu Trinity**

The eternal Creator, Preserver and Destroyer—Brahma, Vishnu and Shiva—of the Hindu Trinity parallel the Western concept of the Father, Son and Holy Spirit. Vishnu, the Second Person of the Trinity, is the immortal Son, the Preserver of the divine design, the Restorer of the universe by Wisdom's light.

As the Preserver, Vishnu preserves divine design conceived in Wisdom's flame. He restores the universe by Wisdom's all-healing light. As the Son, Vishnu embodies Cosmic Christ wisdom. He is also the mediator, or bridge, between the human consciousness and Brahman, Absolute Reality.

According to the teachings of Hinduism, whenever the forces of darkness would get the upper hand on earth, Vishnu would come to the aid of humanity by taking incarnation as an avatar. (In this sense of the word, Jesus Christ is an incarnation of Vishnu. So are Lord Maitreya, Lord Gautama Buddha, Lord Sanat Kumara. All come in the lineage of the Second Person of the Trinity, the Universal Christ.) The avatar would vanquish evil and establish the religion of the age in which he was born.

Vishnu was thus incarnated nine times, most notably as Rama and Krishna (his eighth incarnation). Vishnu's divine consort, Lakshmi, took human form to serve as his consort in each of his incarnations. Lakshmi's incarnations included Sita, the faithful wife of Rama; the cow girl Radha, beloved of Krishna; and Rukmini, the princess whom Krishna later married.

❖ **VULCAN, God of Fire**

The God Vulcan is a cosmic being devoted to the sacred fire and the implementation of the divine plan by the action of the fire of the Christ consciousness. He, together with his legions, serves diligently to consume those grotesque forms and impure vibrations that are released by the brothers of shadow, the powers of Antichrist, against the sons of God and the manifestation of the divine plan. He also assists those who are striving to overcome, to perfect the caduceus action and to use the creative fire in the service of God and man.

Those who would become alchemists of the sacred fire and masters of the fire element may call to the God Vulcan, who serves with Prince Oromasis and Diana in the training of the fiery salamanders as obedient servants of angels and unascended masters.

❖ **THE WHITE GODDESS (TARA),** *See also* **Kuan Yin** *and* **Mother of the World**

The White Goddess is one of the many images of the Mother of the World. She is a principle, and yet a living being.

In Tibet, the White Goddess is especially loved and worshiped as Tara, the saviouress. Tibetan Buddhists understand that the one who is going to save the world is the Mother, and that she comes to save the world in the end of the age of the Kali Yuga.

Tara is said to have been born from a lotus that grew in the water of a tear shed by Avalokiteshvara, who, as the ancient text records, "saw that however many migrating beings he removed from samsara, they grew no fewer, and he wept." Thus Tara is considered the counterpart of feminine Avalokiteshvara or his divine consort, and like Kuan Yin, she is a bodhisattva of compassion. The relationship between Tara and Kuan Yin has been the subject of much speculation. Some say that Kuan Yin is Tara's Chinese counterpart and others believe that the two are really one and the same being.

The principle symbol of White Tara is the fully-opened lotus, representing the opening of the petals of the chakras. Statues of the White Goddess often show the richness of her raiment. Her crown and earrings symbolize the manifest expression of the abundant life of the Buddha and the Christ. The Mother symbolizes that all things in the Matter universe belong to her children, and so that abundant sense is part of her manifestation. She also shows the renunciate that the real wealth of the cosmos is in the spiritual qualities. The Mother is the one who owns nothing but owns everything, and in this balance we find the discipline of the Buddha.

She is often seated in the full lotus posture, Padmasana, permitting the free flow of the Kundalini. Her left hand is over the heart, and her right hand is extended in the gesture of giving, embodying generosity and the blessing of all life. The knot on the top of her head symbolizes the opening of the crown chakra. The elongated ears and the presence of the third eye symbolize the full use of the inner senses. The large ear is seen on all of the Buddhas, and it indicates the contact with God through the inner ear and the inner sound.

The White Tara is a manifestation of the Divine Mother, the cosmic principle of the Mother. Whether you call her Mother Mary or Isis or the White Tara of Tibet or Kuan Yin or Kali or Durga, she is still the Mother force, the shakti. She also lives within you. She is the Mother light within us all. She is ascended master and unascended master. The White Goddess is the white-fire core of our chakras as the Mother light, the Kundalini energy, the white light in the center of every ray. As you give adoration to that presence within yourself through the rosary, you are raising the energies of the Kundalini and connecting with the cosmic principle of Mother.

In a dictation with the White Goddess in 1977, Serapis said: "Precious hearts, the way of the White Tara is the way of those who see the ultimate need of humanity and are willing to make the ultimate sacrifice. Because of their sense of timing, they read the timing of the Lord. They are mathematicians with me. They are architects of a vast destiny. They see the timing of the enemy. And they know that for the game of point/counterpoint, they must be as a shaft of sacred fire, as the point of diamond, as the discipline of energy. And this is all of their joy, all of their play and laughter condensed in an intense sphere of light. Whirling in that sphere, they actually enjoy with God-delight every pleasure that other disciples take along the wider spiral."[521]

❖ ZADKIEL AND HOLY AMETHYST, Archangels of the Seventh Ray

Zadkiel is the archangel of the seventh ray. Together with his twin flame, Holy Amethyst, and the violet-flame angels, he serves mankind from the Temple of Purification. This temple, once physical, is now in the etheric realm over the island of Cuba. Priests of the sacred fire on Atlantis took their training under the order of Lord Zadkiel here, and their service to life drew the momentum that prevented the island from sinking.

Archangel Zadkiel and Holy Amethyst embody God's freedom, alchemy, transmutation, forgiveness and justice, the very same qualities embodied by Saint Germain and his twin flame. Their work corresponds to the seat-of-the-soul chakra, and their color is violet. The day of the seventh ray is Saturday, which means we can receive a greater release of light, energy and cosmic consciousness from the causal bodies of Zadkiel and Amethyst on that day.

The name Zadkiel means "righteousness of God." In rabbinic tradition, Zadkiel is known as the angel of benevolence, mercy and memory. In some traditions, he was the angel who held back Abraham's hand when Abraham was about to sacrifice his son Isaac. Holy Amethyst, Zadkiel's divine complement, was one of the angels who ministered to Jesus in the Garden of Gethsemane.

In his retreat, Archangel Zadkiel prepares children of God to become priests and priestesses in the Order of Melchizedek. In the days of Atlantis both Jesus and Saint Germain studied at Zadkiel's retreat. Zadkiel anointed both of them into this priesthood.

Zadkiel and Holy Amethyst are here for one purpose: to help us secure our individual freedom so that when we are free, we can free our households, our towns, our nations, our planet. The main block to our freedom is our negative karma. We can transmute it with the violet-flame decrees. We can also balance negative karma by sending forth divine love and compassionately-human love and calling upon the law of mercy and forgiveness.

Archangel Zadkiel describes what he and the ascended hosts see when a devotee of God calls forth the sacred fire of the violet flame: "We see from inner levels the tremendous effort you make to transmute the layers upon layers of karma you have made in this and past lives. It is truly a marvelous thing for us to behold. In one moment you sit surrounded with every kind of negative thought revolving in your aura. In the next, you decide to invoke the violet flame.

"And lo! the mighty power of the seventh ray, as a giant electrode of cosmic energy, begins to form around your person. The violet-flame angels gather around you. With palms outstretched, they direct across your four lower bodies and your aura an arc of the violet ray. As that arc flashes across your being, it vaporizes the negative conditions. They literally disappear from heart and mind!"[522]

Zadkiel refers to the violet flame as the universal solvent that the alchemists have sought throughout the ages.* He says: "I possess in my heart the secrets of alchemy. Invoke them, if you will. And I shall release them to you in answer to your call."[523]

The violet flame can also give you a physical boost. Zadkiel and Holy Amethyst tell us: "Why will you wait while the candle of your life burns low? You can recharge your body with the violet flame. Do you think that God is

---

*Alchemy was a medieval science. The early alchemists sought to transmute base metals into gold and to discover a universal cure for disease and a means of prolonging life. In a broader sense, *alchemy* is defined as "a power or process of transforming something common into something special" or "an inexplicable or mysterious transmuting." Alchemy is the science of self-transformation.

incapable of vitalizing the atoms, the molecules and the cells of your body? He can flood them with violet fire and give you the glow of eternal youth!"[524]

Saint Germain tells us that joy is the motor of life, and the violet flame is the fuel. Forgiveness and mercy are qualities of this flame. To receive the greatest benefit of its power of transmutation, it is important to send the violet flame to all whom you have ever wronged as far back as you can remember in this life. And if you don't know where the person is, write a letter to that person, ask their forgiveness and then burn the letter. You must also give that violet flame to all who have ever wronged you, so that there is forgiveness in both directions. Put all hurts and heartaches into the violet flame! Then let go of the cause, the effect, the record and the memory of those hurts and heartaches. And call upon the law of forgiveness.

The angels can create miracles in our lives, but we have to call them into action to do just that. Zadkiel explains that according to cosmic law the angels may not intercede in the affairs of men unless people pray to them and give them specific assignments. At this very moment angels are waiting for your direction. This law is based on our Father-Mother God's recognition of free will. Unless you ask God to intercede in your behalf, he, by his own decree, will not, and does not, break that covenant of free will and enter into your life uninvited.

Zadkiel says: "When you invoke the light of our violet-flame legions, know that millions of angels of the seventh ray respond to your call immediately. We see the rise, the fall and the ebb of the tide of world karma daily as Keepers of the Flame worldwide do invoke the violet flame and therefore mitigate the effects of mass karma."[525]

How can we be effective in creating miracles to change world conditions? "The violet-flame legions of light are warriors of the Spirit who can meet any condition of planet Earth. We are reinforcements…nearest the physical octave because the violet flame is the most physical flame."[526]

Second, be specific. Archangel Zadkiel and Holy Amethyst say: "The world is filled with many injustices. Examine the world scene and determine what causes are worth fighting for. Choose one or two, and then work on them relentlessly with your violet-flame decrees, your meditations and your active involvement in alleviating the burdens of your cities. Join with others in giving your violet-flame decrees to save our civilization."[527]

"In answer to your call, we send missiles of violet flame to save planet Earth. I tell you, with God all things are possible!"[528]

Third, "The saints in embodiment must anchor divine intercession in the earth by saturating their auras with violet flame. This is the way to make the difference in turning negative world prophecy into positive world prophecy."[529]

Lord Maitreya tells us that miracles are the alchemy of the violet ray and the gift of Saint Germain. The momentum of violet flame that you build in your aura as you decree day by day without fail will enable you to build a storehouse of violet flame that will be available to you in time of emergency—just when you need a miracle. How many times have you heard yourself or someone say: "O God, I really need a miracle now!"

A miracle is sudden transmutation. And sudden transmutation takes place because someone in the universe has garnered enough light, enough violet flame to inject such a momentum, such a quotient of energy that the violet flame applied to a specific problem causes instantaneous change in the etheric plane, the mental plane, the emotional plane and the physical plane.

The final key that Zadkiel gives is to get involved: "The open door to light in the physical octave is you,...is the power of the spoken Word to protest, to demonstrate, to decree. Pray at the altar, then go forth and take your stand in all areas where life is threatened. You are the open door to safety and salvation in the earth."[530]

Through the amethyst crystal, the twin flame of Lord Zadkiel focuses the mother aspect of freedom to the evolutions of this planet. The amethyst is worn by all who serve on the seventh ray and their devotees. All jewels are actually precipitates or condensations of the flame that the jewel focuses. Thus, the amethyst is the focus of the freedom flame, and those jewels that have been consecrated by lightbearers contain in the center a replica of the flame that they represent.

The musical keynote of Holy Amethyst is the "Beautiful Blue Danube," by Johann Strauss.

❖ ZARATHUSTRA, Initiate of the Sacred Fire

This office in hierarchy is presently held by one who was embodied as the founder of Zoroastrianism in ancient Persia. He is the highest initiate of the sacred fire on the planet and the governing authority of the energies of fohat. He is over the priests of the sacred fire and the priesthood of Melchizedek.

All members of the Great White Brotherhood serve in the Order of Melchizedek even as they serve the sacred fire, but only those who have reached a certain level of initiation may be called Priests of the Order of Melchizedek. Other members serve the purposes of the Order but do not bear the title of priest. Zarathustra has many disciples serving under him, and when the most advanced of these reaches a certain attainment, he will qualify for the office, and the teacher will go on to cosmic service.

Zarathustra

Zoroastrianism is the one of the oldest of the world's religions. Zarathustra, its founder, was a prophet who spoke to his God face-to-face. Zarathustra lived in a nonliterate society, whose people did not keep records. His teachings were passed down by oral tradition, and much of what was later written down about his life and teachings has been lost or destroyed. What scholars have been able to piece together about him comes from three sources: the study of the historical milieu prior to and during the time Zarathustra is believed to have lived, tradition, and seventeen sacred hymns called Gathas. Scholars concur that Zarathustra composed these hymns. The Gathas are recorded in the Avesta, the sacred scriptures of Zoroastrianism.

It is believed that Zarathustra was born in what is now east central Iran, but that is not certain. Zarathustra's date of birth is even more difficult to establish. Scholars place it sometime between 1700 B.C. and 600 B.C. The consensus is that he lived around 1000 B.C. or earlier. The Gathas say that Zarathustra was of the Spitama family, a family of knights. The Greek name for Zarathustra is Zoroaster, meaning "Golden Star," or "Golden Light." He was one of the priest class who formulated mantras.

Tradition holds that at the age of twenty, Zarathustra left his father, mother and wife to wander in search of Truth. Ten years later he had the first of many visions. "He saw on the bank a shining Being, who revealed himself as Vohu Manah 'Good Purpose'; and this Being led Zoroaster into the presence of Ahura Mazda and five other radiant figures, before whom 'he did not see his own shadow upon the earth, owing to their great light'."[531]

Ahura Mazda means "Wise Lord." Zarathustra recognized Ahura Mazda as the one true God, the Creator of the universe. Shortly after his first vision, Zarathustra became a spokesman for Ahura Mazda and began to proclaim his message. He instituted a religious reform that was far-reaching. His main objective was to stamp out evil, and he preached against the *daevas* (demons) of the old religion.

At first Zarathustra had little success in spreading his message. He was persecuted by the priests and followers of the daevas, and according to tradition, they tried to kill him a number of times. It took ten years for Zarathustra to make his first convert, his cousin. He was then divinely led to the court of King Vishtaspa and Queen Hutaosa.

Vishtaspa was an honest, simple monarch but was surrounded by the *Karpans,* a group of self-seeking, manipulative priests. They convened a council to challenge the revelations of the new prophet and successfully conspired to have him thrown in jail. As the story goes, Zarathustra won his freedom by miraculously curing the king's favorite black horse. Vishtaspa granted him permission to teach the new faith to his consort, Queen Hutaosa. The beautiful Hutaosa became one of Zarathustra's greatest supporters and assisted him in converting Vishtaspa.

After two long years, the monarch was finally converted. But Vishtaspa required one final sign before he would totally embrace the faith. He asked to be shown what role he would play in the heaven-world. In response, Ahura Mazda sent three archangels to the court of Vishtaspa and Hutaosa. They appeared as effulgent knights in full armour, riding on horseback. According to one text, they arrived in such glory that "their radiance in that lofty residence seemed...a heaven of complete light, owing to their great power and triumph;...when he thus looked upon [them], the exalted king Vishtaspa trembled, all his courtiers trembled, all his chieftains were confused."[532]

Radiating a blinding light and the sound of thunder, they announced that they had come on behalf of Ahura Mazda in order that the king might receive the fullness of the message of Zarathustra. They promised Vishtaspa a life span of 150 years and that he and Hutaosa would have an immortal son. The archangels warned, however, that if Vishtaspa should decide not to take up the religion, his end would not be far away. The king embraced the faith, and the entire court followed suit. The scriptures record that the archangels then took up their abode with Vishtaspa.

In a dictation given January 1, 1981, the ascended master Zarathustra spoke of King Vishtaspa and Queen Hutaosa: "I AM come to deliver the sacred fire of the Sun behind the sun to raise you up and to establish in you the original teaching of Ahura Mazda, Sanat Kumara, delivered long ago in the land of ancient Persia unto me and unto the king and queen who received the conversion of archangels and of the sacred fire and of holy angels by the descent of light. Thus, by their lifestreams' acceptance of my prophecy, there came to pass the multiplication of the bread of life from the heart of Sanat Kumara, whose messenger I was, whose messenger I remain....

"The teaching of the hosts of the LORD and the coming of the great avatar of light, the teaching of betrayal and the consequent warfare of his hosts against the evil ones, was understood and propagated. The law of karma, the law of reincarnation, and even the vision of the last days when evil and the Evil One would be vanquished—all of this went forth by the conversion of the king and the queen and the reaching out of the faith to all of the subjects of the land. Thus, the tests were given by the archangels through my office unto these two chosen ones. Thereby passing the tests, they became blessed as secondary emissaries of Sanat Kumara. And therefore, I the prophet and they holding the balance in the earth manifested a trinity of light and the figure-eight flow.

"Realize the necessary ingredients for the propagation of the faith throughout the earth. The archangels send their messenger with a gift of prophecy that is the Word of Sanat Kumara to every culture and in every age. Thus, the prophet comes forth with the vision, with the anointing and with the sacred fire. But unless the prophet find the fertile field of hearts aflame and receptive, the authority of the Word does not pass unto the people."[533]

According to tradition, when Zarathustra was seventy-seven, he was assassinated by a priest of the old Iranian religion. Some accounts say that he perished by lightning, or a flame from heaven. Much of what happened after Zarathustra's death is shrouded in mystery. Scholars say that his successors reintroduced back into the system the old gods that he had dethroned.

By the time the Medes came to power in the seventh century B.C., Zoroastrianism was a major force in Persia. When Alexander the Great conquered Persia in 331 B.C., he killed the priests and burned down the royal palace, destroying whatever may have been recorded of Zoroastrian tradition.

About A.D. 225, Zoroastrianism reemerged in Persia and was the state religion until around 651, when the Muslims conquered Persia. Although Zoroastrianism was officially tolerated, the Arab conquerors encouraged conversion to Islam through societal pressures, economic incentives or force. Many Zoroastrians converted or went into exile. Loyal Zoroastrians who remained in Persia were taxed for the privilege of practicing their faith. In later centuries, persecution of Zoroastrians escalated. As of 1976, there were only 129,000 Zoroastrians in the world. However, much of what Zarathustra taught lives on in Judaism, Christianity and Islam.

Today Zarathustra is an ascended master whose consciousness bears as an auric emanation of fire that is an all-consuming love, a piercing light that goes to the core of whatever is unreal. We call him a Buddha because he has the attainment of the expansion of the threefold flame and of the Christ mind at the level of initiation that we call the buddhic level.

Being in the presence of Zarathustra is like being in the presence of the physical sun itself. The mastery he has of spiritual fire and physical fire is, if not the highest, among the highest of any adept ascended from this planet. If you want to keep the flame of Zarathustra, visualize him keeping the flame, the divine spark, in your own heart. He is the greatest 'firetender' of them all, if you will. And when you call to him, remember that when you are engaged in the battle of Light and Darkness and you give your call for the binding of the forces of Antichrist, there is no greater devourer of the dark forces than Zarathustra himself. He is an ascended master with buddhic attainment whose auric emanation is one of an all-consuming love.

Zarathustra's retreat is patterned after the secret chamber of the heart, which is the place where the threefold flame burns on the altar of being. Your high priest, who is your Holy Christ Self, retires to that secret chamber to keep that flame. He and other ascended masters can and do visit you there and tutor your soul. Zarathustra has said that we may be welcomed in his retreat when you have the necessary development of the heart. He has not revealed its location.

The Retreats of the
Ascended Masters

Man has dreamed of visiting
the legendary Shamballa, the fabled Shangri-La, and
sacred enclaves of the lost continents of Lemuria and Atlantis.
And once he could—if he knew the secret pathways and
mountain passes and was willing to brave the trek.

Then darkness fell, the temples were desecrated, mankind
entered an age of barbarism, and all but a few adepts were
cut off from the ascended masters of the Great White
Brotherhood, the Eternal Order of the saints East and West.
Their retreats were withdrawn to the etheric plane beyond the physical
realm, reachable only by the most advanced initiates.

With the dawning of the Aquarian age, lightbearers were
again given the opportunity to enter these retreats.
This time by soul travel—apart from the physical body.
And the ascended masters welcomed seekers
to their etheric temples deep in the heart of the Himalayas,
the Andes, or in the center of the earth.

Their purpose is to teach the sons and daughters of God the
Ancient Wisdom long withheld and to assist them to balance
their karma through service to life and violet-flame mantras
invoking the sacred fire of the Holy Spirit.

This is only the beginning of the gifts that come from
contact with the Great White Brotherhood—
an opportunity lost thousands of years ago, renewed
once again to the modern seeker.

The Web of Life

There is a web of life around the planet, an antahkarana of light.* Imagine a spider web, with beautiful dewdrops glistening upon it in the early dawn light. Then imagine that web in the third and fourth dimensions, radiating out in all directions. You have just begun to visualize the beauty and majesty of the web of life.

All of life is interconnected through this great grid of light. There are grids and forcefields of light for every person in embodiment. These connect to all

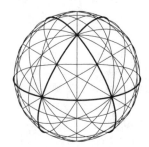

other forms of life—the trees and plant life, animal life, even to the center of the earth and to the auras of the masters themselves. All of this forms a vast and complex filigree pattern of interconnected light.

In this beautiful pattern, the etheric retreats of the Great White Brotherhood appear as giant balls of light. They are centers of infinite lines of force that emanate from one retreat and radiate out to connect with other retreats, both in the earth and expanding into space. Each retreat is a very important nucleus of energy, with a specific purpose to sustain a certain action that trembles through the entire warp and woof of the planetary body to nourish life and sustain the action of the sacred fire.

The locations of the masters' retreats have only recently been revealed, and we are fortunate in this time that the masters have given us this knowledge. They do not have to give us these revelations, but they do so because they are walking the last mile with us, wanting to give us every opportunity to progress spiritually.

The masters understand that when people know where these retreats are, they will center their attention upon them, and some of that attention becomes the conduit for the misqualified energy that all mankind have in their subconscious. So, at the price of some loss of privacy and having the attention of the world upon them, the masters have released the location of their retreats for the benefit of mankind.

The Purposes of the Retreats of the Masters

The heavenly hierarchy functions through its retreats, and the retreats of the ascended masters of the Great White Brotherhood serve many purposes. They are the homes of the masters in the heaven-world—the etheric

*Antahkarana [Sanskrit, "internal sense organ"]: the web of life; the net of light spanning Spirit and Matter connecting and sensitizing the whole of creation within itself and to the heart of God.

body of planet Earth. The masters also use the retreats to anchor certain energies throughout the earth on behalf of mankind. Records of past civilizations and golden ages are stored there. And perhaps most importantly, the masters serve in their retreats as the teachers of mankind.

Souls of light in embodiment who desire to be trained on the spiritual path may journey to the retreats in their soul consciousness while their bodies sleep at night. The retreats are centers of study and learning as well as places for training. Many of the saints—Mother Mary, Jesus, Saint Francis and many of our great leaders and religious teachers—studied in these retreats to prepare for their mission. Similarly, many among mankind today are trained there, consciously working at inner levels to prepare for their mission and divine plan in this age.

The Maha Chohan

The Maha Chohan has said: "The instruction in our retreats continues, and our doors will remain open as long as there are some among humanity who are willing to make both the trek and the sacrifice that are necessary to enter in at the strait gate of the Christ consciousness....

"After you have studied in my retreat for a certain period and after you have attained a certain mastery in the use of the seven rays under the seven chohans, you will be invited to serve with the white-fire and the flaming pink angels as they minister to the needs of humanity twenty-four-hours a day at all levels of the human consciousness. And they, in the Spirit of the God whom they serve, are no respecter of persons. They serve as the Christ did—wherever the need is greatest, seeking to save the sinners as well as the righteous from all forces that oppose the immaculate image of the Cosmic Virgin made manifest in the four lower bodies. For they are dedicated to the preservation of these vehicles as opportunities for the Christ to reveal his flame in time and space."[534]

Cities of the Brotherhood in the Etheric Realm

As well as the retreats of the masters, there are great cities of light in the etheric plane located at various points on the planet. In these cities we find lifestreams who are preparing to reembody, who have petitioned the Lords of Karma and must wait for the opportune moment when the gates of birth are opened to them and they can once again come forth to work out their destiny in the world of form. These waiting souls live and work and serve in situations not unlike those they have left on the planet, with the exception that the etheric cities hold the pattern for what the physical is intended to be in a golden age.

Here are Universities of the Spirit, great temples of light and homes similar to those we know on earth. There are temples of worship, of healing, of invocation and purification, of ideal forms of government, of education, of art and of music.

Those who spend their time between embodiments in these cities have a great worth to contribute in their succeeding lives. Those who carry the flame of idealism in their next embodiment do so out of the remembrance of the joy and happiness they experienced in living, perhaps for centuries, in these etheric homes of light. They come "trailing clouds of glory" in the great hope that somewhere on this green earth they can recreate the beauty and peace they have known in the higher octaves.

Unfortunately, there are also many who do not reach the etheric octaves between embodiments. They live on the other side as they do in this world, without higher aspirations and caught up in lower desires. They reembody from these levels, having risen no higher than the astral plane, and thus have no recollection of anything but a meager, puny existence. These must be led by those of a higher vision, and only those who have some momentum of light are able to reach the etheric cities after they pass on.

Remembering that we have in the neighborhood of six billion lifestreams in embodiment and that ten billion are assigned to this planet who have not yet ascended, we must realize that in the etheric cities, in the retreats of the Brotherhood and on the astral and mental planes, four billion souls are evolving and waiting for the privilege of once again having a physical form that they might continue to work out their karma, balance their debts to life and gain their self-mastery.

The etheric cities show us what the previous golden ages on earth looked like and how the world can be again in a future golden age. A high percentage of the souls who visit the etheric cities try to outpicture some aspects of these cities when they return to earth. Great training and preparation is given to those souls who live in these cities and spend time in the retreats of the masters. It is the purpose of the hierarchy and the Brotherhood to establish those institutions and facilities of higher education on earth that will enable the incoming souls to outpicture that which they have learned in the higher octaves.

If the Retreats Are Real, Why Don't We Remember Them?

The retreats are very real and our service with the masters on these levels is also real, and yet, most often, there is no outer memory of the retreat experience. A spiritual seeker may visit the retreats for some time before having a waking memory of an experience there. Many have no direct memory, but simply return with a prompting, a feeling or an inner direction about decisions to be made in life.

Many times our retreat experiences and service with the masters on the etheric plane will come to our outer awareness as the recall of a particularly vivid dream. Mark Prophet had one experience of working at inner levels early in his service with the masters. It was confirmed by the Brotherhood in a very interesting way. Mark tells the story in his own inimitable style:

"I remember several years ago, when I was staying at the Blackstone Hotel in Chicago attending a special convention there. I went to bed one night, and as I was leaving my body, I remembered the trip across the face of America as though it were an actual plane ride. And pretty soon I was in New York and circling around, and I came down to the Empire State Building.

"Of course, as you know, there is a huge antenna on top of the Empire State Building. And so I came down on that antenna, and I placed my feet on it—one foot, I should say. And as I placed it on there, I got scared, I don't mind telling you, because I realized that there was the street below. I had not even thought that I was traveling out of the body. I thought that I was actually physically on this tower, and I felt that at any moment, if I slipped, I might crash down to the street and get hurt.

"So, eventually, I did slip. I slipped off it and there I was. It was a fog, and I was falling in this fog. The next thing, I said, 'For goodness' sakes, I don't have to fall.' So we crossed the Atlantic Ocean, went over to Paris, like Lindbergh, you know.

"What did I say to myself on this occasion? I said, 'Why, that's only a dream.' I woke up and I remembered the details. But I said, 'It's only a dream.'

"Then I went down in the elevator the next morning. There right across from me at the breakfast table was a little old lady, probably about seventy-five to eighty, maybe even eighty-five. At that time I was not a vegetarian, and I was having my bacon and eggs with coffee. It tasted pretty good, and I was really enjoying it. This lady had ordered a little breakfast of fruit, and she sat there, sipping her coffee and eating her fruit. And she kept looking at me. She sat there with what you'd call a Mona Lisa smile, you know.

"And I said to myself, 'What in the world is going on with this lady? Why is she looking at me like that?'

"Well, pretty soon she looked at me. 'Ahem.'

"I said, 'Yes? How are you?'

"'I'm fine,' she said. 'By the way, I was really amused last night when your foot slipped off the top of the Empire State Building.'

"Now, was it a dream? You decide.

"The point is, I knew I was not alone because others were with me. And the thing that you have to realize is that God is not limited by your body.

"Just because he created your body does not mean that your soul is in that body like an imp in a bottle, and you can't get out of it. Of course you can get out of it! You get out of it at death, don't you? When you lay your body down at night you can also get out of it. And where do you go? Well, you go where God wants you to go."[535]

Memories of the Retreats

For most of mankind, the knowledge gained during their retreat experiences will manifest only in subtle ways upon awakening. For example, if they were to come into contact with some aspect of the teaching of the Brotherhood or a point of cosmic law that they had learned in the retreats, the memory of the experience there might be activated. They might have a sense that something they have just heard or seen is ringing true in their heart. Somehow they feel that this is not new to them—sometime, somewhere they have heard this before, but they just cannot quite remember where or when.

It may be some time before they actually remember their inner experiences, and in the meantime, the memory becomes the polestar that guides their life and

Purified chakras as seen in the etheric body

helps them to make right decisions day by day. But by and by they may begin to remember. Perhaps they will have flashes and memories, and they will think that it is a dream. But it is not a dream. It is a real experience that they have had in their soul and solar consciousness, in their etheric body at night.

The use of the violet flame can be very helpful in remembering your retreat experiences. As you purify your four lower bodies with the violet flame, as you practice the ritual when you retire at night of asking your God Presence to be taken to the retreats, you will begin to have the dim, faint memory of your experience. And one day, you will awaken in the morning, and you will remember being in a temple. You will remember the room where you sat, and you will remember the teacher who stood before you. It will be one of the greatest experiences of your life, and it is not far away.

It simply takes the clearing of the chakras, the purification of your own mind and soul so that what is impressed upon the soul can filter through to your outer awareness. You have much to look forward to as you apply the teachings of the masters and willingly sacrifice the impurities of the human consciousness into the flame.

What Is It Like to Be in an Ascended Master Retreat?

El Morya has described the experience of one group of students in his retreat in Darjeeling:

"Chelas who knock on the door at Darjeeling are asked if they understand the urgency of world conditions and the crying need of the hour. If they have not yet gained that perspective, we recommend that they seek the disciplines of another retreat. For here at Darjeeling we offer a crash program in chelaship and initiation on the path for those who are willing to follow implicitly the demands of their own Christ Self and to respond with a flame that leaps and with eyes that sparkle with the kindling fires of soul discernment.

"We send forth devotees of the Divine Mother. We train emissaries who will represent the Brotherhood and who will go forth into the large cities of the world to teach the way of the sacrifice of the self, as Saint Francis of old, for the greater glory of the Christ in all.

"Come then; fear not to approach the fire blazing on the hearth here in the library of our retreat. Come now and meditate upon the flames, and see how the fiery salamanders dance to the music of the will of God that is the theme of your soul's reunion with the blueprint of your life, the grand design of destiny. See how the patterns blue and rose and gold woven in the Oriental rug recall the tapestry of the mind of God woven in your soul....

"Now, chelas of the will of God who would become chelas of the ascended masters, with the tenderness of the heart of the will of God, I draw you into the folds of the garment of that will, that you might see that the crystal lining of the sapphire blue is flecked with a golden-pink hue—an intense love of the wisdom of God that inspires the Darjeeling Masters to crack the whip of discipline. So great is our love for the soul of God in man that we would set you free to behold your immortal destiny.

"There be some that come to our retreat for training, but their motives are not pure. They are self-seeking. They want power not to glory in God, but for the vainglory of the synthetic self that they refuse to surrender. They are told politely by the gatekeeper that those who enter must leave the slippers of the lesser self at the door. Those who are unwilling to take off the shoes of the shadowed self may not walk upon this hallowed ground.

"It is time to enter the chamber designed with blue and gold motif where there is a screen and seats arranged in theater style. For to understand your path, your very personal path to salvation, you must have the perspective of your past and how you have created the present—both at personal and planetary levels. Come then; and let us see how we shall, in the magic of the flame, discover the designs of your soul destiny.

"We enter the chamber now and take our places before a large semicircular screen on which there will be projected the experiences of other incarnations in the full dimensions that are portrayed from the akashic record. The group assembled here as I speak consists of unascended chelas—some of whom have an outer connection to the Retreat of the Resurrection Spiral in Colorado Springs, Colorado, and to Summit University in Santa Barbara, California. Others among the group are serving the will of God in their respective nations. These look forward to the day when the teachings of the ascended masters will be published in their language, that they might read and study in their outer, waking consciousness that which they receive here in their finer bodies during sleep....

"Now scenes of life in ancient Thrace appear on the screen, and we find ourselves in the marketplace of a forgotten city in the land that is now Turkey. Two unascended masters walk midst the crowds unnoticed. The people are concerned with the activities of the day, with the purchase of food and supplies at the best prices, while the vendors carefully watch the passing of coins from hand to hand to see how much the day's business will bring.

"A group of devotees including some of the chelas now assembled in our retreat enters the marketplace. In this life they are mystics whose devotion is to the fire as it represents the one true God. Already they have borne the ridicule and the ostracism of their peers.

"At the moment of their appearing, a peculiar astrological configuration aligns certain forces of hatred within the subconscious of the populace with an amalgamation of mass hatred focalized on astral planes. This interaction of forcefields in several dimensions of Matter we portray for the chelas, showing also the alignment of constellations, solar hierarchies, and 'fixed' and 'wandering' stars and how these energy fields amplify both the light and the darkness in mankind and cause the energizing of certain levels of karma in incarnations even prior to the ones now in focus on the screen.

"Suddenly without warning, as if seized by a madness and a frenzy not entirely their own, certain individuals who seem to be at a random relationship to one another converge as a single entity. They act as a single unit—the mob— and with a single mind—the mass mind. They begin to pick up stones and hurl them at the devotees. The devotees are surrounded. Not terrified, but calmly centered in the flame that is the object of their worship, they shield their heads and their bodies. But to no avail.

"The mob is brutal. With a desire for vengeance and a thirst for blood projected from the astral hordes, they descend upon the chelas until they are no more. Their souls take leave of that which remains of their finite forms, and the two unascended masters standing by raise the fohatic energies of their heart chakras to assist the souls in the transition.

"By karmic law they were not allowed to interfere with the circumstances that represented a converging of many forces and nature's demand for balance. Through their love and their mastery, they create a forcefield of light whereby the souls are taken safely to the etheric retreat of Pallas Athena over the island of Crete.

"Now we roll back the drama on the screen so that all may examine the interplay of forces and the lines of karma that converged when the devotees first entered the marketplace. They see how they themselves in a much earlier period of earth's history, while engaged in the practice of a religion of darkness, were drawn into acts of fanaticism and untempered zeal that resulted in the death of those who retaliated that day in the forgotten city of ancient Thrace.

"We review the scene in slow motion. I use the diamond that I wear on the index finger of my right hand to focus the action of the sacred fire on the screen. The violet ray that descends from the heart of my Presence is projected through the diamond and bursts forth as a thousand million flames on that scene on the

screen. The chelas are on the edge of their seats as they watch the violet flame consume the cause and core, the record and memory—both in akasha and in their own subconscious.

"The action of the violet flame intensifies in answer to my invocation made to the I AM Presence of each one: In the name of the Christ Self of the chelas, I invoke the fire of Almighty God to blaze forth the action of transmutation to change darkness into light—fear and hatred into love, envy into understanding, and vengeance into victory. As violet-flame angels from Zadkiel's retreat direct the energies of the flame, it forms coils of fire in the subconscious of each individual who was a party to this unfortunate interplay of energy.

"Coils of fire are formed like the curly shavings that fall from planed wood. These coils rise and fall, rise and fall, intensifying the action of transmutation. And now they burst into a wide circle of energy and then return to the center. All of this is the action-formation of the fires of transmutation, flaming fire moving up and down and in and out; and then, following the circle of the cycles of individual karma in the electronic belt—a scrubbing action, a boiling action, a bubbling and a buoyant energy. Such is the diversity of the violet flame.

"Scene by scene, step by step, the angels of the violet flame remove the record from the etheric body, the concepts from the mental body, the emotions from the feeling body, and the scars upon the physical matrix. Right before their very eyes, chelas of the will of God see what the glorious flame of God can do. They cheer. They applaud. And their bravos express the release of energy in their own hearts and a new freedom of the soul as this ancient record is cleared from their consciousness.

"And now, in answer to the chelas' invocations to the violet flame, the fiery salamanders and the violet-flame angels, working hand in hand, retrace the record of that cycle when the lines of causation were drawn in the previous existence, which is also shown as chelas learn the lesson of blindly following the blind and of failing to invoke the wisdom of the Logos as a balance for the tyranny of the ego....

"Those who attended the viewing in our retreat of the events at Thrace saw firsthand and for the first time in this incarnation the violet flame in action in the transmutation of the records of the past."[536]

The Departments in the Heaven-World

Each retreat in the heaven-world is different in appearance and vibration, but all retreats are based on the same fundamental plan. Each contains buildings based on certain geometric patterns. Each has a temple, and the flame upon the altar is the principle focus of the retreat. There may also be other meeting or council rooms, laboratories and other wings with specific functions depending on the purpose of the retreat.

Different retreats have different purposes, and the vast heaven-world is well organized. There are many departments in heaven to oversee all kinds of activities that relate specifically to all aspects of life on earth. For example, there is a specialized branch that works with those who are thinking of suicide or who become victims of suicide. Another branch works with the control of demons and entities, disembodied spirits that exist on the astral plane. Another department deals with finance and seeks to influence and give advice to those who work with financial institutions. There are retreats devoted to healing, to government and to the balancing of the forces of nature.

There is a branch that works solely with incoming souls and children who are preparing to be born. Another segment of the Brotherhood assists those who are departing the earth in the transition called death. This team arranges for people to be met when they arrive in the heaven-world, almost like being met as you would come out of a bus terminal or a train station. At the moment when the person passes over, arrangements are made to have certain beings of light present. The Great Ones and the angelic hosts receive these people and remove them from all the destructive elements that they may have lived in on earth and take them to the schools of light. Here they are oriented and taught in preparation for their next stages of embodiment. Or if they are ready and worthy, they are taken to Luxor to the Ascension Temple of beloved Serapis Bey to be prepared for their ascension.

In all these avenues and compartments of being, the Brotherhood works for the benefit of mankind, working always to stabilize world conditions, to avert disasters or to prevent catastrophes from happening. For example, the Brotherhood was very active when the great plague came to France and other parts of Europe. They tried to stay the plague and work in conscious cooperation with mankind, but they were limited by the ability of mankind to work in conscious cooperation with them, for the ability of the angels and the masters to intercede is limited by mankind's free will.

When people pray and ask for intercession, when they turn over to God their free will and ask him and his angels to step in, this gives them the authority to act in the physical world. The Brotherhood continues to whisper to people all over the world what are the correct things to do in many situations, but sadly, the world does not always listen.

The Radiation from the Retreats Is Felt in the World

The retreats of the masters are great beacons of light in the antahkarana of the planet, and their effects are often felt quite tangibly from near and far. In many cases, the presence of the retreats accounts for the different "feel" or atmosphere in different places around the globe.

You feel entirely different in New York than you do in California or Colorado or Hawaii. The energy and vibrancy of New York comes from the action of the Temple of the Sun over Manhattan. The purity of areas of Northern California comes from the retreat of Archangel Gabriel and Hope between Sacramento and Mount Shasta and the retreat of the Goddess of Purity over San Francisco. The feeling of peace that one has in the Hawaiian Islands comes from the retreat of Elohim Peace and Aloha.

As you study the various retreats around the world, you will begin to notice that the momentum of a retreat can often be seen in the surrounding land and in the people who live nearby. (There is often seen the outpicturing of the true flame of the retreat, but we sometimes see instead mankind's misuse of the energies of that flame.) The retreat of Purity and Astrea, for example, has a profound impact on Russia. The austerity of the people, the concept of Mother Russia, the ability to work hard, fighting for one's nation, the nature of self-sacrifice—all these qualities come through the flame of purity, the influence of the retreat of the Elohim of the fourth ray.

Traveling to the Physical Locations of the Retreats

Many of the retreats are located in or near mountain ranges, often extending down into the mountains themselves. The mountains are also high above the vibrations of the world, inaccessible places with unpredictable weather. Here the retreats are almost impregnable to mankind, safe from desecration by unaware or uncaring mankind.

Many of the physical locations of the masters' retreats are refreshing places to visit due to the radiation of the retreats. Some of them are vacation or pilgrimage destinations—the retreat of the Elohim Peace and Aloha over the Hawaiian Islands, the Royal Teton Retreat over the Teton range in Wyoming, the retreat of Mother Mary and Archangel Raphael over Fátima, Portugal, and the retreat of Archangel Michael over Banff and Lake Louise, to name just a few. These are places where you can go not only to get a physical recharge, but also to recharge your spiritual batteries.

Many of the masters have visited the locations of the retreats during their lives on earth. For example, the apostle Paul went to Arabia following his conversion on the road to Damascus. (See Gal. 1:11–18.) During this sojourn, Paul's soul was tutored at Jesus' retreat on the etheric plane over Arabia.

When you do travel to these locations, it is always an opportunity to consciously tie into the energy of that retreat and to do spiritual work for the masters. In that moment, you can be like an electrode for the energies of Spirit to be anchored in Matter.

A "Visit" to Zadkiel's Retreat

On many occasions the ascended masters have arranged for their students and chelas to travel physically to the locations of their retreats. Elizabeth Clare Prophet tells of one such an experience when El Morya arranged for her to travel to the location of the etheric retreat of Lord Zadkiel and Holy Amethyst over the island of Cuba in 1974. She had been praying for freedom for the Caribbean nations when the opportunity unexpectedly arose for her to fly over Cuba.

"No sooner had I started my prayer momentum for this section of our hemisphere than El Morya arranged for me to fly there this week, and it was completely arranged in a most unique manner. I found myself the night before last on a private plane leaving the Florida mainland, going over the Florida Keys, and approaching the island of Cuba....

"It was to the site of this retreat that Saint Germain came when he was embodied as Christopher Columbus and he set forth in his ships to discover a new world. He was magnetized by the flame of freedom in that etheric temple where he had studied between embodiments and also during his embodiments while leaving his body in periods of sleep. Coming to those islands to chart a new course for a new land, the impetus was freedom.

"We wonder why a focus of freedom can be centered over an area of such darkness—why Communism, dictatorship and the suppression of the individual worth should mushroom right there where the highest concentration of energies for freedom are in this entire hemisphere. The reason is simple. The fallen ones, the archdeceivers, those who are organized against freedom, against the light of man and woman, always gather nearest the greatest light. And so they seek to usurp that light as it is released for the benefit of mankind. Other temples of freedom on the planet, such as the Temple of Mercy of Kuan Yin in Peking and the Rakoczy Mansion in Romania are in the same predicament.*

"We find, then, that in order for the energies of these etheric retreats to be anchored in our world, in the physical plane for action, there must be those in embodiment who know the Law and understand that the calls must be made, the flame must be invoked, that those who are in physical bodies must give the authority to the masters to lower their energies into manifestation....

"One of the things the Brotherhood teaches is that going physically to the area of a retreat and to a physical location near a retreat gives the disciple access to expand greater energies and to do a greater work for the Brotherhood. And if you study the locations of the retreats, you find that many times you come in proximity to them.

"So I found that when I had this opportunity to fly right over Cuba to go to the Cayman Islands, that I would not only be in physical proximity to the island of Cuba to make invocations for the freedom of the people, but I would also, in terms of time and space, be passing through the exact area where the retreat is anchored in the etheric plane above the island. And this is one reason why so many people like to fly, to get up in the air. You do get above what is

---

*In 1974, at the time of this lecture, Romania was behind the Iron Curtain and ruled as a Communist dictatorship.

called the mass consciousness into those planes where the ascended masters in another dimension do have their focuses. So it was a wonderful experience to know that I was actually passing right through—in another plane—a retreat, a focus, a flame of freedom, a retreat of the Brotherhood. And it was very, very tangible, as was the presence of Lord Zadkiel and Holy Amethyst.

"We were in a plane of about ten people, and as we approached the island of Cuba, I was able to stand behind the pilot and copilot and have a complete view of the island. And as I was making my invocations to the hierarchy and to Mother Mary to release those energies necessary for the freedom of this people, there came pouring forth out of heaven lightning and thunder—physical lightning and thunder—descending and crashing into the island, lighting up the island. And this was at night, so that I could see every portion of it and the cities, and the large part of this lightning was concentrated in Havana itself. So I felt that the elemental forces, forces of nature, were there to receive the energies invoked and to make them tangible....

"My experience for the day that followed was to be aware of those energies that actually oppose the divine family as the basic unit of society as they are anchored in that central focus in the islands of the Caribbean. This opposition to the light of the Christ in man and woman and child is energy that is spawned by the dark ones. It is the tearing down of the Real Self, the True Self, to make of people anything but the Christ, to make of them animals or humanists or philosophers or successful businessmen and women—all kinds of involvements in this world that take people's energies away from that central flame into the peripheral living that is continual gratification of the senses and that bottomless pit of desire.... Whether it is food or wealth or sex or continual pleasure, continual enjoyment of something new, it is that constant craving of the ego that sets up a forcefield of antichrist in the individual, and that is the beginning of the tearing down of the family.

"So as I left the Caribbean, I realized that my work had only begun, and that I had literally stirred up a hornets' nest of many forces that were determined not to be moved by the flame of the Christ."[537]

The Ancient Equation of Light and Darkness

Wherever there is a retreat, there is contained the mandala or perfect pattern for the civilization that is under the jurisdiction of that retreat. This may include more than one nation, usually an entire continent. The immediate area around that retreat is intended to outpicture exactly what is in that retreat, "as Above, so below." And yet, wherever a focus of light is held, there is also attracted to it the opposite kind of energy, which is drawn in for balance and transmutation. The more we understand the science of the etheric retreats, the more we can see how scientific also is the perversion of the correct application of energy, for those who misuse energy also follow a science.

We see one example of this in the retreat of Zadkiel and Holy Amethyst, which contains the highest concentration of energies for freedom in the entire hemisphere. And yet it is centered over an area where Communism and the denial of individual freedom is found.

China is another example of the interplay of these forces. There has come forth from the retreats over that ancient land, the retreats of Archangel Jophiel and Christine, of Kuan Yin and Elohim Cyclopea and Virginia, the delicate gentleness, the holiness of the family and the high degree of education in the true culture of China, sustained long before Western man was civilized. The true illumination of the crown chakra is the Father principle within man. But unfortunately we see that in China the Father principle has been eclipsed by the superstate, the perversion of the crown chakra, the perversion of the Father. The government has replaced the true image of the Father, the energies of the retreats of illumination over this nation are eclipsed, and man is not allowed to become the Christ or to raise his energies to attain Christ-mastery.

Yet this can be overcome through conscious cooperation with the very energies of these etheric retreats. When the people learn to invoke the full power of the energy of these retreats, the spell of the hypnotic state of consciousness can be broken. This work has been called the mighty work of the ages.

The Universities of the Spirit

In recent eras, few among mankind have entered the retreats and temples of the Great White Brotherhood. The retreats, once physical on the lost continents of Lemuria and Atlantis, were withdrawn to the etheric plane, reachable only by the most advanced initiates. With the dawning of the Aquarian age, however, lightbearers were given again opportunity to enter these retreats—this time by soul travel, apart from the physical body.

In the twentieth century, a number of the retreats were opened to unascended students of the masters, and on January 1, 1986, Gautama Buddha announced that the seven chohans of the rays had been granted approval by the Lords of Karma to open "Universities of the Spirit in each of their etheric retreats where they might welcome not dozens or hundreds but thousands and tens of thousands of students who will diligently pursue the path of self-mastery on the seven rays systematically, mastering most especially the first and the seventh rays....

"The plan, therefore, is for students to spend fourteen

days in Darjeeling and fourteen days with Saint Germain at the Royal Teton Retreat and to alternate these fourteen days as they weave a balance and restore themselves to the commitment of the beginning and the ending of the cycles of life.

"Having successfully passed certain levels, albeit beginning levels, nevertheless strong levels of accomplishment in the use of these rays, they will have a turn also with Lord Lanto and Confucius here at the Royal Teton and Paul the Venetian, who prefers to use in this hour the Temple of the Sun of the Goddess of Liberty, who is the Divine Mother of beloved Paul....

"Beloved ones, this training, then, will be for the rounding out of the threefold flame in the wisdom of the Path and especially in the development of the path of the sacred heart, the expansion of love that they might rid themselves of fear and hardness of heart and records of death surrounding that heart.

"Then, you see, comes the path of ministration and service, which is the logical manifestation of love and a balanced threefold flame. Through ministration and service in the retreat of Nada in Arabia, they will find, then, a place where they can give the same dynamic decrees you give here for all those untoward conditions in the area of the Middle East. And this shall be their assignment at inner levels even as they study the true path of Jesus Christ on that sixth ray as it has never been taught to them before.

"Having come through these retreats, they are now ready to be washed in the purity of the sacred fires of the ascension temple for a beginner's course and for the first baptism by water of the Divine Mother. Then they proceed to Crete with Paul the apostle, and there Hilarion shows them the Truth of all ages, and the science of Being is unfolded layer upon layer.

"Thus, having completed a round in all of these retreats—cycling fourteenday cycles, some repeated in the same retreat, some interchanging—they will come again to second and third levels of training on those seven rays."

The Opening of the Doors of the Retreats of the Archangels

After you have attended the retreats of the lords of the seven rays, you may also attend the retreats of the seven archangels. In a dictation given May 28, 1987, Jesus Christ spoke of the archangels as "teachers of Christhood par excellence." He said, "When you have done visiting even the retreats of the lords of the seven rays, may you perchance be invited to a series of studies in the retreats of the archangels. This, beloved, is my prayer unto the Father, who has responded by saying, 'My Son, let them prove themselves with thy brothers, the seven masters of light, and then they shall truly know the divine interchange with archangels.' So, beloved, rejoice that not alone Archangel Michael, who has called you in his service, but all of the seven may one day host you in their retreats for the accelerated initiations of life unto eternity."

On February 27, 1988, Archangel Raphael announced that he and Mother Mary, archangels of the fifth ray, were presenting to the world the opening of the doors of their temple "as the first opening in general of a retreat of the archangels to those who have passed beyond the levels of the mystery schools of the lords of the seven rays."

The Retreats of the Elohim

The retreats of the Elohim in the body of the earth and the focuses of the flame therein are like the seven major chakras in the body of man. They are the key focuses for the seven rays upon the planetary body. Unascended lifestreams are seldom taken into the retreats of the Elohim, for these are kept as pure, vibrating electrodes to infuse the body of Virgo and Pelleur with life and to attune it with cosmos. But we can call for the release of the concentrated momentum of the seven rays focused by the Elohim to be released into the planetary body at large, through the elemental kingdom and through the seven chakras in man as well as through the flame of the seven Elohim that is a focus in the forehead of every lifestream.

When visualizing this focus, think of the flame in the retreat of Cyclopea and Virginia, the triangle with the All-Seeing Eye in the center. Visualize a triangle with an All-Seeing Eye in the center of the forehead. See the green precipitation flame blazing through the triangle, and the eye and the radiance of the seven rays swirling around it. The green flame rises in the center, and the seven rays come out from the forehead at the angle of a shield on a cap, in all directions.

Since the Elohim have a cosmic consciousness and a cosmic service throughout the galaxies of the cosmos and on beyond the Great Central Sun, they appoint representatives to be the hierarchs, the administrators of their retreats. The retreats of the Elohim are like touchstones where they place their feet now and then, and where they anchor their consciousness as they are in and out of cosmic service. The Elohim can place an Electronic Presence of their being in their retreats, a replica of themselves, the full blazing Reality of their God consciousness focused there, and just as God himself can be everywhere in cosmos all at once, so they too can be everywhere in the consciousness of God.

Heaven is definitely coalesced and intermeshed with the planet Earth. The only problem that mankind really have is tuning in to the light that is already here in these retreats. There is that lie of separation between Spirit and Matter, and the only way it can be bridged is through invocation, calling forth the light in the name of the Christ, in the name of the I AM Presence. When the call is made, the light floods forth and is anchored. But unless the calls are made daily, the flame, which is the frequency of perfection, seeks its own level and returns to the plane of Spirit. That is why daily invocation is necessary, to continue to bring that perfection and hold it at a level that is actually unnatural to its internal forcefield—but only unnatural until the earth itself is assumed into the perfect state of the ascension.

The seven mighty Elohim are the original builders of form who created the planet in response to the mandates of the Godhead. The seven retreats on the earth of these seven spirits of God are keys to the very existence and life of the planet itself. The flames anchored there are most powerful, and many of their activities are known only to ascended masters.

Even the revelation of the name of the Elohim is a dispensation, because there is so much power even in the pronouncement of the these names. Each letter is the release of fohatic energy from the causal body of the Elohim.

Traveling to the Retreats

You can travel to the etheric retreats while your body sleeps at night. You can escape your physical body and leave the bounds of earth, traveling with or without consciousness. And there are things you can do to facilitate this journey.

It is a good idea to avoid heavy foods in the few hours before sleep so that the functions of the body can be at rest and the soul more easily ascend to higher octaves. It is also best to avoid violent or negative movies or television shows in the hours before sleep. These can magnetize the soul to lower levels

of consciousness instead of the highest levels of the etheric plane. A period of spiritual attunement before sleep, perhaps reading the words of the master, helps attune your consciousness with the intended destination. Where we are in consciousness before we sleep will often determine where we go.

And most important is to make the call—simply ask to be taken by Archangel Michael to the retreat nearest you or the retreat of your choice. Here is a short prayer you can give before you go to sleep to ask to be taken to the retreats. You can use it, for example, to

attend the two-week training sessions with the chohans of the rays. Make this call nightly, and see how the angels will swiftly take you, clothed in your finer bodies, to the ascended masters' classroom to learn important soul lessons.

Father, into thy hands I commend my spirit.

Mighty I AM Presence and Holy Christ Self, I call to Archangel Michael and his legions of blue-lightning angels to protect and transport my soul clothed in her finer bodies to the retreat of the ascended master _____ at _____ this night. Escort me, instruct me, guide and protect me as I work to set free all life on earth. I ask this be done in accordance with the holy will of God.

The Royal Teton Retreat is the most important retreat for newcomers and a very good place to start your conscious experiments with journeying to the retreats.

Some have asked what happens if they live in a different time zone and they are awake while others are asleep and visiting the retreats. Will they miss their classes? The answer is no. The retreats operate twenty-four hours a day in another dimension of time and space.

You may wish to keep a notebook by your bed and write down impressions or ideas that come to you on waking.

A Sense of Self-Worth

The masters have told us that sometimes the only barrier to our attending the retreats is a lack of the sense of self-worth. Like the prodigal son, we have been away so long that we hesitate at the threshold. Will I still be welcome after all this time?

Remember that God dwells in you, and God in you is worthy to attend the retreats of light. The master Morya addresses this subject and invites you to the Retreat of Good Will at Darjeeling: "I say to you again, the welcome mat is out. Here in Darjeeling we await the coming of those chelas who will recognize their spiritual prerogative—their right, if they choose to make themselves ready—to cast aside those human deep feelings and momentums of the past and, in the wonder of regeneration, to generate within themselves the tender feelings of love and compassion for the will of God, beholding in that will the same embodied thought that beloved Jesus beheld: 'Not my will, O mighty I AM Presence, but thine be done.'

"In this wondrous concept embraced, men shall find their freedom. Standing apart, standing backward and beholding it as a mere vision, as a possibility at some distant time, as a myth, as a hallucinatory grail that does not exist, men shall not find it. Recognizing that it is as close as hands and feet and heartbeat, men shall find it within themselves, and discovering it there, shall discover it everywhere.

"How then shall Darjeeling be closed against them? How shall any retreat of the ascended masters be closed against them? Those worthy to come to one are worthy to come to all. Those worthy to come to none are worthy to come to none. Unworthiness, beloved ones, is only the human concept that is not willing to recognize in God the freeing power whereby they may enter into the very heart of each ascended master retreat and draw from those retreats the fullness of that immortal love that shall lead them progressively forward, day after day, to that place upon the Path where the will of God can be known, loved, adored and cherished. And then that will cherish them.

"As the will of God cherishes you in response to your call, you shall find yourself vested from day to day with more of the radiance of the Brothers of the Diamond Heart."[538]

There Are Still Physical Retreats

When Atlantis sank and darkness filled the earth, many of the retreats of the Great White Brotherhood were withdrawn to the etheric plane. However, there are still a number of retreats that are anchored physically in the earth. The Royal Teton Retreat is one of these. It has physical chambers secured within the mountain of the Grand Teton in the Teton range, as well as etheric components beyond the physical plane. Hence it is called a physical/etheric retreat.

The retreat of the Master of Paris is a physical outpost of the Great White Brotherhood in the city of Paris. Godfré Ray King describes this retreat and

The Grand Teton

tells the story of his journey there in *The Magic Presence,* and it remains a place where students of the masters who meet the necessary qualifications may travel physically to assist in the work of the Brotherhood.

The masters have spoken of their desire in this age to once again bring their retreats into the physical. On November 23, 1975, El Morya said: "Saint Germain is not content to train the souls in the etheric retreats of the Great White Brotherhood. No, he is determined to have the focuses such as the focus of the Master of Paris, a home of light in the physical octave, a home of light in the city, a home of light where souls can be received. So then where are the stalwart ones? Where are the builders? Where are the pioneers who will have the courage to enter the canyons of New York City and Chicago and all of the great cities of America and the world?"

The masters have, from time to time, anchored their light in an outer focus dedicated by their chelas to the keeping of the Flame. And thus Pythagoras' mystery school at Crotona, King Arthur's Camelot, and ashrams in the Himalayas have been sponsored by the masters as physical outposts of the Brotherhood. The masters are once more looking for those who will dedicate themselves to the keeping of the Flame—the Flame on the altar that is the central focus of a retreat.

Descriptions of the Retreats of the Masters

On the following pages you will find the descriptions of all of the retreats that the masters have revealed to us thus far. Thirty-three years ago, the masters instructed Elizabeth Clare Prophet to sit down and record the details of these retreats. She sat for many weeks, night and day, as each master came before her to reveal the patterns of their consciousness and their purpose. In many cases they showed her the geometry and architecture of their retreats in such detail that she could have drawn them—their flames, the temples, the libraries, the meeting rooms, all that could be revealed. These original revelations are the core of what you will find here. In some cases, the masters or the messengers have released additional information since that time, and this information has also been included.

Of course, this list does not include every retreat of the Brotherhood, nor has every retreat been fully described. Many of the masters have not yet revealed the locations of their retreats. And for some, only the location is known—but even this knowledge in itself is a dispensation. Nevertheless, what we have received is a great gift, even as there is also much left for our own souls to discover in our journeys to the heaven-world.

Descriptions
of the Retreats

❖ APOLLO AND LUMINA'S RETREAT, The Retreat of the Elohim of the Second Ray

The Crown Chakra

The retreat of Apollo and Lumina is located in the etheric plane over Lower Saxony, Germany. Here the Elohim of the second ray focus the energies of the crown chakra of the planet.

On the outside of the building are three pillars in the formation of a triangle. These pillars are electrodes focusing a yellow star at the top of each one. There are three stories in the round dome of this etheric retreat, built in a parabolic curve. The first floor is the largest, the second and third are progressively smaller. A spherical focus of the flames of Apollo and Lumina is in the center of each of these three levels.

In the center of the first floor is a golden-yellow ball resembling a whirling galaxy, its component star clusters whirling at such a high frequency that they appear to be at perfect rest. In the center of the second floor is an identical sphere of brilliant sapphire blue. In the center of the upper room is another golden sphere like the one on the first floor. On each floor there is a spherical meditation room having as its focal point the spherical flame.

Each of these rooms accommodates approximately one thousand angels serving under Apollo and Lumina. Their glorious golden-yellow auras and robes make those who behold them feel as if they are in the center of the Great Hub. Classrooms, laboratories, libraries and archives form a radial pattern out from the center of the meditation room on each of the three floors. At the first level there is a circular hallway following the circumference of the building. On either side of the hall are three-dimensional exhibits showing the operation of the law of cycles throughout the earth. There are several thousand such displays atop square pillars about four feet high.

When the Elohim responded to the great command to go forth and create the earth, they did so through the initiation of cycles. The many cycles that are the components of our world actually make up its individuality. The cycles of earth, air, fire and water, of the mineral and plant kingdoms, of time and space—all of these are illustrated. These cycles are based on the law of the twelve illustrated in the twelve bands of the causal body and the twelve signs of the zodiac, also known as the twelve hierarchies of the Sun.

Also illustrated are the cycles of cosmic beings and their releases of light to the planet, the cycles of civilizations, the cycles of photosynthesis and precipitation. The electronic forcefield within the square blocks allows these displays to be suspended in air and to have "live parts," moving flames, spirals, showing the endless complexities of our world and making them simple through illustrations. One could easily spend a hundred years studying these displays and being tutored by the great cosmic scientists who serve in this retreat.

In preparation for the coming golden age, tremendous tides of illumination's flame are being released from this temple. The millions of angels who serve under Apollo and Lumina are ready to go forth to raise the consciousness of the entire earth to the level of the Christ in answer to the calls of the students. These, together with those angels serving at the retreats of Jophiel and Christine, Lord Lanto, the God and Goddess Meru, Lord Gautama Buddha, Lord Himalaya, Lord Maitreya and the World Teachers, should be called upon on behalf of the enlightenment of all mankind, for they are equal in every respect to the tremendous task at hand.

Apollo's flame is a golden yellow with a blue sheath. The action of the blue flame is a protective forcefield for the wisdom of the Christ. It precedes the manifestation of wisdom in the world of form, cutting through the density of human error and misqualified energy, paving the way for the manifestation of the Christ mind. Lumina's flame is a golden yellow, which follows after the flame of Apollo in the manifestation of the seven aspects of the Christ mind.

❖ **THE ARABIAN RETREAT, The Retreat of Jesus and Nada**

Jesus is in charge of the retreat of the Brotherhood in the Arabian Desert, northeast of the Red Sea. Raphael, Mother Mary and Nada also serve from this retreat with legions of angels of peace.

The Arabian Retreat is in a complex of buildings that were hermetically sealed by the masters before a cataclysm covered

The Arabian desert

them with desert sands. The tops of the buildings are now 125 feet beneath the surface.

Every seven years the International Council of the Great White Brotherhood is held in this subterranean city. The retreat is entered through an opening wide enough to admit cars, which drive down an incline into a parking lot and service area two hundred feet in diameter. When the jaws of the earth close, all that can be seen is desert, with no indication of the location of the retreat.

Descending almost four hundred feet by elevator, we enter a huge chamber with large columns, three hundred feet high and decorated with hieroglyphs. We proceed into an adjoining council chamber two hundred feet square, having a single great column in the center supporting the arched ceiling. At the base of the column inlaid in the floor are the cosmic symbols of the twelve houses of the sun. We note that they are different from the signs of the zodiac currently in use in the outer world. The entire architecture, as well as the interior design of this subterranean city, is of an ancient style resembling that which we think of as Greek and Roman.

As we are shown the marvels of the retreat, we enter the television chamber where there is a large reflector upon which one may observe, by the mere turn of a dial, the activities occurring at any given point upon the globe. In the adjoining radio chamber, completely proofed against sound and vibration, there is an instrument that is used to tune into sounds or conversations occurring anywhere on the planet. Thus, the masters have immediate contact with the activities of the outer world. The master K-17, head of the Cosmic Secret Service, frequents this retreat and uses these instruments to gain firsthand knowledge of the activities of the brothers of the shadow and their plots against individual and national freedom.

There is a chemical laboratory where initiates learn how to counteract germ warfare, poisonous gases and chemicals when such are released on a large scale for controlling the masses. In the cosmic-ray chamber, students are taught the use of the seven rays and how to direct them for the blessing of mankind. In the chambers of art, music and state, new techniques are being developed and will be released for the advancing culture and progressive forms of government that will be used in the golden age. In other chambers, the riches and records of ancient civilizations are kept and will one day be released for the edification and blessing of the people.

❖ **ARCTURUS AND VICTORIA'S RETREAT, The Retreat of the Elohim of the Seventh Ray**

The seat-of-the-soul chakra

The retreat of Arcturus and Victoria is on the etheric plane near Luanda, Angola, Africa. This retreat focuses the energies of the seat-of-the-soul chakra of the planet.

Approaching the retreat of these Elohim, we have the feeling that we are entering a mighty fortress. Occupying the space of approximately four city blocks, this massive four-story building reminds us of an ancient fortress built by one of the Mogul emperors. At the same time, the large towers at either of the front corners remind us of the Tower of London. These towers are large and round, with several tiers raised above the top story. The building is actually composed of a rough purple stone having the appearance of velvet. The personal flames of Arcturus and Victoria are anchored therein: the purple of Arcturus to our left, the violet and pink of Victoria to our right.

We are led through the front entrance in the center, and we enter the great hall, which is two stories high and is finished with a highly polished purple and white stone. There are twenty-four pillars evenly distributed in the hall. The ceiling is a darker shade of purple, and the floor a lighter shade. In the center is the magnificent focus of the violet-purple-pink flame. Intensely brilliant, yet gentle in radiation, it permeates the entire hall. It is the "Welcome Home!" of the Elohim—the AUM of their white-fire bodies, which they have chosen to focus as the comfort of the mercy flame to their guests.

At the second-story level of the hall is a balcony. Both above and below, one may enter chambers where council meetings are held under the direction of the Elohim. There is an audience room with thrones for Arcturus and Victoria composed of a purple crystalline substance, one darker than the other. The conference table and chairs, which nearly fill the room, are of a violet-colored marble.

The planetary focus of the purple flame is located over the etheric retreat, an intense and fiery emanation from the heart of the Elohim precipitated from the great house. Its influence extends over the entire planetary body and can be seen from a great distance, rising as a jet d'eau high into the sky, a literal pillar of fire by night and a cloud of witness by day.

The retreat of Arcturus and Victoria is dedicated to the freedom of all mankind through the alchemical action of the flame, the mercy of the Great Law, and the love of the Father-Mother God. Legions of violet, pink and purple-flame angels serve from here; and there is an intense activity of elemental life, who come and go as though this were truly their home on earth.

Other foci where Arcturus and Victoria have flames (but no retreats) are over Australia, the South Pole, the Pyrenees Mountains, Siberia, Victoria Island in northern Canada, and the southern tip of South America.

❖ **THE ASCENSION TEMPLE AND RETREAT AT LUXOR, The Retreat of Serapis Bey**

The Ascension Temple is at Luxor on the Nile River in Egypt. The Temple is a part of the retreat at Luxor, which is presided over by Serapis Bey. Archangel Gabriel and Hope also serve here.

The etheric retreat of the Brotherhood of Luxor is superimposed upon the physical retreat, which is composed of a large, square, white stone building with a surrounding wall and courtyard, and an underground building including the Ascension Temple and Flame Room.

A few miles from the focus is a pyramid, also superimposed with etheric activity. Here in the upper room of the pyramid is the king's chamber, where the initiations of the transfiguration and the resurrection take place. Other rooms within the pyramid are used for initiations given by the Council of Adepts to the devotees who come to Luxor prepared for the most severe disciplines and the total surrender of their human consciousness.

The focus of the ascension flame was carried by Serapis Bey to this location just before the sinking of Atlantis. In succeeding embodiments, he and the brothers who had served in the Ascension Temple on Atlantis built the retreat, which was originally above ground. Here in an underground building is the circular courtroom where the last judgment is conducted by the Council of Adepts. Nearby is the Flame Room, a square building having doors on two sides. One enters here only as a candidate for the ascension, after all initiations have been passed.

Forming another square within the room are twelve white pillars, decorated in gold relief at the base and the top, which surround the central dais on which the ascension flame blazes. They represent the twelve hierarchies of the Sun and the twelve Godly attributes. Each one who ascends from this Temple is ascending because he has attained God-mastery through the disciplines and the tutelage of one of these twelve hierarchies, the hierarchy under whom he was born in the embodiment in which he was destined to ascend.

The candidate for the ascension is bidden by the hierarch of the retreat to pass through the pillars and to stand in the center of the ascension flame. At that point, the individual's cosmic tone is sounded and the flame from Alpha is released from the circle on the ceiling, while the flame from Omega rises from the base. The moment the individual's tone is sounded and simultaneous with the action of the flame, the seraphim in the outer court trumpet the victory of the ascending soul with the most magnificent rendition of the "Triumphal March" from Aïda that anyone will ever hear. The discipline that is the keynote of this retreat is felt in their precise, golden-tone rendition of the piece.

In the underground complex there are other flame rooms for the meditation of the devotees who serve there. There is a focus of the resurrection flame, and there are chambers for the preparation of various initiations, including those of the transfiguration and the resurrection.

Serapis Bey's methods of discipline are tailor-made for each candidate for the ascension. After an initial interview by himself or one of the twelve adepts, devotees who come here are assigned in groups of five or more to carry out projects with other initiates whose karmic patterns lend themselves to the maximum friction between the lifestreams. Each group must serve together until they become harmonious, learning that those traits of character that are most offensive in others are actually the polarity of their own worst faults, and what one criticizes in another is likely to be the root of his own misery. Aside from this

Ruins of the Temple at Luxor

type of group discipline, individuals are placed in situations that provide them with the greatest challenge, according to their karmic pattern. In this retreat one cannot simply up and leave a crisis, a circumstance or an individual that is not to his liking. He must stand, face and conquer his own misqualified energy by disciplining his entire consciousness in the art of nonreacting to the human creation of others, even as he refuses to be dominated or influenced by his own human creation.

The ascension flame is an intense fiery white with a crystal glow. The Easter lily is the symbol of the flame and its focus in the nature kingdom, and the white diamond is its focus in the mineral kingdom. The melody of the flame is the "Triumphal March" from *Aïda*, and the keynote of the retreat is "Liebestraum," by Franz Liszt.

Serapis Bey writes: "I am announcing to all candidates of the ascension and to all who desire to be candidates for the ascension flame at the close of this or their next embodiment that we have arranged classes at our retreat that may be attended by those aspiring after Purity's matrix.

"To those who have said in their hearts, 'I desire above all to be perfect in the sight of God, to have that perfect mind in me which was also in Christ Jesus,'[539] to those who yearn to merge with the flame of God's identity and to find themselves made in the image and likeness of God, to those in whom this desire burns day and night—to you I say, Come and be tutored in those precepts of the Law that perhaps have escaped you in this life or which perhaps you have overlooked in previous embodiments.

"For we are here to fill in the missing links in the chain of Being so that when the hour of your transition comes and you find yourself as the rose on the other side of the wall, you will have the momentum and the inner soul-direction that will carry you to this or one of the other retreats of the Brotherhood either for final preparation for the ascension or for preparation for reembodiment."[540]

❖ **BLUE FLAME, SACRED RETREAT OF THE,** *See* **The Sacred Retreat of the Blue Flame**

❖ **BLUE LOTUS, RETREAT OF THE,** *See* **Retreat of the Blue Lotus**

❖ **THE CATHEDRAL OF NATURE, The Retreat of Kuthumi in Kashmir**

The Cathedral of Nature is the retreat of the ascended master Kuthumi. It is found just above Dal Lake in Srinagar, Kashmir. The physical focus of the etheric retreat is in the beautiful gardens that grace the environs of the lake. These gardens were designed and executed under the direction of Kuthumi in his embodiment as Shah Jahan, the emperor who also built the Taj Mahal in Agra between 1632–1650.

The house where it is said Kuthumi was born

In one of the gardens is a house that is said to be the birthplace of Kuthumi in his last embodiment. Nearby there is another house with a spring of pure water, said to heal many forms of incurable diseases. Pilgrims come from all over to partake of the waters of this spring. Behind the gardens is a mountain, the physical anchoring point for the etheric retreat of beloved Kuthumi, whose flame of illumined peace can be felt throughout the region.

The massive center hall of the retreat is built of a substance resembling marble, combined with sparkling white stones. The giant dome over the hall is composed of the same material. Marble benches form a circular pattern around the center of the room, while on the periphery, they are perpendicular to the sides in a ray-like pattern. The benches are at some distance from one another, leaving room for the masters to gather a group of their disciples around each of these benches.

The colors of the causal body are introduced into this great white hall in the cushions on the seats of the benches; the masters and their disciples wear golden robes, being of the Order of the Brothers of the Golden Robe. Twenty-four-hours a day, groups of disciples with their teacher gather in this great hall. At intervals during each twelve-hour cycle, either the Lord of the World, the Representative of the Cosmic Christ, or one of the World Teachers enters the hall and stands on the raised dais in the center to

address the masters and their disciples. On the
occasion when one of the aforementioned masters gives a discourse, the smaller groups unite
into one large group facing the center.

Adjacent to the great white hall is a flame
room where the focus of the flame of illumination is guarded. Here the Brothers of the
Golden Robe come and sit in the lotus posture
to meditate, to pray and to expand the action of
the flame on behalf of their brothers and sisters
both in and out of embodiment. Other buildings form a part of the complex of this retreat,
including libraries containing scrolls of wis-

Gardens above Dal Lake

dom, guarded by the angels of illumination. In these buildings, the usual
functions of a retreat are carried on by the administrators under the hierarch. These include the programming of education for the entire planet and
the enlisting of souls, either in embodiment or who are preparing for
embodiment, to study these plans and then go forth to implement them in
the world of form.

Kuthumi writes: "I am known as a master of peace, but I prefer to be
called simply a Brother of the Golden Robe. That holy order, which was
founded long ago by one who saw true knowledge as the peace that pas-
seth understanding, still functions today; and we count among our band
ascended ones who have espoused the golden flame of illumination as a
means of imparting peace to mankind as well as those unascended brothers and sisters who desire to become the peaceful presence of His wisdom
to all mankind.

"We are looking for recruits. Therefore I write to you to apprise you
of the fact that there are openings in our chambers, in our libraries and in
our retreats—openings for those who diligently call and are willing to be

Gardens in Srinagar with
Dal Lake in the distance

the allness of the All to hearts hungry
for the flame, never chary. Yes, we have
openings for those who are not chary in
their use of the flame as they call with a
mighty fervor upon His name....

"If you would attend our University
of the Spirit to learn the way to teach
men how to pray, then I say, Call to me
and ask the angelic hosts to accompany
you to my retreat in Kashmir. And we

shall receive you here to hear the Word—not mine alone, but of the masters of the Himalayas, who have outlined a course of instruction for the teachers of the race."[541]

❖ THE CATHEDRAL OF THE VIOLET FLAME

On October 11, 1975, in San Francisco, Archangel Zadkiel announced the transfer from the priests and priestesses of the Violet Planet of the Cathedral of the Violet Flame. He said: "In this moment it is being transported by angelic hosts as they carry this giant cathedral to be placed in the etheric plane of earth's atmosphere for the consecration of the violet flame and as another focal point for souls desiring to be free to frequent while their bodies sleep at night. And therefore, the Cathedral of the Violet Flame is placed in the heart of the Rocky Mountains in commemoration of the light of freedom of the Ruler of the Violet Planet, Omri-Tas, who does respond to the calls of men and women who pursue the light of freedom, yet do not know of the violet flame. Hail unto the children of light! Hail to the elementals! For they are invited also to enter into the Cathedral of the Violet Flame to be saturated with that light, to be cleared of all of the burdens of the planes of mankind's consciousness....

"The focuses of light in this Cathedral are the jewels of the amethyst and violet crystals of many varieties that also hold the action of the violet flame. And these crystals are not native to Terra but come from the Violet Planet as specimens of that which coalesces there as the crystallization of the Christ mind....

"Remember to enter the Violet Flame Cathedral. You will find violet-flame angels tending there, tending the flame of sacred fire, and you will also find on the altar, the central altar, a focus of jade, the gift of the Angel Deva of the Jade Temple, placed there as the offering of healing for those who come to have their substance transmuted—a focus of jade, healing jade, for the removal of the cause and core of that sin and that struggle that produce disease in mind, in souls, in bodies.

"And you will see also certain angels, twelve in number, who come from the Temple of the Angel Deva. You will also see an arc of light from that temple in China to the temple in North America. And if you are fortunate in the flame of living Truth, you may also find the Angel Deva standing there also officiating at the altar with the violet-flame angels.

"So I have come in the midst of the judgment to tell you of this gift of the priests and priestesses of the sacred fire. So make your way to the Cathedral of the Violet Flame and be blessed as you carry that flame north and south and east and west."[542]

❖ **THE CAVE OF LIGHT, The Retreat of the Great Divine Director in the Himalayas**

The Cave of Light is the retreat of the Great Divine Director in the heart of the Himalayas in India. His second spiritual home of light is the Rakoczy Mansion in the Carpathian Mountains of Transylvania. Chananda is the hierarch of the Cave of Light, which is located in the mountain behind his retreat, the Palace of Light.

The Himalayas

The Great Divine Director is a great initiator on the path of the ascension, and one of the purposes of the Cave of Light is to conduct activities to prepare and accelerate candidates for the ascension. Here, the Great Divine Director uses his authority to purify the four lower bodies of advanced initiates of a portion of their remaining karma, to give them purified vehicles to render a cosmic service in the world of form prior to their ascension.

On occasion, unascended lifestreams are taken in their finer bodies to the retreats of the Brotherhood in order to be trained for special service in the world of form that requires superhuman strength and certain disciplines that can only be imparted to the unascended initiate in the retreats. Thus, Jesus was taken into the retreat in Luxor and into the Temple of the Blue Lotus prior to his final three-year ministry.

Some who have been commissioned to go forth in the name of the Brotherhood and who had not yet transmuted their remaining karma received the assistance that was given in the Cave of Light to Godfre, Rex and Nada Rayborn, and Bob and Pearl Singleton whereby their four lower bodies were purified and aligned in order that they might be the immaculate receptacles of the Christ consciousness. When this dispensation is accorded worthy chelas, their remaining service to life is magnificently accomplished because their consciousness has become the perfect focal point in the world of form for the release of the entire Spirit of the Great White Brotherhood. Miracles, demonstrations of alchemy, and the control of natural forces and elemental life become the mark of those who are so blessed by the opportunity of being "perfected" prior to their final initiation and ascension in the light.

In *The Magic Presence*, Godfré Ray King describes being escorted to the Cave of Light by Chananda, along with Rex, Nada, Bob and Pearl. He describes the retreat as a cave of "wondrous beauty" encrusted with dazzling crystalline substance similar to the Cave of Symbols in America. Going far into the cave, they came to doors of solid gold. Inside, it looked like the white heat of a great furnace. Two days and two nights later, they emerged from this Eternal Flame wearing "new bodies of immortal endurance."[543]

The Great Divine Director has spoken of some of the magnificent focuses of light within his retreat: "Do you know also that even in the Cave of Light in India there are replicas of light-magnificence concerning liberty and freedom? Do you know that the replicas and symbols of divine light for and on behalf of America were created by the ascended masters, and they are talismans of great power. Out of these talismans, beamed by the angelic beings and focused by a greater power than in the ancient Atlantean crystals, manifests the intention of Almighty God for this nation!"[544]

Mother Mary has spoken of the Cave of Light as symbolizing the secret chamber of the heart. The Blessed Mother explains that "only in the secret chamber is there safety when outer turmoil prevails in the seven bodies of earth, in the seven layers, even above the surface of the earth. Therefore, you see, my secret chamber is also as a secret chamber in a great pyramid, a secret chamber in the mountain of God.

"In all eras, initiates processioning into the interior place prepared have signified that the hour is come when for the individual and even for a civilization there is the great inbreath—not that which draws in all of a cosmos, but that drawing in, beloved, of the seven rays of attainment that these might be condensed into the crystal that is formed in this interior castle.

"There comes the hour when the expansive manifestations of attainment, of God-mastery, even the accumulation of abundance must now be condensed. And that which is the heart and the essence of the harvest then becomes the nucleus of crystal, harder than rock or diamond. This substance, beloved, begins to form the cave of light.

"Now you understand the use of the term 'Cave of Light' by the Great Divine Director. Blessed ones, his Cave of Light is a consecration to the eighth-ray chakra and the secret chamber of the heart. Not only is it a place of safety, a haven of initiation, not only is it the place where the soul puts on, enters into [the Christ consciousness], but as Christ assimilates her, so the soul and the Christ become one. Thus, in the next round, when going forth from the secret chamber as from the tomb itself, beloved, the soul steps forth fully the manifestation of Christ, the Body and Blood of Christ, the Sacred Heart of Christ.

"Thus may you understand a mother's teaching in this hour of the commencement of initiation of the five secret rays—five levels, then, of the secret chamber of the heart, as though five spherical, interlocking chambers.

May you enter. May you understand. May you know.

"Going to the Heart of the Inner Retreat is another symbolical and actual entering in. Blessed ones, I bring this initiation to your attention, for the hour is coming when you will know the meaning of the word 'safety in the ark of the Lord.' The secret chamber of my heart is the place of safety."[545]

Many ascended masters frequent the Cave of Light. Saint Germain spends a great deal of time there. Chananda tells us that he will be there to welcome us also, in the name of the Great Divine Director. Leto also calls us to this retreat, describing it as "a home of light that you will scarcely desire to leave. The Cave of Light is a forcefield incomparable; an invitation to be there is worth gold itself.... Forget not to call to me in the hour of your journey to the Cave of Light, and I will come with angels shining with a purple light to arc your soul to the special room and the special chair."[546]

The Great Divine Director himself invites us to his retreat, but asks us to first prepare ourselves by devotion to the will of God. He says: "I bid you to come to the Cave of Light when you are ready. And I say, do not come until you are ready, for the doors will not open and the welcome mat will not be out unless you have fully prepared to surrender your all, your life, your service, your will to the will of God. And then we may require that you serve a time in another retreat before you are accepted into that Cave of Light.

"Thus realize that the disciplines of our branch of the hierarchy involve the tethering of the soul to divine direction. If you cannot hear that direction, you will not be ready for our retreat. Thus, you see, you must he tutored in developing the sensitivities of the soul consciousness so that you can be certain when the Lord God, through one of his emissaries, places the rod of power upon you and gives you the key of light and the rod of power that you will detect that direction and follow it to the fullest capability of your consciousness.

"Thus, discerning God-direction is a science in itself, and you will learn much of that science at the ascended masters' university. You will also learn it in the retreats of the violet flame presided over by Lord Zadkiel and by Saint Germain, for these prepare souls for the Cave of Light. And thus these hierarchs should be appealed to. As you retire each night and take your leave of your physical body, the soul travels in its etheric envelope. And if you invoke these masters ere you leave, they will guide you unerringly to the place prepared, the manger, the haven of light in one of the retreats of the Brotherhood where the Christ can be born in you and where you can bear the Christ for all mankind."[547]

❖ **THE CAVE OF SYMBOLS, The Retreat of Saint Germain in the Rocky Mountains**

The Cave of Symbols is the retreat of Saint Germain in Table Mountain in North America's Rocky Mountains. This is an important focus, and many inventions are to be released from this retreat. Saint Germain uses this retreat along with the Rakoczy Mansion in Transylvania, the Cave of Light and the Royal Teton Retreat.

One enters through a cavern in the mountain lined with pink and white crystal and then moves on into a vaulted chamber two hundred feet wide covered with stalactites of rainbow hue in the formation of occult symbols. As focuses of the rainbow rays of God and geometric keys to the release of fohat, the energy that blazes through these symbols extends throughout the United States and has a most significant influence upon her people, keying into their consciousness the matrix of the golden age and the remembrance of their lost inheritance. The cave derives its name from these symbols.

On the opposite wall, at the far side of the chamber, there are three arches, spaced twenty feet apart: the first a deep rose, the second a penetrating white and the third a cobalt blue. These are the focuses of great cosmic beings for the victory of the Christ consciousness in America.

Accompanied by the master Saint Germain, who raises his hand toward the center archway, we gain entrance to a tunnel that opens at his command. After several hundred feet, he shows us through a door on which there are more ancient symbols into a twelve-sided, domed room sixty feet in diameter. Immediately we notice that four of the twelve sides are a brilliant white (focusing the purity of the Christ consciousness in the four elements and the four lower bodies of the planet). The remainder are the pastel hues of the rays.

In this room we are shown the fantastic radio invented by the ascended lady master Leonora, by which one can communicate with other planets in this solar system, with the center of the earth, or with any point on the surface of the earth. There are chemical and electrical laboratories where scientists are perfecting formulas and inventions they have been permitted to take from the hermetically sealed cities at the bottom of the Atlantic Ocean that have been protected since the sinking of Atlantis. These discoveries will be brought forth for mankind's use in the golden age, just as soon as man has learned to harness greed, selfishness and the desire to control others through war and dishonest financial policies.

When the Sons of God are once again in control of the great nations of the world, the ascended masters will step forth with a tremendous wealth of information that has been guarded in their retreats for ages. Here, unascended scientists come forth in their finer bodies while asleep or between embodiments. Students of the light can also ask to be taken there. Saint Germain is training a large cadre of souls devoted to the Christ and to the science of the Christ, who at the proper time will have lowered into the outer consciousness all that they have learned in this and other retreats of the Brotherhood.

There is even what is called an "atomic accelerator"—a golden chair through which are passed electronic currents that quicken the vibratory pattern of the atoms and electrons within the four lower bodies. Initiates of the Brotherhood who have proven their merit by service and devotion to the light and who have already balanced a considerable amount of their karma are allowed to sit in this chair for a length of time prescribed by the master Saint Germain and the Lords of Karma. By accelerating the light frequency in the four lower bodies, a portion of one's karma is balanced and a portion of one's misqualified substance is thrown off by the centrifugal action produced by the revolving electrons and transmuted by the sacred fire.

Thus, the individual's four lower bodies can be accelerated in ascension currents and the soul raised into the ascension. Under the sponsorship of Saint Germain, many lifestreams have ascended from this very room.

Entering an elevator, we descend a hundred feet into the heart of the mountain, emerging in a circular room having a diameter of twenty feet. We are led through a door into a huge hall equipped with furnaces and machines for the production of materials used in the experimental work carried on in the chemical and electrical laboratories in the upper level of the retreat.

Returning to the upper level, we are shown a reception hall with a domed ceiling, adjoining sleeping quarters, and an audience hall also with a domed ceiling of sky blue with painted clouds, giving the impression of being in the open air. Here there is a magnificent organ and piano that is used by the masters to focus the harmonizing currents of the music of the spheres on behalf of the freedom of sons and daughters of God on earth.

The Cosmic Mirror is on the east wall of the Crystal Chamber. When the disciple has reached a certain degree of attainment, he is taken by the master before the Cosmic Mirror, which keys into his etheric body and reflects his past lives, including the cause and effect upon his world of every thought, feeling, word and deed he has ever manifested. The Cosmic Mirror also reflects the original blueprint of his divine plan that is placed upon the etheric body when the soul is born in the heart of God. In viewing his past lives, the disciple then may learn what portion of the divine plan he has outpictured. He may see what conditions in his world must be corrected and what good momentums he has developed that he can now use to overcome the difficulties of the past and the present and thus fulfill his divine plan in the very near future.

At the far end of the audience hall, through a concealed door, one enters the Sphere of Light, a spherical-shaped room where the focus of the sacred fire is used to intensify the expansion of the light within those who are permitted to enter there. The function of this room correlates with the action of the light in the Cave of Light in the charge of the Great Divine Director in India. Together with the Atomic Accelerator, these focuses serve to bring the disciples of the masters closer to their ascension and to provide them with the assistance to accelerate the process that could not be achieved in the outer world.

It is a very real and enlivening experience to stand before the Cosmic Mirror in this retreat. The disciple needs to be ready to look through the illusions, the fantasies and the synthetic self. He must be able to own up to the deceits that the ego continually practices against itself. It is not possible to hide anything from God. The sincere student who would like to get rid of these illusions may call to Saint Germain to be taken to stand before the Cosmic Mirror.

❖ LE CHÂTEAU DE LIBERTÉ, The Retreat of Paul the Venetian in Southern France

In the south of France on the river Rhône is a focus of the flame of liberty and the retreat presided over by Paul the Venetian, chohan of the third

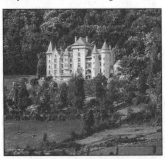

A château in Southern France

ray. The description of Paul's retreat contained herein is of the etheric focus, which is congruent with and extends far beyond a physical castle now owned and maintained by a private French family. Much of the physical surroundings resemble the etheric counterpart; however, the master rarely manifests in the lower octave. The castle itself contains many great works of art and at certain times during the year it is open to the public, even as the great halls in the etheric retreat are open to students of the Venetian who come to study art and culture and the true concepts of liberty.

This vast retreat lends itself to the function of gallery, museum and archives of art and artifacts from many cultures and civilizations. A Versailles of its own splendor, it contains endless classrooms where great works of art of all ages are displayed. Paintings by Paul, his students and other masters abound. Here workshops for musicians, writers, sculptors, students of voice as well as crafts of all kinds have been held, and ascended masters of all the rays have introduced new techniques in every field of art.

The art of beauty and the art of liberty are everywhere in evidence. When one is present upon its surrounding landscape, one enjoys the rise and fall of the waters from the marble fountains, the musical trills of the birds of multicolored plumage, the water lilies on the ponds, the beautiful and fragrant roses that bedeck the graceful marble columns, and the magnificent statuary from the many centuries past.

Within the walls one is also exposed to an exhibit of the grandeur of expression in sculpture, painting and music—the piano, cello, organ, harp and the caroling of the many voices of the choirs. Those who are accomplished in and are exponents of the fine arts—music, writing, sculpture— frequent the Château as guests to imbibe the radiation of its beauty.

But one sees not only the sculpture of genius and hears the music of the spheres, but also the crude attempts of the hopeful amateurs—the timid endeavors of the beginners who have taken their first cautious steps upon the ladder of attainment. It is easy to enjoy the beauty and the fragrance of the flower once its petals are unfolded, but it is the tender shoot first appearing above ground that needs the nourishment of divine love.

Within the Château walls, therefore, the crudest of expressions have an honored place. For to the least of these aspirants, the ascended master Paul extends his loving care, lest their first attempts be shriveled and the bud fall from the stem. Within the circumference of his consciousness, he welcomes all those sons with motives pure; for he considers each man's heart a "Château de Liberté" within which is enshrined the flame of liberty, pulsating to expand some talent, gift or grace—the individual facet of the God-intent for each lifestream. He sees each one's potential and esteems it his reason for being to help each one refine his crude expressions into beautiful designs—whether in statesmanship, in education, in the fine arts, in science, in medicine, in ministration or in the understanding of pure Truth.

As host at his retreat, he greets—with the dignity and majesty of an ascended one—all these chelas of his heart. Beyond the entrance to the etheric retreat, they enter an expansive hall where they are held spellbound by the radiation from the canvas on the wall ahead. This is Paul's painting of the Holy Trinity. Its vibrant emanations throughout the entrance chamber inspire in each beholder such reverent awe, he dare not move nor speak for quite some time. The heavenly Father is portrayed by a majestic figure. The likeness of Jesus depicts the Son, and an impressive white dove with a nine-foot wingspan focuses the Holy Spirit. Begun before his ascension and completed thereafter, this great work of art focuses both dimensions of Paul's service to the earth. Beneath the painting Paul inscribed in gold letters, "Perfect love casteth out fear."

As they become accustomed to this exalted state, the students move across the tessellated floor and descend the stairs, passing through the corridor that leads to the auditorium known as the Flame Room. The threefold flame of liberty is in the center of the room, focused within a golden chalice. Within the base of the chalice is a concentration of the crystal fire mist, the white light out of which the threefold flame proceeds. The focus of the flame of liberty was brought by the Goddess of Liberty from the Temple of the Sun near what is now Manhattan just before the sinking of Atlantis, when the physical structure of the Temple of the Sun was destroyed by cataclysmic action.

The radiance from the flame renders the room as bright as the sun. Paintings done by Paul depicting the saints and sages of all times grace the circular walls of the room. Devotees enter the Flame Room to pay their respects to the flame and to briefly absorb its pulsations, which expand as the rhythm of a giant heartbeat. The focus is so intense that they are asked to meditate in other rooms of the retreat provided for that purpose. The entire retreat vibrates to the rhythm of the liberty flame.

The fleur-de-lis design that we see in the retreat is the symbol of the threefold flame. It is no mere coincidence that the crowned heads of France adopted this symbol as their emblem, for the real liberty flame blazed upon their native soil.

For centuries Paul has felt that beauty is a necessary part of the thought and feeling processes of those who desire spiritual progress, who desire to obtain their freedom and the liberty to do the will of God. He feels that one's capacity to appreciate eternal beauty is expanded in accordance with one's adoration to his own God Presence. Speaking to his chelas, he has said:

"I come as the lord of the third ray of God's divine love, to strengthen the children of God by the power of the Lord's strength wherewith he strengthened his prophet of old....

"I would impress upon you the very patterns that issue from the heart of God—patterns that, as floral cups, are made up of the exact geometry that is required to sustain a momentum of love upon the planet in the last days.

"Precious hearts, it is one thing to have in the mind an idea of love, to think of love, to accept love when all is going well; but I would train you to magnetize love as a vortex of pulsating light-essence that is not moved—that cannot be moved—come what may. To sustain a focus of love when all the world is confounded by the volleying of their hatreds is the calling of the avatars and of their chelas who count not the cost as they give their all for the salvation of a planet and its people.

"Now then, I would take you into my drill sessions. Yes indeed, we do drill in my retreat. Those of you who think that we spend all our days and nights in painting and sculpture and divine arts must realize that each of the seven rays issues forth from the white-fire core of God's Being, and in that white-fire core is the full complement of his consciousness. And so, I have an army of beauty-bearers, those who bear the consciousness of beauty to mankind; and they do march in formation and most lovingly come under the disciplines of Serapis Bey. For they see that out from the flaming center of ordered purity comes forth the pattern whereby they can not only precipitate beauty, but they can also release it to mankind and impress it upon the consciousness of the race.

"Patterns of loveliness are the salvation of mankind, for each perfect design that originates as divine blueprint within the fiery center of life and is then embellished by the adoration of the cherubim and the flaming-pink angels presents to the consciousness of mankind a passion for living, for striving and for reaching the ultimate goal of reunion with the God Self....

"In our drill exercises we impress upon the neophytes as well as the advanced disciples in our retreat the necessity of discipline in outpicturing beauty. We drill the mind through meditation upon perfect forms. We drill the emotions of God-control; and we show how each one may command the perfect feelings of God to be the receptacles of God's light within his consciousness and how he can, in the name of the risen Christ, refuse to admit aught else, especially the teeming emotions of the mass mind.

"This can be done, precious hearts. Do not doubt that you, even in your present state, can rise quickly—no matter what your level of attainment—to greater self-mastery and greater control of the fires of creation. For when you come right down to it, the fires of creativity held within the forcefield of man determine what he can accomplish in his earthly span.

"If you are ready for the disciplines of love, then I invite you to come to France, to the Château de Liberté. Come on wings of song and wings of glory."[548]

❖ **COMFORT, TEMPLE OF,** *See* **The Temple of Comfort**

❖ **CRYSTAL-PINK FLAME, TEMPLE OF,** *See* **The Temple of the Crystal-Pink Flame**

❖ **CYCLOPEA AND VIRGINIA'S RETREAT, The Retreat of the Elohim of the Fifth Ray**

The retreat of Cyclopea and Virginia focuses the energies of the third-eye chakra of the planet and is located high in the Altai Range where China,

The third-eye chakra

Siberia and Mongolia meet, near Tabun Bogdo. The entire retreat is in the etheric realm, although congruent with the mountains.

The massive emerald crystal front resembles a church, having a high central steeple and two lesser steeples on either side. We enter a room that appears as though it has been carved out of the mountain, out of a deep jade colored rock. A Gothic vaulted ceiling, with pillars of green crystal and others of a marble stone effect, seems to support the very mountain itself. A circular sunken room within a larger square room is the focus for the emerald ray. The blazing consciousness of the Elohim suspends therein an all-seeing eye within a triangle. The six pillars surrounding the central altar are five-sided, crystal green. They remind us that we are in a temple dedicated to precipitation.

We note a very active silence in the retreat, a reverence for the science to which all who serve here are dedicated. Our host takes us into several of

Tabun Bogdo, Altai Range

the most important rooms, and as we walk, we note the hieroglyphs on the walls, which we are told are ancient records deciphered only for the most advanced initiates.

We enter a gold room, the precipitation room, decorated in green and gold velvet with jade, pulsing with the flame of green and gold.* Here the great masters gather in council meetings to discuss the very destiny of the planet and to formulate plans for the implementation of the higher science

---

*The green of the precipitation flame is a Chinese green, which has more yellow in it and is tinged with gold, whereas the emerald green of the All-Seeing-Eye is more of a blue-green.

through and among embodied mankind.

We are shown a fountain of healing in an indoor garden with some of the world's most beautiful flowers and tropical birds and one of the most rare botanical collections we have ever seen, including some specimens now extinct and others that are yet to be brought forth. Only advanced initiates are taken through the remaining rooms, laboratories, libraries and chambers where angels and masters serve the evolutions of the planet through their devotion to the cosmic science taught by the Elohim.

❖ **THE DARJEELING RETREAT,** *See* **The Temple of Good Will**

❖ **DIVINE MOTHER, RETREAT OF THE,** *See* **The Retreat of the Divine Mother**

❖ **DJWAL KUL'S RETREAT IN TIBET**

Djwal Kul has an etheric retreat in Tibet where he maintains the focus of his golden flame of illumination. From that point he assists in the raising of the consciousness of India through her embodied teachers, the yogic masters of the Himalayas. In 1972 it was revealed that this retreat was one of many that were receiving students.

❖ **EL MORYA'S RETREAT IN EL CAPITAN, YOSEMITE VALLEY**

In addition to his principal retreat in Darjeeling, El Morya has a retreat in the mountain known as El Capitan, in Yosemite Valley, California. This retreat is situated close to the retreat of his guru, Hercules, which is found in Half Dome, Yosemite Valley.

El Capitan (left) and Half Dome

❖ **ERIEL'S RETREAT IN ARIZONA**

The ascended master Eriel maintains his etheric retreat over the state of Arizona. The etheric retreat is not far from the etheric city over the Arizona deserts, and there is a physical outpost of the retreat in the mountains. Classes in the Light and Sound Rays are held in this retreat. These classes are open only to qualified students, initiates of the ascended masters who are deemed worthy by the Lords of Karma to receive this instruction.

Eriel's retreat is a haven of light apart from worldly vibrations, a retreat in the true sense of the word. Here one learns the beauties of solitude, of aloneness, or all-oneness in God. Those who like to hike in the mountains and meditate upon God will appreciate the Spirit that permeates this retreat. These should call to be taken there while their bodies sleep, for

Arizona desert

only in this atmosphere of complete separation from the world can one learn the involved science of the Light and Sound Rays.

The flame focus in his retreat is purple with a sheath of pink; the radiance from the retreat is that of divine love. To this home of light, Eriel draws children who have made the transition. Young children up to the age of twelve and even those in their teens are taken there for adjustment to the new octave in which they often so suddenly find themselves by accidents, diseases and other causes. Here, Eriel assists them in developing some facet of their divine plan in preparation for reembodiment.

The music "To a Wild Rose," from *Woodland Sketches*, by Edward MacDowell, captures the flame of Eriel's retreat.

❖ THE ETHERIC CITIES

There are fourteen etheric cities over the earth, seven over the seven seas, seven over the seven deserts. These etheric cities are places where souls of light or souls who have the assistance of the ascended masters can go between embodiments or during sleep. These cities are intact at the etheric level; they are as they were in the golden age. John's vision of the New Jerusalem found in the Book of Revelation is derived from his vision of the etheric cities, which establish the inner blueprint of the City Foursquare to be outpictured in the civilizations of the earth.

The God of Gold describes these cities: "In the etheric octave, seven major etheric cities of light—gold is everywhere, light is streaming. Angels walk freely with masterful sons and daughters of God. Children are God-free, realizing the fullness of their causal body. You can see the transparency of the suggestion of the Christ and causal body and I AM Presence visible above these lifestreams. The streets are golden.

"Gold is the conveyor and conductor of the light of the sun, the balance of health in the physical body and the precipitated sunlight from each one's own causal body of earned supply of previous incarnations on earth and service in heaven. Therefore you see, all are not equally wealthy, even in the etheric cities of light, but each demonstrates by his adeptship, love and God-mastery the precipitation of that abundance of gold and beauty and light, culture and soul development and all of the many facets of God-mastery of the seven rays.

"One hears, by a soundless sound and the inner attunement of the chakras, the keynotes of all of the masters of cosmos. One can tune in through meditation through one's chakras to various wavelengths of sound, light, beauty, inspiration and the mystery schools and retreats of other planets and far-off worlds.

"The beauty of nature is resplendent and many-colored—the crystal-clear streams, the freshness of the air, the piercing vitality of the stars, the sense of the permeation of life with the blue ray of the will of God. There is peace and balance, equanimity. There is the sense of well-being and not the irritations and nervousness of the denser bodies we wear, the diets we eat, the vibrations of death and hell in the earth plane.

"Apart from these seven major cities of light, there are the open spaces of the etheric plane where there are isolated temples, edifices of learning, other communities and types of gatherings of students of the masters."[549]

One of the greatest cities in the world for outpicturing the alabaster cities of light is Washington D.C. This is due to Saint Germain and George Washington, who lowered this matrix into form. The plan of this city goes back to the great cities of light that were in the Amazon basin in the great golden age of South America; the key buildings of the city are in white, and in many of them you will see something very much like what is seen in the etheric cities.

❖ **FAITH AND PROTECTION, TEMPLE OF,** *See* **The Temple of Faith and Protection**

❖ **GABRIEL AND HOPE'S RETREAT, The Retreat of the Archangels of the Fourth Ray**

The retreat of Archangel Gabriel and Hope is located in the etheric plane between Sacramento and Mount Shasta and is extended for the protection of San Francisco through the retreat of the Goddess of Purity. The retreats of the archangels have a vast energy field of concentration, and the presence of these retreats accounts for the great purity of this area of Northern California. The retreat was present long before the sinking of Lemuria and was destined to show forth the pristine pattern of purity for the entire continent of Mu and for the Western Hemisphere.

❖ **THE GODDESS OF PURITY'S RETREAT OVER THE ISLAND OF MADAGASCAR**

The Retreat of the Goddess of Purity is on the island of Madagascar, which has survived numerous cataclysms and has been above water hundreds of thousands of years. There is a physical focus that is entered through the side of a mountain and an etheric retreat above it. The latter is designed with a central dome, onion-shaped, and four smaller domes projected from the corners of the square building.

The flame of purity is ministered by the angels of purity under the direction of the Goddess of Purity, who is the hierarch of the retreat. The physical part of the retreat is maintained as a school where students may travel in their finer bodies, but the etheric retreat is frequented only by masters or advanced initiates of the fourth ray.

The maintenance of this focus of purity is essential to the balance of currents on the planet. Angels of purity carry light rays from the flame to the four corners of the earth, to mankind and to elemental life who drink in the radiance of purity with the hope that they, too, might one day inherit immortal life.

Sisters of purity tend the physical focus and the flame, which is a counterpart of the great flame in the etheric temple. The flame is a transparent white, so pure is its essence. The sisters of purity in the physical focus have maintained life in the physical form for over a hundred years. They are unascended adepts of the flame of purity.

The Goddess of Purity speaks of the flame of purity in her retreat: "Purity, beloved ones, begins with a single crystal—the crystal of your own consciousness. And from the point of the flame within the center of the crystal begins the expansion of the consciousness of purity. The pure in heart see God through the crystal of their own consciousness, which they have made God's consciousness. When you have mastered the many facets of the single crystal, then other crystals are added unto you with many more facets; and each crystal denotes another step of initiation to the brothers and sisters of my retreat here in Madagascar. In our beautiful island in the sea, we have consecrated the crystal diadem of purity, which is the consciousness of God; and as the flame passes through the crystal—the mingling of the mist and the crystal, the unformed and the formed—there is the release of the Cosmic Christ consciousness to the earth."[550]

"Here in our temple,...the focus of God-purity is a testimony of the grand design of the universe on behalf of every lifestream evolving upon this planetary home. And do you know, precious hearts of light, that in our focus is a replica of the diamond of identity of each soul destined to evolve upon this planet? This is the service of the brothers and sisters of our retreat, to nourish the divine design."[551]

The Retreats of the Goddess of Light (in the Andes), the Queen of Light (above Sicily) and the Goddess of Purity focus an action of the Trinity to the earth, and together these hierarchs draw the action of the cosmic threefold flame on behalf of her evolutions.

❖ **THE GODDESS OF PURITY'S RETREAT OVER SAN FRANCISCO**

The Goddess of Purity holds the focus of one of the ancient temples of Lemuria in the seven hills of the San Francisco area. The intensity of the flame of purity held in this magnificent retreat is beyond what man can realize. It is a focus of the Mother flame of Mu as well as a focus of the ascension flame.

San Francisco is one of five ancient focuses of Lemuria that today are the five secret-ray chakras of the state of California. These cities are San Juan Capistrano, Santa Barbara, San Luis Obispo, Monterey and San Francisco. The secret rays anchored at these points are for the holding of the balance on the coast against cataclysm and for the transition to a golden-age culture. (The seven main chakras of California, from the base to the crown, are San Diego, Los Angeles, Bakersfield, Fresno, Sacramento, Redding, Mount Shasta.)

The retreat of Archangel Gabriel and Hope, located between Sacramento and Mount Shasta, is extended for the protection of San Francisco through the retreat of the Goddess of Purity.

❖ **GOOD WILL, TEMPLE OF,** *See* **The Temple of Good Will**

❖ **HERCULES AND AMAZONIA'S RETREAT, The Retreat of the Elohim of the First Ray**

The retreat of Hercules and Amazonia is located in the etheric plane in and over Half Dome, a magnificent focus that rises nearly a mile from the

The throat chakra

floor of Yosemite Valley on the west side of California's Sierra Nevada mountain range. The etheric retreat is superimposed within the rock. There Hercules and Amazonia focus the energies of the will of God in this focus of the power center, the throat chakra of the planet.

We enter through a large portal graced by two immense white pillars. The entrance hall is shaped as an octagon, each side leading to another room. We are immediately impressed by the fact that this is a busy retreat—blue-flame angels ten feet high, mighty seraphim, cherubim, angel devas, as well as those ministering to all of the seven rays are coming and going, each intent on rendering a specific service for the Brotherhood. This octagon room glows with the intense love of the Elohim and the angels for the will of God. A bright blue permeates the atmosphere and is both inviting and invigorating to those who are privileged to enter here.

Half Dome

Crossing this hall, we descend a flight of stairs to a circular room. In the center is the focus of a large blue-white diamond with the flame of Hercules and Amazonia blazing through it. In every retreat of the Great White Brotherhood, there is a focus of a flame, and usually the flame is anchored physically in some form of jewel. The jewel of the first ray and the first-ray masters is the diamond. The will of God coalesces as the hardness of the diamond because it is unflinching devotion to the inner pattern, the fiery core of each man's identity. The diamond also symbolizes the crystal clarity of the soul and the precipitation of the Christ.

A circular stairway ascends around the periphery of this room to another round council chamber on the floor above. This room is built on a series of circular platforms, and at one side are the thrones of Hercules and Amazonia. There are accommodations for several hundred guests—members of the Great White Brotherhood—who often meet with the Elohim to discuss ways and means of implementing the power of the will of God in the world of form. Behind the thrones of Hercules and Amazonia is a passageway leading to another room. Those who attend council meetings pass through other doors to the right and to the left of the thrones into another circular chamber that contains the main focus of the flame of the will of God.

As you meditate on the will of God, you can allow your consciousness to move to this retreat because you have knowledge of its existence and an awareness of this octagonal forcefield. In your decrees to Hercules and your invocations, you can fill your aura and the sphere of light around the heart with the energies of the retreat of Hercules and Amazonia.

❖ **HEROS AND AMORA'S RETREAT, The Retreat of the Elohim of the Third Ray**

The Elohim of the third ray, Heros and Amora, focus the energies of the heart chakra of the planet in their retreat located in the etheric plane over Lake Winnipeg, Manitoba, Canada.

The forcefield of this temple and the temple itself are designed after the pattern of a budding lotus whose petals are not quite expanded. The temple is square, made of rose quartz, with giant petals rising at each corner and a tall steeple at the entrance. From the tip of each petal to the center of the sides of the temple extend two bands of a metallic-like substance that serve as conductors of light. There are three petal-shaped doors at the entrance of the retreat, which is in the tall spire in the center of one of the four sides.

The heart chakra

Going through the entrance down a central hallway, we approach the sunken altar of the love ray. Here the pink plume of the love flame burns in the center of the first floor. Three tiers descending into the floor form the bowl for the flame, which is surrounded by carved petals. Three other arteries proceed away from the altar to petal-shaped classrooms that are within the four squares into which the first floor is evenly divided.

There are four levels in this retreat, the second and third floors consisting of chambers used by the pink-flame angels who serve here and the masters who frequent the retreat. On the top floor is the throne of the Elohim in a large round room, an audience chamber, having the appearance of a disc with beautiful carvings in the stone walls.

Throughout the retreat are sculptured art forms that convey the action of divine love to the universe, its cohesive power within the atom and in galaxies. Meditation upon these sculptures infuses the consciousness with the understanding of the laws of love and their operation at every level of consciousness, for they key into the patterns within the atom and the cell of man where the laws of God are written in his inward parts. Therefore, upon seeing these sculptures, the individual ties into that which he already knows, and he becomes that knowledge through meditation.

It is extremely significant to have a retreat of the Elohim of Love as a focus of divine love in the Western Hemisphere. This retreat guides the destiny of North and South America. The radiance of the pink flame from the heart of Heros and Amora together with that of Chamuel and Charity forms an arc of love connecting the retreat over Lake Winnipeg with that of the archangel and archeia of the third ray over St. Louis, Missouri.

This arc of love is for the union of the Western Hemisphere and the bringing in of the golden age. Canada and the United States of America are intended to work together in absolute unity of purpose to defend the Western Hemisphere against all inroads of bondage and all manifestations of anti-love. Canada, the United States of America and South and Central

America are intended to form one cosmic action of the threefold flame—the wisdom of the heart of the United States, the great devotion and love of the people of South and Central America and the unlimited resources of the power ray in Canada.

❖ **ILLUMINATION, TEMPLE OF,** *See* **The Temple of Illumination**

❖ **THE JADE TEMPLE, CHINA**

See the profile of the Angel Deva of the Jade Temple for a description of this retreat.

❖ **JOHN THE BELOVED'S RETREAT OVER THE ARIZONA DESERT**

Arizona desert

The retreat of John the Beloved is located in the etheric plane over the Arizona desert. The flame focused in his retreat is purple and gold. The Elohim Cyclopea has said that from this retreat, John the Beloved "does radiate not only to the United States, but also to Canada, to Mexico, to South America and to the Ural Mountains, to all regions of the world the transcendent vibratory action of the great cup of Christ-love that he partook of in his association with your own beloved Jesus."[552]

❖ **JOPHIEL AND CHRISTINE'S RETREAT, The Retreat of the Archangels of the Second Ray**

The retreat of Archangel Jophiel and Christine is in the etheric realm over the plains of central China, south of the Great Wall near Lanchow.

From the yellow flame of illumination focused here since the first golden ages have come, not only the yellow race and the Yellow River, but also the wisdom of Confucius, Lao

The Great Wall of China

Tzu and the civilizations of ancient China that reached great heights long before there was even a stirring of culture in the West. In those days, China's rulers held mystical contact with the hierarchs of Jophiel's retreat. As long as these initiates held the mandate of heaven—the divine right of rulership—and ruled the land, the civilizations of China grew and prospered under the radiance of the golden sun of cosmic wisdom.

The great science that was brought forth in ancient China came forth under the influence of the retreat of the Elohim Cyclopea and Virginia. The influence of their retreat and that of Jophiel and Christine has brought forth the wisdom of China and the inventive minds of the Chinese people. Their momentum of gentleness, of the family and of service to one another comes from the retreat of Kuan Yin over Peking, the flame of mercy.

❖ KUTHUMI'S RETREAT AT SHIGATSE, TIBET

Kuthumi maintains an etheric retreat at Shigatse, Tibet, where he plays sacred music on a grand organ keyed to the music of the spheres. He

A monastery near Shigatse

directs the vibration of this music to souls at the hour of their death, guiding them to the etheric retreats of the Great White Brotherhood for tutoring in preparation for their next earthly life.

Lord Maitreya describes the music of this organ: "As you know, at Shigatse a great organ has been created by beloved Kuthumi, which he plays for those who are departing from this world and therefore brings to their consciousness the melody and harmony of higher spheres.... The bell-like tones you hear with inner ears are the communion with far-off worlds. They are the melody of the sacred spheres. They are the consummation of the love of planetary bodies ascended. They are the love of cosmic beings, of archangels and their archeiai, of Elohim and sacred-fire beings seldom heard upon this planetary body—composed into a love symphony by your own beloved Kuthumi."[553]

❖ LANELLO'S RETREAT ON THE RHINE

Lanello's retreat is at Bingen on the Rhine River. The vibration of the retreat is felt through the whole town and the surrounding valley.

Lanello describes the retreat as your home away from home: "When you enter our home of light, beloved, you will know indeed that you are home. For our retreat on the Rhine is ever thine.

Bingen and the surrounding valley, circa 1900

"And in those moments or hours when you fancy that as a child you would hang from bowers of trees with flowers—realize that we, too, have swings and fairy gardens and places for children to peekaboo and play hide-and-seek, and waterfalls and fountains and ponds and lilies. And there are swans of light and angels and elementals. And therefore, in our gardens and in the surroundings of our retreat, you will find miniature replicas as well as a cross section of life that comes out of the cooperative venture, and I will say adventure, of our experience together in the service of the Great White Brotherhood.

"There are object lessons here and there, not so obvious but nevertheless there for those who bring some experience of life on earth to interplay with the wisdom of our mystery school. Blessed hearts, how very close are the inner octaves of light—and how much closer many of you are."[554]

Lanello has invited us to his retreat to learn of our divine plan: "Come to our retreat on the Rhine, for we would review with each one of you your divine plan. We are determined to open the scroll of your life and to prove to you by the Word that God has written with his very own finger that you may make your physical ascension in this life. We will show you where you have been and how you have held the line. And we will show you that, with God, this is a victory toward which you must aspire for the glory of God, for the demonstration to the people and for the record of akasha."[555]

The Mouse Tower, on the Rhine at Bingen

Convocations of the ascended masters and unascended mankind are held at Lanello's retreat. K-17 of the Cosmic Secret Service is one master who works from here, and Lanello invites us to attend his courses there: "I invite you to our retreat on the Rhine, to attend courses for fourteen days from today under K-17 in the Cosmic Secret Service.... Come, then, to our retreat and learn how you can be consciously cooperating with the ascended masters in the defense of liberty, the Mother flame and Camelot."[556]

In October 1993, K-17 said: "I welcome you, then, to Lanello's retreat on the Rhine. For we shall hold intense meetings throughout this conference and provide you at inner levels with the intelligence you must have to chart your personal lives and course and to make calls that the course of this nation and many nations shall be for victory, for freedom, for the free-enterprise system, for a solid foundation in God Self-government and a solid foundation in the spiritual path.

"These are wondrous, joyous days. Make the most of them, for one day you will be in temples of light speaking of the many tales, of the many battles and victories and how you were there when the mightiest battle of all was won on planet Earth.

"I am your brother. Call to me. I will give you much insight into the day-to-day decisions of this community as well as in your private lives.

"Beloved ones, mind your respective governments. Mind them well, and let them not lead the course of the earth in a direction that is not upward toward the light. Thus, my motto, with the Mother's, is 'The only way to go is up!'"[557]

Apollo and Lumina have spoken of Lanello's retreat, explaining why it was established in Germany: "I must also tell you that the love of Lanello and his own consort with you was the very cause of the establishment of that retreat on the Rhine as a dedication of the pillar of fire and their sponsorship thirty-three centuries ago in the incarnation of Ikhnaton and Nefertiti. For you see, that Father-Mother flame, that focus also has been for the sponsorship of the reincarnation of the lightbearers of ancient Egypt in the nation of Germany this day."[558]

Lanello invites us to his retreat to be refreshed and recharged. He says: "In our retreat on the Rhine, we have invited seraphic bands to tarry in their ministrations to the earth. And in a special fountain, there the waters are touched by the angels each twenty-four hours. And when you come there, you often go and kneel, and then I bestow the holy water as the sprinkling of the Holy Spirit of our Father Alpha, our Mother Omega, and their sacred-fire emissaries come fresh from the great throne room of the Central Sun. Now I sprinkle you with holy water, sacred fire, dew drops from rose petals in Omega's garden.

"I am Lanello and to you who have not heard, I send the word: Come to our retreat. It is home away from Camelot and another home away from home till we reunite with the Ancient of Days and all of our brothers and sisters and march the grand march to the great Great Central Sun."[559]

❖ **LUXOR, RETREAT AT,** *See* **Ascension Temple and Retreat at Luxor**

❖ **MAITREYA'S RETREAT IN THE HIMALAYAS**

Maitreya established his first mystery school on Lemuria, the ancient continent that sank where the Pacific now is, in order to rescue the lightbearers from a civilization of darkness and of the fallen ones. Since that time, the mystery school of Maitreya has been withdrawn to the etheric octave, to the Himalayas, and only the very few souls of light were allowed to go there to find Maitreya and to study under him.

On April 9, 1971, Maitreya invited the students of the masters to visit his retreat: "Your consciousness may travel on wings of infinite harmony into our domain; and then I am sure that we will be able to teach you in a manner calculated to free you from the dregs of your own human feelings, delusions, confusions and problems.

"Here you will be free to receive the blessing of higher initiation conferred upon you first as an idea, as a concept. You will receive from us the direction to return to your body temples with the understanding that your feet, having walked upon the white marble of our retreat, will have received the blessing of our light—not only your feet, but also your entire consciousness, that you may understand that the way to cosmic initiation is to become involved with those beings of light, that band of holy light ones, who are with me....

"The white-robed ones are in place, and the flame is upon the altar— the flame of initiation, the flame of purity. Many of the cosmic monks, so-called, the devotees of the Spirit (I think you would call them 'cosmic monks'), are now trooping into the vast marble chapel we have erected here in the etheric realm in the Himalayas.

"Come! Let us arise and enter into the temple in the skies over the Himalayas and be at peace. The formation of the cosmic figure of Kuan Yin is upon the altar. She will soon replace it by her gracious presence, and the oil in the lamps of mercy will be lit....

"I extend to you evolving upon this planetary body, from the Far East, from our etheric home of light, a welcome to visit us often in your finer bodies while your physical bodies sleep. And then let your souls awaken within our retreat that you may have the knowledge and the desire and the beautiful concepts we desire to convey to you.

"For initiation is the conferment of mantles of accomplishment, of cosmic achievement. Initiation is the personal accomplishment of the soul, one with the Holy Christ Self, wedded to the God Presence and invoking in the human levels of thought and feeling those transcendental experiences that are the forte of our radiance released unto humanity today."[560]

❖ MAITREYA'S RETREAT OVER TIENTSIN, CHINA

Maitreya maintains an etheric retreat over Tientsin, China, southeast of Peking (Beijing). Tientsin (or Tianjin) is the third largest city in the People's Republic of China. It is located in Hopeh Province in northeast China, about 80 miles southeast of Peking. Tientsin means literally "heavenly ford"; the city is situated 35 miles inland from the Gulf of Chihli, where several streams converge before merging into the Hai Ho (river).

Buddhist Temple
in Tientsin, China

❖ MALTESE CROSS, TEMPLE OF THE, *See* The Rakoczy Mansion

❖ THE MASTER OF PARIS' RETREATS

The Master of Paris has an etheric retreat over the Île de la Cité, which

is the island in the Seine in the very heart of Paris and the birthplace of France. La Sainte-Chapelle is the anchor point of this retreat. The chapel has beautiful stained glass windows with brilliant blues and beautiful rubies. The light filtering through the glass focuses the aspects of the rays of God's consciousness. The halls of justice, the supreme courts and the courts of France, reflecting the justice of Portia and Saint Germain, surround the focus of the Master of Paris.

La Sainte-Chapelle

The Master of Paris also maintains a physical focus in the city of Paris—one of the few physical focuses of the Brotherhood left on the planet—which he often frequents in a physical form. His retreat is a beautiful old castle-like residence with many windows overlooking the city of Paris. This focus is maintained by his disciples and is used frequently by the masters as a meeting place in Paris from which they can direct the energies necessary to hold the balance for the governments of Europe.

Archangel Zadkiel describes the purpose of this retreat in this way: "Take the Master of Paris and that retreat in the very heart of the city. It has always been for the single-eyed purpose of keeping the flame of the seventh ray and thereby using it with Christ-discrimination to aid the blessed servants of God in embodiment who do endeavor to bring about world good—to infuse, then, their work, the work of their hands or their inventions or their art or their pure love for humanity, with a portion of that permanence that comes out of the cycles of the violet flame."[561]

In 1967, Alexander Gaylord explained some of the functions of this retreat of the masters: "Therefore, today, having just come from

The city of Paris

the academy of the Great White Brotherhood that is located on the outskirts of Paris, unknown to any even in the French state, I wish to call to your attention that we are able to assemble at inner levels a number of advanced souls who are taking very specific training in association with the Brotherhood for reembodiment upon the planetary body and to assist Saint Germain in the coming next three decades.

"However, I think it well that this opportunity that is being given to them should also be passed to those of you who are in physical embodiment today. I think it also well if the young men [and women] who are associated with this endeavor would attempt occasionally to attend our academy while their physical form sleeps that they might receive the benefit of the total dedication that is manifest here to the purposes of the Great White Brotherhood...as the august body of world servers and as the emissaries of the Great Central Sun and the Great Central Sun Magnet."562

According to the will of the masters, anyone, anywhere could be invited to enter this retreat as an initiate. No one is barred. We can go there physically, and it is within our grasp, but we bar ourselves, for we cannot enter these retreats until we have a certain attainment.

❖ MERCY, TEMPLE OF, *See* The Temple of Mercy

❖ META'S HEALING RETREAT OVER NEW ENGLAND

The ascended lady master Meta tended the flame of healing in the Healing Temple of Atlantis, which is now focused in the etheric plane over New England. Meta is assisted in her service by priestesses of the sacred fire who have tended the flame of healing for thousands of years. From this focus of healing love have come forth many centers of healing and science that are found today in the New England area.

❖ ORION'S RETREAT IN THE MOUNTAINS OF NORTH AMERICA

Orion, the Old Man of the Hills, maintains a retreat in the mountains of North America. In 1975 he received permission from the Lords of Karma to welcome unascended students of the masters to his retreat: "I maintain a focus of starlight, of the God Star Sirius in the mountains of North America. And now by permission from the Lords of Karma, I am able to welcome you to my abode. And this is a day for me—the opening of my house of light to chelas who will call to be taken to this retreat. And when you come, prepare to be received by angels of freedom, angels who are devotees of Saint Germain! And in my house, my house of light, you will find mementos of patriots of freedom who in every nation have won for the cause of the Great White Brotherhood some noble gain for the

Aquarian cycle, for the Master of Freedom and for the soul of humanity.

"When you come, I will teach you in the way of the mastery of the soul chakra; for my dedication is to all who walk with Godfre and Saint Germain. I serve them in the heart of the mountain. And so I say, come if you will! Classes are beginning, and the first round of souls is being taken for a special training, mine to impart by the grace of God. And you can also expect training in mountain climbing and in survival—survival of the soul and the four lower bodies, survival in transition, survival when energies mount from Sirius, when they intensify.

"And when the step-up of frequency comes and you are required to be in the light, you will have the knowledge of turning the dial of frequency and blending with the new order of the ages. And in that moment, souls who have the flame and the fire and the movement and the mastery of the soul will find themselves elevated to a new consciousness, a new plane where priests and priestesses of Lemuria and sons and daughters of Shasta are gathered, holding the laurel of the Lord of the World."[563]

❖ **OROMASIS AND DIANA'S RETREAT**

Oromasis and Diana have a retreat in the etheric realm over an island in the Bering Sea off the coast of the Kamchatka Peninsula.

❖ **THE PALACE OF LIGHT, The Retreat of Chananda in the Himalayas**

The Palace of Light is the home of Chananda and his sister, the ascended lady master Najah. El Morya, Saint Germain, the Great Divine Director, Daniel and Nada Rayborn and others of the ascended hosts frequent this retreat as guests. The retreat is located in a valley in the Himalayan mountains; the Cave of Light (focus of the Great Divine Director in India) is situated in the mountain behind this retreat.

Godfré Ray King journeyed to the Palace of Light with Alexander Gaylord and Rex, Nada, Bob and Pearl. In *The Magic Presence* he describes a magnificent building of white onyx, four stories high with a great dome in the center. "As we came up the steps, the tones of a beautiful bell announced our arrival and welcomed us as guests of the retreat. In a moment, the great door opened and Najah stood there to greet us.... We were shown to our quarters on the second floor, overlooking the valley."[564]

A Himalayan valley

Godfré describes Chananda's private dining room on the first floor, decorated in white and violet: "Toward one end of the room stood an enormous teakwood table, seating at least twenty people, heavily inlaid with a substance that looked like gold, but was in reality a precipitated metal. Toward the other end of the room was a white onyx table of the same size, the top of which was inlaid in violet and gold, it too being a precipitated substance."[565]

Godfré was taken on a tour of the retreat, seeing a music room, a "Cosmic Observatory" containing scientific instruments not yet known to the outer world, and a council chamber seating seven hundred people. "The walls of this room were of a beautiful milk-white onyx with the most marvelous blue trimmings. On the floor was a thick carpet of the same wonderful blue. There were no windows, and the room occupied almost the entire floor of the palace.... At the side was a dais on which stood an altar and a golden chair.... The main part of the altar was precipitated gold, but the top was made of another precipitated substance, the shade of blue that borders on to violet."[566]

On the ground floor were electrical and chemical laboratories, and in the center of the west wall, the entrance to the half-mile tunnel leading to the Cave of Light.

❖ THE PALACE OF WHITE MARBLE

The Palace of White Marble is a sacred focus of the Great White Brotherhood in the heart of the Himalayas. It has a central gold dome and four minarets proceeding from the corners of the square building. The main council chamber is in the center under the dome, and to the right and the left of the chamber are meditation rooms containing some of the most powerful focuses of the Brotherhood that we have seen in any of their retreats on this planet.

The room to the right of the council hall has a large central altar at the far end of the wall with seats around it in a semicircle, accommodating several hundred people. Three flames grace the altar, which rises in three tiers. Behind each flame, standing out from the wall, is a white stone in the shape of the flame but much larger. Upon each of these three stones behind the three flames are engraved cosmic glyphs focusing such an intense God-power that no mortal eye can gaze upon them and remain mortal.

Therefore only ascended masters are permitted in this meditation room. These symbols are the product of their meditation, their going deep within and contemplating the existence of the very center of being. It is there that these symbols are written, in the very core of each man's being, and they are drawn out only when the individual attains God consciousness as an ascended being. All can look forward to worshiping the very heart of True Being in this room after their ascension.

❖ PEACE, TEMPLE OF, *See* The Temple of Peace

❖ THE PERSIAN RETREAT

In a dictation on July 4, 1979, the ascended lady master Leto spoke of a retreat of the Brotherhood in Persia: "Then, again, you have come with me to the inner retreat of the Brotherhood in Persia where Cha Ara has called you to an understanding of the mysteries of the sacred fire and the path of Zarathustra."

❖ PORTIA'S RETREAT, The Retreat of the Goddess of Justice over Ghana

Portia, the Goddess of Justice and twin flame of Saint Germain, has a retreat over Ghana. This is an important focus, and Portia focuses the flame of justice here. Also on the African continent is the violet-flame retreat of the Elohim Arcturus and Victoria, south of Ghana in Luanda, Angola. This retreat focuses the flame of freedom. In Accra, the capital of Ghana, there is a monument known as the Free-

The Freedom and Justice Arch, Accra, Ghana

dom and Justice Arch—the flames that are focused in these two retreats. This arch focuses as an outer arc of the inner etheric retreat of Portia.

❖ PURIFICATION, TEMPLE OF, *See* The Temple of Purification

❖ PURITY AND ASTREA'S RETREAT, The Retreat of the Elohim of the Fourth Ray

The retreat of Purity and Astrea is located in the etheric plane over the Gulf of Archangel, the southeast arm of the White Sea, Russia. The retreat focuses the energies of the base-of-the-spine chakra of the planet. The etheric focus interpenetrates with the physical on the nearby plains.

One enters the retreat through a large white pyramid that is above ground. Three spires rise through this pyramid and above it. The center spire, extending through the capstone of the pyra-

The base-of-the-spine chakra

mid, is a yellow plume. The smaller spires on either side are pink and blue. One enters the triangular-shaped room and sees, at the far end, three large flame fountains of purity against the backdrop of midnight-blue walls. In the center of the room is the main staircase descending to a very large complex, containing a network of classrooms, flame rooms and a central hall.

Immediately upon descending the stairs, we see another self-sustaining fountain of cosmic purity. Its radiation is so brilliant that we feel we are in the presence of the sun itself. Passing around the fountain, we descend another flight of stairs into the hall of the Elohim. At the far end upon a series of ascending circular platforms is the throne of Purity and Astrea. The domed ceiling is a clear midnight blue mingling with deep violet, while the floor beneath our feet is snow-white stone. Four pillars form a square within the temple, and two more pillars are on the stairs we have just descended.

Stone tables and benches in the same white material are scattered in geometric design throughout the hall. The white stone is used throughout the temple, tinted with the colors of the seven rays in order to focus the purity of the white fire and the Christ consciousness that is expressed through each of the seven rays.

Six flights of stairs, three on either side of this great round hall, lead to other flame rooms and classrooms, one of which emits an intense, sapphire-blue radiance. Descending into this room, we stand at the entrance and observe the magnificent flame of purity in powerful concentration. To the left in midair is the whirling focus of Astrea's circle of blue flame, with the blue-flame sword, the pillar of fire, in the center. The velocity of the flame that forms the circle is so intense that it appears as if it is not moving at all; but we observe from the sparks of blue fire that are thrown off through the centripetal and centrifugal action of the whirling fire that it is indeed moving at great speed and with enough concentrated power of the will of God to cut through the most dense of any humanly misqualified energy.

If we ever needed convincing that the fire of God inherent in the very heart of the earth was sufficient to give mankind salvation, we have abundant proof here that God in us is sufficient to meet every crisis of our existence.

The Elohim have appointed hierarchs in charge of their retreat—masters serving on the blue and white rays. Their legions of white-fire and blue-lightning angels also tend the retreat and minister unto the flames.

❖ THE QUEEN OF LIGHT'S RETREAT OVER THE ISLAND OF SICILY

Messina, Sicily

The Queen of Light maintains an etheric retreat over the island of Sicily, near the town of Messina. Amerissis, the Goddess of Light, uses this retreat, along with the Goddess of Purity's focus in Madagascar and her own focus in the Shrine of Glory in the Andes in South America as anchoring points for a three-fold distribution of the light throughout the world.

❖ THE RAKOCZY MANSION AND THE TEMPLE OF THE MALTESE CROSS, Retreats of the Great Divine Director and Saint Germain

The Rakoczy Mansion is a focus of freedom in the foothills of the Carpathian Mountains in Transylvania, now a part of Romania. Resembling a medieval castle surrounded by woods, this physical focus remains hidden from the eyes of the world.

Ruins of castle of Sztrecsno, Carpathian Mountains

Saint Germain came here before the sinking of Atlantis, carrying the freedom flame under the direct guidance of the Great Divine Director. Saint Germain reembodied here in later centuries, and under the guidance of his guru, rediscovered the flame that he had planted, and then built the Rakoczy Mansion. Here he entertained the heads of state of the European nations, taught the science of alchemy, attempted to unite Europe and expand the freedom flame in the hearts of the people.

The flame room in the center of the mansion seats approximately one hundred persons. It is a rectangular room having entrances at either end, the altar being on the long side of the room with a platform and podium for the officiating hierarch, and the freedom flame in shades of violet blazing on the altar behind the speaker. The physical focus is today for the most part inactive, yet the flame continues to blaze there upon the altar.

A Castle in Transylvania

Saint Germain has transported archives, paintings and collections from this retreat to his focus in the Cave of Symbols. However, just over the House of Rakoczy in the etheric realms, he has recently built an etheric temple in the shape of a Maltese cross. This is a permanent focus of the flame of freedom on behalf of the millions of lifestreams who yearn to drink deeply of the draught of freedom and to taste the elixir of immortal life that has become a legend as the famed fountain of eternal youth, which was sought after by Ponce de Leon and the explorers who came to the New World.

The Great Divine Director has described some of the activities of this retreat: "I am the founder of the House of Rakoczy. And in our mansion in Transylvania, where there has been established on the etheric plane a sacred Temple of the Maltese Cross, there are enshrined records of past civilizations of glory and blueprints for a golden age to come. Some of you have journeyed to that retreat in past embodiments when Saint Germain acted as host, and you came in physical bodies to be entertained there by the Wonderman of Europe, my disciple and your Knight Commander."[567]

The keynote of the retreat is "Tales from the Vienna Woods."

❖ **RAPHAEL AND MOTHER MARY'S RETREAT, The Retreat of the Archangels of the Fifth Ray over Fátima**

The retreat of Raphael and Mother Mary is located in the etheric realm over Fátima, Portugal. The healing flame that blazes on the altar of his retreat was anchored in the physical octave when Mother Mary appeared to the three shepherd children at Fátima in 1917. There is a stream of light that flows like a mighty waterfall from the etheric temple to the physical focus, and to the present hour pilgrims are healed by the "waters" of the healing flame.

Raphael describes one of the halls in his retreat: "I would take you now to what we call the Great Hall of Images. I would permit those of you who are able to see in this mighty hall the mirrors of divine perfection. Have you seen the beauty of Leonardo da Vinci's work? Have you seen the beauty of the mighty sculptors of the Renaissance? Have you seen upon this planet the beautiful radiance of an angel in sculptured marble?

"Let me now ask that you come with me to a place where God is, where, in the magnificent Hall of Images, there are statues, so to speak, made of living spirit fire, beings so majestic as to set your hearts on fire, beings from whose images your soul was framed, beings of such images as by God were named cherubim celestial, seraphim and of the holy order of angels, beings of light and celestial radiance, beings who are unaffrighted by the ideas of mortals but are completely at home with God and with the powers of the great creative essences."[568]

These statues of perfect man and woman, Christed ones, are displayed so that parents can be taken in their finer bodies to see them and meditate on the perfection of the incoming soul or child in the womb for the perfect functioning of the body temple and the flow of light in the chakras.

❖ **THE RESURRECTION TEMPLE, The Retreat of Jesus and Mary over the Holy Land**

The Resurrection Temple is in the etheric realm over the city of Jerusalem in the Holy Land. This retreat, a focus of the resurrection flame, is under the charge of Jesus and Mother Mary.

The temple is located in a round building flanked by two wings. It is white and circular in form, encircled by seven corridors of various or graded degrees of radiation. In the center of the temple is the resurrection flame, an opalescent, mother-of-pearl flame that raises the body to that state just prior to the ascension where the three-fold flame is balanced and the four lower bodies are aligned.

City of Jerusalem

Eight pillars surround the central altar. The paintings on the walls of the circular flame room depict the raising of mankind's consciousness through key individuals' patterns and activities that the Brotherhood of this retreat project as the stages leading to the golden age. We notice on a section of one of the four murals a great patriarch in a pink velvet robe, reading to the people from the book of cosmic law.

Angels of the resurrection flame serve in this retreat, ministering unto the flame and unto those souls who are brought to the resurrection chambers in the wings adjoining the central flame room. Here students are taught how to raise their vibrations to balance the threefold flame and to bring their four lower bodies into alignment in preparation for the ascension, the initiation that follows the resurrection.

There are sections of the retreat where those who have passed prematurely from the screen of life are brought to recuperate from the shock. Here they remain in a state of sleep in their etheric bodies until the action of the resurrection flame resuscitates their consciousness, removes the sting of death, and they awaken of their own free will and come forth to participate in the class work that is carried on in the retreat. After they have adjusted to the change and to their opportunities for service and training between embodiments, they are taken to other retreats of the masters for specialized training and to the etheric cities.

Archangel Uriel and Aurora, together with Gabriel and Hope, frequent this retreat to expand the flame of resurrection on behalf of mankind. By a like token, the Goddess of Spring, beloved Amaryllis, uses the Spirit of the Resurrection Flame each year on behalf of the nature kingdom.

Jesus welcomes us to this retreat: "I welcome you together with Mary the Mother and Saint Germain and the many who have gone before you who are serving here with me in the Temple of the Resurrection, the holy city that pulsates with life abundant above the place where our victory was and is forever one.

"'O Jerusalem, Jerusalem, thou that killest the prophets and stonest them which are sent unto thee, how often would I have gathered thy children together, even as a hen gathereth her chickens under her wings, and ye would not!'[569] Our retreat stands to bear eternal witness to the Truth that we have outpictured in the world of form, and the gates of hell shall not prevail against it!"[570]

❖ **THE RETREAT OF THE BLUE LOTUS, The Retreat of Lord Himalaya**

The Retreat of the Blue Lotus is the focus of God Himalaya in the Himalayan Mountains in Tibet. Here the masculine ray of the Godhead enters the earth, establishing the polarity of Alpha and Omega with the feminine ray of the Godhead that enters at the retreat of the God and Goddess Meru at Lake Titicaca.

In one of the highest mountains of the Himalayan chain, the focus of the manu of the fourth root race is carved, seven chambers, one on top of the other, an impregnable fortress dedicated to individual self-mastery through the flowering of the seven chakras in the body of man. The seven chambers provide a system of initiation whereby one begins his training in the lowest and largest of the chambers and is allowed to ascend to the next chamber only when he has completed certain studies and passed prescribed tests of self-mastery. Each of the seven chambers is separated by hundreds of feet of solid rock. A spiral staircase connects the first three, but beyond that, the initiate must either levitate or adjust his atomic pattern to enter through the walls. These top four chambers are reserved for deep meditation. Here advanced masters and their pupils may leave their bodies and enter the Great Silence (Nirvana) for prescribed periods.

A peak in the Himalayas

Entering the main hall at the base of the complex, we smell the fragrance of the lotus and notice that these flowers are floating in a pool carved in the floor. The Great Hall is frequented by unascended yogic masters who come here out of the body to teach and also to act as scribes, setting forth the Law on scrolls that they then give to their disciples. The chamber seats several hundred disciples who sit in the lotus posture on raised square pads, facing the opposite end of the hall where there is a dais provided for the masters who lecture here. Behind the dais the wall opens into an antechamber, which is the flame room.

Here on an altar is the lotus flame, a focus of the threefold flame. An intense and fiery action of the blue flame forms the petals of the lotus; the golden flame blazes from the center, with the pink radiance emanating therefrom. The hall is rough-hewn, showing

the natural beauty of the rock, the only decoration being the flame itself and a statue of a figure in meditation behind the flame on the opposite side in the antechamber. Because this retreat is devoted to the masculine ray, its emphasis is on going within—on concentration—and so its entire design is conducive to the focusing within the disciples of the yang aspect of the Deity. No outer accouterments or decorations are present, for these would tend to draw the attention of those in meditation outside of themselves. The flame, then, is their sole point of concentration and their only contact outside of themselves with the Spirit of God.

The keynote of the retreat is an Oriental mantra containing the keys to self-mastery and the opening of the seven chakras and the drawing in of the outer mind to the pivot point of the God consciousness within. The action of the retreat is illumination, devotion to the will of God and adoration of his love, the power by which ascended and unascended masters rise into the bliss of nirvanic meditation.

The feeling that permeates the retreat is one of clear light. Truly those who come here must have purified their four lower bodies and regained that clarity of consciousness that was theirs in the beginning and that enables each one to ascend the seven levels of God consciousness in preparation either for the ascension or for the maintaining of life within the physical form over periods of hundreds of years (thus enabling certain key lifestreams to maintain the focus of God in the world of form while their consciousness may come and go at will). These are they who have taken the vow of the bodhisattva to remain in the service of their fellowman until every last man, woman and child is free.

Himalaya invites us to his retreat: "I say, then, daughters of the living flame, invoke the masculine ray as a point of light in the crown chakra, as the magnet that will draw up your feminine energies for the victory. I say to you, sons of flame, invoke the light of Asia, the light of the seventh tier of the Retreat of the Blue Lotus. Let it be the crowning jewel of life. Let it be a frequency and a tone in the crown chakra that impels the rising of soul energies and of Mother flame.

"Strive for oneness, strive for wholeness. Seek the desiring of God and the desirelessness of God. Learn the balance of the twain. Come under the

Law and the rod, and know that I am waiting in the Retreat of the Blue Lotus for you to come up higher and higher, to the pinnacle of your own being. Know, then, that the door of the retreat is open for those who are disciplined in the Law.

"I pray, then, that you will be prepared to be received by the door-keeper and that you will be a part of those who support the masculine ray on behalf of the evolutions of Asia, so many of whom know not their identity in God. So then, may the light of far-off worlds be the star of your crown. And may you meditate upon that blue-sapphire star, a five-pointed star. I seal it on the brow for the protection of the opening of the third eye and the perception of the will of God.

"Come. Come to the Retreat of the Blue Lotus. Come, for there is work to be done. There is action and interaction. There is a civilization to be forged. I am the law of the life—the crown of life—and I AM the masculine ray for the lifewaves of Terra. I extend my hands, for I would pass to you, each one, these mighty currents of Alpha that you might understand what vigor and verve and energy can be yours for the fulfillment of cycles of being."[571]

The flame flower of the retreat is the blue lotus, and the brothers who serve here wear white linen robes.

❖ THE RETREAT OF THE DIVINE MOTHER

The Royal Teton Ranch

The Retreat of the Divine Mother is the retreat of Lady Master Venus. It is in the etheric octave in the Rocky Mountains on the northern border of Yellowstone National Park. The physical focus of the retreat is the Royal Teton Ranch, a property secured by students of the masters under their guidance as an outer focus of the Great White Brotherhood.

On December 15, 1985, Sanat Kumara announced the opening of the door of the Temple of the Divine Mother: "The Mother has waited long for the coming of the Buddha out of the heart of Shamballa. She has waited long for your coming. And she does hold the balance of ancient civilizations that have occurred, both on Lemuria and Atlantis and those long forgotten upon this continent as well as in other areas of the earth.

"This great and vast temple of light, beloved, has been prepared over aeons. It is the place of the gathering of the culture of all nations and peoples. It is the place of the drawing together of many lifewaves. Therefore, minister to them, understand them, feed them the teachings of the path of their own soul's resolution, their own soul's calling, and their own soul's tradition.

"In the heart of Lady Venus, who keeps the flame of Mother Earth with you, the flame of the Divine Mother of Love does abide. Thus Venus, initiator with the holy Kumaras of your souls on the path of the ruby ray, does position herself in this hour in the etheric retreat of the Divine Mother over this Ranch, arcing her heart's love to the retreats of the earth, to the Goddess of Liberty, and to every soul who must journey there."[572]

In 1986 Gautama Buddha spoke of this retreat and of his own, the Western Shamballa, also established in this location: "Almighty ones of light I AM THAT I AM, now you understand that the Western Shamballa, sealed over the Heart of the Inner Retreat and extending for many miles radiating out therefrom, is a consecration of a shrine made holy by the footsteps of archangels long ago. Now you understand that the white-fire/blue-fire sun that has come in the establishment of the Retreat of the Divine Mother, with Lady Master Venus presiding over the Ranch, is also the polarity of that Western Shamballa. As you have heard, then, and understood, you can see that for aeons heaven has been banking upon this area as a place preserved, reserved, then, for evolutions who will come apart because they have been taken to the inner retreats of the Great White Brotherhood."[573]

❖ **THE ROCKY MOUNTAIN RETREAT FOR TEENAGERS**

There is a special retreat for teenagers in the Rocky Mountains over the state of Colorado. It is an entirely new wing that is part of an ancient retreat.

The wing of this retreat is specifically dedicated to teenagers who have died violent deaths or drug-related deaths. Here teenagers can join other teenagers for rehabilitation. Inhabitants of this retreat are assisted in adapting to the shocking experience of suddenly being out of their bodies.

When we hear of teenagers and young people who pass on for these reasons, we can remember that there is a place where they can go. It is very important to make fervent calls for these souls to be taken to their right place. Give a novena, a nine-day ritual of prayers, where each day you return, light a candle and say the calls to Archangel Michael or Astrea to cut these souls free and take them to this level.

❖ **THE ROSE TEMPLE, Nada's Retreat over New Bedford, Massachusetts**

The Rose Temple, retreat of the Lady Master Nada, is located above New Bedford, Massachusetts. Designed after the pattern of a rose, each petal is a room representing an initiation in the flame of love. This retreat is the etheric counterpart of the Temple of Love on Atlantis where Nada once served as a priestess. In the center of the retreat there burns the flame of divine love, tended by brothers and sisters of the third ray for the healing of earth's evolutions by love.

❖ **THE ROYAL TETON RETREAT, Principal Retreat of the Great White Brotherhood in North America**

The Teton Range

The Royal Teton Retreat, congruent with the Teton Range near Jackson Hole, Wyoming, is the principal retreat of the Great White Brotherhood on the North American continent. Confucius is the hierarch of this physical/etheric retreat in the Grand Teton mountain. This retreat is an ancient focus of great light where the seven rays of the Elohim and archangels are enshrined.

The Lords of Karma, Gautama Buddha and all members of the Great White Brotherhood frequent this gathering place of the ascended masters and their disciples, while also maintaining the specialized functions of their own retreats.

This is a very ancient retreat. It was at this spot that the first and second root races descended into form, sponsored by Archangel Michael and the other archangels. As the members of the first root race completed their individual plan and began to ascend, they assumed the positions in hierarchy to reinforce the momentums gathered below in the creative scheme above. Retreats and focuses of the Great White Brotherhood were gradually established as members of the first root race arose to fill the positions necessary for an ever-expanding and transcending magnetization of light upon the planetary body. In the early days of the first root race, the Royal Teton Retreat was opened as the home of the manu and the focus of the seven beloved archangels and their complements, who had also anchored their flames across the planetary body.

Twice a year—at winter and summer solstice—the Lords of Karma convene in the council chambers of this retreat to act upon the petitions of sons and daughters of God and to deliver the cosmic dispensations that come forth from the heart of Alpha and Omega in the Great Central Sun— allotments of energy for the enlightenment and progress of humanity. Each New Year's Eve, the thoughtform for the year is released from the Silent Watcher of this solar system to the Lord of the World, Gautama Buddha, who in turn releases it to earth's unascended evolutions from the Royal Teton Retreat. The thoughtform contains the keys to the outpicturing of the will of God for the planet for the coming twelve-month cycle.

We approach the hidden entrance of the Royal Teton Retreat accompanied by an ascended master, for whom large boulders on the mountainside part and great bronze doors open wide. We descend in an elevator two thousand feet into the heart of the mountain. Entering the reception hall, we behold a magnificent tapestry heavily embroidered with silk and jewels, depicting the founders of the retreat in the act of invoking tremendous power from the sun.

Accompanied by the ascended master Saint Germain, Guy W. Ballard (now the ascended master Godfre) visited the Royal Teton Retreat earlier in the twentieth century. He recorded his experiences there and in the Cave of Symbols in his books *Unveiled Mysteries* and in *The Magic Presence*.

He described being taken to a great council hall two hundred feet long and one hundred feet wide whose ceiling is fifty feet high. White onyx forms part of the walls, others are of highly polished blue and rose granite. A vein of gold left in its natural state in the rock of one wall enhances the setting.

In the center of the arched ceiling is a disc of gold, twelve feet in diameter. A seven-pointed star formed entirely of dazzling, yellow diamonds fills the center of the disc and emits a brilliant golden light. Surrounding this focus of the Central Sun are two twelve-inch rings—the inner ring is rose pink and the outer is a deep iridescent violet. Seven smaller discs also surround the Central Sun focusing the seven rays of the Elohim that contact and invigorate the seven chakras in man and the ganglionic centers in animal life. The currents the Elohim direct through these focuses also benefit the elemental kingdom and plant life on earth. The tremendous currents released by the Elohim are stepped down by the ascended masters and made available to mankind and the elementals.

Focused in the wall at the far end of this hall is a large eye, representative of the All-Seeing Eye of God. Through it, mighty currents are directed for the realignment of the forces upon earth with the immaculate pattern God holds for all of his creation. The seven rays of the Elohim are enshrined at this retreat, and the rays are concentrated and anchored in this large image of the All-Seeing Eye of God in the great council hall.

On another wall is a panel of precipitated substance used as a mirror for the instruction of initiates of the ascended masters and members of the

Brotherhood. Here the masters project the akashic records of activities upon earth or any other planet on which they may desire to give instruction—past, present and future.

Also in this retreat are record rooms containing spindles on which are recorded in pressed gold the records of many civilizations that have existed upon the earth since its earliest days. Other rooms contain gold and jewels that the ascended masters have rescued from the lost continents and civilizations that have fallen.

In the center of the room where the gold is kept is a focus for the precipitation of sunlight. In another room, the threefold flame is focused. There is also a violet-flame chamber as well as departments of science and rehabilitation and council halls where there is continual planning and development of projects to be carried out by souls in embodiment.

In many classrooms those who attend this retreat in their finer bodies during sleep are received. Other areas are provided for those who, after passing from physical embodiment, must remain in a state of sleep until it is time for them to be awakened to make preparation for their next embodiment. A music room with beautiful instruments that have been perfected by the ascended masters sends forth to the world the music of the spheres. The perfected patterns of some of these instruments have been released as ideas into the minds of some musicians in the world, and more will be released in the golden age. Many new inventions, scientific formulas, techniques in art and in every field of human endeavor—already developed by the ascended masters—will also be released from this retreat when mankind have demonstrated their predisposition to use them honorably and morally according to the golden rule.

The Royal Teton Retreat is the focus for the precipitation of the culture of the Divine Mother. Precipitation is necessary in order to have a golden age, and the flame of precipitation is anchored here—Chinese green tinged with gold and yellow, the flame of illumination focused by Confucius and Lord Lanto. This retreat, working in conjunction with the illumination of the retreat of Elohim Apollo and Lumina in Western Europe, gives impetus to the scientific inventions of the Western Hemisphere.

Conclaves are held at the Royal Teton Retreat attended by thousands of lifestreams from every continent who journey here in their finer bodies through soul travel while they sleep. There are also smaller classes and tutorials. Saint Germain and Lord Lanto with the ascended master Confucius conduct their Universities of the Spirit here—courses of instruction being given by the lords of the seven rays and the Maha Chohan at their respective retreats for tens of thousands of students who are pursuing the path of self-mastery on the seven rays. In the etheric realm over this retreat, a large amphitheatre has been built to accommodate those lifestreams who, by recent dispensation, have been permitted to come to the retreat in their finer bodies for instruction.

Confucius has expanded on some of the purposes of attending the retreat: "In coming to the Royal Teton Retreat many purposes are served, notably that many of the evolutions of ancient China have reembodied here in America. These ones are the quiet Buddhic souls, the diligent ones, the ones who have also laid the foundation of the family in America and of the basic loyalty of the family, the code of ethics, the gentleness, the sweetness and the desire for learning as the means to God-awareness.

"Many of these have responded also to the teachings from Tibet and from Gautama and Maitreya. Out of the East they have come. They have come for an embodiment that their wisdom might be fired with freedom, that they might assist America in the grand turn of the centuries whereby the mechanization of a false materialism might be turned about and there might manifest instead an etherealization, a spirituality, a conquering of self, of society and of the energies of time and space."[574]

Lanto also invites us to attend the classes in this retreat: "In the chambers of the Royal Teton, where the golden hue of victory saturates the atmosphere hallowed by the victorious ones, I stand to lecture to those who keep the flame of the World Mother and to the remnant of her seed who have forsaken the ways of the world in preference for her mantle. I invite all who pursue Wisdom—though her veils and garb be varied as she passes through all levels of learning—all who seek her knowledge as that true knowledge that comes forth from the fertile mind of the Creator. To you I say, Come to Wisdom's fount and make ready while there is yet time for you to become all that Wisdom has held in store for you throughout the ages. And with the holy oil of deodar, the Mother shall anoint you to consecrate you for reunion in the Flame."[575]

The music of the retreat is "Song to the Evening Star" from *Tannhäuser*.

❖ **THE SACRED RETREAT OF THE BLUE FLAME, The Retreat of Surya and Cuzco at Fiji**

The Sacred Retreat of the Blue Flame is near Suva, the capital of the Fiji chain in the South Pacific. This retreat is in an island northeast of Viti Levu (the largest of the Fiji Islands) and is both under the sea and within the mountains. This focus of the God Star Sirius on earth was founded by the cosmic being Surya, who was in charge of the retreat when the third and fourth root races came into embodiment on the continent of Mu in the location of the Fiji Islands, which were then among the highest mountain ranges of the entire continent of Lemuria.

The flame focus is of the power of love, an intense blue lined with pink. It is the action of this flame that enables the ascended master Cuzco, the hierarch of the retreat, to hold the balance of the magnetic forcefield of the poles of the earth. The focus of this flame from Sirius, including the magnetic field of the God Star, enables the hierarch, with the assistance of scientific instruments and computers, to keep the planet Earth in its exact orbit around the Sun. These precision instruments are sensitive to the slightest raising or lowering of the light patterns of the earth and make the necessary adjustments for atomic explosions or the weight of human effluvia that rises and falls, either of which might put the earth out of its orbit.

Beloved Cuzco has legions of white-fire, pink-flame and blue-lightning angels in his command. They maintain an entire city in the island under the ocean. The entrance to the underground complex is through a building on the island's surface, and there are branches of the retreat in several of the nearby islands.

The work of the Brotherhood of Suva is so specialized that only masters and certain of their chelas who have specialized in the fields of magnetics and the physical sciences are admitted. The currents from Sirius and the service that the Brotherhood renders at this retreat are absolutely essential to the existence of the earth. The adjustment of atmospheric conditions and infringements upon the four elements must be balanced through the work of these cosmic scientists, otherwise the tremendous weight of human karma would not allow the functions of nature to go on, and mankind could no longer inhabit this planet.

On December 23, 1973, Cuzco gave further insight into the workings of his retreat: "My retreat, then, is concerned with such matters as planetary cataclysm, its possibility, its prevention, with the straightening of the axis of the earth, with climatic conditions and with the evolutions of souls migrating from one continent to another in order to gain awareness of all of the facets of the Christ consciousness in preparation for mastery.

"As I stand in my retreat, cosmic instruments available to me enable me to perceive the aura of any individual lifestream walking the earth at any place, at any hour of the day or night. For it is my responsibility to determine whether the energy, the weight of darkness, released through the aura of the individual increases the total karmic weight of a planet, and thereby increases the possibility of cataclysm....

"I come to show you that the preservation of a planet, a people, of lifewaves and root races is most scientific and is carried on by the ascended masters for this one purpose—to preserve the opportunity for evolution. For you see, if the planet Earth were destroyed, it would take thousands, tens of thousands of years for your souls to complete their evolution on other planetary homes amongst other lifewaves at different levels of evolution. Therefore, hierarchy is concerned with the preservation of the platform of planet Earth."

On another occasion, Cuzco spoke of the work of the department of earth sciences at his retreat: "I concern myself with every aspect of the earth body—the planes of the earth, the seas and the depths of the deep.... I have many, many scientists working with me on various planes. And I am overshadowing physical scientists in the earth who are attempting to determine what are the next burdens that shall come upon this planet in the form of earth changes.

"I have brought with me today twenty-four ascended masters who are masters of the earth sciences. They know everything there is to know regarding earth changes—whether it be of pole shifts, volcanoes, floods, or the rising and sinking of land masses or islands. All of this is under their control. At my retreat at Viti Levu, these masters head the department of the earth sciences. The members of this department keep watch over the slightest changes in the energies of the earth.

"You may call to these twenty-four scientists who oversee this work at my retreat, and they may directly transfer to your hearts and minds information that you might not otherwise have had. I have not previously made these scientists accessible to the members of this organization, though they have overshadowed the greatest scientists on earth who are aware of earth changes and measure them.

"Now you, the devotees of Saint Germain, are given the opportunity to call to them in your decrees, giving them your energy and your cooperation to assist them as they attempt to hold the balance for earth changes.

"This, then, is my message to you this day, beloved: You have made a great difference. Continue to make that difference! One day you may find that because you held the fort, a golden age was born. This is the matrix that I hold and the vision that I cherish. All is in flux. Therefore, everything is possible! To the realm of the possible I commend you!"[576]

❖ **SHAMBALLA, Ancient Home of Sanat Kumara**

Shamballa, the ancient home of Sanat Kumara and Gautama Buddha, is located in the etheric realm over the Gobi Desert in China. This retreat, once physical, has since been withdrawn to the etheric octave, or heaven-world.

The retreat was originally built for Sanat Kumara, hierarch of Venus, who long ago came to earth in her darkest hour, when all light had gone out in her evolutions and there was not a single individual on the planet who gave adoration to the God Presence or the Inner Buddha. Sanat Kumara was accompanied on this mission by a band of one hundred and forty-four thousand souls of light, who, with him, had volunteered to keep the flame of life on behalf of earth's people. This they vowed to do until the children of God, who had been turned away from their first love by fallen angels, would respond to the love of God and turn once again to serve their mighty I AM Presence.

The Gobi Desert

Four hundred who formed the avant-garde went before Sanat Kumara to build, on the White Island in the brilliant-blue Gobi Sea (where the Gobi Desert now is), the magnificent retreat that was to become for all time the legendary Shamballa. This city was originally a physical replica of the Venusian city of the Kumaras. The volunteers from Venus focused here the one hundred forty-four virtues of the flames of the elements, composing a diamond replica of the focus in the Great Hub. The "City of White" was approached from the mainland by a beautiful marble bridge.

The main temple of Shamballa is marked by a golden dome and is surrounded by terraces, flame fountains and seven temples—one for each of the seven rays—situated on a wide avenue resembling the Champs-Elysées, lined with trees and flowers, flame fountains and tropical birds including bluebirds of happiness. The altar of the threefold flame is in the main temple, where the star of Sanat Kumara is hung from the ceiling over the altar. This, the principal focus of the threefold flame upon the planet, was established by Sanat Kumara when he came long ago. Through it, he connected a ray from his heart to every lifestream evolving on the planet, and thus assisted their Holy Christ Selves to raise mankind's consciousness back to the place where they could be taught the laws of self-mastery. In past ages, people would come each year from many miles to witness the visible, physical sacred fire and to take home a piece of wood consecrated by Sanat Kumara to light their fires through the coming year. Thus began the tradition of the Yule log, commemorating the return to the fire of Christhood.

Sanat Kumara founded the activities of the Great White Brotherhood on the planetary level, and their headquarters remain here today. Here the masters train messengers to go forth with the teachings of the Christ, adapted to every level of human consciousness. Each year the fruits of all endeavors made by angels, elementals and representatives of the Brotherhood in the world of form are returned to Shamballa in the Fall and are brought to the feet of the Lord of the World. The angels come on Saint Michael's day, September 29th. The elementals come at the end of October and representatives of the Brotherhood at the end of November, when in America the feast of gratitude is celebrated at Thanksgiving.

In the legends of the East, Shamballa is the name of a mythical kingdom, an earthly paradise, said to exist somewhere between the Himalayas and the Gobi desert. Ancient Tibetan texts describe the kingdom as a beautiful place in an inaccessible part of Asia, formed of eight regions, each surrounded by a ring of snow-capped mountains and therefore looking like an eight-petaled blossom. It is an idyllic country free of strife and crime, whose inhabitants have attained great spiritual development and powers.

The kingdom of Shamballa plays a central role in Tibetan Buddhism. Author Edwin Bernbaum writes that the sacred texts of the Tibetans speak of Shamballa as "a mystical kingdom hidden behind snow peaks somewhere north of Tibet. There a line of enlightened kings is supposed to be guarding the most secret teachings of Buddhism for a time when all truth in the world outside is lost in war and the lust for power and wealth. Then, according to prophecy, a future King of Shamballa will come out with a great army to destroy the forces of evil and bring in a golden age. Under his enlightened rule, the world will become, at last, a place of peace and plenty, filled with the riches of wisdom and compassion.

"The texts add that a long and mystical journey across a wilderness of deserts and mountains leads to Shamballa. Whoever manages to reach this distant sanctuary, having overcome numerous hardships and obstacles along the way, will find there a secret teaching that will enable him to master time and liberate himself from its bondage. The texts warn, however, that only those who are called and have the necessary spiritual preparation will be able to get to Shamballa; others will find only blinding storms and empty mountains—or even death."[577]

Gautama Buddha was the first initiate to serve under Sanat Kumara, hence the one chosen to succeed him in the office of Lord of the World. On January 1, 1956, Sanat Kumara placed his mantle on Lord Gautama, whereupon the chela par excellence of the Great Guru also became the hierarch of Shamballa. Today, Gautama Buddha sustains the tie to the threefold flames of all mankind. It will be sustained until each individual makes his ascension in the light.

Sanat Kumara, retaining the title of Regent Lord of the World, returned to Venus and to his twin flame, Lady Master Venus, who had kept the home fires burning during his long exile. There he continued his service with the Great White Brotherhood and the advanced evolutions of his home star on behalf of planet Earth.

❖ **THE SHRINE OF GLORY, The Retreat of the Goddess of Light in the Andes**

Christ of the Andes, on the border of Argentina and Chile

The Shrine of Glory is the etheric retreat of the Goddess of Light in the Andes Mountains in South America. This retreat emits a glow of soft white light with the colors of the seven rays delicately filtering through.

One enters through a portal graced by four pillars. The architecture is in what we know as the Greek tradition, but actually it is Atlantean. We enter a great hall that is hewn out of the mountain, and there is a fountain that emits the radiance of the Goddess of Light. We descend six steps and enter a marble hall fifty feet high with doorways on either side leading to classrooms and council halls where members of the Brotherhood meet.

Hanging from the vaulted ceiling is a large chandelier made of white diamonds that reflects the flame of light focused here by the Brotherhood who serve with the Goddess of Light. Wearing robes of white, these brothers and sisters of the retreat work with the pure white light, the precipitation of the elixir, the action of the light rays and the direction of their currents throughout nature and the evolutions of the planet. The vibration of light is so intense in this retreat that noise does not register, and only the pure emanations that come forth through the throat chakras of those who serve here are audible. In the same manner, all discordant vibrations, thoughts and feelings are filtered by the intensity of the light waves, and only harmony is sustained within the retreat.

The forcefield of light from this retreat extends over the entire planet as an antahkarana, a network of filigree light patterns from the heart of the Goddess of Light herself and her flame that is focused there. The filigree pattern of radiation that emanates from the retreat connects with the Holy Christ Selves of all mankind and gives impetus to men's longings for greater light.

This retreat has a physical focus in a beautiful home in the mountains not far removed from the etheric retreat.

❖ TABOR'S RETREAT IN THE ROCKY MOUNTAINS

The ascended master Tabor, the God of the Mountains, has a retreat in North America's Rocky Mountains.

The walls of Tabor's Retreat are jeweled and lined with crystal. There is a fountain of light with a rainbow action of the sacred fire. Waves of rainbow colors illumine the retreat, a perpetual focus of the seven rays of the hierarchy.

Through this retreat and through his focus in the front range above Colorado Springs, Lord Tabor radiates the protection of the first ray and the action of the will of God through North and Central America, with a special protective action to the emerging Christ consciousness in the sons of God, the youth and the elemental kingdom.

In 1977, the God of Gold spoke of God Tabor and his retreat: "It is the desire of the God Tabor to convey to you the message that within his retreat, that certain retreat that is kept hidden from the eyes of the world, there is a focal point of gold as well as books upon the subject of gold, which are ancient. These are manuscripts and they have set forth the intricacies of the Law, the wisdom of the Christed ones, the plots of the fallen ones and all that you require in an understanding of how it will be necessary to defeat them and to reestablish the light consciousness upon earth.

"I ask that you will make calls, then, to Saint Germain, to the God Tabor and to myself to be allowed to enter this retreat in your etheric body to study these volumes and therefore to draw forth from them in your waking consciousness the necessary solutions that will be given to you by the Master Alchemist Saint Germain."[578]

❖ THE TEMPLE OF COMFORT, The Retreat of the Maha Chohan over Sri Lanka

The Temple of Comfort is the retreat of the Maha Chohan in the etheric realm over the island of Sri Lanka (formerly known as Ceylon). It has a physical focus in a large home overlooking a tea plantation.

Portraits of the seven chohans hang in the room where the flame of the Holy Spirit is focused. Through their portrait focuses, these ascended masters radiate the complementary qualities of the seven rays they direct on behalf of the evolutions of earth. The council

A tea plantation in Sri Lanka

chamber where the seven chohans meet with the Maha Chohan is in this retreat, the headquarters for their joint service to earth.

In the central altar of the retreat is the comfort flame. In an adjoining flame room, there is anchored in a crystal chalice bordered with crystal doves a white flame, tinged in pink, with gold at its base, emitting a powerful radiance of divine love. Angels carry the emanations of these flames to the four corners of the earth to the hearts of all who yearn for comfort and purity from the Father-Mother God.

❖ **THE TEMPLE OF THE CRYSTAL-PINK FLAME, The Retreat of Archangels of the Third Ray**

Archangel Chamuel and Charity maintain an etheric retreat over St. Louis, Missouri, "on the south side" of North America. The retreat is called the Temple of the Crystal-Pink Flame. An arc of divine love forms a bridge between this retreat and that of the Elohim of the third ray, Heros and Amora, in the etheric realm near Lake Winnipeg in Manitoba, Canada.

The city's most prominent landmark, the 630-foot high stainless steel Gateway Arch, stands on the banks of the Mississippi River and symbolizes St. Louis as the gateway to the West. So, too, the Gateway Arch, inspired by the inner design of the retreat, is intended as a sign to quicken the awareness of all who behold it that here is the open door to the etheric retreat of beloved Chamuel and Charity.

The Gateway Arch, St. Louis

The emanation of the love ray from this retreat is a flow of creativity. It has been misused in dissonant forms of art and music as well as a certain momentum of prejudice and narrow-mindedness that is the perversion of the true flame of love. Nevertheless, the flame of love from this retreat promotes the generosity of heart, the givingness and forgivingness of the people on the North American continent. The enormous energy of love simply flushes out all else and assists the people to retain that concern for the world and for humanity. The altar and flame of the retreat are dedicated to the flow of life from the heart of God to the heart of Christ to the heart of man.

❖ **THE TEMPLE OF FAITH AND PROTECTION, The Retreat of Archangel Michael and Faith**

The Temple of Faith and Protection is in the etheric realm over Banff and Lake Louise in the Canadian Rockies in Alberta, Canada. Archangel Michael and Faith are the hierarchs of this retreat, the home of legions of blue-lightning angels who come from the four corners of the universe to serve a planet in travail. Bands of angels serving under the archangels of the other six rays also gather here, where great conclaves of the angelic hosts are held under the sponsorship of Michael, the Prince of the Archangels.

Lake Louise

The temple is round, inlaid with gold, diamonds and sapphires. There are four entrances marking the twelve, three, six and nine o'clock lines of the focus, forming a square platform beneath the temple. Each entrance has a forty-foot golden door, approached by forty-nine steps. Blue sapphires adorn the golden doors and the golden dome in a radial pattern. Beautiful gardens, fountains and white marble benches surround the temple.

The pyramid-shaped altar is made of white and blue diamonds; the color of the flame ranges from a deep sapphire blue to a pastel, almost white shade. The seats that surround the altar in concentric rings accommodate thousands of angels. Two large balconies form circular rings inside the temple, as Archangel Michael says, "for standing room only." The flame in the center rises towards the golden dome, which is studded with blue sapphires on the outside and blue diamonds on the inside.

After the coming of the first root race to the planet, when the archangels acted as chohans of the rays until these were appointed from among mankind, the retreat was hewn out of the mountain, a physical focus to which all might come to renew their energies, their faith in the divine plan for their lifestreams and their enthusiasm to serve the will of God. After the descent of mankind's consciousness into duality and the coming of the Luciferians and the laggards, the physical temple was destroyed, but the etheric focus lived on, as tangible as a physical temple ever was to those who travel there in their finer bodies.

When men departed from their original state of innocence and perfection, they lost their own innate protection. Archangel Michael tells us that when his angels enter the atmosphere of earth, when they descend into the dimensions of time and space, they "wear a crystalline helmet of light substance that is harder than the diamond." He says, "We do this because we wish no penetration to ensue that would bring into our world the power of darkness and shadow or misqualified substance. Yet, you have heard the statement made, 'Fools rush in where angels fear to tread.' And therefore, mankind today often go without their tube of light, without any form of protection whatsoever into...those places of iniquity where the dark spirits assemble to vampirize mankind, [where] individuals pick up in their feeling world those negatives that then linger long afterward as the seeds of disease and produce those unhallowed states of consciousness and unhappiness that sometimes produce a terrible manifestation of the suicide entity."[579]

Archangel Michael and Faith invite unascended lifestreams to come to this retreat while their bodies sleep to recharge and repolarize their lifestreams with the battery of the flame of faith. Angels and elementals do likewise, for all know what an invigorating experience it is to meditate in the flame room in the center of the temple and draw in the essence of the power of the will of God.

At a certain time every evening, the legions of Archangel Michael who have been recharged in the flame go forth in formation from this retreat. Legions of angels perpetually go forth from and return to the retreat, recharged for their service to mankind, for protection and the overcoming of discarnates and entities from the astral plane that would attempt to interfere with the fulfillment of the plan of God.

Archangel Michael tells us that he charges us with the faith to complete our inner vows, our divine mission. He says, "Each and every one of you has stood before the Lords of Karma before coming into embodiment, promising to render a service for the Christ. And I have stood with you, and I have also pledged my energies and those of my legions in the defense of your faith.

"And so, in our temple of light at Banff, our angels do come to receive the fires of protection. There they dip in and they are recharged for the service to mankind that they perform twenty-four hours a day. Angels of Archangel Michael's band would never go forth to do battle without the armour of light and the full protection of the Law. I charge you then to learn a lesson from your angel of faith: to put on that armour, the whole armour of God, as you have been taught, and then to go forth as you shall go forth with the legions of fearlessness flame."[580]

The keynote of this retreat is the "Soldiers' Chorus" from *Faust*, by Charles Gounod.

❖ **THE TEMPLE OF GOOD WILL, The Retreat of El Morya at Darjeeling**

The Temple of Good Will is the etheric retreat of the master El Morya. It is located in the etheric realm in the foothills of the Himalayas above the city of Darjeeling, India. Magnificent, radiant currents of light pour from his retreat, which also has a physical focus in the hills surrounding the city.

The etheric retreat is a glistening white building in Moorish architecture, square with minarets at the four corners and a large central flame-shaped dome. The walls are as thick as a medieval castle. The apertures are also flame or dome-shaped, delicately shaded in a pale blue as are the doorways, the apertures atop the minarets and the carvings that mark the divisions of the four stories of the retreat.

Darjeeling, India

As we enter this headquarters of the inner-world government, on the first floor, we are shown the main auditorium. At the far end is the focus of the diamond heart, ministered unto by the devas and Brothers of the Diamond Heart. On a raised altar there is a pale-blue diamond with a delicate blue flame encompassing the white flame that is visible in the center of the diamond.

The Brothers of the Diamond Heart who serve at this retreat under the master El Morya assist humanity's endeavors by organizing, developing, directing and implementing the will of God as the foundation for all successful organized movements. Within this main auditorium and the adjoining council rooms, the brothers, in their royal-blue robes of oriental design finished with light blue sashes, meet to discuss the plans of the Brotherhood for the most effective release of the flame of the will of God into the arena of action. Their great love for the will of God emanates the feeling of great compassion for humanity and of concern for their welfare, that they go not astray as they attempt in good faith to carry out the vows they have made at inner levels to further the divine plan and the onward-moving tide of the Father's will for the coming golden age.

The diamond-shining mind of God is the focus, the very heart, of any endeavor. Thus, these servants of the will of God, through their devotion to the diamond in the Great Hub and its focus here on the altar at Darjeeling, assist the Holy Christ Selves of any group who come together for service in maintaining a focus of that diamond as a magnet that will draw to the group the energies required for the completion of a particular project or community service. These brothers direct the angel ministrants of the flame, the devas and the angels of white fire and blue lightning to go forth with the creative essence of the sacred fire focused here to carry it daily to the many centers of action across the face of the earth.

In rooms adjoining the main auditorium, public servants, world and community leaders and holders of public office are schooled between embodiments and in their finer bodies during sleep. All lifestreams on the first ray come here at one point or another in their embodiments, as well as between embodiments, to renew the charge of Morya's thrust for a purpose in the world of form and to refresh their own understanding of the intricacies of the will of God in politics, in religion, in business, in finance and in education.

On the second floor we are shown the private quarters of our beloved master, his study, libraries and formal meeting rooms for members of the Darjeeling Council. Another great hall is fully equipped to accommodate several hundred ascended and unascended masters who meet frequently to discuss international problems and the means to their solution.

We are taken to the third floor where we notice more of the intricate carvings in Indian and Tibetan designs engraved in the white marble. The theme of the blue lotus recurs throughout the halls, whereas in the interior of the master's quarters we see his favorite flower, the forget-me-not, clustered here and there. We learn that these carvings can be changed at will, for they are engravings of the diamond-shining mind of God, which the brothers of this retreat reflect to a remarkable degree and use as a function of the Christ mind and its ability to precipitate and to heal at will.

As we approach this floor, our hearts are expectant and quickened by the pulsations of the focus of the will of God. The doors to the flame room are opened by our host who bids us enter. Sparkling white walls are contrasted by royal-blue floor and ceiling. The flame of the will of God is adorned in the center of the room by an inlaid design, a cosmic pattern in mosaic, a focus of the divine geometry. The flame has a royal-blue center with deeper and lighter shades flowing without as facets of the will of God.

The third and fourth floors of the retreat have many prayer and meditation rooms. Here, worship is conducted, and special ceremonies are even held upon the roof under the stars where there is also an astronomical observatory.

There are great lessons to be learned on the path of initiation, and they begin even at the very door of Morya's retreat in Darjeeling. Morya is a very stern guru, and he has an interesting sense of humor. At the entrance to this retreat, he keeps a very gruff chela. This gatekeeper has no appearance whatsoever of mastery or of even being worthy to stand at the gate of the master's retreat. He speaks gruffly and is not dressed in the best of attire. If those who knock at the door of the retreat have disdain for the gatekeeper, then the master determines that they are not worthy to be received at his retreat.

The master himself addresses the subject of his seeming sternness and of his great love for us: "For a long period of time individuals have intimated to mankind that I, Morya El, am extremely stern. This may be true, in a sense, that I am stern because the first ray in itself represents the will of God. And I ask you, beloved hearts, if I, as the chohan of the first ray, am to flinch from the will of God, then where is the foundation and basis for all that is to follow? But I tell you that my love is as real and tangible as any of the other chohans of the rays, and they will be the first to witness to its reality and tangibility. If you contact any other master of light, whether you are sleeping or awake in your finer bodies, they will verify the great love. But I know, my chelas, it is not necessary that you ask, for you know, who know the light, that I love you. You know that I have stood beside you when you needed me. And you know that I will continue to do so as long as you revere in your hearts and minds the will of God, even when sometimes you seem to fall short of it.

"However, I do not condone falling short of the will of God. I hope that the day will soon come when every one of you will be so firm that nothing can break you or shake you or change you. I await that day. I await the day when you are ready to give your all to the light as we have done."[581]

Morya opens his doors constantly to different lifestreams who desire to come closer to the will of God. He invites you to his retreat where he and the brothers of the diamond heart open their arms and say, "Come to our fireside, warm yourselves upon the sacred fires, partake of our holy communion."

A portion of the Temple of Good Will

Morya says: "Gracious ones, as I gaze upon the minarets here at Darjeeling, as I see the gleaming white marble so unlike and yet like the Taj Mahal, as I see our art treasures resplendent in hope of the will of God, how I would share with you some glimpse of all that herein remains as a monumental achievement to the Temple of Good Will. How I would share with you the soft carpets of our retreat. How I would share with you the musical tinkle of our fountain. How I would share with you the pleasant hours by the fireside, contemplating the immortal purpose.

"How I would share with you myself and all that God has wrought through me. How I would share with you the love of the shining faces round about our council table. How I would share with you the deliberations of our council. How I would share with you the communion of saints and the communion with heaven. How I would share with you the mighty pillar of good will, the great blue flame that pulsates upon our altar. How I would share with you every gift of good will, this season and eternally."[582]

❖   **THE TEMPLE OF ILLUMINATION, The Retreat of the God and**
    Goddess Meru at Lake Titicaca

The Temple of Illumination is the etheric retreat of the God and Goddess Meru. It is the focus of the feminine ray of the Godhead to the earth,
poling with the masculine ray anchored in the Himalayas in the retreat of

Lord Himalaya. This vast retreat is
located over Lake Titicaca high in
the Andes mountains on the Peru-
Bolivia border. Jesus, the Blessed
Mother and many saints have studied in this retreat.

Lake Titicaca is 3,205 square
miles and, at 12,500 feet, is the
world's highest navigable lake. The

Lake Titicaca

retreat covers a good portion of the lake and is centered over the remains
of an ancient temple to the Sun on the Island of the Sun. According to legend, the ruins mark the spot where the two founders of the Inca dynasty
were sent down to the earth by the Sun.

The etheric focus of the God and Goddess Meru, a beautiful white and
gold Atlantean temple with columns gracing the entrance, reminds us of the
magnificent physical focus that was here in the days of Lemuria. The
emblem of the retreat is a golden sun, and the golden-pink flame, a focus
of the flame of Helios and Vesta, is in the flame room to the right of a great
hall, decorated in gold with great pillars through which we pass on the way
to the focus of the flame.

The God and Goddess Meru serve directly under Helios and Vesta—
thus, the pink and gold theme of their retreat. The flame of Helios and
Vesta is focused in the center of the room, and around it pilgrims gather,
kneeling on pink and yellow cushions or simply meditating in the lotus posture. Going back through the main hall through which we came, we notice
that the far end opposite the entrance to the retreat is a focus of the golden
flame of illumination.

Branches of the building contain classrooms, council halls and the
private quarters of the God and Goddess Meru. This is the focus for
the coming golden age; for in their sponsoring of the sixth root race, as
the manus thereof, the God and Goddess Meru recognize their role as
preparing the way for the incoming seventh root race in South America
under the guidance of the Great Divine Director. To this retreat have been
transferred the records of ancient civilizations from many other retreats in
the world. The focus of Kuthumi in Kashmir also contains a library with

these records, as does the Royal Teton Retreat.

The focuses of Apollo and Lumina, Jophiel and Christine, Lord Maitreya and all who serve the golden flame of illumination are connected with each other and this retreat by their mutual service on behalf of the illumination of mankind and the raising of their consciousness to the level of the Christ—Universal and individual—as the voice within, the teacher that shall no longer be hid into a corner as the great golden age dawns.

The World Teachers, Jesus and Kuthumi, frequent this retreat and give instruction to the pilgrims who journey here while their bodies sleep and between embodiments. The creativity and culture of the golden age will be brought forth by the entire Spirit of the Great White Brotherhood through this focus of the feminine ray, the Mother aspect, and the activity of the expansion of Spirit in Matter.

The Temple of Illumination and the Royal Teton Retreat form the arc of the yellow flame of illumination for the golden age in the West. This golden flame is a tangible, almost physical flame. It has influenced the founding of the form of government in the United States of America that has endured for two centuries. This system was inspired by the Brotherhood; through it the government is intended to be through the consciousness of the Christ in those who govern and in the people. The problems in government arise when people misuse or take advantage of the form of government. Similarly, the free-enterprise system works well when people practice the golden rule and do not desire to exploit one another. When people have, instead, a sense of sharing and abundance, the West will prosper.

Reed boat, Lake Titicaca

Our greatest initiations come in our day-to-day contact with our fellow man. These initiations are calculated to help us to develop self-mastery. We are intended to use our initiative in the free-enterprise system to draw forth from our causal body the divine plan for our life and those things that will benefit our fellow man. As we do this, we automatically enter the spirals of initiation. It takes hard work and striving to build a business, for example, and right motive is important. The system behaves correctly when we use our energies to develop self-mastery instead of the gain of worldly money and power. If we operate on our initiative to bring forth creative ideas in business, education and all areas of human endeavor, we will pass the initiations that have been transferred from the inner retreats from the Brotherhood of Light.

In a dictation given December 22, 1973, Goddess Meru invited us to make the call to hear the lectures she and the God Meru have given at their retreat. She said: "Of the many lectures and addresses that the God Meru and I have given before multitudes on the etheric plane, there are specific ones that may be heard by you if you but make the call and the attunement. It is as though you were to take a tape recording of one of your messengers' lectures, to play it back and to hear it. So you can, by tuning in to our retreat, receive these lectures that we have given. And therefore, our message to you this day can be an unending one. For if you so desire, and if you make the invocation each day, all through your life, you can be receiving the words of the God and Goddess Meru into your etheric body.

"Your outer mind may not have the full awareness of these lectures, these teachings, but step by step as you rise higher, you will have that awareness of the mind that was also in Christ Jesus. And you will know because you are known of God. You will know because the known laws of God are anchored within your forcefield, within your consciousness, being and world.

"This is a sacred opportunity, one that ought not to be taken lightly or forgotten. May I suggest, then, that you make note of this dispensation and that each night before retiring, each morning before getting out of bed you remember to make the call for the continuing release of wisdom from the heart of the God and Goddess Meru."[583]

❖ **THE TEMPLE OF THE MALTESE CROSS,** *See* **The Rakoczy Mansion**

❖ **THE TEMPLE OF MERCY, Kuan Yin's Retreat near Peking, China**

Beijing, China

The Temple of Mercy, etheric focus of the Goddess of Mercy, Kuan Yin, is situated in the foothills above Beijing (Peking), China.

In this retreat, a central pagoda with golden dome rises above twelve surrounding pagodas, each of which focuses the yin and yang qualities of the twelve hierarchies of the Sun. The plus and minus factors of each of the lines of the cosmic sundial are reproduced here musically by the representatives of each of the hierarchies serving in each of the twelve lesser pagodas. The cosmic hum that comes forth from the Great Hub is reproduced in the central tower as the music of the spheres. It is a combination of these plus and minus factors of Alpha and Omega in unique combination in each of the twelve houses that produces the action of the mercy flame that is in the central focus under the golden dome. This music is the origin of Chinese and oriental music. It is the focus of this retreat that makes oriental art so completely different from our Western modes and conceptions.

Hanging above the entrance to each of the twelve temples are pieces of crystal and precipitated metal that chime the notes of the temples as the wind blows through them. A circular stairway spiraling along the periphery takes us to the top of each pagoda. There are landings at four levels where the tones of the yin and yang aspects of the hierarchy represented are released.

In the central pagoda, where silence has been observed for centuries, there is an altar, carved in ivory, where the flame of mercy pulsates within a golden urn. The central pagoda is six stories high, an imposing building with many flame rooms, council chambers and classrooms where the brothers and sisters of mercy serve and receive from the world those souls who require respite and a saturation of the forgiveness flame before they are able to return once again to embodiment, to fulfill their divine plan and to balance the debts they owe to life.

Kuan Yin is truly a cosmic mother; the tenderness of her heart's love for all who come here melts even the most dense of human creation and spurs those with even the heaviest karma to renewed service and an invocation of the flame. So great is Kuan Yin's compassion and forgiveness that none who come here leave without knowing that because they are loved, they can go forth to try again and to succeed.

The momentums of gentleness, of devotion to family, of service to one another that are so special in the Chinese people come from the action of the mercy flame of this retreat.

❖ **THE TEMPLE OF PEACE, The Retreat of the Elohim of the Sixth Ray**

The solar-plexus chakra

Peace and Aloha focus the energies of the solar-plexus chakra of the planet in their retreat located in the etheric plane over the Hawaiian Islands. From the Temple of Peace, the Elohim radiate ribbons of Cosmic Christ peace over the entire earth as a network of the Cosmic Christ consciousness. In addition to purple and gold flames, Mighty Cosmos' secret rays are focused in this retreat.

The forcefield of the Temple of Peace may be visualized as a purple and gold heart, with a magnetic forcefield of alternating purple and gold concentric heart-shaped rings. The flame in the center of the heart is the flame of Cosmic Christ peace. This forcefield is superimposed over the temple.

One enters the etheric temple in the etheric body, and immediately the eternal presence of the flame of peace is felt. The entrance hall leads into a round room; ten pillars grace the circular walls, which reflect the pulsations of the secret rays anchored in the center of the room. The altar of the secret

Hawaii

rays is sunken in the center of the room. Three steps lead to a circular pathway surrounding the altar in which the secret rays are anchored.

Proceeding on past the altar of the secret rays and down a hallway, we descend a flight of stairs leading to the great Hall of Peace. This is actually in the center of the temple, architecturally patterned after the hall we have just passed through, except on a larger scale. There are twelve pillars on the circuit, evenly spaced on the circular walls, which reflect the purple and gold of the Elohim of Peace anchored in the center dais. Descending the three steps and walking around the focus, we come to the thrones of Peace and Aloha. Between the twelve pillars that adorn the sides of the temple are twelve doors leading to twelve circular anterooms, one of which is the room through which we just passed where the secret rays are focused. The flame of peace, being at the fulcrum of the Christ consciousness, is in the center of the temple, the throne of Peace and Aloha at the twelve o'clock line and the secret rays at the six o'clock line.

Initiates on the sixth ray study at the Temple of Peace under the careful guidance of the Elohim who are in charge. Those who are preparing to embody on the sixth ray will spend some time here before reembodying in order to learn how the Elohim focus the flame of peace through the Holy Spirit in nature and the activities of the builders of form. Prior to his embodiment as Saint Francis, when he prayed, "Lord, make me an instrument of thy peace!" beloved Kuthumi studied under the Great Initiator, Lord Maitreya, in his retreat in the Himalayas; but before taking on a physical body, he was brought to the Temple of Peace where his development of the flame of peace was tested through ordered steps of initiations that are

Hawaii

conducted under the auspices of the hierarchy of that retreat.

Outside the great Hall of Peace, there are three other buildings (at the nine, twelve, and three o'clock lines). Here the Brotherhood of Peace works diligently, drawing up plans for the implementation of peace throughout the world. Volunteers who study there while their body temples sleep or who are between embodiments come to the retreat to study the plans for peace, and here they take vows before Peace and Aloha to go forth as their representatives in the world of form to carry the flame of peace and to implement the plans of the Brotherhood of Peace.

Those who have journeyed to the Hawaiian Islands can attest to the great peace they feel here, which extends throughout the Pacific Ocean.

❖ **THE TEMPLE OF PURIFICATION, The Retreat of the Archangels of the Seventh Ray**

The Temple of Purification is in the etheric realm over the island of Cuba. It is presided over by Archangel Zadkiel and Holy Amethyst. The retreat is also the place of the Order of Melchizedek and of the eternal priesthood of all religions of the world.

Before the sinking of Atlantis, the Temple of Purification was a physical retreat for the priests and priestesses of the Order of Zadkiel. These Masters of Invocation used not only the focus of the flame but also the accumulated good of their causal bodies for the transmutation of misqualified energies on earth. Journeying to and fro, even into the astral realms, these dedicated servants were, and are, a self-appointed clean-up committee who remove the debris, especially in the large cities of the world, so that mankind may continue to function.

There are seven temples at this retreat. The complex is composed of a central temple with seven pillars surrounded by six lesser temples. The architecture and design of the central temple is very similar to that of Archangel Michael and Faith at Banff. The temple is circular with a golden dome, having four entrances with a pyramid-shaped altar in the center where the focus of the violet flame blazes. The decoration throughout the temples is effected with amethyst inlaid in gold, while the golden dome is plain.

At the time of Atlantis, Saint Germain served in the Order of Lord Zadkiel as a high priest in the Temple of Purification. Prior to the sinking of the continent he was called by his own teacher, the Great Divine Director, to carry the flame of freedom from this temple to a place of safety in the Carpathian foothills in Transylvania. When Atlantis sank, the Temple of Purification was withdrawn to the etheric plane.

Saint Germain later returned to the location of this retreat when he was embodied as Christopher Columbus, who set forth in his ships to discover a new world. He was magnetized to this retreat by the flame of freedom in the etheric Temple of Purification and by the inner memory of serving in that temple on Atlantis. He studied here between embodiments and also during his embodiments while leaving his body in periods of sleep. The impetus for coming to those islands was the impetus of freedom, helping him to chart a new course for a new land.

The keynote of the retreat is the "Blue Danube Waltz," inspired upon Johann Strauss by Saint Germain.

❖ **THE TEMPLE OF THE SUN, The Retreat of the Goddess of Liberty**

While embodied on Atlantis, the Goddess of Liberty erected the Temple of the Sun where Manhattan Island now is. With the sinking of the continent, the physical temple was destroyed, but its etheric counterpart remains a major world center focusing the flames of the twelve hierarchies of the Sun. The temple, which was the West gate of Atlantis, has become the East gate

Liberty Island

of the New World. It is one of the most important retreats on the planet.

The central altar of the Temple of the Sun is over the Statue of Liberty on Liberty (Bedloe's) Island in New York Harbor, the spread of the focus extending over Manhattan Island and parts of New Jersey. The temple is a replica of the temple of Helios and Vesta in the

sun of our solar system. In the central flame room of the temple, we find the pattern that is reproduced over and over again throughout the universe from the heart of the Great Hub to the Flaming Yod, to the sun of each solar system and each God Star. Every planetary home has a Sun Temple where the central altar is dedicated to the Father-Mother God, the pure white essence of the creative fire of Alpha and Omega, and the twelve surrounding altars are tended by the representatives of the twelve hierarchies of the Sun who focus their flames on behalf of the evolutions of that planet.

Tiers of flame rooms proceed out from this center room. In these flame rooms, the brothers in white attend other flames of the one hundred and forty-four. The flame of liberty, the fleur-de-lis of pink, blue and gold, blazes from one of these outer courts. The aura of the retreat is saturated with the golden flame of illumination, and as the Château de Liberté in France (also a focus of the threefold flame of liberty) emits a pink aura, so we find that the twin flames of Helios and Vesta are represented in perfect balance in these two retreats dedicated to the liberation of all mankind. The gold and the pink reflect the wisdom and the love of our Sun God and Goddess.

The Goddess of Liberty says, "Give me your tired, your poor, your huddled masses yearning to breathe free, the wretched refuse of your teeming shore. Send these, the homeless, tempest-tossed to me. I lift my lamp beside the golden door."[584] Her Temple of the Sun is the open door of

America from Europe, opening the door to all facets of the consciousness of humanity through the twelve aspects of the twelve solar hierarchies. The many millions who have come from Europe and Asia are the people who are destined to become a part of the mandala, or pattern, of the golden age.

New Jersey and Manhattan,
Liberty Island at far left

The great diversity of virtues proceeding forth from the Temple of the Sun accounts for the great immigration that has been drawn to the Eastern shores of the United States. The melting pot that has created the nation of America has occurred through the grid and the forcefield of this retreat. Every evolution associated with this planet can be found on Manhattan Island. Every form of endeavor of science, art, music and everything under the sun that mankind have imagined—either to amplify the attributes and virtues of the twelve hierarchies or as perversions of the same—all can be found within a few miles of this retreat.

The flame of this retreat inspired the creation of the Statue of Liberty. The book she holds is the Book of the Law that is destined to come forth in America, the teachings of the great masters of wisdom, the teachings of the ascended masters.

❖ **THE TEMPLE OF THE SUN, The Retreat of Helios and Vesta in the Center of the Sun**

In the center of the sun of this solar system is the great Temple of the Sun of Helios and Vesta. On a number of occasions the masters have invited us to journey there. On July 6, 1984, Godfre said: "And now, this evening as you take your leave from your physical body temples, Helios and Vesta receive you with open arms of light and love and vast wisdom of the spheres in their retreat in the Temple of the Sun. White angels with fiery shields and helmets and swords held, seraphim, legions of Justinius, of Uriel, Helios and Vesta, my own bands and others shall accompany you now into the heart of the sun known as Victory.

"Thus, Mighty Victory himself takes his name from the sun of this system, and it is to the Victory Retreat of Helios and Vesta that we go."[585]

Holy Amethyst has also described a journey to this retreat: "I come to you in the flame of the World Mother and in a chariot of fire, of violet fire, and I would take with me those who are ready for the ascent.... Are you ready? Step, then, inside with me. For now we shall ascend to the heights of the sun. And our wings shall not melt, for they are made of burnished gold, tried in the very fires of the sun, in the heart of Helios and Vesta.

"Now we ascend over the treetops and over the clouds and over the effluvia of the air. We rise higher into the blue and we know that God is truly everywhere I AM. There come into view celestial hues and angelic choirs, elementals who serve the outer reaches of space....

"And so we come, then, closer to Helios and Vesta. We find not greater heat but greater light, and there is a coolness and a delight. And we see, standing in the center of the sun, our Father-Mother God—representatives thereof, twin flames of pink and gold, standing arms outstretched....

"As our chariot approaches in a spiral—for we enter the sun according to the spirals of the sun that form cosmic highways for billions of lifewaves and angels and the Elohim, too—so we come in on a pathway of golden-pink light. And the angels who have suspended and guided our chariot now bring us to a place of rest. We have had no sense of movement, only that we have seen the seas and the great panorama of the highways of the Infinite.

"Gently we disembark and we walk the pathway to the throne room and to the inner temple. Our hearts are expectant and leap within. For in the anthem of the free that we hear the trumpets playing (trumpets of mighty seraphim and cherubim and mighty beings we have not known before who are dancing in paeans of praise), in the flowers we have never seen and in the crystal lights in all directions, we know truly this is the heart, the very heart of hearts, the very heart of Being....

"We approach swiftly, lightly. And upon the golden stairway we enter. We are bidden welcome by the keeper of the gate. We take from off our feet our sandals. And we enter as children, much in the same manner that we left....

"We are received down the long corridor covered by a golden-pink flame, as it were, a flame beneath our feet. And we approach, then, the arms of Helios and Vesta. Each one is embraced, and the kiss of the Father-Mother God is placed upon the forehead. We kneel in utter adoration and we receive the blessing of the Infinite One."[586]

❖ **THE TEMPLE OF TRUTH, The Retreat of Hilarion**

The Temple of Truth is located in the etheric realm over the island of Crete, where the ruins of the original physical Temple of Truth remain from the period when the island was part of the mainland of Greece.

The ascended master Hilarion is the hierarch of the retreat, and Pallas Athena, the Goddess of Truth, is the Patroness. Together they direct the activities of the Brotherhood of Truth, angelic hosts serving on the fifth ray, and unascended lifestreams who come in their finer bodies between embodiments and also during sleep to learn the truth of all teachings, especially of cosmic law, of the science of healing, mathematics, music, the divine geometry and the science of engrammic rhythms, the laws of alchemy and precipitation.

Crete

The Brotherhood of Truth caters to souls who have been disillusioned by false teachings, who have become skeptics and agnostics, even atheists. They also sponsor all teachers of Truth, servants of God, religious leaders and missionaries, working steadfastly to draw their consciousness into a greater appreciation of the fullness of Truth, of which they may have only experienced a part, which part they thought to be the whole and taught as such.

The Brotherhood also works tirelessly to introduce matrices of Truth into the consciousness of mankind, wherever imperfection or error appears. They survey the scene in an attempt to find one or more contacts who will be receptive to the higher vibration of Truth that will draw the perfect plan, pattern or idea for a particular endeavor or service.

The ruins of the temple are just one more reminder that wherever light is raised and virtue is espoused, the hordes of darkness gather to destroy and to tear down, lest the flame rise above the mediocrity of their consciousness and consume it. Subsequent to the rape of the Temple of Truth, the Delphic order under the Lady Vesta (twin flame of Helios and the first Goddess of Truth to the earth) and Pallas Athena directed the release of messages through embodied lifestreams, called the Oracle of Delphi. The wisdom released through them gave great assistance to those embodied who were keeping the flame of wisdom and truth on behalf of mankind. Eventually one member of the order betrayed their service, and so the dispensation was withdrawn.

The etheric temple is a replica of the physical focus built on the scale of the Parthenon. Long marble steps lead to the columned building decorated in gold frieze. The classrooms and council halls of the Temple of Truth are located in the immense area beneath the ascending marble steps. The hundred-foot altar in the center of the temple, a single beautifully carved pillar, holds the focus of the flame of truth in a golden brazier.

The brothers and sisters who minister unto the flame and serve in this retreat form concentric squares at the base of the pillar. Their places are marked by mosaic designs, and between the innermost square and the pillar are mosaic patterns depicting great masters and cosmic beings who have served the cause of Truth throughout the ages.

The flame of Truth is an intensely bright and fiery green, the color that compels precipitation, actualization, alchemy, practicality, healing and rejuvenation. The abstract, the ephemeral, the intangible, all are made concrete by the flame of Truth and the service rendered by all who are devoted to the life of God, of which it is a focus.

Hilarion invites us to attend classes in his retreat: "When you come then to the Temple of Truth, be prepared for the reception of Lanello, our newly ascended Brother of Truth who by attainment wears the robe of our retreat and lectures in our halls, teaching and preaching as of old after the gospel of Jesus the Christ, who taught his disciples to become fishers of men.

"If you would be fishers of men, if you would carry the sword of Truth and wear our robe, then come and be initiated, and receive a just portion of the fires of Truth. For our God is a consuming fire, and he shall consume in this hour all that is allied with error and that defiles the image of the Holy Virgin."[587]

❖ **URIEL AND AURORA'S RETREAT, The Retreat of the Archangels of the Sixth Ray**

The retreat of Uriel and Aurora is located in the etheric realm over the Tatra Mountains south of Cracow, Poland. Uriel and Aurora also serve with legions of Peace from the Retreat of Jesus in Saudi Arabia.

❖ **VAIVASVATA MANU'S RETREAT IN THE HIMALAYAS**

Vaivasvata Manu, the manu of the fifth root race, maintains a focus in the Himalayas. The flame focused in his retreat magnetizes the souls evolving within the fifth root race to the pattern of the Christ consciousness that he holds on their behalf.

In 1994 the Great Divine Director announced that this retreat and the retreats of all of the manus had been opened to some among mankind: "The upper tenth of the members of all root races who have incarnated and those who are not of the root races but of the angelic kingdom who have taken incarnation in order to teach those root races—the upper tenth, then, began at summer solstice...to attend an accelerated course at the etheric retreats of the manus: at my own retreat and the retreats of the God and Goddess Meru, Lord Himalaya and Vaivasvata Manu."[588]

❖ VICTORY'S TEMPLE

On June 3, 1960, El Morya announced a dispensation from the Karmic Board and from Helios and Vesta for a temple of the Great White Brotherhood to be built on earth. He said: "The grant to mankind from the ascended host is to give to the world a genuine outer focus of the Great White Brotherhood without concealment or secrecy. A mighty Temple of Victory is to be built in this nation for all mankind, dedicated to the presence of Almighty God. It shall be called "I AM" the Temple of Life's Victory.... The pattern for this vast temple is now being lowered from the blessed Silent Watcher into the etheric realms and the action will be completed by July 1.... We are affirming the freedom of earth by establishing the first temple of the Great White Brotherhood known to the outer world since Atlantean days."

Saint Germain has given a description of the temple and its function: "Surely if temporal government can demand of mankind the material substance to arm the earth with instruments of destruction, the lovers of peace and freedom, who are multitudinous in every land, will respond to the great privilege of laying many stones in this outer temple designed in such lofty spiritual grandeur at inner levels! When it is complete I am planning on giving my greatest gift to America and the world, for therein I am going to actually anchor the full focus of my freedom flame!...

"The first floor of the temple (and there are three above the earth level) is Victory's Temple. It is the largest and is completely circular, surrounded by huge Corinthian columns on the outside and granite artwork as lovely as the Taj Mahal itself, all within the beauty of its towering columns. Around the circular amphitheater will be glorious paintings of the great chohans themselves and also including beloved Jesus and Mary, the archangels and many others of the familiar members of the ascended host. Services here will be open to all mankind without restriction as to creed or race in keeping with the traditions of the Brotherhood.

"The second floor is dedicated to the Holy Spirit and as such is an 'upper room,' vast though it may be, dedicated to the magnificent Lord the Maha Chohan. Here the most sacred rituals shall be performed, including those that are calculated to represent the ceremonial action of this age over which I now preside. The anchoring of the freedom flame here is a gift of divine wisdom. A huge focus of a snow-white dove will also be anchored in this temple, within which the masters of light shall precipitate several sacred tokens and foci of the sacred fire to assist in amplifying the action of the Holy Spirit within the lives of mankind....

"The third floor is closed to all except the most advanced chelas and is under the direction of the great ascended master Serapis, whose stricter disciplines lead to the freedom of the ascension. It is circular, too, but smaller than the other temples. We expect to permit here the use of an ascension chair—located directly above the freedom flame focus on the second floor, which is, in turn, above Victory's altar on the first floor. This temple is strictly dedicated to the ascension and is for the use of those nearing that achievement. In this temple we will actually step through the veil in our tangible bodies and assist in completing the earthly victory of our most faithful chelas as we did in the Cave of Symbols and other sacred retreats.

"Thus this circular 'pyramid' of victory honors the name of God by a means whereby the various stages of evolution may come into a practical focus that will not be too sharply delineated so as to separate men from one another, except to inspire them and elevate them by world-renowned beauty and the vibratory action of the great Brotherhood itself as it now moves once again into fiery world action in the outer visible unconcealed realm."[589]

The design for this temple came from Mighty Victory. The temple exists in all its pristine beauty in the etheric realm and may be visited by unascended mankind while they sleep. We yet await the full manifestation of this dispensation through the physical building of the temple.

❖ **THE WESTERN SHAMBALLA, Gautama Buddha's Retreat in North America**

On New Year's Eve 1976 Gautama Buddha prophesied the future transfer of the forcefield of his retreat to America. He said that America "is indeed the place where all shall return to the cause and core of the Dharma ([i.e.,] the Teaching) and the Sangha. For here we will transfer Shamballa, here we will transfer that City of Light one day. But for now, it will be the implementation of a secondary forcefield, the Omega aspect of Shamballa, as the Alpha aspect remains positioned where it is."

The Heart of the Inner Retreat

In 1981 Gautama established his Western Shamballa over "the Heart" of what his devotees call the "Inner Retreat." On April 18, he said, "From Shamballa I arc a light. I would establish the ground of the Ancient of Days…. In this hour I contemplate—note it well—the arcing of the flame of Shamballa to the Inner Retreat as the Western abode of the

Buddhas and the bodhisattvas and the bodhisattvas-to-be who are the devotees of the Mother light."

So, the "yang" presence of Gautama Buddha remains at that point of Shamballa in the East in the etheric octave over the Gobi Desert, and his "yin" presence is in the West in the etheric octave over the Gallatin Range in the Northern Rockies focused at the Heart of the Inner Retreat. This property, known as the Royal Teton Ranch, a cathedral of nature bordering on Yellowstone Park, is the physical coordinate of the Western etheric retreat of the Lord of the World. Here we contemplate the mysteries of the Inner Buddha and the Inner Christ and lend our threefold flames to anchor in the Western Hemisphere the forcefield of Shamballa.

❖ ZARATHUSTRA'S RETREAT

Zarathustra has said that we are "candidates to come to his retreat." He calls it the place prepared, a mighty retreat that is a replica of the secret chamber of the heart, your very own heart. The location of Zarathustra's retreat has not been released. Zarathustra explains why:

"I look forward to welcoming you there, beloved ones, yet I have not released the whereabouts of this retreat, nor shall I. For when you make attunement with your own heart, beloved ones, and when you are in that heart as the devotee of the God within your heart, then so know and so understand: you shall not be able to avoid reaching that retreat of mine that is the replica of the secret chamber of the heart. Thus, I will tell you one thing. It is deep within the mountains. But which mountains, beloved, you will have to discover for yourselves."[590]

Conclusion:
Bringing Heaven to Earth

An Ascended Master in the Making

Now *you* have been on the journey that Elizabeth Clare Prophet went on all those years ago. You may wonder, "Well what has all this to do with me? My life has so many challenges. I have so much to do. It is hard enough for me to keep up with paying the bills, working my job and finding time for my family, let alone myself. What about the world? There are so many problems on earth, too many to mention, let alone to solve. The heaven-world sounds wonderful, but it seems so different to the one in which I live."

But is it?

There are no accidents in the universe. The masters, your Higher Self and your guardian angel have placed this book in your hands for a very simple reason: You, too, have a fiery destiny. You have a Higher Self. You have a mission that was ordained from the beginning. You have a twin flame on earth or somewhere in cosmos. And whether you realize it or not, you are an ascended master in the making.

As your older brothers and sisters, the masters are way-showers, pointing the way on the path home to God and your reunion with your own God Presence. Many walked the earth, just as you do—some quite recently. They know the challenge of life on earth. They know the path home, the pitfalls along the way and the rough places on the climb up the mountain of being. They, too, had knotty problems and difficult karmic circumstances to overcome. They are not far removed from you.

Now, at the cusp of a new age, they beckon from just beyond the veil. They stand at the threshold where heaven meets earth, and they say, "We did it! So can you! Yes, there are steps to be taken and assignments to fulfill. But we can help you. We have known you since the dawn of time and beyond. We desire to see you return to our Father's home of light, the eternal city.

"Call to us. We know the way. We have the tools that you need to make it over the crevasse and the icy river. Come to our retreats. Let us teach you and tell you those things that can make a difference in your life. Let us help you bring heaven to earth."

Their offer is very real and their intercession and presence is powerful. Take advantage of it.

Won't you pause for a moment, right now, and ask your Higher Self to guide you to the master who can most help you on your spiritual path?

Perhaps you know who your master is. Perhaps you were drawn to a master as you read the book. If you are not sure, go first to the master El Morya. He takes on many new students and prepares them to meet their master.

Find the master who speaks to your heart, and invite that master into your life. Go to their retreat at night. Pray to that one, use their prayers or decrees. Ask them to enter your world, to teach you and train you at night as you sleep. Ask them to help you to bring heaven to earth. This master may begin by transforming a little corner of your own world, the one in which you live.

The Retreats Are Real

After journeying to the retreats of the masters in her finer body and returning to write about them, Elizabeth Clare Prophet said, "I want you to know that these retreats are real, that the ascended masters are real, that the Elohim, the archangels and the chohans are real. The information that we have been given is so fantastic and so startling that, at the same time we hear it, we feel the carnal mind and the whole momentum of the hordes of darkness resisting the reality and the tangibility of this knowledge and the practicality of it and what can be done with it. We must realize the implications of this knowledge."

God has set up these forcefields of the etheric retreats as highly concentrated centers of light so that we could appeal to the masters and invoke their light for the liberation of the planet. It has been said that there is enough violet-flame energy anchored in the retreats of the violet-flame masters on the planet to free the earth entirely and bring it into the golden age of Aquarius. It only remains for mankind to invoke that energy and that flame. Nothing else stands in the way of the victory.

The key is the invocation. For God is already here, but by comic law, the forces of light cannot interfere in this plane unless we ask them to help, unless we call to them for assistance.

Why is that? Because we are given free will to function in this physical plane. This plane of being was turned over to us. And in order for God and the masters to enter into this, our domain, we have to give them the authority to do so, consciously and by our own free will. Free will means that we have the opportunity to return to God the authority in this level that he gave to us. We have to say:

"In the name of the Christ, I call forth the seven mighty Elohim, the archangels, and the chohans of the rays to release the full-gathered momentum of the flames anchored in their retreats into my being and world and throughout the planet Earth for the victory of the light."

Such invocations need to be made daily. As they are given, we will see enlightenment, liberation, freedom, the fulfillment of the law of being and ultimately a golden age upon our beloved planet.

Heaven on Earth

There are many ways to make such calls. For example, Jesus taught his disciples to pray, "Thy will be done. Thy kingdom come on earth as it is in heaven." And this is the goal. There is already a kingdom of light—a kingdom of "heaven"—on this planet in the etheric octave. And the more we know about the retreats and the etheric cities and what they look like, the more we remember of our experiences there, the more we can begin to outpicture them in our homes and work environment, in our cities and nations. As we create more heavenly environments for life on earth, eventually we will bring heaven to earth.

The master Hilarion says: "A place must be prepared on earth for the masters, for their coming and for the disciples attending their coming. As each home of light resembles more and more the etheric retreats of the Brotherhood, so there is the meeting of heaven and earth and there is the open door to the path of the ascension whereby worlds are transcended and the soul that is born in Matter is born again in Spirit. Thus prepare the place, prepare the manger for the birth of the Christ. Prepare the home where the eagles will gather together."[591]

You can walk in the footsteps of the masters who have gone before you. You can walk the earth as an ascending one. You can bring the aura of the masters and their retreats to those whom you meet each day. You can change your life and the lives of those around you. And at the conclusion of a life of service, you can reunite with God in the ritual of the ascension. You can become an ascended master and return to your home in the etheric cities and retreats of light.

There Is Another Retreat

In his book *Unveiled Mysteries,* Godfré Ray King tells of going into the mountains southeast of Tucson, making camp in a canyon and falling asleep. He dreams of a young man, and when he awakes, the young man is there.

He follows the young man to a cliff. The youth places his hands on a rock, presses against it, and a section of the wall slides to one side. They enter a tunnel that was an ancient underground watercourse. They go through another door and come to a beautiful valley. The young man turns to him and says, "My friend, you have returned home after a long absence."

These are the words that will be spoken to you by the doorman at the retreat of you and your twin flame when you arrive in your mansion in the heaven-world—for you and your twin flame also have a mansion on the etheric plane. It will be your home when you ascend.

You have been evolving for thousands and hundreds of thousands of years upon this planet. You have been coming and going to and from the retreats of the Brotherhood in between embodiments and while you have been in embodiment. And you have your own home of light.

The messenger says, "I want you to expect to journey to that retreat, to your own home of light. It is one thing to be a guest in the retreats and mansions of the masters. But sometime, someplace, you want to feel at home in your own home where you can sink down in your chair, take off your shoes and put your feet up and do what you want to do.

"Now how many of you have consciously asked to be taken to your own mansion, to your own etheric retreat?... Well, what are you waiting for?

"Why are you depressed, not knowing your divine plan or which way to go? Don't you realize all of that is just bogging you down and distracting you from these crystal moments and experiences you could be having? It is weighing on you, when you could be having your meditation time before going to sleep.

"Fifteen minutes before you fall asleep, meditate on the Buddha, go within, call to your I AM Presence and the I AM Presence of your twin flame and ask for your reunion in higher octaves."[592]

So, what are you waiting for? Try it tonight. A whole new world awaits you.

❖

Charts and Maps

Rays of the Flames Magnetized on the Days of the Week	God-Qualities Amplified through Invocation to the Flame	Chakras, or Centers: Chalices of Light Sustaining the Frequencies of the Rays in the Four Lower Bodies; World Religion of This Ray
First Ray Will of God (Blue) Magnified on Tuesday	Omnipotence, perfection, protection, faith, desire to do the will of God through the power of the Father	**Throat** (Blue) **Judaism**
Second Ray Wisdom of God (Yellow) Magnified on Sunday	Omniscience, understanding, illumination, desire to know God through the mind of the Son	**Crown** (Yellow) **Buddhism**
Third Ray Love of God (Pink) Magnified on Monday	Omnipresence, compassion, charity, desire to be God in action through the love of the Holy Spirit	**Heart** (Pink) **Christianity**
Fourth Ray Purity of God (White) Magnified on Friday	Purity, wholeness, desire to know and be God through purity of body, mind and soul through the consciousness of the Divine Mother	**Base of the Spine** (White) **Hinduism**
Fifth Ray Science of God (Green) Magnified on Wednesday	Truth, healing, constancy, desire to precipitate the abundance of God through the immaculate concept of the Holy Virgin	**Third Eye** (Green) **Confuciansim**
Sixth Ray Peace of God (Purple and Gold) Magnified on Thursday	Ministration of the Christ, desire to be in the service of God and man through the mastery of the Christ	**Solar Plexus** (Purple and Gold) **Islam**
Seventh Ray Freedom of God (Violet) Magnified on Saturday	Freedom, ritual, transmutation, transcendence, desire to make all things new through the application of the laws of alchemy	**Seat of the Soul** (Violet) **Taoism**
Eighth Ray Liberator of the Sacred Fire of the Seven Rays / All Days	Integration, wholeness, transition to the five secret rays	**Secret Chamber of the Heart** (Between Pink and Gold; a Peach Color) **Zoroastrianism**

and the Beings Who Ensoul Them

Chohans, or Lords, Focusing the Christ Consciousness of the Ray; Location of Their Retreats	Archangels and Divine Complements Focusing the Solar Consciousness of the Ray; Location of Their Retreats	Elohim and Divine Complements Focusing the God Consciousness of the Ray; Location of Their Retreats
El Morya Darjeeling, India	**Michael** **Faith** Banff and Lake Louise, Canada	**Hercules** **Amazonia** Half Dome, Sierra Nevada, California, U.S.A.
Lanto Grand Teton, Teton Range, Wyoming, U.S.A.	**Jophiel** **Christine** South of the Great Wall near Lanchow, North Central China	**Apollo** **Lumina** Western Lower Saxony, Germany
Paul the Venetian Southern France Temple of the Sun, New York City	**Chamuel** **Charity** St. Louis, Missouri, U.S.A.	**Heros** **Amora** Lake Winnipeg, Canada
Serapis Bey Luxor, Egypt	**Gabriel** **Hope** Between Sacramento and Mount Shasta, California, U.S.A.	**Purity** **Astrea** Near Gulf of Archangel, southeast arm of White Sea, Russia
Hilarion Crete, Greece	**Raphael** **Mother Mary** Fátima, Portugal	**Cyclopea** **Virginia** Altai Range where China, Siberia and Mongolia meet, near Tabun Bogdo
Nada Saudi Arabia	**Uriel** **Aurora** Tatra Mountains south of Cracow, Poland	**Peace** **Aloha** Hawaiian Islands
Saint Germain Transylvania, Romania Table Mountain, Rocky Mountains, U.S.A.	**Zadkiel** **Amethyst** Cuba	**Arcturus** **Victoria** Near Luanda, Angola, Africa
The Maha Chohan Sri Lanka (Ceylon)	**Uzziel** **His Twin Flame** (Not Yet Revealed)	(Not Yet Revealed)

Map of retreat locations

Note: For retreats marked *, the exact location has not been revealed and the number on the map indicates the general area where the retreat is situated.

1. Heros and Amora's Retreat, Lake Winnipeg, Canada *
2. The Temple of Faith and Protection, Banff and Lake Louise, Canada
3. The Western Shamballa and the Retreat of the Divine Mother, Royal Teton Ranch, Southwest Montana, U.S.A.
4. The Royal Teton Retreat, Teton Range, Wyoming, U.S.A.
5. Orion's Retreat, Mountains of North America *
6. Gabriel and Hope's Retreat, between Sacramento and Mt. Shasta, California
7. Four retreats in the Rocky Mountains: the Cathedral of the Violet Flame, the Cave of Symbols, the Retreat for Teenagers and Tabor's Retreat, all located in the Rocky Mountains of North America *
8. The Goddess of Purity's Retreat over San Francisco
9. El Morya's Retreat in El Capitan and Hercules and Amazonia's Retreat in Half Dome, Yosemite Valley, California
10. Tabor's Retreat in the Mountains above Colorado Springs, U.S.A.
11. John the Beloved's Retreat over the Arizona Desert and Eriel's Retreat in Arizona *
12. The Temple of the Crystal-Pink Flame, St. Louis, Missouri, U.S.A.
13. Meta's Healing Retreat over New England, U.S.A. *
14. The Rose Temple, New Bedford, Massachusetts, U.S.A.
15. The Temple of the Sun, Manhattan and New Jersey, U.S.A.
16. The Temple of Peace, Hawaiian Islands *
17. The Temple of Purification, Cuba *
18. The Temple of Illumination, Island of the Sun, Lake Titicaca, Bolivia
19. The Shrine of Glory, Andes Mountains, South America *
20. Purity and Astrea's Retreat, Gulf of Archangel, Russia
21. Apollo and Lumina's Retreat, West Lower Saxony, Germany
22. Lanello's Retreat on the Rhine, Bingen, Germany
23. The Master of Paris' Retreats in Paris, France
24. Le Château de Liberté, Rhône River, South of France *
25. Raphael and Mother Mary's Retreat, Fátima, Portugal

26. Uriel and Aurora's Retreat, Tatra Mountains, South of Cracow, Poland

27. The Rakoczy Mansion and the Temple of the Maltese Cross, Carpathian Mountains, Romania

28. The Queen of Light's Retreat, Messina, Sicily

29. The Temple of Truth, Crete, Greece *

30. The Resurrection Temple, Jerusalem

31. The Persian Retreat *

32. The Ascension Temple and Retreat at Luxor

33. The Arabian Retreat, Arabian Desert *

34. Portia's Retreat, Ghana *

35. Arcturus and Victoria's Retreat, near Luanda, Angola

36. The Goddess of Purity's Retreat over the Island of Madagascar *

37. Oromasis and Diana's Retreat, an Island off the Kamchatka Peninsula, Bering Sea *

38. Cyclopea and Virginia's Retreat, Altai Range, where Russia, Mongolia and China meet

39. Shamballa, Gobi Desert *

40. The Temple of Mercy, Foothills above Peking (Beijing), China

41. Maitreya's Retreat over Tientsin, China

42. Jophiel and Christine's Retreat, South of the Great Wall, near Lanchow, China

43. The Jade Temple, China *

44. The Cathedral of Nature, Srinagar, Kashmir

45. The Palace of Light and the Cave of Light, Himalayas *

46. Djwal Kul's Retreat in Tibet *

47. Kuthumi's Retreat at Shigatse, Tibet

48. Four retreats somewhere in the Himalayas: Maitreya's Retreat, the Palace of White Marble, the Retreat of the Blue Lotus and Vaivasvata Manu's Retreat *

49. The Temple of Good Will, Darjeeling, India

50. The Temple of Comfort, Sri Lanka

51. The Sacred Retreat of the Blue Flame, Island Northeast of Viti Levu, Fiji Islands

Zarathustra's Retreat – location not revealed

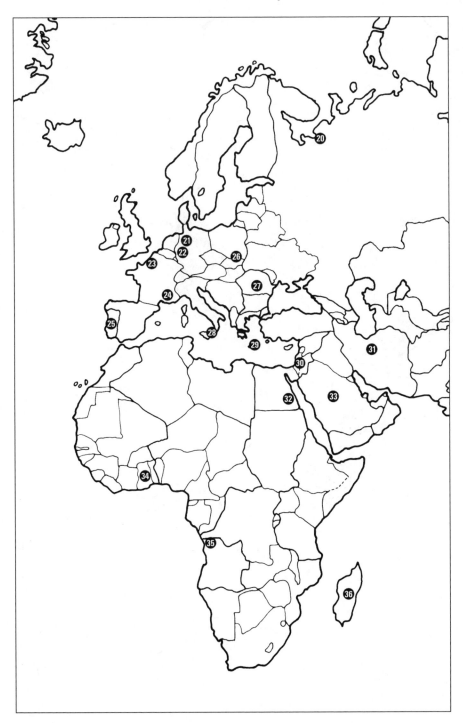

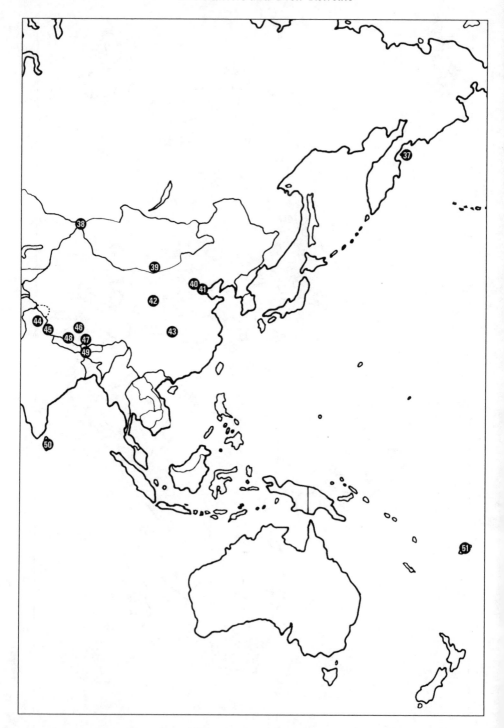

Notes

Books referenced here are published by Summit University Press unless otherwise noted.

1. Acts 1:9.
2. Rev. 7:9, 10, 13–17.
3. Gen. 1:28.
4. Heb. 10:7, 9.
5. Gen. 1:3.
6. Ps. 8:5.
7. Gen. 4:9.
8. Elizabeth Clare Prophet, *Afra: Brother of Light* (Corwin Springs, Mont.: The Summit Lighthouse Library, 2003), pp. 25–26.
9. Ibid., pp. 29–30.
10. Ibid., p. 35.
11. Godfré Ray King, *The Magic Presence,* 5th ed. (Chicago: Saint Germain Press, 1982), pp. 187–214.
12. Mark L. Prophet and Elizabeth Clare Prophet, *Climb the Highest Mountain: The Path of the Higher Self* (1986), pp. 129–30.
13. For a description of the Hub and the Great Central Sun, see Mark L. Prophet and Elizabeth Clare Prophet, *The Masters and the Spiritual Path* (2000), pp. 221–24.
14. Jer. 31:33; Heb. 8:10; 10:16.
15. Rev. 1:8, 11; 21:6; 22:13.
16. Alpha, "A Replica of the Crystal Atom," *Pearls of Wisdom*, vol. 25, no. 51, December 19, 1982.
17. Archangel Zadkiel, "An Hour of Great Need in the Planetary Body," *Pearls of Wisdom*, vol. 27, no. 46A, September 19, 1984.
18. Amaryllis, March 21, 1971.
19. Amen Bey, "An Ancient Temple of Luxor," *Pearls of Wisdom*, vol. 34, no. 29, June 27, 1991.
20. Goddess of Light, July 4, 1972.
21. Goddess of Light, October 16, 1966.
22. Goddess of Light, January 20, 1980.
23. Goddess of Light, October 16, 1966.
24. The Goddess of Light, "Be Aware! Be Vigilant!" *Pearls of Wisdom*, vol. 32, no. 54, November 10, 1989, quoted by Elizabeth Clare Prophet, June 28, 1996.
25. Goddess of Light, July 2, 1995.
26. The Mighty Angel Clothed with a Cloud and a Rainbow Upon His Head and in His Hand a Little Book, "Joy Is Timeless, Spaceless Energy," March 22, 1978.
27. Angel Deva of the Jade Temple, "Rivers of Living Water," October 10, 1969.

28. Ibid.

29. Angel of Gethsemane, "To Strengthen the Body of God Upon Earth," April 12, 1979.

30. Angel of Listening Grace, "In the Hour of Overcoming," *Pearls of Wisdom*, vol. 19, no. 47, November 21, 1976.

31. Luke 22:42.

32. Mother Mary, "The Consecration of Russia to the Immaculate Heart of Mary," *Keepers of the Flame Lesson 14*, p. 54.

33. Angel of the Agony, "The Hour of Love's Reunion," *Pearls of Wisdom*, vol. 44, no. 40, October 7, 2001.

34. Ibid.

35. Angel of the Cosmic Cross of White Fire, "Angels of the Cosmic Cross of White Fire Minister unto the Sons and Daughters of God in the Hour of Their Crucifixion," *Pearls of Wisdom*, vol. 23, no. 21, May 25, 1980.

36. Angels of the Cosmic Cross of White Fire and the Ruby Ray, "The Joy of Forgiveness," *Pearls of Wisdom*, vol. 40, no. 37, September 14, 1997.

37. Matt. 28:6.

38. Angel of the Resurrection, "From the Tomb of Mater to the Open Door of the Spirit," April 8, 1977.

39. Angel of the Revelation of Saint John the Divine, "The Message of Alpha and Omega to the Seven Churches," October 10, 1976.

40. The Angel Who Rolled Away the Stone, "Roll Away the Boulders of Pride!" *Pearls of Wisdom*, vol. 40, no. 28, July 13, 1997.

41. Elizabeth Clare Prophet, *The Great White Brotherhood in the Culture, History and Religion of America* (1987), p. 269–70.

42. The Great Divine Director, "A Path of Karma Yoga," *Pearls of Wisdom*, vol. 31, no. 73, October 30, 1988.

43. Sanat Kumara with the Seven Holy Kumaras, "Let the Wall of Fire Descend!" *Pearls of Wisdom*, vol. 35, no. 49, November 4, 1992.

44. Arcturus and Victoria, "Rub the Violet Flame Lamp and See What Happens." *Pearls of Wisdom*, vol. 36, no. 30, July 25, 1993.

45. Ibid.

46. Mark Prophet, "An Introduction to the Elementals," October 12, 1964.

47. E. L. Gardner, intro. to Geoffrey Hodson, *Fairies at Work and at Play* (London: The Theosophical Publishing House LTD, 1976), p. 21. First published in 1925.

48. Aries and Thor, "The Servants of God and Man in the Air Element," *Pearls of Wisdom*, vol. 23. no. 16, April 20, 1980.

49. Mighty Victory, "Victory's Torch Passed unto the Messengers of Truth in Science and Religion," December 31, 1976, quoted by Elizabeth Clare Prophet, June 30, 1995.

50. Paramahansa Yogananda, *Autobiography of a Yogi* (Los Angeles: Self-Realization Fellowship, 1977), pp. 348, 355.

51. Ibid., pp. 348–49.

52. Ibid., p. 349.

53. Surya, "Passing Through," *Pearls of Wisdom*, vol. 31, no. 5, January 31, 1988.

54. Babaji, "The Radiant Word," *Pearls of Wisdom*, vol. 30, no. 51, November 20, 1987.

55. Archangel Michael, "On the Defense of the Path and the Platform of Soul Liberation," October 10, 1977.

56. Elizabeth Clare Prophet, *The Greater Way of Freedom* (1976), pp. 73, 74.

57. Cardinal Bonzano, November 24, 1963.

58. Vaivasvata Manu, "Torrents of Divine Love," "The Radiant Word," *Pearls of Wisdom*, vol. 15, no. 48, November 26, 1972.

59. The Maha Chohan, "I Will Be Brahma/Vishnu/Shiva Where I AM," October 5, 1978.

60. Lord Brahma, "Light Up the World!" *Pearls of Wisdom*, vol. 36, no. 46, October 6, 1993.

61. Sanat Kumara, "The Warning," *Pearls of Wisdom*, vol. 31, no. 4, January 24, 1988.

62. Buddha of the Ruby Ray, "A Dewdrop Rare of Ruby Ray," *Pearls of Wisdom*, vol. 31, no. 69, October 16, 1998.

63. Ibid.

64. Casimir Poseidon, "Defend Peace and Do Not Accept Cataclysm," December 29, 1996, quoted by Elizabeth Clare Prophet, October 11, 1999.

65. Celeste, July 24, 1964.

66. Ibid.

67. Gen. 11:1–9.

68. Elizabeth Clare Prophet, March 10, 1996.

69. Chananda, May 16, 1965.

70. Godfré Ray King, *The Magic Presence* (Santa Fe, N.M.: Saint Germain Press, 1974), pp. 386–89.

71. Chananda, "India in Her Darkest Hour," *Pearls of Wisdom*, vol. 24, no. 23, June 7, 1981.

72. John 21:22.

73. Exod. 28:36; Jer. 2:3; Zech. 14:20, 21.

74. Thérèse of Lisieux, "A Bird That Takes Flight," *Pearls of Wisdom*, vol. 24, no. 44, November 1, 1981.

75. Clara Louise, "The Central Temple of Ancient Lemuria," *Pearls of Wisdom*, vol. 34, no. 30, June 28, 1991.

76. Astrea and Purity, "The Word Must Be Spoken: Make the Call!" *Pearls of Wisdom*, vol. 45, no. 43, October 27, 2002.

77. Gautama Buddha, "The Torch Is Passed!" *Pearls of Wisdom*, vol. 26, no. 22, May 29, 1983.

78. Elizabeth Clare Prophet, October 25, 1981.

79. Clara Louise Kieninger, *Ich Dien* (1975), p. 176.

80. Confucius, *The Doctrine of the Mean*, trans. James Legge.

81. Confucius, *Analects*, 15:20, trans. Arthur Waley.

82. Confucius, *Analects*, 4:23.

83. The Duke of Chou, quoted in Herrlee G. Greel, *The Origins of Statecraft in China* (Chicago: University of Chicago Press, 1970), 1:98.

84. Confucius, *Analects*, 7:13, trans. James Legge.

85. Robert Eno, *The Confucian Creation of Heaven: Philosophy and the Defense of Ritual Mastery* (Albany: State University of New York Press, 1990), p. 2.

86. Ibid., p. 3.

87. Ibid., p. 5.

88. Confucius, *Analects*, 7:5.

89. Confucius, "The Golden Light of the Golden Age of China," June 13, 1976.

90. Confucius, July 3, 1962.

91. A Cosmic Being from out the Great Silence, "Summoned to the Highest and Noblest Purpose," *Pearls of Wisdom*, vol. 30, no. 71, December 10, 1987.

92. Eccles. 1:2.

93. Mighty Cosmos, "The Secret Rays Are Released to the Earth from the Heart of Alpha and Omega," *Pearls of Wisdom*, vol. 16, no. 22, June 6, 1973.

94. Mighty Cosmos, July 1, 1995.

95. Decree 0.10 in *Prayers, Meditations and Dynamic Decrees for the Coming Revolution in Higher Consciousness*.

96. Cuzco, "The Wisdom of God Parents," *Pearls of Wisdom*, vol. 32, no. 2, January 8, 1989.

97. James 1:8.

98. Matt. 6:22.

99. Cyclopea, November 22, 1964.

100. Decree 50.05 in *Prayers, Meditations and Dynamic Decrees for the Coming Revolution in Higher Consciousness*.

101. Cyclopea, "The Beacon of the All-Seeing Eye of God Be with You!" *Pearls of Wisdom*, vol. 40, no. 19, March 26, 1997.

102. Godfré Ray King, *The Magic Presence* (Chicago: Saint Germain Press, 1935), p. 2.

103. Ibid., pp. 5, 8.

104. Ibid., pp. 62, 64–65, 86.

105. Ibid., p. 106.

106. Ibid., pp. 248–49.

107. Serapis Bey, *Dossier on the Ascension* (1979), pp. 158, 176.

108. David Lloyd, "From Glory unto Glory, even as by the Spirit of God," December 30, 1971.

109. Annie Besant and C. W. Leadbeater, *The Lives of Alcyone*, ch. 47.

110. Djwal Kul, *Pearls of Wisdom*, vol. 15, no. 15, April 9, 1972, "The Radiant Word."

111. God Tabor, "The Earth Declares the Glory of the Lord," *Pearls of Wisdom*, vol. 16, no. 40, October 7, 1973.

112. Mark L. Prophet, quoted by Elizabeth Clare Prophet, "Renewal for Elemental Life," October 9, 1998.

113. Gen. 3:17.

114. Geoffrey Hodson, *Fairies at Work and at Play* (London: The Theosophical Publishing House LTD, 1976), p. 103. First published in 1925.

115. *Pearls of Wisdom*, 1969, pp. 263, 264.

116. Oromasis and Diana, "Call for the Rainbow Fire!" *Pearls of Wisdom*, vol. 33. no. 32, August 19, 1990.

117. Lanello, "In the Sanctuary of the Soul," *Pearls of Wisdom*, vol. 40, no. 52, December 28, 1997.

118. Mark Prophet, "The Kingdom of the Elements: Fire, Air, Water, Earth," July 2, 1972.

119. Oromasis and Diana, "Call for the Rainbow Fire!" July 8, 1990, quoted by Elizabeth Clare Prophet, October 9, 1998.

120. Matt. 11:14; 17:12.

121. 2 Kings 2:11.

122. John 3:30.

123. John the Baptist, "The Proclamation of the Heralds of All Time," *Pearls of Wisdom*, vol. 19, no. 22, May 30, 1976.

124. Anthony Kenny, *Thomas More* (New York: Oxford University Press, 1983), p. 2.

125. El Morya, "Clean House!" *Pearls of Wisdom*, vol. 38, no. 26, June 18, 1995.

126. Genesis 5:24.

127. Enoch, "Transfigured by Christ's Immortality," June 17, 1962.

128. Enoch, "The Walk with God," April 5, 1969.

129. Enoch, "I Have Chosen to Walk the Earth..." *Pearls of Wisdom*, vol. 30, no. 9, March 1, 1987.

130. Ibid., pp. 299, 300.

131. Ernon, Rai of Suern, "Lessons Learned," *Pearls of Wisdom*, vol. 34, no. 61, November 27, 1991.

132. Rom. 1:16.

133. Hope, "A Cosmic Sense of Space and Time," *Pearls of Wisdom*, vol. 12, no. 5, February 2, 1969.

134. Bhikshu Sangharakshita, *A Survey of Buddhism*, rev. ed. (Boulder, Colo.: Shambhala with London: Windhorse, 1980), p. 372.

135. Detlef Ingo Lauf, *Secret Doctrines of the Tibetan Books of the Dead*, trans. Graham Parkes (Boston: Shambhala, 1989), p. 105; *Tibetan Sacred Art: The Heritage of Tantra* (Berkeley: Shambhala, 1976), p. 120.

136. Vairochana, "Balance Your Karma: Take the High Road," *Pearl of Wisdom*, vol. 37, no. 3, January 16, 1994.

137. Indrabhuti, *Jnanasiddhi*, quoted in Lama Anagarika Govinda, *Insights of a Himalayan Pilgrim* (Berkeley: Dharma Publishing, 1991), p. 113.

138. Akshobhya, "Becoming Real!" *Pearls of Wisdom*, vol. 37, no. 4, January 23, 1994.

139. Ratnasambhava, "Elements of Being," *Pearls of Wisdom*, vol. 37, no. 6, February 6, 1994.

140. Lama Anagarika Govinda, *Foundations of Tibetan Mysticism* (1960; reprint, New York: Samuel Weiser, 1969), p. 262; *Insights of a Himalayan Pilgrim* (Berkeley: Dharma Publishing, 1991), p. 84.

141. John 10:10.

142. Fortuna, October 16, 1966.

143. Rev. 4:4. See also Rev. 4:10, 11; 5:5–14; 7:11–17; 11:15–18; 14:1–3; 19:4.

144. Goddess of Liberty, "God Has Decided to Save the Earth," *Pearls of Wisdom*, vol. 44, no. 39, September 30, 2001.

145. Cyclopea, "Only God-Free Being Is Real," *Pearls of Wisdom*, vol. 38, no. 14, March 26, 1995.

146. The Spirit of Freedom in the Fourteen Ascended Masters Who Govern the Destiny of America, November 22, 1975.

147. The Fourteen Ascended Masters Who Govern the Destiny of America, July 1, 1996.

148. Goddess of Freedom, "Play to Win!" *Pearls of Wisdom*, vol. 35, no. 46, October 25, 1992.

149. Fun Wey, "Be at Peace," April 16, 1972.

150. Fun Wey, April 23, 1967.

151. Luke 1:28.

152. Archangel Gabriel, September 10, 1963.

153. *Pearls of Wisdom*, 1984, Book One, Introduction One, pp. *19–20*.

154. Edwin Arnold, *The Light of Asia* (London: Kegan Paul, Trench, Trubner & Co., 1930), p. 96.

155. The God of Gold with God Tabor, "The Flow of Energy in the City Foursquare: Children of God, Demand and Supply the Abundance of the Mother!" October 10, 1977.

156. The Great Divine Director, "Crisis Resolved in the Cosmic Cross of White Fire," *Pearls of Wisdom*, vol. 23, no. 11, March 16, 1980.

157. Cyclopea, "The Wrapping of the Earth in the Swaddling Garment of Crystal," October 5, 1979.

158. Cyclopea and Virginia, "I Will Stand upon My Watch!" *Pearls of Wisdom*, vol. 25, no. 13, March 28, 1982.

159. Lanello and God Harmony, October 7, 1978.

160. God Harmony, "The Initiation of Our Chelas in the Flame of God Harmony: The Scientific Method for a Greater Area of Self-Mastery," *Pearls of Wisdom*, vol. 23, no. 24, June 15, 1980.

161. Ibid.

162. Lanello and God Harmony, October 7, 1978.

163. God Harmony, July 1, 1995.

164. Ibid.

165. Ibid.

166. God Harmony, "The Initiation of Our Chelas in the Flame of God Harmony."

167. God Harmony, "On Keeping the Harmony," *Pearls of Wisdom*, vol. 32, no. 53, November 9, 1989.

168. Helios, "The God Behind the Physical Sun." Part 2, *Pearls of Wisdom*, vol. 13, no. 30, July 26, 1970.

169. Hercules, "Brace Yourself to Carry the Earth," *Pearls of Wisdom*, vol. 17, no. 4, January 27, 1974.

170. Hercules and Amazonia, June 29, 1995, quoted in Elizabeth Clare Prophet, "The Empowerment of Elohim," *Pearls of Wisdom*, vol. 41, no. 42, October 18, 1998.

171. Hercules and Amazonia, "Our Primary Concern: To Remove the Fallen Ones from the Planet," *Pearls of Wisdom*, vol. 45, no. 51, December 22, 2002.

172. Archangel Michael, "Hail, Excalibur!" *Pearls of Wisdom*, vol. 32, no. 45, November 1, 1989.

173. Gen. 6:4; Num. 13:32–33; I Enoch 7–16; 68:1–20, 39–41; 105:16; Book of the Secrets of Enoch (II Enoch) 18:1–4; Book of Jubilees 5:1–3; 7:21–23; Testament of Reuben 2:18, 19.

174. El Morya, "I Am Unbenched!" *Pearls of Wisdom*, vol. 32, no. 33, August 13, 1989.

175. James Campbell Brown, *A History of Chemistry from the Earliest Times till the Present Day* (London: J. & A. Churchill, 1913).

176. Hargrave Jennings, *The Divine Pymander of Hermes Mercurius Trismegistus* (San Diego, Calif.: Wizards Bookshelf, 1985), p. x.

177. Hermes Mercurius Trismegistus, "The Emerald Tablet of the Heart," *Pearls of Wisdom*, vol. 24, no. 73, August 1981.

178. El Morya, "The Gemini Mind: For the Governing of Society and the Self," *Pearls of Wisdom*, vol. 24, no. 43, October 25, 1981.

179. Hermes Trismegistus, "The Guild of God Mercury: The Sword and the Pen," *Pearls of Wisdom*, vol. 36, no. 42, September 22, 1993.

180. Heros and Amora, "Bricks of Ruby Ray Planted in the Earth for the Restabilization of the Planet," *Pearls of Wisdom*, vol. 38, no. 40, September 17, 1995.

181. "The Elohim and Their Retreats," *Pearls of Wisdom*, 1978, p. 351.

182. Mark L. Prophet and Elizabeth Clare Prophet, *Lords of the Seven Rays* (1986), book 2, pp. 171–73.

183. Hilarion, "The Revolution of Truth," *Pearls of Wisdom*, vol. 36, no. 45, October 3, 1993.

184. Hilarion, "Preach the Gospel of Salvation in Every Nation!" *Pearls of Wisdom*, vol. 33, no. 39, October 7, 1990.

185. Hilarion, "The Revolution of Truth," *Pearls of Wisdom*, vol. 36, no. 45, October 3, 1993.

186. Mark L. Prophet and Elizabeth Clare Prophet, *Lords of the Seven Rays* (1986), book 2, p. 181.

187. Ibid., p. 185.

188. Lord Himalaya, "Your Love Is the Essence of Yourself," *Pearls of Wisdom*, vol. 34, no. 5, February 3, 1991.

189. Igor, "The Drama of One Life Touched by God," The Radiant Word, *Pearls of Wisdom*, vol. 15, no. 53, December 31, 1972.

190. Mother Mary, July 3, 1966.

191. Igor, "The Drama of One Life Touched by God."

192. R. S. Nathan, comp., *Symbolism in Hinduism* (Bombay: Central Chinmaya Mission Trust, 1983), p. 13.

193. *Encyclopedia of Eastern Philosophy and Religion* (Boston: Shambhala, 1994), s.v. "Ishvara."

194. Klaus K. Klostermaier, *A Survey of Hinduism* (Albany, N.Y.: State University of New York Press, 1989), p. 377.

195. Swami Prabhavananda and Christopher Isherwood, *How to Know God: The Yoga Aphorisms of Patanjali* (New York: Harper & Brothers, 1953), pp. 53–54.

196. Ishvara, "The Quivering of a Cosmos," September 4, 1977.

197. Gen. 6:5.

198. Gen. 4:25, 26.

199. Ps. 16:10.

200. Mark 9:13.

201. For the story of Jesus' journey to the East, along with translations of these manuscripts, see Elizabeth Clare Prophet, *The Lost Years of Jesus* (1987).

202. Decree 60.01 in *Prayers, Meditations, Dynamic Decrees for the Coming Revolution in Higher Consciousness*.

203. Elizabeth Clare Prophet and Staff of Summit University, *Walking with the Master: Answering the Call of Jesus* (Corwin Springs, Mont.: The Summit Lighthouse Library, 2002).

204. Jesus, "From the Temples of Love: The Call to the Path of the Ascension," *Pearls*

of Wisdom, vol. 30, no. 27, July 5, 1987.

205. Heros and Amora, "A Heart of Undefiled Love," *Pearls of Wisdom*, vol. 36, no. 22, May 30, 1993.

206. *Keepers of the Flame Lesson 10*, p. 24.

207. Johannes, January 25, 1987.

208. Johannes, "The Initiation of the Mother within the Church: To Receive the Body of the Lord," July 3, 1977.

209. John 19:27.

210. Dan. 3:20–26.

211. Archangel Jophiel. "An Era of Unprecedented Enlightenment," *Pearls of Wisdom*, vol. 32, no. 5, January 29, 1989.

212. Archangel Jophiel, "The Power of the Angels of Illumination," *Pearls of Wisdom*, vol. 25, no. 46, November 14, 1982.

213. Archangel Jophiel and Christine, *Pearls of Wisdom*, vol. 32, no. 22, May 28, 1989.

214. Elizabeth Clare Prophet, "How Angels Help You to Contact Your Higher Self," February 20, 1993.

215. Ibid.

216. Saint Germain, "For the Victory!" *Pearls of Wisdom*, vol. 35, no. 44, October 18, 1992.

217. James H. Charlesworth, ed., *The Old Testament Pseudepigrapha*, 2 vols. (Garden City, N.Y.: Doubleday and Company, 1983–85), 1:281.

218. Isa. 6:1–7.

219. Justinius, "Called to God," *Pearls of Wisdom*, vol. 28, no. 22, June 2, 1985.

220. Justinius, "Appeal to the Seraphim: We Are Bigger than Life!" Part 2, *Pearls of Wisdom*, vol. 40, no. 11, March 16, 1998.

221. Sanat Kumara, "The Warning," *Pearls of Wisdom*, vol. 31, no. 4, January 24, 1988.

222. Justinius, "The Army of the Hosts of the Lord," March 6, 1977.

223. Serapis Bey, *Dossier on the Ascension* (1978), p. 130.

224. Justinius, "Legions of Purity in Defense of the Mother Flame," December 8, 1974.

225. Serapis Bey, *Dossier on the Ascension* (1978), pp. 130–31.

226. The Keeper of the Scrolls, April 22, 1962.

227. Ibid.

228. Ibid.

229. Swami Prabhavananda and Christopher Isherwood, trans., *Bhagavad Gita* (Hollywood, Calif.: Vedanta Press, 1987), p. 58; Juan Mascaro, trans., *The Bhagavad Gita* (New York: Penguin Books, 1962), pp. 61–62.

230. Elizabeth Clare Prophet has released an audiocassette of devotional songs, *Krishna: The Maha Mantra and Bhajans*, that can be used in this exercise.

231. Sanat Kumara, *The Opening of the Seventh Seal* (Corwin Springs, Mont.: The Summit Lighthouse Library, 2001), pp. 234–35.

232. Lady Kristine, "My Beloved, Let Us Deliver the Word!" *Pearls of Wisdom*, vol. 25, no. 34, August 22, 1982.

233. K-17, "Agents for the Cosmic Christ," *Pearls of Wisdom*, vol. 17, nos. 11 and 12, March 17 and 24, 1974.

234. Ibid.

235. *Kuan Yin's Crystal Rosary: Devotions to the Divine Mother East and West* is a New-Age ritual of hymns, prayers, and ancient Chinese mantras that invoke the merciful presence of Kuan Yin, Bodhisattva of Compassion, and of Mary, mother of Jesus. Includes a booklet and three audiocassettes that you may offer singly or in sequence. (Available from Summit University Press.)

236. Kuan Yin, "The Quality of Mercy for the Regeneration of the Youth of the World," *Pearls of Wisdom*, 1982, Book II, pp. *120–21*.

237. Kuan Yin, "A People and a Teaching Whose Time Has Come," September 18, 1976.

238. Kuan Yin, "The Sword of Mercy," October 10, 1969.

239. Kuan Yin, "Karma, Mercy, and the Law," *Pearls of Wisdom*, 1982, Book II, p. *106*.

240. Kuan Yin, "A Mother's-Eye View of the World," *Pearls of Wisdom*, 1982, Book II, p. *87*.

241. Isa. 1:18.

242. Kuan Yin, "Mercy: The Fire that Tries Every Man's Works," *Pearls of Wisdom*, 1982, Book II, p. *95*.

243. Kuan Yin, "A Mother's-Eye View of the World," *Pearls of Wisdom*, 1982, Book II, p. *87*.

244. Kuan Yin, "Mercy: The Fire that Tries Every Man's Works," *Pearls of Wisdom*, 1982, Book II, p. *96*.

245. Kuthumi, "Remember the Ancient Encounter," *Pearls of Wisdom*, vol. 28, no. 9, March 3, 1985.

246. Ibid.

247. David Kinsley, *The Goddesses' Mirror: Visions of the Divine from East and West* (Albany N.Y.: University of New York Press, 1989), p. 66.

248. See Rev. 11:3 and Dan. 12:5.

249. Matt. 10:41.

250. Matt. 26:48.

251. Ps. 136.

252. 1 Cor. 3:19.

253. Acts 9:5; Mark L. Prophet and Elizabeth Clare Prophet, *Understanding Yourself* (1999), p. 153.

254. Leonora, "Mind Control," *Pearls of Wisdom*, vol. 13, no. 34, August 23, 1970.

255. Mother Mary, August 15, 1962.

256. Godfré Ray King, *The Magic Presence*, 5th ed. (Chicago: Saint Germain Press, 1982), pp. 187–214.

257. Leto, "Do You Remember? The Crown of the Divine Mother," January 2, 1972.

258. Leto, "Welcome to the Cave of Light," July 4, 1979.

259. From the poem "The New Colossus," by Emma Lazarus, inscribed on the pedestal of the Statue of Liberty.

260. Henry Wadsworth Longfellow, "Santa Filomena," Stanza 10.

261. The Goddess of Liberty, "The Awakening," *Pearls of Wisdom* 1986, Book Two, p. 7.

262. The Goddess of Liberty, *Liberty Proclaims* (1975), pp. 13, 15–16.

263. Queen of Light, July 3, 1969.

264. Acts 7:22.

265. Exod. 2:11–12.

266. Exod. 3:2, 7, 10, 14.

267. Sanat Kumara gives a detailed account of this episode in Moses' mission in *The Opening of the Seventh Seal* (Corwin Springs, Mont.: The Summit Lighthouse Library, 2001), pp. 33–39.

268. Num. 20:3–12.

269. John 21:16, 17.

270. Lord Ling, "The Code of Life for the Initiate," *Pearls of Wisdom*, vol. 34, no. 32, June 30, 1991.

271. Listening Angel, "Teach the Children!" *Pearls of Wisdom*, vol. 35, no. 60, December 4, 1992.

272. Magda, "Transmute the Past and the Future," *Pearls of Wisdom*, vol. 40, no. 36, September 7, 1997.

273. Lotus, "The Mantle of My Authority," *Pearls of Wisdom*, vol. 17, no. 2, January 13, 1974.

274. For further information about Aimee and her life, see Aimee Semple McPherson, *This is That* (New York: Garland, 1985); *Aimee: Life Story of Aimee Semple McPherson* (Los Angeles: Foursquare Publications, 1979).

275. Magda, "Transmute the Past and the Future," *Pearls of Wisdom*, vol. 40, no. 36, September 7, 1997.

276. Jesus and Magda, "A Torch of Responsibility," *Pearls of Wisdom*, vol. 27, no. 62, December 26, 1984.

277. Acts 2:3.

278. Matt. 3:16.

279. Mark L. Prophet and Elizabeth Clare Prophet, *Climb the Highest Mountain: The Path of the Higher Self,* (1986), pp. 386–87.

280. The Maha Chohan, "A Tabernacle of Witness for the Holy Spirit in the Final

Quarter of the Century," July 1, 1974.

281. W. Y. Evans-Wentz, ed., *The Tibetan Book of the Great Liberation* (London: Oxford University Press, 1954) p. xxvii.

282. Kenneth K. S. Ch'en, *Buddhism in China: A Historical Survey* (Princeton, N.J.: Princeton University Press, 1964), pp. 405–6.

283. Marilyn M. Rhie and Robert A. F. Thurman, *Wisdom and Compassion: The Sacred Art of Tibet* (San Francisco: Asian Art Museum of San Francisco, 1991), pp. 20, 21.

284. Manjushri, "You Have the Mind of God!" *Pearls of Wisdom*, vol. 37, no. 21, May 22, 1994.

285. Ibid.

286. Mother Mary, January 1, 1974.

287. Mother Mary, "To Prick the Conscience of the Nations," *Pearls of Wisdom*, vol. 27, no. 48, September 30, 1984.

288. Mother Mary, February 24, 1980.

289. Mother Mary, "The Continuity of Being," *Pearls of Wisdom*, vol. 27, no. 63, December 30, 1984,

290. Francis Johnston, *Fatima: The Great Sign* (Washington, N.J.: AMI Press, 1980), p. 139.

291. Mark L. Prophet and Elizabeth Clare Prophet, *My Soul Doth Magnify the Lord!* (1986), pp. 261, 263.

292. Mother Mary, "Behold the Handmaid [Shakti] of the Lord!" December 31, 1977.

293. "But whoso shall offend one of these little ones which believe in me, it were better for him that a millstone were hanged about his neck, and that he were drowned in the depth of the sea." Matt. 18:6.

294. Mother Mary, "The Right Arm of the Mother," January 28, 1979.

295. Maximus, "The Energy of the Great Central Sun," *Pearls of Wisdom*, vol. 20, no. 29, July 17, 1977.

296. Maximus, "I AM Maximus," August 11, 1979.

297. Archangel Michael, "The Chela of the First Ray," *Pearls of Wisdom*, vol. 30, no. 35, August 30, 1987.

298. Mother Mary, "Light of My Heart, I Give to Thee," *Pearls of Wisdom*, vol. 24, no. 58, March, 1981.

299. Lord Ling, October 13, 1963.

300. Heb. 6:20.

301. Heb. 5:6.

302. John 3:30.

303. Archangel Zadkiel, "The Priesthood of the Order of Melchizedek," *Pearls of Wisdom*, vol. 29, no. 57, November 9, 1986.

304. God Meru, August 28, 1966.

305. God Meru, "To Plead the Cause of Youth," *Pearls of Wisdom*, vol. 30, no. 19, May 10, 1987.

306. God Meru, September 1, 1973.

307. Hilarion, "Dispensations from the Healing Masters," December 30, 1974.

308. Exod. 13:21–22; 14:21–30.

309. *Saint Germain On Alchemy* (1993), pp. 142–51.

310. Elizabeth Clare Prophet, "A Meditation for Unity," *Pearls of Wisdom*, vol. 41, no. 44, November 1, 1998.

311. Ibid.

312. Ibid.

313. *Sacred Ritual for the Creation of the Cloud by the Ascended Master Saint Germain* (1983), audiocassette tape and booklet. An abbreviated version of this ritual can be found in Elizabeth Clare Prophet, *Creative Abundance* (1998), pp. 103–15.

314. Dan. 12:1.

315. Rev. 12:7–9.

316. Elizabeth Clare Prophet, "How Angels Help You to Protect Yourself and Those You Love," February 21, 1993.

317. Archangel Michael, "Hail, Children of the White-Fire Sun," July 4, 1971.

318. Archangel Michael, "When the Heart Cries Out to God," *Pearls of Wisdom*, vol. 13, no. 35, August 30, 1970.

319. Ibid.

320. Archangel Michael, "A Divine Mediatorship," *Pearls of Wisdom*, vol. 25, no, 45, November 7, 1982.

321. See W. Y. Evans-Wentz, ed., *Tibet's Great Yogi Milarepa: A Biography from the Tibetan*, 2d ed. (1951; reprint, New York: Oxford University Press, Galaxy Books. 1976).

322. Ibid., p. 91.

323. Ibid., p. 105.

324. Ibid., pp. 106, 128.

325. Ibid., pp. 133, 134–35.

326. Lanello, "I Am Sent to Father You and to Mother You," *Pearls of Wisdom*, vol. 38, no. 37, August 27, 1995.

327. Ibid.

328. *Letters of Helena Roerich*, vol. II (New York: Agni Yoga Society, 1954), p. 18.

329. Helena Roerich, *Mother of the World* (New York City: Agni Yoga Society, 1956), pp. 10, 12.

330. Mother of the World, May 13, 1979.

331. God Harmony, July 25, 1968.

332. Isa. 40:31.

333. Nada, "Life Is Still Sweet," *Pearls of Wisdom*, vol. 23, no. 6, February 10, 1980.

334. Mark L. Prophet and Elizabeth Clare Prophet, *Lords of the Seven Rays* (1986), Book Two, p. 229.

335. Nada, "The Practice of Law in the Feminine Ray," July 5, 1974.

336. The Nameless One from out the Great Central Sun, "The Dilemma of Being," *Pearls of Wisdom*, vol. 34, no. 37, July 28, 1991.

337. Jesus and Kuthumi, *Corona Class Lessons* (1986), p. 375.

338. Rev. 15:2.

339. Neptune and Luara, *Pearls of Wisdom*, vol. 23, no. 17, April 27, 1980.

340. Claude Bragdon, Introduction, in Nicholas Roerich, *Altai-Himalaya: A Travel Diary* (Brookfield, Conn.: Arun Press, 1929), p. xix.

341. Nicholas Roerich, *Himalayas: Abode of Light* (Bombay: Nalanda Publications, 1947), p. 21, in Jacqueline Decter, *Nicholas Roerich: The Life and Art of a Russian Master* (Rochester, Vt.: Park Street Press, 1989), p. 141.

342. Nicholas Roerich, *Himalayas*, p. 13, in Decter, *Nicholas Roerich,* p. 203.

343. Nicholas Roerich, *Heart of Asia* (New York: Roerich Museum Press, 1929), pp. 7, 8.

344. Roerich, Notovotch and Abhedananda all published their translations of these texts describing Jesus' journey to the East. All three accounts are included in Elizabeth Clare Prophet, *The Lost Years of Jesus* (1987).

345. Svetoslav Roerich, "My Father," in *Nicholas Roerich* (New York: Nicholas Roerich Museum, 1974), p. 15.

346. Nicholas Roerich, "Be the Unextinguishable Ones!" *Pearls of Wisdom*, vol. 33, no. 44, November 11, 1990.

347. Ibid.

348. Omri-Tas, July 6, 1963.

349. Omri-Tas, "A Violet Flame Sea of Light," *Pearls of Wisdom*, vol. 34, no. 26, June 24, 1991.

350. The Old Man of the Hills, "Fiery Vortices of Consciousness Becoming God," in Elizabeth Clare Prophet, *The Great White Brotherhood in the Culture, History and Religion of America* (1987), p. 217.

351. Ibid., pp. 218–20.

352. Ibid., pp. 221–22.

353. Oromasis and Diana, *Pearls of Wisdom*, vol. 23, no. 15, April 13, 1980.

354. Oromasis and Diana, "Call for the Rainbow Fire!" *Pearls of Wisdom*, vol. 33, no. 32, August 19, 1990.

355. Lord Maitreya, "To Restore the Christhood of America!" *Pearls of Wisdom*, vol. 35, no. 42, October 11, 1992.

356. Padma Sambhava, "Initiation—The Transfer of the Fivefold Secret-Ray Action of the Buddhas to All Who Will to Be Both Hearers and Doers of the Word," December 5, 1977.

357. Luke 6:46.
358. Padma Sambhava, "God Is Just: All Will Receive Their Just Reward," *Pearls of Wisdom*, vol. 38, no. 36, August 20, 1995.
359. Kenneth L. Woodward, *Making Saints: How the Catholic Church Determines Who Becomes a Saint, Who Doesn't, and Why* (New York: Simon & Schuster, 1996), pp. 156–57.
360. Laura Chandler White, trans., *Who is Padre Pio?* (Rockford, Ill.: Tan Books, 1974), p. 41.
361. Ibid., pp. 39–40.
362. Stuard Holroyd, *Psychic Voyages* (London: Danbury Press, 1976), pp. 44–45.
363. *The Greater Way of Freedom* (1976), p. 60.
364. Jophiel and Christine, "For Europe: A Dispensation and a Cycle," *Pearls of Wisdom*, vol. 24, no. 12, March 22, 1981.
365. Herbert Thurston, S. J., and Donald Attwater, eds., *Butler's Lives of the Saints*, rev. ed. (New York: P. J. Kenedy & Sons, 1956), 1:612–17.
366. Sanat Kumara, "The Judgment of Serpent and His Seed," *Pearls of Wisdom*, vol. 22, no. 46, November 18, 1979; also published in Sanat Kumara, *The Opening of the Seventh Seal* (Corwin Springs, Mont.: The Summit Lighthouse Library, 2001), pp. 294–97.
367. Oliver St. John Fogarty, *I Follow Saint Patrick* (London: Rich & Cowan, 1938), p. 298.
368. Saint Patrick, April 3, 1977.
369. Paul the Venetian, "The Art of Love," *Pearls of Wisdom*, vol. 27, no. 3, January 15, 1984.
370. Ibid.
371. Paul the Venetian, July 6, 1963.
372. Mark L. Prophet and Elizabeth Clare Prophet, *Lords of the Seven Rays* (1986), Book Two, pp. 112–13.
373. Peace and Aloha, "I Came Not to Send Peace, but a Sword," *Pearls of Wisdom*, vol. 21, no. 16, April 16, 1978.
374. Elohim Peace, January 3, 1965.
375. Elohim Peace, "Peace Be Still!" April 17, 1966.
376. Elohim Peace, "I Inaugurate a Thirty-Three-Tiered Spiral of Peace in The Summit Lighthouse," *Pearls of Wisdom*, vol. 34, no. 48, October 13, 1991.
377. Elohim Peace, February 15, 1959, quoted in Elizabeth Clare Prophet, "Teachings of the Elohim Peace and Aloha," Part 1, *Pearls of Wisdom*, vol. 44, no. 48, December 2, 2001.
378. Elohim Peace, January 3, 1965, quoted in Elizabeth Clare Prophet, "Teachings of the Elohim Peace and Aloha," Part 1.
379. Elohim Peace, January 3, 1965, quoted in Elizabeth Clare Prophet, "Teachings of the Elohim Peace and Aloha," Part 2, *Pearls of Wisdom*, vol. 44, no. 49,

December 9, 2001.

380. Elohim Peace and Aloha, "The Path of True Love," *Pearls of Wisdom*, vol. 36, no. 21, May 23, 1993.

381. Peace and Aloha, "I Came Not to Send Peace, but a Sword," *Pearls of Wisdom*, vol. 21, no. 16, April 16, 1978.

382. Elohim Peace, March 26, 1978.

383. Elohim Peace, "The Crown Jewel of Peace," *Pearls of Wisdom*, vol. 35, no. 43, October 14, 1992.

384. Peace and Aloha, *Pearls of Wisdom*, vol. 32, no. 14, April 2, 1989.

385. Peace and Aloha, "I Came Not to Send Peace, but a Sword."

386. Elohim Peace and Aloha, "The Path of True Love," *Pearls of Wisdom*, vol. 36, no. 21, May 23, 1993.

387. Ibid.

388. Goddess of Peace, *Pearls of Wisdom*, vol. 6, no. 32, August 9, 1963.

389. Phylos the Thibetan, *A Dweller on Two Planets* (Los Angeles: Borden Publishing Company, 1940), p. 194.

390. The *Ashram Notes*, by El Morya, includes six Ashram rituals designed to link "hearts worldwide in a ritual of scheduled group meditations": The Unison Ritual; Great Central Sun Ritual: O Cosmic Christ, Thou Light of the World!; Sacred Ritual for Attunement with God's Holy Will; Sacred Ritual for Soul Purification; Sacred Ritual for Transport and Holy Work; and Sacred Ritual for Oneness. The rituals are also published in a separate booklet called *Ashram Rituals*.

391. The Ascended Master Phylos the Tibetan, "We Are Winners and We Win with Joy!" *Pearls of Wisdom*, vol. 34, no. 25, June 23, 1991.

392. *Pearls of Wisdom* 1978, pp. 390–91.

393. Madame d'Adhémar's diaries are excerpted in Isabelle Cooper-Oakley, *The Count of Saint Germain* (Blauvelt, N.Y.: Rudolph Steiner Publications, 1970).

394. Portia, October 10, 1964.

395. Portia, "The Mercy and Justice of the Law in the Mother Flame of Freedom," July 1, 1978.

396. Matt. 17:14–21.

397. Astrea, *Keepers of the Flame Lesson 23*, p. 39.

398. Astrea, "The Purging of the Company of the Saints—Go and Sin No More," *Pearls of Wisdom*, vol. 17, no. 16, April 21, 1974.

399. Astrea, "I Enlist Your Help!" *Pearls of Wisdom*, vol. 34, no. 13, March 31, 1991.

400. Astrea, "The Purging of the Company of the Saints."

401. Ra Mu, "You Becoming the All—For Thou Art Mother Also," *Pearls of Wisdom*, vol. 24, no. 76, November 1981.

402. Sanat Kumara, "The Warning," *Pearls of Wisdom*, vol. 31, no. 4, January 24,

1988.

403. Archangel Raphael, "The Day of the Coming of the Lord's Angel," *Pearls of Wisdom*, vol. 29, no. 32, June 29, 1986.

404. Mother Mary, "The Vow to Heal a Planet," *Pearls of Wisdom*, vol. 30, no. 7, February 15, 1987.

405. John 9:4, 5; 12:35, 36.

406. Archangel Raphael, "Healing, Karma and the Path," *Pearls of Wisdom*, vol. 29, no. 32, June 29, 1986.

407. Archangel Raphael, "Healing, Karma and the Violet Flame," *Pearls of Wisdom*, vol. 30, no. 7, February 15, 1987.

408. Mother Mary, "The Vow to Heal a Planet."

409. Ray-O-Light, circa 1959.

410. Mark 5:1–15; 9:17–27; 2:3–12; Matt. 8:5–13, 16.

411. Ray-O-Light, "Keep Moving!" *Pearls of Wisdom*, "The Radiant Word," vol. 25, no. 29, July 18, 1982.

412. Ray-O-Light, circa 1959.

413. Ray-O-Light, "Keep Moving!"

414. *Keepers of the Flame Lesson 31*, p. 54.

415. Rex with Pearl, Bob and Nada, "The Physical Ascension," *Keepers of the Flame Lesson 31*, pp. 70, 72.

416. *Keepers of the Flame Lesson 31*, p. 56.

417. Rose of Light, "The Call to the Practice of Love," *Pearls of Wisdom*, vol. 33, no. 22, June 10, 1990.

418. Rose of Light, "The Opening of the Rose of Light," *Pearls of Wisdom*, vol. 32, no. 52, November 8, 1989.

419. Rose of Light, "The Call to the Practice of Love."

420. Saint Germain, "I Have Chosen to Be Free," *Pearls of Wisdom*, vol. 18, no. 30, July 27, 1975.

421. For more information about this ancient golden age, see Godfré Ray King, *Unveiled Mysteries* (Chicago: Saint Germain Pres, 1934), pp. 33–71.

422. Gen. 14:18, 19; Ps. 110:4; Heb. 5:6, 10; 6:20; 7.

423. 1 Sam. 7:3.

424. 1 Sam. 8:5.

425. 1 Sam. 8:7.

426. Henry Thomas and Dana Lee Thomas, *Living Biographies of Great Scientists* (Garden City, N.Y.: Nelson Doubleday, 1941), p. 15.

427. David Wallechinsky, Amy Wallace and Irving Wallace, *The Book of Predictions* (New York: William Morrow and Co., 1980), p. 346.

428. Clements R. Markham, *Life of Christopher Columbus* (London: George Philip and Son, 1892), pp. 207–8.

429. *Encyclopaedia Britannica*, 15th ed., s.v. "Columbus, Christopher."

430. Ibid.

431. See Virginia Fellows, *The Shakespeare Code* (1stBooks Library, 2000).

432. Voltaire, *Œuvres*, Lettre cxviii, ed. Beuchot, lviii, p. 360, quoted in Isabel Cooper-Oakley, *The Count of Saint Germain* (Blauvelt, N.Y.: Rudolf Steiner Publications, 1970), p. 96.

433. For further information on the embodiments of Saint Germain and his sponsorship of the United States, see "The Mystical Origins of the United States of America," in *Saint Germain On Alchemy* (1985), pp. 101–26.

434. Saint Germain, "Keep My Purple Heart," *Pearls of Wisdom*, vol. 31, no. 72, October 29, 1988.

435. Sanat Kumara, *The Opening of the Seventh Seal* (Corwin Springs, Mont.: The Summit Lighthouse Library, 2001), pp. 11–15.

436. Maurice Walsh, trans., *Thus Have I Heard: The Long Discourses of the Buddha Digha Nikaya* (London: Wisdom Publications, 1987), pp. 295–96.

437. Dan. 7:9.

438. Rigveda 2.41.16, 1.3.12, quoted in David Frawley, *Gods, Sages and Kings: Vedic Secrets of Ancient Civilization* (Salt Lake City, Utah: Passage Press, 1991), pp. 70, 71.

439. Serapis Bey, "The Mobilization of Spiritual Forces," *Pearls of Wisdom*, vol. 25, no. 60.

440. Jesus and El Morya, "The Order of the Good Samaritan," *Pearls of Wisdom*, vol. 27, no. 52, October 28, 1984.

441. Matt. 21:44; Luke 20:18.

442. Serapis Bey, *Dossier on the Ascension* (1979), pp. 158, 176–77.

443. Ibid., p. 89.

444. Rev. 16:10–11. See also Elizabeth Clare Prophet, *Vials of the Seven Last Plagues* (1980), ch. 9.

445. Servatus, "Healing in the New Jerusalem," April 6, 1977.

446. Ibid.

447. Ibid.

448. Ibid.

449. Elizabeth Clare Prophet, *The Great White Brotherhood in the Culture, History and Religion of America* (1987), p. 269.

450. Sanat Kumara, "Raising the Consciousness of the Mother Flame," *Pearls of Wisdom*, vol. 42, no. 24, June 13, 1999.

451. Sanat Kumara with the Seven Holy Kumaras, "Let the Wall of Fire Descend!" *Pearls of Wisdom*, vol. 35, no. 49, November 4, 1992.

452. Stella Kramrisch, *The Presence of Shiva* (Princeton, N.J.: Princeton University Press, 1981), p. 439.

453. Ibid., pp. 439–40.

454. Lord Shiva, "The Power of Change," *Pearls of Wisdom*, vol. 34, no. 62, December 1, 1991.

455. Lord Shiva, "The Touch of Shiva: The Initiation of Love," Part 2, *Pearls of Wisdom*, vol. 21, no. 47, November 19, 1978.

456. David R. Kinsley, *Hindu Goddesses* (Berkeley and Los Angeles: University of California Press, 1988), pp. 96–97.

457. Gautama Buddha, "Making Choices," *Pearls of Wisdom*, vol. 26, no. 39, September 25, 1983.

458. Purity and Astrea, "The Electronic Fire Rings Placed on Earth's Latitudinal Lines by the Seraphim," December 30, 1979.

459. Lanello, "The Spirit of Christmas," *Pearls of Wisdom*, vol. 25, no. 68.

460. The Spirit of Selflessness, "From Out the Great Central Sun Magnet," October 14, 1974.

461. Archangel Michael and the Goddess of Liberty, "I Have a Plan," *Pearls of Wisdom*, vol. 30, no. 26, June 28, 1987.

462. The Maha Chohan, "A Flame of Selflessness to Keep," April 15, 1976.

463. Mark 14:3–8; John 12:3–7.

464. The Spirit of the Resurrection, March 17, 1974.

465. The Spirit of the Resurrection, December 5, 1976.

466. The Spirit of the Resurrection, March 17, 1974.

467. Sponsors of Youth from out the Great Central Sun, "A Call for an All-Out Commitment to the Cause of Youth," December 28, 1977, quoted by Elizabeth Clare Prophet, July 2, 1996.

468. Ibid.

469. Sponsors of Youth from out the Great Central Sun, "Save the Children!" *Pearls of Wisdom*, vol. 35, no. 59, December 2, 1992.

470. Mark L. Prophet and Elizabeth Clare Prophet, *Understanding Yourself* (1999), p. 130.

471. John 14:2–3.

472. Surya, "Turning Points in the Earth," *Pearls of Wisdom*, vol. 37, no. 36, September 4, 1994.

473. Sanat Kumara, *The Opening of the Seventh Seal* (2001), p. 232.

474. Decree 10.13 in *Prayers, Meditations, Dynamic Decrees for the Coming Revolution in Higher Consciousness* (Corwin Springs, Mont.: The Summit Lighthouse, 1994).

475. Astrea and Purity, *Pearls of Wisdom*, vol. 32, no. 18, April 30, 1989.

476. Surya, *Pearls of Wisdom*, vol. 32, no. 19, May 7, 1989.

477. "Our Precious Pearl's Discourse," April 6, 1937, in *Ascended Master Discourses* (Chicago: Saint Germain Press, 1937), p. 321.

478. God Tabor and Mother Mary, "Help Elementals Gain Their Threefold Flame," *Pearls of Wisdom*, vol. 41, no. 46, November 15, 1998.

479. God Tabor, March 27, 1964.

480. Theosophia, "Signs of the Soul's Longing for Christ," *Pearls of Wisdom*, vol. 33, no. 25, July 1, 1990.

481. Theosophia, "A Page in the Mother's Book of Healing," Part I, *Pearls of Wisdom*, vol. 20, no. 8, February 20, 1977.

482. Theosophia, "Educate the Children!" *Pearls of Wisdom*, vol. 34, no. 36, July 21, 1991.

483. T. N. Taylor, ed., *Soeur Thérèse of Lisieux, the Little Flower of Jesus* (New York: P. J. Kennedy & Sons, n.d.), pp. 339–40.

484. Cindy Cavnar, ed., *Prayers and Meditations of Thérèse of Lisieux* (Ann Arbor, Mich.: Servant Publications, 1992), p. 172.

485. Ibid., p. 16.

486. *Story of a Soul: The Autobiography of St. Thérèse of Lisieux*, trans. John Clarke, 2d ed. (Washington, D.C.: ICS Publications, 1976), pp. 222–23.

487. Saint Bernadette (1844–1879), a devout peasant to whom the Blessed Virgin appeared 18 times in a grotto near Lourdes, France, when she was 14, endured the painful and debilitating disease of tuberculosis of the bone for more than seven years while she served as a Sister of Notre Dame at the Convent of Saint-Gildard. During the last two years of her life she developed a large tumor on her knee, which she kept a secret as long as she could so she would not be relieved of her duties, as portrayed in the film *The Song of Bernadette* (1943) based on Franz Werfel's novel by the same name.

488. Saint Thérèse of Lisieux, "Outside the Church," Part II, *Pearls of Wisdom*, vol. 31, no. 39, July 13, 1988.

489. For more information on the cosmic clock, see Elizabeth Clare Prophet, *The Great White Brotherhood in the Culture, History and Religion of America* (1987), ch. 15.

490. Acts 1:10.

491. Two Men Who Stood by in White Apparel, "The Ascension of Jesus the Christ," April 19, 1976.

492. Ibid.

493. Ibid.

494. The Unknown Master of the Himalayas, "The Spiritual Defense of the Soul," *Pearls of Wisdom*, vol. 28, no. 31, August 4, 1985.

495. Archangel Uriel, "'Thus Far and No Farther!' Saith the LORD," December 29, 1985, quoted by Elizabeth Clare Prophet, March 23, 1996.

496. Archangel Uriel, "The Hour of the Fulfillment of Your Christhood," February 27, 1988, quoted by Elizabeth Clare Prophet, March 23, 1996.

497. 1 Cor. 6:1–3.

498. Archangel Uriel, *Exhortations out of the Flame of the Ark of the Covenant*, no. 3, p. 4.

499. Archangel Uriel, "Look to the Mountain!" *Pearls of Wisdom*, vol. 25, no. 23, June 6, 1982.

500. Rom. 12:19.

501. Archangel Uriel, "The Sealing of This Cycle of the Lord's Resurrection," April 15, 1979.

502. Ibid.

503. Archangel Uriel, "Overcome by the Power of Light!" *Pearls of Wisdom*, vol. 26, no. 23, June 5, 1983.

504. Archangel Uriel, "Walk the Earth as Christs!" *Pearls of Wisdom*, vol. 25, no. 50, December 12, 1982.

505. Elizabeth Clare Prophet, "Saint Germain's Prophecy for the Aquarian Age," March 23, 1996.

506. Rev. 14:6.

507. Rev. 1:4, 11, 20; 5:1, 2, 5, 9; 6:1; 20:12.

508. Archangel Uzziel, "The Sign of the Coming of the Eighth Ray of Integration," December 30, 1979.

509. Archangel Uzziel with Clara Louise, "You Must Open the Heart Chakra of America," April 8, 1977.

510. Helena Blavatsky, *Collected Writings,* vol. 4: 1882–1883 (Wheaton, Ill.: Theosophical Press, 1969), pp. 577, 578.

511. C. W. Leadbeater, *The Masters and the Path* (Adyar, Madras, India: Theosophical Publishing House, ca.1959), pp. 40–41.

512. Vaivasvata Manu, "Nurturing the Souls of a Planet," October 12, 1973.

513. Vajrasattva, Spokesman for the Five Dhyani Buddhas, "Becoming the Gentle Ones," *Pearls of Wisdom*, vol. 36, no. 40, September 15, 1993.

514. Ibid.

515. *The "I AM" Discourses by the Great Cosmic Being Mighty Victory* (Chicago, Ill.: Saint Germain Press, 1949), pp. 3–4, 272.

516. Virgo and Pelleur, *Pearls of Wisdom*, vol. 23, no. 14, April 6, 1980.

517. Ezek. 1; 10; Rev. 4.

518. Deut. 25:4; 1 Cor. 9:9; 1 Tim. 5:18.

519. Virgo and Pelleur, *Pearls of Wisdom*, vol. 23, no. 14, April 6, 1980.

520. Virgo and Pelleur, "A Desperate Plea: Invoke the Violet Flame on Behalf of the Elementals," *Pearls of Wisdom*, vol. 34, no. 42, September 1, 1991.

521. Serapis Bey and the White Goddess, "Disciplines of the Sacred Centers of God-Awareness (Chakras) for Discipleship East and West," December 30, 1977.

522. Archangel Zadkiel, December 31, 1968, quoted by Elizabeth Clare Prophet, "Saint Germain's Prophecy for the Aquarian Age," March 2, 1996.

523. Archangel Zadkiel, December 30, 1980, quoted by Elizabeth Clare Prophet, "Saint Germain's Prophecy for the Aquarian Age," March 2, 1996.

524. Holy Amethyst, December 31, 1960, quoted by Elizabeth Clare Prophet, "Saint

Germain's Prophecy for the Aquarian Age," March 2, 1996.

525. Archangel Zadkiel, October 6, 1987, quoted by Elizabeth Clare Prophet, "Saint Germain's Prophecy for the Aquarian Age," March 2, 1996.

526. Archangel Zadkiel, *Pearls of Wisdom*, vol. 32, no. 17, April 23, 1989.

527. Archangel Zadkiel and Holy Amethyst, "Vials of Freedom," December 30, 1974, quoted by Elizabeth Clare Prophet, "Saint Germain's Prophecy for the Aquarian Age," March 2, 1996.

528. Archangel Zadkiel, March 24, 1989, quoted by Elizabeth Clare Prophet, "Saint Germain's Prophecy for the Aquarian Age," March 2, 1996.

529. Ibid.

530. Archangel Zadkiel, "My Gift of the Violet Flame," *Pearls of Wisdom*, vol. 30, no. 58, November 27, 1987.

531. Mary Boyce, *Zoroastrians, Their Religious Beliefs and Practices* (London: Routledge and Keegan Paul, 1979), p. 19.

532. Dinkart 7.4.75–76, quoted in Bernard H. Springett, *Zoroaster, the Great Teacher* (London: William Rider and Son, 1923), p. 25.

533. Zarathustra. "A Moment in Cosmic History—The Empowerment of Bearers of the Sacred Fire," *Pearls of Wisdom*, vol. 24, no. 13, March 28, 1981.

534. The Maha Chohan, "The Opening of the Temple Doors," *Pearls of Wisdom*, vol. 16, no. 19, May 13, 1973.

535. Mark L. Prophet, "The Secret Places of God in the Earth," December 24, 1972.

536. El Morya, *The Chela and the Path* (1976), pp. 36–42, 43.

537. Elizabeth Clare Prophet, "Karma, Reincarnation and the Family," June 15, 1974.

538. Mark L. Prophet and Elizabeth Clare Prophet, *Morya I* (Corwin Springs, Mont.: The Summit Lighthouse Library, 2001), pp. 193–94.

539. Phil. 2:5.

540. Serapis Bey, "The Opening of the Temple Doors IV," *Pearls of Wisdom*, vol. 16, no. 13, April 1, 1973.

541. Kuthumi, "The Opening of the Temple Doors II," *Pearls of Wisdom*, vol. 16, no. 11, March 18, 1973.

542. Archangel Zadkiel, "The Cathedral of the Violet Flame," October 11, 1975.

543. See Godfré Ray King, *The Magic Presence*, 4th ed. (Chicago: Saint Germain Press, 1974), pp. 392–96.

544. Great Divine Director, October 15, 1966

545. Mother Mary, March 11, 1987.

546. Leto, "Welcome to the Cave of Light," July 4, 1979.

547. Great Divine Director, September 1, 1973.

548. Paul the Venetian, "The Opening of the Temple Doors III," *Pearls of Wisdom*, vol. 16, no. 12, March 25, 1973.

549. Godfre, September 3, 1984.

550. The Goddess of Purity, "The Flame in the Center of the Crystal," September 13, 1970.

551. The Goddess of Purity, "Purity Is the Key," October 12, 1970.

552. Cyclopea, "The Divine Intent," October 22, 1965.

553. Lord Maitreya, "The Call to Come to Our Retreat in the Far East," *Pearls of Wisdom*, vol. 27, no, 38, July 22, 1984.

554. Lanello, "The Positioning of the Chelas on the 360 Degrees of the Circle of Life," *Pearls of Wisdom*, vol. 24, no. 2, January 11, 1981.

555. Lanello, April 8, 1979.

556. Lanello and K-17, "An Intelligence Report," October 8, 1977.

557. K-17, October 6, 1993.

558. Apollo and Lumina, "The New Flame of Joy," November 25, 1983.

559. Lanello, "Light of My Heart Burning in the Lighthouse," July 4, 1979.

560. Lord Maitreya, "The Call to Come to Our Retreat in the Far East," *Pearls of Wisdom*, vol. 27, no. 38, July 22, 1984.

561. Archangel Zadkiel, "God Has Sent the Seven Archangels for the Rescue of the People of Light on Earth," *Pearls of Wisdom*, vol. 24, no. 6, February 8, 1981.

562. Alexander Gaylord, January 22, 1967.

563. The Old Man of the Hills, "Fiery Vortices of Consciousness Becoming God," in Elizabeth Clare Prophet, *The Great White Brotherhood in the Culture, History and Religion of America* (1987), pp. 220–21.

564. Godfré Ray King, *The Magic Presence*, 4th ed. (Chicago: Saint Germain Press, 1974), pp. 377–78.

565. Ibid., p. 379.

566. Ibid., pp. 384–85.

567. The Great Divine Director, "God-Direction for the Coming Cycle," *Pearls of Wisdom*, vol. 16, no. 42, October 21, 1973.

568. Archangel Raphael, November 3, 1966.

569. Matt. 23:37.

570. Jesus the Christ, "The Opening of the Temple Doors VII," *Pearls of Wisdom*, vol. 16, no. 16, April 22, 1973.

571. Himalaya, "The Masculine Ray in the Aquarian Age," February 22, 1975.

572. Elizabeth Clare Prophet, "The Message of the Inner Buddha: 'Some Will Understand,'" *Pearls of Wisdom*, vol. 32, no. 30, July 23, 1989.

573. Gautama Buddha, "The Teaching Is for the Many," *Pearls of Wisdom*, vol. 29, no. 21, May 25, 1986.

574. Confucius, "In the Golden Light of the Golden Age of China," June 13, 1976.

575. Lanto, "The Opening of the Temple Doors IX," *Pearls of Wisdom*, vol. 16, no. 18, May 6, 1973.

576. Cuzco, "Make the Difference!" *Pearls of Wisdom*, vol. 38, no. 27, June 25, 1995.

577. Edwin Bernbaum, *The Way to Shambhala* (Garden City, N.Y.: Anchor Press/Doubleday, 1980), pp. 4–5.

578. The God of Gold with God Tabor, "The Flow of Energy in the City Foursquare: Children of God, Demand and Supply the Abundance of the Mother!" October 10, 1977.

579. Archangel Michael, July 5, 1968.

580. Archangel Michael, "Charge! Charge! Charge! And Let Victory Be Proclaimed!" *Pearls of Wisdom*, vol. 17, no. 15, April 14, 1974.

581. Mark L. Prophet and Elizabeth Clare Prophet, *Morya I* (Corwin Springs, Mont.: The Summit Lighthouse Library, 2001), p. 56.

582. Mark L. Prophet and Elizabeth Clare Prophet, *Morya: The Darjeeling Master Speaks to His Chelas on the Quest for the Holy Grail* (1983), p. 334.

583. Goddess Meru, "A Fiat of Solstice: A Petition for Quickening and for Judgment," December 22, 1973.

584. Words by Emma Lazarus, from "The New Colossus."

585. Godfre, "Allegiance to the Honor of God," *Pearls of Wisdom*, vol. 27, no. 50, October 14, 1984.

586. Holy Amethyst, "Journey to the Sun in a Chariot of Fire," July 3, 1971.

587. Hilarion, "The Opening of the Temple Doors V," *Pearls of Wisdom*, vol. 16, no. 14, April 8, 1973.

588. The Great Divine Director, "I Come to Sound the Alarm: Save Souls Who Will Be Lost without Your Intercession," *Pearls of Wisdom*, vol. 37, no. 29, July 19, 1994.

589. Saint Germain, *Pearls of Wisdom*, vol. 3, no. 24, June 10, 1960.

590. Zarathustra, "Thou Purging Fire!" *Pearls of Wisdom*, vol. 35, no. 36, September 6, 1992.

591. Matt. 24: 28; Hilarion, "The Challenges of Apostleship," *Pearls of Wisdom*, vol. 20, no. 17, April 24, 1977.

592. Elizabeth Clare Prophet, November 6, 1975.

Picture Credits

Pages 41, 230, 242, 247, 256, 383, 395, maps: Brad Davis; 236, 245, 247: Nicholas Roerich Museum, New York, N.Y. Used by permission; 432, 445, 449 (top): Library of Congress, Prints and Photographs Division, LC-DIG-ppmsc-04925, LC-DIG-ppmsca-00782, LC-DIG-ppmsc-05193; 487: Ian Swindale. Some images © 2003 www.clipart.com.

Glossary

Terms set in *italics* are defined elsewhere in the glossary.

Adept. An initiate of the *Great White Brotherhood* of a high degree of attainment, especially in the control of *Matter,* physical forces, nature spirits and bodily functions; fully the alchemist undergoing advanced initiations of the s*acred fire* on the path of the *ascension.*

Akashic records. The impressions of all that has ever transpired in the physical universe, recorded in the etheric substance and dimension known by the Sanskrit term *akasha.* These records can be read by those with developed *soul* faculties.

Alchemical marriage. The soul's permanent bonding to the *Holy Christ Self,* in preparation for the permanent fusing to the *I AM Presence* in the ritual of the *ascension.* See also *Soul; Secret chamber of the heart.*

Angel. A divine spirit, a herald or messenger sent by God to deliver his *Word* to his children. A ministering spirit sent forth to tend the heirs of *Christ*— to comfort, protect, guide, strengthen, teach, counsel and warn. The fallen angels, also called the dark ones, are those angels who followed Lucifer in the Great Rebellion, whose consciousness therefore "fell" to lower levels of vibration. They were "cast out into the earth" by Archangel Michael (Rev. 12:7–12)—constrained by the karma of their disobedience to God and his Christ to take on and evolve through dense physical bodies. Here they walk about, sowing seeds of unrest and rebellion among men and nations.

Antahkarana. The web of life. The net of *Light* spanning *Spirit* and *Matter,* connecting and sensitizing the whole of creation within itself and to the heart of God.

Archangel. The highest rank in the orders of *angels.* Each of the *seven rays* has a presiding Archangel who, with his divine complement or Archeia, embodies the God consciousness of the ray and directs the bands of angels serving in their command on that ray.

Archeia (pl. Archeiai). Divine complement and *twin flame* of an *Archangel.*

Ascended Master. One who, through *Christ* and the putting on of that mind which was in Christ Jesus (Phil. 2:5), has mastered time and space and in the process gained the mastery of the self in the *four lower bodies* and the four quadrants of *Matter,* in the *chakras* and the balanced *threefold flame.* An Ascended Master has also transmuted at least 51 percent of his karma, fulfilled his divine plan, and taken the initiations of the ruby ray unto the ritual of the *ascension*—acceleration by the *sacred fire* into the Presence of the I AM THAT I AM (the *I AM Presence*). Ascended Masters inhabit the planes of *Spirit*—the kingdom of God (God's consciousness)—and they may teach unascended souls in an *etheric temple* or in the cities on the *etheric plane* (the kingdom of heaven).

Ascension. The ritual whereby the *soul* reunites with the *Spirit* of the living God, the *I AM Presence*. The ascension is the culmination of the *soul's* God-victorious sojourn in time and space. It is the process whereby the soul, having balanced her karma and fulfilled her divine plan, merges first with the *Christ* consciousness and then with the living Presence of the I AM THAT I AM. Once the ascension has taken place, the soul—the corruptible aspect of being—becomes the incorruptible one, a permanent atom in the Body of God. See also *Alchemical marriage*.

Aspirant. One who aspires; specifically, one who aspires to reunion with God through the ritual of the *ascension*. One who aspires to overcome the conditions and limitations of time and space to fulfill the cycles of karma and one's reason for being through the sacred labor.

Astral plane. A frequency of time and space beyond the physical, yet below the mental, corresponding to the *emotional body* of man and the collective unconscious of the race; the repository of mankind's thoughts and feelings, conscious and unconscious. Because the astral plane has been muddied by impure human thought and feeling, the term "astral" is often used in a negative context to refer to that which is impure or psychic.

Atman. The spark of the divine within, identical with *Brahman*; the ultimate essence of the universe as well as the essence of the individual.

AUM. See *OM*.

Avatar. The incarnation of the *Word*. The avatar of an age is the *Christ*, the incarnation of the Son of God. The *Manus* may designate numerous Christed ones—those endued with an extraordinary *Light*—to go forth as world teachers and wayshowers. The Christed ones demonstrate in a given epoch the law of the *Logos*, stepped down through the Manu(s) and the avatar(s) until it is made flesh through their own word and work—to be ultimately victorious in its fulfillment in all souls of light sent forth to conquer time and space in that era.

Bodhisattva. (Sanskrit, 'a being of *bodhi* or enlightenment.') A being destined for enlightenment, or one whose energy and power is directed toward enlightenment. A Bodhisattva is destined to become a *Buddha* but has forgone the bliss of *nirvana* with a vow to save all children of God on earth. An Ascended Master or an unascended master may be a Bodhisattva.

Brahman. Ultimate Reality; the Absolute.

Buddha. (From Sanskrit *budh* 'awake, know, perceive.') "The enlightened one." Buddha denotes an office in the spiritual *hierarchy* of worlds that is attained by passing certain initiations of the *sacred fire*, including those of the *seven rays* of the Holy Spirit and of the five secret *rays*, the raising of the feminine ray (sacred fire of the *Kundalini*) and the "mastery of the seven in the seven multiplied by the power of the ten."

Caduceus. The Kundalini. See *Sacred fire.*

Causal Body. Seven concentric spheres of *light* surrounding the *I AM Presence*. The spheres of the Causal Body contain the records of the virtuous acts we have performed to the glory of God and the blessing of man through our many incarnations on earth. See also *Chart of Your Divine Self.*

Central Sun. A vortex of energy, physical or spiritual, central to systems of worlds that it thrusts from, or gathers unto, itself by the Central Sun Magnet. Whether in the *microcosm* or the *Macrocosm*, the Central Sun is the principal energy source, vortex, or nexus of energy interchange in atoms, cells, man (the heart center), amidst plant life and the core of the earth. The Great Central Sun is the center of cosmos; the point of integration of the *Spirit-Matter* cosmos; the point of origin of all physical-spiritual creation; the nucleus, or white-fire core, of the *Cosmic Egg*. (The God Star, Sirius, is the focus of the Great Central Sun in our sector of the galaxy.) The Sun behind the sun is the spiritual Cause behind the physical effect we see as our own physical sun and all other stars and star systems, seen or unseen, including the Great Central Sun.

Chakra. (Sanskrit, 'wheel, disc, circle.') Center of *light* anchored in the *etheric body* and governing the flow of energy to the *four lower bodies* of man. There are seven major chakras corresponding to the *seven rays*, five minor chakras corresponding to the five secret rays, and a total of 144 light centers in the body of man.

Chart of Your Divine Self. There are three figures represented in the Chart. The upper figure is the *I AM Presence*, the I AM THAT I AM, the individualization of God's presence for every son and daughter of the Most High. The Divine Monad consists of the I AM Presence surrounded by the spheres (color rings) of *light* that make up the body of First Cause, or *Causal Body*.

The middle figure in the Chart is the Mediator between God and man, called the *Holy Christ Self*, the *Real Self* or the *Christ* consciousness. It has also been referred to as the Higher Mental Body or one's Higher Consciousness. This Inner Teacher overshadows the lower self, which consists of the *soul* evolving through the four planes of *Matter* using the vehicles of the *four lower bodies*—the *etheric* (memory) *body*, the *mental body*, the *emotional* (desire) *body*, and the *physical body*—to balance karma and fulfill the divine plan.

The three figures of the Chart correspond to the Trinity of Father, who

The Chart of Your Divine Self

always includes the *Mother* (the upper figure), Son (the middle figure) and Holy Spirit (the lower figure). The latter is the intended temple of the Holy Spirit, whose *sacred fire* is indicated in the enfolding *violet flame*. The lower figure corresponds to you as a disciple on the *Path*.

The lower figure is surrounded by a *tube of light*, which is projected from the heart of the I AM Presence in answer to your call. It is a cylinder of white light that sustains a forcefield of protection twenty-four hours a day, so long as you guard it in harmony. The *threefold flame* of life is the divine spark sent from the I AM Presence as the gift of life, consciousness and free will. It is sealed in the *secret chamber of the heart* that through the love, wisdom and power of the Godhead anchored therein the *soul* may fulfill her reason for being in the physical plane. Also called the Christ flame and the liberty flame, or fleur-de-lis, it is the spark of a man's divinity, his potential for Christhood.

The silver cord (or *crystal cord*) is the stream of life, or *lifestream*, that descends from the heart of the I AM Presence to the Holy Christ Self to nourish and sustain (through the *chakras*) the *soul* and its vehicles of expression in time and space. It is over this 'umbilical cord' that the energy of the Presence flows, entering the being of man at the crown and giving impetus for the pulsation of the threefold flame as well as the physical heartbeat.

When a round of the soul's incarnation in Matter-form is finished, the I AM Presence withdraws the silver cord (Eccles. 12:6), whereupon the threefold flame returns to the level of the Christ, and the soul clothed in the etheric garment gravitates to the highest level of her attainment, where she is schooled between embodiments until her final incarnation when the Great Law decrees she shall go out no more.

The dove of the Holy Spirit descending from the heart of the Father is shown just above the head of the Christ. When the son of man puts on and becomes the Christ consciousness as Jesus did, he merges with the Holy Christ Self. The Holy Spirit is upon him, and the words of the Father, the beloved I AM Presence, are spoken: "This is my beloved Son, in whom I AM well pleased" (Matt. 3:17).

Chela. (Hindi *celā* from Sanskrit *ceta* 'slave,' i.e., 'servant.') In India, a disciple of a religious teacher or *guru*. A term used generally to refer to a student of the *Ascended Masters* and their teachings. Specifically, a student of more than ordinary self-discipline and devotion initiated by an Ascended Master and serving the cause of the *Great White Brotherhood*.

Chohan. (Tibetan, 'lord' or 'master'; a chief.) Each of the seven *rays* has a Chohan who focuses the *Christ* consciousness of the ray. Having ensouled and demonstrated the law of the ray throughout numerous incarnations, and having taken initiations both before and after the *ascension*, the candidate is appointed to the office of Chohan by the Maha Chohan (the "Great Lord"), who is himself the representative of the Holy Spirit on all the rays.

Christ. (From the Greek *Christos* 'anointed.') Messiah (Hebrew, Aramaic 'anointed'); 'Christed one,' one fully endued and infilled—anointed—by the *Light* (the Son) of God. The *Word*, the *Logos*, the Second Person of the Trinity. In the Hindu Trinity of Brahma, Vishnu and Shiva, the term "Christ" corresponds to or is the incarnation of Vishnu, the Preserver; Avatāra, God-man, Dispeller of Darkness, *Guru*.

The term "Christ" or "Christed one" also denotes an office in *hierarchy* held by those who have attained self-mastery on the *seven rays* and the seven *chakras* of the Holy Spirit. Christ-mastery includes the balancing of the *threefold flame*—the divine attributes of power, wisdom and love—for the harmonization of consciousness and the implementation of the mastery of the seven rays in the chakras and in the *four lower bodies* through the Mother flame (the raised *Kundalini*).

At the hour designated for the *ascension*, the *soul* thus anointed raises the spiral of the threefold flame from beneath the feet through the entire form for the transmutation of every atom and cell of her being, consciousness and world. The saturation and acceleration of the *four lower bodies* and the soul by this transfiguring light of the Christ flame take place in part during the initiation of the *transfiguration*, increasing through the resurrection and gaining full intensity in the ritual of the ascension.

Christ Self. The individualized focus of "the only begotten of the Father, full of grace and Truth." The *Universal Christ* individualized as the true identity of the *soul*; the *Real Self* of every man, woman and child, to which the soul must rise. The Christ Self is the Mediator between a man and his God. He is a man's own personal teacher, master and prophet.

Color rays. See *Seven rays*.

Cosmic Being. (1) An *Ascended Master* who has attained cosmic consciousness and ensouls the *light*/energy/consciousness of many worlds and systems of worlds across the galaxies to the Sun behind the *Great Central Sun;* or, (2) A being of God who has never descended below the level of the *Christ*, has never taken physical embodiment, and has never made human karma.

Cosmic Christ. An office in *hierarchy* currently held by Lord Maitreya under Gautama *Buddha*, the *Lord of the World*. Also used as a synonym for *Universal Christ*.

Cosmic Clock. The science of charting the cycles of the *soul's* karma and initiations on the twelve lines of the clock under the Twelve Hierarchies of the Sun. Taught by Mother Mary to Mark and Elizabeth Prophet for sons and daughters of God returning to the Law of the One and to their point of origin beyond the worlds of form and lesser causation.

Cosmic Egg. The spiritual-material universe, including a seemingly endless chain of galaxies, star systems, worlds known and unknown, whose center, or white-fire core, is called the *Great Central Sun*. The Cosmic Egg has both a spiritual and a material center. Although we may discover and observe the Cosmic Egg from the standpoint of our physical senses and perspective, all of the dimensions of *Spirit* can also be known and experienced within the Cosmic Egg. For the God who created the Cosmic Egg and holds it in the hollow of his hand is also the God flame expanding hour by hour within his very own sons and daughters. The Cosmic Egg represents the bounds of man's habitation in this cosmic cycle. Yet, as God is everywhere throughout and beyond the Cosmic Egg, so by his Spirit within us we daily awaken to new dimensions of being, soul-satisfied in conformity with his likeness.

Cosmic Law. The Law that governs mathematically, yet with the spontaneity of Mercy's flame, all manifestation throughout the cosmos in the planes of *Spirit* and *Matter*.

Crystal cord. The stream of God's *Light*, life and consciousness that nourishes and sustains the *soul* and her *four lower bodies*. Also called the silver cord (Eccles. 12:6). See also *Chart of Your Divine Self*.

Deathless solar body. See *Seamless garment*.

Decree. A dynamic form of spoken prayer used by students of the *Ascended Masters* to direct God's *light* into individual and world conditions. The decree may be short or long and is usually marked by a formal preamble and a closing or acceptance. It is the authoritative *Word* of God spoken in man in the name of the *I AM Presence* and the living *Christ* to bring about constructive change on earth through the will of God. The decree is the birthright of the sons and daughters of God, the "Command ye me" of Isaiah 45:11, the original fiat of the Creator: "Let there be light: and there was light" (Gen. 1:3). It is written in the Book of Job, "Thou shalt decree a thing, and it shall be established unto thee: and the light shall shine upon thy ways" (Job 22:28).

Dictation. A message from an *Ascended Master*, an *Archangel* or another advanced spiritual being delivered through the agency of the Holy Spirit by a *Messenger* of the *Great White Brotherhood*.

Divine Monad. See *Chart of Your Divine Self*; *I AM Presence*.

Electronic Presence. A duplicate of the *I AM Presence* of an *Ascended Master*.

Elohim. (Hebrew; plural of *Eloah*, 'God.') The name of God used in the first verse of the Bible: "In the beginning God created the heaven and the earth." The Seven Mighty Elohim and their feminine counterparts are the builders of form. They are the "seven spirits of God" named in Revelation 4:5 and the "morning stars" that sang together in the beginning, as the Lord revealed them to Job (Job 38:7). In the order of *hierarchy*, the Elohim and *Cosmic Beings* carry the greatest concentration, the highest vibration of *Light* that we can comprehend in our present state of evolution. Serving directly under the Elohim are the four hierarchs of the elements, who have dominion over the elementals—the gnomes, salamanders, sylphs and undines.

Emotional body. One of the *four lower bodies* of man, corresponding to the water element and the third quadrant of *Matter*; the vehicle of the desires and feelings of God made manifest in the being of man. Also called the astral body, the desire body or the feeling body.

Entity. A conglomerate of misqualified energy or disembodied individuals who have chosen to embody evil. Entities that are focuses of sinister forces may attack disembodied as well as embodied individuals.

Etheric body. One of the *four lower bodies* of man, corresponding to the fire element and the first quadrant of *Matter*; called the envelope of the *soul*, holding the blueprint of the divine plan and the image of *Christ*-perfection to be outpictured in the world of form. Also called the memory body.

Etheric octave or etheric plane. The highest plane in the dimension of *Matter*; a plane that is as concrete and real as the physical plane (and even more so) but is experienced through the senses of the *soul* in a dimension and a consciousness beyond physical awareness. This is the plane on which the *akashic records* of mankind's entire evolution register individually and collectively. It is the world of *Ascended Masters* and their *retreats,* etheric cities of *light* where *souls* of a higher order of evolution abide between embodiments. It is the plane of Reality.

The lower *etheric plane,* which overlaps the astral/mental/physical belts, is contaminated by these lower worlds occupied by the false hierarchy and the mass consciousness it controls.

Fallen angels. See *Angels*.

Four Cosmic Forces. The four beasts seen by Saint John and other seers as the lion, the calf (or ox), the man and the flying eagle (Rev. 4:6–8). They serve directly under the *Elohim* and govern all of the *Matter* cosmos. They are transformers of the Infinite Light unto souls evolving in the finite. See also *Elohim*.

Four lower bodies. Four sheaths of four distinct frequencies that surround the *soul* (the physical, emotional, mental and etheric bodies), providing vehicles for the soul in her journey through time and space. The etheric sheath, highest in vibration, is the gateway to the three higher bodies: the *Christ Self*, the *I AM Presence* and the *Causal Body*. See also P*hysical body*; *Emotional body*; *Mental body*; *Etheric body*.

Great Central Sun. See *Central Sun*.

Great Hub. See *Central Sun*.

Great White Brotherhood. A spiritual order of Western saints and Eastern adepts who have reunited with the *Spirit* of the living God; the heavenly hosts. They have transcended the cycles of karma and rebirth and ascended (accelerated) into that higher reality that is the eternal abode of the soul. The *Ascended Masters* of the Great White Brotherhood, united for the highest purposes of the brotherhood of man under the Fatherhood of God, have risen in every age from every culture and religion to inspire creative achievement in education, the arts and sciences, God-government and the abundant life through the economies of the nations. The word "white" refers not to race but to the aura (halo) of white *light* surrounding their forms. The Brotherhood also includes in its ranks certain unascended *chelas* of the *Ascended Masters*.

Guru. (Sanskrit.) A personal religious teacher and spiritual guide; one of high attainment. A guru may be unascended or ascended.

Hierarchy. The universal chain of individualized God-free beings fulfilling the attributes and aspects of God's infinite Selfhood. Included in the cosmic hierarchical scheme are Solar Logoi, *Elohim*, Sons and Daughters of God, ascended and unascended masters with their circles of *chelas, Cosmic Beings,* the Twelve Hierarchies of the Sun, *archangels* and *angels* of the *sacred fire,* children of the *light*, nature spirits (called elementals) and *twin flames* of the Alpha/Omega polarity sponsoring planetary and galactic systems.

This universal order of the Father's own Self-expression is the means whereby God in the *Great Central Sun* steps down the Presence and power of his universal being/consciousness in order that succeeding evolutions in time and space, from the least unto the greatest, might come to know the wonder of his love. The level of one's spiritual/physical attainment—measured by one's balanced self-awareness "hid with *Christ* in God" and demonstrating his Law, by his love, in the *Spirit/Matter* cosmos—is the criterion establishing one's placement on this ladder of life called hierarchy.

Higher Mental Body. See *Chart of Your Divine Self*.

Higher Self. The *I AM Presence;* the *Christ Self;* the exalted aspect of selfhood. Used in contrast to the term "lower self," or "little self," which indicates the *soul* that went forth from and may elect by free will to return to the Divine Whole through the realization of the oneness of the self in God. Higher consciousness.

Holy Christ Self. See *Christ Self.*

Hub, The Great. See *Central Sun.*

Human monad. The entire forcefield of self; the interconnecting spheres of influences—hereditary, environmental, karmic—which make up that self-awareness that identifies itself as human. The reference point of lesser- or non-awareness out of which all mankind must evolve to the realization of the *Real Self* as the *Christ Self.*

I AM Presence. The I AM THAT I AM (Exod. 3:13–15); the individualized Presence of God focused for each individual *soul.* The God-identity of the individual; the Divine Monad; the individual Source. The origin of the soul focused in the planes of *Spirit* just above the physical form; the personification of the God flame for the individual. See also *Chart of Your Divine Self.*

I AM THAT I AM. See *I AM Presence.*

Kali Yuga. (Sanskrit.) Term in Hindu mystic philosophy for the last and worst of the four yugas (world ages), characterized by strife, discord and moral deterioration.

Keepers of the Flame Fraternity. Founded in 1961 by Saint Germain, an organization of *Ascended Masters* and their *chelas* who vow to keep the flame of life on earth and to support the activities of the *Great White Brotherhood* in the establishment of their community and mystery school and in the dissemination of their teachings. Keepers of the Flame receive graded lessons in *Cosmic Law* dictated by the *Ascended Masters* to their *Messengers* Mark and Elizabeth Prophet.

Kundalini. See *Sacred fire.*

Lifestream. The stream of life that comes forth from the one Source, from the *I AM Presence* in the planes of *Spirit,* and descends to the planes of *Matter* where it manifests as the *threefold flame* anchored in the secret chamber of the heart for the sustainment of the *soul* in *Matter* and the nourishment of the *four lower bodies.* Used to denote souls evolving as individual "lifestreams" and hence synonymous with the term "individual." Denotes the ongoing nature of the individual through cycles of individualization.

Light. The energy of God; the potential of the *Christ.* As the personification of *Spirit,* the term "Light" can be used synonymously with the terms "God" and "Christ." As the essence of Spirit, it is synonymous with *"sacred fire."* It is the emanation of the *Great Central Sun* and the individualized *I AM Presence*—and the Source of all life.

Logos. (Greek, 'word, speech, reason.') The divine wisdom manifest in the creation. According to ancient Greek philosophy, the Logos is the controlling principle in the universe. The Book of John identifies the *Word*, or Logos, with Jesus Christ: "And the *Word* was made flesh, and dwelt among us" (John 1:14). Hence, Jesus Christ is seen as the embodiment of divine reason, the Word Incarnate.

Lord of the World. Sanat Kumara held the office of Lord of the World (referred to as "God of the earth" in Rev. 11:4) for tens of thousands of years. Gautama Buddha recently succeeded Sanat Kumara and now holds this office. His is the highest governing office of the spiritual *hierarchy* for the planet— and yet Lord Gautama is truly the most humble among the *Ascended Masters*. At inner levels, he sustains the *threefold flame,* the divine spark, for those *lifestreams* who have lost the direct contact with their *I AM Presence* and who have made so much negative karma as to be unable to magnetize sufficient *Light* from the Godhead to sustain their *soul's* physical incarnation on earth. Through a filigree thread of light connecting his heart with the hearts of all God's children, Lord Gautama nourishes the flickering flame of life that ought to burn upon the altar of each heart with a greater magnitude of love, wisdom and power, fed by each one's own *Christ* consciousness.

Macrocosm. (Greek, 'great world.') The larger cosmos; the entire warp and woof of creation, which we call the *Cosmic Egg.* Also used to contrast man as the *microcosm* ('little world') against the backdrop of the larger world in which he lives. See also *Microcosm.*

Mantra. A mystical formula or invocation; a word or formula, often in Sanskrit, to be recited or sung for the purpose of intensifying the action of the *Spirit* of God in man. A form of prayer consisting of a word or a group of words that is chanted over and over again to magnetize a particular aspect of the Deity or of a being who has actualized that aspect of the Deity. See also *Decree.*

Manu. (Sanskrit.) The progenitor and lawgiver of the evolutions of God on earth. The Manu and his divine complement are *twin flames* assigned by the *Father-Mother God* to sponsor and ensoul the Christic image for a certain evolution or lifewave known as a root race—*souls* who embody as a group and have a unique archetypal pattern, divine plan and mission to fulfill on earth.

According to esoteric tradition, there are seven primary aggregations of souls—that is, the first to the seventh root races. The first three root races lived in purity and innocence upon earth in three Golden Ages before the fall of Adam and Eve. Through obedience to *Cosmic Law* and total identification with the *Real Self*, these three root races won their immortal freedom and ascended from earth.

It was during the time of the fourth root race, on the continent of Lemuria, that the allegorical Fall took place under the influence of the fallen angels known as Serpents (because they used the serpentine spinal energies to beguile the soul, or female principle in mankind, as a means to their end of lowering the masculine potential, thereby emasculating the Sons of God).

The fourth, fifth and sixth root races (the latter soul group not having entirely descended into physical incarnation) remain in embodiment on earth today. Lord Himalaya and his beloved are the Manus for the fourth root race, Vaivasvata Manu and his consort are the Manus for the fifth root race, and the God and Goddess Meru are the Manus for the sixth root race. The seventh root race is destined to incarnate on the continent of South America in the Aquarian age under their Manus, the Great Divine Director and his divine complement.

For further information about the root races, see Book 4 of the *Climb the Highest Mountain* series, *The Path of Brotherhood*, pp. 19–21.

Manvantara. (Sanskrit, from *manv*, used in compounds for *manu*, + *antara*, 'interval, period of time.') In Hinduism, the period or age of a *Manu*, consisting of 4,320,000 solar years; one of the fourteen intervals that constitute a *kalpa* (Sanskrit), a period of time covering a cosmic cycle from the origination to the destruction of a world system. In Hindu cosmology, the universe is continually evolving through periodic cycles of creation and dissolution. Creation is said to occur during the outbreath of the God of Creation, Brahma; dissolution occurs during his inbreath.

Mater. (Latin, 'mother.') See *Matter; Mother*.

Matter. The feminine (negative) polarity of the Godhead, of which the masculine (positive) polarity is *Spirit*. Matter acts as a chalice for the kingdom of God and is the abiding place of evolving *souls* who identify with their Lord, their *Holy Christ Self*. Matter is distinguished from matter (lowercase m)—the substance of the earth earthy, of the realms of maya, which blocks rather than radiates divine *light* and the Spirit of the *I AM THAT I AM*. See also *Mother; Spirit*.

Mental body. One of the *four lower bodies* of man, corresponding to the air element and the second quadrant of *Matter*; the body that is intended to be the vehicle, or vessel, for the mind of God or the *Christ* mind. "Let this [Universal] Mind be in you, which was also in Christ Jesus" (Phil. 2:5). Until quickened, this body remains the vehicle for the carnal mind, often called the lower mental body in contrast to the Higher Mental Body, a synonym for the *Christ Self* or *Christ* consciousness.

Messenger. Evangelist. One who goes before the *angels* bearing to the people of earth the good news of the gospel of Jesus Christ and, at the appointed time, the Everlasting Gospel. The Messengers of the *Great White Brotherhood* are anointed by the *hierarchy* as their apostles ("one sent on a mission"). They deliver through the *dictations* (prophecies) of the *Ascended Masters* the testimony and lost teachings of Jesus Christ in the power of the Holy Spirit to the seed of *Christ*, the lost sheep of the house of Israel, and to every nation. A Messenger is one who is trained by an *Ascended Master* to receive by various methods the words, concepts, teachings and messages of the *Great White Brotherhood*; one who delivers the Law, the prophecies and the dispensations of God for a people and an age.

Microcosm. (Greek, 'small world.') (1) The world of the individual, his *four lower bodies,* his aura and the forcefield of his karma; or (2) The planet. See also *Macrocosm.*

Mother. "Divine Mother," "Universal Mother" and "Cosmic Virgin" are alternate terms for the feminine polarity of the Godhead, the manifestation of God as Mother. *Matter* is the feminine polarity of *Spirit*, and the term is used interchangeably with Mater (Latin, 'mother'). In this context, the entire material cosmos becomes the womb of creation into which Spirit projects the energies of life. Matter, then, is the womb of the Cosmic Virgin, who, as the other half of the Divine Whole, also exists in Spirit as the spiritual polarity of God.

Nirvana. The goal of life according to Hindu and Buddhist philosophy: the state of liberation from the wheel of rebirth through the extinction of desire.

OM (AUM). The Word; the sound symbol for ultimate Reality.

Path. The strait gate and narrow way that leadeth unto life (Matt. 7:14). The path of initiation whereby the disciple who pursues the *Christ* consciousness overcomes step by step the limitations of selfhood in time and space and attains reunion with Reality through the ritual of the *ascension.*

Pearls of Wisdom. Weekly letters of instruction dictated by the *Ascended Masters* to their *Messengers* Mark L. Prophet and Elizabeth Clare Prophet for students of the sacred mysteries throughout the world. *Pearls of Wisdom* have been published by *The Summit Lighthouse* continuously since 1958. They contain both fundamental and advanced teachings on *cosmic law* with a practical application of spiritual truths to personal and planetary problems.

Physical body. The most dense of the *four lower bodies* of man, corresponding to the earth element and the fourth quadrant of *Matter*. The physical body is the vehicle for the *soul's* sojourn on earth and the focus for the crystallization in form of the energies of the *etheric, mental* and *emotional bodies.*

Rays. Beams of *Light* or other radiant energy. The light emanations of the God-head that, when invoked in the name of God or in the name of the *Christ,* burst forth as a flame in the world of the individual. Rays may be projected by the God consciousness of ascended or unascended beings through the *chakras* and the third eye as a concentration of energy taking on numerous God-qualities, such as love, truth, wisdom, healing, and so on. Through the misuse of God's energy, practitioners of black magic project rays having negative qualities, such as death rays, sleep rays, hypnotic rays, disease rays, psychotronic rays, the evil eye, and so on. See also *Seven rays.*

Real Self. The *Christ Self*; the *I AM Presence*; immortal *Spirit* that is the animating principle of all manifestation. See also *Chart of Your Divine Self.*

Reembodiment. The rebirth of a *soul* in a new human body. The soul continues to return to the physical plane in a new body temple until she balances her karma, attains self-mastery, overcomes the cycles of time and space, and finally reunites with the *I AM Presence* through the ritual of the *ascension.*

Root race. See *Manu.*

Sacred fire. The Kundalini fire that lies as the coiled serpent in the base-of-the-spine *chakra* and rises through spiritual purity and self-mastery to the crown chakra, quickening the spiritual centers on the way. God, *light,* life, energy, the *I AM THAT I AM.* "Our God is a consuming fire" (Heb. 12:29). The sacred fire is the precipitation of the Holy Ghost for the baptism of souls, for purification, for alchemy and transmutation, and for the realization of the *ascension,* the sacred ritual whereby the *soul* returns to the One.

Samadhi. (Sanskrit, literally "putting together": "uniting") In Hinduism, a state of profound concentration or absorption resulting in perfect union with God; the highest state of yoga. In Buddhism, samadhis are numerous modes of concentration believed to ultimately result in higher spiritual powers and the attainment of enlightenment, or *nirvana.*

Seamless garment. Body of *Light* beginning in the heart of the *I AM Presence* and descending around the *crystal cord* to envelop the individual in the vital currents of the *ascension* as he invokes the holy energies of the Father for the return home to God. Also known as the deathless solar body.

Secret chamber of the heart. The sanctuary of meditation behind the heart *chakra,* the place to which the *souls* of *lightbearers* withdraw. It is the nucleus of life where the individual stands face to face with the inner *Guru,* the beloved *Holy Christ Self,* and receives the soul testings that precede the alchemical union with that Holy Christ Self—the marriage of the *soul* to the Lamb.

Seed Atom. The focus of the Divine *Mother* (the feminine ray of the Godhead) that anchors the energies of *Spirit* in *Matter* at the base-of-the-spine *chakra*. See also *Sacred fire*.

Seven rays. The *Light* emanations of the Godhead; the seven *rays* of the white Light that emerge through the prism of the *Christ* consciousness.

Siddhis. Spiritual powers such as levitation, stopping the heartbeat, clairvoyance, clairaudience, materialization and bilocation. The cultivation of siddhis for their own sake is often cautioned against by spiritual teachers.

Soul. God is a *Spirit*, and the soul is the living potential of God. The soul's demand for free will and her separation from God resulted in the descent of this potential into the lowly estate of the flesh. Sown in dishonor, the soul is destined to be raised in honor to the fullness of that God-estate which is the one Spirit of all life. The soul can be lost; Spirit can never die.

The soul remains a fallen potential that must be imbued with the reality of Spirit, purified through prayer and supplication, and returned to the glory from which it descended and to the unity of the Whole. This rejoining of soul to Spirit is the *alchemical marriage* that determines the destiny of the self and makes it one with immortal Truth. When this ritual is fulfilled, the highest Self is enthroned as the Lord of Life, and the potential of God, realized in man, is found to be the All-in-all.

Spirit. The masculine polarity of the Godhead; the coordinate of *Matter*; God as Father, who of necessity includes within the polarity of himself God as *Mother*, and hence is known as the *Father-Mother God*. The plane of the *I AM Presence*, of perfection; the dwelling place of the *Ascended Masters* in the kingdom of God. (When lowercased, as in "spirits," the term is synonymous with discarnates, or astral *entities*; "spirit," singular and lowercased, is used interchangeably with soul.)

Spoken Word. The *Word* of the Lord God released in the original fiats of Creation. The release of the energies of the Word, or the *Logos*, through the throat *chakra* by the Sons of God in confirmation of that lost Word. It is written, "By thy words thou shalt be justified, and by thy words thou shalt be condemned" (Matt. 12:37). Today disciples use the power of the Word in *decrees*, affirmations, prayers and *mantras* to draw the essence of the *sacred* fire from the *I AM Presence*, the *Christ Self* and *Cosmic Beings* to channel God's *light* into matrices of transmutation and transformation for constructive change in the planes of *Matter*.

The Summit Lighthouse. An outer organization of the *Great White Brotherhood* founded by Mark L. Prophet in 1958 in Washington, D.C., under the direction of the *Ascended Master* El Morya, Chief of the Darjeeling Council, for the purpose of publishing and disseminating the teachings of the ascended masters.

Threefold flame. The flame of the *Christ*, the spark of life that burns within the *secret chamber of the heart* (a secondary *chakra* behind the heart). The sacred trinity of power, wisdom and love that is the manifestation of the *sacred fire*. See also *Chart of Your Divine Self*.

Transfiguration. An initiation on the path of the *ascension* that takes place when the initiate has attained a certain balance and expansion of the *threefold flame*. Jesus' transfiguration is described in Matthew 17:1–8.

Tube of light. The white *Light* that descends from the heart of the *I AM Presence* in answer to the call of man as a shield of protection for his *four lower bodies* and his *soul* evolution. See also *Chart of Your Divine Self*.

Twin flame. The *soul's* masculine or feminine counterpart conceived out of the same white-fire body, the fiery ovoid of the *I AM Presence*.

Unascended master. One who has overcome all limitations of *Matter* yet chooses to remain in time and space to focus the consciousness of God for lesser evolutions. See also *Bodhisattva*.

Universal Christ. The Mediator between the planes of *Spirit* and the planes of *Matter*. Personified as the *Christ Self*, he is the Mediator between the Spirit of God and the *soul* of man. The Universal Christ sustains the nexus of (the figure-eight flow of) consciousness through which the energies of the Father (Spirit) pass to his children for the crystallization (*Christ*-realization) of the God Flame by their soul's strivings in the cosmic womb (matrix) of the *Mother* (Matter).

Violet flame. Seventh-ray aspect of the Holy Spirit. The *sacred fire* that transmutes the cause, effect, record and memory of sin, or negative karma. Also called the flame of transmutation, of freedom and of forgiveness. See also *Decree; Chart of Your Divine Self*.

Word. The Word is the *Logos*: it is the power of God and the realization of that power incarnate in and as the Christ. The energies of the Word are released by devotees of the Logos in the ritual of the science of the *spoken Word*. It is through the Word that the Father-Mother God communicates with mankind. The Christ is the personification of the Word. See also *Christ; Decree*.

World Teacher. Office in *hierarchy* held by those Ascended Beings whose attainment qualifies them to represent the universal and personal *Christ* to unascended mankind. The office of World Teacher, formerly held by Maitreya, was passed to Jesus and his disciple Saint Francis (Kuthumi) on January 1, 1956, when the mantle of *Lord of the World* was transferred from *Sanat Kumara* to Gautama *Buddha* and the office of *Cosmic Christ* and Planetary Buddha (formerly held by Gautama) was simultaneously filled by Lord Maitreya. Serving under Lord Maitreya, Jesus and Kuthumi are responsible in this cycle for setting forth the teachings leading to individual self-mastery and the *Christ* consciousness. They sponsor all *souls* seeking union with God, tutoring them in the fundamental laws governing the cause-effect sequences of their own karma and teaching them how to come to grips with the day-to-day challenges of their individual dharma, the duty to fulfill the Christ potential through the sacred labor.

Other Titles from
SUMMIT UNIVERSITY ◖ PRESS®

Fallen Angels and the Origins of Evil

Saint Germain's Prophecy for the New Millennium

The Lost Years of Jesus

The Lost Teachings of Jesus (4 vols.)

The Human Aura

Saint Germain On Alchemy

The Science of the Spoken Word

Kabbalah: Key to Your Inner Power

Reincarnation: The Missing Link in Christianity

Quietly Comes the Buddha

Lords of the Seven Rays

Prayer and Meditation

The Chela and the Path

Mysteries of the Holy Grail

Dossier on the Ascension

The Path to Your Ascension

Understanding Yourself

Keys to the Kingdom

Mary's Message for a New Day

Mary's Message of Divine Love

CLIMB THE HIGHEST MOUNTAIN SERIES

The Path of the Higher Self

The Path of Self-Transformation

The Masters and the Spiritual Path

The Path of Brotherhood

The Path of the Universal Christ

The Masters and Their Retreats

Predict Your Future:
Understand the Cycles of the Cosmic Clock